"Information through Innovation"

Mastering and Using

WORDPERFECT 6.0 for DOS

H. ALBERT NAPIER
Rice University and Napier & Judd, Inc.

PHILIP J. JUDD
Napier & Judd, Inc.

boyd & fraser publishing company

Acquisitions Editor: Anne E. Hamilton
Production Editor: Barbara Worth
Production Services: Rebecca Evans & Associates
Cover Design: Hannus Design Associates
Manufacturing Coordinator: Tracy Megison

bf © 1994 by boyd & fraser publishing company
A Division of South-Western Publishing Co.
One Corporate Place • Ferncroft Village
Danvers, Massachusetts 01923

I(T)P International Thomson Publishing
boyd & fraser publishing company is an ITP company.
The ITP trademark is used under license.

Manufactured in the United States of America

Library of Congress Cataloging-in-Publication Data

Napier, H. Albert, 1944-
    Mastering and using WordPerfect 6.0 for DOS / H. Albert Napier, Philip J. Judd.
        p.   cm.
    Includes index.
    ISBN 0-87709-426-8 (pbk.) ISBN 0-877( )-466-7 (hard cover)
    1. WordPerfect (Computer file) 2. Word rocessing.   I. Judd, Philip J., 1953-   .   II. Title.
    Z52.5.W65N369 1994   93-34938
    652.5'536—dc20   CIP

1 2 3 4 5 6 7 8 9 10 H 7 6 5 4 3

Dedication

This book is dedicated to the staff at NJI.

BRIEF CONTENTS

CONTENTS

Chapter Three
Creating and Editing a Document   35

Chapter Four
Additional Editing Features   59

Chapter Five
Using the WordPerfect Button Bar   83

Appendix A
Proofreader's Marks
617

Appendix B
Converting To/From WordPerfect 6.0 for DOS
619

Appendix C
Using the Sound, Fax, and Shell Features in WordPerfect 6.0 for DOS
621

Index
623

PREFACE

■ INTRODUCTION

Today there are literally millions of people using personal computers. One of the most popular applications of personal computers is document preparation. Today, most organizations use word processing software to prepare all kinds of documents, from simple one-page letters to multi-page newsletters and brochures. WordPerfect 6.0 for DOS was chosen as the framework for this book because it is one of the best-selling word processing software packages currently available under the DOS environment for IBM PCs and compatible personal computers.

■ OBJECTIVES OF THIS BOOK

This book has been developed for an introductory course on word processing that utilizes IBM PCs or compatible hardware on which WordPerfect 6.0 for DOS is used. The objectives of this book are:

- To acquaint the student with the process of using personal computers to prepare a variety of documents with word processing software.

- To provide a working knowledge of the basic and advanced capabilities of WordPerfect 6.0 for DOS.

- To permit learning through examples using an exercise-oriented approach.

- To provide students with an excellent source of reference to advance their knowledge of WordPerfect 6.0 for DOS.

■ AUTHORS' EXPERIENCE

The authors have worked with personal computers since PCs came to the market in the late 1970s. More than 40,000 people have attended personal computer training classes for which the authors have been responsible. This book is based on proven materials that have been used extensively in these training activities. In addition, the authors have more than 40 years of combined teaching and consulting experience.

■ DISTINGUISHING FEATURES

Access Methods for WordPerfect 6.0 for DOS

This book features a unique parallel treatment of WordPerfect's user interfaces. The use of pull-down menus, *with or without a mouse*, is available in WordPerfect 6.0 for DOS. WordPerfect 6.0 for DOS also allows the student to use the traditional keyboard function and combination keys to access its features. This book shows the student how to access WordPerfect 6.0 for DOS features using either the pull-down menu or the keyboard methods.

New and Improved WordPerfect 6.0 for DOS Features

A number of new features appear in WordPerfect 6.0 for DOS. One of these features is the ability to quickly access commands using the Button Bar. The File Manager is available to handle file and disk management tasks. Each of these new features is covered in this book.

Many important features in WordPerfect 5.1 for DOS have been changed in WordPerfect 6.0 for DOS. Some of the features that have been modified are font selection, merging documents, macros, graphics, and WordPerfect characters. Each of these features is comprehensively covered in this book.

Quick Start Approach

In Chapter 1, the student is introduced to the basics of WordPerfect 6.0 for DOS. Chapter 2 provides a quick start to the "create-edit-print" cycle in WordPerfect. After completing Chapter 2, the student can 1) create a document, 2) edit the document, 3) save the document on a floppy or hard disk, 4) print the document, 5) close the document, 6) open and edit a document, and 7) exit WordPerfect.

Learning Through Examples

The book is designed for students to learn through examples rather than learning a series of features or commands. The materials are built around a series of example problems. The student learns commands for one example, then the commands are reinforced in others. New features are covered in subsequent examples.

Step-by-Step Instructions and Screen Illustrations

All examples in this text include step-by-step instructions. Screen illustrations are used extensively to assist the student while learning WordPerfect 6.0 for DOS. The authors have found this approach very useful for the novice student as well as more advanced users, who may consider the book as a reference tool.

Extensive Exercises

At the end of each chapter, realistic exercises provide comprehensive coverage of the topics introduced in the chapter. Each chapter typically includes eight to ten exercises. There are more than 200 pages of exercises in the book.

Student Keyboard Template and Command Summary Card

The book includes a punch-out version of the WordPerfect 6.0 for DOS keyboard template for student use. A Command Summary page is also provided.

Instructor's Manual and Resources

An Instructor's Manual, which includes additional exercises and Transparency Masters, is available to adopters of this text. A set of Instructor's Resource Disks with complete solutions to all examples and exercises, and a Test Item File are also available.

■ LEVEL OF INSTRUCTION

This book is designed to introduce the beginning, intermediate, and advanced capabilities of WordPerfect 6.0 for DOS. First, the basic skills needed to create, change, save, and print a new or existing document are introduced. Subsequent chapters cover more advanced subjects, and build on previously presented concepts and developed skills. Each chapter contains eight to ten exercises that will help students improve their skills. A variety of practical examples provide an understanding of how WordPerfect can be used. The book assumes the student has little or no word processing background.

However, individuals with some previous experience can also advance their knowledge of WordPerfect 6.0 for DOS. This book is characterized by its continuity, simplicity, and practicality. This book does not replace the WordPerfect 6.0 for DOS Reference Manual that accompanies the software package. Used in conjunction with the Reference Manual, this book will provide the user with a complete understanding of the capabilities of WordPerfect 6.0 for DOS.

■ ORGANIZATION/FLEXIBILITY

This book is designed to first take the student through the fundamentals of WordPerfect 6.0 for DOS. After developing a solid foundation, the student learns more advanced features. The book is useful for college courses, professional schools, training classes, individual learning, and as a reference tool.

Chapter 1 describes the WordPerfect 6.0 for DOS software package and the process of accessing the WordPerfect 6.0 for DOS software. The pull-down menu and keyboard methods of accessing WordPerfect 6.0 for DOS features are discussed and illustrated.

The important "create-edit-print" cycle is covered in Chapter 2. After completing Chapter 2, the student can 1) create a document, 2) edit the document, 3) save the document on a floppy or hard disk, 4) print the document, 5) close the document, 6) open and edit a document, and 7) exit WordPerfect.

More extensive coverage of the process for creating a document appears in Chapter 3. Methods for inserting and replacing text are covered. The select feature and steps for deleting and undeleting text are shown. The help feature is also described.

Additional editing features are covered in Chapter 4. The use of File Manager to open a file is discussed. Important features such as revealing codes, searching for and replacing text, changing the case of letters, and moving and copying text are demonstrated.

The WordPerfect Button Bar is covered in Chapter 5. Methods for using, creating, editing, formatting, and selecting a Button Bar are demonstrated. The use of the Speller, Thesaurus, and Grammatik features is covered in Chapter 6.

When a document is created or edited, it may need to be formatted in a specific manner. Chapter 7 shows the basic formatting features such as fonts, margins, tabs, line spacing, justification, hyphenation, and indent. The use of the Ribbon for additional formatting is also demonstrated. Additional formatting features such as headers and footers, page numbering, and page breaks are illustrated in Chapter 8.

WordPerfect includes many features for enhancing the text in a document. Chapter 9 contains instructions for using the right flush, center, bold, underline, and italics features. Additional text enhancement features such as using superscripts and subscripts, changing font size, and changing font appearance are also shown. The use of the WP Characters feature and the Hidden Text feature is also discussed in Chapter 9.

The printing capabilities are illustrated in Chapter 10. The steps for printing a document that appears on a screen, printing a document from a disk, and previewing a document are specified. Printer options are also discussed in this chapter.

WordPerfect allows the use of more than one document window on the screen at a time. The methods for arranging, moving, and sizing multiple document windows are discussed in Chapter 11.

In many situations, it may be necessary to merge two documents. For example, a form letter may need to be sent to all customers of a company. The steps for merging a file containing the document with another file containing addresses are covered in Chapter 12. The processes for merging a document with input from the keyboard and creating a merged list are discussed in Chapter 13.

Rather than repeat the same actions for certain tasks each time they are performed, a macro can be created in WordPerfect. The steps necessary for creating and using a macro are demonstrated in Chapter 14. The process for creating an interactive macro is also discussed.

When documents are prepared, envelopes and labels may be needed. Methods for printing envelopes and labels are shown in Chapter 15. The document merge technique learned in Chapter 13 is also used to merge address labels in Chapter 15.

Sometimes it may be necessary to place information in a specific order within a document. The process for sorting information is covered in Chapter 16. Part of this chapter presents information on sorting text used in a document merge. The process for selecting text that matches certain information is also demonstrated.

Documents may require the use of newspaper-style or parallel columns. The steps for using these types of columns are demonstrated in Chapter 17. Creating newspaper-style columns using the Ribbon is also covered.

Some documents require a table of information, such as sales data. In Chapter 18, the steps to create and edit a table are shown. Chapter 19 provides the steps for using the advanced table features of WordPerfect. These features include using functions in formulas, and creating range names.

WordPerfect includes some desktop publishing capabilities. The method for including a graphic in a document is illustrated in Chapter 20. Other features such as specifying the graphics caption, attachment type, vertical position, horizontal position, and size are demonstrated. Options related to border style, border space, caption location, and gray shading are shown

Graphics can be rotated, scaled, and moved within a graphics box. These features are covered in Chapter 21.

Advanced graphic features such as using graphics lines, placing a graphic on another graphic or in a text box, and placing a watermark graphic on a document page are demonstrated in Chapter 22.

A complex mathematical equation may need to be included in some technical documents. Chapter 23 describes the processes for creating an equation, printing an equation, using the equation palette, saving an equation, using an equation in a document, retrieving an equation, and editing an equation.

Many documents use the same style or format. The processes for creating, editing, saving, retrieving, and deleting a style are illustrated in Chapter 24. WordPerfect's advanced typesetting features such as leading adjustment, word and letter spacing, and kerning are also demonstrated.

Outlines are used in preparing many types of documents. Chapter 25 covers the steps for creating and editing an outline. The procedures for hiding and showing outline families is also illustrated. The use of the Outline Edit Mode is demonstrated.

Endnotes and footnotes are used in reports to document the author's sources of information. These features are illustrated in Chapter 26.

Long reports may require a table of contents, index, and list of figures. The methods for creating, defining, and generating such items are illustrated in Chapter 27.

The File Manager feature and the QuickFinder are discussed in Chapter 28. These features provide alternative methods for finding and opening documents.

This book includes three appendices. A selection of proofreader's marks is included in Appendix A. Appendix B discusses the methods for converting a document to and from WordPerfect 6.0 for DOS. Appendix C describes the Sound, Fax, and Shell features new to WordPerfect 6.0 for DOS.

■ ACKNOWLEDGEMENTS

We would like to thank and express our appreciation to the many fine individuals who have contributed to the completion of this book. We have been fortunate to have a reviewer whose constructive comments have been so helpful in completing this book; special thanks go to Cristal Ewald, Iowa State University.

We also appreciate the copy editing completed by Sheryl Rose.

As noted earlier, an extensive set of exercises is included in this book. The authors are particularly appreciative to Professor Robert R. Zilkowski of William Rainey Harper College for his assistance in preparing most of the exercises for the chapters.

No book is possible without the motivation and support of an editorial staff. Therefore, we wish to acknowledge with great appreciation the following people at boyd & fraser: Tom Walker, Publisher; James H. Edwards, Senior Acquisitions Editor; Anne Hamilton, Acquisitions Editor; Barbara Worth, Production Editor; Peggy Flanagan, Production Manager; and Becky Herrington, Director of Production, for their keen assistance in preparing this book.

We are very appreciative of the personnel at Napier & Judd, Inc., who helped prepare this book. We acknowledge, with great appreciation, the assistance provided by Nancy Onarheim, Joyce Sarahan, and Robyn Yahola in preparing and checking the many drafts of this book.

H. Albert Napier
Philip J. Judd
Houston, Texas

CHAPTER ONE

GETTING STARTED WITH WORDPERFECT 6.0 FOR DOS

OBJECTIVES

In this chapter, you will learn to:

■ Define the term *word processing*
■ Determine the hardware and software requirements for WordPerfect 6.0
■ Access the WordPerfect 6.0 program
■ Use the WordPerfect 6.0 template
■ Use the pull-down menus
■ Change the default directory
■ Exit the WordPerfect program

■ CHAPTER OVERVIEW

This chapter tells you how to access WordPerfect 6.0 for DOS (hereafter called WordPerfect 6.0). The items that appear on the WordPerfect 6.0 screen are discussed. The WordPerfect 6.0 template and the menu structure are explained and illustrated. The procedures for changing directories and for exiting WordPerfect 6.0 are shown.

■ WHAT IS WORD PROCESSING?

Word processing is the preparation and production of documents using automated equipment. Today, most word processing activities are done with personal computers and a computer program that is called **word processing software**. Personal computers allow people to complete word processing tasks as well as a host of other duties, including desktop publishing. In many organizations today, you need to know a word processing program in order to get a job.

■ WHAT IS WORDPERFECT 6.0?

WordPerfect 6.0 for DOS is a word processing software package. WordPerfect 6.0 allows you to create and change documents. You can save a document on a storage device so you can retrieve it at a later time.

WordPerfect 6.0 allows you to see your document on the screen as it will look when it is printed. This popular software is used by organizations as well as by individuals.

WordPerfect 6.0 can be used to create and edit:

Letters	Mailing labels
Memos	Forms
Reports	Address lists
Book manuscripts	Brochures
Newsletters	

■ HARDWARE REQUIREMENTS

To use the version of WordPerfect covered in this book, you must have an IBM or compatible personal computer. It is recommended that your computer be an 80386 or higher processor, and that it have at least 520K of RAM and 16 MB of available hard disk space. Your personal computer also needs an EGA, VGA, 8514/A, or high resolution graphics adapter and monitor. It is also recommended that you use DOS 6.0 or an earlier version of DOS with a memory management program. Consult your DOS reference manual for details on this topic.

■ SOFTWARE REQUIREMENTS

This book focuses on WordPerfect 6.0. When you purchase the WordPerfect 6.0 software, you are given a set of diskettes on which the programs are stored. You will install the software from the diskettes on the hard disk of a computer. Then you will access the programs on the hard disk. For instructions on how to install WordPerfect 6.0 on a hard disk, see the reference manual that comes with the software.

■ SUPPLIES

When using a personal computer, you will need several items. First, you should have access to the WordPerfect 6.0 reference manual that comes with the software.

You will also need to have some floppy diskettes on which to store documents. Make sure you have the proper type of diskette for the computer you are using. You can purchase diskettes at office supply stores and campus bookstores. If you have never used diskettes, follow the instructions for handling that come with them. You may also want a disk storage box to protect your diskettes when you are not using them.

You will need to format the diskettes before you store documents on them. Refer to your DOS reference manual for the procedures to format a diskette.

■ ACCESSING WORDPERFECT 6.0

Before you attempt to access WordPerfect 6.0 and place it into the memory of your personal computer, check all connections.

Turn on   the computer

You may access WordPerfect 6.0 from DOS or through the Windows program.

The steps for loading the software from DOS are listed below.

Type   CD\WP60

Press   [↵Enter]

Type   WP

Press   [↵Enter]

Type   WP

Press   Enter

The WordPerfect 6.0 copyright screen appears on your monitor. In a few seconds, your screen should look similar to Figure 1-1.

■ THE WORDPERFECT DOCUMENT SCREEN

Figure 1-1 is an example of a WordPerfect 6.0 document screen. This window contains a blank document.

Figure 1-1

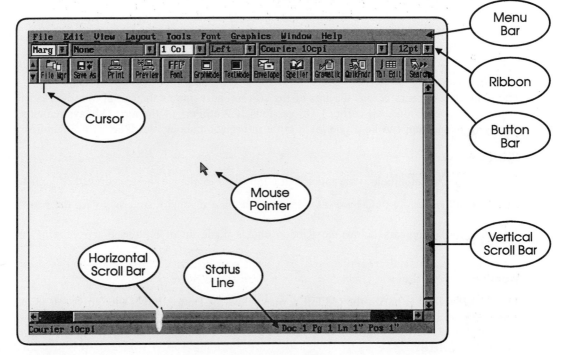

Your screen may not look the same as Figure 1-1 which displays the Graphics Mode that permits you to view your document in a WYSIWYG format. WYSIWYG is an acronym for *What You See Is What You Get* and it means that your text will appear on the screen as it will appear when printed. In addition, graphical figures will be visible on the screen. You may change the view on your screen to the Graphic Mode by using the View Graphics Mode command. WordPerfect 6.0 also has two other screen modes—Text Mode and Page Mode. The Text Mode screen displays your text in monospaced characters and does not display the contents of graphics boxes. In this mode, you must use Print Preview to see what your printout will look like. The Page Mode screen displays text and graphics like the Graphics Mode, but you can also see the layout of your page including headers, footers, and page numbers. Page Mode will be discussed further in Chapter 8.

In This Chapter

The use of the menus with a mouse and with a keyboard are shown in two columns. The directions in the left column are for the menus using a keyboard. They appear in normal type. The instructions in the right column are for accessing the menus with a mouse. They appear in *italic* type.

Press and hold	Alt		**Move**	*the mouse pointer to the View menu choice*
Press	V for View		**Click**	*the mouse button*
Press	G for Graphics Mode		**Move**	*the mouse pointer to the Graphics Mode option*
			Click	*the mouse button*

Elements of the WordPerfect 6.0 screen are described below. Some of these items may not appear on your screen at this time. You will be shown later how to include them.

Menu Bar

The menu bar appears across the top of the screen and contains the initial WordPerfect 6.0 commands available to you. Unlike the earlier DOS versions of WordPerfect, the menu always remains on the screen. The Help menu item can help you learn more information about WordPerfect 6.0 features.

Ribbon

The Ribbon is located below the menu and allows you to change the appearance of your text.

Button Bar

The Button Bar appears below the Ribbon and is made up of buttons that represent commonly used commands.

Cursor

The blinking vertical bar in the top left corner below the Button Bar is the cursor. It marks the location where text will be entered on the screen.

Mouse Pointer

The mouse pointer appears as an arrow on the screen and can be used to make selections from the menus, Button Bar, and Ribbon. It can also be used to move the cursor to a new position within existing text.

Scroll Bars

A vertical and/or horizontal scroll bar may appear on the right side and bottom of the document area. These scroll bars include scroll arrows as well as the scroll box. The scroll bars allow you to move the cursor to various parts of the document.

Status Bar

The status bar appears at the bottom of the screen. It indicates the font or filename, the current document, the current page number (Pg), the vertical position of the cursor (Ln), and the horizontal position of the cursor (Pos).

■ DEFAULT SETTINGS

Some initial settings, called **defaults**, apply to the documents you prepare. You will learn ways to change the settings in later chapters.

In WordPerfect, margins are measured from the edges of a page. WordPerfect 6.0 adjusts the text to fit within the current margins. The default setting is a 1-inch margin for the top, bottom, left, and right side of a page.

Line spacing determines the amount of space between lines. WordPerfect 6.0 single spaces your document unless you change the line spacing.

Justification refers to alignment of text. Left justification is the default setting. When left justification is used, WordPerfect 6.0 aligns the text in your document on the left margin and has a "ragged right" margin.

Tabs are an exact measurement for indenting text in a document. A tab is displayed on the screen as a certain amount of blank space. The WordPerfect 6.0 default setting for tabs is every 1/2 inch.

WordPerfect 6.0 uses inches as the standard unit of measurement to position text on a page.

■ METHODS FOR ACCESSING WORDPERFECT 6.0 FEATURES

WordPerfect 6.0 provides three interface methods for accessing its features:

1. Keyboard function keys
2. Menus using the keyboard
3. Menus using the mouse

When the keyboard function keys method is used, you place a template on the keyboard. The template specifies which WordPerfect 6.0 features are performed by each function key.

WordPerfect 6.0 features may also be accessed by selecting words from the menu at the top of the screen using the keyboard. You may access the menu using the keyboard by pressing the ALT key and the corresponding underlined letter of the desired menu item.

When a mouse is used with the menu bar, you select WordPerfect 6.0 features by pointing at the item with the mouse pointer and clicking the mouse button. **Clicking** means to press the mouse button and then release it. There are two other basic mouse operations: double-clicking and dragging. **Double-clicking** means to press the mouse button twice quickly. **Dragging** means to press and hold down the mouse button while moving the mouse.

■ TEMPLATE

A **template** is a diagram of the function keys. It includes a list of WordPerfect 6.0 features that can be executed by using the function keys. The function keys, labeled F1 through F10 or F12, can be used by themselves or with the CTRL, ALT, or SHIFT keys. The WordPerfect 6.0 template is color-coded. **Black** commands are issued by pressing only the function key. **Green** commands are issued by pressing the function key while pressing the SHIFT key. **Blue** commands are issued by pressing the function key while pressing the ALT key. **Red** commands are issued by pressing the function key while pressing the CTRL key. Figure 1-2 displays the WordPerfect 6.0 template.

Figure 1-2

Student Template for use with WordPerfect® for DOS	Shell	Speller	Screen	Move	Ctrl	Outline	Decimal Tab	Notes	Font	Ctrl	Merge/Sort	Record Macro	Tab Set	Save
Bold Ctrl+B Page Number Ctrl+P Compose Ctrl+A Paste Ctrl+V Copy Ctrl+C Play Sound Clip Ctrl+S Cut Ctrl+X Repeat Ctrl+R Cycle Ctrl+Y Set QuickMark Ctrl+Q Find QuickMark Ctrl+F Toggle Text Ctrl+T Italics Ctrl+I Undo Ctrl+Z Outline Edit Ctrl+U WP Characters Ctrl+W	Writing Tools	Replace	Reveal Codes	Block	Alt	Mark Text	Flush Right	Columns/Tables	Styles	Alt	Graphics	Play Macro	Table Edit	Envelope
	Setup	◆Search	Switch	◆Indent◆	Shift	Date	Print/Fax	Format		Shift	Merge Codes	Open/Retrieve	WP Characters	Bookmark
	Help	◆Search	Switch To	◆Indent		File Manager	Bold	Exit	Underline		End Field	Save As	Reveal Codes	Block
boyd & fraser publishing company	**F1**	**F2**	**F3**	**F4**		**F5**	**F6**	**F7**	**F8**		**F9**	**F10**	**F11**	**F12**

> ### In This Book
>
> The keyboard function key interface method is referred to as the keyboard method in the rest of the text.
>
> When you use the WordPerfect 6.0 features with the keyboard method, you will often be asked to press one key, and while still holding the key down, to press another key. For example, you may be asked to hold down the SHIFT key, and then press the F7 key to select the Print feature. This type of instruction will appear in the text as:
>
> **Press**   `Shift` + `F7`

■ MENUS

You will practice the methods for accessing the menus with a keyboard and with a mouse in this section.

Selecting Menus

The method you use to select a menu option from the menu bar depends on whether you are using the keyboard or a mouse.

> ### In This Book
>
> For mouse instructions, if you are right handed, the left mouse button will be referred to as the mouse button. If the right mouse button is to be used, it will be referred to as the alternate mouse button. If you are left handed, the buttons may be switched.

For example, to select the Layout menu from the menu bar:

Press and hold   Alt

Press   L for Layout

To select an option from the menu displayed using the keyboard, press the underscored letter associated with the menu option. Or, press arrow keys to highlight the option of your choice and press ←Enter .

Move   *the mouse pointer to the Layout menu*

Click   *the mouse button*

To select an option from the menu using the mouse, move the mouse pointer to the menu option and click the mouse button. Or, press and hold down the mouse button, drag the mouse pointer to an option, and then release the mouse button.

For example, to select the Columns option from the Layout menu:

Press   ↓ to move to the Columns option

Press   ←Enter

or

Press   C for Columns

Move   *the mouse pointer to the Columns option*

Click   *the mouse button*

The Text Columns dialog box appears. Your screen should look like Figure 1-3.

Figure 1-3

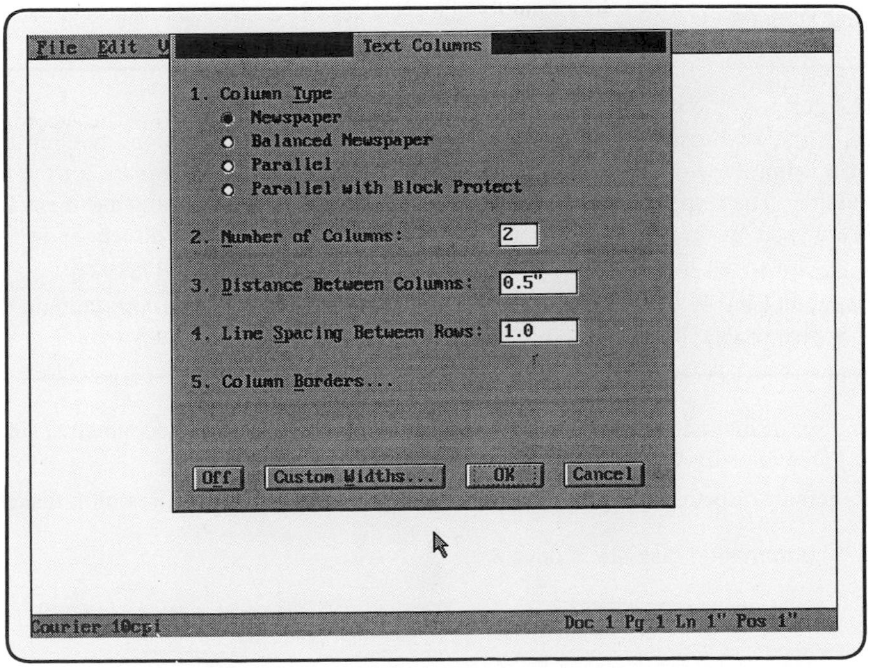

```
 File  Edit  V              Text Columns

      1. Column Type
         ● Newspaper
         ○ Balanced Newspaper
         ○ Parallel
         ○ Parallel with Block Protect

      2. Number of Columns:        [2 ]

      3. Distance Between Columns:  [0.5"]

      4. Line Spacing Between Rows: [1.0 ]

      5. Column Borders...


         [Off]  [Custom Widths...]  [  OK  ]  [Cancel]

                            ▶

 Courier 10cpi                      Doc 1 Pg 1 Ln 1" Pos 1"
```

Exiting Menus

To leave the menus, press ESC or click on the Cancel command button.

To exit the Layout menu:

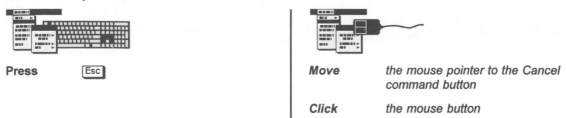

Press   Esc

Move   *the mouse pointer to the Cancel*
                  command button

Click   *the mouse button*

■ CHANGING THE DEFAULT DIRECTORY

A **directory** is a file that holds the names of a group of files. It helps you group your files to keep them organized. A directory name can have up to eight characters. The name should include only letters and numbers. Do not use special characters such as $, or %, and do not include spaces in a directory name. You may enter the alphabetic characters in a directory name using lowercase and uppercase letters. You can organize your directories and files with the File Manager feature. This feature is discussed in Chapter 28.

All of the material you prepare with WordPerfect 6.0 is saved on document files. Each time you start WordPerfect 6.0, the computer selects a directory for saving and opening document files. This directory is called the **default directory**.

You can determine which directory is the default by pressing SHIFT+F1 and choosing the Location of Files option or by using the File, Setup, Location of Files command sequence. The directory listed in the Documents text box is the current default directory. WordPerfect 6.0 automatically creates a subdirectory called "WPDOCS".   Once you change the default directory, WordPerfect 6.0 will refer to that directory until you change it again.

In This Book

The use of the keyboard function keys and the use of the menus with and without a mouse are shown using three columns. The directions in the left or first column are for the function key method. They appear in normal type. The instructions for using the menus with a keyboard appear in the second column. They appear in italics. The directions in the third column are for using the menus with a mouse. They appear in normal type.

If a command cannot be performed using one of the three methods, the column for that method appears empty.

In the following set of instructions, if you are using a hard disk to store your documents, simply substitute the hard drive letter (usually C:) in place of A:.

To change the default directory to drive A so you can save your document files on a diskette:

Insert   a formatted diskette in drive A

Many options are available under the Setup command. To access the Setup command:

Press	Shift + F1	**Press and hold**	Alt	**Move**	the mouse pointer to the File menu
Press	5 or L for Location of Files	**Press**	F for File	**Click**	the mouse button
		Press	T for Setup	**Move**	the mouse pointer to the Setup option
		Press	L for Location of Files	**Click**	the mouse button
				Move	the mouse button to the Location of Files option
				Click	the mouse button

The Location of Files dialog box appears on the screen. Your screen should look like Figure 1-4.

Figure 1-4

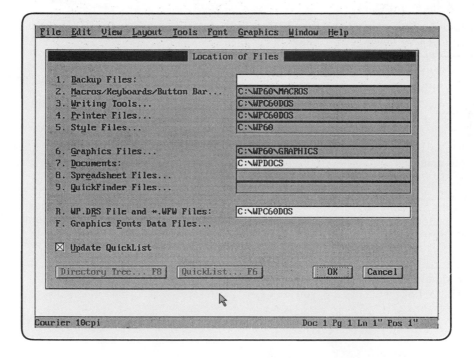

A **dialog box** provides options within a command. If a menu command is followed by an ellipsis (...), that command will provide a dialog box.   Dialog boxes often contain option buttons, check boxes, list boxes, text boxes, and command buttons.

Option buttons are round buttons. Whenever these round buttons appear in a dialog box, only one can be active. You can select the appropriate option button by pressing the underlined letter associated with that option or by clicking on the option button.

Check boxes are small square boxes in which you can check or place an X. In Figure 1-4, a check box appears in the lower left corner. If a check box contains an X, then that feature is on or active. If the check box is blank, then that feature is off or inactive. To activate a check box, press the underlined letter associated with that check box until an X appears or click on the box until an X appears.

List boxes provide a list of names from which you can make a selection. Sometimes you cannot see the entire list. If you cannot see the entire list, scroll bars appear next to the list for you to view the remaining options. To select an item from a list box using the keyboard, press the underlined letter associated with the list box, then press arrow keys to select the proper item. To select an item from a list box using the mouse, click on the item in the list box.

Text boxes allow you to type an option in them. For example, in Figure 1-4 the Documents text box allows you to type the directory for document files. To select the text box, press the underlined letter associated with the text box or move the mouse pointer to the text box option and click the mouse button.

Command buttons are rectangular buttons. Common command buttons are the OK and Cancel buttons, both of which are shown in Figure 1-4. To select a command button with the keyboard, press the TAB key until the desired command button has a blue outline. Then press the ENTER key. You could also click the command button with the mouse.

To change the location where files are being stored:

Press	7 or D to select the Documents text box	*Type*	*7 or D to select the Documents text box*	**Move**	the mouse pointer to the Documents option
Type	A:\WPDOCS	*Type*	*A:\WPDOCS*	**Click**	the mouse button
				Type	A:\WPDOCS

To accept the name:

Press	[←Enter] to select the OK command button	*Press*	*[←Enter] to select the OK command button*	**Move**	the mouse pointer to the OK command button
				Click	the mouse button

Your screen should now look like Figure 1-5.

Figure 1-5

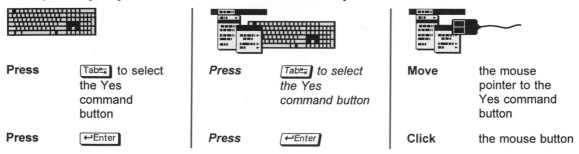

When you are prompted whether or not to create the directory "A:\WPDOCS":

Press	Tab⇥ to select the Yes command button	*Press*	*Tab⇥ to select the Yes command button*	**Move**	the mouse pointer to the Yes command button
Press	↵Enter	*Press*	↵Enter	**Click**	the mouse button

You have created a directory named "WPDOCS" on the diskette in the A drive. You may store your document files on the diskette using this directory. These same steps can be applied when you are creating a default directory on the hard disk (usually the C drive).

If you are using keyboard commands, to close the Location of Files dialog box and the Setup dialog box:

Press   ↵Enter twice

■ EXITING WORDPERFECT 6.0

When you finish using WordPerfect 6.0, you need to exit the software.

To exit WordPerfect 6.0:

Press	F7	*Press and hold*	*Alt*	**Move**	the mouse pointer to the File menu
Press	N to select the No command button	*Press*	*F for File*	**Click**	the mouse button
Press	Y to select the Yes command button	*Press*	*E for Exit*	**Move**	the mouse pointer to the Exit option
		Press	*Tab to select the No command button*	**Click**	the mouse button
		Press	*←Enter*	**Move**	the mouse button to the No command button
		Press	*Tab to select the Yes command button*	**Click**	the mouse button
		Press	*←Enter*	**Move**	the mouse button to the Yes command button
				Click	the mouse button

Your screen should return to a DOS prompt.

EXERCISE 1

INSTRUCTIONS: Define the following concepts:

1.   Cursor _____

_____

2.   Function keys _____

_____

3.   Status bar _____

_____

4.   Mouse pointer _____

_____

5.   Template _____

_____

6.   Default directory _____

_____

7.   Menus _____

_____

EXERCISE 2

INSTRUCTIONS:		Circle T if the statement is true and F if the statement is false.
T	F	1. The blinking vertical bar on the screen is the cursor.
T	F	2. The status bar appears at the bottom of the screen. It shows the font you are using, the current page number, and the vertical position of the cursor.
T	F	3. A template is a diagram of the function keys and their operations.
T	F	4. **Black** commands are issued by pressing the SHIFT key and then pressing the corresponding function key.
T	F	5. **Green** commands are issued by pressing only the function key.
T	F	6. The vertical scroll bar permits you to view different parts of the document.
T	F	7. A menu can be accessed with a mouse or the keyboard.
T	F	8. The names for a group of files can be stored in a special location called a directory.
T	F	9. A dialog box usually appears when any menu command or function key is chosen.

EXERCISE 3

INSTRUCTIONS: Identify the circled items on Figure 1-6.

Figure 1-6

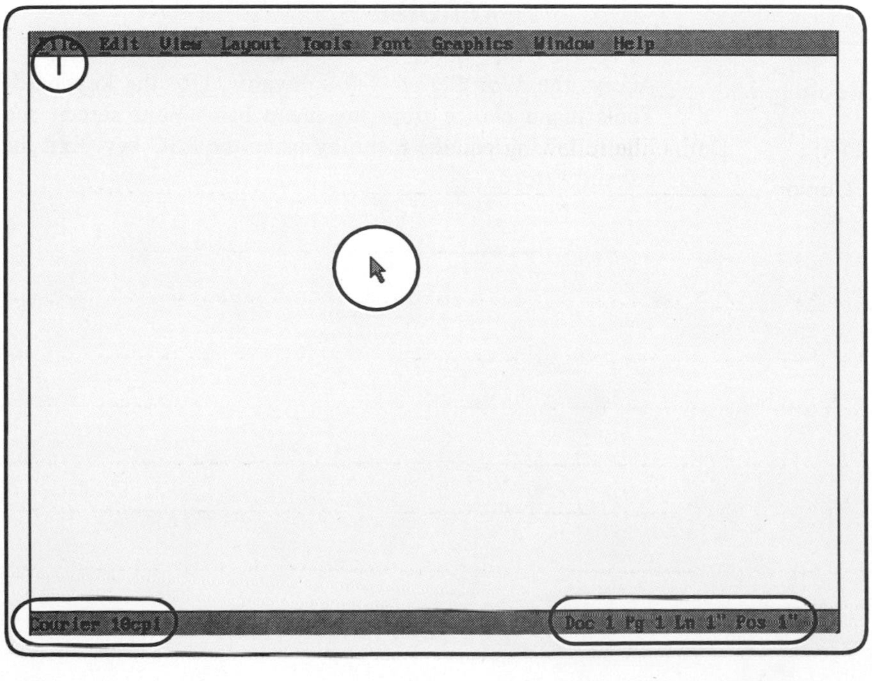

EXERCISE 4

INSTRUCTIONS: Access the WordPerfect 6.0 software. Use the mouse to access the Tools menu choice from the menu bar. Your screen should look like Figure 1-7. Close the menu by clicking in the document area. Exit the WordPerfect 6.0 software.

Figure 1-7

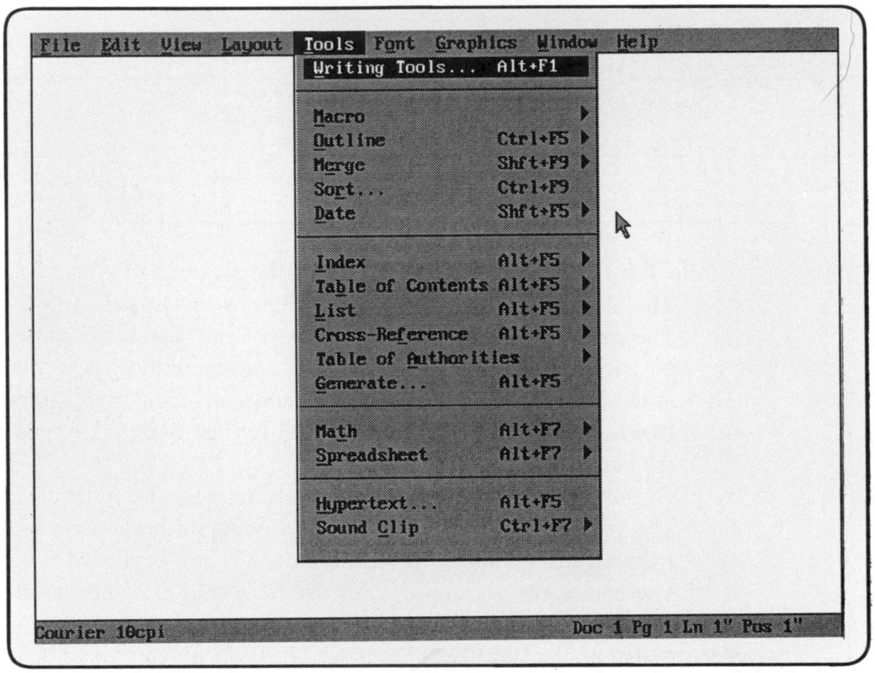

EXERCISE 5

INSTRUCTIONS: Access the WordPerfect 6.0 software. Use the keyboard to access the Tools menu choice from the menu bar. Your screen should look like Figure 1-7. Close the menu by using the ESC key. Exit the WordPerfect 6.0 software.

EXERCISE 6

INSTRUCTIONS: Access the WordPerfect 6.0 software. Use the mouse to access the Size/Position option from the Font menu appearing on the menu bar. Your screen should look like Figure 1-8. Close the menu by clicking in the document area. Exit the WordPerfect 6.0 software.

Figure 1-8

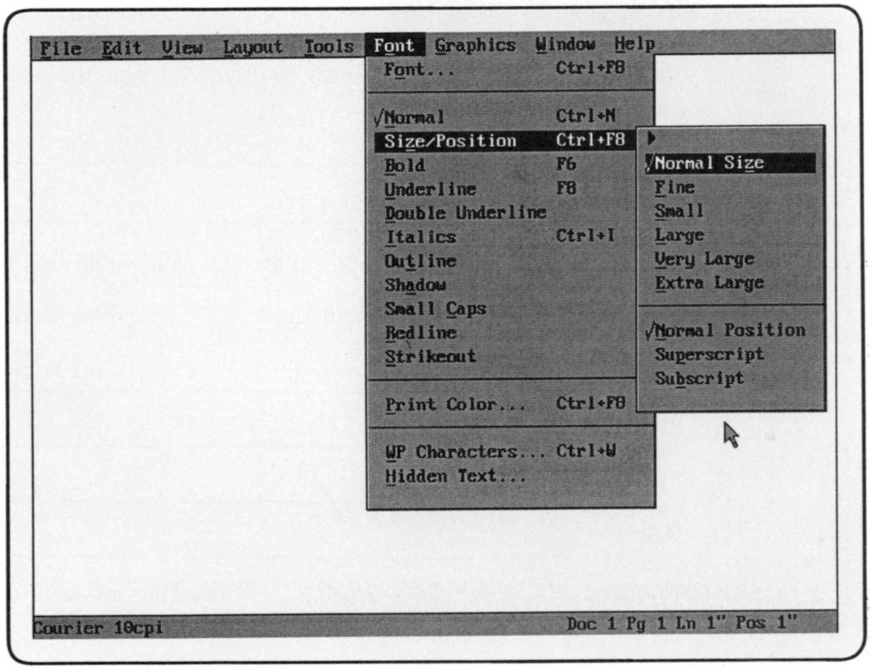

EXERCISE 7

INSTRUCTIONS: Access the WordPerfect 6.0 software. Use the keyboard to access the Size/Position option from the Font menu appearing on the menu bar. Your screen should look like Figure 1-8. Close the menu by using the ESC key. Exit the WordPerfect 6.0 software.

EXERCISE 8

INSTRUCTIONS: Access the WordPerfect 6.0 software. Create a new default directory named "WPLETTER" on a floppy diskette in drive A. Exit the WordPerfect 6.0 software.

EXERCISE 9

INSTRUCTIONS: Access the WordPerfect 6.0 software. Create a new default directory named "WPREPORT" on the floppy disk drive. Exit the WordPerfect 6.0 software.

EXERCISE 10

INSTRUCTIONS: Access the WordPerfect 6.0 software. Create a new default directory named "WPMEMOS" on a floppy diskette in drive A. Exit the WordPerfect 6.0 software.

EXERCISE 11

INSTRUCTIONS: Use the template and the menus to identify where you would find the following:

	Menu Used	Function Key Used
A. Setup	_____	_____
B. Print/Fax	_____	_____
C. Reveal Codes	_____	_____
D. Help	_____	_____
E. Exit	_____	_____

EXERCISE 12

INSTRUCTIONS: Use the template to identify which keys you would use to implement the following:

	Function Key
A. Date	_____
B. Font	_____
C. Speller	_____
D. Format	_____

CHAPTER TWO

QUICK START FOR WORDPERFECT 6.0

OBJECTIVES

In this chapter, you will learn to:
- Create a document
- Edit a document
- Save a document
- Print a document
- Close the WordPerfect 6.0 document
- Open an existing document
- Exit WordPerfect 6.0

■ CHAPTER OVERVIEW

When you create a document using WordPerfect 6.0, you will probably go through the following steps:

1. Access the WordPerfect 6.0 software
2. Create the document by keying in the material
3. Make modifications or changes to the document
4. Save the document in a file on a disk
5. Print the document

In other situations, you might open an existing document from a disk and make changes to it on your screen. After completing the changes, you save the document again. You might also print it.

When you are finished using one document, you will probably choose to close the document before you start working on another document. You must exit the WordPerfect 6.0 software when you are completely finished.

In this chapter, you are given a quick overview of the processes of creating, editing, printing, and saving a document. You are also introduced to the process of closing a WordPerfect 6.0 document. You will then open an existing document, make some changes, and save the document again. The procedure for exiting WordPerfect 6.0 is also presented.

■ CREATING A SIMPLE DOCUMENT

Access the WordPerfect 6.0 software on your computer.

In this exercise you will type a short paragraph. As you type, the text will be displayed on the monitor screen and will reside in the memory of your computer. If you make a typing error, press BACKSPACE to delete the error and then enter the characters again. (You will learn other methods for correcting errors later.)

Word Wrap

You can type without worrying about how much text fits on a line. As you type, words automatically wrap to the next line. Do not press ENTER at the end of each line. Press ENTER only to create a blank line, to end a paragraph, or to end a short line.

Type the paragraph displayed in Figure 2-1 including the errors. Remember, do not press ENTER at the end of each line. You will make some needed changes in the next section. Your text may not appear exactly like the text in Figure 2.1.

Figure 2-1

```
With WordPerfect, you do not have too worry about pressing
enter the end of each line.  WordPerfect decides how much text
can fit on a line.  As you type, words automatically wrap to
the next line.
```

■ EDITING A DOCUMENT

After you complete the process of creating a document, you may need to edit the document. In the paragraph you typed, the word "at" needs to be inserted in the first sentence. Also, the second letter "o" in the word "too" on the first line needs to be deleted.

To edit the first sentence:

Press	⬆ and ⬅ to move the cursor before the "t" in "the" in the first sentence	**Press**	*⬆ and ⬅ to move the cursor before the "t" in "the" in the first sentence*	**Move**	the mouse pointer before the "t" in "the" in the first sentence
				Click	the mouse button

The top part of your screen should look like Figure 2-2.

Figure 2-2

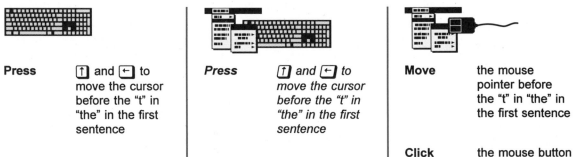

```
File  Edit  View  Layout  Tools  Font  Graphics  Window  Help
With WordPerfect, you do not have too worry about pressing enter
the end of each line.  WordPerfect decides how much text can fit
on a line.  As you type, words automatically wrap to the next
line.
```

To insert the word "at":

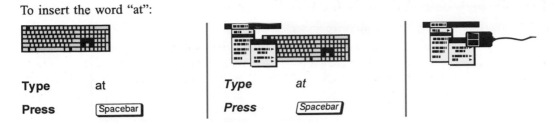

| **Type** | at | **Type** | at |
| **Press** | Spacebar | **Press** | Spacebar |

The top part of your screen should look like Figure 2-3.

Figure 2-3

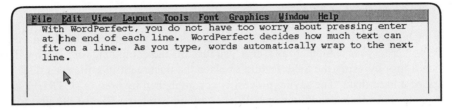

```
File  Edit  View  Layout  Tools  Font  Graphics  Window  Help
With WordPerfect, you do not have too worry about pressing enter
at the end of each line.  WordPerfect decides how much text can
fit on a line.  As you type, words automatically wrap to the next
line.
```

To delete the second "o" in the word "too" on the first line:

| **Press** | ↑ and → to move the cursor before the second "o" in the word "too" on the first line | **Press** | *↑ and → to move the cursor before the second "o" in the word "too" on the first line* | **Move** | the mouse pointer before the second "o" in the word "too" on the first line |
| | | | | **Click** | the mouse button |

The top part of your screen should look like Figure 2-4.

Figure 2-4

```
File  Edit  View  Layout  Tools  Font  Graphics  Window  Help
With WordPerfect, you do not have too worry about pressing enter
at the end of each line.  WordPerfect decides how much text can
fit on a line.  As you type, words automatically wrap to the next
line.
```

| **Press** | Delete | **Press** | Delete | Press | Delete |

An alternative for correcting the spelling of "too":

Move	*the cursor after the second "o" in "too"*	**Move**	*the cursor after the second "o" in "too"*	**Move**	the mouse pointer after the second "o" in "too"
Press	←Backspace	**Press**	←Backspace	**Click**	the mouse button
				Press	←Backspace

No matter which method you used, the top part of your screen should look like Figure 2-5.

Figure 2-5

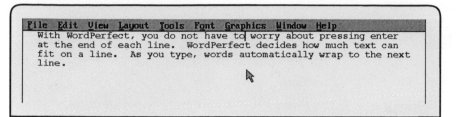

Additional editing features are presented in Chapters 3 and 4.

■ SAVING A DOCUMENT

While creating or editing a document, any changes you make are stored temporarily in your computer's memory. If the power to your computer fails, or if you turn off the computer, your work will be lost. You can prevent such a loss by using the Save feature to place the document in a file on a disk. The disk can be a floppy disk or a hard disk. The saving process is accomplished by pressing CTRL+F12 or F10 or by selecting Save or Save As from the File menu. When you are naming a file for the first time, it does not matter whether you choose Save or Save As. Regardless of which you choose, the Save Document 1 dialog box will appear on your screen. Once you have specified the default directory for saving your documents, you will type the name of the document in the Filename text box. A document name can have up to eight characters. Use only letters and numbers in a filename. Do not include special characters such as $, or @.

As you work, it is a good idea to save the document every 10 to 15 minutes. The CTRL+F12 or File Save feature allows you to save a previously named document without losing your place on the screen, and then to continue creating or editing the document. Once a file has a name, the only time you will use the F10 or File Save As choice is when you wish to change the filename or change its location. For simply saving your work periodically, it is faster to use the Save choice. No dialog box will appear and your file is quickly saved with its original filename in its previous location.

Since you have not saved this document yet, use F10 or the File Save As command to save the document using the filename "PRACTICE":

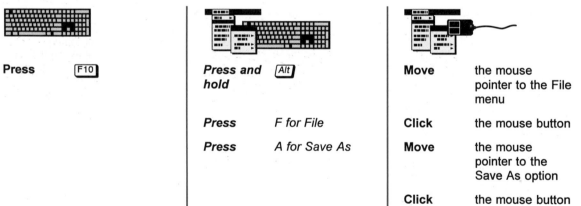

Press	F10	**Press and hold**	Alt	**Move**	the mouse pointer to the File menu
		Press	F for File	**Click**	the mouse button
		Press	A for Save As	**Move**	the mouse pointer to the Save As option
				Click	the mouse button

The Save Document 1 dialog box appears. Your screen should look like Figure 2-6.

Figure 2-6

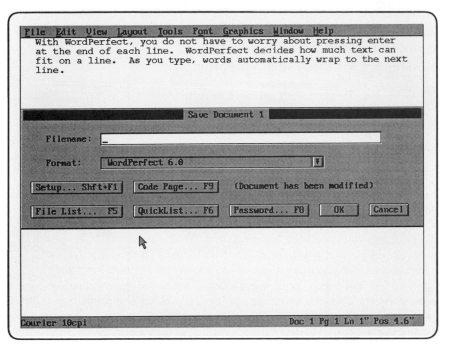

To save the file with the name "PRACTICE":

 **Type**	PRACTICE	 *Type*	*PRACTICE*	 **Type**	PRACTICE

When you type a filename in WordPerfect 6.0, you may use upper or lowercase.

To accept the filename and return to your document:

Press	⏎Enter to select the OK command button	*Press*	*⏎Enter to select the OK command button*	**Move**	the mouse pointer to the OK command button
				Click	the mouse button

The bottom part of your screen should look like Figure 2-7.

Figure 2-7

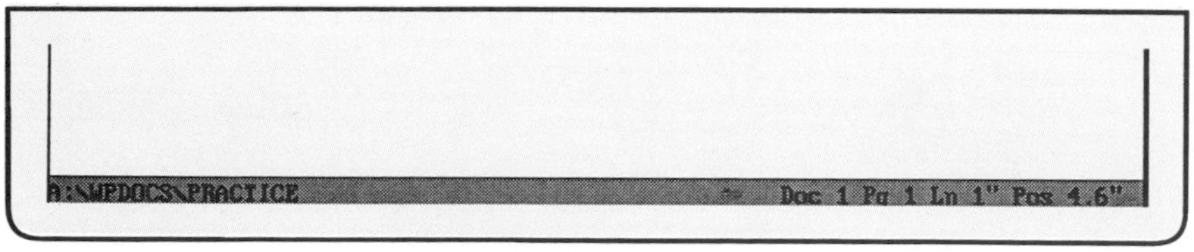

A:\WPDOCS\PRACTICE   Doc 1 Pg 1 Ln 1" Pos 4.6"

Notice that the document name appears in the status bar.

If you are using a floppy diskette and are saving to the directory created in Chapter 1, you will have "A:\WPDOCS\PRACTICE" on the status bar. If you are using a hard disk, "A:" will be replaced by "C:".

■ PREVIEWING AND PRINTING A DOCUMENT

After you create a document, you often print it. Before printing a document, you can view it to see what it will look like when it is printed.

To view the document as it will appear when you print it:

Press	Shift + F7	***Press and hold***	*Alt*	**Move**	the mouse pointer to the File menu
Press	7 or V for Print Preview	***Press***	*F for File*	**Click**	the mouse button
		Press	*V for Print Preview*	**Move**	the mouse pointer to the Print Preview option
				Click	the mouse button

To view your document at 100%:

Press	V for View	***Press***	*V for View*	**Move**	the mouse pointer to the Zoom 100% button on the Button Bar
Press	1 or ↵Enter to select 100% View	***Press***	*1 or ↵Enter to select 100% View*	**Click**	the mouse button

A preview of the document appears on the screen. Your screen should look like Figure 2-8.

Figure 2-8

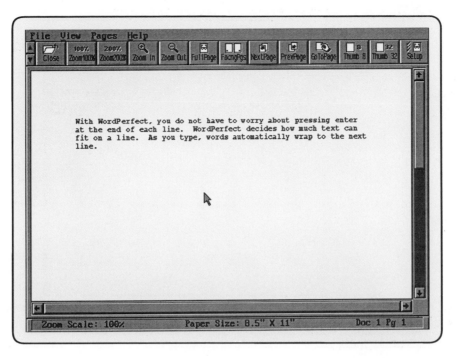

To return to your document:

Press   `F7`

Press   F for File

Press   C for Close

Move   the mouse pointer to the Close button on the Button Bar

Click   the mouse button

When you have finished viewing the document, you can then print it. You do not have to view the document before printing it. However, it is a good idea to see how the document appears before you print it.

To print the entire "PRACTICE" document:

Press   `Shift`+`F7`

Press and hold   `Alt`

Press   F for File

Press   P for Print/Fax

Move   the mouse pointer to the File menu

Click   the mouse button

Move   the mouse pointer to the Print/Fax option

Click   the mouse button

The Print/Fax dialog box should appear on your screen. Your screen should look like Figure 2-9.

Figure 2-9

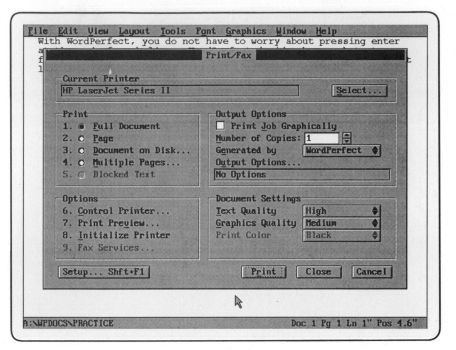

To print the document:

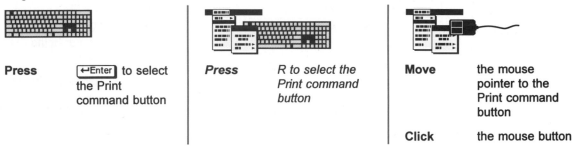

| **Press** | ⌐←Enter⌐ to select the Print command button | *Press* | *R to select the Print command button* | **Move** | the mouse pointer to the Print command button |
| | | | | **Click** | the mouse button |

Additional printing features are presented in Chapter 10.

■ CLOSING A DOCUMENT

When you have finished working on a document, you should save it. You may also choose to close the document before starting to work on another document. You can close a document by pressing F7 or by selecting Close from the File menu.

To close the document and clear the screen:

| **Press** | ⌐F7⌐ | *Press and hold* | ⌐Alt⌐ | **Move** | the mouse pointer to the File menu |
| **Press** | N for No | *Press* | *F for File* | **Click** | the mouse pointer |

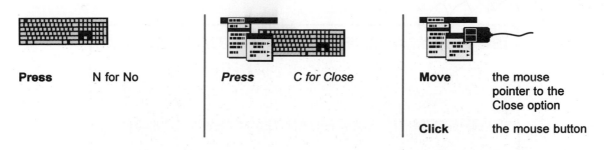

Press	N for No	*Press*	*C for Close*	**Move**	the mouse pointer to the Close option
				Click	the mouse button

If changes to the document had not been saved, you would be prompted with a dialog box to save the document before closing it.

■ OPENING A DOCUMENT

The documents you create in WordPerfect 6.0 are saved in files. When you want to edit a document, you need to open a copy of the file from a disk and place it in the memory of your computer. A copy of the file appears on the computer screen.

The document is then active in your computer's memory and you can edit it. However, the changes you make will affect only the document on the screen. They will not be recorded on the disk until you save them.

You can open a document from any directory. If the document is stored in the current directory, just enter the document name. If the document is stored in a different directory, you must include the drive and directory name before the document name.

To open your "PRACTICE" document:

Press	Shift + F10	*Press and hold*	*Alt*	**Move**	the mouse pointer to the File menu
		Press	*F for File*	**Click**	the mouse button
		Press	*O for Open*	**Move**	the mouse pointer to the Open option
				Click	the mouse button

The Open Document dialog box appears. Your screen should look like Figure 2-10.

Figure 2-10

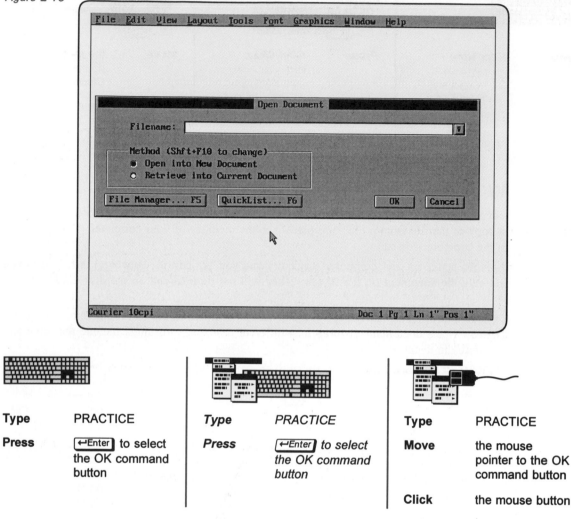

Type	PRACTICE	***Type***	*PRACTICE*	**Type**	PRACTICE
Press	`←Enter` to select the OK command button	***Press***	*`←Enter` to select the OK command button*	**Move**	the mouse pointer to the OK command button
				Click	the mouse button

Your screen should look like Figure 2-11.

Figure 2-11

> File Edit View Layout Tools Font Graphics Window Help
> With WordPerfect, you do not have to worry about pressing enter
> at the end of each line. WordPerfect decides how much text can
> fit on a line. As you type, words automatically wrap to the next
> line.

To insert additional text:

Press	`Home`, `Home`, `↓` to move the cursor to the end of the document	***Move***	*the cursor to the end of the document*	**Move**	the mouse pointer to the right of the last character in the document
Press	`←Enter` twice	***Press***	*`←Enter` twice*	**Click**	the mouse button

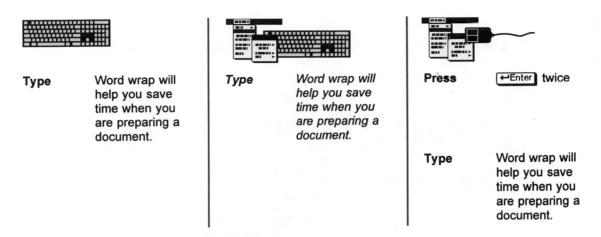

Type	Word wrap will help you save time when you are preparing a document.	*Type*	*Word wrap will help you save time when you are preparing a document.*	**Press**	⏎Enter twice
				Type	Word wrap will help you save time when you are preparing a document.

When you finish, your screen should look like Figure 2-12.

Figure 2-12

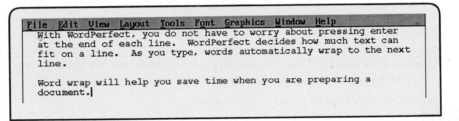

After changing a document, you usually save it again using the same name for the document file. Since you have already named this file, you can use the CTRL+F12 keys or the File Save command. The File Save command saves the file under the same name and automatically replaces the old file.

To save the document with the same name:

Press	Ctrl + F12	***Press and hold***	*Alt*	**Move**	the mouse pointer to the File menu
		Press	*F for File*	**Click**	the mouse button
		Press	*S for Save*	**Move**	the mouse pointer to the Save option
				Click	the mouse button

■ EXITING WORDPERFECT 6.0

When you finish using WordPerfect 6.0, you will need to exit the software.

To exit WordPerfect 6.0:

Press	F7

Press and hold	Alt
Press	*F for File*
Press	*E for Exit*

Move	the mouse pointer to the File menu
Click	the mouse button
Move	the mouse pointer to the Exit option
Click	the mouse button

Before ending your use of the software, WordPerfect gives you a chance to save your current document. This feature can be very helpful if you have made some changes to your document and have not saved them, before entering your request to exit WordPerfect. In this example, we have already saved our last changes and therefore do not need to save them again.

To show the present document does not need to be saved:

Press	N for No

Press	*N for No*

Move	the mouse pointer to No
Click	the mouse button

To specify that you want to exit WordPerfect:

Press	Y for Yes

Press	*Y for Yes*

Move	the mouse pointer to Yes
Click	the mouse button

EXERCISE 1

INSTRUCTIONS: Define the following concepts:

1.   Insert _____

_____

2.   Delete _____

_____

3.   Word wrap _____

_____

4.   Save As feature _____

_____

5.   Exit feature _____

_____

6.   Save feature _____

_____

7.   Open feature _____

_____

8.   Print/Fax feature _____

_____

9.   Close feature _____

_____

EXERCISE 2

INSTRUCTIONS: Circle T if the statement is true and F if the statement is false.

T   F   1.   In WordPerfect 6.0, you do not need to press ENTER at the end of each line of a paragraph.

T   F   2.   When you are creating or editing a document, any changes you make are stored temporarily in your computer's memory.

T   F   3.   The Save feature saves a document and clears the screen.

T   F   4.   You can use letters, numbers, $, and % in a filename.

T   F   5.   When only a filename is typed, it is automatically saved in your default directory.

T   F   6.   When you finish typing a document, and then print it, the document is automatically saved.

T   F   7.   You must preview a document before printing it.

T   F   8.   When you want to edit a document, you need to open a copy of the file from a disk and place it in the memory of your computer so it will appear on your screen.

T   F   9.   You can open a document only if it is found in the default directory.

T   F   10.   When you finish using WordPerfect 6.0, you need to exit from the software.

In The Remaining Chapters of This Book

In the exercises, you are sometimes instructed to create a document. Your text may word wrap differently from the text in the illustration. Do not press ENTER at the end of a line of text to force it to wrap like the exercise illustration.

EXERCISE 3

INSTRUCTIONS:
1. Create the following document.
2. Save the document in a file using the name "CH02EX03".
3. Use the Print Preview feature to see how the document will appear when you print it.
4. Print the document.
5. Close the document.

> Word processing provides an individual with an effective and efficient means of preparing documents. You can create documents and quickly make needed changes prior to printing the document. The software allows your to save the document in a file for later use.

EXERCISE 4

INSTRUCTIONS:
1. Open the file "CH02EX03".
2. Insert the word "**software**" on the first line between "**processing**" and "**provides**".
3. Delete the "**r**" in "**your**" in the last sentence.
4. Save the document with the same name.
5. Print the document.
6. Close the document.

EXERCISE 5

INSTRUCTIONS:
1. Create the following document.
2. Save the document in a file using the name "CH02EX05".
3. Use the Print Preview feature to see how the document will appear when you print it.
4. Print the document.
5. Close the document.

> Thank you very much for attending our recent training class on WordPerfect 6.0 for DOS. We hope you enjoyed the class and are successfully using the software in your work.
>
> Our company also provides training on products such as Lotus 1-2-3, Microsoft Excel, dBASE IV, and Paradox. A brochure is enclosed that describes these courses and includes our class schedule for the next months. We look forward too having you attend more of our classes.

EXERCISE 6

INSTRUCTIONS:

1. Open the file "CH02EX05".

2. Insert the word **"three"** in the second sentence of the second paragraph between **"next"** and **"months"**.

3. Delete the extra "**o**" in "**too**" in the third sentence of the second paragraph.

4. Save the document with the same name.

5. Print the document.

6. Close the document.

EXERCISE 7

INSTRUCTIONS:

1. Create the following document.

2. Save the document in a file using the name "CH02EX07".

3. Use the Print Preview feature to see how the document will appear when you print it.

4. Print the document.

5. Close the document.

```
The World Economic Summit was held in Houston, Texas.  Rice
University was the meeting site for the chiefs of state from the
industrialized nations of the worlds.  The conference lasted three
days.

During the conference, the Rice University campus was closed to the
public.  Professors and students were not allowed on the campus
during the formal sessions.  Many of the buildings on the campus were
used as temporary offices for the delegations from the various
countries.
```

EXERCISE 8

INSTRUCTIONS:

1. Open the file "CH02EX07".

2. Insert the words **"last summer"** at the end of the first sentence of paragraph one.

3. Delete the "**s**" in "**worlds**" in the second sentence of the first paragraph.

4. Save the document with the same name.

5. Print the document.

6. Close the document.

EXERCISE 9

INSTRUCTIONS:

1. Create the following document.
2. Save the document in a file using the name "CH02EX09".
3. Use the Print Preview feature to see how the document will appear when you print it.
4. Print the document.
5. Close the document.

> Each year on July 4, people in the United States celebrate the Independence Day holiday. Many individuals have picnics with their friends. Often people watch fireworks displays. In some cases, people purchase their own fireworks and create their own shows. Parades are held in many communities.
>
> Sometimes people may take advantage of the day off to travel to the beach for a day of sun and swimming. Other individuals may travel to a relative's house. Family celebrations may include games, fireworks, and preparation of special foods.

EXERCISE 10

INSTRUCTIONS:

1. Create the following document.
2. Save the document in a file using the name "CH02EX10".
3. Print the document.
4. Close the document.

> I need information on the total number of graduates of full-time students attending community colleges in the states of Illinois, Florida, and California.
>
> This information can probably be obtained from the U.S. Department of Education.
>
> Tuition and fees from these students affect the taxes of the above states. Can you find how it affects your state.

EXERCISE 11

INSTRUCTIONS:

1. Open the file "CH02EX10".
2. In the first line, delete "**I need**" and replace with "**Find**".
3. In the first sentence, delete the words "**graduates of**".
4. Also, in the first sentence insert "**and part-time**" after the words "**full-time**".
5. In the second paragraph delete the word "**probably**".
6. In the third paragraph, delete "**Tuition and fees from**" and capitalize the "**T**" in the word "**these**".
7. At the end of the third paragraph, change the period ("**.**") to a question mark ("**?**").
8. Save the document in a file using the name "CH02EX11".
9. Close the document.

EXERCISE 12

INSTRUCTIONS:

1. Create the following document.
2. Save the document in a file using the name "CH02EX12".
3. Preview the document, then print it.
4. Close this document.
5. Open the file "CH02EX12".
6. In the first sentence after the word "**their**" insert the words "**two-months**" to the sentence.
7. In the second sentence of the first paragraph, delete the words "**supervised by**" and replace them with the phrase "**under the supervision of**".
8. In the third sentence of the first paragraph, change the word "**learn**" to "**learned**".
9. Also in the third sentence of the first paragraph, insert "**we follow**" after the word "**procedures**" (place the cursor before the comma and type the insert).
10. At the end of the second paragraph, insert two spaces after the period and insert the following text: "**These trainees are very proficient in basic WordPerfect 6.0.**"
11. After making the changes, save the document with the same name.
12. Preview the document, then print it.
13. Close the document.

On September 1, four trainees will have finished their training and
will be ready to begin working on the regular staff. They have been
supervised by T. James Crawford, our training director. Each person
has learn the procedures, our company policies, and their rights and
responsibilities as a member of our company.

These people may be placed as soon as openings develop. The
trainees are Sue Schneider, Betty Zilkowski, Ryan Bradley, and Scott
Roberts.

CHAPTER THREE

CREATING AND EDITING A DOCUMENT

OBJECTIVES

In this chapter, you will learn to:

- Use the mouse and arrow keys for cursor movement
- Prepare a document
- Insert the current date
- Use the Zoom feature
- Insert and replace text
- Use the Block feature to highlight text
- Delete and undelete text
- Use the Help feature

■ CHAPTER OVERVIEW

In the previous chapter, the basics of preparing, editing, saving, printing, and opening a document were presented. You mastered the use of these WordPerfect 6.0 activities using the function key or menu methods. The processes for creating and editing documents are discussed in more detail in this chapter. Cursor movement is explained for the keyboard and mouse methods. Methods for inserting, replacing, deleting, and undeleting text are described and illustrated. The Help feature is presented.

> **In This Book**
>
> To this point in the book, the software has been referred to as WordPerfect 6.0 or WordPerfect 6.0 for DOS. In most situations in the rest of the book, the software is simply called WordPerfect.

■ MOVEMENT TECHNIQUES

The **cursor** is the blinking vertical bar on your screen. It marks the location where text will be entered on the screen. You can use either the keyboard or a mouse to move the cursor through your document.

The cursor can move only through text or lines that already exist in your document. When you reach a point where there are no text or blank lines, the cursor stops moving.

The Keyboard Method

As you move the cursor up or down through your document, the cursor retains its current horizontal position, if possible. For example, if the cursor is at position 5 inches on one line, it stays at position 5 inches in all the lines unless they are shorter than 5 inches long, in which case the cursor moves to the right

---

In This Book

In some situations, you will be asked to press several keys in succession to move the cursor to a specific place on the screen. For example, you may be directed to move the cursor to the top of the screen by pressing the HOME key and then the UP ARROW key. This type of instruction will appear in the text as:

Press Home , ↑

If the keystrokes must be pressed simultaneously, the instructions will appear in the text as:

Press Ctrl + ↑

The following table lists the keystrokes you can use to move the cursor through the document.

Movement	Cursor Keys
Left one character	←
Right one character	→
Word left	Ctrl + ←
Word right	Ctrl + →
Left side of screen (after any formatting codes)	Home , ←
Left side of screen (before any formatting codes)	Home , Home , ←
Far right of line (even when the line extends beyond the right edge of the screen)	End , or Home , Home , Right
Up one line	↑
Down one line	↓
Top of current screen	Home , ↑
Bottom of current screen	Home , ↓
Top of previous page	Page Up
Top of next page	Page Down
Up one paragraph	Ctrl + ↑
Down one paragraph	Ctrl + ↓
Beginning of a document (after any formatting codes)	Home , Home , ↑
Beginning of a document (before any formatting codes)	Home , Home , Home , ↑
End of a document	Home , Home , ↓
Go to a specific page	Ctrl + Home , type number of desired page and press ←Enter

---

<u>User Tip</u>

WordPerfect 6.0 offers a new feature called the Bookmark. It is used to mark a position in your document so that you can quickly return to that location. When you save your document, a QuickMark is automatically placed at the position of the cursor. The benefit of this mark is that you can quickly return to the last point of editing the next time you open that document.

To manually place a QuickMark at the current position of the cursor, press ALT+F5 and 5 or B. Then press Q to select the Set QuickMark command button. If you are using the menu, you would choose Bookmark from the Edit menu and then select the Set QuickMark command button. There is also a quick keystroke method for creating a QuickMark. Press CTRL+Q and the QuickMark is placed in the document at the location of the cursor. You can see the [Bookmark] code in Reveal Codes.

You may only have one QuickMark in a document at a time. When you create a new one, the original is automatically erased. It is possible to create more than one Bookmark in a document by naming each one. For more details on this feature, consult the WordPerfect 6.0 Reference manual.

To use a QuickMark, press ALT+F5 and 5 or B. Then press I to select the Find QuickMark command button. If you are using the menu, you would choose Bookmark from the Edit menu and then select the Find QuickMark command button. The quick keystroke method for finding a QuickMark is CTRL+F.

The Mouse Method

To position the cursor using a mouse, move the mouse pointer to a specific location, then click the mouse button.

There are three basic mouse operations: clicking, double-clicking, and dragging. **Clicking** means to press the mouse button and then release it. **Double-clicking** means to press the mouse button twice quickly. **Dragging** means to press and hold down the mouse button while moving the mouse.

If you want to scroll to parts of the document that are not displayed, use the **vertical and horizontal scroll bars** to view different parts of your document. If the **vertical or horizontal scroll bars** are not visible on the screen, you may view them by selecting the View option on the menu bar and then selecting the desired scroll bar.

To view the scroll bars:

Press and hold	[Alt]	**Choose**	View
Press	V for View	**Choose**	Horizontal Scroll Bar
Press	H for Horizontal Scroll Bar	**Choose**	View
Press and hold	[Alt]	**Choose**	Vertical Scroll Bar
Press	V for View		
Press	V for Vertical Scroll Bar		

The **vertical scroll bar** appears on the right side of the screen. Use the vertical scroll bar to scroll up or down in your document.

The **horizontal scroll bar** appears above the status bar and allows you to scroll from the left side of the document to the right side of the document.

A scroll bar has two directional arrows. These arrows are separated by a gray shaded area containing a **scroll box**. The position of the scroll box represents the current position of the cursor in the document. For example, if the vertical scroll box appears in the middle of the vertical scroll bar, you are viewing the middle of your document. The appearance of the scroll box in the vertical scroll bar depends on the size of the document. If you have a blank screen, the vertical scroll box fills the entire scroll bar. Figure 3-1 illustrates the parts of the vertical scroll bar and horizontal scroll bar.

Figure 3-1

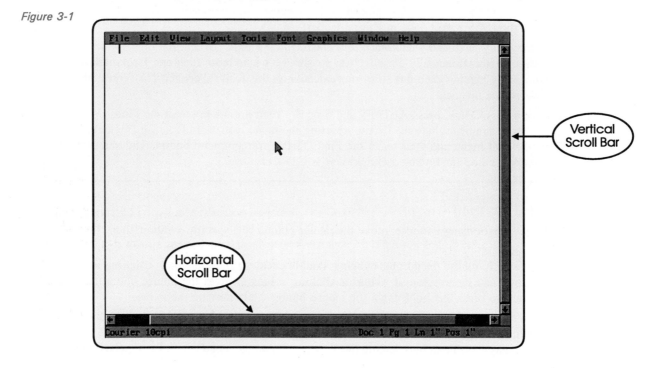

Using the scroll bar moves the position of your cursor. The following table lists the mouse techniques you can use to move the cursor.

Movement	Mouse Technique
Up one line	Click the up scroll arrow on the vertical scroll bar
Down one line	Click the down scroll arrow on the vertical scroll bar
Top of present screen	Click the gray shaded area above the vertical scroll box
Bottom of present screen	Click the gray shaded area below the vertical scroll box
Beginning of a document	Drag the vertical scroll box to the top of the vertical scroll bar
End of a document	Drag the vertical scroll box to the bottom of the vertical scroll bar

Movement	Mouse Technique
Left one character	Click the left scroll arrow on the horizontal scroll bar
Right one character	Click the right scroll arrow on the horizontal scroll bar
Left margin of document	Click the gray shaded area to the left of the horizontal scroll box
Right margin of document	Click the gray shaded area to the right of the horizontal scroll box
Left side of document	Drag the horizontal scroll box to the left side of the horizontal scroll bar
Right side of document	Drag the horizontal scroll box to the right side of the horizontal scroll bar

■ PREPARING A DOCUMENT

In This Book

Up to this point, you have been instructed to move the mouse pointer to a particular menu item and then click the mouse button. The keyboard alternative has been to press the ALT key and type the underlined letter of the desired menu item. From this point forward, you will simply be instructed to choose the desired command. The symbols representing the mouse and the keyboard are omitted from the keystroke columns in the rest of this book.

You can mix the use of the mouse, keyboard, and function key methods.

At this point, change the default directory to "A:\WPDOCS" or "C:\WPDOCS." Suppose you want to create the letter in Figure 3-2.

Figure 3-2

```
current date



Mr. Ernest Johnson
10001 Central Avenue
New York, NY 11566

Dear Mr. Johnson:

Congratulations on your new business.  I wish you many years of
success.

I would appreciate the opportunity to discuss with you how your
company could benefit from our unique solution to your financial
deadlines.

I hope to hear from you soon.

Sincerely,



Tommy Jones
```

■ INSERTING THE DATE

To begin the letter, you want to create the date. Rather than typing the date manually, you can have WordPerfect insert the date. To insert the current date as text:

Press	Shift + F5	*Select*	*Tools*	**Choose**	Tools
Press	3 or F to select the Date Format option	*Select*	*Date*	**Choose**	Date
		Select	*Format*	**Choose**	Format

The Date Formats dialog box appears. Your screen should look like Figure 3-3.

Figure 3-3

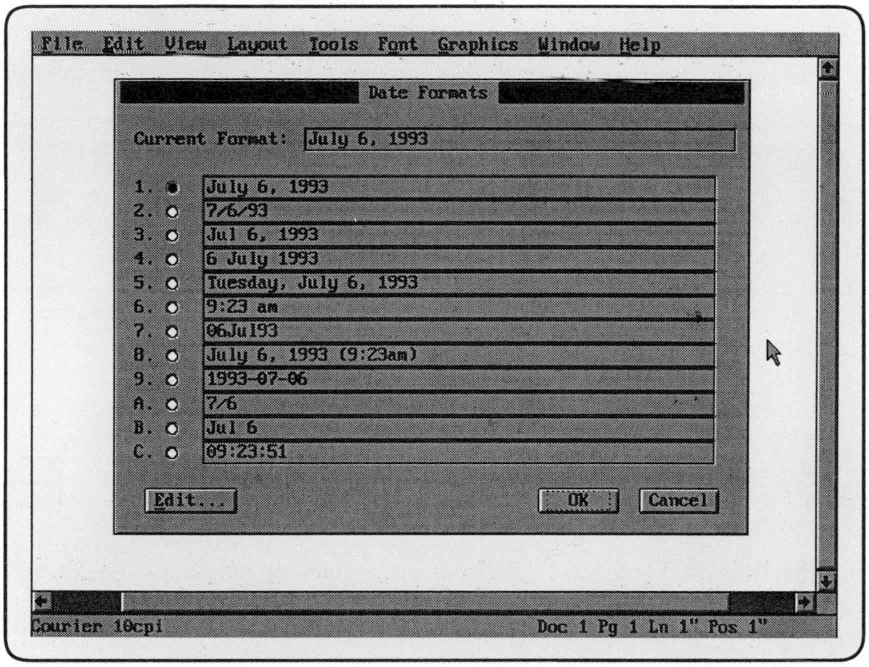

You may select one of the predefined choices or you may create your own format by selecting the Edit command button. You may include words, spaces, and punctuation to create a custom date format. The default date format appears as the first choice in the Date Formats dialog box.

To select a different format:

Press	any number from 1 to 9 or A through C to select the desired format	Press	any number from 1 to 9 or A through C to select the desired format	Choose	one of the twelve choices visible on the screen
	or		or		or
Press	E to create a customized date format	Press	E to create a customized date format	Click	the Edit command button to create a customized date format

To accept the default date format or the format you specify:

Press	⏎Enter	Press	⏎Enter	Click	the OK command button

If you do not choose a date format, WordPerfect defaults to inserting the date using the month-day-year format.

To insert the date as text:

Press	Shift + F5	Select	Tools	Choose	Tools
Press	1 or T to accept the date as text	Select	Date	Choose	Date
		Select	Text	Choose	Text

If you select the Date Code option instead of Date Text, the date on the screen appears to be the same. The difference is that with Date Code, the date is a variable and will change each time you open the document. The top part of your screen should look like Figure 3-4, except that you have a different date.

Figure 3-4

To leave three blank lines after the date:

Press	⏎Enter four times	**Press**	⏎Enter four times	**Press**	⏎Enter four times

Continue typing the letter in Figure 3-2, inserting blank lines as necessary. Save the document as "JOHNSON.LTR".

■ USING THE ZOOM FEATURE

Once a letter is typed, you may need to view it to be sure it is not too high or too low on the page. In earlier versions of WordPerfect, this was only possible in Print Preview. The appearance could not be edited in the Print Preview mode. Using a new feature in WordPerfect 6.0 called Zoom, you are permitted to view a reduced or enlarged image of the text. You may also edit the text while using the Zoom feature. Thus, in 50% Zoom the document appears miniature and you can adjust margins or line spacing to make the document appear as desired. Viewing in a mode greater than 100% enlarges the text on the screen but will not print it in the larger font. This capability can be helpful to users who are visually challenged or who are working with a very small font. The changing of margins, line spacing, and fonts is discussed in greater detail in later chapters. In this section, you will practice changing to a larger and smaller Zoom view of the document.

Select	View		**Choose**	View
Select	Zoom		**Choose**	Zoom
Select	50%		**Choose**	50%

Your screen should look like Figure 3-5.

Figure 3-5

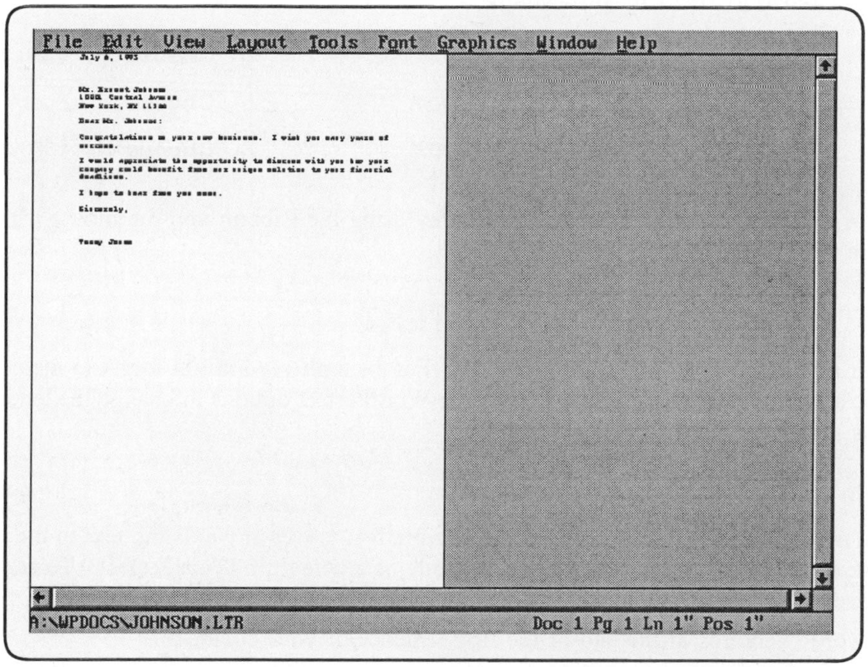

To see the document in an enlarged view:

Select	View	Choose	View
Select	Zoom	Choose	Zoom
Select	150%	Choose	150%

Your screen should look like Figure 3-6.

Figure 3-6

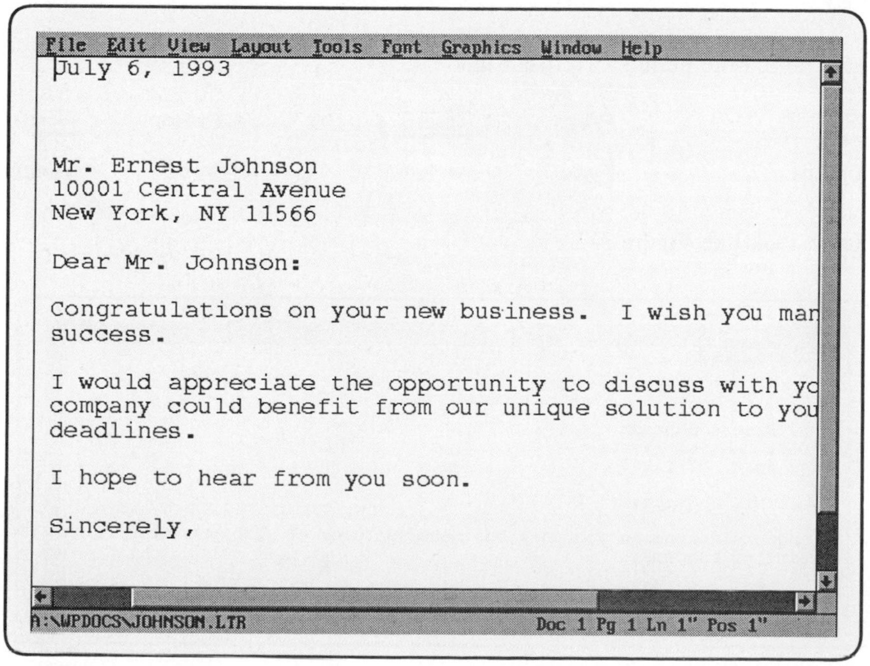

To return the document to 100% magnification:

Select	View		**Choose**	View
Select	Zoom		**Choose**	Zoom
Select	100%		**Choose**	100%

It is possible to change to a different magnification by using the Ribbon and the mouse. The Ribbon is discussed more thoroughly in Chapter 7.

■ INSERTING AND REPLACING TEXT

After you enter a document, you may need to edit it. For example, you might forget to include a word, or you might type a word incorrectly. You will now use WordPerfect options to change the letter you created in the previous section.

Insert Mode

When you add new text to an existing document, WordPerfect moves any existing text to the right to make room for the new text. This feature, called **insert mode**, is a default in WordPerfect. To add text to your document, move the cursor to the location where you want to insert text and begin typing.

To insert the word "venture" at the end of the first sentence of your document:

Move	the cursor to some character in the word "Congratulations"		*Move*	the cursor to some character in the word "Congratulations"		**Move**	the mouse pointer before the period after the word "business"
Press	`Ctrl`+`→` four times		*Press*	`Ctrl`+`→` four times		**Click**	the mouse button
Press	`→` until the cursor is before the period		*Press*	`→` until the cursor is before the period			

The cursor is now before the period. To insert the text:

Press	`Spacebar`		*Press*	`Spacebar`		**Press**	`Spacebar`
Type	venture		*Type*	venture		**Type**	venture

Your screen should look like Figure 3-7.

Figure 3-7

```
File  Edit  View  Layout  Tools  Font  Graphics  Window  Help
July 6, 1993

Mr. Ernest Johnson
10001 Central Avenue
New York, NY 11566

Dear Mr. Johnson:

Congratulations on your new business venture.  I wish you many
years of success.

I would appreciate the opportunity to discuss with you how your
company could benefit from our unique solution to your financial
```

Typeover Mode

Typeover mode allows you to write over existing text with new text. The INSERT key allows you to **toggle**–to change from Insert mode to Typeover mode and back again. To enter Typeover mode, press the INSERT key. When you are in Typeover mode, any character you type replaces the character to the right of the cursor. As long as you are in Typeover mode, the word "Typeover" appears at the left end of the status bar. When you want to return to Insert mode, press the INSERT key again.

To replace the word "Avenue" with "Parkway" in the inside address of your document:

Press	Home , Home , ↑	**Press**	Home , Home , ↑	**Move**	the mouse pointer before the "A" in "Avenue"
Press	↓ five times	**Press**	↓ five times	**Click**	the mouse button
Press	Ctrl + → twice	**Press**	Ctrl + → twice		

Your screen should look like Figure 3-8.

Figure 3-8

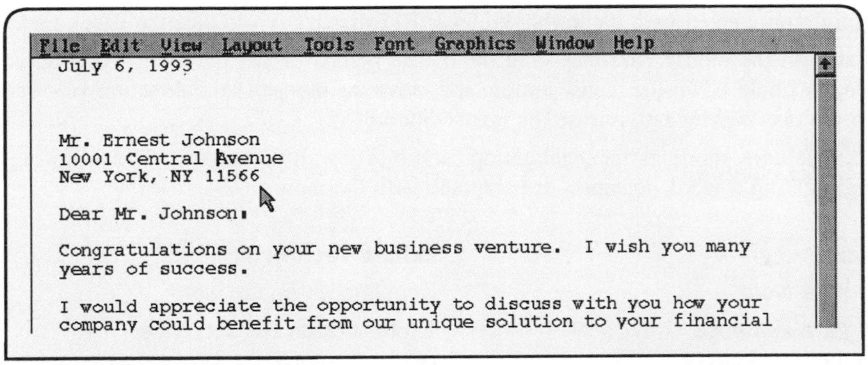

To enter Typeover mode:

Press	Insert	**Press**	Insert	**Press**	Insert
Type	Parkway	**Type**	Parkway	**Type**	Parkway

The bottom of your screen should look like Figure 3-9.

Figure 3-9

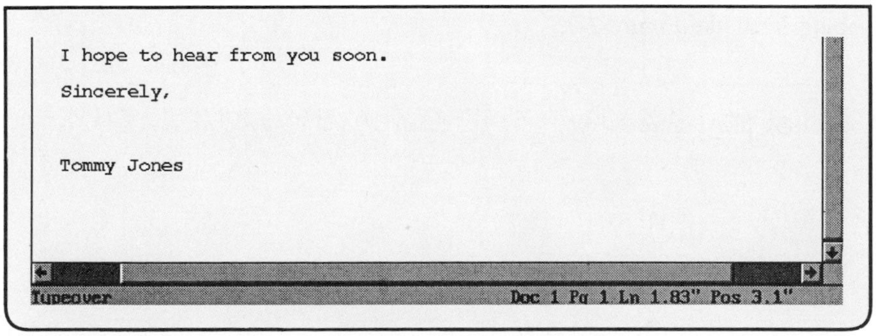

Notice that the word "Typeover" appears on the status bar, indicating you are in the Typeover mode.

To return to Insert mode:

Press   [Insert] | *Press*   [Insert] | Press   [Insert]

Notice that the word "Typeover" no longer appears on the status bar. You have returned to the default Insert mode.

■ USING THE BLOCK FEATURE

The Block feature is used to highlight text within your document. After you highlight text using the Block feature, you can apply many other WordPerfect features to the highlighted text. For example, you may want to underline all letters in a group of words. You first need to highlight the words using the Block feature. Then you can underline the words using the Underline feature available in WordPerfect. Throughout the book, you will see several examples of how to use highlighted text.

Highlighting Text with the Keyboard and the Mouse

You can highlight text from the keyboard by pressing F12 or ALT+F4 and then pressing an arrow key, text character, or punctuation character. For example, if you wanted to highlight a word, move the cursor to the beginning of the word, and press F12 or ALT+F4 to turn on the Block feature. Then press CTRL plus the RIGHT ARROW key to highlight the word.

To remove highlighting created with the keyboard, press F12 or ALT+F4 to turn the Block feature off.

To highlight text with the mouse, you may drag the mouse pointer across the text. To drag, you click at the beginning of the text, hold down the mouse button, and move the mouse in the direction you want to highlight. When you have the text highlighted, release the mouse button.

WordPerfect also includes shortcuts for highlighting certain text with the mouse. The following table lists the shortcuts for highlighting a word, sentence, or paragraph with the mouse.

Selection	Mouse Technique
Highlight a word	Double-click on the word
Highlight a sentence	Triple-click on the sentence
Highlight a paragraph	Quadruple-click on the paragraph

To remove the highlighting from the text, click anywhere inside the document area.

To practice highlighting the first paragraph of your document:

Move   the cursor before the "C" in "Congratulations" | *Move*   the cursor before the "C" in "Congratulations" | **Move**   the mouse pointer before the "C" in "Congratulations"

Click   the mouse button

Your screen should look like Figure 3-10.

Figure 3-10

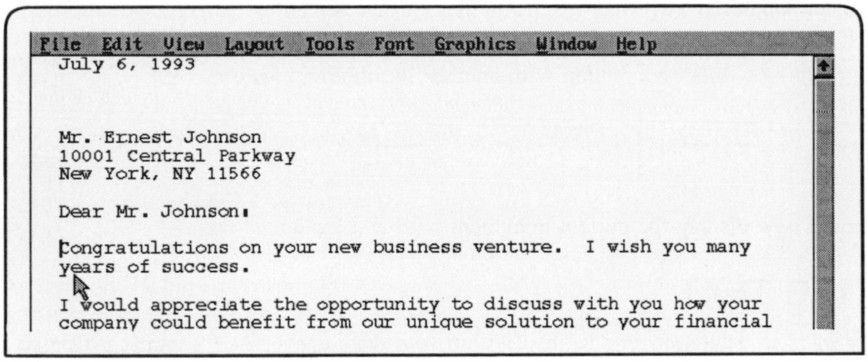

```
File  Edit  View  Layout  Tools  Font  Graphics  Window  Help
July 6, 1993

Mr. Ernest Johnson
10001 Central Parkway
New York, NY 11566

Dear Mr. Johnson:

Congratulations on your new business venture.  I wish you many
years of success.

I would appreciate the opportunity to discuss with you how your
company could benefit from our unique solution to your financial
```

To highlight the first paragraph:

Press	F12 or Alt + F4	*Select*	*Edit*	**Drag**	the mouse until you have highlighted the first paragraph
Press	↓ until you have highlighted the first paragraph	*Select*	*Block*	**Release**	the mouse button
		Press	←Enter *(this will highlight all text until a hard return is encountered)*		

Your screen should look like Figure 3-11.

Figure 3-11

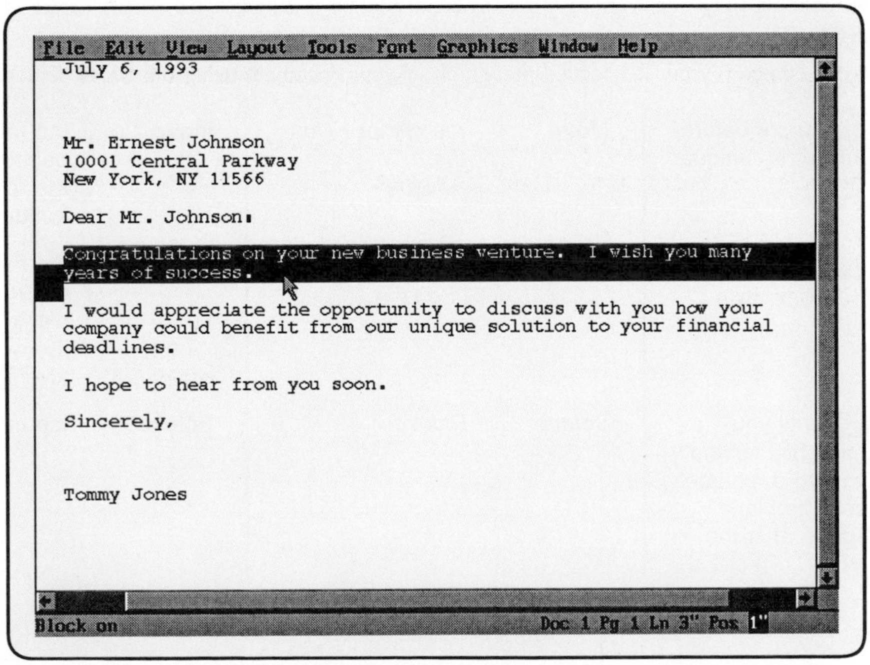

```
File  Edit  View  Layout  Tools  Font  Graphics  Window  Help
July 6, 1993



Mr. Ernest Johnson
10001 Central Parkway
New York, NY 11566

Dear Mr. Johnson:

Congratulations on your new business venture.  I wish you many
years of success.

I would appreciate the opportunity to discuss with you how your
company could benefit from our unique solution to your financial
deadlines.

I hope to hear from you soon.

Sincerely,



Tommy Jones


Block on                                    Doc 1 Pg 1 Ln 3" Pos 1"
```

Notice that the text "Block On" appears on the status bar.

You now can select another WordPerfect feature to apply to the selection. In some situations, you may need to stop using the Block feature.

To turn off highlighting without continuing with another WordPerfect feature:

Press	F12 or Alt + F4	*Press*	*the Esc key*	**Click**	on the document area

Your screen should now display the current document with no highlighted text.

■ DELETING TEXT

There are many ways to **delete**, or remove, text within your document. The following table lists the keystrokes to delete text.

Deletion	Keystrokes
Character to the left of the cursor	←Backspace
Character to the right of the cursor	Delete
Word at the cursor	Ctrl + ←Backspace or Ctrl + Delete
From the cursor to the end of the line	Ctrl + End
From the cursor to the end of the page	Ctrl + Page Down
Highlighted text	Select the text, press Delete

Suppose you need to delete the word "unique" from the second paragraph of your document. One method of deleting a word or group of words is to highlight the text using the Block feature and then press the DELETE key. If you are deleting only one word, a more efficient method is to place the cursor in the word and press CTRL+BACKSPACE.

To delete the word "unique" from the second paragraph of your document using the Block feature:

Move	the cursor before the "u" in "unique	*Move*	*the cursor before the "u" in "unique"*	**Move**	the mouse pointer before the "u" in "unique"
Press	F12 or Alt + F4	*Select*	*Edit*	**Drag**	the mouse until the word and the blank space after the word "unique" are highlighted
Press	→ until you have highlighted the word "unique" and the blank space after the word	*Select*	*Block*	**Release**	the mouse button

		Press	Ctrl + → *until*	
or			*you have highlighted the word "unique" and the blank space after the word*	
Press	Spacebar			

The bottom of your screen should look like Figure 3-12.

Figure 3-12

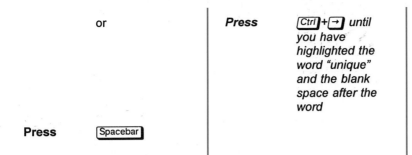

```
Congratulations on your new business venture.  I wish you many
years of success.

I would appreciate the opportunity to discuss with you how your
company could benefit from our unique solution to your financial
deadlines.

I hope to hear from you soon.

Sincerely,


Tommy Jones
```
Block on   Doc 1 Pg 1 Ln 3.33" Pos 4.8"

To delete the word "unique":

Press	Delete	*Press*	Delete	**Press**	Delete

The word "unique" and the blank space after it should now be removed from your document.

Another method for deleting the word "unique" is:

Move	the cursor before the "u" in "unique"	*Move*	*the cursor before the "u" in "unique"*	**Move**	the mouse pointer before the "u" in "unique"
Press	Ctrl + ←Backspace	*Press*	Ctrl + Delete	**Double-click**	the word "unique"
				Press	Delete

■ UNDELETING TEXT

If you mistakenly delete text, it is not lost at that moment. WordPerfect stores your last three text deletions. You can display them on your screen in reverse order at any time and restore, or **undelete**, the deletion of your choice. The text is restored at the current location of the cursor.

To restore the word "unique":

Move	the cursor before the "s" in "solution"	*Move*	*the cursor before the "s" in "solution"*	Move	the mouse pointer before the "s" in "solution"
Press	Esc	*Select*	*Edit*	Click	the mouse button
		Select	*Undelete*	Choose	Edit
				Choose	Undelete

The Undelete dialog box appears.   Your screen should look like Figure 3-13.

Figure 3-13

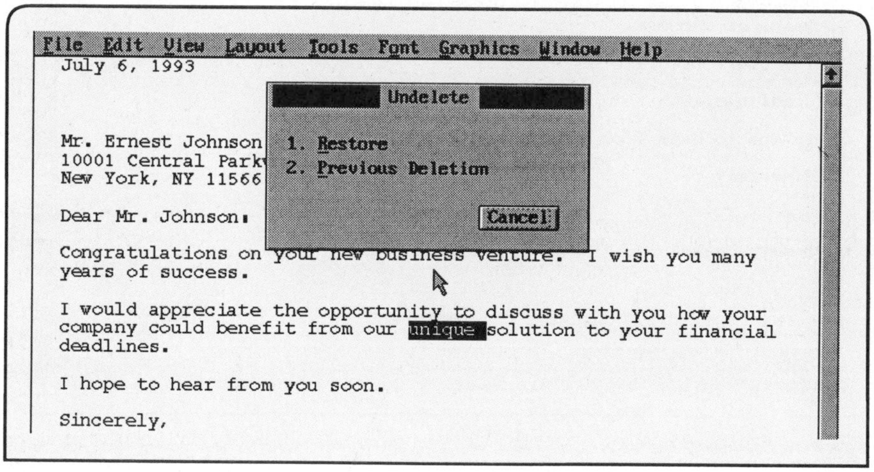

To restore the highlighted text:

Press	1 or R to select the Restore option	*Press*	*1 or R to select the Restore option*	Click	the Restore option

Your screen should look like Figure 3-14.

Figure 3-14

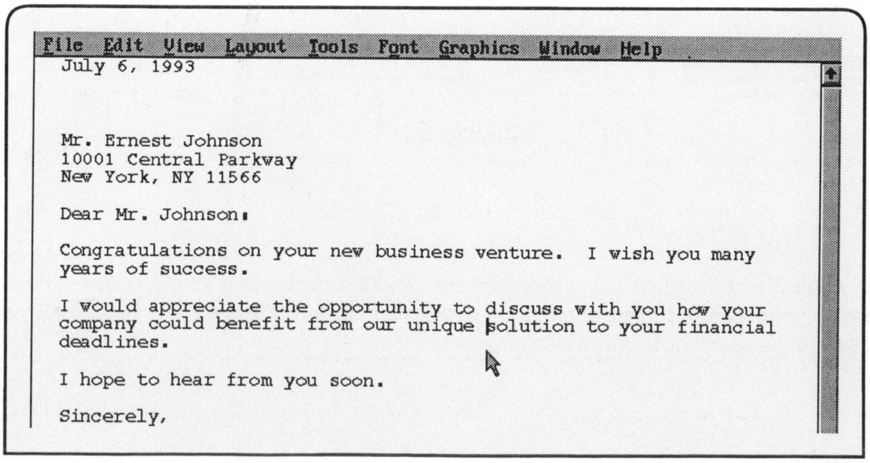

Save your document, replacing the old contents with the current document. Close the document.

WordPerfect also offers a feature called Undo. It is found in the Edit menu above the Undelete command. Undo permits you to cancel almost any action done immediately prior to selecting the Undo command. Thus, if used immediately, it could also have restored the word "unique." The Undo feature is good for canceling mistakes in formatting changes and other choices. It only works immediately after an action and, unlike Undelete, it only recalls the single most recent action.

■ USING THE HELP FEATURE

The Help feature allows you to learn more about WordPerfect quickly on your screen.

Use the Help feature to display any of these items on your screen:

1. An alphabetical listing of WordPerfect features and their keystrokes

2. Descriptions of WordPerfect features and menu options

3. Information about the current feature you are using

To access the Help Contents feature:

Press F1	**Select** Help	**Choose** Help
	Select Contents	**Choose** Contents
Use arrow keys to select any feature about which you need information.	Use arrow keys to select any feature about which you need information.	Click on any topic shown in a different color about which you need information.
Press ←Enter	**Press** ←Enter	**Choose** the Look command button

Pressing the F1 key or choosing Contents from the Help menu while you are in the normal editing screen displays the main Help Contents. You can then select any jump term by pressing arrow keys or by double-clicking on it to highlight it and then pressing ENTER. A **jump term** moves you to a detailed description of the feature. A jump term is text that appears in another color or boldfaced. For example, if you select Index you see an alphabetical listing of topics.

If you cannot see all of the jump terms on the screen, use the arrow keys or scroll bars to view the additional topics.

Pressing F1 after you have initiated a WordPerfect feature provides a description of that particular feature. To exit the Help feature:

Press Esc	**Press** Esc	**Choose** Cancel

EXERCISE 1

INSTRUCTIONS: Define the following concepts:

1. Cursor _____

_____

2. Insert mode _____

_____

3.   Undeleting text _____

_____

4.   Movement techniques _____

_____

5.   Block feature _____

_____

6.   Date feature _____

_____

7.   Deleting text _____

_____

8.   Typeover mode _____

_____

9.   Zoom _____

_____

EXERCISE 2

INSTRUCTIONS: Circle T if the statement is true and F if the statement is false.

T	F	1.	When you are in Insert mode and enter new text, WordPerfect pushes forward any existing text and moves it to the right to make room for the new text.
T	F	2.	WordPerfect defaults to inserting the date using the month-day-month format.
T	F	3.	Typeover mode allows you to replace existing text with new text.
T	F	4.	To enter the Typeover mode, press INSERT.
T	F	5.	WordPerfect stores your last four deletions.
T	F	6.	The Block feature is used to highlight text within your document.
T	F	7.	The words "Block On" appear on the status bar to indicate you are using the Block feature.
T	F	8.	You cannot restore text that has been deleted.
T	F	9.	The cursor can move only through text that already exists in your document.
T	F	10.	WordPerfect automatically defaults to Typeover mode.
T	F	11.	Zoom only permits viewing in 100% or 200% modes.

EXERCISE 3

INSTRUCTIONS:
1.   Create the following document. As you type the text, use the movement techniques and insert/delete functions available in WordPerfect to correct any errors.
2.   Save the document in a file using the name "CH03EX03".
3.   View the document in 75% Zoom mode. Then return to 100% mode.
4.   Use the Print Preview feature to see how the document will appear when you print it.

5.   Print the document.
6.   Close the document.

Word processing provides an individual with an effective and
efficient means of preparing documents. You can create documents and
quickly make needed changes prior to printing the document. The
software allows you to save the document in a file for later use.

EXERCISE 4

INSTRUCTIONS:

1.   Open the file "CH02EX05" created in the previous chapter.
2.   Practice using the cursor movement keys as follows:
   a.   Move the cursor to the end of the document using the `Home`,`Home`,`↓` keys.
   b.   Move the cursor to the beginning of the document using the `Home`,`Home`,`↑` keys.
   c.   Move the cursor to the word "**recent**" in the first line of the first paragraph.
   d.   Move the cursor to the end of the first line of the first paragraph using the `End` key.
   e.   Move the cursor to the beginning of the first line of the first paragraph using the `Home`,`↑` key.
   f.   Move the cursor to the second paragraph (down one paragraph) using the `Ctrl`+`↓` keys.
   g.   Move the cursor to the first paragraph (up one paragraph) using the `Ctrl`+`↑` keys.
   h.   Move the cursor to the top of the screen using the `Page Up` key.
3.   Close the document.

EXERCISE 5

INSTRUCTIONS:

1.   Create the following document. Use the Date Tool to insert the current date as text. As you type the letter, use the movement techniques and insert/delete functions to correct any errors.
2.   Save the document in a file using the name "CH03EX05".
3.   View the document in 200% View mode. Return the view to 100% mode.
4.   Use the Print Preview feature to see how the document will appear when you print it.
5.   Print the document.
6.   Close the document.

```
current date


FBN Software Company
2100 Skyview Way
Ventura, CA 91015

Dear Sir:

Please send by return mail all of your product brochures, technical
specifications and price lists for your software related to
accounting for IBM and IBM compatible personal computers.

Additionally, please add our name on your mailing list to update us
on any future changes in your product line.

Sincerely,


Jane Mitchell
```

EXERCISE 6

INSTRUCTIONS:

1. Open the file "CH03EX05".
2. Using the Typeover mode, replace the word **"Way"** in the inside address with **"Avenue"**.
3. Using the Insert mode, insert the word **"yours"** after **"Sincerely"** in the complimentary closing.
4. Save the document in a file using the name "CH03EX06".
5. Print the document.
6. Close the document.

EXERCISE 7

INSTRUCTIONS:

1. Open the file "CH03EX06".
2. Using the Block feature, delete the words **"IBM and IBM compatible"** in the first paragraph.
3. Delete the **"s"** in **"computers"** in the first paragraph.
4. Print the document.
5. Restore the words **"IBM and IBM compatible"** in the first paragraph.
6. Restore the **"s"** in **"computer"** in the first paragraph.
7. Save the document in a file using the name "CH03EX07".
8. Print the document.
9. Close the document.

EXERCISE 8

INSTRUCTIONS:

1. Create the following document. Insert the current date as text.
2. Save the document in a file using the name "CH03EX08".
3. Use the Print Preview feature to see how the document will appear when you print it.
4. Print the document.
5. Close the document.

current date

Ms. T. J. Jackson
Travel Coordinator
Ace Travel Services
820 Gessner, Suite 1135
Houston, TX 77024

Dear Ms. Jackson:

Thank you for helping plan vacation trip to Europe this summer. I am really looking forward to seeing England, Ireland and Scotland. Your courtesy is really appreciated. This is my first trip to Europe and you were quite patient in answering my questions.

Sincerely yours

Thomas Alexander

EXERCISE 9

INSTRUCTIONS:
1. Open the file "CH03EX08".
2. Make the corrections displayed below. The marks on the sheet are proofreader's marks. If you are not familiar with proofreader's marks, Appendix A in this book contains a list of proofreader's marks and their meanings.
3. Save the document in a file using the name "CH03EX09".
4. Print the document.
5. Close the document.

```
current date


Ms. T.J. Jackson
Travel Coordinator
Ace Travel Services
820 Gessner, Suite 1135
Houston, TX 77024

Dear Ms. Jackson:
                            me    my
Thank you for helping plan vacation trip to Europe this summer.
I am really looking forward to seeing England, Ireland, and
Scotland.  Your courtesy is really appreciated. ¶ This is my first
trip to Europe and you were quite patient in answering my
questions.

Sincerely yours,


            w.
Thomas Alexander
```

EXERCISE 10

INSTRUCTIONS:
1. Create the following document. Insert the current date as text.
2. Save the document in a file using the name "CH03EX10".
3. Use the Print Preview feature to see how the document will appear when you print it.
4. Print the document.
5. Close the document.

current date

Dr. George Mills
205 Wildwood Lane
Baton Rouge, LA 70806

Dear Dr. Mills:

It is my disagreeable job to remind you of your balance of $163.90.
You have been on time with your payments before; therefore, I find it
difficult to ask you to pay your balance promptly. If you cannot
make your payments, please let me know. I am always open to the
possibility of extending the time within reason. Perhaps you have
overlooked this bill or maybe some crisis has occurred that will not
permit you to pay at this time.

Please phone me at my office at 555-9812 and let me know your
situation. I have enclosed a self-addressed envelope for your
convenience. I await your phone call or your payment.

Most cordially yours,

John Rich

EXERCISE 11

INSTRUCTIONS:

1. Create the following document. Make the corrections shown. Refer to Appendix A for the proofreader's marks if you need help.
2. Insert the current date as text.
3. Save the document in a file using the name "CH03EX11".
4. Use the Print Preview feature to see how the document will appear when you print it.
5. Print the document.
6. Close the document.

```
current date


Mrs. Eva Johnson, President                 Insert above street line
1220 Algonquin Road ←              AAA Computer Services
Missoula, MT 59801

Dear Mrs. Johnson

Where is the best place to communicate with your workers?  On
their paychecks--it's the one thing they receive from you that
they never throw away. What kinds of messages can you give them?
                                              eral
You can indicate that payroll deductions (like Fed  Taxes, State
Taxes, F.I.C.A., Union Dues, Health Insurance, etc.) are made in
their his  interest.  You can also talk about paid vacations, education
benefits, stock investments you make on his/her behalf.
     produce                              their
We make checks and stubs to fit all occasions.  We make room for
you to include extra information deemed beneficial to the your
employee.  This innovative idea is just one of many that our
company, INFOCHECKS, has available for your use. Give us a call.
Let us help you communicate quickly and efficiently with all your
employees.

Very sincerely yours,

INFOCHECKS, Inc.



Jan Underwood, President
Sales Specialists
```

EXERCISE 12

INSTRUCTIONS:

1. Open the file "CH03EX10".
2. Using the Typeover mode, replace the word "**Lane**" in the inside address to "**Road**".
3. Using the Block feature, delete the words "**disagreeable job**" in the first line of the message.
4. In place of the words deleted in direction 3, insert "**duty**".
5. Create a new paragraph by adding two returns at the end of the second sentence. The new paragraph will start "**If you cannot...**".
6. Using the Block feature, delete the sentence "**I am always open to the possibility of extending the time within reason.**"
7. In the last paragraph, first sentence, using the Block feature, delete "**and let me know your situation**".
8. In the last paragraph, first sentence, using the Insert mode after "**555-9812**" insert "**and discuss the many options for payment available**".
9. Save the document in a file using the name "CH03EX12".
10. Print the document.
11. Close the document.

CHAPTER FOUR

ADDITIONAL EDITING FEATURES

OBJECTIVES

In this chapter, you will learn to:
- Use the File Manager to open a file
- Use the Reveal Codes feature
- Search for and replace text
- Change the case of text
- Move and copy text

■ CHAPTER OVERVIEW

In this chapter, additional editing features are discussed. You are shown an alternative method for opening files. The Reveal Codes feature is introduced. The methods of searching for and replacing text are described and illustrated. The process for changing letters from lowercase to uppercase and vice versa is also presented. Finally, the uses of the move and copy features are discussed.

■ USING THE FILE MANAGER TO OPEN A FILE

At this point, you need to open the "JOHNSON.LTR" document created in Chapter 3. There may be times that you do not remember the exact name of a file or do not remember the location of the file. WordPerfect 6.0 offers a feature called the File Manager to help you locate and manage your files.

Before beginning this exercise, change the default directory to "A:\WPDOCS" or "C:\WPDOCS".

To open the "JOHNSON.LTR" file using the File Manager:

Press [F5]

Choose *File*

Choose *File Manager*

The Specify File Manager List dialog box appears. Your screen should look similar to Figure 4-1.

Figure 4-1
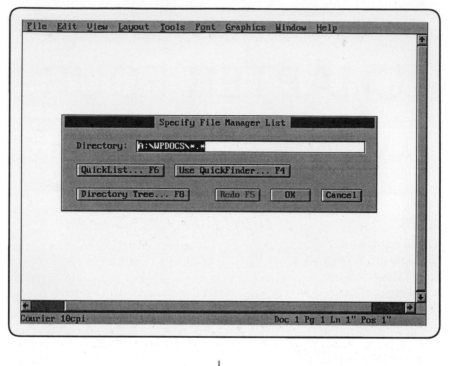

| Press | ⌐Enter to accept the current directory | | *Click* | *the OK command button to accept the current directory* |

The File Manager dialog box appears and lists all the files in the default directory. Your screen should look similar to Figure 4-2.

Figure 4-2

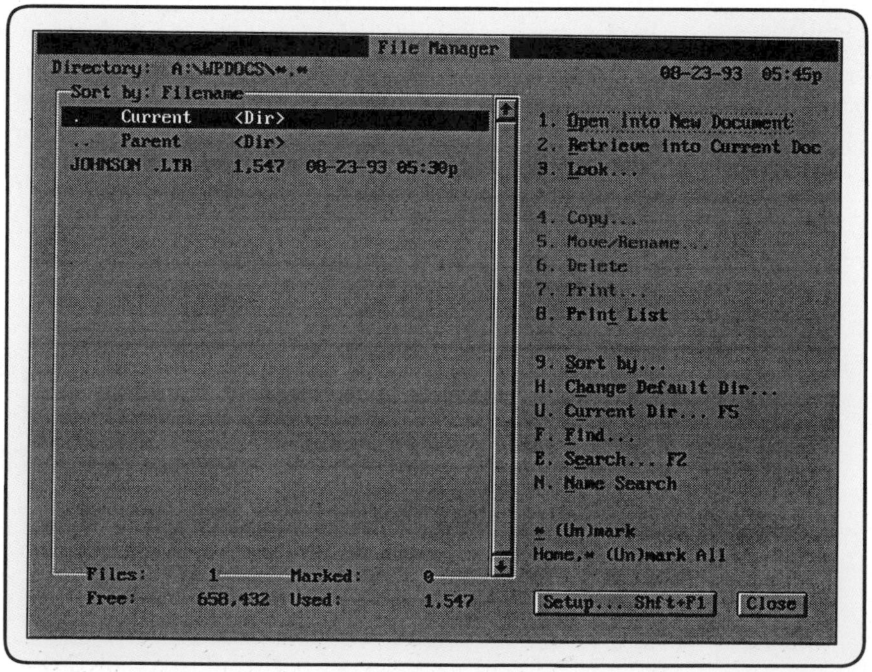

To open the "JOHNSON.LTR" file:

Press	⬇ until "JOHNSON.LTR" is highlighted	***Click***	*on "JOHNSON.LTR"*
Press	1 or O to select the Open into New Document option	***Click***	*the Open into New Document option*

The "JOHNSON.LTR" file should appear on the screen. The File Manager is used to preview documents before opening them. In addition, you can use the File Manager to copy, move, delete, or print files. These and other File Manager features are discussed in Chapter 28.

■ REVEAL CODES

WordPerfect tries to show your document on the screen as it will appear when printed. This makes it easy for you to quickly see the results of any changes and improvements that you make.

But there is much happening "behind the scenes" in WordPerfect. Nearly every time you use a feature to change the appearance of your document, a special code that you cannot see is placed in the document. These codes tell WordPerfect what to do when it is printing your document. For example, suppose you want to make a sentence stand out when printed. You could do this by formatting the sentence in bold letters (how to do this will be discussed later). The sentence stands out on the screen in darker letters. But you have also inserted "Bold On" and "Bold Off" codes before and after the sentence.

The Reveal Codes feature allows you to see these codes on the screen. When you press F11 or ALT+F3 or select the Reveal Codes option from the View menu, the screen is split into two sections. The top section is the normal screen that you always see when you are editing.

The bottom part of the screen is the Reveal Codes section. The text is shown with the codes. As you move the cursor or click the mouse pointer through the codes and text in the Reveal Codes section, the cursor also moves through the same text in the top section. You can edit the text in the Reveal Codes section just as you would in the top section. The menu and function keys can also be used when Reveal Codes is present on the screen. You can also delete a code if you wish.

In This Book

For the remainder of this book, instructions will appear in two columns. The left column has instructions for issuing the commands from the keyboard using the function keys. The right column contains instructions for issuing commands using the menus. You may choose these commands using either the mouse or the ALT key and underlined letter.

You can mix the use of the mouse, keyboard, and function key methods.

To display the codes for your document:

Press	Alt + F3 or F11	***Choose***	*View*
		Choose	*Reveal Codes*

The Reveal Codes feature appears on the screen. Your screen should look like Figure 4-3.

Figure 4-3

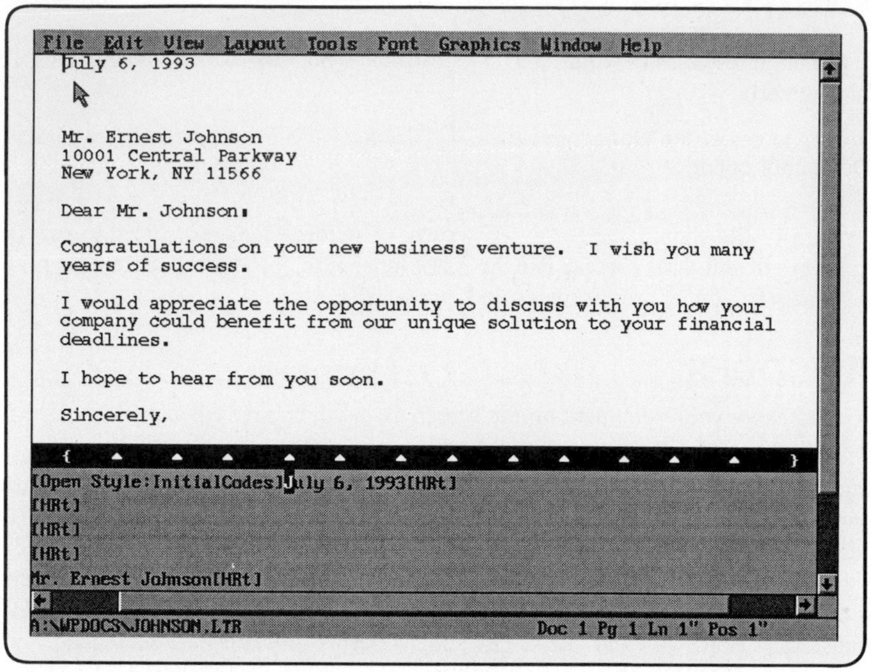

The first code will always be the [Open Style:InitialCodes] code. In this code are stored any special preferences you have designated. You may not delete this code. The [HRt] code stands for a hard return. A **hard return** code is inserted whenever you press ENTER in the text. This causes the text following the cursor to begin on a new line, and the cursor is placed at the front of that line.

The [SRt] code represents a soft return. A **soft return** code is inserted by WordPerfect at the end of every line where there is no hard return. This code allows WordPerfect to word wrap throughout the paragraph as you add or delete text. You can see a soft return code by moving the cursor down so the body of the letter appears in the Reveal Codes section.

A full list of Codes appears in "Appendix B" of the WordPerfect Reference manual.

To remove the document codes from your screen:

Press   Alt + F3 or F11   **Choose**   View

                                          Choose   Reveal Codes

Your screen should now show the current document as it was before you used the Reveal Codes feature.

■ SEARCHING FOR AND REPLACING TEXT

You can use the **Search feature** to locate specific text in your document. A **Replace feature** exists to help you replace any particular text with new text.

Using the Search feature, you can locate a word, phrase, or code each time it occurs in your document. You can search forward from your position in the document by pressing F2 or by selecting the Search option from the Edit menu. You can search backward in your document by pressing SHIFT+F2 or by changing the direction option in the Search dialog box.

In the Search dialog box, you are asked to enter the text that WordPerfect should locate. This text is called a **search string**. If the search string contains only lowercase letters, then WordPerfect will look for matching text that is in lowercase and uppercase. If the search string contains one or more uppercase letters, then WordPerfect looks for an exact match on the uppercase letters. For example, if the search string is "sum", then WordPerfect will find such words as "sum", "Sumaria", and "resume". If the search string is "Sum", then WordPerfect will find only "Sumaria".

If your search string is a short word, such as "sum", you may wish to choose the "Find Whole Words Only" option. In this way, only the word will be located, and no larger words containing the search string will be found. For example, if the search is told to find only the whole word "sum", then WordPerfect will not find "Sumaria" or "resume".

In This Book

When using a mouse, it is common practice to move the cursor in the document by moving the mouse pointer to the desired location and clicking the mouse button. In the remaining portion of this book, you are instructed to simply *click* at the appropriate location rather than be given the set of instructions to move the mouse pointer to the location and press or click the mouse button.

Searching Forward

To search forward for the word "you" in the document:

Press	Home , Home , ↑		***Click***	*at the beginning of the document*
Press	F2		***Choose***	*Edit*
Type	you		***Choose***	*Search*
Press	←Enter		***Type***	*you*
Press	4 or W to place an X in the Find Whole Words Only check box		***Click***	*in the Find Whole Words Only check box until an X appears*

The bottom part of your screen should look like Figure 4-4.

Figure 4-4

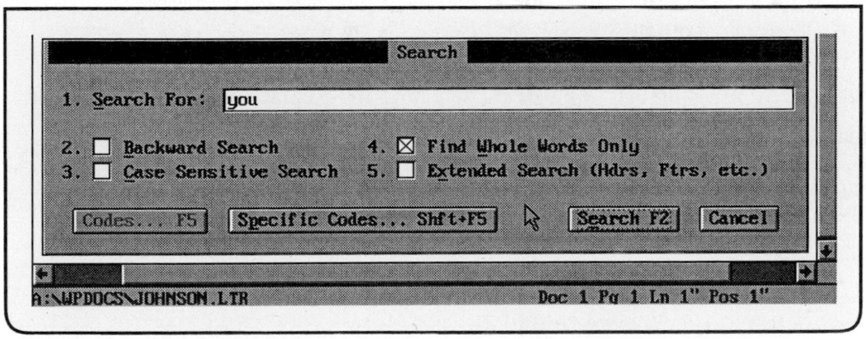

To begin the search:

Press	F2		***Click***	*the Search command button*

The Search dialog box disappears. The top part of your screen should look like Figure 4-5.

Figure 4-5

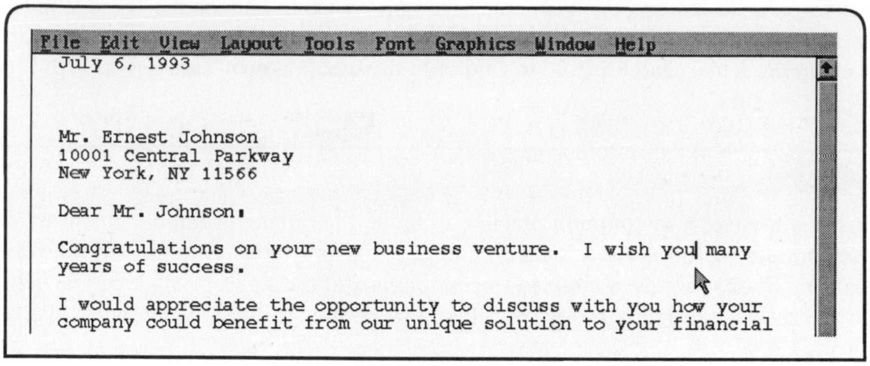

```
File  Edit  View  Layout  Tools  Font  Graphics  Window  Help
July 6, 1993                                                          ↑


Mr. Ernest Johnson
10001 Central Parkway
New York, NY 11566

Dear Mr. Johnson:

Congratulations on your new business venture.  I wish you many
years of success.
                                                      ▶

I would appreciate the opportunity to discuss with you how your
company could benefit from our unique solution to your financial
```

Notice the text that is being sought is always immediately before the location of the cursor.

To continue searching for the same occurrence of the text:

Press	[F2] twice		**Choose**	*Edit*
			Choose	*Search*
			Click	*the Search Command button*

Continue repeating the process for finding the next occurrence of the text you specified. Eventually, the message "Not found" will appear on the screen, showing there are no more occurrences of that text. Accept the message by pressing the ENTER key or clicking on the OK command button.

In the event your cursor is near the end of the document, you could conduct a backward search. Follow the same steps as those for a forward search. When the Search dialog box appears, press B to place an X in the Backward Search check box or click the Backward Search option. If numbers do not appear next to the choices and selected characters are not underlined, you may press the ENTER or TAB key to display the numbers and underlined characters for the purpose of selecting options.

Replacing Text

You can replace text by pressing ALT+F2 or by selecting the Replace option from the Edit menu.

To replace "financial" with "accounting":

Press	[Home],[Home],[↑]		**Click**	*at the beginning of the document*
Press	[Alt]+[F2]		**Choose**	*Edit*
			Choose	*Replace*

The Search and Replace dialog box appears. Notice the "Find Whole Words Only" check box remains marked. The bottom part of your screen should look like Figure 4-6.

Figure 4-6

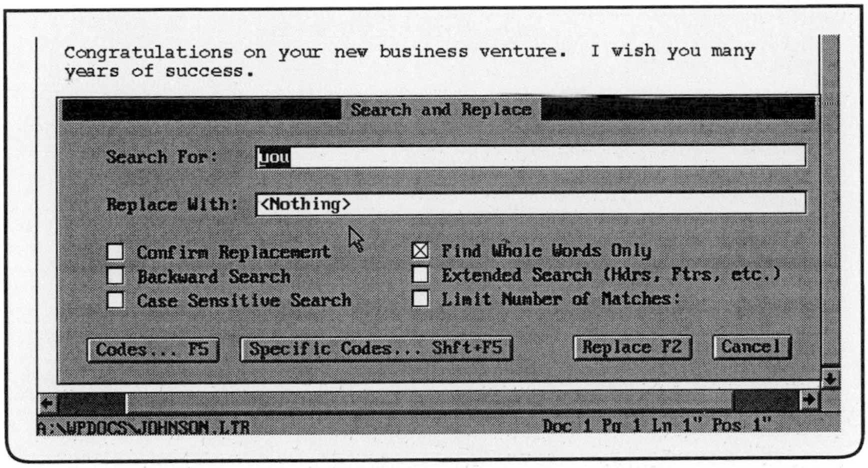

```
┌─────────────────────────────────────────────────────────┐
│  Congratulations on your new business venture.  I wish you many  │
│  years of success.                                                │
│                                                                   │
│  ████████████████████████ Search and Replace ███████████████████ │
│                                                                   │
│  Search For:  ▐you▌                                               │
│                                                                   │
│  Replace With: <Nothing>                                          │
│                                                                   │
│        ☐ Confirm Replacement     ⌧ Find Whole Words Only         │
│        ☐ Backward Search          ☐ Extended Search (Hdrs, Ftrs, etc.) │
│        ☐ Case Sensitive Search    ☐ Limit Number of Matches:     │
│                                                                   │
│   │Codes... F5│ │Specific Codes... Shft+F5│   │Replace F2│ │Cancel│ │
│                                                                   │
│  A:\WPDOCS\JOHNSON.LTR                Doc 1 Pg 1 Ln 1" Pos 1"     │
└─────────────────────────────────────────────────────────┘
```

To specify you want to search for the word "financial":

| **Type** | financial | **Type** | *financial* |

The bottom part of your screen should look like Figure 4-7.

Figure 4-7

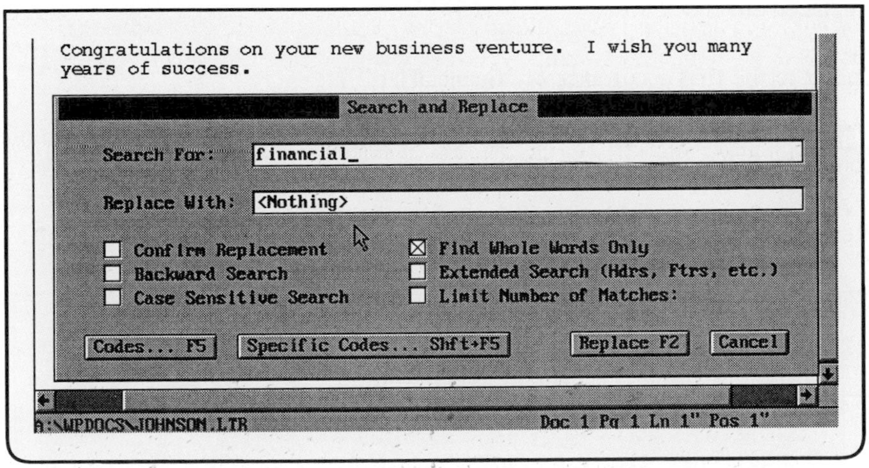

```
┌─────────────────────────────────────────────────────────┐
│  Congratulations on your new business venture.  I wish you many  │
│  years of success.                                                │
│                                                                   │
│  ████████████████████████ Search and Replace ███████████████████ │
│                                                                   │
│  Search For:  financial_                                          │
│                                                                   │
│  Replace With: <Nothing>                                          │
│                                                                   │
│        ☐ Confirm Replacement     ⌧ Find Whole Words Only         │
│        ☐ Backward Search          ☐ Extended Search (Hdrs, Ftrs, etc.) │
│        ☐ Case Sensitive Search    ☐ Limit Number of Matches:     │
│                                                                   │
│   │Codes... F5│ │Specific Codes... Shft+F5│   │Replace F2│ │Cancel│ │
│                                                                   │
│  A:\WPDOCS\JOHNSON.LTR                Doc 1 Pg 1 Ln 1" Pos 1"     │
└─────────────────────────────────────────────────────────┘
```

To replace the word "financial" with "accounting":

| **Press** | Tab↹ to move the cursor to the Replace With text box | *Click* | *the Replace With text box* |
| **Type** | accounting | *Type* | *accounting* |

The bottom part of your screen should look like Figure 4-8.

Figure 4-8

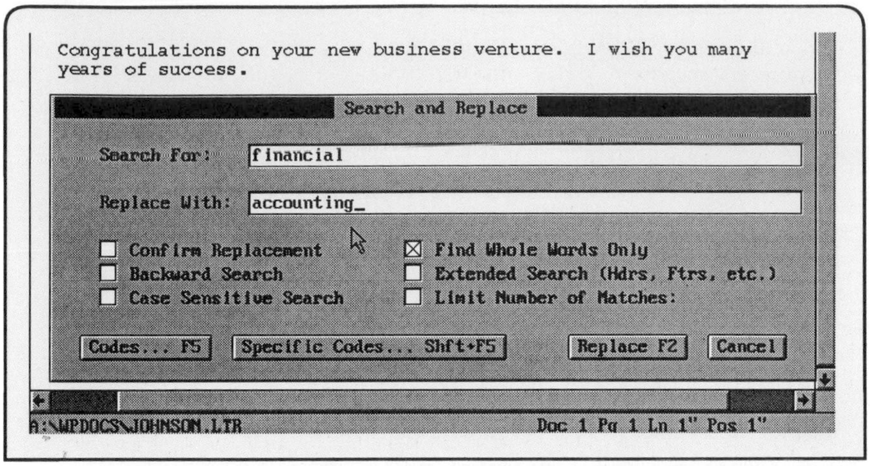

```
Congratulations on your new business venture.  I wish you many
years of success.
┌────────────────────── Search and Replace ──────────────────────┐

  Search For:  │financial                                        │

  Replace With: │accounting_                                     │

    ☐ Confirm Replacement    ☒ Find Whole Words Only
    ☐ Backward Search        ☐ Extended Search (Hdrs, Ftrs, etc.)
    ☐ Case Sensitive Search  ☐ Limit Number of Matches:

  ┌ Codes... F5 ┐ ┌ Specific Codes... Shft+F5 ┐    ┌ Replace F2 ┐ ┌ Cancel ┐

A:\WPDOCS\JOHNSON.LTR                          Doc 1 Pg 1 Ln 1" Pos 1"
```

To have the Replace command stop on each instance, permitting you to confirm whether you want to replace the old text and continue the search and replace routine:

Press [Tab⇄] or [↵Enter] | ***Click*** *in the Confirm Replacement check box until an X appears*

Press F to place an X in the Confirm Replacement check box

To move the cursor to the first occurrence of "financial":

Press [F2] to select the Replace command button | ***Click*** *the Replace command button*

The Confirm Replacement dialog box appears. The bottom of your screen should look like Figure 4-9.

Figure 4-9

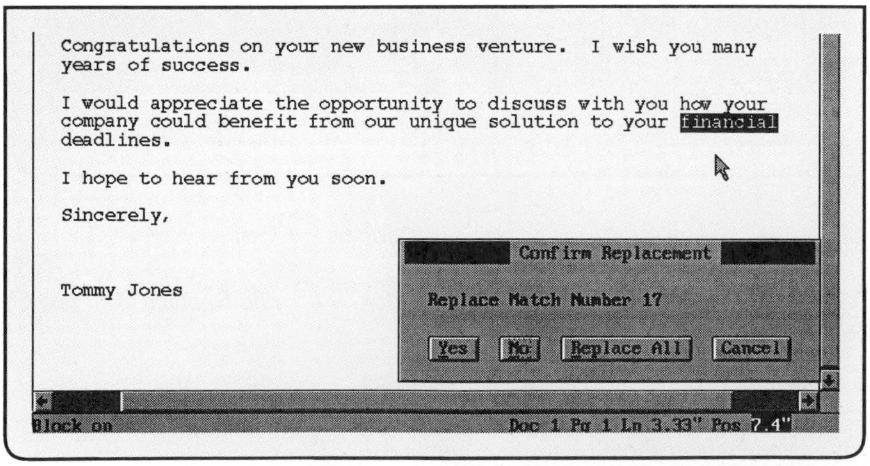

```
Congratulations on your new business venture.  I wish you many
years of success.

I would appreciate the opportunity to discuss with you how your
company could benefit from our unique solution to your ▐financial▌
deadlines.

I hope to hear from you soon.

Sincerely,

                          ┌──────── Confirm Replacement ────────┐
Tommy Jones
                            Replace Match Number 17

                            ┌ Yes ┐ ┌ No ┐ ┌ Replace All ┐ ┌ Cancel ┐

Block on                                    Doc 1 Pg 1 Ln 3.33" Pos 7.4"
```

The dialog box appearing in the lower right corner of the screen indicates that you may answer "Yes" to confirm the replacement, "No" to skip this occurrence, or "Replace All" which will automatically change all occurrences in the text.

To change "financial" to "accounting", answer Yes by typing a "Y" or by clicking on it.

If another match is found, it is immediately highlighted. The dialog box appears again in the lower right corner. When no more matches exist, a box appears on the screen indicating how many occurrences were found and how many were replaced.

To close the dialog box:

Press	⏎Enter		*Click*	*the OK command button*

Save your document. This action replaces the old contents of the file with the current document.

■ CHANGING THE CASE

The Convert Case feature lets you change highlighted characters to uppercase or lowercase letters. Highlight the text that you want to change. Then press SHIFT+F3 or choose the Convert Case option from the Edit menu.

To change the word "Congratulations" to uppercase in the first paragraph of your document:

Move	the cursor before the "C" in the word "Congratulations"		*Double-click*	*the word "Congratulations"*
Press	F12 or Alt + F4			
Press	Ctrl + →			

The top part of your screen should look like Figure 4-10.

Figure 4-10

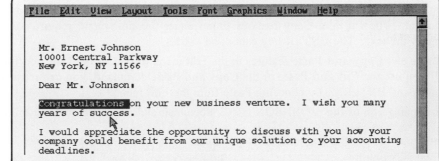

To switch to uppercase:

Press	Shift + F3		*Choose*	*Edit*
Press	1 or U to select the Uppercase option		*Choose*	*Convert Case*
			Choose	*Uppercase*

The top part of your screen should look like Figure 4-11. The rest of the characters in the word "Congratulations" have been converted to uppercase.

Figure 4-11

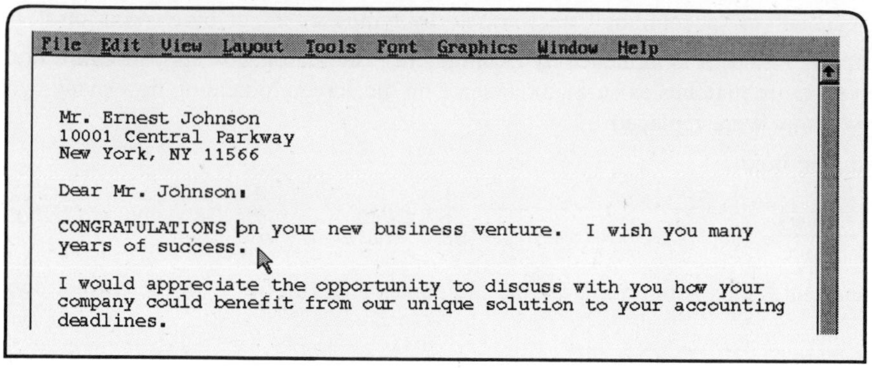

```
 File  Edit  View  Layout  Tools  Font  Graphics  Window  Help

    Mr. Ernest Johnson
    10001 Central Parkway
    New York, NY 11566

    Dear Mr. Johnson:

    CONGRATULATIONS on your new business venture.  I wish you many
    years of success.

    I would appreciate the opportunity to discuss with you how your
    company could benefit from our unique solution to your accounting
    deadlines.
```

Save your document. This action replaces the old contents of the file with the current document.

■ MOVING AND COPYING TEXT

WordPerfect 6.0 allows you to move and copy text from one area of the document to another or into a different document. Several methods are available for moving and copying text.

To move text using the keyboard, highlight the desired text and press CTRL+X.   To copy text using the keyboard, highlight the desired text and press CTRL+C. To place the cut or copied text into the document, place the cursor at the desired location and press ENTER or CTRL+V. The text appears in the new location. You can also move or copy text by highlighting the text and pressing CTRL+F4.

To move or copy text using the mouse, use the Cut, Copy, and Paste commands located in the Edit menu. To move or copy text using the mouse, highlight the text that you wish to move or copy. Then choose Cut or Copy from the Edit menu. These commands move or copy text, respectively, to a temporary holding area.

To place the cut or copied text in the document, move the cursor to the desired location and choose Paste from the Edit menu. The Cut and Copy features found under the Edit menu require using the Paste command to regain the text. The ENTER key cannot be used.

The **Cut and Paste** and **Copy and Paste** features in the Edit menu provide a third method for moving or copying text. If you use the **Cut and Paste** or the **Copy and Paste** command, you can retrieve the cut or copied text by pressing ENTER or by choosing Paste from the Edit menu.

To move the first paragraph of the "JOHNSON.LTR" document and place it below the third paragraph:

Move	the cursor before the first letter of the first paragraph	**Click**	*in the first paragraph*
Press	F12 or Alt+F4	**Quadruple-click**	*the paragraph*
Press	←Enter twice to highlight the paragraph and the extra hard return code	**Choose**	*Edit*
Press	Ctrl+X	**Choose**	*Cut*

The top part of your screen should look like Figure 4-12.

Figure 4-12

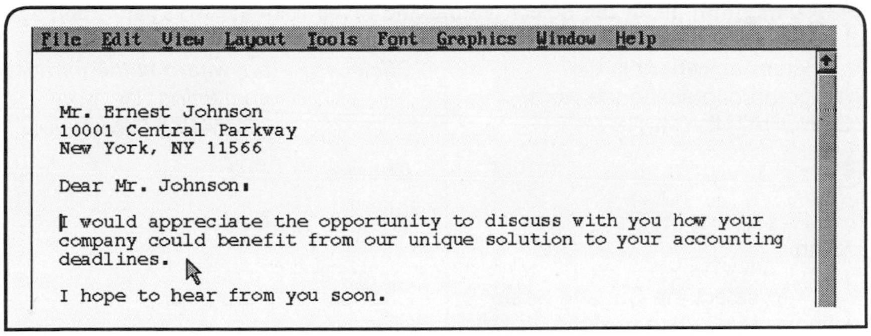

Notice that the first paragraph no longer appears in your document.

To place the paragraph you removed at the proper location in your document:

Move	the cursor before the "S" in "Sincerely"		*Click*	*before the "S" in "Sincerely"*
Press	Ctrl +V		*Choose*	*Edit*
			Choose	*Paste*

Your screen should look like Figure 4-13. You may need to add hard returns to improve the appearance of the document.

Figure 4-13

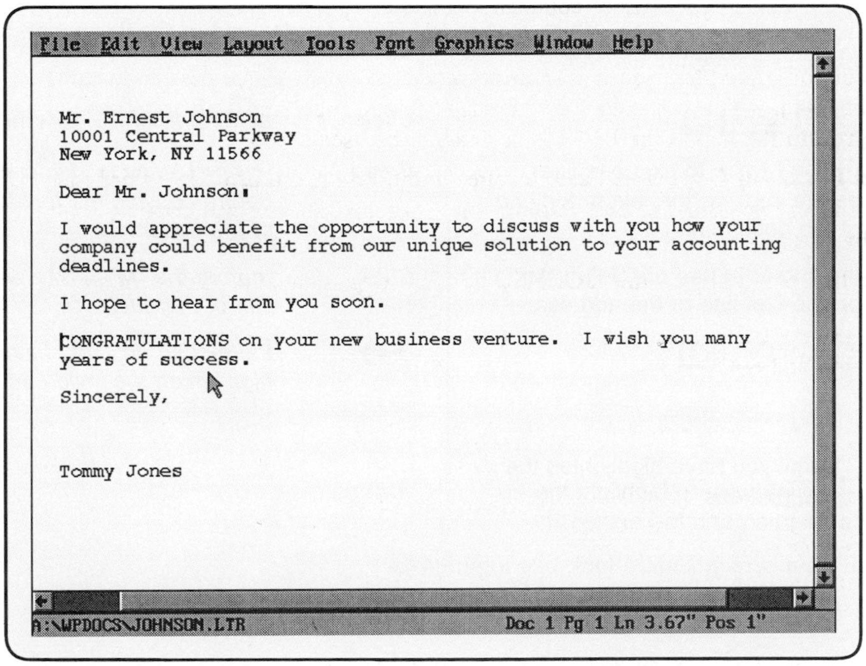

Another method for highlighting text is to use the Select option under the Edit menu. It allows you to quickly highlight a sentence, paragraph, or page in your document.

To move the third paragraph using the Select feature and place it as the first paragraph again:

Move	the cursor anywhere in the paragraph containing the word "CONGRATULATIONS"		*Click*	*anywhere in the paragraph containing the word "CONGRATULATIONS"*
Press	Ctrl + F4		*Choose*	*Edit*
Press	2 or R to select the Paragraph option		*Choose*	*Select*
Press	1 or T to select the Cut and Paste option		*Choose*	*Paragraph*
			Choose	*Edit*
			Choose	*Cut*

The paragraph should be gone from the document.

To place the paragraph you removed at the original location in your document:

Move	the cursor before the "I" in the first paragraph		*Click*	*before the "I" in the first paragraph*
Press	←Enter		*Choose*	*Edit*
			Choose	*Paste*

To copy the inside address using the Block feature and place it at the end of the document, first add some additional blank lines below the closing:

Press	Home , Home , ↓		*Click*	*at the end of the document*
Press	←Enter twice to skip one line before copying the text to the end of the document		*Press*	*←Enter twice to skip one line before copying the text to the end of the document*
Move	the cursor before the "M" in "Mr." on the first line of the address		*Click*	*before the "M" in "Mr." in the first line of the address*
Press	F12 or Alt + F4		*Drag*	*the mouse until you have highlighted the inside address*
Press	↓ until you have highlighted the inside address			

The top part of your screen should look like Figure 4-14.

Figure 4-14

File Edit View Layout Tools Font Graphics Window Help
July 6, 1993
Mr. Ernest Johnson
10001 Central Parkway
New York, NY 11566
Dear Mr. Johnson:
CONGRATULATIONS on your new business venture. I wish you many years of success.
I would appreciate the opportunity to discuss with you how your company could benefit from our unique solution to your accounting deadlines.

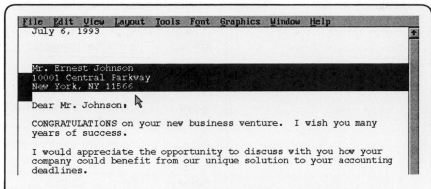

To use the Copy feature:

Press	Ctrl+F4	***Choose***	*Edit*
Press	2 or C to select the Copy and Paste option	***Choose***	*Copy*

To paste the address at the end of the letter:

Press	Home, Home, ↓	***Click***	*at the end of the document*
Press	↵Enter	***Choose***	*Edit*
		Choose	*Paste*

The bottom part of your screen should look like Figure 4-15.

Figure 4-15

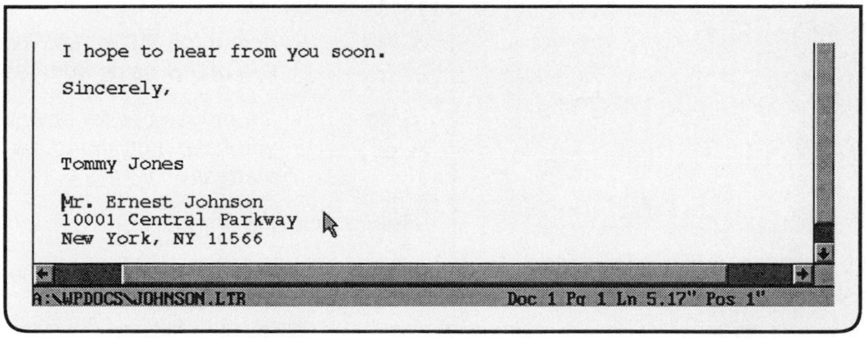

I hope to hear from you soon.
Sincerely,
Tommy Jones
Mr. Ernest Johnson
10001 Central Parkway
New York, NY 11566
A:\WPDOCS\JOHNSON.LTR
Doc 1 Pg 1 Ln 5.17" Pos 1"

Note: To demonstrate the Drag and Drop feature in the next section, please delete the inside address that now appears at the bottom of the letter.

Drag and Drop

The **Drag and Drop feature** allows you to move and copy text by simply using the mouse. To move text using the Drag and Drop feature, highlight the text, drag the cursor to the desired location, and release the mouse button. The text leaves its original position and moves to the position of the cursor. When using the mouse to drag the highlighted text to its new location, the mouse appears to have a tiny piece of paper attached to it. It is important to watch for the location of the cursor. When the cursor is in the desired location, release the mouse button.

To move the first paragraph of your document and place it below the third paragraph using the Drag and Drop feature:

Click	in the first paragraph
Quadruple-click	the paragraph
Move	the mouse pointer over the highlighted text
Drag	the mouse pointer before the "S" in "Sincerely"
Release	the mouse button

The bottom part of your screen should look similar to Figure 4-16.

Figure 4-16

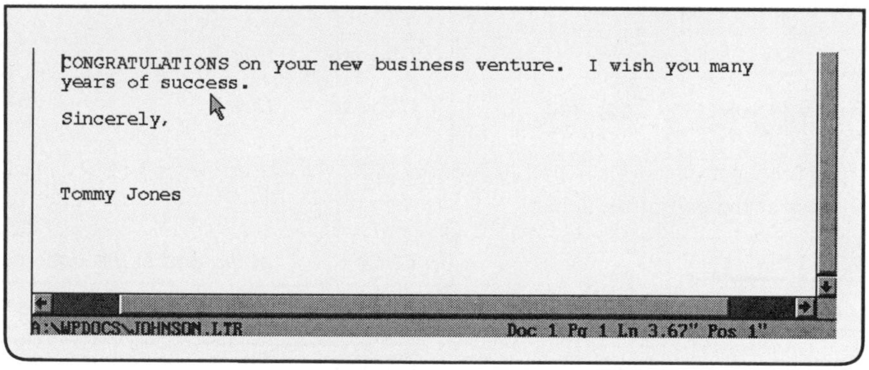

You can also copy text using the Drag and Drop feature. To do so, hold down the CTRL key before dragging the text.   Release the CTRL key after you release the mouse button.

To copy the inside address using the Drag and Drop feature and to place it at the end of the document:

Click	before the "M" in "Mr." on the first line of the inside address
Drag	the mouse pointer downward until you have highlighted the inside address
Hold down	the [Ctrl] key
Drag	the inside address to the bottom of the document
Release	the mouse button
Release	the [Ctrl] key

The bottom part of your screen should look like Figure 4-17.

Figure 4-17

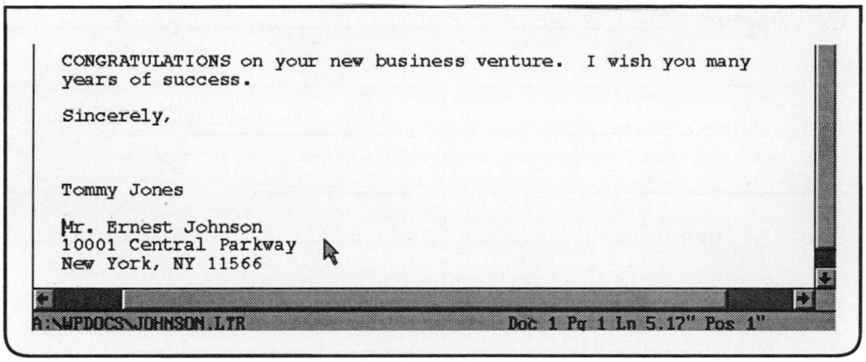

```
CONGRATULATIONS on your new business venture.  I wish you many
years of success.

Sincerely,


Tommy Jones

Mr. Ernest Johnson
10001 Central Parkway
New York, NY 11566
```
A:\WPDOCS\JOHNSON.LTR   Doc 1 Pg 1 Ln 5.17" Pos 1"

For more information on the various cut and copy options, see the WordPerfect Reference manual. Close your document without saving the changes.

EXERCISE 1

INSTRUCTIONS: Define the following concepts:

1. File Manager _____

_____

2. Replace feature _____

_____

3. Search feature _____

_____

4. Reveal codes _____

_____

5. Cut feature _____

_____

6. Select feature _____

_____

7. Block feature _____

_____

8. Soft return _____

_____

9. Convert Case feature _____

_____

10. Search string _____

_____

11.   Copy feature _____

   _____

12.   Paste feature _____

   _____

13.   Drag and Drop feature _____

   _____

14.   Hard return _____

   _____

EXERCISE 2

INSTRUCTIONS:				Circle T if the statement is true and F if the statement is false.
T	F	1.		The File Manager only allows you to open a specified file.
T	F	2.		The Replace feature allows you to locate a word, phrase, or code in a document and replace it with another word, phrase, or code.
T	F	3.		You use the Copy feature to highlight a sentence, paragraph, or page of text.
T	F	4.		When you use the Search feature, you must be at the beginning of the document because you can only search from the cursor forward.
T	F	5.		When you use the Cut feature, the text always stays on the screen.
T	F	6.		If the search string contains only lowercase letters, then WordPerfect will look for matching text that is in lowercase and uppercase.
T	F	7.		The Block feature is used to highlight text within your document.
T	F	8.		The codes that WordPerfect uses are not visible on your normal editing screen.
T	F	9.		When you press ENTER, a hard return code is inserted into the document.
T	F	10.		The Convert Case feature allows text to be changed only from uppercase to lowercase.

EXERCISE 3

INSTRUCTIONS: 1.   Create the following document.
      2.   Save the document in a file using the name "CH04EX03".
      3.   Display the document codes using the Reveal Codes feature. Notice the hard return [HRt] and the soft return [SRt] codes that appear in the document.
      4.   Close the document.

current date

Mr. T. J. Smith
11134 Moss Spring Street
Houston, TX 77081

Dear Mr. Smith:

Please remit your payment that is currently past due as soon as
possible. Your prompt attention to this matter will be appreciated.

We have sent you three letters advising you of the need to complete
payment for the furniture you purchased from us last year.

If you need any additional information at this time, please contact
me at 672-1901.

Sincerely,

Nora Thompson
Accounts Receivable

EXERCISE 4

INSTRUCTIONS:

1. Create the following document.
2. Save the document in a file using the name "CH04EX04".
3. Display the document codes using the Reveal Codes feature. Notice the hard return [HRt] and the soft return [SRt] codes that appear in the document.
4. Close the document.

```
current date


Ms. S. K. Garza
Business Forms Company
2304 Gessner, Suite 798
Miami, FL 33433

Dear Ms. Garza:

Congratulations on your new job.  I know that you will enjoy your
position with Business Forms Company.

If you have any questions about your new position with Business
Forms Company, please contact your supervisor, Ms. Susan Johnson, at
792-4000, extension 7784.

Sincerely,



Mary K. Scanlan
Office Supervisor
```

EXERCISE 5

INSTRUCTIONS:

1. Open the file "CH04EX03" using the File Manager.
2. Search the document from the beginning of the document forward to find each occurrence of the word "**to**".
3. Search the document from the end of the document backward to find each occurrence of the word "**you**".
4. Use the Replace feature to search the document for the name "**Smith**" and replace it with "**Jones**".
5. Search the document for the word "**furniture**" and replace it with the word "**appliances**".
6. Save the document in a file using the name "CH04EX05".
7. Print the document.
8. Close the document.

EXERCISE 6

INSTRUCTIONS:

1. Open the file "CH04EX04" using the File Manager.
2. Search the document from the beginning of the document forward to find each occurrence of the word "**with**".
3. Search the document from the end of the document backward to find each occurrence of the word "**your**".
4. Use the Replace feature to search the document for the name "**Business Forms**" and replace it with "**Graphics Art**".
5. Save the document in a file using the name "CH04EX06".
6. Print the document.
7. Close the document.

EXERCISE 7

INSTRUCTIONS:

1. Create the following document.
2. Save the document in a file using the name "CH04EX07".
3. Print the document.
4. Change the case of the words "**General Computer Corporation**" to uppercase.
5. Change the case of the word "**wonderful**" to uppercase.
6. Change the case of the word "**SUCCESS**" to lowercase.
7. Change the case of the word "**ME**" to lowercase.
8. Print the document.
9. Save the document using the same filename.
10. Close the document.

```
current date


Dear Shirley,

Thank you for your recent letter regarding your new job at General
Computer Corporation.  I think the SUCCESS you are enjoying is
wonderful.

Please keep ME informed about your activities in your new position.

With all my love,


Aunt Jan
```

EXERCISE 8

INSTRUCTIONS:

1. Create the following document. Note that you will move information around in the exercise so the document will make more sense.
2. Save the document in a file using the name "CH04EX08".
3. Print the document.
4. Move the third paragraph so it appears as the first paragraph in the document.
5. Move the second paragraph so it appears as the third paragraph in the document.
6. Print the document.
7. Save the document using the same name.
8. Close the document.

```
current date


Mr. A. J. Bohem
West Coast Production Company
11235 Anaheim Blvd.
Los Angeles, CA 90014

Dear A. J.:

Thanks again for your recent order from us.

We hope that you find our products to be the best quality available.

Thank you for your recent letter in which you requested we send you
10 of our best water pumps.  I am sure you will enjoy using these
fine products.

Sincerely,


T. J. Chin
```

EXERCISE 9

INSTRUCTIONS:

1. Create the following document. Note that you will move information around in the exercise so the document will make more sense.
2. Save the document in a file using the name "CH04EX09".
3. Print the document.
4. Move the third paragraph so it appears as the second paragraph in the document.
5. Create a fourth paragraph. Copy the contents of the first paragraph **(FANTASTIC NEWS!!!)** to create a fourth paragraph.
6. Print the document.
7. Save the document using the same name.
8. Close the document.

```
current date


Mr. C. S. Baker
Midway Distribution Company
9225 Golden Arch Way
Chicago, IL 60606

Dear Carl:

FANTASTIC NEWS!!!

We will serve dinner for a maximum of four people any evening
between now and the end of the month.  Please call me at 758-4700 so
we can make arrangements for the dinner.

You have been selected as a winner in our special drawing for a
dinner.  Your name was selected from business cards left in our
restaurant.

Cordially,



Susan K. Thomas
Chicken Delight Restaurant
```

EXERCISE 10

INSTRUCTIONS:

1. Create the following document.
2. Save the document in a file using the name "CH04EX10".
3. Change the words "**Global Marketing**" to uppercase.
4. Change the word "**newest**" to uppercase.
5. Change words "**Special Delivery**" to uppercase.
6. Search the document from beginning to end for each occurrence of the word "**the**".
7. Move the second paragraph so it appears as the first paragraph in the document.
8. Change the case of the words "**EXAMINATION COPY**" to lowercase.
9. Print the document.
10. Save the document using the same name.
11. Close the document.

```
current date

Special Delivery

Dr. Don Sedik
William Rainey Harper College
1200 Algonquin Road
Palatine, IL 60067

Dear Dr. Sedik:

We would like to invite you to preview Global Marketing, the newest
text for the International Marketing Courses.  Global Marketing will
bring the European Common Market and the Asian markets right to your
classroom.

Global Marketing is just off the press.  Global Marketing is written
by two professors who have studied global markets from inside the
Common Market.

Return the enclosed card to receive Global Marketing as an
EXAMINATION COPY.

Sincerely,



Mark Healy
Director of Marketing
```

EXERCISE 11

INSTRUCTIONS:

1. Create the following document.
2. Save the document in a file using the name "CH04EX11".
3. Print the document.
4. Move the third paragraph so it appears as the first paragraph.
5. Search the document from the beginning forward to find each occurrence of the word "**your**".
6. In the second paragraph, delete the words "**future litigation**" and insert "**income tax fraud**".
7. Search the document from the end of the document backwards and replace "**Accountants Association**" with "**CPAs**".
8. In the first paragraph, insert "**$100**" after the word "**enclosed**".
9. Preview the document.
10. Save the document using the same name.
11. Print the document.
12. Close the document.

```
current date


Dr. Dan Danis
Dewey, Cheatum & Howe
616 North Michigan
Albuquerque, NM 87100

Dear Dr. Danis:

It was kind of you to address the Albuquerque Accountants
Association.  Your talk on white-collar fraud was very informative
and entertaining.

The Albuquerque Accountants Association will long remember your talk
and its implications for future litigation.

On behalf of the members of the Albuquerque Accountants Association,
please accept the enclosed check for your March 25 speech.

Thank you,



Robert Held, President
Albuquerque Accountants Association
```

EXERCISE 12

INSTRUCTIONS:

1. Create the following document.
2. Save the document in a file using the name "CH04EX12".
3. Display the Reveal Codes. Notice the hard return [HRt] and the soft return [SRt] codes that appear in the document.
4. Print the document.
5. Use the Replace feature to delete the company name **"ROSS, ANDERSON & COMPANY, INC."** and replace it with the name **"WORLDWIDE ACCOUNTING"**.
6. Move the first sentence of the first paragraph so it appears as the second sentence of the first paragraph in the document.
7. Search the document for the word **"auditor"** and replace it with **"director of financial resources"**.
8. Proofread the document and correct the errors created with changing **"auditor"** to **"director of financial resources"**.
9. Change the case of the words **"Certified Mail"** to uppercase.
10. Preview and print the document.
11. Save the document using the same name.
12. Close the document.

current date

Certified Mail

Mrs. Rose Trunk
5999 North Meridian Street
Indianapolis, IN 46206

Dear Mrs. Trunk:

Your name has been suggested as a possible auditor for a position that involves extensive foreign travel. We are very interested in an individual who is willing to travel in Europe, the Far East, and Australia.

The position involves representing us as an auditor in areas where we have operations, sales representatives, and regional offices.

The initial salary for an auditor is negotiable. If you would be interested in talking about this position further, contact Mr. Charles Norris, Director of Financial Operations.

Very cordially yours,

ROSS, ANDERSON & COMPANY, INC.

James Seeck
Vice President

CHAPTER FIVE

USING THE WORDPERFECT BUTTON BAR

OBJECTIVES

In this chapter you will learn to:
- Use the Button Bar to perform tasks
- Create a Button Bar
- Customize a Button Bar
- Change the format of the Button Bar
- Select a different Button Bar

■ CHAPTER OVERVIEW

In this chapter, the WordPerfect Button Bar is discussed. The View Button Bar feature is introduced. The methods for using a Button Bar to create and edit a document are described. Finally, the process for creating, customizing, and formatting the Button Bar are presented.

■ USING THE BUTTON BAR TO PERFORM TASKS

This book has presented three methods for selecting features: using the keyboard function keys, using the mouse with the menus, and selecting from the menu with the keyboard. WordPerfect provides an alternative method to quickly access commands with the mouse. This feature is called the Button Bar.

The **Button Bar** is made up of buttons that represent commands. Each command has a predefined button. The most commonly used commands have been placed on the default Button Bar. The default Button Bar has 15 buttons. Thirteen buttons are visible. The other two buttons are accessed by clicking the down arrow on the left side of the Button Bar. The buttons can only be accessed using the mouse. By default, the Button Bar appears above the document area on the screen. Changing its position is discussed later in this chapter. To view the Button Bar if it is not presently visible on your screen:

> **Choose**   *View*
>
> **Choose**   *Button Bar*

Notice that Print is one of the buttons on the default Button Bar. Instead of pressing SHIFT+F7 or choosing File Print/Fax from the menu, you can click the Print button to select the command. To save the document, you may choose the Save As button instead of pressing F10 or choosing Save As from the File menu.

To preview a document using the Button Bar:

> **Click**   the Preview button on the Button
> Bar

> **Click**   the Zoom 100% button on the
> Button Bar

The Preview window appears on the screen displaying your document in 100% Zoom mode. Your screen should look like Figure 5-1.

Figure 5-1

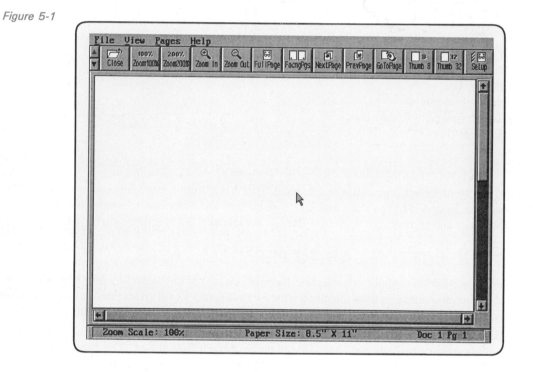

To close the Preview window:

> **Click**   the Close button on the Button
> Bar

To save a document using the Button Bar:

> **Click**   the Save As button on the Button
> Bar

The Save Document 1 dialog box appears on the screen. Your screen should look like Figure 5-2.

Figure 5-2

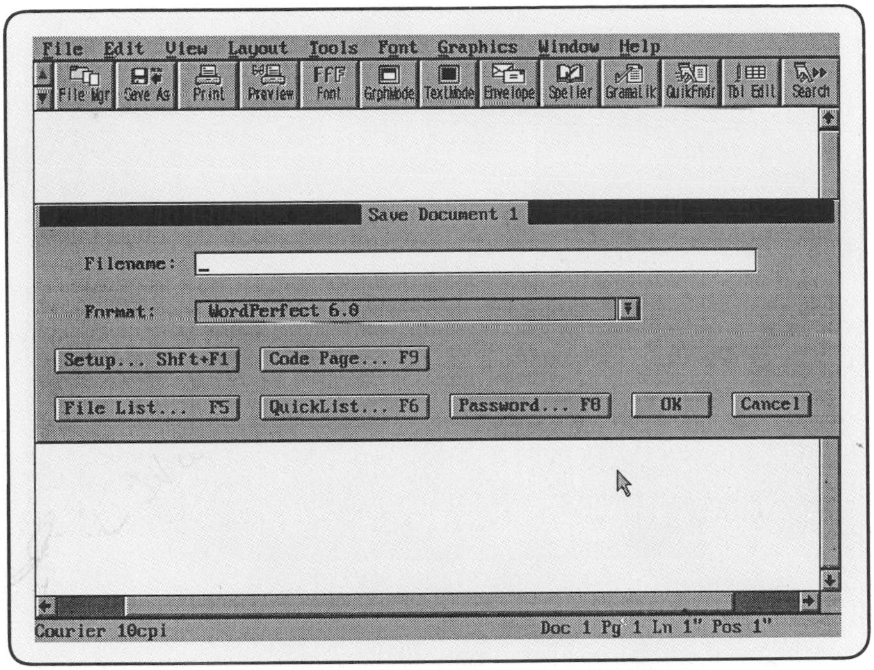

Click on the Cancel command button to remove the dialog box from the screen.

■ CREATING A BUTTON BAR

WordPerfect 6.0 has seven Button Bars built into it. You may select one of these Button Bars or you may choose to create your own Button Bar. You can create your own Button Bar by selecting the Button Bar Setup, Select command in the View menu. **Note:** Some of the commands in this chapter may be issued from the keyboard. However, because the Button Bar is primarily a tool to be used only with the mouse, you will only be given mouse instructions in this chapter.

To create a new Button Bar:

Choose	*View*
Choose	*Button Bar Setup*
Choose	*Select*

The Select Button Bar dialog box appears. Your screen should look like Figure 5-3.

Figure 5-3

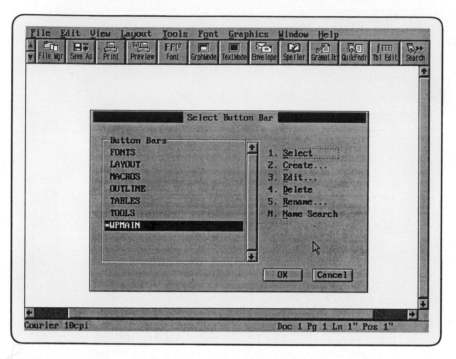

To create a custom Button Bar:

Choose	the Create option
Type	MYBUTTON in the Button Bar Name box
Click	the OK command button

The Edit Button Bar dialog box appears.   Your screen should look like Figure 5-4.

Figure 5-4

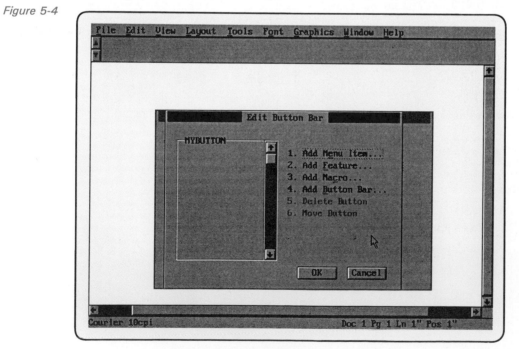

To add a command to the bar, choose Add Menu Item and then select the specific command from the menu. You may use the keyboard or mouse to select items from the menu.

To add a button for the File Open command:

Choose	*Add Menu Item*
Choose	*File*
Choose	*Open*

Your screen should look like Figure 5-5.

Figure 5-5

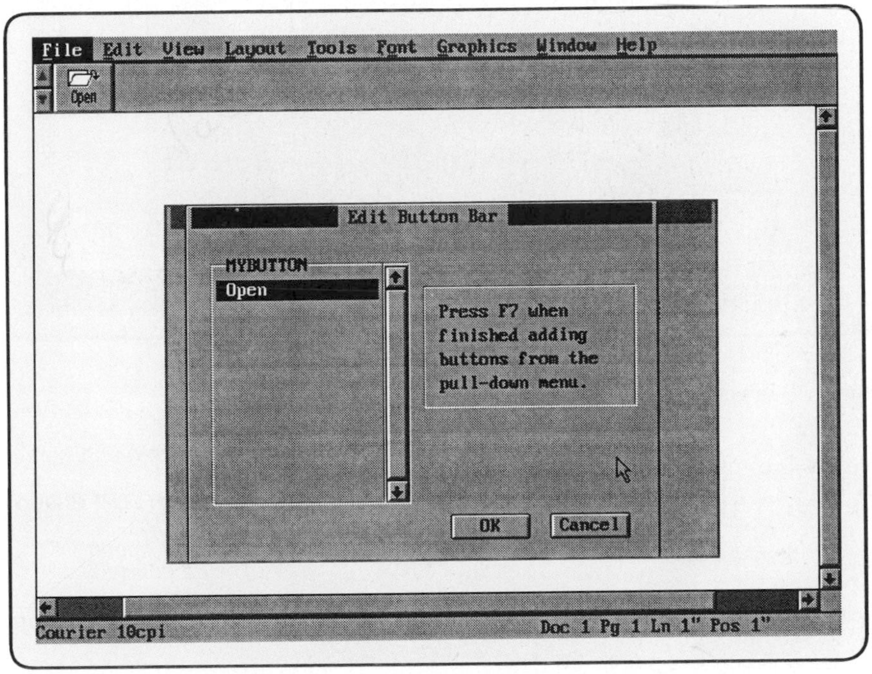

The Open command appears at the beginning of the Button Bar. To complete the Button Bar, add the following menu items:

> File Close
>
> File Save
>
> File Print
>
> Edit Undelete
>
> Edit Convert Case Uppercase
>
> Edit Convert Case Lowercase
>
> Edit Replace
>
> View Reveal Codes

Your screen should look like Figure 5-6.

Figure 5-6

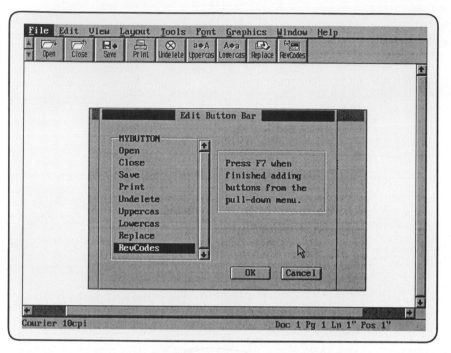

To use the Button Bar you created:

Click	*the OK command button*
Choose	*the MYBUTTON Button Bar*
Choose	*the Select option*

The newly created Button Bar appears on the screen. The top part of your screen should look like Figure 5-7.

Figure 5-7

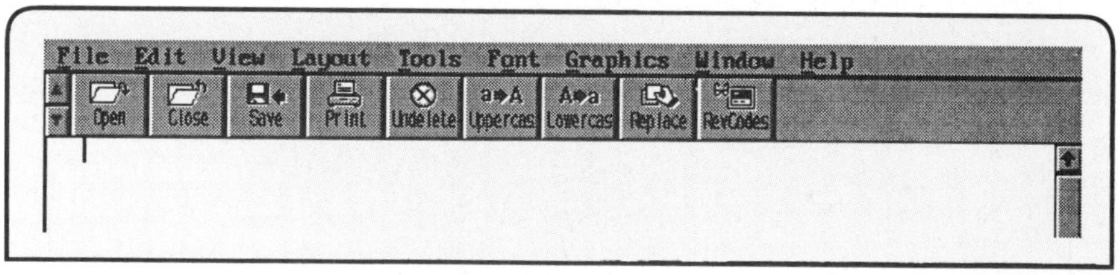

■ CUSTOMIZING A BUTTON BAR

You might use different commands from those appearing on the Button Bar. You can customize the Button Bar by selecting the Button Bar Setup, Edit command in the View menu.

Deleting a Button

To delete a button, highlight the button and choose the Delete command. To delete the "Replace" button:

Choose	*View*
Choose	*Button Bar Setup*
Choose	*Edit*
Select	*the Replace command in the MYBUTTON list box*
Choose	*the Delete Button option*
Choose	*the Yes command button*

The "Replace" command button is gone from the Button Bar. Your screen should look like Figure 5-8.

Figure 5-8

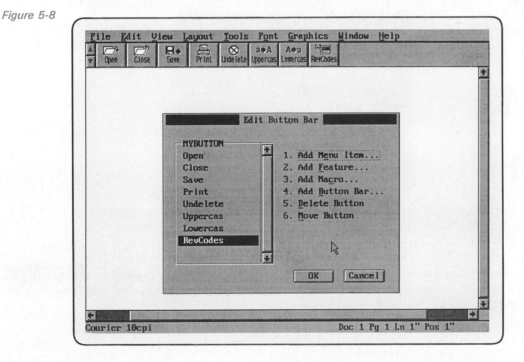

Adding a Button

You should still be in the Button Bar Edit mode. To return the "Replace" button to the Button Bar:

Choose	*Add Menu Item*
Choose	*Edit*
Choose	*Replace*
Click	*the OK command button*

The Replace button reappears at the end of the Button Bar.

Moving a Button

To move the position of a button, highlight the command in the list box by clicking on it or by pressing arrow keys to select it. Once the desired command is highlighted, select the Move Button option. The selected command will disappear from the list. Highlight the command appearing in the place you want to move the selected command and select the Paste Button option.

Remaining in the Button Bar Edit mode, to move the "Replace" button back to its original location:

> **Select**   *the Replace command in the MYBUTTON list box*
>
> **Choose**   *the Move Button option*

Your screen should look like Figure 5-9.

Figure 5-9

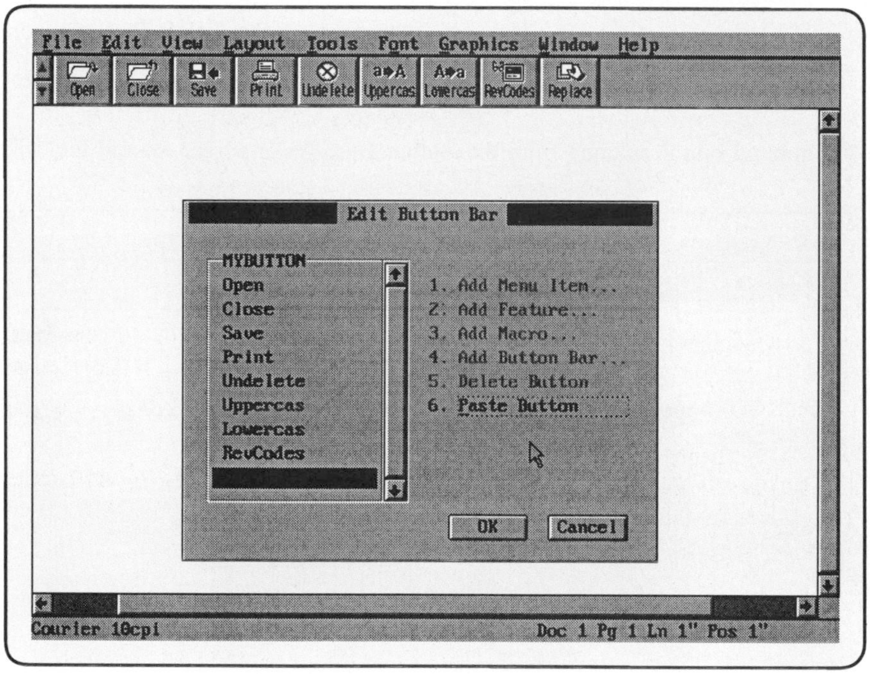

Notice that the "Replace" selection is gone from the list. In addition, the Move Button option has been replaced by a Paste Button option. To place the Replace button before the "RevCodes" command and close the dialog box:

> **Select**   *the RevCodes command in the MYBUTTON list box*
>
> **Choose**   *the Paste Button option*
>
> **Click**   *the OK command button*

The top part of your screen should look like Figure 5-10.

Figure 5-10

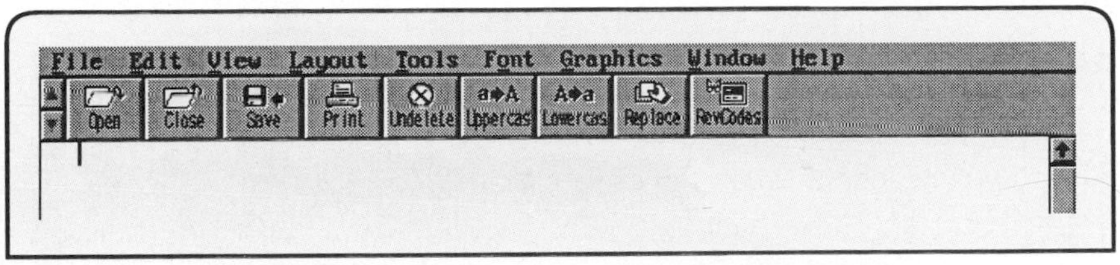

The "Replace" button appears to the left of the "RevCodes" button on the Button Bar. Any of the buttons may be placed in different positions.

Removing the Button Bar from Display

When you close a document, the Button Bar remains on the screen. To remove the Button Bar from the screen:

Choose	*View*
Choose	*Button Bar*

The Button Bar no longer appears on the screen. Return the Button Bar to the screen by selecting the View Button Bar command again.

■ FORMATTING THE BUTTON BAR

You can change the location of the Button Bar on the screen or the appearance of the buttons. Use the Button Bar Setup Options command from the View menu to change the Button Bar format.

By default, the Button Bar appears at the top of the WordPerfect screen and displays a graphic and text. You can change the location of the Button Bar to any border of the screen.

You can also change the appearance of the buttons. As an alternative to viewing both text and graphics, you can display text only or graphics only.

To change the placement and appearance of the Button Bar:

Choose	*View*
Choose	*Button Bar Setup*
Choose	*Options*

The Button Bar Options dialog box appears. Your screen should look like Figure 5-11.

Figure 5-11

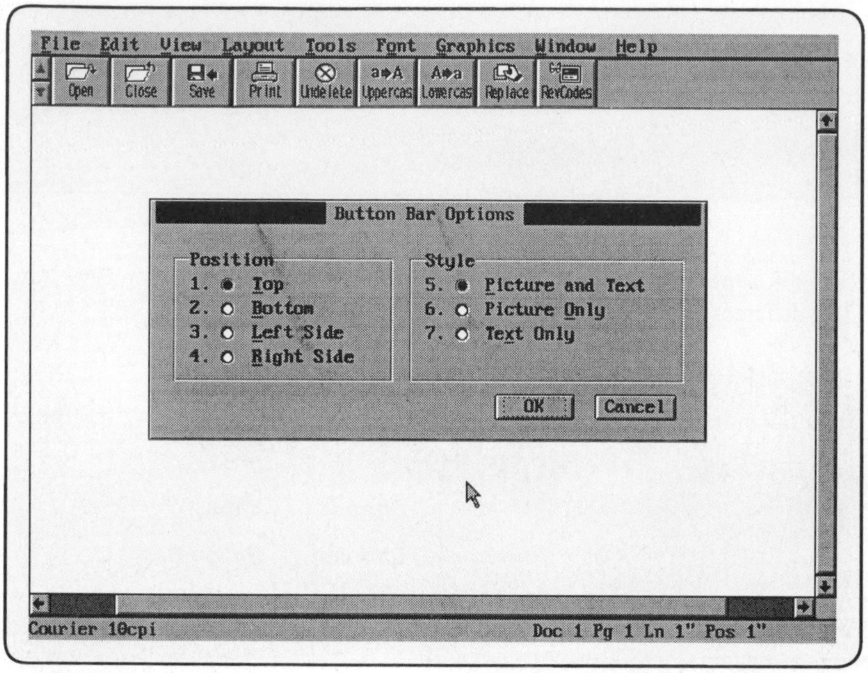

To change the position of the Button Bar to the right side of the screen:

Click   *the Right Side option button in the Position option box*

To change the appearance of the Button Bar to Picture Only:

Click   *the Picture Only option button in the Style option box*

To accept the changes to the Button Bar and close the dialog box:

Click   *the OK command button*

Your screen should look like Figure 5-12.

Figure 5-12

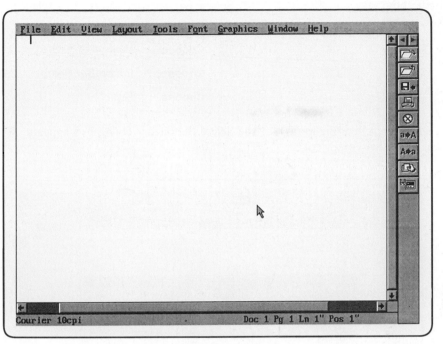

The Button Bar appears at the right of the screen. Each button contains only the picture representing that command. The individual buttons are smaller. The smaller buttons allow more buttons to be placed on the bar. However, without the text, some of the pictures are difficult to understand.

To change the Button Bar back to the defaults:

Choose	*View*
Choose	*Button Bar Setup*
Choose	*Options*

To change the position and style settings:

Click	*the Top option button in the Position option box*
Click	*the Picture and Text option button in the Style option box*

To accept the changes:

Click	*the OK command button*

■ SELECTING A DIFFERENT BUTTON BAR

WordPerfect has seven Button Bars already created to assist with creation of tables, macros, and other features. Use the Button Bar Setup Select command sequence from the View menu to choose a different Button Bar.

You should currently have the "MYBUTTON" Button Bar on your screen. To select the "WPMAIN" Button Bar:

Choose	*View*
Choose	*Button Bar Setup*
Choose	*Select*

Your screen should look like Figure 5-13. The Select Button Bar dialog box appears. The Button Bar choices appear in the list box.

Figure 5-13

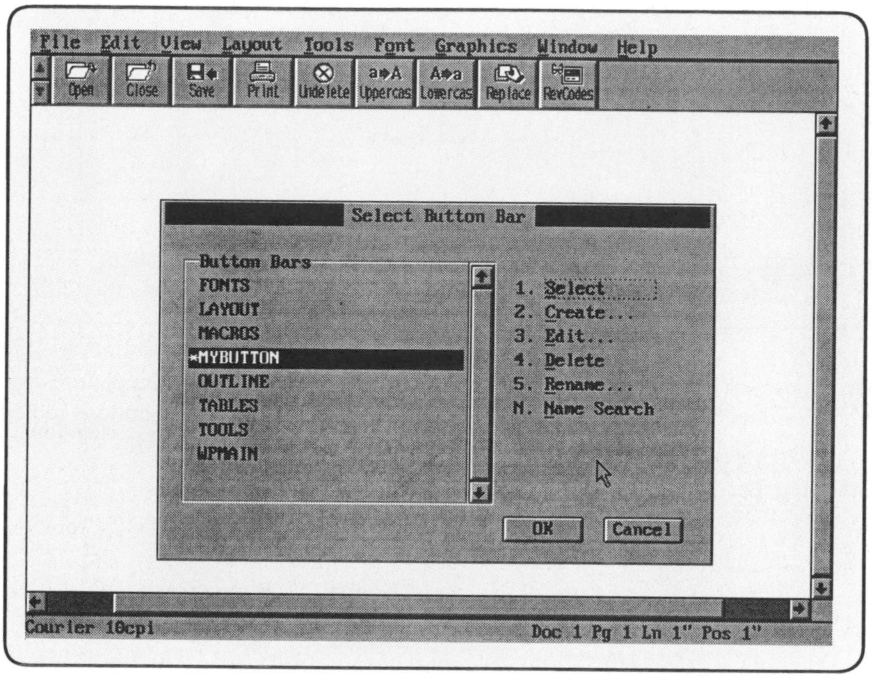

To select the "WPMAIN" Button Bar:

Choose	*the WPMAIN choice in the Button Bars list box*
Choose	*the Select option*

The "WPMAIN" Button Bar appears on your screen. The top part of your screen should look like Figure 5-14.

Figure 5-14

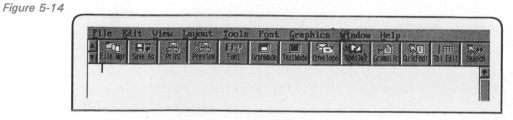

EXERCISE 1

INSTRUCTIONS: Define the following concepts:

1. View Button Bar feature _____

    _____

2. Button Bar Setup Edit feature _____

    _____

3. Button Bar Setup Options feature _____

    _____

4. Button Bar Setup Select feature _____

    _____

EXERCISE 2

INSTRUCTIONS: Circle T if the statement is true and F if the statement is false.

T	F	1.	The Button Bar feature allows you to perform commands quickly by clicking on buttons that represent commands.
T	F	2.	The default Button Bar is called "WPMAIN".
T	F	3.	You can customize a Button Bar by using the View Button Bar command.
T	F	4.	The Print feature has a button on the default Button Bar.
T	F	5.	When you use the Button Bar Setup Options command, you can move the buttons on the Button Bar.
T	F	6.	The Button Bar Setup Options command allows you to change the position of the Button Bar.
T	F	7.	Buttons can contain text, pictures, or text and pictures.

EXERCISE 3

INSTRUCTIONS:
1. Open the "JOHNSON.LTR" file.
2. Display the default Button Bar.
3. Print the document using the Button Bar.
4. Close the document using the Button Bar.

EXERCISE 4

INSTRUCTIONS:
1. Open the "JOHNSON.LTR" file.
2. Display the default Button Bar.
3. Using the Button Bar, search the document for the word "**business**".
4. Using the Button Bar, preview the document.
5. Using the Button Bar, close the document. Do not save changes to the document.

EXERCISE 5

INSTRUCTIONS: 1. Create a Button Bar using the name "CH05EX05".
2. The Button Bar should be able to perform the following commands:
File Save As
File Open
File Close
Edit Replace
Edit Copy
Edit Paste
Edit Undelete

EXERCISE 6

INSTRUCTIONS: 1. View the "CH05EX05" Button Bar.
2. Using the Button Bar, open the "JOHNSON.LTR" file.
3. Using the Button Bar, replace each occurrence of the word "**Johnson**" with the word "**Smith**".
4. Using the Button Bar, copy and paste the inside address to the bottom of the document.
5. Using the Button Bar, save the document as "CH05EX06".
6. Using the Button Bar, close the document.

EXERCISE 7

INSTRUCTIONS: 1. Edit the "CH05EX05" Button Bar.
2. Delete the Undelete button.
3. Move the Open button to the first position on the Button Bar.
4. Add a File Save button to the Button Bar.
5. Move the Save As button to the end of the Button Bar.
6. Save the changes to the Button Bar.

EXERCISE 8

INSTRUCTIONS: 1. Change the options for the "CH05EX05" Button Bar.
2. Place the Button Bar on the bottom of the screen.
3. Change the button style to text only.
4. Save the changes to the Button Bar.
5. Change the Button Bar position to the left of the screen.
6. Change the button style to picture only.
7. Return the Button Bar to its original location at the top of the screen. Make it display text and picture.
8. Change to the "WPMAIN" default Button Bar.

CHAPTER SIX

THE SPELLER, THESAURUS, AND GRAMMATIK FEATURES

OBJECTIVES

In this chapter, you will learn to:
- Use the Speller feature
- Use the Thesaurus feature
- Use the Grammatik feature

■ CHAPTER OVERVIEW

In this chapter, the Speller, Thesaurus, and Grammatik features are discussed and demonstrated.

■ USING THE SPELLER FEATURE

You can use the WordPerfect Speller feature to check for spelling errors in your document. The Speller can also find repeated words, words that contain numbers, and words with irregular capitalization.

To access any of the three features, press ALT+F1 or select the Writing Tools option from the Tools menu. A dialog box displays options for using the Speller, the Thesaurus, Grammatik or Document Information. To use the Speller, press 1 or S, or click on the selection. The Speller dialog box appears. You may check a word, page, document, or from the cursor to the end of the document. You may also look up a particular word or edit the existing Supplemental dictionary.

When WordPerfect finds a word that it does not recognize, it tries to find all the possible words that you could have meant to write. These words are displayed in the Suggestions list box, and you can select one to replace the word in your text. You can also edit the unrecognized word, or you can choose to ignore the Speller and continue with the spell check.

> **In This Book**
>
> Earlier in this book, you were given instructions on how to create and use a subdirectory. For the remainder of this book, it will be assumed that you know where you are saving your files and where they are stored for purposes of retrieval. You will simply be told to save or retrieve a file.

Open the "JOHNSON.LTR" document created in Chapter 3.

To show the use of the Speller feature, you need to intentionally make some errors in the letter. Before you proceed with this chapter, make the following changes to the document:

Add "**, Suite 3A**" to the end of the street address.

Change the case on "**CONGRATULATIONS**" to "**COngratulations**".

Misspell "**appreciate**" by removing a "**p**".

Misspell "**opportunity**" by removing the first "**o**".

Misspell "**from**" by removing the "**r**".

In the last sentence of the letter, add an extra "**to**" next to the original "**to**" with a space in between them.

To start the Speller feature:

Press   Ctrl + F2

Click   *the Speller button on the Button Bar*

The Speller dialog box appears on the screen. Your screen should look like Figure 6-1.

Figure 6-1

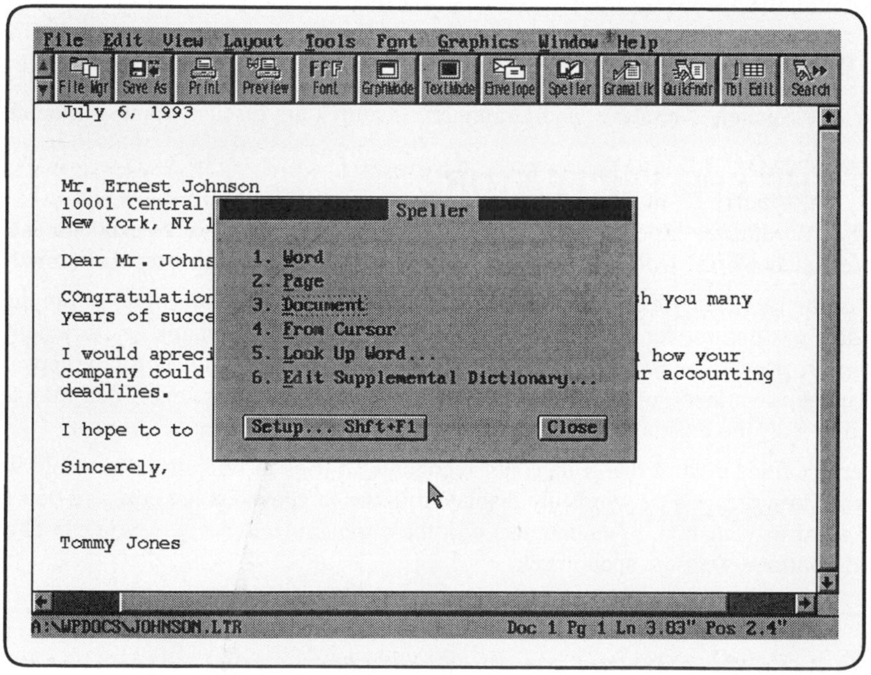

To select the option for spell checking the entire document:

Press   3 or D to select the Document option

Choose   *the Document option*

When the Speller feature does not find a word in the dictionary, it highlights the word in the document and displays a list of possible choices in the Suggestions list box. The most likely correct word appears in the Word text box.

The commands you may use to continue the Speller feature are described below:

Skip Once - WordPerfect has found a word that it does not know. This option allows you to tell WordPerfect to skip this occurrence of the word, and continue with the spell check. In choosing this option, WordPerfect will stop again on this word if it is found later in the document. In the "JOHNSON.LTR" document, you will want to skip the word "3A".

Skip in this Document - This option allows you to tell WordPerfect not only to skip this one occurrence of this word, but to skip this word every time it occurs in the rest of the document.

Add to Dictionary - Add this word to the supplemental dictionary so that it is valid for every document that you spell check.

Edit Word - This option permits you to manually alter the spelling of a word. When you are finished editing the word, press F7 or ENTER to resume the spell checking operation.

Look Up - There may be times when you cannot begin to know how to spell a certain word. This option enables you to look up a word based on a few letters and a pattern symbol. A "?" stands for a single letter that you do not know. An "*" stands for zero or more letters after the pattern. For example, "so?p*" lists such words as soap, soapier, soapbox, soup, and soupy.

Ignore Numbers - This option permits you to globally ignore number and letter combinations common in inventory lists.

Replace Word - This option replaces the incorrect word in the document with the text that appears in the Word text box of the Speller. If the suggested word is incorrect, you may highlight the correct word in the Suggestions list box and it will appear in the Word text box.

Select Dictionary - With this option, you may specify a different supplemental dictionary. See the "Speller" section in the WordPerfect Reference manual for more information.

To skip the word "3A":

Press	1 or O to select the Skip Once option	*Choose*	the Skip Once option

To correct the case on "COngratulations":

Press	⬇ to highlight "Congratulations" in the Suggestions list box	*Choose*	"Congratulations" in the Suggestions list box
Press	3 or R to replace the word	*Choose*	the Replace Word option

To select the proper spelling of "apreciate":

Press	arrow keys to select the word "appreciate" in the Suggestions list box (if it is not already the suggested word)		*Choose*	*the word "appreciate" in the Suggestions list box (if it is not already the suggested word)*
Press	7 or R or ↵Enter to select the Replace option		*Choose*	*the Replace Word option*

To correct the misspelled word "pportunity":

Press	4 or W to select the Edit Word option		*Choose*	*the Edit Word option*
Type	o		*Type*	*o*
Press	F7 or ↵Enter to return to the spell checking procedure		*Press*	*F7 or ↵Enter to return to the spell checking procedure*

To select the proper spelling of "fom", follow the same steps as those used above for correcting "appreciate". You may need to use the scroll bar in the Suggestions list box in order to see the correct spelling of "from."

To delete the second occurrence of the word "to":

Press	3 or D to select the Delete Duplicate Word option		*Choose*	*the Delete Duplicate Word option*

Some portion of a name may become highlighted because it is not found in a dictionary. The Speller feature does not recognize most proper names.

To indicate "Tommy" is spelled correctly and that you wish to add it to the dictionary:

Press	3 or T to select the Add to Dictionary option		*Choose*	*the Add to Dictionary option*

Your screen should look like Figure 6-2.

Figure 6-2

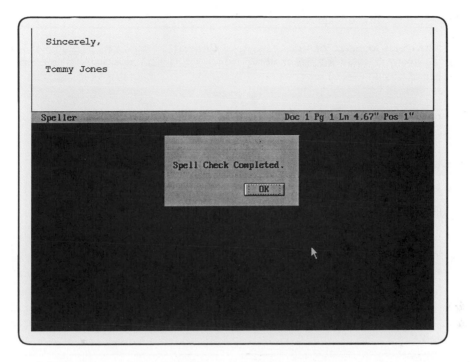

A dialog box is displayed with the message "Spell check completed."

To close the dialog box:

| **Press** | [←Enter] | **Click** | *the OK command button* |

You can also access the Speller feature through the "TOOLS" Button Bar.

■ USING THE THESAURUS FEATURE

The Thesaurus feature displays words with the same or very similar meaning as that of the word at the cursor.

To show a list of words that mean the same as "benefit" in the second paragraph:

Move	the cursor anywhere in the word "benefit"	**Click**	*on the word "benefit"*
Press	[Alt] + [F1]	**Choose**	*Tools*
Press	2 or T to select the Thesaurus option	**Choose**	*Writing Tools*
		Choose	*Thesaurus*

The Thesaurus dialog box appears on the screen. Your screen should look like Figure 6-3.

Figure 6-3

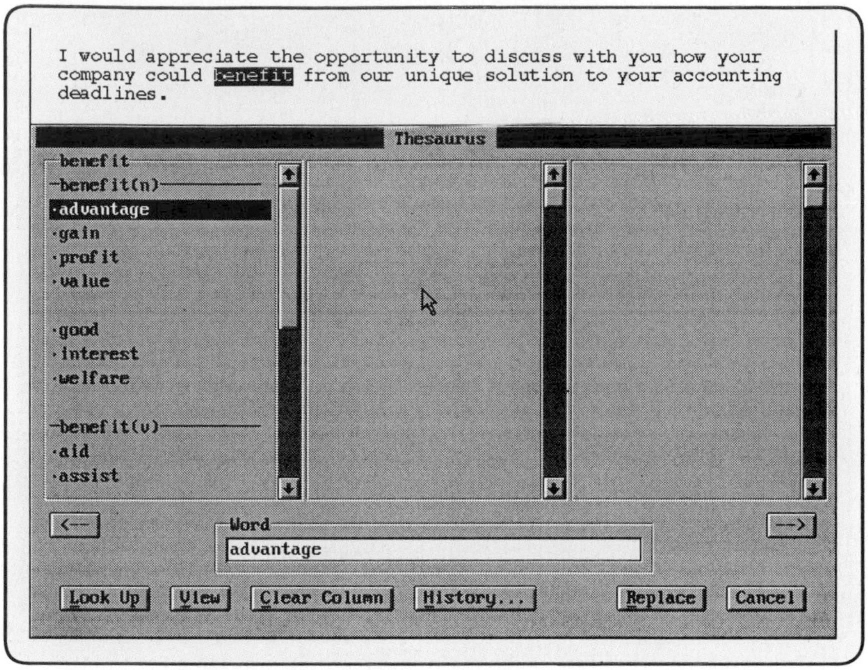

To replace "benefit" with "profit":

Press	arrow keys until "profit" is highlighted	*Click*	on the word "profit" in the benefit box
Press	R to select the Replace command button	*Click*	the Replace command button

The word "benefit" is now replaced by "profit".

You can also access the Thesaurus feature through the "TOOLS" Button Bar.

■ USING THE GRAMMATIK FEATURE

WordPerfect 6.0 offers a grammar checker called Grammatik. With this tool, you can examine sentence structure and identify many errors, including incomplete sentences, run-on sentences, and sentences ending in prepositions and other errors in language usage. Consult the WordPerfect Reference manual for more details about the errors Grammatik can correct.

Before using the Grammatik feature, it is helpful to have the desired document already on the screen. For our purposes, we will continue to use the "JOHNSON.LTR" file.

To start the Grammatik feature:

Press	Alt + F1	*Click*	the Grammatik button on the Button Bar 
Press	3 or G to select Grammatik		

In a moment or two, the Grammatik software introduction screen appears. You may use items from the menu or select a quick option from the bottom on the screen. Press "I" or click on "Interactive check" to begin an interactive check. The Error Detection Screen appears below the document. Your screen should look like Figure 6-4.

Figure 6-4

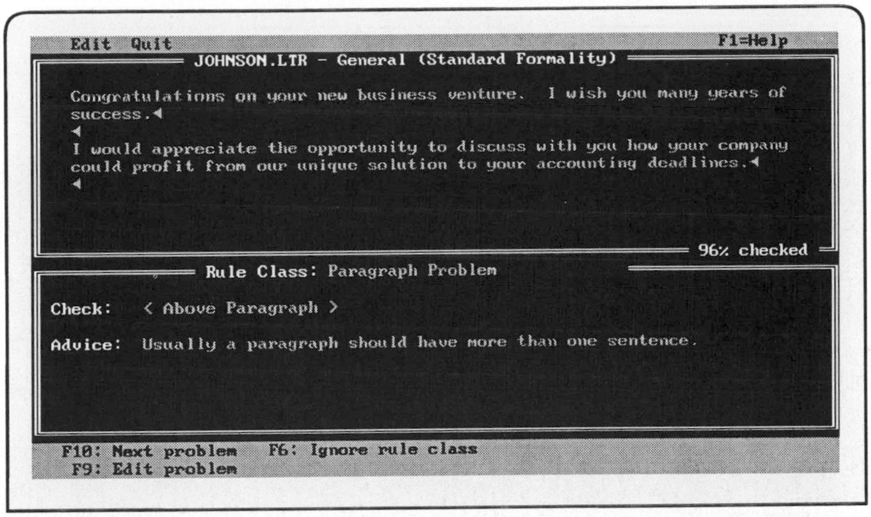

A Rule Class appears describing the type of problem found. You are offered advice about the problem.

The following options appear at the top and bottom of the screen to assist you with either correcting the error or ignoring it:

> **F1 Help** - This command takes you to the Help feature, explains in detail why the error is being noted, and suggests what you can do to correct it.

> **Quit** - This command closes Grammatik.

> **Edit** - This command displays a list of the various commands listed below. In addition, with the F8 key, you are able to mark a problem and return to fix it later. With the F4 key, you may display information about parts of speech.

> **F6 Ignore rule class** - When you select this command, you are telling Grammatik to skip all occurrences of this type of error for the rest of this proofreading session.

> **F9 Edit problem** - When you select this command, you are permitted to edit the existing text. When finished, you may press F9 to have the text reviewed again or F10 to resume on the next problem.

> **F10 Next problem** - This command is used after the **Replace** button or can be used to ignore the advice about a particular problem.

As we examine the "JOHNSON.LTR" file, we will be alerted to single sentence paragraphs and starting too many sentences with the word "I". In every error, select the option for **Next Problem** to ignore making any corrections.

When Grammatik is finished examining the entire document, you are returned to the opening Grammatik screen. You may view Readability Statistics or set other Preferences related to the Grammatik feature by pressing ALT and a highlighted letter at the top of the screen or by clicking on the desired option. For more information about Grammatik, consult the WordPerfect Reference manual.

To return to the document editing screen, press Q for Quit or click on the Quit Grammatik command in the bottom of the screen. The document remains on the screen. You will need to resave the document with any changes made during the Grammatik check.

You can also access the Grammatik feature through the "TOOLS" Button Bar.

Save your document, replacing the old contents of the file with the current document. Close the document.

EXERCISE 1

INSTRUCTIONS: Define the following concepts:

1.   Speller feature _____

_____

2.   Thesaurus feature _____

_____

3.   Grammatik feature _____

_____

EXERCISE 2

INSTRUCTIONS: Circle T if the statement is true and F if the statement is false.

T   F   1.   The WordPerfect Speller feature only checks for spelling errors in your document.

T   F   2.   The Speller feature can only spell check a word or page.

T   F   3.   When a word is not found by the Speller feature, it is highlighted and a list of possible choices is displayed.

T   F   4.   The Speller feature recognizes proper names as words.

T   F   5.   When a spell check is complete, a count of the number of words is shown at the bottom left of the screen.

T   F   6.   The Thesaurus feature displays words with the same or very similar meaning as that of the word at the cursor.

T   F   7.   The Grammatik feature will alert you to "run-on" sentences.

EXERCISE 3

INSTRUCTIONS:

1.   Create the following document. Prepare the document exactly as it appears. You will correct the errors using the Speller feature.

2.   Correct the spelling errors using the Speller feature.

3.   Use the Thesaurus feature to select another word for **"comparing"** in the first paragraph.

4.   Use the Thesaurus feature to choose another word for **"approach"** in the second paragraph.

5.   Use the Thesaurus feature to pick another word for **"purchase"** in the second paragraph.

6.   Save the document in a file using the name "CH06EX03".

7.   Print the document.

8.   Close the document.

```
current date


Ms. Betty Smith
3457 Tanglewood Drive
Seattle, WA 99703-4596

Dear Ms. Smith:

I recently read your article comparing wrd processing software
packages in a personal computer magazine.

As I read through the article, I really appreciated the ojeciv
approach you took in preparin the materials.  It helped me decide to
purchase WordPerfect 6.0 for DOS.

Cordially,



Thomas J. Tucker
```

EXERCISE 4

INSTRUCTIONS:

1. Create the following document. Prepare the document exactly as it appears. You will correct the errors using the Speller feature.
2. Correct the spelling errors using the Speller feature.
3. Use the Thesaurus feature to select another word for "**document**" in the first paragraph.
4. Use the Thesaurus feature to choose another word for "**contact**" in the third paragraph.
5. Save the document in a file using the name "CH06EX04".
6. Print the document.
7. Close the document.

current date

Ms. Jo Ann Garza
1717 W. 43rd St.
Seattle, WA 93712

Dear Ms. Garza:

Per our conversation, enclosed is a credit application for our
departent stor. Please complete all qustions and return the
document to me at yore ealiest convenince.

We are sure that yu will enjy using our credet card.

If you have any questions concernng the credit application, please
contact me.

Sincerely yours,

T. W. House

EXERCISE 5

INSTRUCTIONS:

1. Create the following document. Prepare the document exactly as it appears. You will correct the errors using the Speller feature.
2. Correct the spelling errors using the Speller feature.
3. Once the spelling errors are corrected, use the Thesaurus feature to select another word for "**recommendation**" in the first paragraph.
4. Use the Thesaurus feature to select another word for "**inconvenience**" in the third paragraph.
5. Save the document using the name "CH06EX05".
6. Print the document.
7. Close the document.

```
current date


Mrs. Barbara Radebaugh
243 Missisippi Avenue
Richmond, VA 23200

Dear Mrs. Radebaugh:

Has it ever occured to you that our recomendation for your credit
card has long been delaid.

Please axcept our appology for this.  We enadvertently sent your
file to Washinton D.C.

We will reemburse you for any inconveneince this may have caused.

Sincerely yours,



Lawrence King
```

EXERCISE 6

INSTRUCTIONS:

1. Create the following document. Prepare the document exactly as it appears. You will correct the errors using the Speller feature.
2. Correct the spelling errors by using the Speller feature. ("**Eva**" is spelled correctly.)
3. Once the spelling errors are corrected, use the Thesaurus feature to select another word for "**fantastic**" in the first paragraph.
4. Use the Thesaurus feature to select another word for "**freakish**" in the first paragraph.
5. Use the Thesaurus feature to select another word for "**praised**" in the second paragraph.
6. Save the document in a file using the name "CH06EX06".
7. Print the document.
8. Close the document.

```
current date


Mrs. Eva Groft
249 Sentree Avenue
Charllotte, NC 28214

Dear Mrs. Groft:

You realise, of course, that sales of your new book are seting
fantactic records.  HOT WINDS is a well-docummented story of freskish
summer storms.

Congradulations on the reseption your book is recieving.  I am sure
it gives you great satisfation to have your book praeised by many
readers.

Sincerly,



Edith Hagan
```

EXERCISE 7

INSTRUCTIONS:
1. Create the following document. Prepare the document exactly as it appears. You will correct the errors using the Speller feature.
2. Check for proper spelling by using the Speller feature.
3. Use the Thesaurus feature to select another word for "**information**" in the first paragraph.
4. Use the Thesaurus feature to select another word for "**treatment**" in the second paragraph.
5. Use the Thesaurus feature to select another word for "**happy**" in the second paragraph.
6. Use the Grammatik feature to review the readability of the document. You may ignore the suggested changes.
7. Save the document in a file using the name "CH06EX07".
8. Print the document.
9. Close the document.

```
current date


Dr. Georgia Miller
Brown County Pike
Buffalo, NY 14210

Dear Dr. Miller:

We would greatley appresiate recieving any information you can give
us about the diagnose, treatment, and progress the patient (Mr.
Wayne Goebert) maide in the hosiptal.

If you have any other pertenint information about this patient that
would help us in his treatment, we should be most happy to recieve
it.

Sincerely yours,



Xi Se Chung, M.D.
```

EXERCISE 8

INSTRUCTIONS:

1. Create the following document. Prepare the document exactly as it appears. You will correct the errors using the Speller feature.
2. Correct the spelling errors using the Speller feature.
3. Use the Thesaurus feature to change "**beautiful**" in the first paragraph.
4. Change the words "**Registered Mail**" to all uppercase letters.
5. Use the Thesaurus feature to change the word "**parties**" in the second paragraph.
6. At the end of the first paragraph, delete the semicolon and the remainder of the line. Replace the semicolon with a period.
7. Search for and replace "**$10,000**" with "**$12,500**".
8. Use the Grammatik feature to review the readability of the letter. You may ignore the suggestions offered.
9. Save the document in a file called "CH06EX08".
10. Print the document.
11. Close the document.

current date

Registered Mail

Mrs. Halina Polakowski
12600 Review Drive
Portland, OR 97203

Dear Mrs. Polakowski:

The Carney Company which you recomended to me has done a beuatiful job on our covered patio. The outdoor custom brick has been layed smoothley, and the grass was not hurt with all the diging and traffic. When we first talked to Pat Carney, the owner, we were somewhat apprehinsive about the estimate given for doing th work; but the total bill was very fair.

We can hopefuly treat big partys on our spaceious, covered patio. Thank you for your loan of $10,000 to cover the cost of building the patio and your advice.

Our check to repay you the $10,000 is incloused.

Sincerely,

Barb Bednarz
Executive Vice President

CHAPTER SEVEN

FORMATTING A DOCUMENT

OBJECTIVES

In this chapter, you will learn to:
- Change the font
- Set margins, tabs, line spacing, and text justification
- Use the hyphenation feature
- Use the indent feature
- Use the Ribbon to format a document

■ CHAPTER OVERVIEW

In this chapter, the procedures for formatting a document are discussed. The procedure for changing the base font is explained. Methods for setting margins, tabs, line spacing, and text justification are described and illustrated. The indent and hyphenation features are demonstrated.

■ DEFAULT SETTINGS

WordPerfect has default settings for several of the most commonly used formatting features. These default settings are already defined when you begin preparing a document.

Some of WordPerfect's default settings for a document are:

Feature	Initial Setting
Footers	None
Headers	None
Hyphenation	No
Justification	Left
Line Spacing	1
Margins	
Top Margin	1"
Bottom Margin	1"
Left Margin	1"
Right Margin	1"

Feature	Initial Setting
Page Numbers	No Page Numbers
Tabs	Relative to Left Margin, every 0.5"
Unit of Measure	Inches (")
Paper Orientation	Portrait

In this chapter you will create the document in Figure 7-1. Several formatting choices will be made first. Do not begin to type it yet.

Figure 7-1

```
     The company recently hired an executive secretary to support
growing activities.  Chris Jones accepted responsibilities on
November 5.  Previously with a marketing management company, Jones
brings a wide range of business and community experience to the
organization.
     On another topic, the results of the survey for a location for
next year's annual meeting are as follows:
     Las Vegas          33%              $75.00
     Santa Monica       25%
     Orlando            35%              $125.00
     New York           17%
     A runoff vote will be held next month between Las Vegas and
Orlando.  Please keep in mind that personal expenses for each
location have been estimated to be $75 and $125, respectively.
     The final topic for this newsletter concerns plans for the
community service project.  Here are the details:
1.   Arrive promptly at Hamilton Stadium at 9:00 AM on Saturday,
     December 5.
2.   Wear layered clothing for warmth in the morning with anticipated
     higher temperatures through the afternoon.
3.   Bring tools, including shovels, rakes, and other available
     gardening equipment.
4.   The mayor and her assistant will meet us at the site along with
     other members of the Chamber of Commerce.
```

■ FONTS

Fonts are sets of printed characters with the same size and appearance. A font can be described in four ways: typeface, weight, style, and point size.

1. **Typeface** refers to the design and appearance of printed characters on a page. Examples of typefaces are:

Roman-WP	Helvetica
Courier	**Bodoni Bold**

2. **Weight** refers to bold, medium, or light print density or darkness of the characters. Normal print is in medium weight. **This is bold print.**

3. **Style** refers to upright or italic print. Normal print is upright. *This is italic.*

4. **Point size** refers to the size of the printed characters.

11 point   12 point

14 point   8 point

Your printer comes with the capability to print in at least one font.

The font that is used for normal printing is called the **initial font** or **base font**. The initial font depends on the fonts in your printer and what your printer can do with them. Whenever your printer has only one font available, any text that you print will use this font.

Your printer has a specific font that it uses initially. You have several ways to change the base font selection.

One way to set the initial font is to press SHIFT+F8 and choose the Document option or select Document from the Layout Menu. Fonts selected using this method do not appear in the Reveal Codes. This method allows you to use a different font for each document. To permanently change the initial font to a different default, choose the Select command from the Print/Fax choice under the File menu.

Another way you can select the font is to press CTRL+F8 or select Font from the Font menu. When this option is used, a code is inserted and the font is changed. The font choice is displayed in Reveal Codes. The new font is applied from the current cursor location forward in your document. With this method, you could change fonts several times in the same document. Instructions on how to set fonts using this method are discussed below.

In this section, it is assumed that your computer is connected to a Hewlett Packard LaserJet Series II. If you have some other printer, the list of available fonts may vary. Regardless of your printer setup, you can go through the following steps and make selections that you consider appropriate for your printer.

To change the document font:

Press   Ctrl + F8

Click   the Font button on the Button Bar   FFF Font

The Font dialog box appears. The top part of your screen should look like Figure 7-2.

Figure 7-2

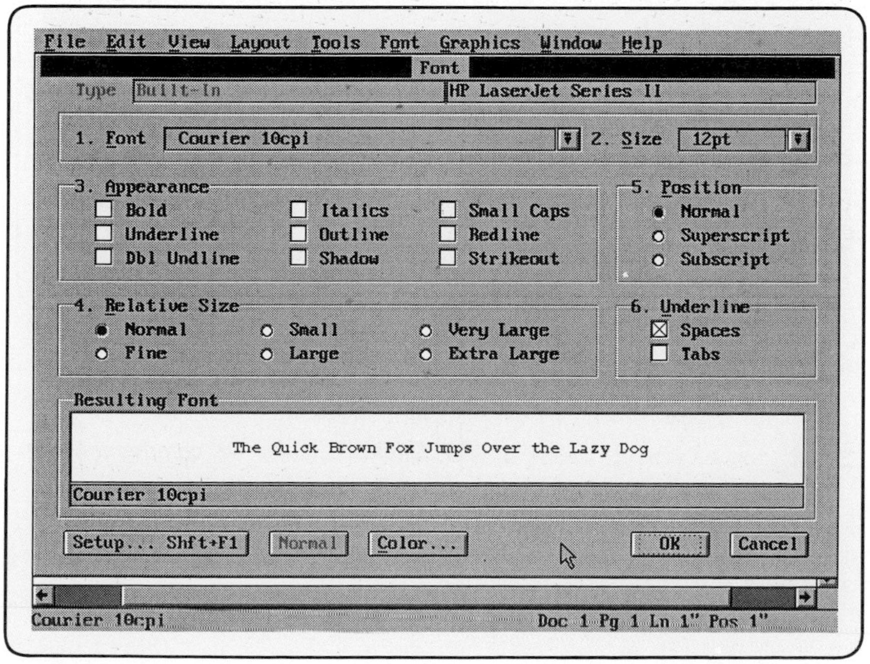

To specify Roman-WP (Type 1) as the base font:

Press	1 or F to display the drop down list of available fonts in the Font text box	*Click*	*the down arrow on the Font drop down list to the right of the current font choice*
Press	⬇ until the Roman-WP (Type 1) option is highlighted in the Font list box	*Click*	*the down scroll arrow until the Roman-WP (Type 1) option is displayed in the Font list box*
Press	[←Enter]	*Double-click*	*the Roman-WP (Type 1) option*

To specify the point size as 10:

Press	2 or S to select the Point Size text box	*Click*	*the down arrow on the Size drop down list to the right of the current Size choice*
Type	10	*Double-click*	*on 10*

Your screen should look like Figure 7-3.

Figure 7-3

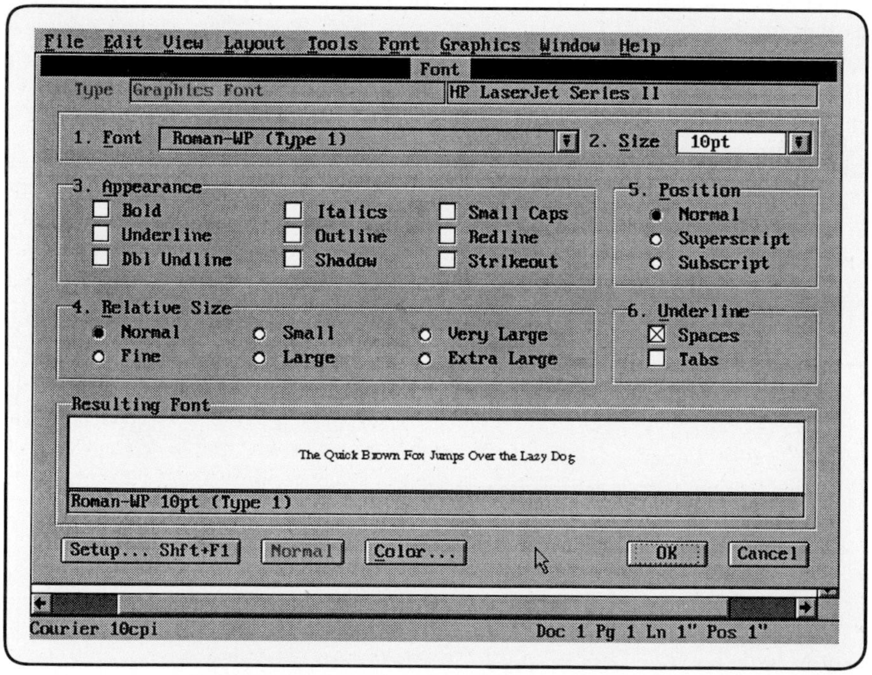

Notice the Resulting Font box shows a preview of how the font will appear in the document. To accept Roman-WP (Type 1) 10 point as the font and remove the dialog box from your screen:

Press	[←Enter]	*Click*	*the OK command button*

Notice Roman-WP 10pt (Type 1) appears on the status bar. To use the default Courier font again:

Press	Ctrl + F8	***Click***	*on the Font button on the Button Bar*
Press	1 or F to display the drop down list of available fonts	***Click***	*the down arrow on the Font drop down list to the right of the current font choice*
Press	↑ until the Courier 10cpi option is highlighted in the Font list box	***Click***	*↑ until the Courier 10cpi option in the Font list box is displayed*
Press	↵Enter	***Double-click***	*the Courier 10cpi option*

To accept Courier as the font and return to your document:

Press	↵Enter three times	***Click***	*the OK command button twice*

Notice Courier 10cpi appears on the status bar. A code is inserted in Reveal Codes and the font is changed. The new font is applied from the current cursor location forward in your document. With this method, you could change fonts several times in the same document.

■ MARGINS

Margins refer to the distance from the top, bottom, left, and right sides of the page. All text in a document appears within the margins you specify. The initial setting specified by WordPerfect for the top, bottom, left, and right margins is 1" from each edge of the page.

Whenever you modify the margins, a code is placed in the document. New settings for the left and right margins affect the current paragraph and all text entered after the location of the code. New settings for the top and bottom margins affect the current page and all subsequent pages after the location of the code. Text appearing above the codes on earlier pages or paragraphs uses previously defined margin settings.

The fact that the margin code is placed at the beginning of the paragraph or at the beginning of the page is new to WordPerfect 6.0. The feature is called Auto Code Placement. It means that when you select some formatting choices your cursor does not need to be at the beginning of the document, page or paragraph. The software will determine the placement of the code, positioning it not at the present position of the cursor but rather at the beginning of the document, page, or paragraph. Auto Code Placement is an important feature because certain codes must be at the very beginning of a document, page, or paragraph to take affect.

To change the margins for this document:

Press	Shift + F8	***Choose***	*Layout*
Press	2 or M to select the Margins option	***Choose***	*Margins*

The Margin Format dialog box appears. Your screen should look like Figure 7-4.

Figure 7-4

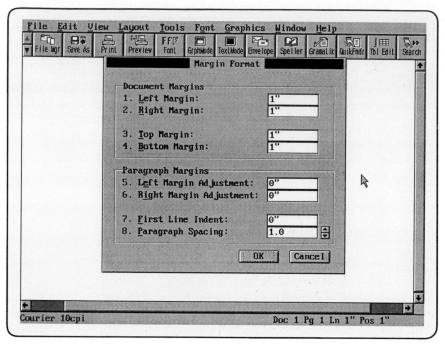

You can enter either a fraction or a decimal number as the new value for a margin. For example, you can enter 1.75 or 1 3/4 to change the margin to 1.75 inches. If you use a fraction, it will be converted to the decimal equivalent for the number.

To change the left margin to 1 1/2":

| **Press** | 1 or L to select the Left Margin text box | *Click* | *in the text box containing the current left margin* |
| **Type** | 1.5 or 1 1/2 | *Type* | *1.5 or 1 1/2* |

You do not need to type the inch (") mark.

To change the right margin to .75":

| **Press** | [Tab⇆] or [↓] to select the Right Margin text box | *Click* | *the Right Margin text box* |
| **Type** | .75 or 3/4 | *Type* | *.75 or 3/4* |

To change the top margin to 1 1/2":

| **Press** | [Tab⇆] or [↓] to select the Top Margin text box | *Click* | *in the Top Margin text box* |
| **Type** | 1.5 or 1 1/2 | *Type* | *1.5 or 1 1/2* |

Your screen should look like Figure 7-5.

Figure 7-5

```
 File  Edit  View  Layout  Tools  Font  Graphics  Window  Help
┌───┐ ┌───┐ ┌───┐ ┌───┐ ┌───┐ ┌───┐ ┌───┐ ┌───┐ ┌───┐ ┌───┐ ┌───┐ ┌───┐ ┌───┐ ┌───┐
File Mgr Save As Print Preview Font GrphMode TextMode Envelope Speller Gramatik QuikFndr Tbl Edit Search
```

```
                        Margin Format
    ┌─Document Margins──────────────────────────────┐
    │   Left Margin:              1.5"               │
    │   Right Margin:             0.75"              │
    │                                               │
    │   Top Margin:               1.5_              │
    │   Bottom Margin:            1"                 │
    └───────────────────────────────────────────────┘
    ┌─Paragraph Margins─────────────────────────────┐
    │   Left Margin Adjustment:   0"                │
    │   Right Margin Adjustment:  0"                │
    │                                               │
    │   First Line Indent:        0"                │
    │   Paragraph Spacing:        1.0      ▲▼        │
    └───────────────────────────────────────────────┘
                        [  OK  ]    [ Cancel ]
```

```
Courier 10cpi                          Doc 1 Pg 1 Ln 1" Pos 1"
```

To leave the bottom margin at 1" and return to your document:

Press   [←Enter] three times   **Click**   *the OK command button*

Notice the status bar on your computer screen. The Ln indicator has changed from 1" to 1.5", indicating the top margin is now 1.5". The Pos indicator has changed from 1" to 1.5", indicating that the left margin is now 1.5".

You can also change margins through the "LAYOUT" Button Bar.

At this time, type the information in Figure 7-6. Press TAB once to begin each paragraph. Press TAB *once* before each city's name. Press TAB *once* between each city and percentage. Notice in Figure 7-6 that the percentages will not line up under each other. Do not force them to line up with extra tabs or spaces. If you force the text to line up with extra spaces or tabs, you could be creating problems later if you decide to change to a different font or need to change the position of the tabbed data. Customizing the tab settings is covered in the next section.

Figure 7-6

```
     The  company  recently  hired  an  executive  secretary  to  support
growing activities.  Chris Jones accepted responsibilities on November
5.   Previously  with  a  marketing  management  company,  Jones  brings  a
wide range of business and community experience to the organization.
     On  another  topic,  the  results  of  the  survey  for  a  location  for
next year's annual meeting are as follows:
     Las Vegas  33%
     Santa Monica    25%
     Orlando    35%
     New York   17%
     A  runoff  vote  will  be  held  next  month  between  Las  Vegas  and
Orlando.   Please keep in mind that personal expenses for each location
have been estimated to be $75 and $125, respectively.
```

■ TABS

Tabs are used to move text a certain number of spaces in a document. Tabs are also used to keep columns of text straight and ordered. You can define where each tab should occur on the page and how much space is defined for each one.

WordPerfect has four types of tab settings: Left, Center, Right, and Decimal. When you press the TAB key to move to a new location, the type of tab used at that location depends on whatever tab code was specified.

The following table lists the type of tab stop settings available in WordPerfect.

Selection	Type of Tab Stop Setting
Left	Text is left-aligned at the tab stop.
Center	Text is centered over the tab stop.
Right	Text is right-aligned at the tab stop.
Decimal	Text is aligned at the align character, usually a decimal point.

A dot leader may be applied to any of the tab styles. A dot leading tab will place dots in the blank area between tabs. Dot leaders are often used in a Table of Contents or for phone lists in which the eye may need assistance for seeing items on the same line.

One method for changing the type of tab and the position of a tab is to press SHIFT+F8, Line and Tab Set. The Tab Set feature changes the tab settings from the cursor forward in the document.

Another way to insert a new tab setting is through the use of hard tabs. A hard tab sets a tab for one line, not the entire document. You can use the information in the following table to create hard tabs:

Type of Tab	Keystroke
Left Tab	[Home], [Tab]
Center Tab	[Home], [Shift]+[F6]
Decimal Tab	[Home], [Ctrl]+[F6]
Right Tab	[Home], [Alt]+[F6]

Absolute or Relative Tabs

Tabs are controlled on the page in one of two ways. Normally, tabs are set relative to the margins and will adjust accordingly if the margins change. However, at times you may want to place tabs a specific distance from the left edge of the page. Absolute tabs do not vary with margin changes. When an absolute tab is used, current margin settings are ignored. For example, if you set an absolute tab at 2", then the tab will be 2" from the left edge of the page. Changes to the left margin do not affect the location of absolute tabs.

Relative tabs are set in relation to the left margin. You can change the left margin any number of times, but the tabs will always remain the same distance from the left margin. For example, if the left margin is 1" and you set the first tab at 0.5", then the tab will be located at 0.5 inches to the right of the left margin or 1.5" from the left edge of the page. If you change the left margin to 2", your tab setting will still be 0.5" to the right of the new left margin or 2.5" from the left edge of the page.

To change the current relative tab settings, it is important to place the cursor at the appropriate location.

Turn on the Reveal Codes feature to see where to place the cursor:

Press	F11 or Alt + F3		*Choose*	*View*
Place	the cursor on the first [Lft Tab] code before the word "Las Vegas"		*Choose*	*Reveal Codes*
			Click	on the first [Lft Tab] code before the word "Las Vegas"

Your screen should look like Figure 7-7.

Figure 7-7

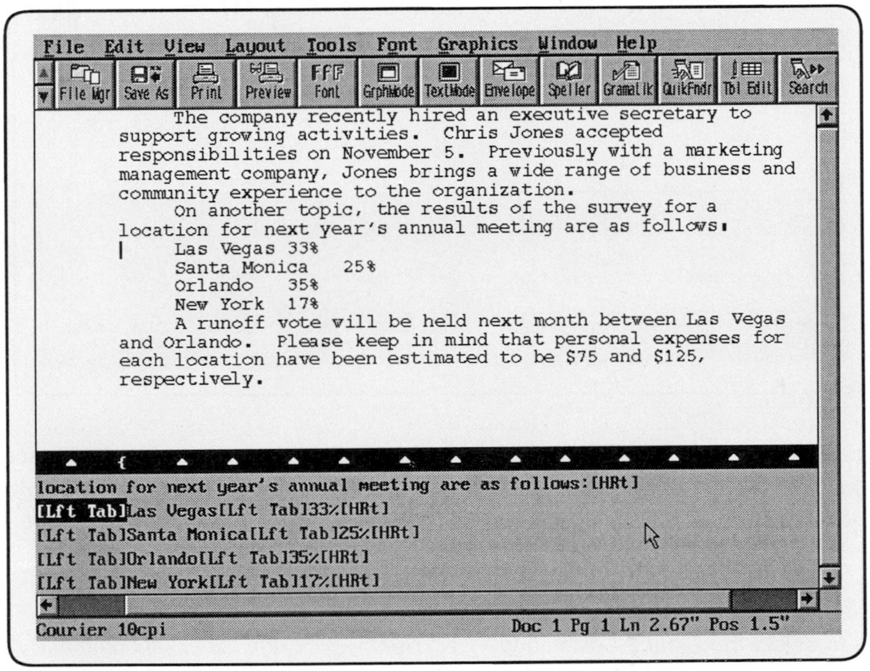

```
 File  Edit  View  Layout  Tools  Font  Graphics  Window  Help

 File Mgr Save As Print Preview Font GrphMode TextMode Envelope Speller GramatIk QuikFndr Tbl EdiIt Search

        The company recently hired an executive secretary to
support growing activities.  Chris Jones accepted
responsibilities on November 5.  Previously with a marketing
management company, Jones brings a wide range of business and
community experience to the organization.
        On another topic, the results of the survey for a
location for next year's annual meeting are as follows:
        Las Vegas 33%
        Santa Monica   25%
        Orlando   35%
        New York  17%
        A runoff vote will be held next month between Las Vegas
and Orlando.  Please keep in mind that personal expenses for
each location have been estimated to be $75 and $125,
respectively.


location for next year's annual meeting are as follows:[HRt]
[Lft Tab]Las Vegas[Lft Tab]33%[HRt]
[Lft Tab]Santa Monica[Lft Tab]25%[HRt]
[Lft Tab]Orlando[Lft Tab]35%[HRt]
[Lft Tab]New York[Lft Tab]17%[HRt]

Courier 10cpi                          Doc 1 Pg 1 Ln 2.67" Pos 1.5"
```

To change the current relative tab settings:

Press	Shift + F8		*Choose*	*Layout*
Press	1 or L to select the Line option		*Choose*	*Line*
Press	1 or T to select the Tab Set option		*Choose*	*Tab Set*

The Tab Set dialog box appears. Your screen should look like Figure 7-8.

Figure 7-8

```
 File  Edit  View  Layout  Tools  Font  Graphics  Window  Help
                              Tab Set                              ▶▶
   >                                                               rdt
  |....|....+0"...|....+1"....|....+2"....|....+3"....|....+4"....|....+5"....|...|  ↑
     L    L    L    L    L    L    L    L    L    L    L    L    L
                Las Vegas 33%
                Santa Monica    25%
                Orlando    35%
                New York   17%
                A runoff vote will be held next month between Las Vega
        and Orlando.  Please keep in mind that personal expenses fc
        each location have been estimated to be $75 and $125,
        respectively.




    ○ Absolute    ● Left   ┌─Relative to Margin─────┐
    ● Relative    ○ Right  │ Set Tab:  0"      │  │ Repeat Every:  0.5" │
                  ○ Center
    □ Dot Leader  ○ Decimal  [ Clear One ]  [ Clear All ]  [   OK   ]  [ Cancel ]

←
 A:\WPDOCS\FIG7-7.DOC                        Doc 1 Pg 1 Ln 2.67" Pos 1.5"
```

Notice the bottom of the dialog box. The Relative and Left option buttons are chosen. Notice also that the ruler displayed across the top of the screen displays an L every half inch. Each L is a left tab setting and is set in 1/2" increments. When you set right or center tabs, an R or C will appear on the ruler, respectively.

To delete all existing tabs from the current location of the cursor forward:

Press	A to select the Clear All command button	*Click*	*the Clear All command button*

All of the tab settings in the ruler have been removed. Notice that the city names and percentages have all run together. This will change shortly.

To set a left tab at 1/2" so that the city names line up under the paragraphs:

Press	S to select the Set Tab box	*Click*	*in the Set Tab box*
Type	.5	*Type·*	*.5*
Press	[↵Enter]	*Press*	*[↵Enter]*

The letter "L" appears at the 1/2" position on the ruler.

By default, WordPerfect creates left tabs. To specify a different type of tab setting, you must first enter the number of the tab position and then select the tab type.

For example, to set a right tab at 4" so that the percent symbols line up under each other:

Press	S to select the Set Tab box	*Click*	*in the Set Tab box*
Type	4	*Type*	*4*

| Press | ←Enter | | Click | *the Right option button* |

| Press | R to select the Right option button |

Your screen should look like Figure 7-9.

Figure 7-9

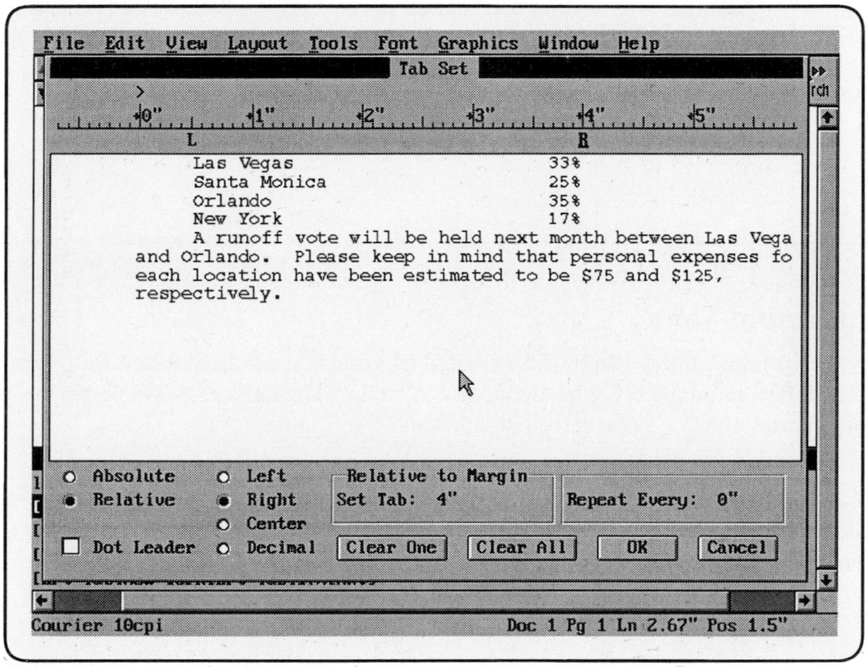

```
 _____
|  File  Edit  View  Layout  Tools  Font  Graphics  Window  Help  |
|  _____  Tab Set  _____  |▶▶|
| |                                                             |  |rch|
| |   >                                                         |  |   |
| | .|.0".|...|.1".|...|.2".|...|.3".|...|.4".|...|.5".|...|.    |▲|
| |      L                          R                           |  |
| |          Las Vegas                33%                       |  |
| |          Santa Monica             25%                       |  |
| |          Orlando                  35%                       |  |
| |          New York                 17%                       |  |
| |          A runoff vote will be held next month between Las Vega|
| |    and Orlando.  Please keep in mind that personal expenses fo|
| |    each location have been estimated to be $75 and $125,    |  |
| |    respectively.                                            |  |
| |                                                             |  |
| |                            ▯                                |  |
| |                                                             |  |
|1|                                                             |▼|
|↓|  ○ Absolute   ○ Left   ─Relative to Margin─                 |  |
||  ● Relative   ● Right   Set Tab: 4"    Repeat Every: 0"      |  |
||                ○ Center                                     |  |
|↑| □ Dot Leader  ○ Decimal [Clear One] [Clear All] [ OK ] [Cancel]|
| |_____|▼|
|←|_____|→|  |
| Courier 10cpi                          Doc 1 Pg 1 Ln 2.67" Pos 1.5"|
|_____|
```

To close the dialog boxes and return to the document:

| Press | Tab until the OK command button contains a blue rectangle | | Click | *the OK command button twice* |

| Press | ←Enter three times |

The cities and percentages are now spaced apart. When you remove Reveal Codes from the screen, the top part of your screen should look like Figure 7-10.

Figure 7-10

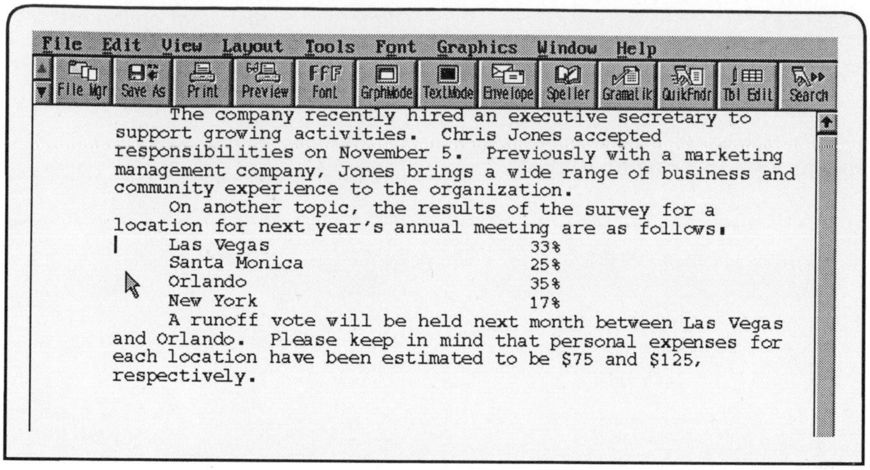

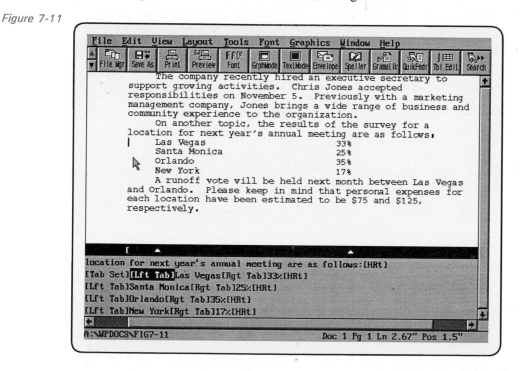

Modifying Existing Tabs

Assume you wish to change the position of the current tabs and add another tab setting. Turn Reveal Codes on and place the cursor immediately *after* the [Tab Set] code. The cursor should be on the [Lft Tab] code before the word "Las Vegas". Your screen should look like Figure 7-11.

Figure 7-11

You may remove the Reveal Codes from the screen. Then enter the Tab Set dialog box with either SHIFT+F8, Line, and Tab Set choices or the Layout, Line, Tab Set option on the menu.

To quickly move the cursor along the ruler to a different tab setting, press the UP or DOWN ARROW keys. To move the cursor to the beginning or end of the ruler, use the HOME, HOME, LEFT ARROW or HOME, HOME, RIGHT ARROW key combination, respectively.

To change the positions of a tab setting, place the cursor on the tab setting and press CTRL+RIGHT ARROW or CTRL+LEFT ARROW to move the tab right or left, respectively.

Move the right tab set at 4" to 3".

Press	↑ twice to move the cursor to the right tab setting
Press	Ctrl + ← several times until the R appears below the 3" mark on the ruler

To place a decimal tab at 5" so that the dollar amounts will line up properly:

Press	S to select the Set Tab box		*Click*	*in the Set Tab box*
Type	5		*Type*	*5*
Press	↵Enter		*Click*	*the Decimal option button*
Press	D to select the Decimal option button			

To return to the document:

Press	Tab until the OK command button contains a blue rectangle		*Click*	*the OK command button twice*
Press	↵Enter three times			

To use the new decimal tab:

Move	the cursor to the end of the line containing Las Vegas information		*Click*	*at the end of the line containing Las Vegas information*
Press	Tab once		*Press*	*Tab once*
Type	$75.00		*Type*	*$75.00*

Repeat the above steps for the Orlando data using $125.00 as the amount. As you type, the numbers should move backward until you type the decimal point to accommodate for larger or smaller numbers. Your screen should look like Figure 7-12.

Figure 7-12

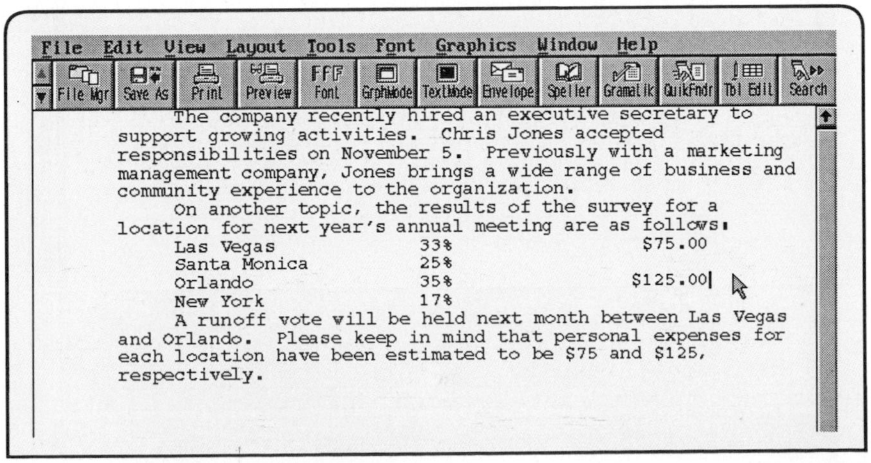

Evenly Spaced Tabs

After typing column data such as the cities, percentages, and dollar amounts, you may wish to add more paragraph text. To do so, you should return to the default tab settings. By default, WordPerfect documents have tabs set at every 1/2". To return to those evenly spaced tabs, you can use the Repeat Every option in the Tab Set dialog box.

Be sure your cursor is on a blank line *after* the data for the cities and their percentages. Enter the Tab Set dialog box with either SHIFT+F8, Line, and Tab Set choices or the Layout, Line, Tab Set option on the menu.

First, you will clear the existing tabs:

Press	A to select the Clear Tabs command button	**Click**	the Clear All command button

To set evenly spaced tabs every 1/2" beginning at position 0":

Press	S to select the Set Tab box	**Click**	in the Set Tab box
Type	0	**Type**	0
Press	⏎Enter	**Choose**	the Left option to be sure the default tabs will be left aligned
Press	L to be sure the default tabs will be left aligned	**Click**	in the Repeat Every box
Press	P to select the Repeat Every box	**Type**	.5 or 1/2
Type	.5 or 1/2		
Press	⏎Enter	**Press**	⏎Enter

Your screen should look like Figure 7-13.

Figure 7-13

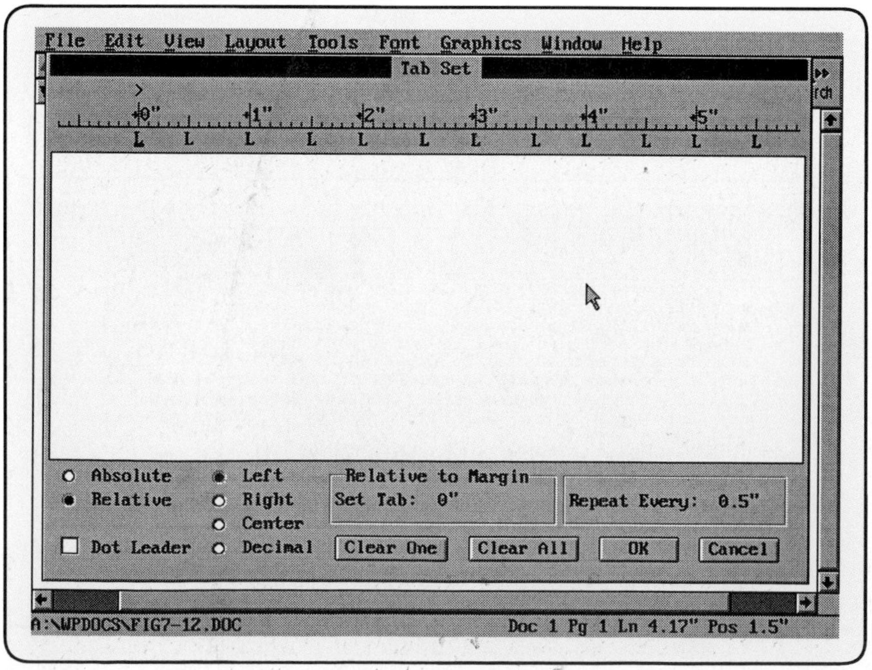

Return to the document screen.

You can also set tabs through the "LAYOUT" Button Bar.

■ LINE SPACING

The Line Spacing feature is used to specify the number of lines to move down each time WordPerfect word wraps to a new line or the ENTER key is pressed. The default setting for line spacing in WordPerfect is single spacing.

Whenever you change the line spacing in a document, any text entered following the location of the line spacing code will be affected. Any text appearing before the point in the document where you change the line spacing will not be modified.

To change the line spacing in your document:

Press	Home , Home , ↑	**Click**	*at the beginning of the document*
Press	Shift + F8	**Choose**	*Layout*
Press	1 or L to select the Line option	**Choose**	*Line*

To select Line Spacing:

Press	3 or S to select the Line Spacing text box	**Click**	*in the Line Spacing text box*

You can enter any whole number, decimal increment, or fraction to change the line spacing.

To change the line spacing to double:

Type	2	**Type**	*2*
Press	↵Enter	**Press**	*↵Enter*
			or
		Click	*the up triangle button several times until 2.00 appears*
		Double-click	*on the 2.00 to accept it*

Your screen should look like Figure 7-14.

Figure 7-14

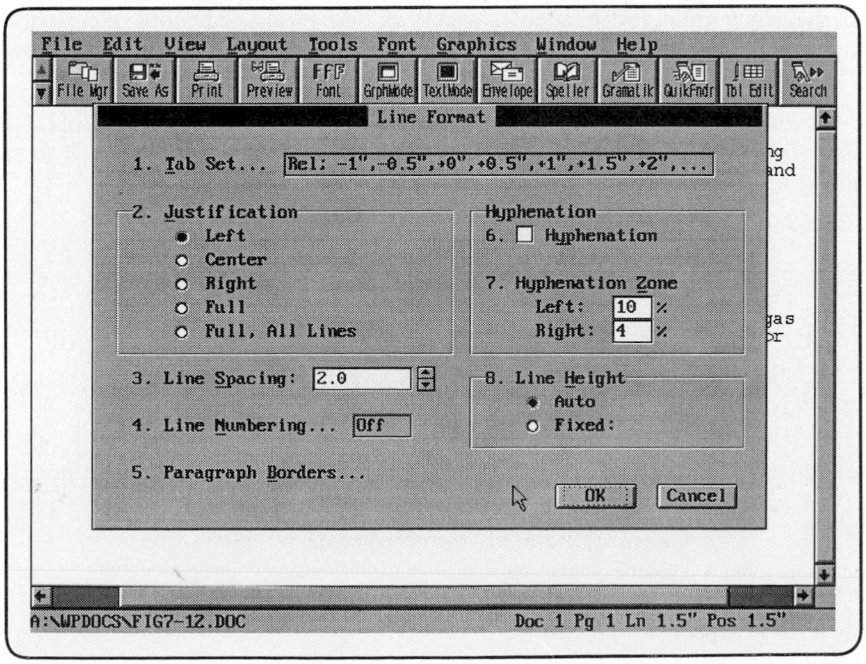

To return to your document:

| **Press** | [←Enter] twice | | **Click** | the OK command button |

Notice that the spacing between each line of text has increased to two lines. Your screen should look like Figure 7-15.

Figure 7-15

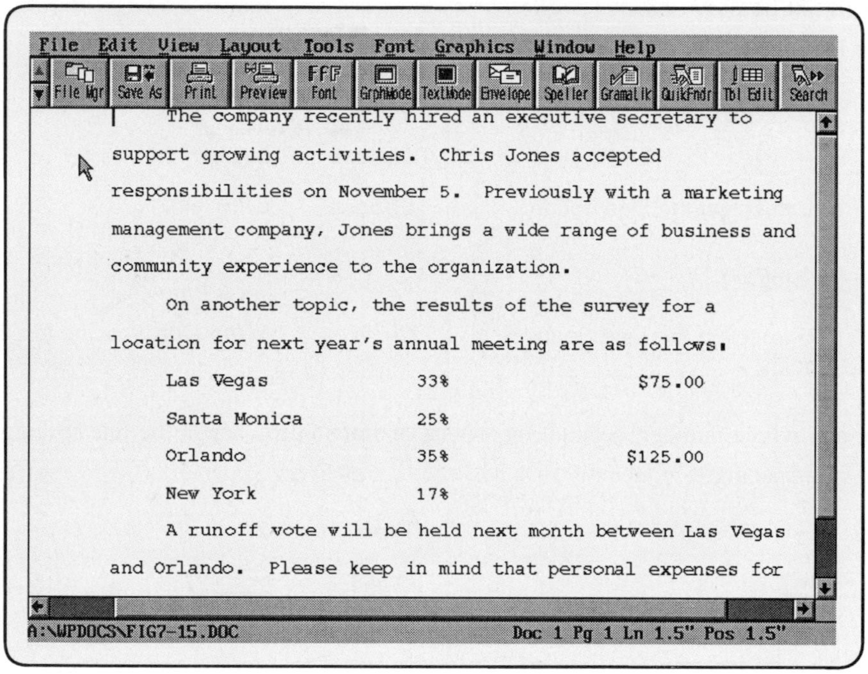

■ JUSTIFICATION

Text can be aligned to your requirements by using the Justification feature. There are four types of justification. They are left, right, full, and center. The default in WordPerfect 6.0 is left justification.

When left justification is used, your text is aligned along the left margin and the result is a ragged-right margin. Similarly, when right justification is specified, text is aligned along the right margin and a ragged-left margin appears on your screen. If you use center justification, the text is centered between the margins.

When you use full justification, the text is aligned along both the left and right margins. The paragraphs in this book use full justification. Spaces among words are compressed or expanded to spread the text evenly between the left and right margins.

To change justification to Full:

Press	[Shift]+[F8]		**Choose**	*Layout*
Press	1 or L to select the Line option		**Choose**	*Line*
Press	2 or J to select the Justification option box		**Choose**	*Justification*

Notice that the option button next to Left is selected. This indicates that the current justification is left.

To change the justification to Full:

Press   4 or F to select the Full option   ***Click***   *the Full option button*
button

Notice that the justification selection is now Full. Your screen should look like Figure 7-16.

Figure 7-16

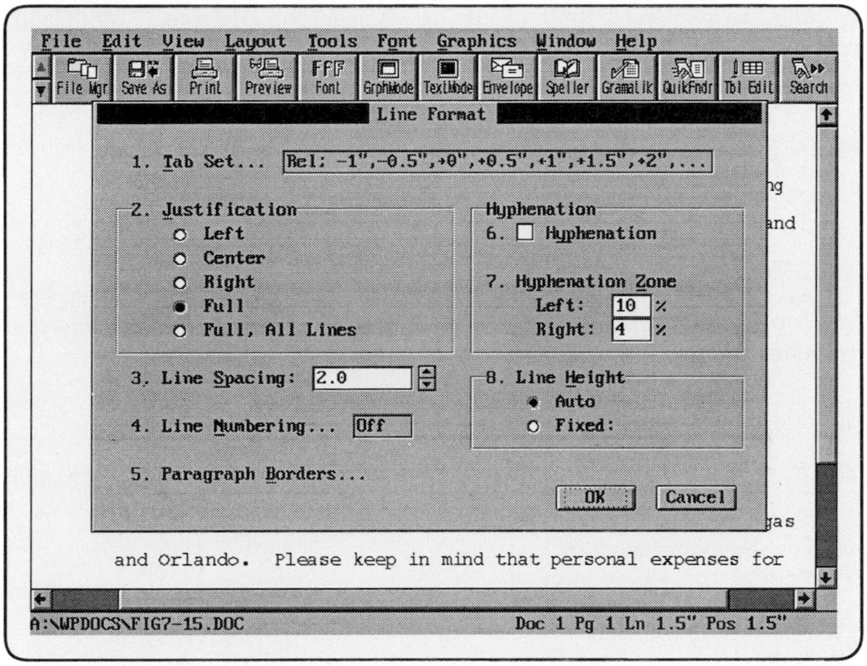

To remove the dialog box and return to the document:

Press   [←Enter] twice   ***Click***   *the OK command button*

If you want right, left, or center justification, you can specify the new justification by pressing the appropriate number or letter or by choosing the appropriate option from the Justification option under the Layout menu.

You can also change the justification through the "LAYOUT" Button Bar.

■ HYPHENATION

WordPerfect uses the word wrap feature to move a word to the next line whenever the word would extend beyond the right margin. The Hyphenation feature allows you to hyphenate these words in your document.

Three items must be considered when the Hyphenation feature is used. The elements include: the hyphenation zone, the hyphenation dictionary, and the hyphenation prompt option.

The **hyphenation zone** is a special area that WordPerfect uses to test whether a word should be hyphenated. This test is done "behind the scenes" and you are never aware of it. Suppose WordPerfect finds a word that is a candidate for hyphenation. If the word fits into this special area, the hyphenation zone, then the word is not hyphenated. If the word does not fit, then it is hyphenated. You can set the size of the hyphenation zone. If you make it larger, fewer words are hyphenated.

The **hyphenation dictionary** is a special dictionary that WordPerfect uses to "look up" words and find out where a word can contain hyphens.

The **hyphenation prompt** option tells WordPerfect whether it should ask you how to hyphenate a word, or use the special hyphenation dictionary to find out where the hyphen should be placed. The three options available for the hyphenation prompt are Never, When Required, and Always. "Never" tells WordPerfect to always use the hyphenation dictionary. "When Required" tells WordPerfect to first use the hyphenation dictionary, but if the word does not exist in the dictionary, then WordPerfect asks you what to do. "Always" tells WordPerfect to always ask you how to hyphenate a word. The hyphenation prompt and hyphenation dictionary features can be changed by pressing SHIFT+F1, and selecting the Environment option or by selecting Environment from the Setup option under the File menu. By default, WordPerfect prompts for hyphenation when required.

To use the Hyphenation feature:

Press	Shift + F8	***Choose***	*Layout*
Press	1 or L to select the Line option	***Choose***	*Line*

To use the Hyphenation feature:

Press	6 or Y to place an X in the Hyphenation check box	***Click***	*the Hyphenation check box until an X appears*

To return to your document:

Press	←Enter twice	***Click***	*the OK command button*

Some words may now be hyphenated.

■ INDENT

The TAB and INDENT features are similar to the extent that they both move text to the next tab setting. However, if you press the TAB key, WordPerfect moves only the first line of a paragraph to the next tab setting. If you use the INDENT feature, the entire paragraph moves to the next tab setting. It appears as if a new left margin is set at the next tab setting. However, this margin is not permanent. The indent is terminated whenever you press ENTER. The Indent feature uses whatever existing tab settings are present in the document.

There are three types of indents: Left, Double, and Hanging. In a left indent, the lines in a paragraph are indented from the left margin. A double indent allows you to indent text an equal distance from both the left and right margins. Whenever you use a hanging indent, the first line of a paragraph is placed at the left margin and the remaining lines of text are indented using the next tab setting. Hanging indents are most commonly used in bibliographies.

Move the cursor to the bottom of the document and type the paragraph shown in Figure 7-17 below.

Figure 7-17

```
    The final topic for this newsletter concerns plans for the

community service project.  Here are the details:

1.
```

To left-indent the first item in the list at the first tab stop from the left margin:

Press F4

Choose Layout

Choose Alignment

Choose Indent →

Your screen should look like Figure 7-18.

Figure 7-18

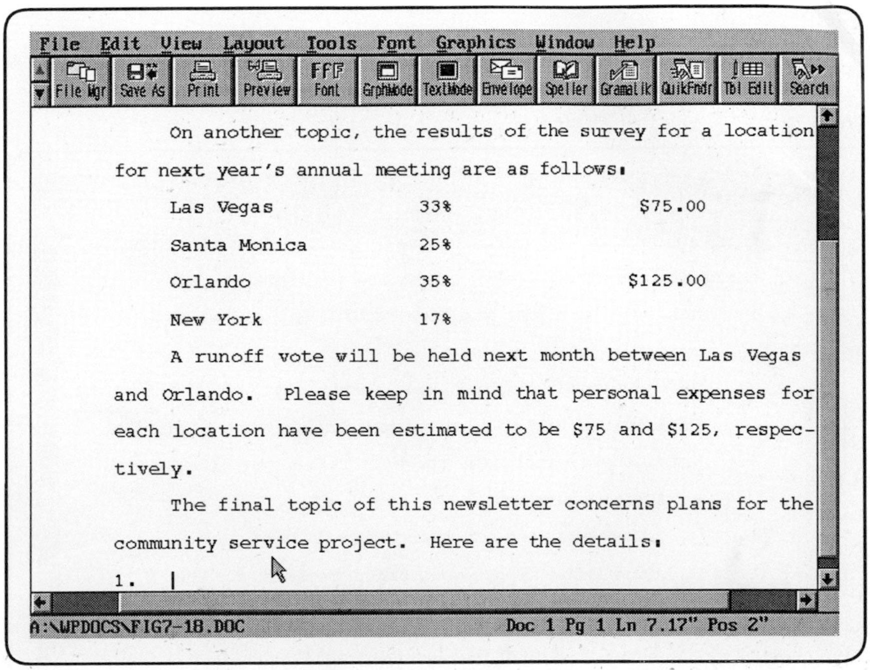

```
 File  Edit  View  Layout  Tools  Font  Graphics  Window  Help
File Mgr Save As Print Preview Font GrphMode TextMode Envelope Speller Gramatik QuikFndr Tbl Edit Search

          On another topic, the results of the survey for a location
     for next year's annual meeting are as follows:
          Las Vegas          33%              $75.00
          Santa Monica       25%
          Orlando            35%             $125.00
          New York           17%
          A runoff vote will be held next month between Las Vegas
     and Orlando.  Please keep in mind that personal expenses for
     each location have been estimated to be $75 and $125, respec-
     tively.
          The final topic of this newsletter concerns plans for the
     community service project.  Here are the details:
          1.  |
A:\WPDOCS\FIG7-18.DOC                    Doc 1 Pg 1 Ln 7.17" Pos 2"
```

Refer to Figure 7-1 at the beginning of this chapter to type the text for the first item on the list. Let the words wrap normally. If you can watch the screen as you type, you will see the second line of text wrap under the text on the first line, not back at the left margin. After typing the information for the first item, press the ENTER key. Notice the cursor returns to the left margin under the number one. Type a two and a period. Then follow the instructions above by pressing the F4 again or choosing Layout Alignment Indent → from the menu before typing the information for the second item on the list. Continue typing the third and fourth items, using the F4 key or the menu method to keep the text aligned properly.

When all four items are completed, turn Reveal Codes on to see the INDENT code. The bottom of your screen should look like Figure 7-19.

Figure 7-19

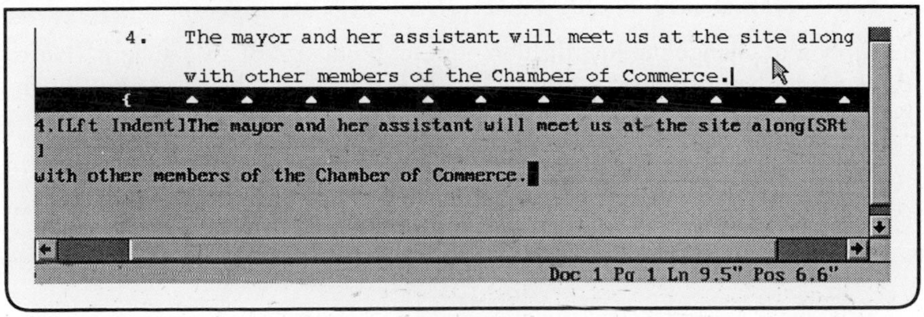

```
     4.    The mayor and her assistant will meet us at the site along
           with other members of the Chamber of Commerce.|
4.[Lft Indent]The mayor and her assistant will meet us at the site along[SRt
]
with other members of the Chamber of Commerce.
                                    Doc 1 Pg 1 Ln 9.5" Pos 6.6"
```

You may turn Reveal Codes off. To double-indent the fourth item to the second tab stop from both margins:

Move	the cursor before the first word of the fourth item		*Click*	*before the first word of the fourth item*
Press	Shift + F4		*Choose*	*Layout*
			Choose	*Alignment*
			Choose	*Indent* →←←

Notice the text has moved in an additional 1/2" from the left margin and has moved in from the right margin as well. Your screen should look like Figure 7-20.

Figure 7-20

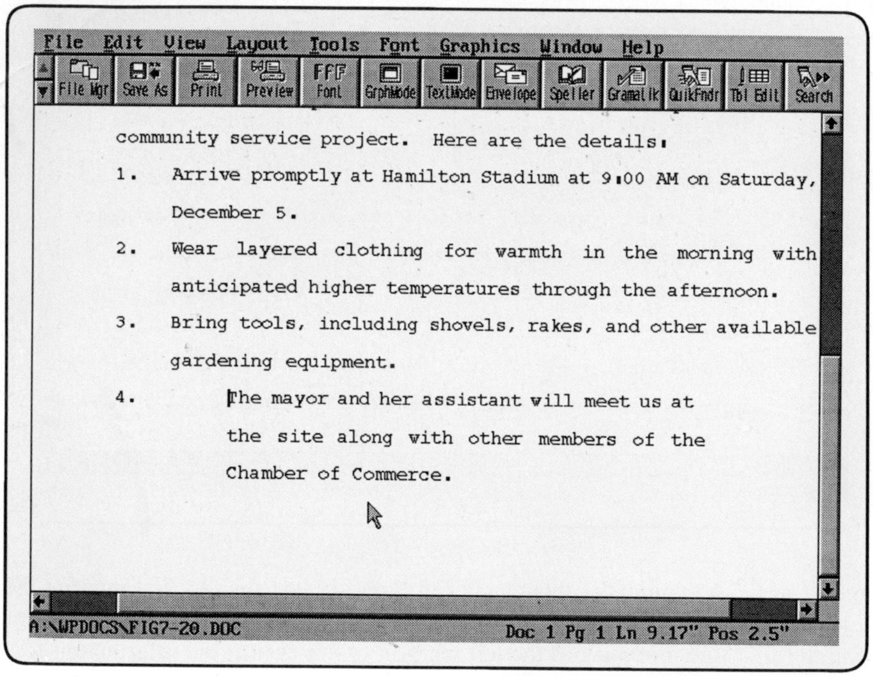

To remove the Double-Indent code, highlight the [Lft/Rgt Indent] code in Reveal Codes and delete it.

While this example used a numbered list to demonstrate indenting, you might also wish to use indenting for bulleted items.

Save the document as "REPORT.DOC".

■ USING THE RIBBON FOR FORMATTING

You can use the Ribbon to change the justification, font, or point size of a document. **Note**: Some of the commands in this section may be issued from the keyboard. However, because the Ribbon is primarily a tool to be used only with the mouse, you will only be given mouse instructions in this section. To display the Ribbon on the screen:

Choose	*View*
Choose	*Ribbon*

Figure 7-21 identifies the parts of the Ribbon.

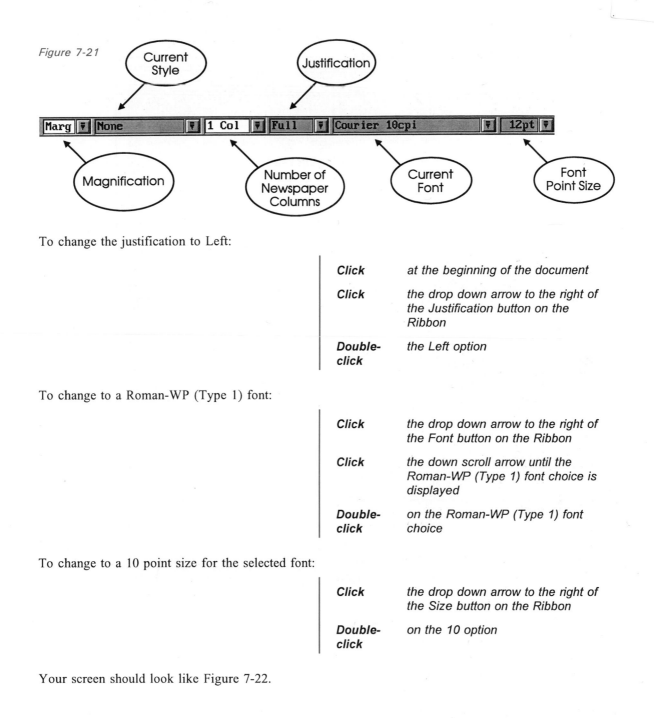

Figure 7-21

To change the justification to Left:

Click	*at the beginning of the document*
Click	*the drop down arrow to the right of the Justification button on the Ribbon*
Double-click	*the Left option*

To change to a Roman-WP (Type 1) font:

Click	*the drop down arrow to the right of the Font button on the Ribbon*
Click	*the down scroll arrow until the Roman-WP (Type 1) font choice is displayed*
Double-click	*on the Roman-WP (Type 1) font choice*

To change to a 10 point size for the selected font:

Click	*the drop down arrow to the right of the Size button on the Ribbon*
Double-click	*on the 10 option*

Your screen should look like Figure 7-22.

Figure 7-22

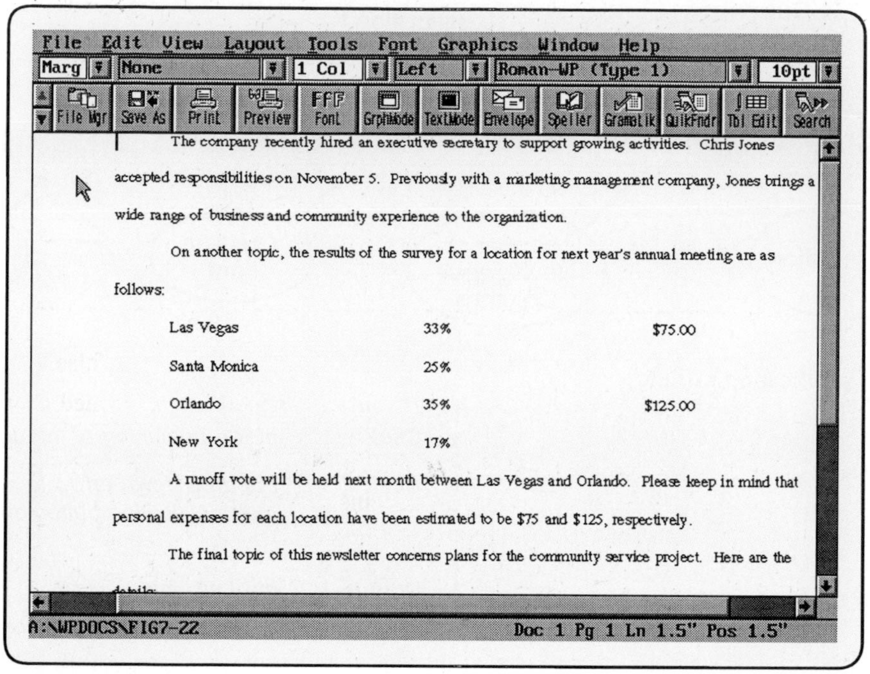

File Edit View Layout Tools Font Graphics Window Help
Marg ▼ None   ▼ 1 Col ▼ Left ▼ Roman-WP (Type 1)   ▼ 10pt ▼

File Mgr Save As Print Preview Font GrphMode TextMode Envelope Speller Gramatik QuikFndr Tbl Edit Search

The company recently hired an executive secretary to support growing activities. Chris Jones accepted responsibilities on November 5. Previously with a marketing management company, Jones brings a wide range of business and community experience to the organization.

On another topic, the results of the survey for a location for next year's annual meeting are as follows:

Las Vegas	33%	$75.00
Santa Monica	25%	
Orlando	35%	$125.00
New York	17%	

A runoff vote will be held next month between Las Vegas and Orlando. Please keep in mind that personal expenses for each location have been estimated to be $75 and $125, respectively.

The final topic of this newsletter concerns plans for the community service project. Here are the details:

A:\WPDOCS\FIG7-22   Doc 1 Pg 1 Ln 1.5" Pos 1.5"

Additional Ribbon features will be discussed in later chapters.
Close the document without saving any changes.

EXERCISE 1

INSTRUCTIONS: Define the following concepts:

1.   Indent _____

_____

2.   Justification _____

_____

3.   Fonts _____

_____

4.   Hyphenation _____

_____

5.   Line spacing _____

_____

6.   Default settings _____

_____

7.   Tabs _____

_____

8.   Margins _____

_____

EXERCISE 2

INSTRUCTIONS: Circle T if the statement is true and F if the statement is false.

T   F   1.   A font typeface is the design and appearance of printed characters on the page.

T   F   2.   A font consists of four elements: typeface, pound, style, and point size.

T   F   3.   The default setting for margins in WordPerfect is 1 1/2".

T   F   4.   Current margin settings are ignored when using relative tabs.

T   F   5.   Left, Center, Right, Decimal, and Dollar are the five types of tab settings available in WordPerfect.

T   F   6.   A left margin tab is one that is set relative to the left edge of the page.

T   F   7.   Default tab settings are pre-set at one-half inch intervals.

T   F   8.   WordPerfect double spaces your document unless you change the line spacing.

T   F   9.   Full justification means that text is aligned with the right margin of the document.

T   F   10.   When you use the Indent feature, you have to press TAB to indent each line of text.

EXERCISE 3

INSTRUCTIONS: 1.   Create the following document. The format settings for the document are listed below:

Initial Font:	Roman-WP (Type 1) 12 point
Margins:	
Left	1.5"
Right	1.0"
Top	2.0"
Bottom	1.0"
Relative Left tabs:	0.5", 1.0", 2.0", and 4" left-aligned tabs
Line spacing:	Double. Use single line spacing for the paragraph listing the stores.
Justification:	Full
Hyphenation:	None

2.   Enter the information about each store at the 2" and 4" tab stops.

3.   Preview the document.

4.   Save the document in a file using the name "CH07EX03".

5.   Print the document.

6.   Close the document.

As you already know, sales in District A were level from last November to March of this year, and have started to decline since March. A research group was created in late April to study the situation in District A. The group consists of Maria Alvarez, Senior Market Analyst, Jennifer Chang, Financial Advisor to the HQ Sales Department, and Sharon Jackson, Senior Sales Analyst for the Southern Division.

There are five stores in District A. The five stores and their locations are listed below:

Store A1	Bering Street
Store A2	Bookman Avenue
Store A3	Taft Street
Store A4	Howard Street
Store A5	Oliver Boulevard

This district is managed by Howard Smith, who has been with the company for 35 years. Mr. Smith has been the manager of District A for 10 years.

EXERCISE 4

INSTRUCTIONS:

1. Create the following document. The format settings for the document are listed below:

Initial Font:	Courier 10cpi
Margins:	
Left	1.5"
Right	1.0"
Top	2.0"
Bottom	0.5"
Relative Left tabs:	.75" and 1.75" left-aligned tabs
Justification:	Full
Line spacing:	Single
Hyphenation:	Yes

2. Preview the document.
3. Save the document in a file using the name "CH07EX04".
4. Print the document.
5. Close the document.

```
TO:      J. Chang
         S. Jackson
         M. Alvarez

FROM:    Hector Garcia
         Division Manager

DATE:    current date

RE:      Meeting on District A


There will be a meeting on June 11 at 8:30 am in Conference Room 1109.
At this time, you will present the results of your preliminary study
on District A sales problems.  Approximate length of the meeting will
be 1 1/2 hours.

Present at this meeting will be Robert Chambers, Regional Manager;
Marla Johnson, HQ Sales Manager; James Gonzalez, Personnel Manager;
and myself.

You will each have 20 minutes to present each of your topics.  Topics
are assigned in the following manner:

         Alvarez --
         Market Analysis for District A; include comparison with other
         districts.

         Chang --
         Financial analysis for District A; include graphs with your
         spreadsheets.

         Jackson --
         Sales analysis for District A; also present possible cause(s)
         of sales problems.

If you have any questions, please contact me at Ext. 8099.
```

EXERCISE 5

INSTRUCTIONS:

1. Open the document in file "CH07EX04".
2. Make the left and right margins 1.0" for the entire document.
3. Change the line spacing to 2 beginning with the first sentence of the first paragraph below the memo headings. Delete the extra [HRt] codes at the end of the memo text paragraphs.
4. Make the three paragraphs concerning the topic assignments for Alvarez, Chang, and Jackson single-spaced.
5. Make the entire document left justified.
6. Preview the document.
7. Save the document in a file using the name "CH07EX05".
8. Print the memo.
9. Close the document.

EXERCISE 6

INSTRUCTIONS: 1.   Create the following document. The format settings for the document are listed below:

Initial Font:	Courier 10cpi
Margins:	
Left	1.5"
Right	1.0"
Top	1.5"
Bottom	1.0"
Hyphenation:	None
Line spacing:	Single
Tabs:	Set your own tabs. The column titles "**1991**", "**1992**", and "**1993(est.)**" should be centered over each column. The dollar amounts should be right-aligned in each column.

2.   Preview the document.
3.   Save the document in a file using the name "CH07EX06".
4.   Print the document.
5.   Close the document.

```
              1991           1992          1993(est.)

District A    $150,000       $151,000       $90,000
District B     209,000        215,000       218,000
District C      80,000         90,000        95,000
District D      92,000         98,000       102,000
District E     180,000        187,000       197,000
```

EXERCISE 7

INSTRUCTIONS: 1.   Create the following document. The format settings for the document are listed below:

Initial Font:	Roman-WP (Type 1) 10 point
Margins:	
Left	1.5"
Right	1.0"
Top	2.0"
Bottom	1.0"
Relative Left tabs:	0.5", 1.0", and 2.0" left-aligned tabs
Line spacing:	Double. Use single line spacing for the paragraphs that are numbered 1 and 2.
Justification:	Full
Hyphenation:	None

2.   Preview the document.
3.   Be sure that the paragraphs numbered 1 and 2 are single-spaced. All other paragraphs should be double-spaced.
4.   Note that the paragraphs numbered 1 and 2 are indented from both margins.

5. Save the document in a file using the name "CH07EX07".
6. Print the document.
7. Close the document.

Various investigative tools were used to study the stores in District A. Extensive interviews were conducted by myself and the staff. We interviewed the store managers and various sales personnel. A marketing research firm, Sanchez and Locken, was contracted to interview repeat customers. Customers were queried about service and product satisfaction. A private retail investigator, Sam Malone of Malone Investigations, was contracted to secretly observe store activities. This investigation was done before we arrived to audit the stores. The accounting firm Jackson, Johnson & James was hired to perform a full audit on the district. This audit is still in progress and is expected to be complete in four weeks.

The results of the preliminary study indicate two possible causes for the sales decline in the District:

1. Surveys and interviews with customers indicate that service has declined in the past few months. Customers cite instances where sales personnel were unwilling to solve problems with products or assist customers at the desk. Telephone support has also declined. Numerous complaints concerned poor telephone support. Stores A3 and A5 were especially lax in these areas.

2. Customers and the retail investigator noticed the shoddy appearance of the stores. Products were in disarray on the shelves while sales personnel "loafed in back." Parking lots were strewn with trash in some cases. Stores A2, A3, and A5 needed building repairs. The investigator noted a ceiling leak in Store A5.

However, customer comments and investigative reports indicate that Store A4 may be an exception to the problems listed above. Several compliments were given concerning this store, and the investigators thought this store to be adequately organized. However, it is recommended that all stores be thoroughly inspected by company personnel.

EXERCISE 8

INSTRUCTIONS:
1. Create the following document. Define your own format settings. However, you must define the initial font to be Helve-WP (Type 1) 12 point.
2. The items in column "**Size Type 1**" are decimal aligned. The items in column "**Size Type 2**" are right aligned. In the third column, the items are left aligned. In the last column, they are centered. The headings of each column are centered.
3. Preview the document.
4. Save the document in a file using the name "CH07EX08".
5. Print the document.
6. Close the document.

Please fill out the information below using a pencil. Please print legibly.

NAME:

ADDRESS:

TELEPHONE NUMBER: AGE: SEX:

Please circle the sizes desired:

Size Type 1	Size Type 2	Size Type 3	Size Type 4
1,200.34	150	Octagon	One
299.11	2,900	Square	Round
25.09	10	Triangle	Parallel
7.1	2	Box	3-D

EXERCISE 9

INSTRUCTIONS:

1.   Create the following document. The format settings for the document are listed below:

Initial Font:	Helve-WP (Type 1) 10 point
Margins:	
Left	1.5"
Right	1.5"
Top	1.75"
Bottom	1.75"
Left tabs:	1.25" and 3.5" left-aligned tabs
Line spacing:	Double spacing for the table only. Then change back to single spacing.
Justification:	Left
Hyphenation:	On

2.   Spell check the document.
3.   Preview the document.
4.   Save the document in a file called "CH07EX09".
5.   Print the document.
6.   Close the document.

current date

Mr. Charles Harrington
119 Ferndale Road
Atlanta, GA 30327

Dear Mr. Harrington:

I have just seen your current picture, "Skyway Paradise." As a result of this startling film, I would like to invite you to participate in a Senior Film Seminar to be held November 15 at the Oak Street Theater in Chicago. During this seminar, we will discuss the following films you have made:

"Date with Desire"	1960
"Remembering Africa"	1970
"Chicago Byline"	1980
"Moonbeam"	1989

At this seminar, you will be expected to present some remarks comparing and contrasting your changes in cinematic style. Of course, questions from the audience will be accepted. The whole program will last only two hours. During this time you may wish to comment about your latest releases.

Sincerely,

John Muchmore
Film Critic

EXERCISE 10

INSTRUCTIONS:

1. Create the following document. The format settings for the document are listed below:

Initial Font:	Courier 10cpi
Margins:	
Left	1.5"
Right	1.5"
Top	0.75"
Bottom	0.75"
Line spacing:	Change to double spacing for the first and last paragraphs only.
Relative Left tabs:	.25", .625", 1" left-aligned
Justification:	Left
Hyphenation:	On

2. Use a left indent after typing the numbers.
3. Use a left indent after the a, b, and c items.

4.   Spell check the document.
5.   Save the document in a file called "CH07EX10".
6.   Print the document.

Division of words at the end of a line should be avoided, but when it is unavoidable in order to have as even a right margin as possible, the following rules should be followed:

1. WordPerfect 6.0 will frequently present hyphenated words that you must not hyphenate if you are to follow the rules. A word of six or more letters containing two or more syllables may be divided between syllables, provided such division does not violate other standard word division rules or guides. The division is indicated by a hyphen at the correct point of division at the end of the line.

2. A word division guidebook should be consulted if there is any doubt about the point of division.

3. One-syllable words, such as wrapped, through, planned, height, or strolled, must not be divided.

4. Do NOT separate from the remainder of the word:

    a.   A one-letter syllable at the beginning of a word, such as abandon, enough, or enormous.

    b.   A one- or two-letter syllable at the end of a word, such as already, mighty, or teacher.

    c.   A syllable that does not contain a vowel, such as a contraction.

5. Avoid dividing proper names, abbreviations, and numbers. A date may, if necessary, be divided between the day and the year (the hyphen is not used).

6. Avoid the division of words at the end of two or more successive lines, or the final word on a page, or the word at the end of the last complete line of a paragraph.

    More guides for dividing words properly can be found in any word division guidebook found in bookstores.

CHAPTER EIGHT

ADDITIONAL FORMATTING FEATURES

OBJECTIVES

In this chapter, you will learn to:
- Create headers and footers
- Create page numbers
- View a document in Page Mode
- Create page breaks

■ CHAPTER OVERVIEW

This chapter discusses how to create headers, footers, page numbers, and page breaks. The steps for viewing your document in Page Mode are also illustrated.

■ HEADERS AND FOOTERS

Headers and footers are pieces of text that help identify the pages of a document. **Headers** appear at the top of each page. **Footers** appear at the bottom of each page. A blank line separates them from the main body of the text. You can adjust the placement of headers and footers on the page by adjusting the top and bottom margins.

Headers and footers are created only once for a document. You can tell WordPerfect if you want headers or footers to print on only certain pages. For example, if you want headers and footers printed on every page, define a header code and a footer code at the top of the first page. If you want a header to print from page 10 to the end of your document, define the header code at the top of page 10. If you want a footer to print from page 10 to page 20, define a footer code at the top of page 10, and discontinue the code on page 21.

You can also suppress header and footer codes for certain pages. This is helpful when you are creating a report with a cover letter. You do not want headers or footers on the cover letter. In that case, you would suppress the headers and footers for the first page. Suppression is discussed again later in this chapter.

Open the "REPORT.DOC" document created in the previous chapter.

Before creating a header, be sure your cursor is at the top of the document.

To create a header:

Press	Shift + F8	**Choose**	*Layout*

Press	5 or H to select the Header/ Footer/Watermark option	**Choose**	*Header/Footer/Watermark*

The Header/Footer/Watermark dialog box appears on the screen. Your screen should look like Figure 8-1.

Figure 8-1

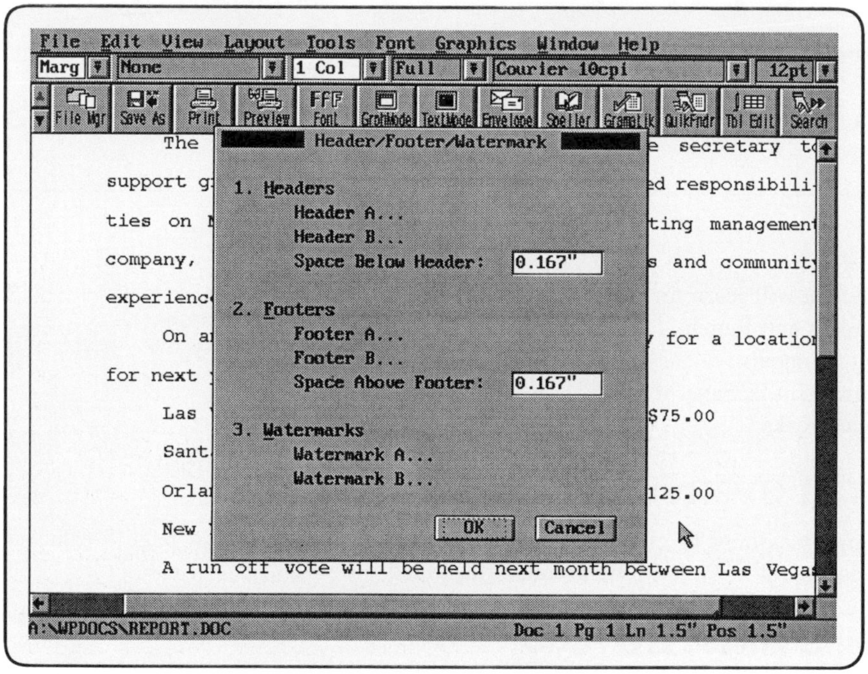

Watermarks are drawings that appear behind the printed text. Watermarks are discussed more thoroughly in Chapter 22.

To select Headers:

Press	1 or H to select the Headers option	**Choose**	*Headers*

WordPerfect allows you to create two different headers or footers in a document (Header A and Header B). If you are printing a one-sided document, you will probably only need Header or Footer A. If you are printing a two-sided document, you might want to use a different header or footer for the odd and even pages. In this situation, you might choose to place Header A on the odd pages and Header B on the even pages.

To select Header A:

Press	1 or A to select the Header A option	**Choose**	*the Header A option*

The Header A dialog box appears on the screen. Notice that the default is for the Header to appear on all pages. To accept the Header on all pages and to create it:

Press	[←Enter] to select the Create command button	**Click**	*the Create command button*

Your screen should look like Figure 8-2.

Figure 8-2

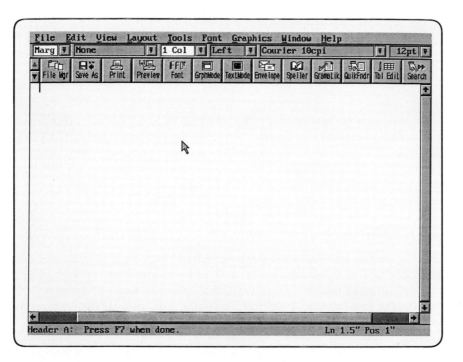

Notice that "Header A:" appears in the status bar. Also notice that the "Pos" indicator on the status bar shows the left margin to be 1". The left margin of the document is 1 1/2". By default, WordPerfect places the header or footer code before the left or right margin code. Therefore, you may need to set margins in the header or footer screen to match those in the document. To do so, you can use the usual method discussed in the previous chapter using the SHIFT+F8, Margins option or the Layout Margins option in the menu. Change the left margin to 1 1/2" and the right margin to .75".

To enter the header text:

Type Company Newsletter	*Type* *Company Newsletter*

The top part of your screen should look like Figure 8-3.

Figure 8-3

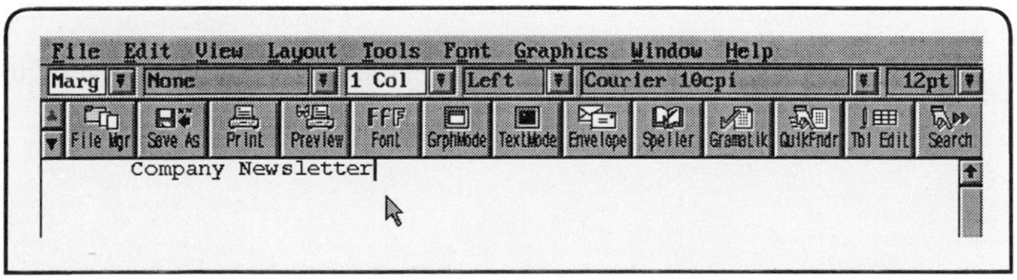

To close the Header:

Press F7	*Press* F7

You cannot see the headers or footers on the screen when you are editing your document. You can see them if you use the Print Preview feature or choose to view your document in Page Mode. After adding page numbering, you will be instructed to view the header and page numbers.

Footers are created in the same way as headers.

User Tip

WordPerfect 6.0 permits you to insert the filename in a document. This would most typically be done in a header or footer. To insert the filename, press SHIFT+F8, select Other, and Insert Filename or choose Layout, Other, Insert Filename. Then select 1 or 2 to insert just the filename or the path and filename, respectively. Pressing ENTER three times will return you to the document screen.

■ PAGE NUMBERING

The Page Numbering feature lets you attach page numbers to each page in your document. The page numbers appear in one of five styles: Arabic (1, 2, 3...), lowercase letters (a, b, c...), uppercase letters (A, B, C...), lowercase Roman numerals (i, ii, iii...), and uppercase Roman numerals (I, II, III...). Page numbers may be in one of four formats. Basic page numbering is discussed in this section. Secondary page numbering is another option. It allows you to keep track of a second set of page numbers. The third and fourth alternatives are Chapter and Volume page numbering. Either of these types of numbering would be used in documents where the page numbering pattern changes in each section. For more information about Secondary, Chapter, and Volume page numbering, consult the WordPerfect Reference manual.

To insert a page number at the top right of every page:

Move	the cursor to the beginning of the document		*Click*	*at the beginning of the document*
Press	Shift + F8		*Choose*	*Layout*
Press	3 or P to select the Page option		*Choose*	*Page*

The Page Format dialog box appears on the screen.

Press	1 or N to select the Page Numbering option		*Choose*	*Page Numbering*

The Page Numbering dialog box appears on the screen. Your screen should look like Figure 8-4.

Figure 8-4

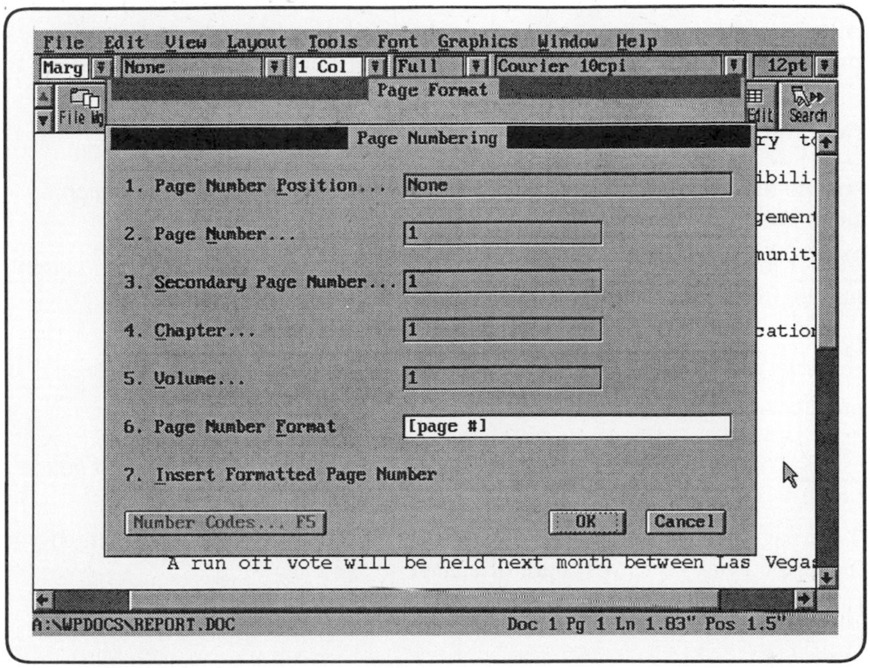

To select the Page Number Position:

Press   1 or P to select the Page Number   *Choose*   *Page Number Position*
                 Position option

The Page Number Position dialog box appears. Your screen should look like Figure 8-5.

Figure 8-5

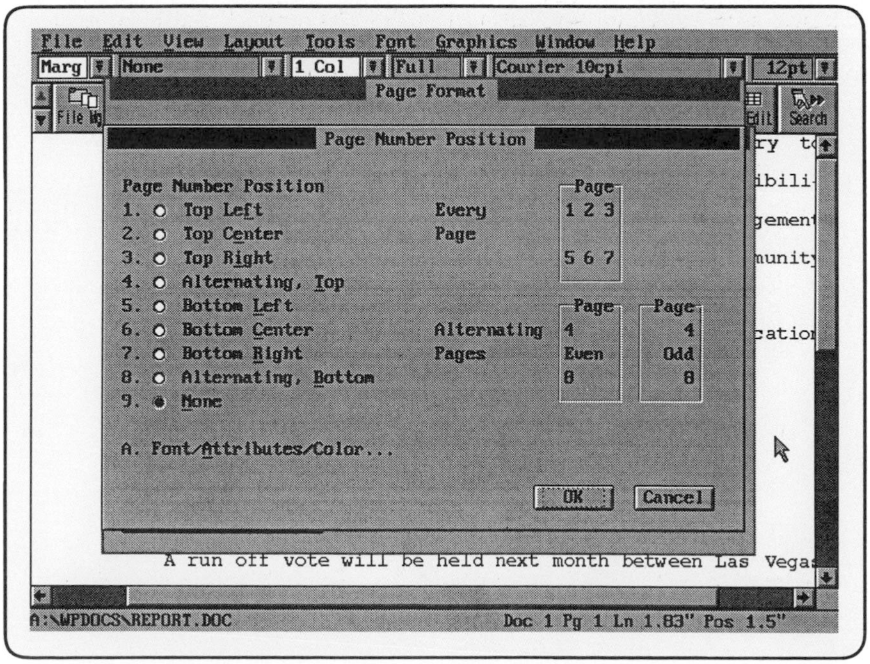

WordPerfect shows you eight possible locations for the page number; you may choose one. Make your selection from the list of choices on the left or make a selection based on the miniature pages on the right. If you use the miniature page on the right, selecting a 6 would place the page number in the Bottom Center of the page.

To select the Page Number Position:

Press	3 or I to select the Top Right option button		*Click*	*the Top Right option button*
Press	`←Enter` to accept the Page Number Position		*Click*	*the OK command button*

With the sixth option, you may change the appearance of the page number to be "Page 1", "- 1 -", etc.

To return to your document:

Press	`←Enter` three times		*Click*	*the OK command button twice*

You cannot see the page numbers on the screen when you are editing your document. If you wish to see them, you must use the Print Preview feature or change to the Page Mode.

To view the header and page number in Print Preview:

Press	`Shift` + `F7`		*Click*	*the Preview button on the Button Bar*
Press	7 or V to select the Print Preview option		*Click*	*the Zoom 100% button on the Button Bar*
Press	V for View			
Press	1 to view at 100% magnification			

Your screen should look like Figure 8-6.

Figure 8-6

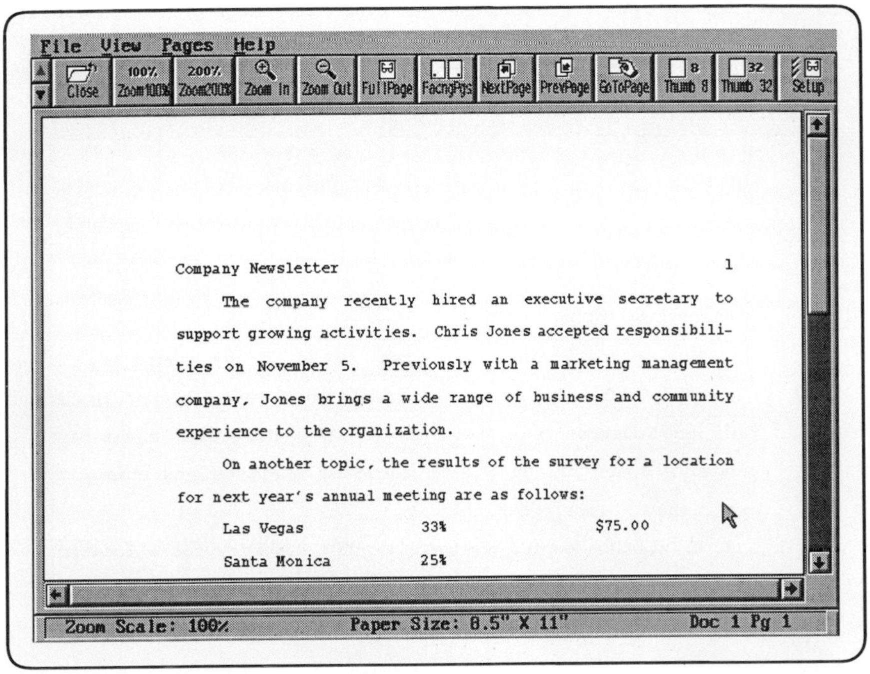

To return to the document screen:

Press   F7

Click   *the Close button on the Button Bar*

■ VIEWING IN PAGE MODE

Page Mode viewing is a new feature in WordPerfect 6.0. You are permitted to see the actual page as it will appear when printed. It is not recommended that you stay in Page Mode. The computer will respond more slowly in this mode and you should only remain in it for final viewing of a document.

To view the header and page number in Page Mode:

Press   Ctrl + F3

Press   4 or P to select the Page option button

Choose   *View*

Choose   *Page Mode*

Your screen should look like Figure 8-7.

Figure 8-7

```
 File  Edit  View  Layout  Tools  Font  Graphics  Window  Help
Marg ▼  None              ▼  1 Col ▼  Full  ▼  Courier 10cpi        ▼    12pt ▼
▲  🗁     🖫      🖶      🖳      FFF      ▢       ▣       🖼       🗗       🗏       🗐       🗒       🔍
▼ File Mgr Save As Print  Preview  Font  GrphMode TextMode Envelope Speller GramatIk QuikFndr Tbl Edit Search


    Company Newsletter

    |    The  company  recently  hired  an  executive  secretary  t
   ▧
        support growing activities.  Chris Jones accepted responsibili-

        ties on November 5.  Previously with a marketing management

        company, Jones brings a wide range of business and communit

        experience to the organization.

            On another topic, the results of the survey for a locatio

        for next year's annual meeting are as follows:
◄                                                                              ►
A:\WPDOCS\REPORT.DOC                          Doc 1 Pg 1 Ln 1.83" Pos 1.5"
```

To return to Graphics Mode:

Press	Ctrl + F3	*Choose*	*View*
Press	3 or G to select the Graphics option button	*Choose*	*Graphics Mode*

Save your document using the filename "REPORT1.DOC".

User Tip

Suppressing headers, footers, and page numbers was mentioned at the beginning of this chapter. Suppressing the appearance of headers, footers, and page numbers is often done for the first page of a document. Suppressing headers and page numbers is done by pressing SHIFT+F8, and then selecting Page, and Suppress or choosing Layout Page Suppress.

An alternative to suppressing the appearance of headers, etc. is to use a new feature in WordPerfect 6.0. It is called Delay Codes. With Delay Codes, the header, footer, and page number codes could all be placed at the top of the first page of the document. You would then use the Delay Codes feature to indicate how many pages to skip before displaying the codes. Enter the Delay Codes feature by pressing SHIFT+F8, and then selecting Page, and Delay Codes or choosing Layout Page Delay Codes. You may indicate how many pages to skip. Then an editing area appears and you would insert the codes you want to be delayed. You can use function key commands or make selections from the menu. When finished, press F7 and then press ENTER to return to the document.

■ PAGE BREAKS

A page break is a code that tells WordPerfect where one page ends and another begins. There are two types of page breaks in WordPerfect: a soft page break ([SPg]) and a hard page break ([HPg]). The program automatically inserts the soft page break. You insert the hard page break.

WordPerfect calculates when the text has filled a page and inserts a **soft page break** code into the document. You can identify a soft page break by a single line that appears in your document. As you make changes to your document, WordPerfect is always coordinating the position of the soft page break codes with each page of text. You have no control over a soft page break. These codes cannot be edited.

However, you do have control over **hard page break** codes. Whenever you want to force a page break in your document, you can place a hard page break into the text. You can identify a hard page break in your document by a double line that appears. You can easily delete this code.

To insert a hard page break in the "REPORT1.DOC" document:

Move   the cursor to the left margin of the fourth paragraph

Press   `Ctrl` + `←Enter`

Your screen should look like Figure 8-8.

Figure 8-8

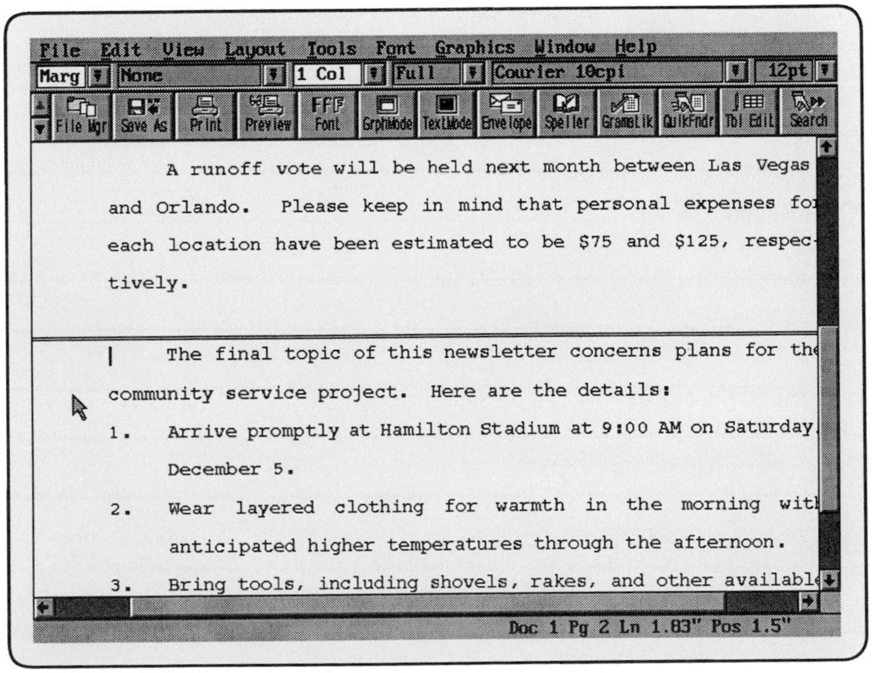

Notice that a double line appears above the fourth paragraph, indicating a hard page break has been inserted. The page indicator in the status bar now displays Pg 2.

To delete a hard page break using the Reveal Codes feature:

Press   `Alt` + `F3` or `F11`   **Choose**   *View*

Move   the cursor to the [HPg] code   **Choose**   *Reveal Codes*

Press	Delete		**Click**	on the [HPg] code
			Press	Delete

You can also delete a hard page break from the normal editing screen. Turn Reveal Codes off. Place the page break above the fourth paragraph again. If you want to delete a hard page break from the normal editing screen:

Move	the cursor above the double line		**Click**	above the double line
Press	Delete		**Press**	Delete

Insert a hard page break in the document again before you save it.

Save your document. Replace the old contents of the file with the current document. Close the file.

EXERCISE 1

INSTRUCTIONS: Define the following concepts:

1. Soft page break _____

    _____

2. Hard page break _____

    _____

3. Headers and footers _____

    _____

4. Delay Code _____

    _____

5. Page numbering _____

    _____

EXERCISE 2

INSTRUCTIONS: Circle T if the statement is true and F if the statement is false.

T	F	1.	Headers appear at the bottom of a page, and footers appear at the top of a page.
T	F	2.	The Page Numbering feature allows you to select where you want the page number to appear on the page.
T	F	3.	You can add or delete soft page breaks.
T	F	4.	A hard page break is used when you want to force a page to end and another to begin at a certain location in a document.
T	F	5.	Once you define a header in your document, you cannot stop the header from printing on every page.

T   F   6.   If you look closely, you can see the tiny footer on the screen when you are editing your document.

T   F   7.   You can identify a soft page break by a single line that appears in the document.

T   F   8.   When using the Page Numbering feature, you can choose between Arabic, Egyptian, and Roman numerals.

T   F   9.   WordPerfect manages the order of the page numbers when you are editing your document.

T   F   10.   You cannot see a hard page break on the screen. You must use the Reveal Codes feature to see it.

EXERCISE 3

INSTRUCTIONS:

1. Create the following document. The format settings for the document are listed below:

Font:	Helve-WP (Type 1) 12 point
Margins:	
Left	1.0"
Right	1.0"
Top	1.0"
Bottom	0.5"
Left Margin tabs:	Use your own discretion.
Justification:	Full
Line spacing:	Single space questions. Double space between questions.

2. Double space the software types in Question 3. Place two hard returns after "**Other**".

3. Copy the software types in Question 3 to Question 4.

4. Place 20 hard returns after Question 7.

5. Place a page break after Question 3, Question 6, and Question 8.

6. Place a page number at the bottom center of every page.

7. Place Header A against the left margin. The first line should be "**ABC CAN COMPANY**". The second line should be the current date.

8. Place one footer against the left margin. It should say "**Survey #1577**".

9. Preview the document.

10. Save the document in a file using the name "CH08EX03".

11. Print the document.

12. Close the document.

NAME: ID#:

JOB TITLE: EXT:

ADDRESS:

1. How long have you been with ABC Can Company?

2. How long have you been in your present job?

3. Indicate the number of hours you spend per week using the following types of software packages:

    Word Processing
    Spreadsheet Analysis
    Graphics
    Operating System
    Electronic Mail
    Calendaring
    Desktop Publishing
    Communications
    Database
    Other - please list below.

4. Circle the type of software package(s) you would like to learn:

5. Do you know how to type?

6. Would you like to improve your typing skills by using a special software package that teaches typing?

7. Briefly describe two or three critical tasks in your position.

8. Are there specific applications of information technology that need to be considered in your work area? If so, then please specify them; otherwise, proceed to the next question.

9. Are there ways information technology can be used to improve your individual efficiency and effectiveness as an employee? If so, then please specify them.

EXERCISE 4

INSTRUCTIONS:

1. Open the document file "CH08EX03".
2. Place an extra hard return between "**ABC CAN COMPANY**" and the current date in Header A.
3. Edit Footer A to say "**Survey: MP8-4**".
4. Move the page number to the bottom right corner of every page.
5. Preview the document.
6. Save the document in a file using the name "CH08EX04".
7. Print the document.
8. Close the document.

EXERCISE 5

INSTRUCTIONS:

1. Create the following document. Prepare the document exactly as it appears.
2. Place the text "**Chapter 8, Exercise 5 Solution**" and a hard return in Header A.
3. Place a footer at the left side of the page. Use your first and last name, followed by a comma and the word "**administrative assistant**" i.e., "**Ann Student, administrative assistant**".
4. Page break after each paragraph.
5. Double space the entire document.
6. Number the pages at the top right corner of each page.
7. Suppress Header A, Footer A, and the page numbers on the first page.
8. Spell check the document.
9. Preview the document.
10. Save the document in a file using the name "CH08EX05".
11. Print the document.
12. Close the document.

I have been involved with three deliberations with the members of the Program Committee to make plans for the forthcoming yearly meeting, to which all supervisors will be summoned. This is the result of the discussions held by the Executive Committee. Each of the meetings proved to be significantly interesting and profitable.

The group unanimously approved an outline including a variety of endeavors, only two of which would be a prescribed talk by some persons considered outstanding in the field of supervision. The meeting will take place at our Northwest Facilities and last all day. Lunch will be catered by the Four French Chefs.

I want you to study the proposed program and let me know at your earliest convenience whether or not you think the suggestions are suitable.

At this meeting, we will map plans for the new products we plan to introduce to the public and the ad campaigns to accompany them.

EXERCISE 6

INSTRUCTIONS:

1. Create the following list of client names, addresses, and paragraph numbers to be used for form letters.
2. Page break after each paragraph listing. Do not page break after the last one.
3. Place a header entitled "**Client letters**".
4. Place page numbers at the top center of each page.
5. Use your name as the footer.
6. Spell check the document.
7. Preview the document.
8. Print the document.
9. Save the document in a file using the name "CH08EX06".
10. Close the document.

```
Bridgette O'Connor
84 Bristol Place
Farmingdale, NY 11735

Paragraphs 1, 3, 15, 14

Kent R. Burnham
582 San Ysidro Road
Shippensburg, PA 17257

Paragraphs 12, 10, 2

Pat Dickey-Olson
1026 Highmont Road
Cheney, WA 89004

Paragraphs 8, 5, 9, 13, 3

Jan Charbaulski
429 Sulgrave Drive
St. Louis, MO 63153

Paragraphs 16, 7, 11, 14, 9, 13

Claudis Orr
512 Mariposa Avenue
Rio Piedras, CA 90012

Paragraphs 6, 2
```

EXERCISE 7

INSTRUCTIONS:

1. Open the document in file "CH08EX06".
2. Delete the page breaks, footer, header, and page numbering codes from the document.
3. Double space the entire document.
4. Preview the document.
5. Print the document.
6. Save the document in a file using the name "CH08EX07".
7. Close the document.

EXERCISE 8

INSTRUCTIONS:

1. Create the following document. Prepare the document exactly as it appears.
2. Use Full justification in the document.
3. Double space the document.
4. Place the header "**Investment Paragraphs**" in the document.
5. Number the pages at the bottom center of each page.
6. Use your name as the footer.
7. Place a page break after each paragraph.
8. Suppress the header on the first page.
9. Spell check the document.
10. Preview the document.
11. Print the document.
12. Save the document in a file using the name "CH08EX08".
13. Close the document.

This is an excellent time for you to take a close look at the income you are receiving from the tax exempt bonds in your portfolio. When you bought the bonds, did you buy fixed income or lifetime maturation?

Essentially any person can earn funds today, but only an informed person will know how to correctly invest her extra money to gain utmost safety of principal and gain the greatest growth in investment appreciation.

To many investors, earnings is the most important purpose of their investment program. It is their maintenance income, their retirement plan, their self-insurance for children and grandchildren, as well as their trust for charities.

CHAPTER NINE

TEXT ENHANCEMENTS

OBJECTIVES

In this chapter, you will learn to:
- Use the Center feature
- Use the Flush Right feature
- Change font appearance
- Boldface text
- Underline text
- Italicize text
- Change the font size/position
- Remove text enhancements
- Add text enhancements to existing text
- Use WP Characters
- Use the Hidden Text feature

■ CHAPTER OVERVIEW

In this chapter, the processes for enhancing text are discussed. The Center and Flush Right features are introduced. Changing font appearance by boldfacing, underlining, and italicizing text are described and illustrated. Procedures for inserting superscripts and subscripts as well as changing font size are discussed. The use of hidden text in documents is also discussed and illustrated.

■ USING THE CENTER FEATURE

The **Center** feature allows you to place text in the center of a line in your document. The text is centered between the left and right margins.

A [Cntr on Mar] code is placed before the text to be centered. To turn on the Center feature, press SHIFT+F6 or choose Center from the Alignment option from the Layout menu. After entering the text, press ENTER to end the Center feature. A hard return code [HRt] is placed in the document after the words to be centered.

Before starting this section, be sure you are in a clean document.

In the following instructions, you will compose the document in Figure 9-1.

Figure 9-1

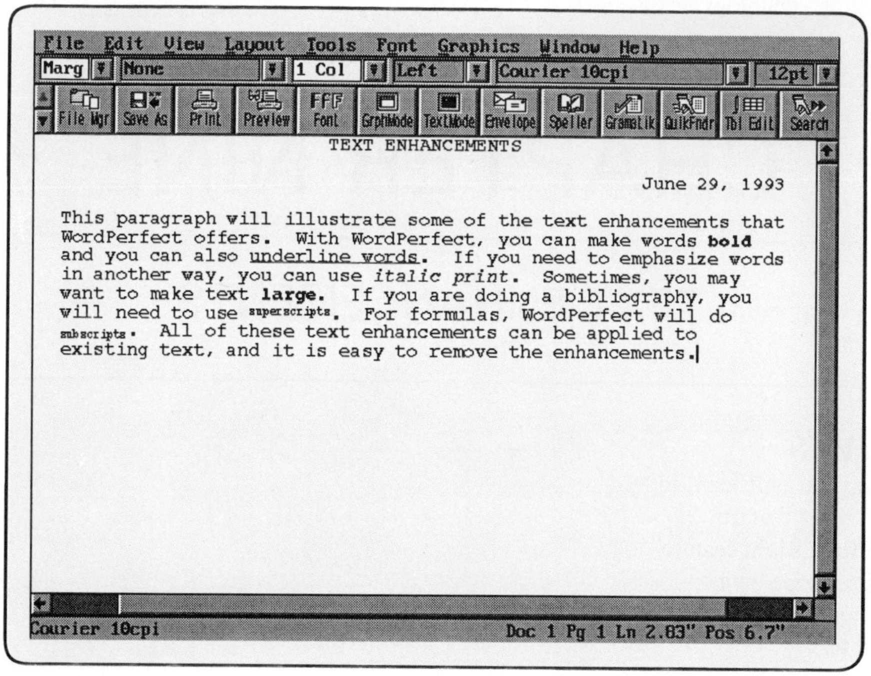

To center the text "TEXT ENHANCEMENTS" between the left and right margins:

Press   Shift + F6

Choose   *Layout*

Choose   *Alignment*

Choose   *Center*

Notice that the cursor is now in the center of the first line on your screen.

Type   TEXT ENHANCEMENTS

Type   *TEXT ENHANCEMENTS*

To end the Center feature:

Press   ←Enter

Press   ←Enter

The top part of your screen should look like Figure 9-2.

Figure 9-2

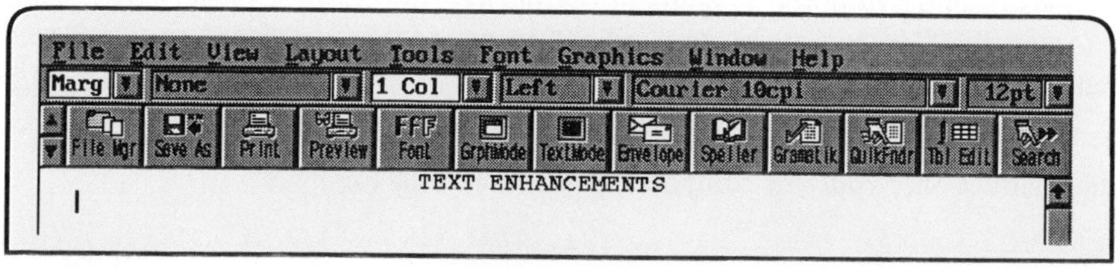

To insert a blank line:

Press   ←Enter

Press   ←Enter

■ USING THE FLUSH RIGHT FEATURE

With the Flush Right feature, you can quickly adjust text so that it is placed against the right margin. The **Flush Right** feature can be used to adjust a word, part of a line, or a group of lines to the right margin.

The Flush Right feature is activated by pressing ALT+F6 or by choosing Flush Right from the Alignment option from the Layout menu. A [Flsh Rgt] code is placed before the adjusted text. Flush Right is turned off by pressing ENTER. A hard return code [HRt] is inserted at the end of the line and the cursor is placed at the beginning of the next line.

To select Flush Right:

Press   Alt + F6

Choose   *Layout*

Choose   *Alignment*

Choose   *Flush Right*

Notice the cursor moves to the right margin.

To insert the current date as text:

Press   Shift + F5

Choose   *Tools*

Press   1 or T to select the Insert Date Text option

Choose   *Date*

Choose   *Text*

Except for a different date, the top part of your screen should look like Figure 9-3.

Figure 9-3

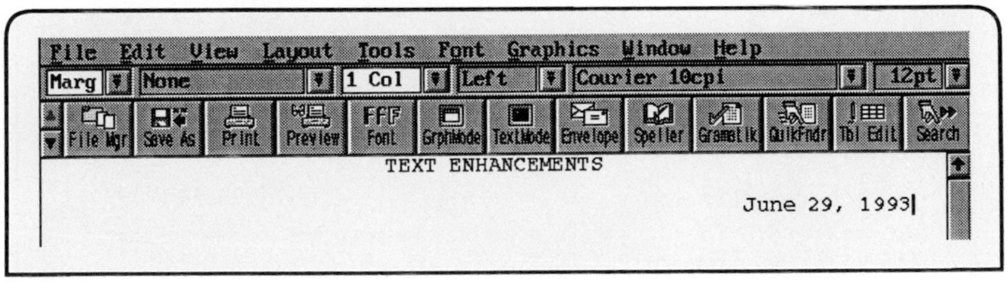

To end the Flush Right feature and add a blank line:

Press   ⏎Enter twice

Press   ⏎Enter *twice*

■ CHANGING FONT APPEARANCE

With the Font feature, you can change the font and point size of text. You can also change the appearance of text to italics, bold, underline, double underline, small caps, strikeout, outline, shadow, or redline. You can alter a font appearance by pressing CTRL+F8 or by choosing the Font menu.

Boldfacing Text

The **Bold** feature lets you print text that is darker than the rest so that it will attract attention on the page. When you use the Bold feature, WordPerfect inserts a [Bold On] and a [Bold Off] code around the selected text in your document.

Type the text in Figure 9-4 to begin the bold exercise.

Figure 9-4

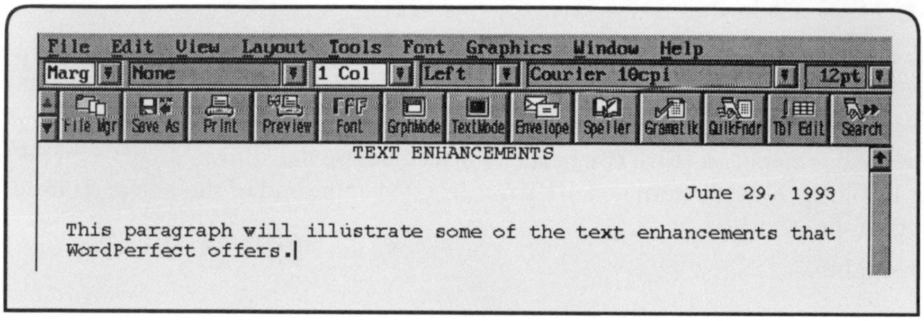

To use the Bold feature:

Press	Spacebar twice		*Press*	*Spacebar twice*
Type	With WordPerfect, you can make words		*Type*	*With WordPerfect, you can make words*
Press	Spacebar		*Press*	*Spacebar*
Press	F6		*Choose*	*Font*
Type	bold		*Choose*	*Bold*
			Type	*bold*

The top part of your screen should look like Figure 9-5.

Figure 9-5

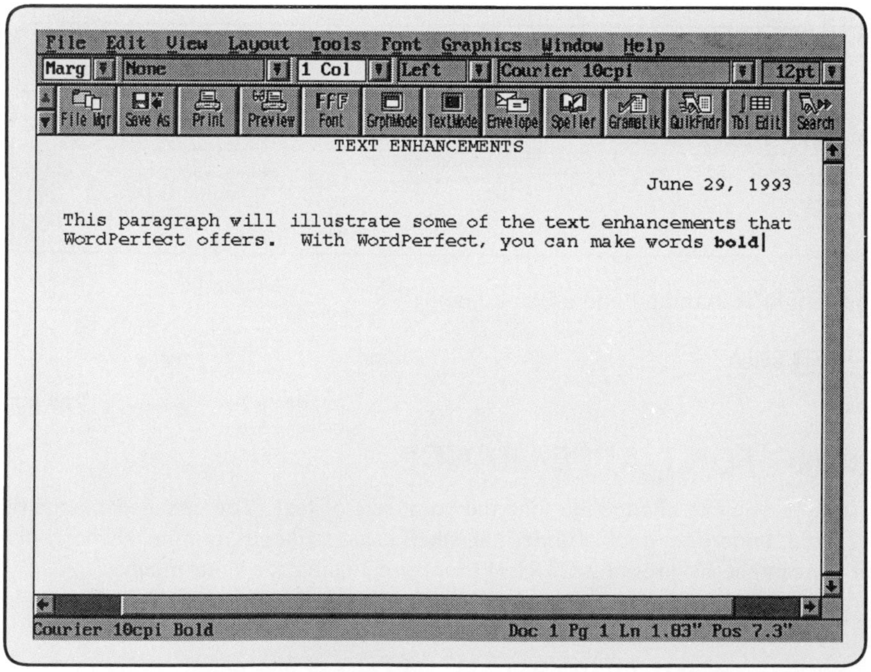

Notice the change in the appearance of the Pos and Font indicators on the status bar. The Pos indicator is darker because Bold is activated. Notice that the name of the Font in the status bar now displays the word "Bold".

To exit the Bold feature:

Press	F6		*Choose*	*Font*
	or		*Choose*	*Bold*
Press	→ to move the cursor beyond the code			*or*
			Press	→ *to move the cursor beyond the code*

Again, notice the change in the appearance of the Pos and Font indicators on the status bar. The intensity has changed back to normal because Bold is no longer active, and the word "Bold" no longer appears in the name of the font.

You can also turn off text enhancements by choosing the Normal option under the Font menu. However, this will turn off all enhancements. For example, if you are boldfacing and underlining a word, using the Normal option will turn off both the bold feature and the underline feature.

You can also boldface text through the "FONTS" Button Bar.

Underlining Text

The **Underline** feature allows you to emphasize text by placing a line under the text. You can choose to underline just the words or underline the words and the spaces between them. The default is to underline words and the spaces.

When you use the Underline feature, the [Und On] code is inserted before the text and the [Und Off] code is inserted at the end of the underlined text in your document.

To use the Underline feature:

Press	Spacebar		*Press*	*Spacebar*
Type	and you can also		*Type*	*and you can also*
Press	Spacebar		*Press*	*Spacebar*
Press	F8		*Choose*	*Font*
Type	underline words		*Choose*	*Underline*
			Type	*underline words*

Notice the change in the appearance of the Pos indicator on the status bar. An underline appears to show that the Underline feature is active.

Your screen should look like Figure 9-6.

Figure 9-6

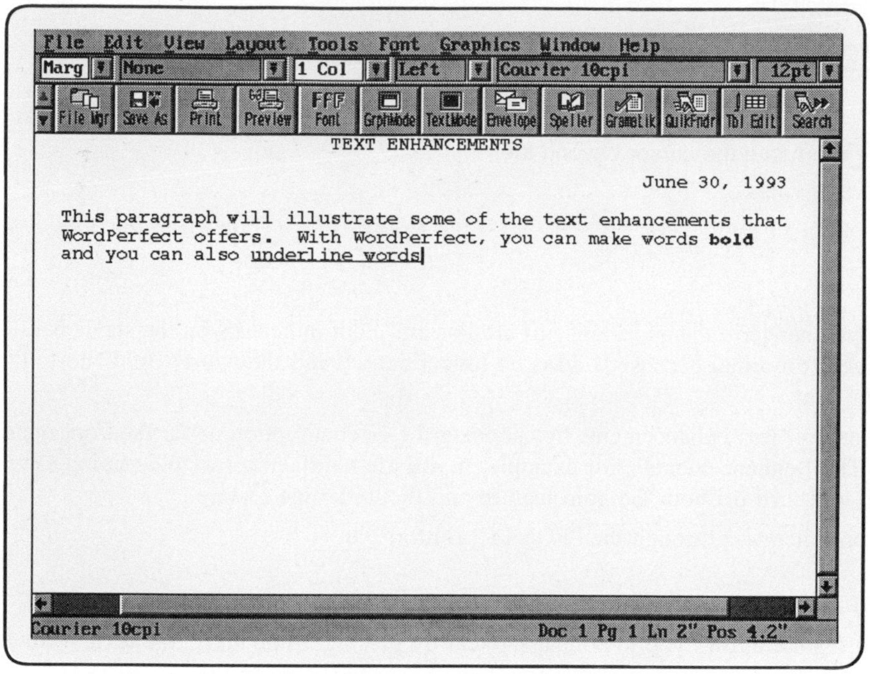

```
 File  Edit  View  Layout  Tools  Font  Graphics  Window  Help
[Marg ▼] None              [▼][1 Col][▼][Left  ▼][Courier 10cpi      ▼][12pt▼]
[File Mgr][Save As][Print][Preview][FFF Font][GrphMode][TextMode][Envelope][Speller][Gramatik][QuikFndr][Tbl Edit][Search]
                          TEXT ENHANCEMENTS                              ▲

                                                June 30, 1993

    This paragraph will illustrate some of the text enhancements that
    WordPerfect offers.  With WordPerfect, you can make words bold
    and you can also underline words|





                                                                        ▼
 Courier 10cpi                              Doc 1 Pg 1 Ln 2" Pos 4.2"
```

To stop using the Underline feature:

Press	F8		***Choose***	*Font*
	or		***Choose***	*Underline*
Press	→ to move the cursor beyond the code			*or*
			Press	*→ to move the cursor beyond the code*

Again, notice the change in the appearance of the Pos indicator on the status bar. The Underline feature is no longer active.

You can also underline text through the "FONTS" Button Bar.

Italicizing Text

The **Italics** feature allows you to emphasize text by making it a different style—text slanted toward the right rather than upright print. When you use the Italics feature, an [Italc On] code and an [Italc Off] code appear around the text.

To change the font appearance to italics:

Type			***Type***	
Press	Spacebar twice		***Press***	*Spacebar twice*
Type	If you need to emphasize words in another way, you can use		***Type***	*If you need to emphasize words in another way, you can use*
Press	Spacebar		***Press***	*Spacebar*
Press	Ctrl + I		***Choose***	*Font*

Type	italic print.	**Choose**	*Italics*
		Type	*italic print.*

Your screen should look like Figure 9-7.

Figure 9-7

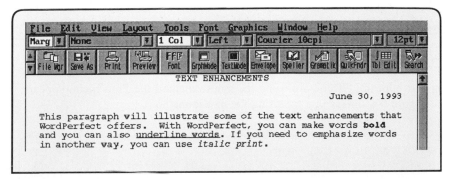

Note that this time the Pos indicator does not change appearance when the Italics feature is active.

To stop using italics:

Press	Ctrl + I	**Choose**	*Font*
	or	**Choose**	*Italics*
Press	→ to move the cursor beyond the code		*or*
		Press	→ *to move the cursor beyond the code*

You can also italicize text with the "FONTS" Button Bar.

■ CHANGING THE FONT SIZE/POSITION

You can use the **Font Size/Position** feature to change the size of printed characters and the position of text on the line. This feature can be used as an alternative to changing the base font every time you want to place text in a new font size.

The Font Size/Position selections are Fine, Small, Large, Very Large, Extra Large, Superscript, or Subscript. These selections are available by pressing CTRL+F8 or choosing the Size/Position option from the Font menu.

WordPerfect adjusts the point sizes of the Fine, Small, Large, Very Large, and Extra Large font sizes depending on the setting for the initial font. For the Superscript and Subscript font sizes, WordPerfect adjusts the text for Fine print and raises or lowers the text on the line. The font sizes available to you are limited to the fonts contained in your printer. For example, if your printer contains Times Roman 10 point and Times Roman 12 point, your document will print only in those two sizes. If your initial font is Times Roman 10 point, then selecting the Large font size will result in Times Roman 12 point text.

Additional information on printing is included in Chapter 10.

Large Text

To begin the process of changing the font size to Large:

Press	[Spacebar] twice		***Press***	[Spacebar] *twice*
Type	Sometimes, you may want to make text		***Type***	*Sometimes, you may want to make text*
Press	[Spacebar]		***Press***	[Spacebar]
Press	[Ctrl]+[F8]		***Choose***	*Font*

The Font dialog box appears. If you are using the mouse method the Font menu appears. Your screen should look like Figure 9-8 unless you are using the mouse method.

Figure 9-8

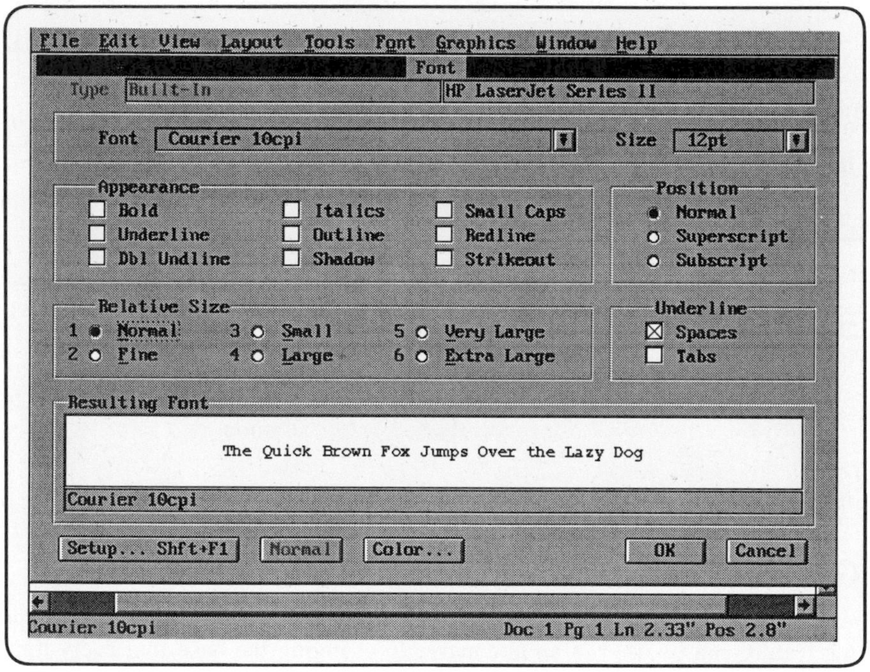

To change the font size to Large:

Press	4 or R to select the Relative Size option		***Choose***	*Size/Position*
Press	4 or L to select the Large option button		***Choose***	*Large*
Press	[←Enter]		***Type***	*large.*
Type	large.			

Notice that the text does not look larger than the surrounding text, but rather it is bold. Remember that the use of the Font Size/Position feature depends upon the fonts within your printer.

To stop using the Large font size:

Press	Ctrl + F8	**Choose**	*Font*
Press	4 or R to select the Relative Size option	**Choose**	*Size/Position*
Press	1 or N to select the Normal option button	**Choose**	*Normal Size*
Press	↩Enter		*or*
	or	**Press**	→ *to move the cursor beyond the code*
Press	→ to move the cursor beyond the code		

You could also turn off the Large font size by pressing CTRL+N or by choosing the Normal option under the Font menu.

The top part of your screen should look like Figure 9-9.

Figure 9-9

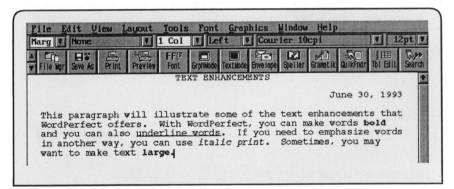

Notice that the "large" text does not appear larger. Instead, it appears boldfaced. When your printer cannot create the desired text enhancement, it will alter the text in some other way.

Superscripts and Subscripts

The **Superscript** feature places smaller text slightly above a line of normal printed text. The **Subscript** feature places smaller text slightly below a line of normal printed text. This is ^{superscript}, and this is $_{subscript}$. WordPerfect inserts a [Suprscpt On] and [Suprscpt Off] code around the text that is raised by the Superscript feature. [Subscpt On] and [Subscpt Off] codes are placed around the text that is lowered by the Subscript feature.

To add text using the Superscript feature:

Press	Spacebar twice	**Press**	Spacebar twice
Type	If you are doing a bibliography, you will need to use	**Type**	*If you are doing a bibliography, you will need to use*
Press	Spacebar	**Press**	Spacebar
Press	Ctrl + F8	**Choose**	*Font*
Press	5 or P to select the Position option	**Choose**	*Size/Position*
Press	2 or S to select the Superscript option button	**Choose**	*Superscript*

Press	⏎Enter		*Type*	*superscripts*
Type	superscripts			

The top part of your screen should look like Figure 9-10.

Figure 9-10

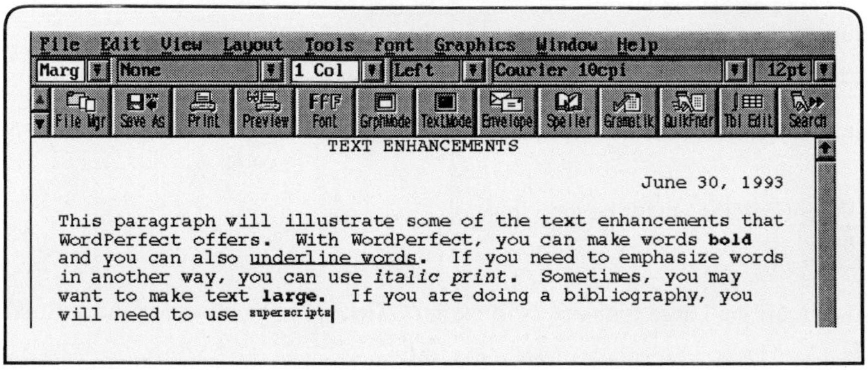

To stop using the Superscript feature:

Press	Ctrl + F8		*Choose*	*Font*
Press	5 or P to select the Position option		*Choose*	*Size/Position*
Press	1 or N to select the Normal option button		*Choose*	*Normal Position*
Press	⏎Enter			*or*
	or		*Press*	→ *to move the cursor beyond the code*
Press	→ to move the cursor beyond the code			

To use the Subscript feature:

Type			*Type*	
Press	Spacebar twice		*Press*	*Spacebar twice*
Type	For formulas, WordPerfect will do		*Type*	*For formulas, WordPerfect will do*
Press	Spacebar		*Press*	*Spacebar*
Press	Ctrl + F8		*Choose*	*Font*
Press	5 or P to select the Position option		*Choose*	*Size/Position*
Press	3 or B to select the Subscript option button		*Choose*	*Subscript*
Press	⏎Enter		*Type*	*subscripts*
Type	subscripts			

The top part of your screen should look like Figure 9-11.

Figure 9-11

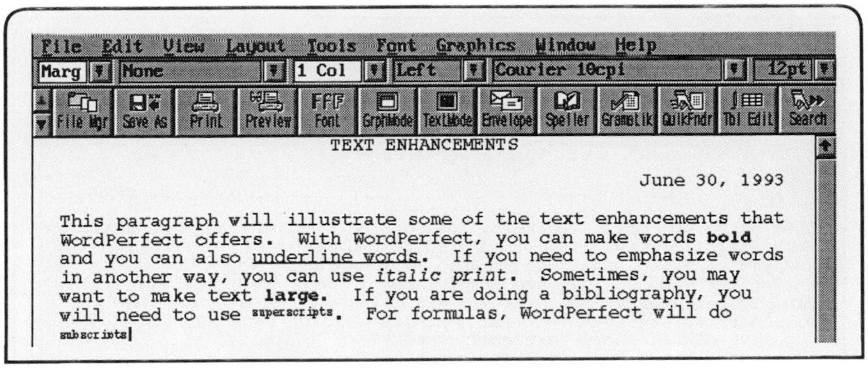

To stop using the Subscript feature:

Press	Ctrl + F8		***Choose***	*Font*
Press	5 or P to select the Position option		***Choose***	*Size/Position*
Press	1 or N to select the Normal option button		***Choose***	*Normal Position*
Press	←Enter			
	or			*or*
			Press	→ *to move the cursor beyond the code*
Press	→ to move the cursor beyond the code			

You can also superscript and subscript text through the "FONTS" Button Bar.

Type a period and press the SPACEBAR twice and type the text displayed in Figure 9-12 to finish the document.

Figure 9-12

```
All of these text enhancements can be applied to existing text,
and it is easy to remove the enhancements.
```

When you have finished typing, your screen should look like Figure 9-13.

Figure 9-13

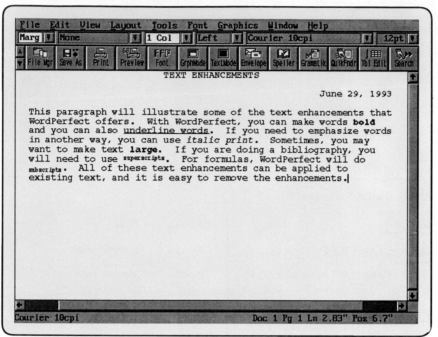

Print the document to see how the text enhancements print. If you used an HP Laser Jet II, your document should look similar to Figure 9-14. Note: The left and right margins were altered for the display of Figure 9-14.

Figure 9-14

TEXT ENHANCEMENTS

June 30, 1993

This paragraph will illustrate some of the text enhancements that WordPerfect offers. With WordPerfect, you can make words **bold** and you can also <u>underline</u> words. If you need to emphasize words in another way, you can use <u>italic print</u>. Sometimes, you may want to make text **large**. If you are doing a bibliography, you will need to use superscripts. For formulas, WordPerfect will do subscripts. All of these text enhancements can be applied to existing text, and it is easy to remove the enhancements.

Notice that the "italicized" text does not appear slanted. Instead, it appears underlined. When your printer cannot create the desired text enhancement, it will alter the text in some other way.

■ REMOVING TEXT ENHANCEMENTS

Each time you apply a text enhancement, WordPerfect places a code for that enhancement into the document. Using Reveal Codes, you can delete these codes and remove the enhancement from the text.

Turn on Reveal Codes and scroll up in the document until you can see the [Subscpt On] code.

Notice that before the word "subscripts" there is a [Subscpt On] code, and at the end of "subscripts" is another code, [Subscpt Off]. These are the codes that tell WordPerfect to make the word "subscripts" appear smaller and lower than surrounding text. Think of these codes as a pair—when you delete one of the codes, they are both deleted.

To remove the Subscript enhancement:

| **Press** | the arrow keys to place the cursor on the [Subscpt On] code | **Click** | on the [Subscpt On] code |
| **Press** | `Delete` | **Press** | `Delete` |

Now the text that was subscripted is the same size and in the same position as the surrounding text.

To remove the Superscript enhancement:

| **Press** | the arrow keys to place the cursor on the [Suprscpt On] code | **Click** | on the [Suprscpt On] code |
| **Press** | `Delete` | **Press** | `Delete` |

Notice that the text is no longer above the surrounding text, and both the [Suprscpt On] and [Suprscpt Off] codes have been removed.

To delete the other text enhancements:

Press	the arrow keys to place the cursor on the [Large On] code	**Click**	on the [Large On] code
Press	`Delete`	**Press**	`Delete`
Press	the arrow keys to place the cursor on the [Italc On] code	**Click**	on the [Italc On] code
Press	`Delete`	**Press**	`Delete`
Press	the arrow keys to place the cursor on the [Und On] code	**Click**	on the [Und On] code
Press	`Delete`	**Press**	`Delete`
Press	the arrow keys to place the cursor on the [Bold On] code	**Click**	on the [Bold On] code
Press	`Delete`	**Press**	`Delete`

To delete the Flush Right and Center codes:

| **Press** | the arrow keys to place the cursor on the [Flsh Rgt] code | **Click** | on the `Fish Rgt` code (you may have to scroll up in the document to see the code) |
| **Press** | `Delete` | **Press** | `Delete` |

Press	the arrow keys to place the cursor on the [Cntr on Mar] code		*Click*	*on the [Cntr on Mar] code (you may have to scroll up in the document to see the code)*
Press	Delete		*Press*	Delete

Notice these text enhancements are different from the bold, underline, italics, large, superscript, and subscript codes because only one code is placed in the document at the beginning of the word. When all the text enhancement codes and Reveal Codes have been removed from the document, your screen will look like Figure 9-15.

Figure 9-15

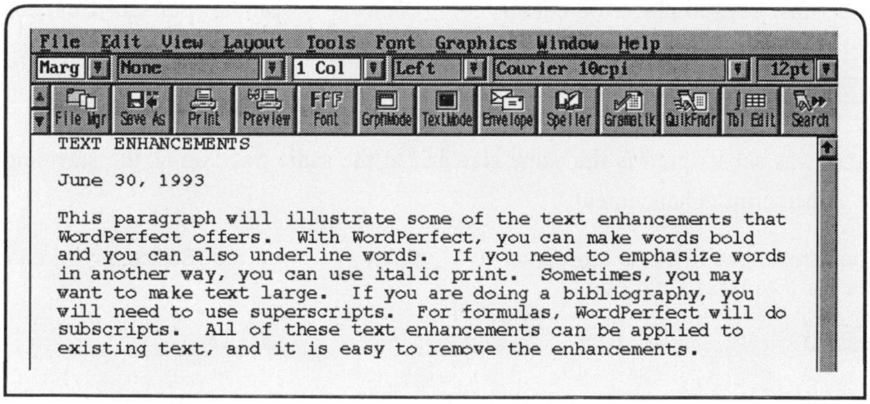

■ ADDING TEXT ENHANCEMENTS TO EXISTING TEXT

Now that you have removed the enhancement codes from the document, you can learn how to apply text enhancements to existing text.

To center the title:

Move	the cursor before the "T" in "TEXT ENHANCEMENTS" (if necessary)		*Click*	*before the "T" in "TEXT ENHANCEMENTS" (if necessary)*
Press	Shift + F6		*Choose*	*Layout*
			Choose	*Alignment*
			Choose	*Center*
				or
			Highlight	*TEXT ENHANCEMENTS*
			Click	*the Justification drop-down list on the Ribbon*
			Double-click	*on the Center option*

Notice that you have to select the text when using the Ribbon.

To make the date flush right again:

Move	the cursor before the beginning of the date	*Click*	*before the beginning of the date*
Press	Alt + F6	*Choose*	*Layout*
		Choose	*Alignment*
		Choose	*Flush Right*
			or
		Highlight	*the date*
		Click	*the Justification drop-down list on the Ribbon*
		Double-click	*on the Right option*

Your screen should look like Figure 9-16.

Figure 9-16

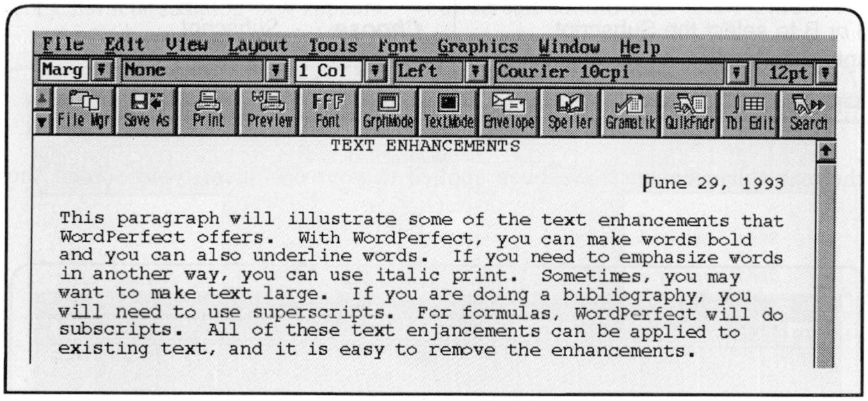

To boldface the word "bold":

Select	the word "bold"	*Highlight*	*the word "bold"*
Press	F6	*Choose*	*Font*
		Choose	*Bold*

Because the bold text enhancement places a code on either side of text, you must highlight the existing text before issuing the bold command.

To reapply the other text enhancements to the existing text:

Select	the word "underline"	*Highlight*	*the word "underline"*
Press	F8	*Choose*	*Font*
Select	the word "italic"	*Choose*	*Underline*
Press	Ctrl + I	*Highlight*	*the word "italic"*
Select	the word "large"	*Choose*	*Font*
Press	Ctrl + F8	*Choose*	*Italics*

Your screen should look like Figure 9-19.

Figure 9-19

The medium filled bullet is the first character in the Typographic Symbols set. Notice the numbers in the Number text box. The medium bullet is number 4,0. The first number in a character number represents the set. The Typographic Symbols set is the fourth character set. The second number represents the character number. Each set of characters begins with the number zero. Because the bullet is the first character, its number is zero. As you become more familiar with the special characters, you will be able to type the number representing the character rather than switching to the character set and highlighting the number.

To insert the bullet in the document at the cursor and close the dialog box:

Press   I to select the Insert command   ***Click***   *the Insert command button*
                   button

Your screen should look like Figure 9-20.

Figure 9-20

To insert a second bullet:

Move	the cursor to the end of the document		***Click***	*at the end of the document*
Press	[←Enter] twice		***Press***	[←Enter] *twice*
Press	[Ctrl]+[W]		***Choose***	*Font*
			Choose	*WP Characters*

Your screen should look like Figure 9-21.

Figure 9-21

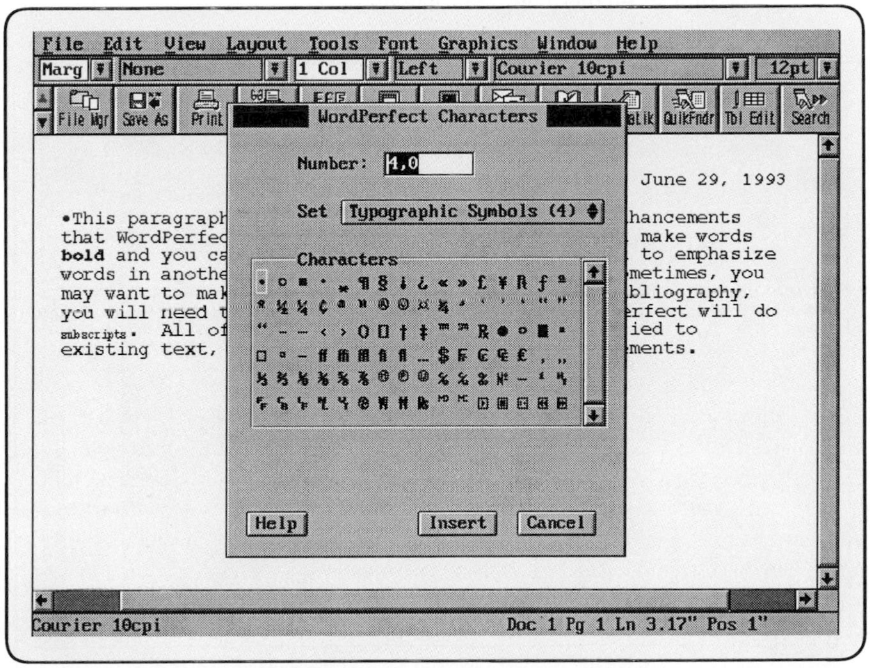

Notice the Typographic Symbols set is still selected. Once you select a set during a session of WordPerfect, the set will appear the next time you enter the WordPerfect Characters feature.

To select the bullet and close the dialog box:

Press	[←Enter] to accept the number in the Number text box		***Click***	*the Insert command button*

The bullet appears in your document. To delete the second bullet:

Press	[Backspace]		***Press***	[Backspace]

■ USING THE HIDDEN TEXT FEATURE

WordPerfect allows you to place text in your document and hide it. For example, you may want to place a question in your document that is not part of your document. You could use the **Hidden Text** feature to hide the question when printing and viewing on the screen. Like the Bold feature, the Hidden Text feature places a [Hidden On] code at the beginning of the text and a [Hidden Off] code at the end of the text.

WordPerfect also offers a feature called Comments which is similar to Hidden Text. The **Comments** feature is different from the Hidden Text feature in four ways. First, Comments cannot be printed with your document, but you can print Hidden Text. Second, Comments are not treated as regular text. Third, Hidden Text affects your page numbering if it is displayed and Comments do not. Fourth, Hidden Text is not enclosed in a border box. Consult your WordPerfect Reference manual for more information about Comments.

Insert two blank lines at the end of your document. To create hidden text:

| **Press** | Alt + F5 | **Choose** | *Font* |

The Mark dialog box appears if you are using the keyboard method, and your screen should look like Figure 9-22. If you are using the mouse method, the Font menu appears.

Figure 9-22

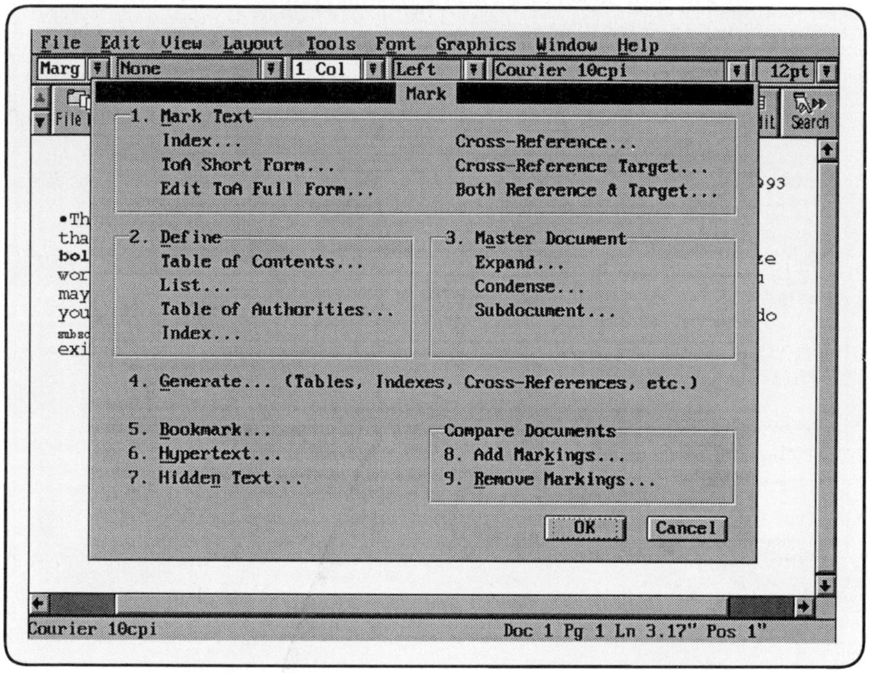

| **Press** | 7 or N to select the Hidden Text option | **Choose** | *Hidden Text* |

The Hidden Text dialog box appears. Your screen should look like Figure 9-23.

Figure 9-23

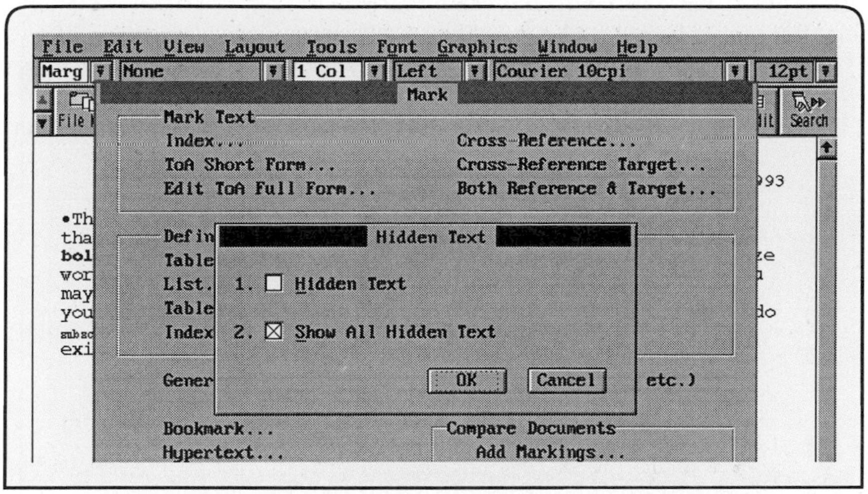

To select Hidden Text:

Press	1 or H to place an X in the Hidden Text check box	*Click*	*the Hidden Text check box until an X appears*
Press	⏎Enter	*Click*	*the OK command button*
Type	This is my hidden text.	*Type*	*This is my hidden text.*

To turn off the Hidden Text feature:

Press	Alt + F5	*Choose*	*Font*
Press	7 or N to select the Hidden Text option	*Choose*	*Hidden Text*
Press	1 or H to remove the X in the Hidden Text check box	*Click*	*the Hidden Text check box until the X disappears*
Press	⏎Enter	*Click*	*the OK command button*
	or		*or*
Press	→ to move the cursor beyond the code	*Press*	*→ to move the cursor beyond the code*

Turn Reveal Codes on. Your screen should look like Figure 9-24.

Figure 9-24

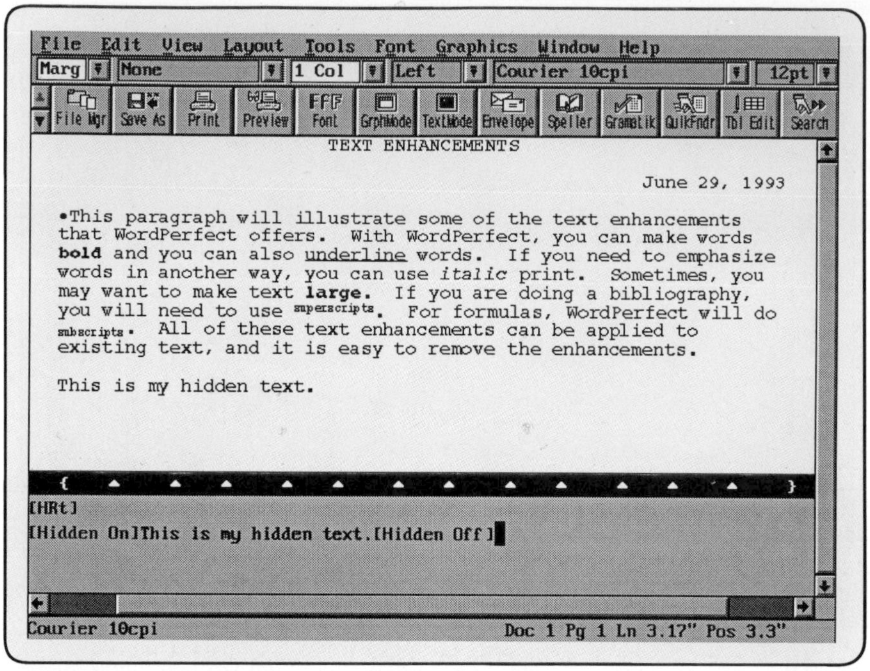

To hide hidden text:

Press	Alt + F5	**Choose**	*Font*
Press	7 or N to select the Hidden Text option	**Choose**	*Hidden Text*
Press	2 or S to remove the X in the Show All Hidden Text check box	**Click**	*the Show All Hidden Text check box until the X disappears*
Press	←Enter	**Click**	*the OK command button*

With your text hidden, your screen should look like Figure 9-25.

Figure 9-25

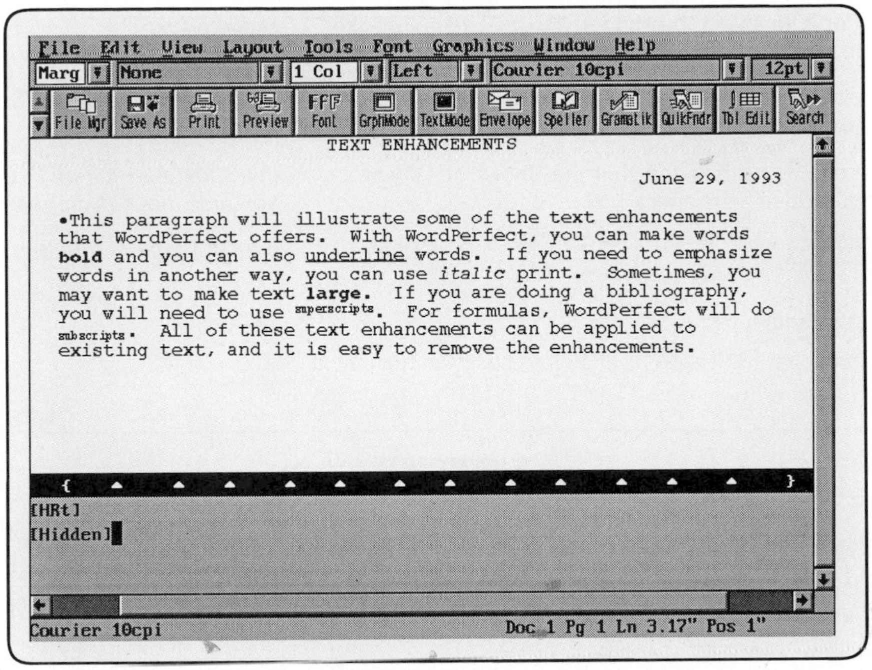

Notice that when your text is hidden, WordPerfect inserts a [Hidden] code in your document.

To display hidden text:

Press	Alt + F5	**Choose**	*Font*
Press	7 or N to select the Hidden Text option	**Choose**	*Hidden Text*
Press	2 or S to place an X in the Show All Hidden Text check box	**Click**	*the Show All Hidden Text check box until an X appears*
Press	←Enter	**Click**	*the OK command button*

Notice that the codes in Reveal Codes have changed back to [Hidden On] and [Hidden Off].

To remove the Hidden Text codes:

Press	the arrow keys to place the cursor on the [Hidden On] code	**Click**	*on the [Hidden On] code*
Press	Delete	**Press**	*Delete*

Turn off the Reveal Codes.

To hide existing text:

Select	This is my hidden text.	**Highlight**	*This is my hidden text.*
Press	Alt + F5	**Choose**	*Font*

The Mark Text dialog box appears if you are using the keyboard method. If you are using the mouse method, the Font menu appears on your screen.

Press	7 or N to select the Hidden Text option	**Choose**	*Hidden Text*
Press	1 or H to place an X in the Hidden Text check box	**Click**	*the Hidden Text check box until an X appears*
Press	2 or S to remove the X in the Show All Hidden Text check box	**Click**	*the Show All Hidden Text check box until the X disappears*
Press	⌐←Enter	**Click**	*the OK command button*

Your text is now hidden again.

Save the document as "ENHANCE.DOC". Close the document.

EXERCISE 1

INSTRUCTIONS: Define the following concepts:

1.   Bold _____

_____

2.   Center _____

_____

3.   Underline _____

_____

4.   Font Size/Position _____

_____

5.   Superscript _____

_____

6.   Font Appearance _____

_____

7.   Flush Right _____

_____

8.   Hidden Text _____

_____

9.   Italics _____

_____

10.   Subscript _____

_____

11. Comments _____

_____

12. WordPerfect characters _____

_____

EXERCISE 2

INSTRUCTIONS: Circle T if the statement is true and F if the statement is false.

T   F   1. You can center text between the margins.
T   F   2. Pressing ENTER ends centering.
T   F   3. You can remove all text enhancements by deleting the appropriate code in Reveal Codes.
T   F   4. The Bold feature allows you to create text that prints lighter than the rest of the text.
T   F   5. The Font indicator on the status bar changes when you use the Bold feature.
T   F   6. WordPerfect defaults to underlining words and spaces.
T   F   7. The Flush Right feature aligns text against the left margin.
T   F   8. The Superscript feature places text slightly below a line of normal printed text.
T   F   9. The Hidden Text feature places text in a box on the screen.
T   F   10. The Font Size selections are Fine, Small, Medium, Very Large, and Extra Large.
T   F   11. The Font Appearance selections are Bold, Underline, Double Underline, Flush Right, Italic, Outline, Shadow, Small Caps, Redline, or Strikeout.
T   F   12. The Flush Right feature is turned off by pressing ENTER.
T   F   13. WordPerfect provides six character sets in the WordPerfect Characters feature.

EXERCISE 3

INSTRUCTIONS: 1. Create the following document.
2. Center the text "**LIBRARY ANNOUNCEMENT**".
3. Boldface the text "**New Additions to the Reference Library:**".
4. Place bullets before each title and indent the title text.
5. Underline the titles of each book.
6. Spell check your document.
7. Preview the document.
8. Save the document in a file using the name "CH09EX03".
9. Close the document.

```
                    LIBRARY ANNOUNCEMENT


New Additions to the Reference Library:

•  Mastering and Using WordPerfect 6.0 for DOS, by H. Albert Napier
   and Philip J. Judd.

•  Mastering and Using Lotus 1-2-3 Release 3.4, by H. Albert Napier
   and Philip J. Judd.

•  Mastering and Using Lotus 1-2-3 Release 2.4, by H. Albert Napier
   and Philip J. Judd.
```

EXERCISE 4

INSTRUCTIONS:
1. Open the "CH09EX03" document.
2. Remove the center, bold, and underline codes.
3. Save the document in a file using the name "CH09EX04".
4. Close the document.

EXERCISE 5

INSTRUCTIONS:
1. Create the following document using the WordPerfect Characters feature.
2. Save the document as "CH09EX05".
3. Print the document.
4. Close the document.

```
                  WORDPERFECT CHARACTERS

The WordPerfect Characters feature offers many symbols that you can
use in documents.  Some of the more commonly used character sets
include the multinational, iconic, and typographic symbols sets.  The
following list describes some uses for these character sets.

Multinational 1          accented letters as in résumé or fiancée

Typographic Symbols      round bullets such as • or squares such as ■

                         copyright symbol ©, trademark symbol ™, or
                         registered symbol ®

Iconic Symbols           special symbols like ☺ or ♥ or ✆

Math/Scientific          special math symbols like ∑ or ≥ or ±

Greek                    Greek letters that can create organization
                         names like ΦBK

All of these symbols and many more are available by choosing WP
Characters from the Font menu.
```

EXERCISE 6

INSTRUCTIONS:

1. Create the following document.
2. Center the last line of the notice.
3. Underline the third sentence.
4. Boldface the words "**Mr. Michael Nguyen**" and "**ext. 5622**".
5. Preview the document.
6. Save the document in a file using the name "CH09EX06".
7. Print the document.
8. Close the document.

DANGER! DANGER! DANGER!

ONLY AUTHORIZED PERSONNEL

MAY PROCEED BEYOND THIS POINT

This area is restricted due to sensitive chemical experiments in process. You must have security clearance level 7 or higher to enter this level. All halls and labs are monitored by surveillance cameras and security guards. If you require assistance, please contact Mr. Michael Nguyen at ext. 5622.

ABC Can Company, R&D Division, Policy #125

EXERCISE 7

INSTRUCTIONS:

1. Create the following document.
2. Use Full justification in the document.
3. Center, bold, and underline the titles and words as indicated.
4. Use a 2" top margin.
5. Indent the description paragraphs beneath each class name.
6. Place bullets before each course title.
7. Spell check the document.
8. Preview the document.
9. Print the document.
10. Save the document in a file using the name "CH09EX07".
11. Close the document.

```
                          HARPER COLLEGE

                            PRESENTS

                 BUSINESS INFORMATION MANAGEMENT

                   A Listing of Fall Courses


•BIM 170 Intro to Information Applications and Technologies

              Provides an overview of business information
              applications -- technology, people, and procedures
              within organizational and environmental contexts.


•BIM 175 Enterprise-Wide Information Analysis

              Collecting and analyzing organizational needs,
              utilizing planning tools, and collecting data for
              assessing the impact of change upon work groups and
              teams.


•BIM 250 Multimedia Business Presentations

              Effective transparencies, slides, and computer
              presentations using a storyboard.  This course will
              be taught by an outstanding educational television
              producer.



                          Sign Up Now!

                For more information, contact:

       COORDINATOR, BUSINESS INFORMATION MANAGEMENT

                         HARPER COLLEGE
```

EXERCISE 8

INSTRUCTIONS: 1.   Create the following document. Read the instructions in steps 2 and 3
                       before you enter the text.
                       The format settings for the document are listed below:

Initial Font:	Helve-WP (Type 1) 10 point
Margins:	
Left	1.0"
Right	1.0"
Top	1.0"
Bottom	1.0"
Tabs:	Set at your discretion.
Justification:	Full
Line spacing:	Single
Hyphenation:	None

    2.   As you type the document, flush right the third paragraph.
    3.   Use the Flush Right feature on the fourth paragraph.

4. Change the last sentence in the fifth paragraph, **"It's really quite simple!"**, to shadow text.
5. Preview the document.
6. Save the document in a file using the name "CH09EX08".
7. Print the document.
8. Close the document.

TO: Jack Fontana
         Accounting Department

FROM: Donna Kainer
         Micro User Support Team (MUST)

DATE: current date

RE: Flush Right Question

Jack, I want to follow up on your WordPerfect question from yesterday. If you have a word, phrase, or paragraph that you want "pushed" to the right margin, then the Flush Right feature is the one to use. You are only creating more work for yourself if you create a right tab at or near the right margin.

You can use the Flush Right feature by pressing the Alt+F6 keys. For example, if you want a word at the right margin, press Alt+F6, type the word, and then press the Enter key to end the Flush Right feature.

Here is an example.

You can flush right an entire paragraph by blocking the paragraph first. Then press the Alt+F6 keys to move it. I entered this paragraph in the normal manner—flush against the *left* margin. Then I made it flush right. It's really quite simple!

The Flush Right feature is especially useful in headers and footers, too.

I hope that I have been of help to you. Please call me at ext. 1500 if you have any more questions.

EXERCISE 9

INSTRUCTIONS: 1. Create the following document. The format settings for the document are listed below:

Initial Font:	Helve-WP (Type 1) 12 point
Margins:	
Left	1.5"
Right	1.5"
Top	1.0"
Bottom	1.0"
Tabs:	Set at your discretion.
Justification:	Full
Line spacing:	Double

2. The title of the document is bold, centered, and in a Large font size.
3. Change the underlined sentences to double underlines.
4. Boldface the first sentence of paragraph five, "**As a result of . . .**". Then change the text to small caps.
5. Preview the document.
6. Save the document in a file using the name "CH09EX09".
7. Print the document.
8. Close the document.

RESULTS OF COMPUTER SKILL INVENTORY

Last month, the Micro User Support Team (MUST) conducted a survey of ABC Can Company personnel. This survey asked users about their computer skills. The results of this survey have been computed and are listed below.

<u>The type of software that is used by the greatest number of people at ABC Can Company is electronic mail.</u> Eighty-seven percent of ABC personnel use electronic mail (E-mail). Users spend an average of 3.2 hours per week sending and receiving messages on E-mail. Since MUST installed E-mail at ABC only a year ago, this statistic is considered quite significant. Second and third in this category are word processing and graphics software.

<u>ABC users spend the most time on word processing software.</u> Average usage time is 22.5 hours per week. Users requested word processing the most as the type of software package that they wanted to learn. Eighty percent of the requests for more training in word processing specified WordPerfect as the package to learn. Second and third in this category are spreadsheet and graphics software.

A small number of users want to learn or improve their typing skills. Nine percent of the respondents to the survey said that they are interested in learning through a typing software program. Three percent of the respondents want a course with a teacher.

As a result of the computer skills survey, MUST is in the process of evaluating the computer training program at ABC Can Company. We are creating new courses and updating old courses to meet ABC's computer needs. We are also hiring an outside training firm, Napier & Judd, Inc., to help us meet the demand for more training.

The Training Services Department will send a notice and schedule of classes in three weeks to all ABC personnel.

EXERCISE 10

INSTRUCTIONS:

1. Create the following document using the font changes as indicated.
2. Use Full justification in the document.
3. Insert the following sentence as hidden text at the top of the document. "**FILE IT RIGHT, TAXES LESS** form letter: **ORGANIZATION UNLIMITED**."
4. Spell check the document.
5. Preview the document.
6. Hide the hidden text.

7. Print the document.
8. Save the document in a file using the name "CH09EX10".
9. Close the document.

---

current date

Mr. William Trunk
1408 Redbud Lane
Bloomington, IN 47401

Dear Mr. Trunk:

DON'T WAIT TILL NEXT YEAR!

Now that the dreaded tax season has passed, start reorganizing your files now. FILE IT RIGHT, TAXES LESS is our **new book just off the press.**

FILE IT RIGHT, TAXES LESS tries to bring every step of the process in preparing your taxes down to its lowest and easiest level. We have been selling this philosophy for years. If 5,000,000 customers use this book, that tells you **we must be on to something worthwhile.**

Remember what the Director of Internal Revenue said about doing your taxes. "File early, keep good records."[1] **Don't be late again with your taxes.** Send in your order **NOW!** The cost of this book is only $10.95, a small price to pay.

Very sincerely yours,

ORGANIZATION UNLIMITED

Rupert James McGrath, Publisher

[1]Speech before Kokomo Tax Preparers, Spring 1993

EXERCISE 11

INSTRUCTIONS:
1. Create the following document.
2. Use Full justification in the document.
3. Insert the following sentence as hidden text at the top of the document. **"Form letter for interactive Video."**
4. Spell check the document.
5. Hide the hidden text.
6. Preview the document.
7. Print the document.
8. Save the document in a file using the name "CH09EX11".
9. Close the document.

```
                        Student's Street Address
                   Student's City, State, and Zip Code



current date



Mr. Bill Liskowske
1776 Freedom Road
Boston, MA 02109

Dear Mr. Liskowske:

        "A little knowledge is a dangerous thing."¹

Since you are in the education business, you must realize that the
above quote reflects a serious problem.  Millions of high school
students drop out of school every day with only a little knowledge.
```

INTERACTIVE VIDEO

```
This is not a buzz word.  It is a whole new concept in teaching.
It combines computers, video, instant replay, and testing on almost
any topic you would like.²
```

For a demonstration and complete discussion of how this works, and
how it has improved the education of some misguided students, CALL
1-800-555-9090.

WE BELIEVE that everyone should be able to reach their greatest
potential for self-fulfillment and have the necessary skills to
start some type of career.

```
DON'T HESITATE!   This opportunity is only for a short time.
Remember "Live every day as if it were your last."³  Make sure this
quote can be your students' dream and your legacy.

Most sincerely yours,



Gary Jacobs, Vice President for Sales

¹Alexander Pope, An Essay on Criticism, Part II, line 15.
²Read our book Education for the Masses.
³Marcus Aurelis (121-180 A.D.).
```

CHAPTER TEN

PRINTING FEATURES

OBJECTIVES

In this chapter, you will learn to:
- Print a document from the screen
- Print a document from a disk
- Set printer options
- Select a printer
- Change Output Options
- Change Document Settings

■ CHAPTER OVERVIEW

In this chapter, the processes for printing a document are discussed. The methods for printing a document from the screen or disk, setting printer options, and viewing a document are described and illustrated. The procedures for canceling, rushing, or stopping a print job are also discussed.

■ PRINTING A DOCUMENT ON SCREEN

The Print/Fax feature allows you to print the document that is currently displayed on the screen. The Fax options are discussed in Appendix C.

There are three options for printing a document that appears on the screen. The **Full Document** option prints the entire document. The **Page** option prints only the page on which the cursor is located. The **Multiple Pages** option prints selected pages of the document.

Before starting this section, be sure you have a clear screen. Then, open the document "REPORT1.DOC".

Note: To complete these exercises and for your screen to match the figures in this chapter, you will need to turn your printer off or take the printer offline. If your computer is not attached to a printer, continue with the instructions.

To print the entire document:

Press   Shift + F7

Click   the Print button on the Button Bar

The Print/Fax dialog box appears. Your screen should look like Figure 10-1.

Figure 10-1

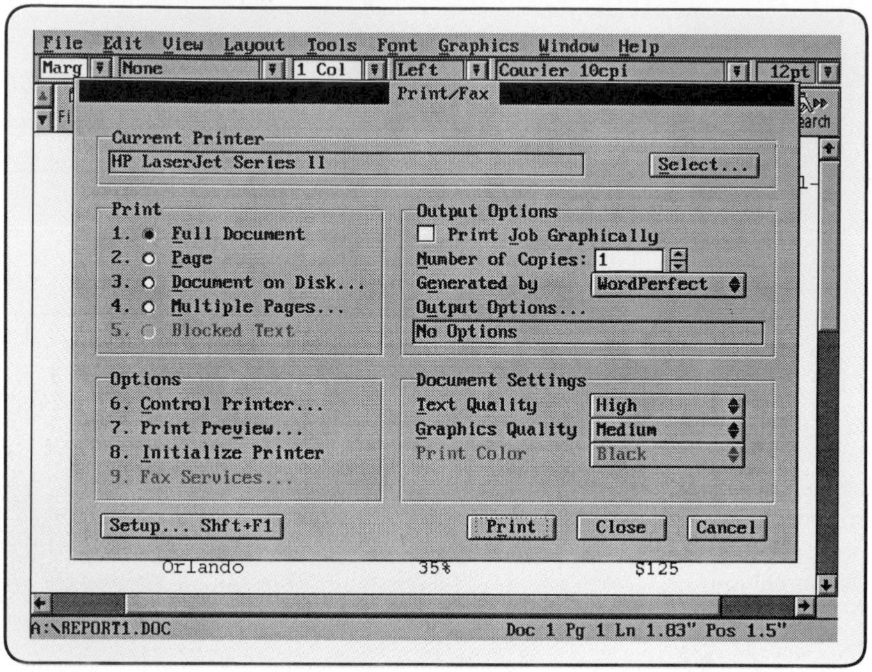

To select Full Document:

Press	1 or F to select the Full Document option button	*Click*	*the Full Document option button*
Press	[←Enter] to select the Print command button	*Click*	*the Print command button*

The print job has been sent to the printer and you can now continue working on your document. WordPerfect does not show you any messages about your print job except in Control Printer (discussed later in the chapter).

To print the page on which the cursor is located:

Press	[Shift]+[F7]	*Click*	*the Print button on the Button Bar* 

To select Page:

Press	2 or P to select the Page option button in the Print box	*Click*	*the Page option button in the Print box*
Press	[←Enter] to select the Print command button	*Click*	*the Print command button*

Again, no message is displayed as your document is printing.

To use the Multiple Pages option:

Press	⌈Shift⌉+⌈F7⌉	*Click*	*the Print button on the Button Bar* 
Press	4 or M to select the Multiple Pages option button in the Print box	*Click*	*the Multiple Pages option button in the Print box*

The Print Multiple Pages dialog box appears. Your screen should look like Figure 10-2.

Figure 10-2

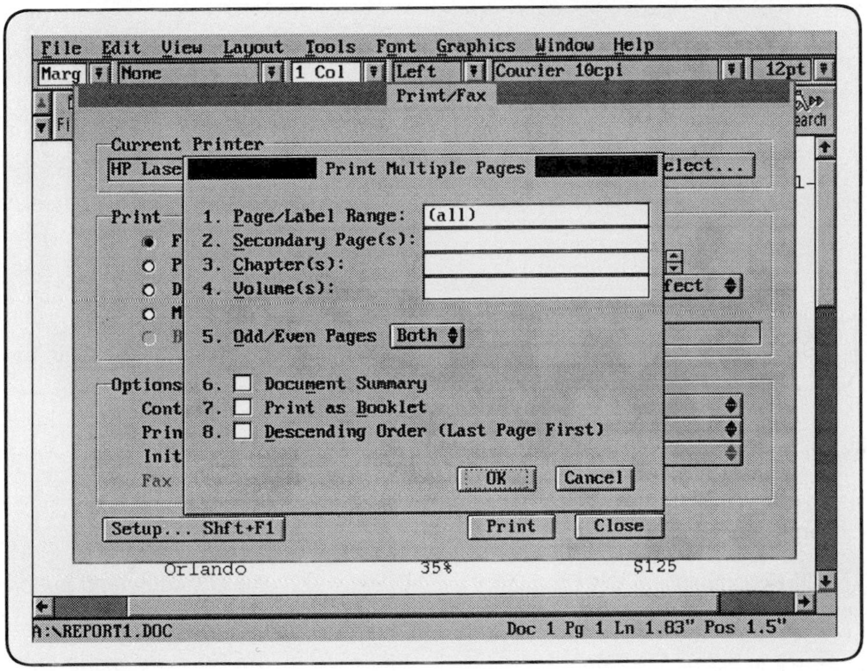

You can specify individual pages or groups of pages to be printed by using the examples presented in the following list:

Page(s)	Page(s) Printed
1	Page 1
1,2 or 1 2	Pages 1 and 2
1-	Page 1 through the end of the document
1-3	Pages 1 through 3
-5	The beginning of the document through page 5

To print only page 2:

Press	1 or P to select the Page/Label Range text box	*Click*	*on the Page/Label Range text box*
Type	2	*Type*	*2*

Your screen should look like Figure 10-3.

Figure 10-3

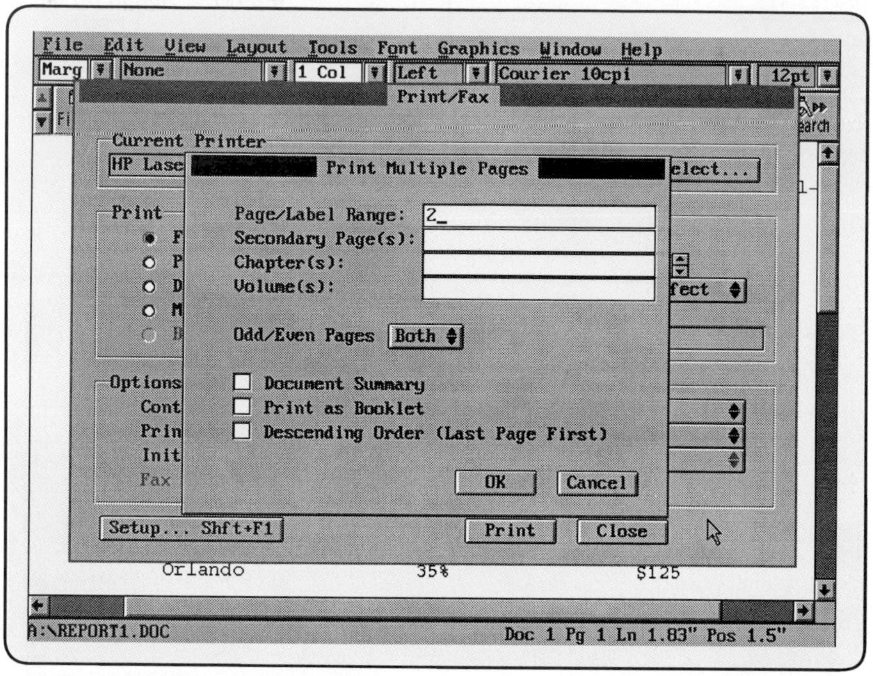

Unless you have set up page numbering for secondary pages, chapters, or volumes, you will not use options 2 through 4.

To begin printing:

Press	⏎Enter to select the OK command button	***Click***	*the OK command button*
Press	⏎Enter to select the Print command button	***Click***	*the Print command button*

WordPerfect also allows you to print odd- or even-numbered pages with the Multiple Pages option.

To print only odd pages:

Press	Shift + F7	***Click***	*the Print button on the Button Bar* 
Press	4 or M to select the Multiple Pages option in the Print box	***Click***	*the Multiple Pages option button in the Print box*
Press	5 or O to select the Odd/Even Pages option	***Click***	*on the Odd/Even Pages option*
Press	O to select Odd	***Choose***	*Odd*

You can also specify a range of pages in your document by entering a range in the Page/Label Range text box. For example, if you wanted to print the odd pages in your document from pages 11-21, you would specify that range in the Page/Label Range text box before pressing ENTER.

To begin printing:

Press	←Enter to select the OK command button	*Click*	*the OK command button*
Press	←Enter to select the Print command button	*Click*	*the Print command button*

Close the document.

■ PRINTING A DOCUMENT ON DISK

The **Document on Disk** feature allows you to print a document that is not currently displayed on your screen. Instead, the document was created in a previous editing session and saved on disk. You can print part or all of a saved document.

To print a document saved on disk:

Press	Shift + F7	*Click*	*the Print button on the Button Bar* 
Press	3 or D to select the Document on Disk option button in the Print box	*Click*	*the Document on Disk option button in the Print box*

The Document on Disk dialog box appears. Your screen should look like Figure 10-4.

Figure 10-4

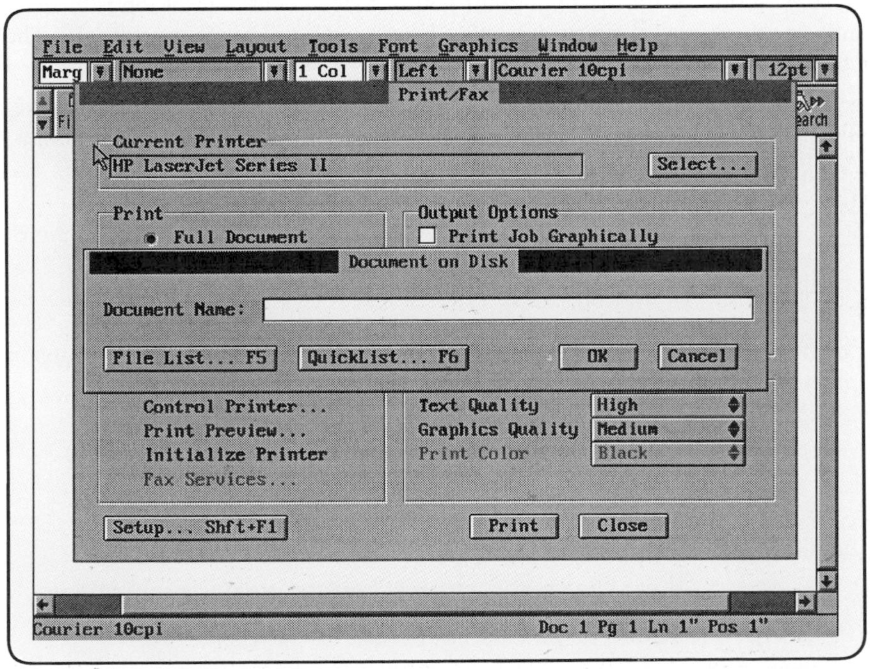

You have three options for specifying the filename. First, you can specify a filename in the Document Name text box. Second, you can press F5 or click on the File List command button. Third, you can press F6 or click on the QuickList command button.

To specify the document name:

Type	"REPORT1.DOC" in the Document Name text box		*Type*	*"REPORT1.DOC" in the Document Name text box*
Press	[←Enter] to select the OK command button		*Click*	*the OK command button*

The Print Multiple Pages dialog box appears. To print "REPORT1.DOC":

Press	[←Enter] to accept the default Page/Label Range		*Click*	*the OK command button to accept the default Page/Label Range*
Press	[←Enter] to select the Print command button		*Click*	*the Print command button*

■ SETTING PRINTER OPTIONS

The Options box in the Print dialog box contains several features that you can use to oversee printing. These options are described in the following pages.   All these options are saved with your document and affect only the current document.

Control Printer

The Control Printer feature allows you to check the progress of a document that is printing and to control any other documents that are waiting to print.

Each time you use the Print features to print all or part of a document, a print job is created. You do not have to wait until one document is finished printing before you send another print job. There is no limit to the number of print jobs you can send to the printer.

WordPerfect assigns each print job a number and holds it in line on a first-come, first-serve basis. When the printer is finished with the first print job, WordPerfect sends the next job to the printer.

To display the Control Printer screen:

Press	[Shift]+[F7]		*Click*	*the Print button on the Button Bar*
Press	6 or C to select the Control Printer option in the Options box		*Choose*	*the Control Printer option in the Options box*

The Control Printer dialog box appears. Your screen should look similar to Figure 10-5.

Figure 10-5

File Edit View Layout Tools Font Graphics Window Help
Control Printer

┌─Current Job──┐
│ Job Number: [None   ]   Page Number: [None   ]   │
│ Status: [Stopped   ]   Current Copy: [None   ]   │
│ Message: [None   ]   │
│ Paper: [None   ]   │
│ Location: [None   ]   │
│ Action: [Fix printer (check cable, make sure printer is turned ON)] │
│   [Press "G" to continue   ]   │
│ Percentage Processed: [0] [   ]   │
│   │
│ ┌─Job─Document────────Destination────────┐ ▲   1. Cancel Job   │
│ │ 6   (Screen)   LPT 1   │ ▓   2. Rush Job   │
│ │ 7   (Screen)   LPT 1   │   3. * (Un)mark   │
│ │ 8   (Screen)   LPT 1   │   4. (Un)mark All │
│ │ 9   (Screen)   LPT 1   │   │
│ │ 10   B:\REPORT.DOC   LPT 1   │ ▼   │
│   │
│ ┌─Text──────Graphics─────Copies─Priority─┐   [Stop] [Go] │
│ │ High   Medium   1   Normal   │   [Network... F8] [Close] │
└───┘
Press Shft+F7, 6 to resume printing   Doc 1 Pg 1 Ln 1" POS 1"

Note that the Job numbers and Document names on your screen may be different.

The top section, or the Current Job box, shows the status information about the current print job. The message area displays notes about the current print job, such as printer problems or printing in progress.

The Job Document Destination box is displayed in the middle of the screen. The current print job and the next jobs waiting in line to be printed are listed in this box. If you have several print jobs, you can press the UP and DOWN ARROW keys or click on the Up and Down scroll bar arrows to see all of the print jobs.

The bottom box shows the Text, Graphics, Copies, and Priority options selected for the current print job. These options are discussed in the Output Options section later in the chapter.

Cancel Job

With the Cancel Job option, you can cancel one or more print jobs. If you want to cancel a print job, highlight the job and select the Cancel Job option. You are asked if you want to cancel the highlighted print job. If you have more than one print job to cancel, you can highlight each job and mark it by pressing a 3 or an asterisk (*), or by clicking on the (Un)mark option. If you want to mark or unmark all the print jobs, use option 4, (Un)mark All.

To cancel the second print job in the Job Document Destination box:

Press	⬇ to move the highlight to the second print job		*Click*	*on the second print job*
Press	1 or C to select the Cancel Job option		*Choose*	*the Cancel Job option*
Press	Y to select the Yes command button		*Click*	*the Yes command button*

Notice that the second print job is no longer listed.

Rush Job

The Rush Job option moves the job you highlight to the front of the print job list. Highlight the print job you want to rush and select the Rush Job option. You are asked if you want to rush the highlighted job. If you answer yes, then the current print job is interrupted and the rush job is printed. WordPerfect then returns to finish the print job that was interrupted. However, the interrupted print job will begin printing from the beginning again.

To rush the last "REPORT1.DOC" print job:

Press	⬇ twice or until the last "REPORT1.DOC" print job is selected	*Click*	*on the last "REPORT1.DOC" print job*
Press	2 or R to select the Rush Job option	*Choose*	*the Rush Job option*
Press	Y to select the Yes command button	*Click*	*the Yes command button*

Notice that the last "REPORT1.DOC" print job is now first in the print job list.

Go

The Go command button restarts the printer after it has been stopped with the Stop command option.

Stop

The Stop command button stops the printer, but no print jobs are terminated. This feature is helpful if there is a printer problem, such as a paper jam. Correct the problem, press G or click the Go command button. A job that has been stopped and then started will begin printing from the beginning again.

To cancel all print jobs and return to your document:

Press	4 to select the (Un)mark All option	*Choose*	*the (Un)mark All option*
Press	1 or C to select the Cancel Job option	*Choose*	*the Cancel Job option*
Press	Y to select the Yes command button	*Click*	*the Yes command button*
Press	G to clear the message in the Current Job box	*Click*	*the Go command button*
Press	⏎Enter to select the Close command button	*Click*	*the Close command button*

Print Preview

With the **Print Preview** feature, you can see on the screen how a document will look when it is printed. Headers, footers, margins, page numbers, text, and graphics are shown on the screen. WordPerfect tries to duplicate the printed page on the screen as closely as possible. You cannot edit your document while using the Print Preview feature.

There are several options on the Print Preview menu. To view the normal size of the document, select 100% from the View menu. Select 200% from the View menu to view the document at twice its normal size. You can use arrow keys or the scroll bars to move around the screen.

The Full Page option under the View menu lets you view the entire page. The Facing Pages option under the View menu displays even-numbered and odd-numbered pages on one screen.

The Thumbnails option under the View menu allows you to look at several pages at once. When you press T or choose Thumbnails, another menu appears listing options for 1, 2, 4, 8, 32, or other numbers of pages to view.

Use the Next Page and Previous Page options under the Pages menu to move between pages in your document.

Open the "REPORT1.DOC" file.

To view the document:

Press	Shift + F7	***Click***	*the Preview button on the Button Bar* 

Press	7 or V to select the Print Preview option

Your screen should look like Figure 10-6.

Figure 10-6

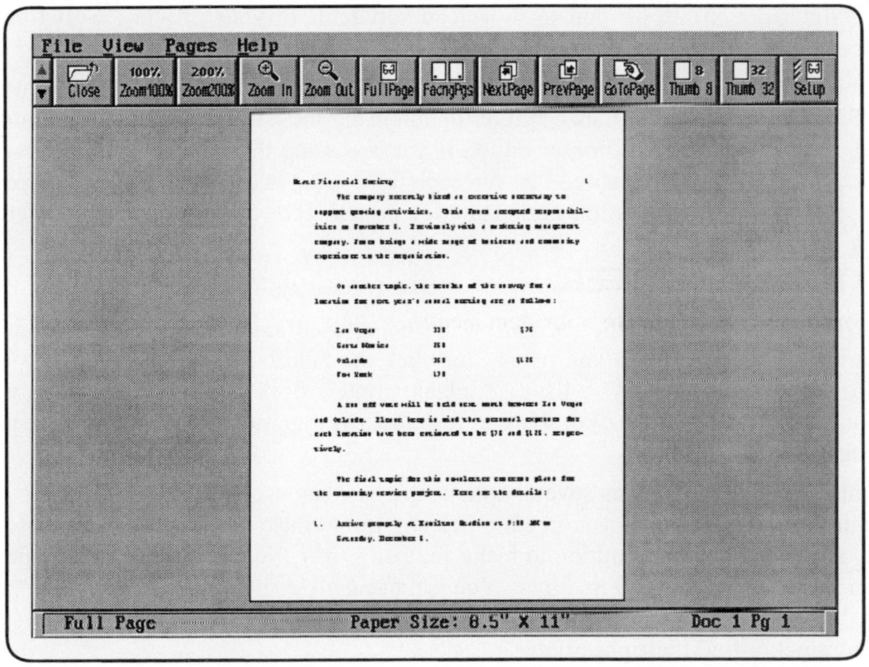

You can use the menu or the Print Preview Button Bar to perform various tasks.

To view your document at 200%:

Press	V for View	***Click***	*the Zoom 200% button on the Button Bar* 

Press	2 for 200% View

To view your document with the Full Page option:

Select	View	*Click*	the Close button on the Button Bar

Select	Full Page		

To return to your document:

Press	F7	*Click*	the Close button on the Button Bar

You can use the Zoom feature in the normal editing screen also to change your view of the document.

Initialize Printer

The Initialize Printer option allows you to download soft fonts to your printer. Soft fonts are special software that contain the design of certain fonts.

You can use this option if you have a printer that supports soft fonts and soft fonts are installed. Press Shift+F7 and 8 or I to select the Initialize Printer option using the keyboard. Choose Print/Fax from the File menu and choose the Initialize Printer option if you are using the mouse. WordPerfect loads these fonts into your printer. This option should be run each time you power up your printer if you plan to use the soft fonts. For more information on initializing the printer, see your WordPerfect Reference manual.

■ SELECTING A PRINTER

The Current Printer box identifies the current printer being used and lets you select a new printer and change your printer settings. When you press S or click the Select command button, the Select Printer dialog box appears. The box displays a list of available printers from which to choose. If your printer is not shown, you may need to run the WordPerfect Installation program again to copy more printer files to your WordPerfect directory.

The Select Printer dialog box contains several options that you can use on a selected printer. You can add printers and edit printer settings. If you need to delete a printer, use the Delete option. Before you edit a printer file, you can use the Copy option to make another printer file. The Information option gives you the information about the printer and its fonts. You can use the Update option to update a *.PRS file, and use the List *.PRS to list all the *.PRS files on your system. If you have a lot of printers, you can use Name Search to quickly find the right printer.

To display the Select Printer options:

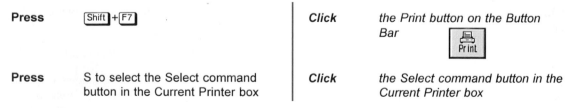

Press	Shift + F7	*Click*	the Print button on the Button Bar

Press	S to select the Select command button in the Current Printer box	*Click*	the Select command button in the Current Printer box

Except for the printer name(s) and the number of printers, which might be different, your screen should look like Figure 10-7.

Figure 10-7

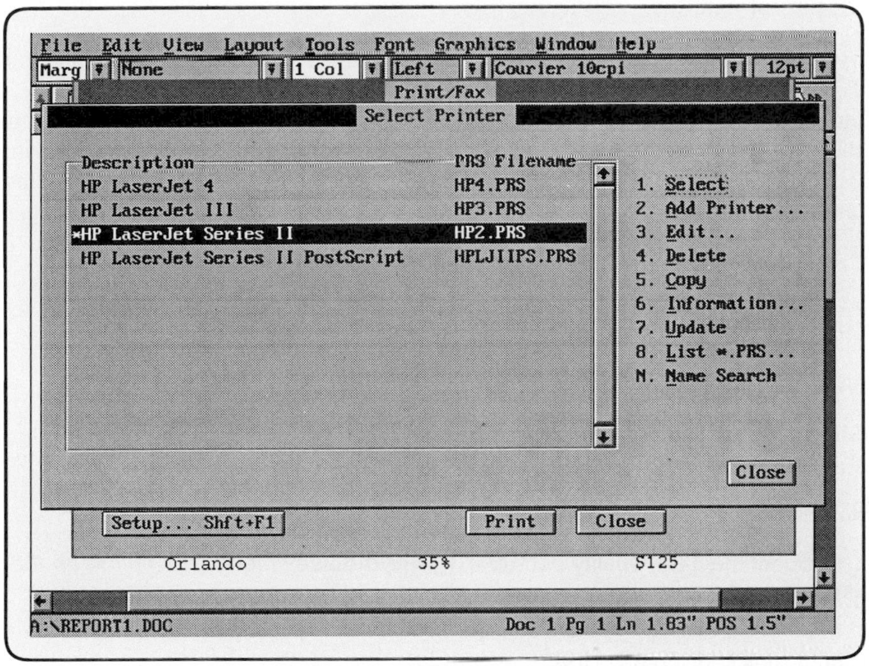

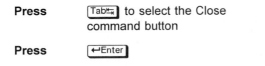

For additional information on selecting a printer, see the "Print: Select Printer" section in the WordPerfect Reference manual.

To return to the Print dialog box:

Press   Tab⇄ to select the Close   ***Click***   *the Close command button*
command button

Press   ←Enter

■ CHANGING OUTPUT OPTIONS

If you only want to change your output options for a particular document, you can use the options in the Output Options box. If you want any options set as defaults, press SHIFT+F1 or click on the Setup command button.

Print Job Graphically

If you are using several graphic images or you want to print text over an image, you may want to use the **Print Job Graphically** option. This option allows you to print your document with graphic images exactly as you see it in Print Preview.

Number of Copies

The Number of Copies option in the Output Options box tells WordPerfect how many copies of your document you want printed. To change the number of copies printed, type the number of desired copies in the Number of Copies text box or click the up or down triangle buttons next to the Number of Copies text box to increase or decrease the number of copies.

Generated By

The **Generated By** option in the Output Options box specifies whether WordPerfect or the printer should make the extra copies.

When WordPerfect creates the copies, the print time is slower because WordPerfect sends the whole document to the printer for each copy. However, the copies are collated. When the printer makes the copies, WordPerfect needs to send only one copy to the printer. The printer prints multiples of each page so the copies are not collated.

Note that your printer may not support this feature.

■ CHANGING DOCUMENT SETTINGS

Text Quality

The **Text Quality** option in the Document Settings box sets the print quality of text within a document. These settings affect the clarity of the printed characters in a document.

To display the Text Quality options:

Press T to select the Text Quality pop-up list button	**Hold down** the mouse button on the Text Quality pop-up list button

Your screen should look like Figure 10-8.

Figure 10-8

The pop-up list displays the options available for text quality. For additional information on the Text Quality options, see the WordPerfect Reference manual.

To close the pop-up list:

Press [Esc]	**Release** the mouse button

Graphics Quality

The **Graphics Quality** option in the Document Settings box determines the print quality of graphics within a document.

To display the Graphics Quality options:

Press	G to select the Graphics Quality pop-up list button	*Click*	*the Graphics Quality pop-up list button*
		Hold down	*the mouse button to view the pop-up list*

Your screen should look like Figure 10-9.

Figure 10-9

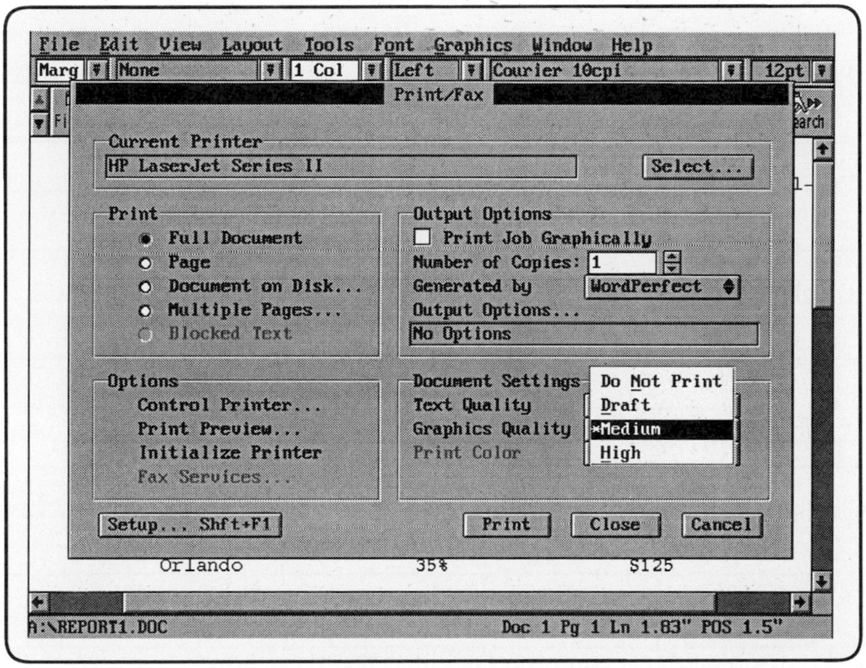

The pop-up list displays the options available for graphics quality. For additional information on the Graphics Quality options, see the WordPerfect Reference manual.

To close the pop-up list and the Print/Fax dialog box:

Press	Esc	*Release*	*the mouse button*
Press	Esc	*Click*	*the Close command button*

Close the document "REPORT1.DOC" without saving changes. *Note: Be sure that you turn your printer back on (put the printer online) if your computer is attached to a printer.*

EXERCISE 1

INSTRUCTIONS: Define the following concepts:

1.   Document on Disk _____

    _____

2.   Print Preview _____

    _____

3.   Multiple Pages _____

    _____

4.   Full Document _____

    _____

5.   Page _____

    _____

6.   Graphics Quality _____

    _____

7.   Text Quality _____

    _____

8.   Print Job Graphically _____

    _____

EXERCISE 2

INSTRUCTIONS: Circle T if the statement is true and F if the statement is false.

T   F   1.   To print the page containing the cursor, you would select the Page option from the Print/Fax dialog box.

T   F   2.   To print the entire document that you are currently editing, you would select the Full Document option from the Print/Fax dialog box.

T   F   3.   When printing multiple pages, if you specify -20 in the Print Multiple Pages dialog box for the Page/Label Range, WordPerfect prints from page 20 to the end of the document.

T   F   4.   The Document on Disk feature allows you to print the document that you are currently editing to a file on your hard disk.

T   F   5.   The Document on Disk feature allows you to print a document without having to open it first.

T   F   6.   Through the Print Preview feature, WordPerfect tries to duplicate the printed page on the screen as closely as possible.

T   F   7.   You can make last-minute changes to your document through the Print Preview feature.

T   F   8.   You can actually see the reveal codes when you select the 200% option from the Print Preview screen.
T   F   9.   You can start and stop your printer by using the Initialize Printer option.
T   F   10.   The Generated By option specifies whether WordPerfect or the printer should make the extra copies.
T   F   11.   The Graphics Quality option determines the print quality of text.

EXERCISE 3

INSTRUCTIONS: 1.   Create the following document.
                       2.   Preview the document.
                       3.   Print the document.
                       4.   Save the document in a file using the name "CH10EX03".
                       5.   Close the document.
                       6.   Print the document without opening it.
                       7.   Open document "CH10EX03".
                       8.   Place a page break before the word "**Sincerely**".
                       9.   Preview the document.
                       10.   Print the second page of the document.
                       11.   Close the document without saving the changes.

```
current date


Mr. Thomas D. Little
3434 Lakeland Drive
Princeton, NJ 02234

Dear Mr. Little:

It has been six months since you had your last dental examination.

Research studies show that with regular checkups and professional
teeth cleaning, you can reduce the incidence of serious dental
problems.  Of course, proper brushing and flossing of your teeth
between your office visits help to lessen the likelihood of any
dental problems.

Please call Darlene at 876-4300 to make an appointment.

Sincerely yours,


Dr. A. Lanham Johnson, D.D.S.
```

EXERCISE 4

INSTRUCTIONS:
1. Open document "CH09EX09". If you have not yet created it, then do so at this time.
2. Print page 2 only using the Multiple Pages option from the Print/Fax dialog box.
3. Save the document in a file using the name "CH10EX04".
4. Close the document.

EXERCISE 5

INSTRUCTIONS:
1. Open document "CH09EX06". If you have not yet created it, then do so at this time.
2. Preview the document at full page.
3. Preview the document at 100%. Scroll down through the document to the bottom.
4. Preview the document at 200%. Scroll to the right margin. Scroll down to the bottom of the document along the right margin.
5. Close the preview screen. Close the document.

EXERCISE 6

INSTRUCTIONS:
1. Open document "CH09EX09". If you have not yet created it, then do so at this time.
2. Preview page 1 of the document at 100%.
3. Preview page 2 of the document at 200%.
4. Close the document.

EXERCISE 7

INSTRUCTIONS:
1. Create the following document using Full justification.
2. Save this document in a file using the name "CH10EX07".
3. Print three copies of this document. Use the Number of Copies option.
4. Close the document.

current date

Mr. John Mogab
1800 Roscoe Lane
Pasadena, TX 77199

Dear Mr. Mogab:

YOU ARE OUR NUMBER ONE CUSTOMER!

I am sure that you were wondering why I asked for your address last Friday evening. Now you know.

I have been the manager of Casa Adobe for the past six years. Never have I seen a customer enjoy our restaurant more than you. It seems that I never fail to see you in our restaurant at least two or three times a week. Of course, you are a "regular" on Friday evenings. Moreover, you bring at least ten or twenty people with you!

Thank you so much for your support! As a gesture of our appreciation, Casa Adobe would like to send you to Cozumel for one week at our expense.

Let's discuss this over lunch (my treat, of course). Please call me at 888-9090.

Sincerely,

Ms. Cynthia Harlowe
Manager, Casa Adobe

EXERCISE 8

INSTRUCTIONS:

1. Open document "CH10EX07".
2. Change the Text Quality to draft.
3. Print one copy of the document.
4. Change the Text Quality to high.
5. Print one copy of the document.
6. Compare the two copies.
7. Close the document.

EXERCISE 9

INSTRUCTIONS:

1. Create the following document using Full justification.
2. Change the Text Quality to draft.
3. Print five copies using the Number of Copies option.
4. Save this document in a file using the name "CH10EX09".
5. Close the document.

```
current date


Mr. Jerry Underwood
4422 Woodburn Road
Bowling Green, KY 42101

Dear Mr. Underwood:

This is an example of using WordPerfect to illustrate how to use
the printer options feature.

This copy was set for a text quality of DRAFT, with five copies
being made from one command.

Sincerely,


Marge Braun
```

EXERCISE 10

INSTRUCTIONS:
1. Create the following document using Full justification.
2. Change the Text Quality to draft.
3. Print three copies using the Number of Copies option.
4. Save the document in a file using the name "CH10EX10".

```
current date


Ms. Erica Drake
300 Jay Street
Upper Montclair, NJ 07043

Dear Ms. Drake:

Your former students are planning an early retirement party for
you on May 25.  We know that you will be having many retirement
parties and want to be sure to get on your calendar.

The party will be held at the Kelsey Road House in the Tea Room at
2 p.m.  I think it's only fair to tell you that this group will be
giving you and your spouse a two-week trip to Europe.  You may
pick the date.

Most respectfully yours,


Michelle Keller
```

CHAPTER ELEVEN

USING MULTIPLE WINDOWS

OBJECTIVES

In this chapter, you will learn to:
- Frame a window
- Size a window
- Move a window
- Open more than one document
- View more than one document window

■ CHAPTER OVERVIEW

In this chapter, the process for using multiple document windows is described and illustrated.

■ FRAMING A WINDOW

Before starting this section, be sure you have a clear screen.

Open the "PRACTICE" document created in Chapter 2.

Notice that, by default, the document is maximized and is displayed as a full screen. When a document is maximized, you cannot see the window frame. To see the window frame, you must first frame it.

To frame the "PRACTICE" document:

Press [Ctrl]+[F3] | ***Choose*** *Window*

The Screen dialog box appears if you are using the keyboard method, and your screen should look like Figure 11-1. If you are using the mouse method, the Window menu appears.

Figure 11-1

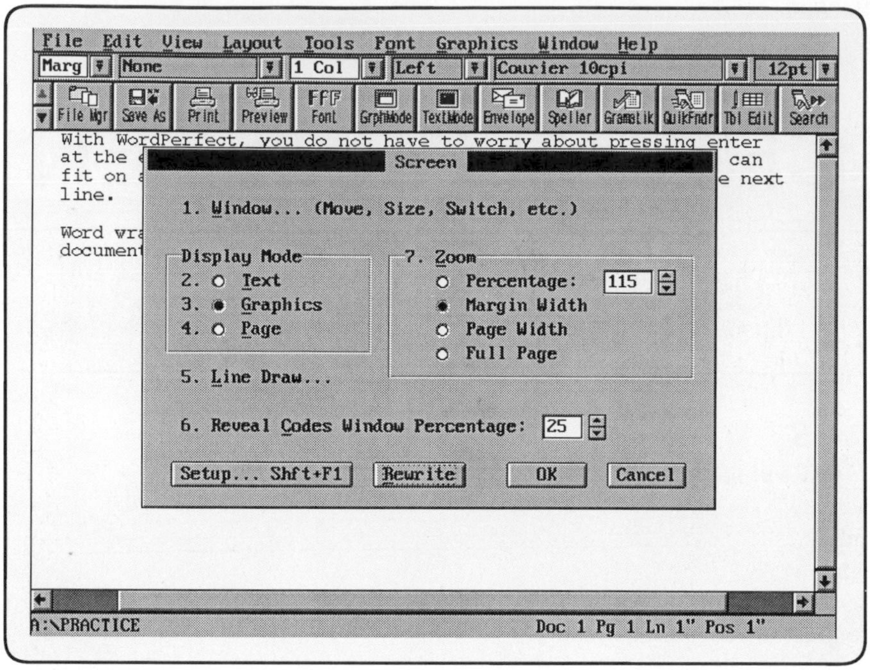

To continue framing the document:

Press   1 or W to select the Window option | ***Choose***   *Frame*

The Window dialog box appears if you are using the keyboard method, and your screen should look like Figure 11-2. If you are using the mouse method, your screen should look like Figure 11-3.

Figure 11-2

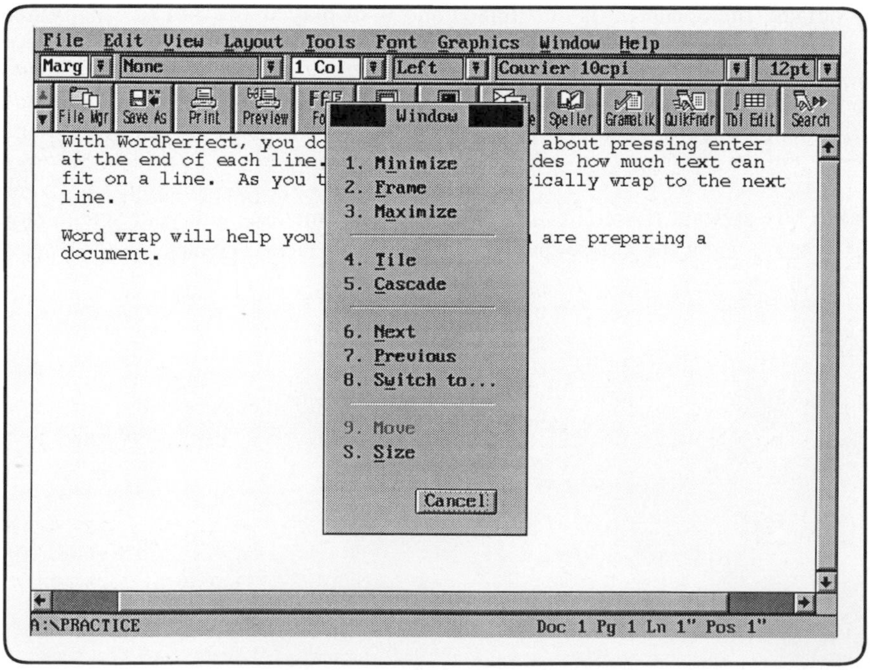

To choose the Frame option:

Press   2 or F to select the Frame option

Notice that you can now see the window frame of the "PRACTICE" document. Your screen should look like Figure 11-3.

Figure 11-3

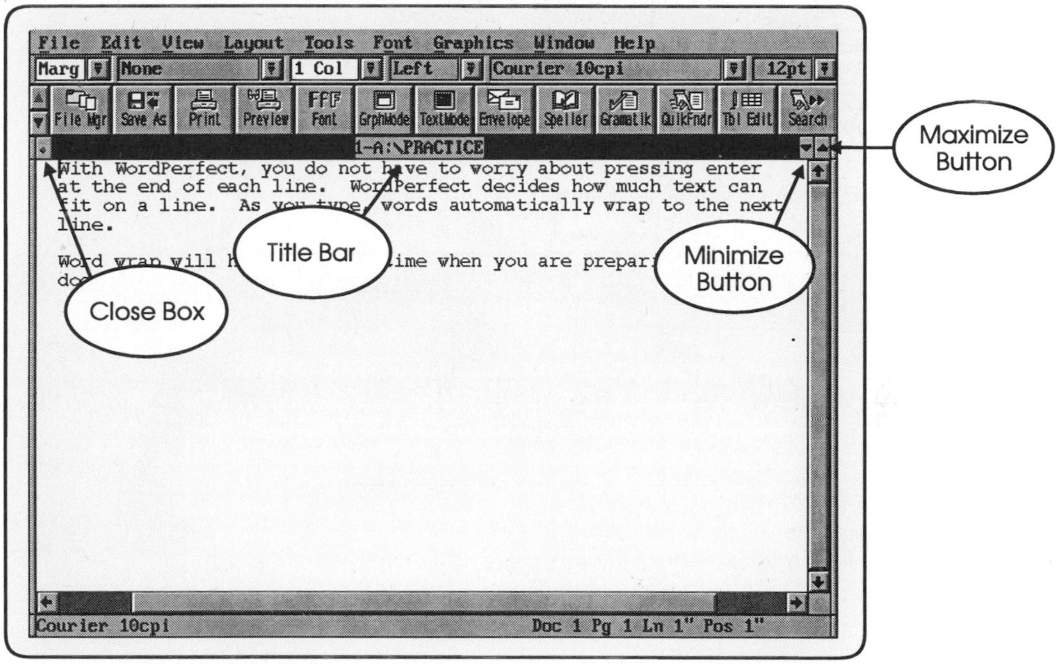

Parts of a Window

A document window has four different parts—the Close Box, the title bar, the Minimize button, the Maximize button, and the frame. The Close Box, in the upper left corner of the document window, can be used to close the document. In the Text mode, the Close Box is a small dot in the upper left corner. The title bar contains the name of the file. The Minimize button, the triangle pointing down in the upper right corner, can be used to make the document window a small rectangle on the screen. The Maximize button can be used to make the document as large as the screen. This button is the up triangle in the top right corner of the document window. The frame is the border around the document window. You can use the frame to size the window. These parts are identified in Figure 11-3 above.

■ SIZING A WINDOW

You can change the size of a window by changing the size of the window frame. You can change the size of the window by pressing CTRL+F3 or by dragging the window frame. To change the size of the "PRACTICE" window:

Press   Ctrl + F3

Press   1 or W to select the Window option

Move   the mouse pointer to the bottom of the "PRACTICE" window until it becomes a double-pointing arrow

Click   on the bottom frame and drag the frame up to make the window smaller vertically

Press	S to select the Size option	*Release*	*the mouse button to accept the window size*
Press	⬆ to make the window smaller vertically	*Click*	*on the right or left side of the frame and drag the frame over to make the window smaller horizontally*
Press	⬅ to make the window smaller horizontally		
Press	⏎Enter to accept the new window size		

Your screen should look similar to Figure 11-4.

Figure 11-4

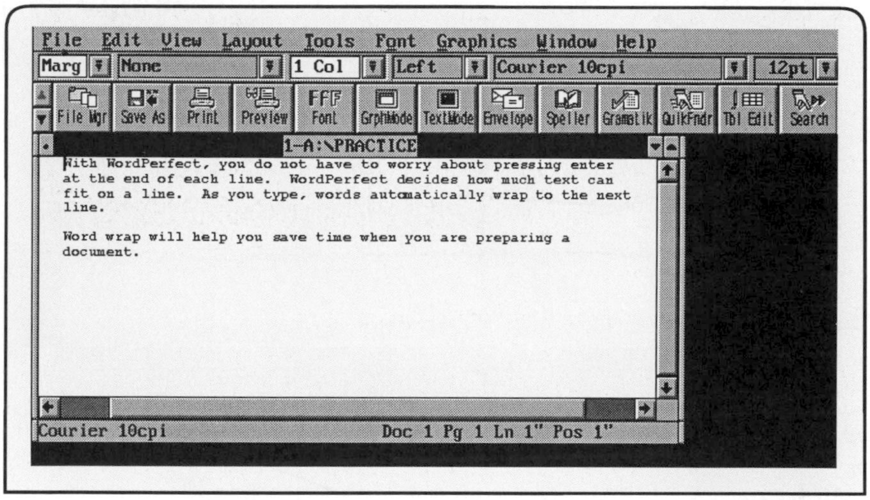

Any one of the four frame sides can be used to change the window size. If you move to a corner of the window frame, you can size the window proportionally.

■ MOVING A WINDOW

At times, you may want to move a document window. To move a window, you can press CTRL+F3 or drag the window title bar.

To move the "PRACTICE" document window to the middle of the WordPerfect window:

Press	Ctrl + F3	*Move*	*the mouse pointer to the "PRACTICE" title bar until it becomes a four-pointing arrow*
Press	1 or W to select the Window option	*Drag*	*the window toward the middle of the screen*
Press	9 or M to select the Move option	*Release*	*the mouse button to accept the new window position*
Press	⬇ and ➡ to move the "PRACTICE" window to the middle of the screen		
Press	⏎Enter to accept the new window position		

Your screen should look similar to Figure 11-5.

Figure 11-5

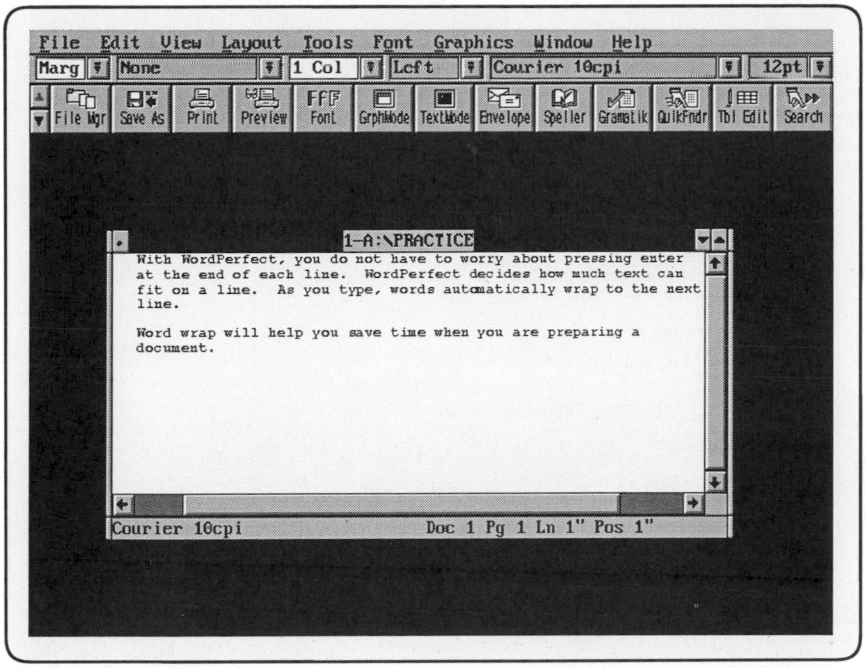

Close the "PRACTICE" document without saving changes.

■ OPENING MORE THAN ONE DOCUMENT

In WordPerfect, you can have a maximum of nine documents open at the same time. Each file appears in a separate window on your screen. When more than one document window is open, you can use the same WordPerfect features that are available when only one document is open.

You can open documents using the Open feature or create new documents using the New feature. The **Open** feature allows you to open a document saved on a diskette or hard disk. To open a document, press SHIFT+F10 or choose Open from the File menu.

The **New** feature allows you to create a blank document. The first blank document is called "1-(Untitled)". When no other documents are open, "1-(Untitled)" automatically appears on the screen. Any subsequent documents that are created are numbered "2-(Untitled)", "3-(Untitled)", and so on. To create a blank document, choose New from the File menu.

Open the "JOHNSON.LTR" document created in Chapter 3. Your screen should look like Figure 11-6.

Figure 11-6

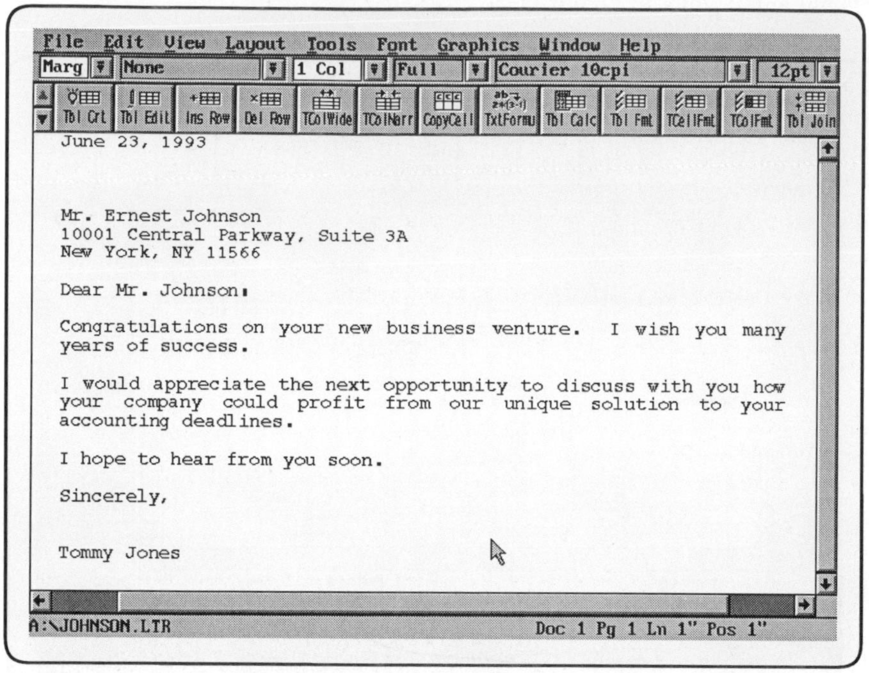

To create a blank document while "JOHNSON.LTR" is on the screen, choose New from the File menu. To create a blank document:

Choose	*File*
Choose	*New*

Your screen should look like Figure 11-7.

Figure 11-7

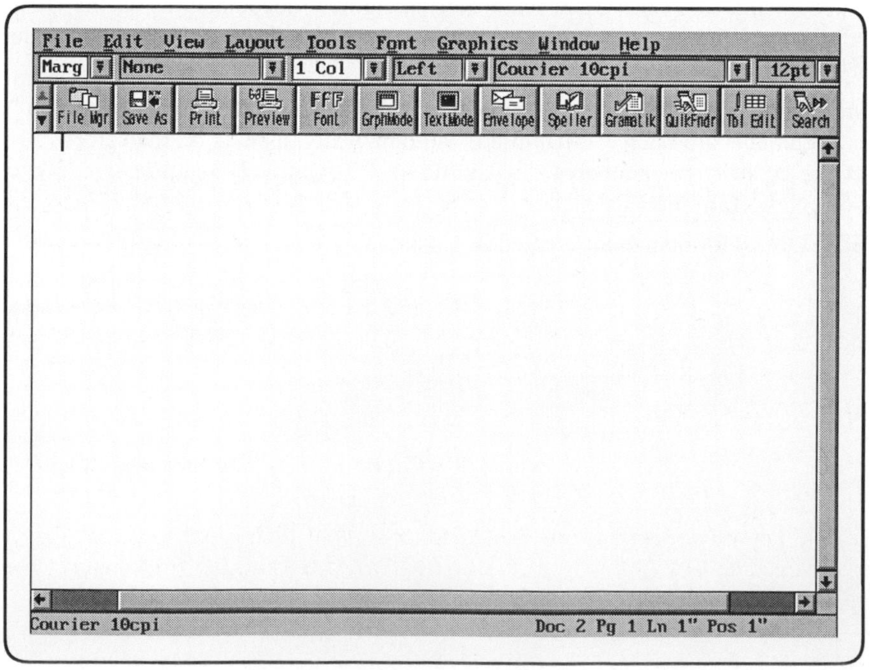

Since each document is maximized, only document 2 is visible on the screen.

■ VIEWING MORE THAN ONE DOCUMENT

With WordPerfect, you can have up to nine documents open at one time. However, you may not be able to see each document. You can use the Window Tile command or the Window Cascade command to view part of each open document.

Tiling Windows

The **Window Tile** command allows you to see all of your open documents by dividing the screen into equal parts.

To split the screen so that you can see both of your documents:

Press	Ctrl + F3		***Choose***	*Window*
Press	1 or W to select the Window option		***Choose***	*Tile*
Press	4 or T to select the Tile option			

Your screen should look like Figure 11-8.

Figure 11-8

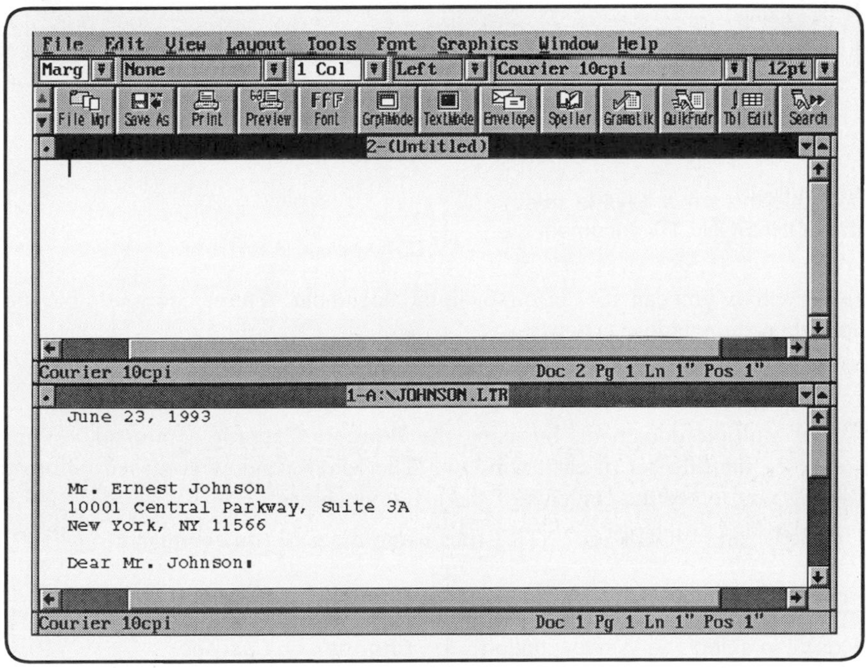

Notice that "2-(Untitled)" appears in the top part of the screen. When the Window Tile command is chosen, the active document appears in the top left window. You can make another document the active document by pressing F3 or CTRL+Y or by clicking on the window.

To make "JOHNSON.LTR" the active window:

Press	F3		***Click***	*on the "JOHNSON.LTR" window*

If you are using the keyboard method, the Switch to Document dialog box appears with a list of open documents. Your screen should look like Figure 11-9. If you are using the mouse method, you are in the "JOHNSON.LTR" document.

Figure 11-9

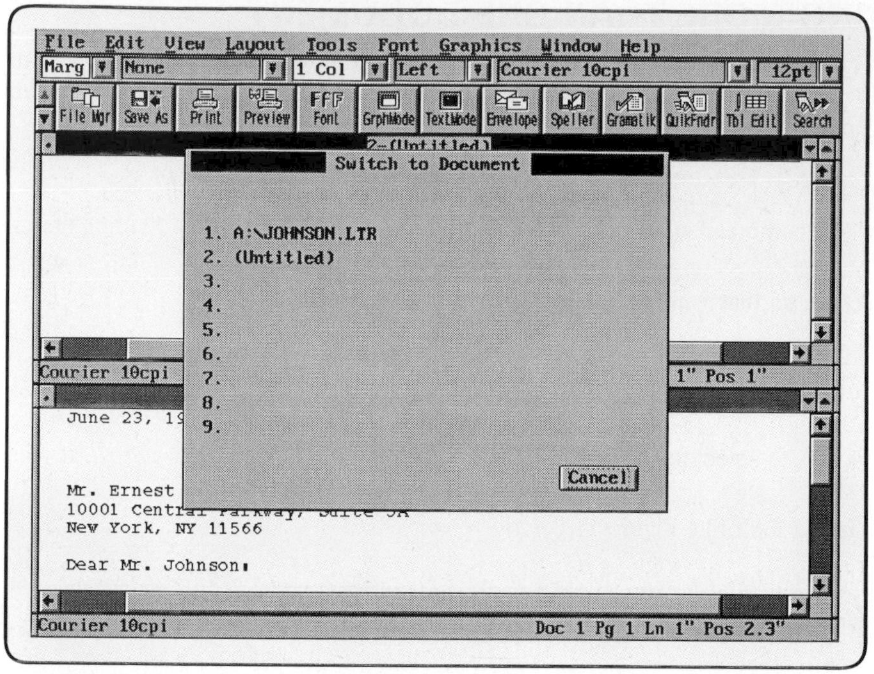

To select the "JOHNSON.LTR" document from the Switch to Document dialog box:

Press   1 or use the arrow keys to select
               the JOHNSON.LTR document

When a window is active, you can see the cursor in the document. The window title bar should appear in a different color when the window is active.

Cascading Windows

You can also view multiple documents by using the **Window Cascade** command. When you cascade windows, you can see the title bar of each window. The active window is placed before the other open documents allowing you to see the contents of the active document.

To view "2-(Untitled)" and "JOHNSON.LTR" files using the Cascade command:

Press   Ctrl + F3   ***Choose***   *Window*

Press   1 or W to select the Window option   ***Choose***   *Cascade*

Press   5 or C to select the Cascade option

Your screen should look like Figure 11-10.

Figure 11-10

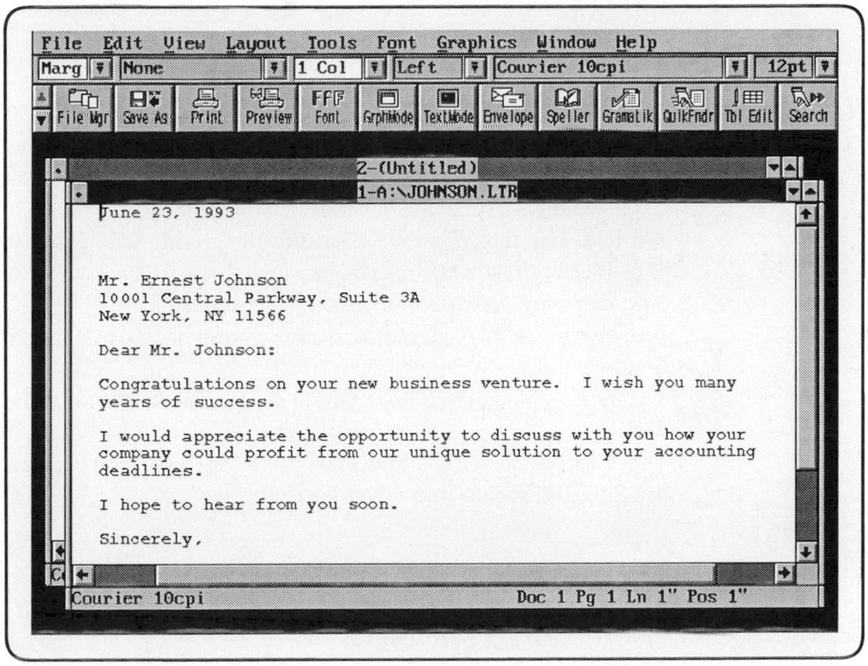

Notice that the active document, "JOHNSON.LTR", is placed before "2-(Untitled)".   Close "JOHNSON.LTR" and "2-(Untitled)". Do not save any changes.

EXERCISE 1

INSTRUCTIONS: Define the following concepts:

1. File New feature _____

    _____

2. Window Tile command _____

    _____

3. Window Cascade command _____

    _____

4. Window Move feature _____

    _____

5. Window Size feature _____

    _____

6. File Open feature _____

    _____

7. Window Frame _____

    _____

EXERCISE 2

INSTRUCTIONS: Circle T if the statement is true and F if the statement is false.

T   F   1.   The Window Tile command allows you to display more than one document on the same screen at the same time.

T   F   2.   Each window contains a separate document.

T   F   3.   While using the Window Cascade command, you can use only certain WordPerfect features.

T   F   4.   You can only size a window using the mouse.

T   F   5.   WordPerfect allows you to have a maximum of three documents open at one time.

T   F   6.   The File New feature allows you to open a file saved on a diskette or a hard disk.

T   F   7.   The Cascade feature allows you to see all of your open documents by dividing the screen into equal parts.

EXERCISE 3

INSTRUCTIONS: 1.   Create the following document.

```
This is a perfect example of changing from one document to another.
You can look at both screens at the same time and make corrections or
additions to two documents.  This is particularly valuable if both
documents are related to each other.  Another valuable benefit of
using multiple windows is that it provides some security for your
document from prying eyes.
```

2.   Create a new document.
3.   Enter the following text in the new document.

```
You can use multiple windows to copy and paste information between
documents.  If you need information in one document and the text
already exists in another document, you can copy and paste the data
using multiple windows.  Multiple windows allow you to see what you
are copying in the first document, and where you want to place the
copied text in the second document.
```

4.   Preview and print "DOCUMENT1".
5.   Preview and print "DOCUMENT2".
6.   Add to "DOCUMENT1" the sentence "**Document security during preparation is very important in many offices.**"
7.   Add to "DOCUMENT2" the sentence "**Copying and pasting are just two of the features that are enhanced with multiple windows.**"
8.   Save "DOCUMENT1" using the name "CH11EX03.01".
9.   Save "DOCUMENT2" using the name "CH11EX03.02".
10.   Close both documents.

EXERCISE 4

INSTRUCTIONS: 1.   Create the following document.

```
current date


Ms. Anna Marie Brummett
507 Burning Tree Lane
Dover, DE 19901

Dear Ms. Brummett:

Enclosed with this letter you will find your contract for submitting
ideas that were used by our company.  We would like to keep you on a
retainer.  We have never had anyone as prolific with ideas as you
are.
```

2.   Create a blank document.
3.   Enter the following text in the blank document.

```
                                MEMO


TO:      Beth Adams
FROM:    Eileen Bannon, Manager
DATE:    current date
SUBJECT: NEW PROMOTION

Beth, let me be the first to congratulate you.  I am promoting you to
Administrative Assistant for Susan O'Brien.  You have shown excellent
work habits, extreme dedication to the job, and the necessary sense
of humor.

Good luck in your new position.  I will tell payroll of your new
increase in salary.

xx
```

4.   Spell check the memo.
5.   Preview and print the memo.
6.   Save the memo in a file using the name "CH11EX04.02".
7.   Continue with the first document adding the following text.

According to our Research and Development department, you have come
up with some very exciting ideas for future development.

Keep up the good work. We are happy to be able to offer you the
retainer.

Sincerely,

Deborah Cook
Vice President

xx

8.   Spell check the letter.
9.   Preview and print the letter.
10.   Save the letter in a file using the name "CH11EX04.01".
11.   Close both documents.

EXERCISE 5

INSTRUCTIONS: 1.   Create the following document.

When you use the multiple windows feature of WordPerfect, you are
giving yourself the advantage of being able to do two things
simultaneously. If you are interrupted by the telephone, you can
switch to a different document and take the message down in
WordPerfect.

2.   Create a new document.
3.   Enter the following text in the new document.

You can use multiple windows to hide confidential documents from
people who shouldn't see them. For example, you can have two
documents open and quickly maximize the non-confidential document so
that it is the only document displayed on the screen. This prevents
a visitor at your desk from seeing something confidential or
sensitive in nature.

4.   Save "DOCUMENT1" in a file using the name "CH11EX05.01".
5.   Save "DOCUMENT2" in a file using the name "CH11EX05.02".
6.   Print both documents.
7.   Close both documents.

EXERCISE 6

INSTRUCTIONS: 1.   Create the following document.

```
current date


Ms. Sharon Perroni
645 Thornwood Court
Naples, FL 33962

Dear Ms. Perroni:

You have been a customer of ours for over 15 years.  In that time you
have always paid your charges on time.

Because you are a good customer
```

2.   Create a new document.
3.   Enter the following text in the blank document.

```
                            MEMORANDUM


TO:      Trish Dostalek, Manager, Store 14001
FROM:    James Suefert, Customer Services
DATE:    current date
SUBJECT: TOO MANY UNSATISFIED CUSTOMERS

Please stop in to see me as soon as possible.  Your office has
received its fourth complaint this week.  What is going on?

I know that "off" locations have their problems, but four complaints
in one week is too many.  Is it because your workers did not receive
the proper indoctrination?

xx
```

4.   Spell check the memo.
5.   Preview and print the memo.
6.   Save the memo in a file using the name "CH11EX06.02".
7.   Continue with the first document adding the following text.

```
we want to give you a 25 percent off coupon to use the next time you
are in our store.  We really appreciate your patronage.

Sincerely,


Linda Breuer, Store Manager

xx
```

8. Spell check the letter.
9. Preview and print the letter.
10. Save the letter in a file using the name "CH11EX06.01".
11. Close both documents.

EXERCISE 7

INSTRUCTIONS:
1. Open the document "CH11EX04.01".
2. Open the document "CH11EX06.02".
3. Delete the first paragraph from "CH11EX04.01".
4. Delete the second paragraph from "CH11EX06.02".
5. Print both documents.
6. Print document "CH11EX05.02" without opening it.
7. Close both documents without saving changes.

EXERCISE 8

INSTRUCTIONS:
1. Open the document "CH11EX04.01".
2. Open the document "CH11EX05.02".
3. Open the document "CH11EX03.02".
4. Tile the documents.
5. Create a new document.
6. Cascade the documents.
7. Size the "DOCUMENT4" window so that it appears very small.
8. Move the "DOCUMENT4" window to the bottom, left corner of the screen.
9. Close all of the documents without saving changes.

EXERCISE 9

INSTRUCTIONS:
1. Open the document "CH10EX03". If you have not created the document yet, do so at this time.
2. Open the document "CH09EX03". If you have not created the document yet, do so at this time.
3. Create a new document.
4. Cascade the documents.
5. Tile the documents.
6. Print the document "CH10EX03".
7. Spell check the document "CH09EX03".
8. Type the following text in "DOCUMENT3".

> The July 24th meeting has been cancelled. Please reschedule any appointments as necessary.
>
> Please advise all staff of the schedule change.

9. Save the note as "CH11EX09".
10. Close all the documents without saving changes.

CHAPTER TWELVE

MERGING DOCUMENTS

OBJECTIVES

In this chapter, you will learn to:
- Create a form file
- Create a data file
- Merge a form and a data file

■ CHAPTER OVERVIEW

In this chapter, the processes for merging documents and for printing merged documents are described and illustrated.

■ CREATING A FORM FILE

A **document merge** is a procedure in which text is combined from several documents and printed as one document. Some applications of the document merge technique are mass-produced form letters, mailing labels, and contracts. Merges are useful when the same text is repeated in many documents.

For example, suppose the same letter must be sent to ABC Can Company's 1,000 customers. The only difference between one letter and the next is the customer's name, address, and salutation. You can work very hard to create 1,000 separate documents. Or you can work very smart by creating only two documents! One document contains the repeated text and special merge codes that take the place of the customer's name, address, and salutation. A second document contains only the text that corresponds to the merge codes in the first document: the names, addresses, and salutations of each customer. You then use the WordPerfect Merge feature to merge these two documents to print 1,000 letters.

The document that contains the merge codes and any repeated text is called the **form file**. This file manages the entire merge operation. The merge codes in the form file call for text to be inserted where each code resides. This text can be supplied from three sources. One source is a **data file**. This file is a WordPerfect document that contains text to be merged, like the document in the example above that contains the names, addresses, and salutations.

Another source for text to be inserted into the form file is the keyboard. As the merge is operating, you can enter data (i.e., names and addresses) from the keyboard. The third source is a DOS delimited text file. This source is useful when you are getting the data from a program other than WordPerfect. Consult the WordPerfect Reference manual for more information about DOS delimited text files.

One of the merge codes in the form file that calls for text to be inserted in its place is the **FIELD** merge code. A **field** is a data item or piece of text, like name, address, salutation, or phone number. In the form file, there can be many field merge codes throughout the document. In the data file, there is a corresponding field of text for each field merge code in the form file. All related fields in the data file make up a **record**.

The following example shows how to create a form file and insert the field merge codes into the document. The next section will show you how to create a data file with text to correspond with each field merge code.

Before starting this section, close any documents on the screen.

To display the Merge Codes screen:

Press	Shift + F9	*Choose*	*Tools*
		Choose	*Merge*
		Choose	*Define*

The Merge Codes dialog box appears. Your screen should look like Figure 12-1.

Figure 12-1

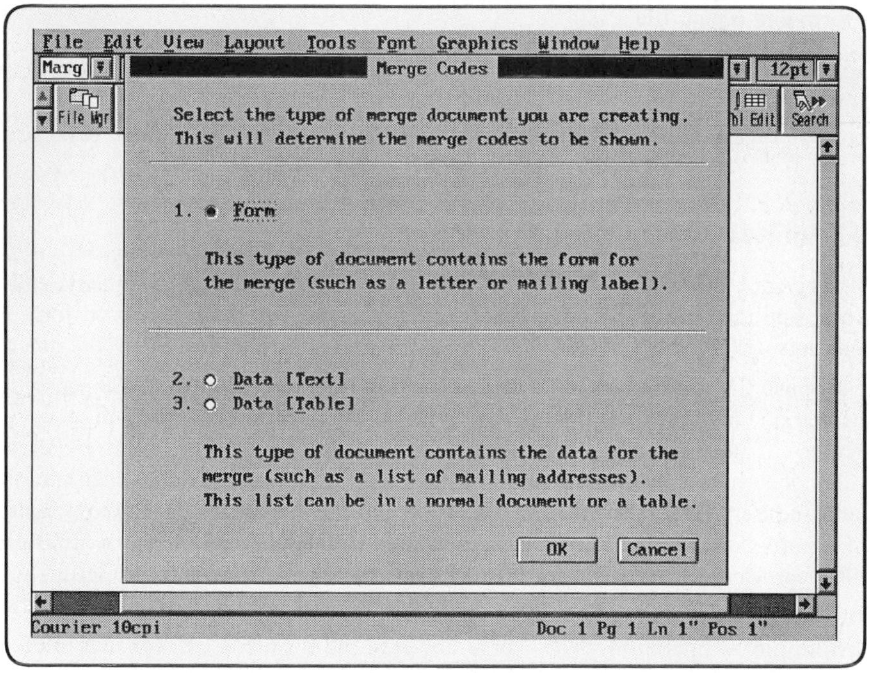

To create the form file:

Press	1 or F to select the Form option button	*Click*	*the Form option button*

The Merge Codes (Form File) dialog box appears. Your screen should look like Figure 12-2.

Figure 12-2

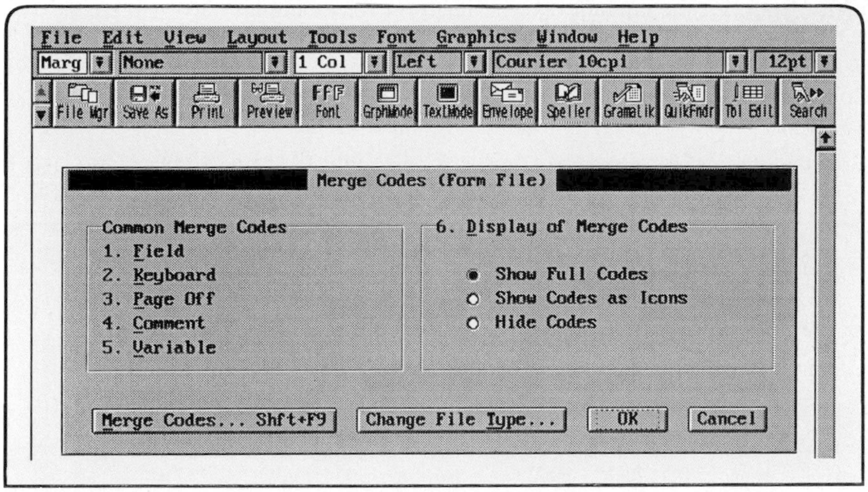

The Merge menu items are described below:

The **Field** option allows you to define which field from the data file you would like inserted at the current position in the form file. You will be prompted for the field name or number.

The **Keyboard** option allows you to insert a merge code that stops the merge and waits for you to input information from the keyboard.

The **Page Off** option allows you to tell WordPerfect not to place each printed merge document on a new page.

The **Comment** option places comments in the form or data files to make them easier to understand.

The **Variable** option allows you to assign a variable for text or numbers. For example, you might use variables to keep track of text or numbers that change during the merge process. For additional information on the Variable option, see the WordPerfect Reference manual, "Appendix K."

The **Display of Merge Codes** box contains several options for viewing your merge codes. The Show Full Codes option is the WordPerfect default, and it allows you to see all of your merge codes. You can also choose to view the merge codes as icons in your document with the Show Codes as Icons option. The icons are small diamond shapes that take the place of the merge codes. The third option, Hide Codes, allows you to hide all the merge codes. You might want to hide your codes so that your document looks neater.

The **Merge Codes** command button allows you to select other merge codes. When you press SHIFT+F9 or click the Merge Codes command button, a dialog box appears containing a list of various merge codes. You can use the arrow keys or the scroll bars to move through the list. For additional information on the list of merge codes, see the WordPerfect Reference manual.

The **Change File Type** command button allows you to change a form file into a data file or a data file into a form file. You can also choose a data table file instead of a data text file. A data text file is a regular document you are using for a merge, while a data table file contains all the field information in a table.

To insert the merge code for the current date in our form file example:

Press	M or Shift + F9 to select the Merge Codes command button	**Click**	the Merge Codes command button

The All Merge Codes dialog box appears. Your screen should look like Figure 12-3.

Figure 12-3

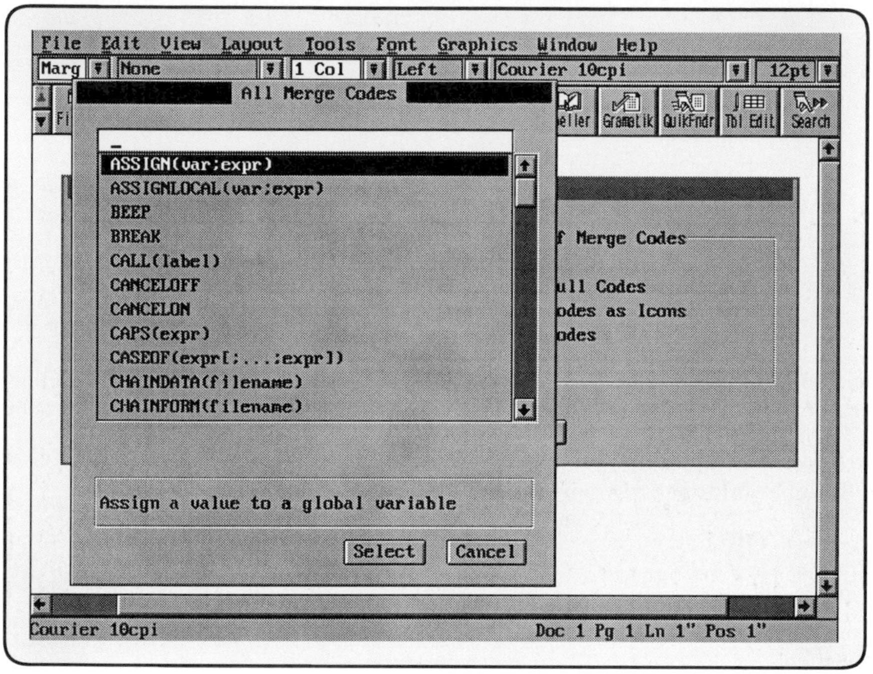

To select the **DATE** merge code:

Press	D	**Click**	the down scroll arrow until the **DATE** option is visible
	or	**Click**	on the **DATE** option
Press	↓ until the **DATE** option is highlighted	**Click**	the Select command button
Press	←Enter to select the Select command button		

The top part of your screen should look like Figure 12-4.

Figure 12-4

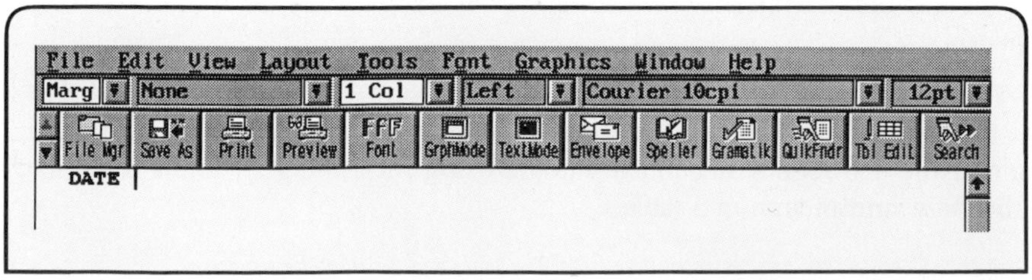

To insert three blank lines:

Press	←Enter four times	**Press**	←Enter four times

To insert a field code:

Press	Shift + F9		*Choose*	*Tools*
Press	1 or F to select the Field option in the Common Merge Codes box		*Choose*	*Merge*
			Choose	*Define*
			Choose	*the Field option in the Common Merge Codes box*

The Parameter Entry dialog box appears. Your screen should look like Figure 12-5.

Figure 12-5

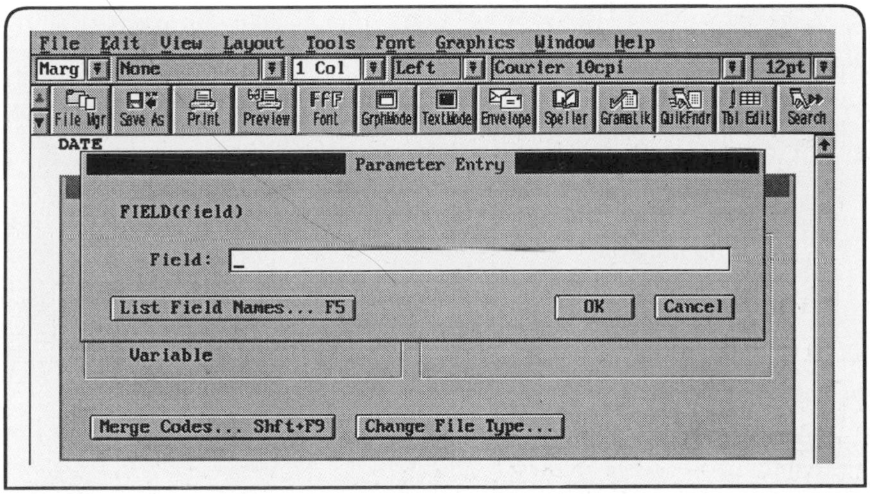

The **FIELD** merge code indicates which field in the data file you want to insert at the current position in the form file. You are prompted for the field, which can be a name or number. If you do not use field names, WordPerfect will number your fields.

To identify the first field as "Title":

Type	Title		*Type*	*Title*
Press	↵Enter		*Click*	*the OK command button*

Your screen should look like Figure 12-6.

Figure 12-6

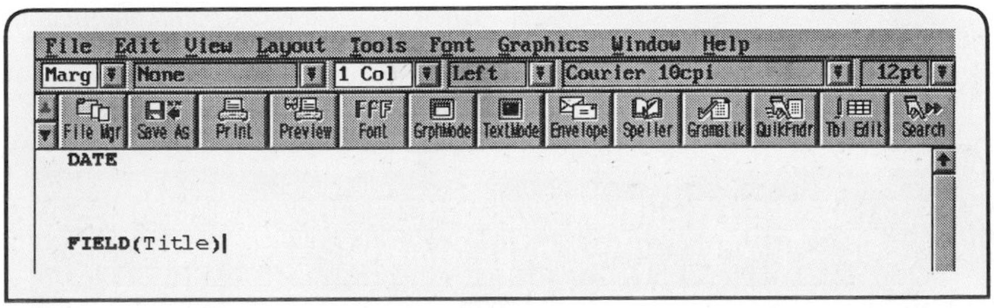

To insert a space between fields:

Press	Spacebar		*Press*	*Spacebar*

To insert the second field code for field "First":

Press	Shift + F9		**Choose**	Tools
Press	1 or F to select the Field option in the Common Merge Codes box		**Choose**	Merge
Type	First		**Choose**	Define
Press	Enter		**Choose**	the Field option in the Common Merge Codes box
			Type	First
			Click	the OK command button

The top part of your screen should look like Figure 12-7.

Figure 12-7

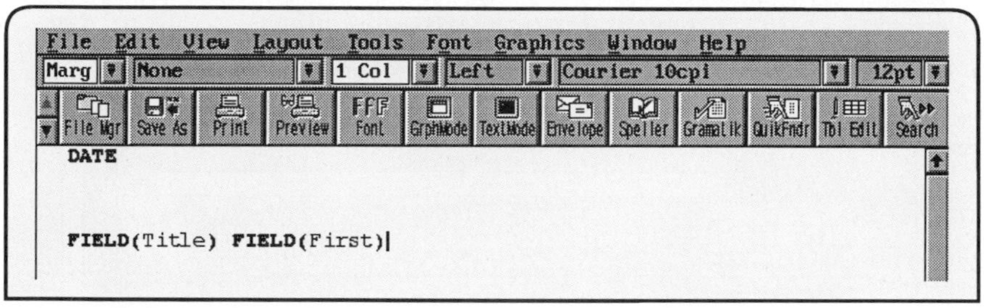

To insert a space between fields:

Press	Spacebar		**Press**	Spacebar

To insert the third field code for the field "Last":

Press	Shift + F9		**Choose**	Tools
Press	1 or F to select the Field option in the Common Merge Codes box		**Choose**	Merge
Type	Last		**Choose**	Define
Press	Enter		**Choose**	the Field option in the Common Merge Codes box
			Type	Last
			Click	the OK command button

The top part of your screen should look like Figure 12-8.

Figure 12-8

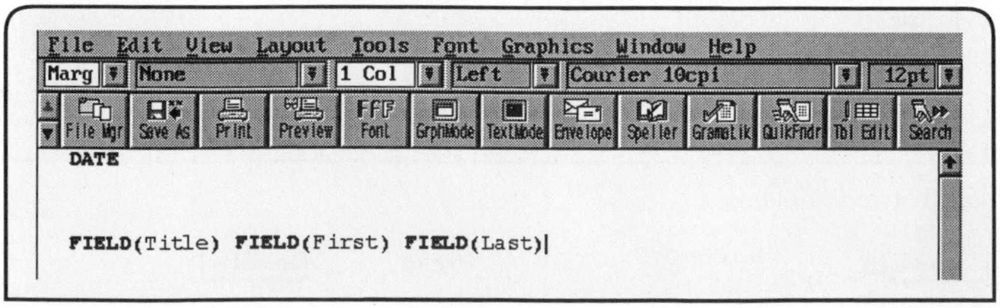

To move to the next line:

Press	[←Enter]		*Press*	[←Enter]

To insert the fourth field code for field "Company":

Press	[Shift]+[F9]		*Choose*	*Tools*
Press	1 or F to select the Field option in the Common Merge Codes box		*Choose*	*Merge*
			Choose	*Define*
			Choose	*the Field option in the Common Merge Codes box*

If one or more fields do not contain text in the data file, spaces or blank lines are printed in the resulting document. You can place a "?" after the field name to avoid blank lines or spaces. When the form and data files are merged, fields in the data file that do not contain text are ignored.

There are a few records that do not include a company name. To avoid blank lines in these locations in the merged document:

Type	Company?		*Type*	*Company?*
Press	[←Enter]		*Click*	*the OK command button*

To move to the next line:

Press	[←Enter]		*Press*	[←Enter]

To insert the fifth field code for field "Address":

Press	[Shift]+[F9]		*Choose*	*Tools*
Press	1 or F to select the Field option in the Common Merge Codes box		*Choose*	*Merge*
Type	Address		*Choose*	*Define*
Press	[←Enter]		*Choose*	*the Field option in the Common Merge Codes box*
			Type	*Address*
			Click	*the OK command button*

The top part of your screen should look like Figure 12-9.

Figure 12-9

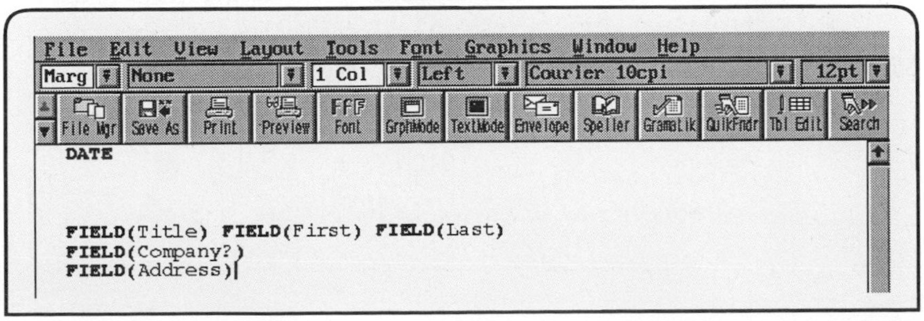

```
 File  Edit  View  Layout  Tools  Font  Graphics  Window  Help
 Marg ▼ None              ▼ 1 Col ▼ Left    ▼ Courier 10cpi        ▼  12pt ▼
 File Mgr Save As Print Preview Font GrphMode TextMode Envelope Speller GramatIk QuikFndr Tbl Edit Search

   DATE


   FIELD(Title) FIELD(First) FIELD(Last)
   FIELD(Company?)
   FIELD(Address)|
```

To insert one blank line:

Press	⊣Enter twice		*Press*	⊣Enter *twice*

To insert the salutation text:

Type	Dear		*Type*	*Dear*
Press	Spacebar		*Press*	*Spacebar*

You can repeat fields in a form file.

To repeat the "Title" field code in the salutation:

Press	Shift + F9		*Choose*	*Tools*
Press	1 or F to select the Field option in the Common Merge Codes box		*Choose*	*Merge*
Type	Title		*Choose*	*Define*
Press	⊣Enter		*Choose*	*the Field option in the Common Merge Codes box*
			Type	*Title*
			Click	*the OK command button*

To insert a space between fields:

Press	Spacebar		*Press*	*Spacebar*

To repeat the "Last" field code in the salutation, add a colon, and skip one line before starting the letter:

Press	Shift + F9		*Choose*	*Tools*
Press	1 or F to select the Field option in the Common Merge Codes box		*Choose*	*Merge*
Type	Last		*Choose*	*Define*
Press	⊣Enter		*Choose*	*the Field option in the Common Merge Codes box*
Type	:		*Type*	*Last*
Press	⊣Enter twice		*Click*	*the OK command button*
			Type	*:*
			Press	*⊣Enter twice*

The top part of your screen should look like Figure 12-10.

Figure 12-10

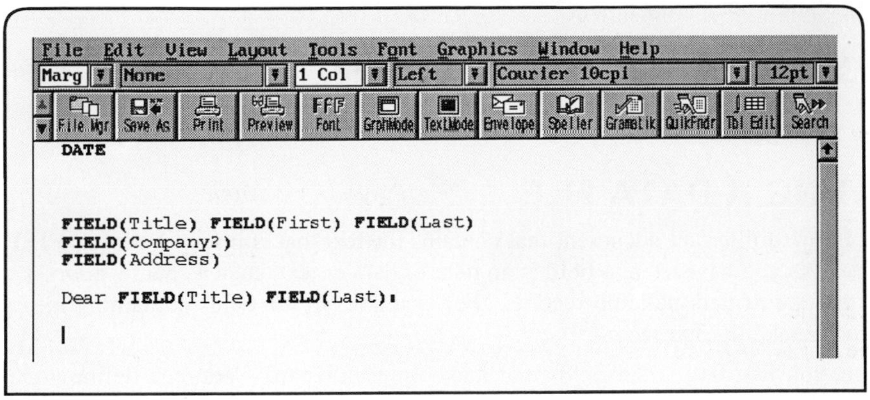

Complete the letter as shown in Figure 12-11.

Figure 12-11

```
Congratulations on your new business venture.  I wish you many years
of success.

My firm is a full-service CPA firm.  We are committed to serving our
clients' needs efficiently and effectively.  We offer all types of
accounting and auditing services, as well as tax counseling and tax
return preparation.  Additionally, we also provide pickup and
delivery service.

I would appreciate the opportunity to discuss with you how your
company could benefit from our unique solution to your financial
deadlines.

I hope to hear from you soon.

Sincerely,



Michael Roberts
```

Save the document as "LETTER.FRM".

To view the beginning of the document:

Press	Home , Home , ↑	***Click***	*at the left margin at the top of the document*

■ CREATING A DATA FILE

The **data file** is a WordPerfect document that contains the text that is inserted at each **FIELD** merge code in the form file. As you have seen, a field is an item of data or text, such as name, address, or title. Fields in a data file that are related make up records. For example, all the fields containing information about a particular person make up one record.

In the data file, you first define the fields that make up each record. You can define a maximum of 255 fields in each record. The form file does not have to use all the fields defined in a record. During the merge operation, the form file will select only the fields it needs to complete the merge document.

You may enter as much data or text for each record as you want. However, every field must be represented in each record, and the fields must be in the same order in each record. The field can contain text or be empty, but the field must exist. For example, suppose a record has fields for name, company, and address. However, not every recipient of the letter will be an employee of a company. When entering text into the data file, all recipients must have a field designated "company". But some of the people will have no text in the company field.

Each field can have varying lines of text. For example, you might have two lines in the address field of one record and three lines in the address field of another record.

You need a blank document to create your data file. To create a blank document:

Choose	*File*
Choose	*New*

Notice that you cannot see the document "LETTER.FRM" when the blank document is open.

To arrange the documents so that you can see both:

Press	Ctrl + F3	***Choose***	*Window*
Press	1 or W to select the Window option	***Choose***	*Tile*
Press	4 or T to select the Tile option		

Your screen should look like Figure 12-12.

Figure 12-12

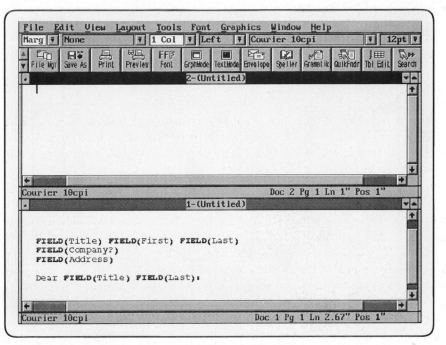

Notice that "2-(Untitled)" is the active window. Any commands that are performed or text that is entered will affect "2-(Untitled)".

The first merge code in the data file should be the **FIELDNAMES** code. This code defines the names of the fields and sets their order in the record. The names of the fields must match the names defined in the form file. This code should be the first line of the data file.

To name the fields in the data file:

Press	Shift + F9		***Choose***	*Tools*
Press	2 or D to select the Data [Text] option button		***Choose***	*Merge*
Press	3 or N to select the Field Names option in the Common Merge Codes box		***Choose***	*Define*
			Click	*the Data [Text] option button*
			Choose	*the Field Names option in the Common Merge Codes box*

The Field Names dialog box appears. Your screen should look like Figure 12-13.

Figure 12-13

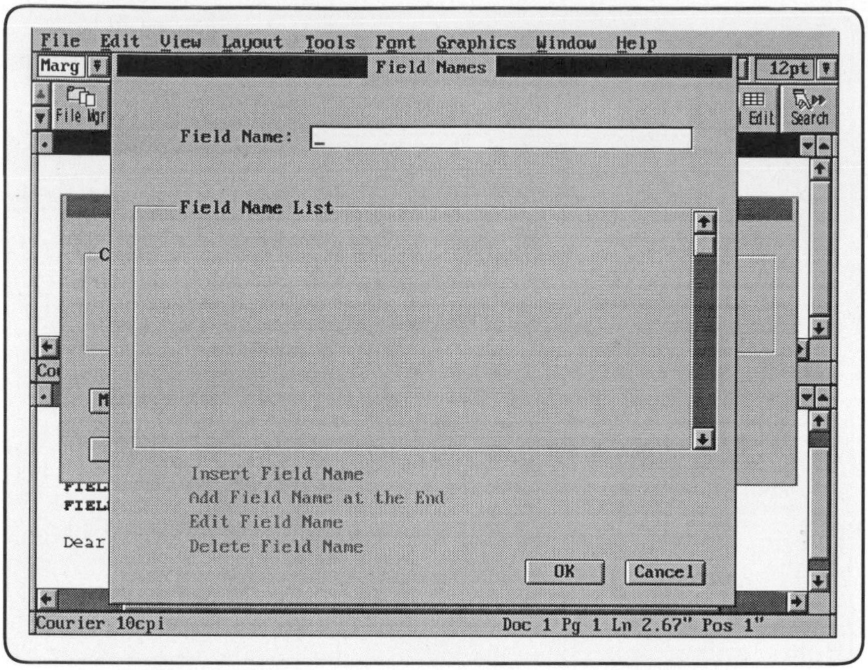

Notice that your cursor is in the Field Name text box waiting for you to enter the first field name.

To enter the first three field names:

Type	Title		*Type*	*Title*
Press	[←Enter]		*Press*	[←Enter]
Type	First		*Type*	*First*
Press	[←Enter]		*Press*	[←Enter]
Type	Last		*Type*	*Last*
Press	[←Enter]		*Press*	[←Enter]

To enter the name for the fourth field "Company":

Type	Company		*Type*	*Company*
Press	[←Enter]		*Press*	[←Enter]

Notice that the "?" is not part of the "Company" field name. The "?" is a variable to be entered in the form file only. *Do not* use the "?" in the data file.

To enter the name for the last field in the record:

Type	Address		*Type*	*Address*
Press	[←Enter]		*Press*	[←Enter]

Notice that the field names are listed in the Field Name List box.

To end the process of naming the fields and close the Merge Codes dialog box:

Press	[←Enter] twice		*Click*	*the OK command button*

Notice that an **ENDRECORD** code is placed at the end of the line to tell WordPerfect that this is the end of the record definition. This code is inserted between each record in the data file.

The top part of your screen should look like Figure 12-14.

Figure 12-14

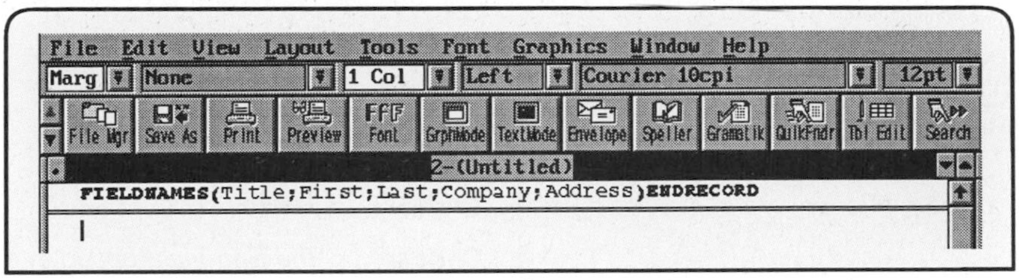

To enter the data for the first field "Title" of record 1:

Type	Mr.		*Type*	*Mr.*

Fields in each record are separated by the **ENDFIELD** code and a hard return.

To end the "Title" field:

Press	F9		*Choose*	*Tools*
			Choose	*Merge*
			Choose	*Define*
			Choose	*the End Field option in the Common Merge Codes box*

Your screen should look like Figure 12-15.

Figure 12-15

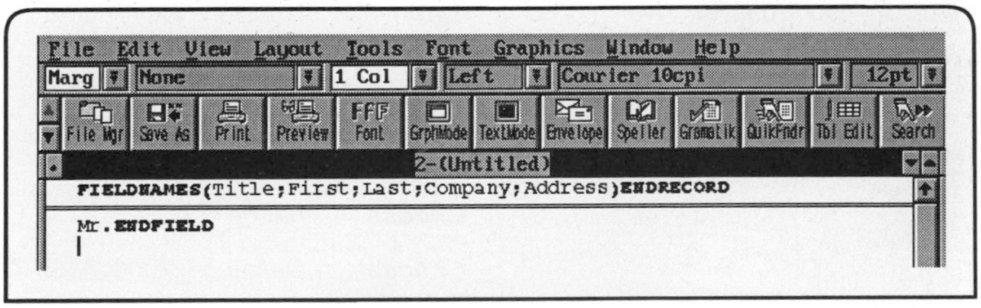

Notice that the next field name appears on the status bar.

To enter the data for the second field "First" of record 1:

Type	John		*Type*	*John*

To end the "First" field:

Press	F9		*Choose*	*Tools*
			Choose	*Merge*
			Choose	*Define*
			Choose	*the End Field option in the Common Merge Codes box*

To enter the data for the third field "Last" of record 1:

Type	Brown	**Type**	*Brown*

To end the "Last" field:

Press	F9	**Choose**	*Tools*
		Choose	*Merge*
		Choose	*Define*
		Choose	*the End Field option in the Common Merge Codes box*

If a field is empty, the field still needs an **ENDFIELD** code.

To enter the code for the empty fourth field "Company" of record 1:

Press	F9	**Choose**	*Tools*
		Choose	*Merge*
		Choose	*Define*
		Choose	*the End Field option in the Common Merge Codes box*

To enter the two-line data for the fifth field "Address" of record 1:

Type	1900 West Road	**Type**	*1900 West Road*
Press	←Enter	**Press**	*←Enter*
Type	Houston, TX 77088	**Type**	*Houston, TX 77088*

To end the "Address" field:

Press	F9	**Choose**	*Tools*
		Choose	*Merge*
		Choose	*Define*
		Choose	*the End Field option in the Common Merge Codes box*

Records are separated by the **ENDRECORD** merge code followed by a hard page break [HPg].

To end record 1:

Press	Shift + F9	**Choose**	*Tools*
Press	2 or E to select the End Record option in the Common Merge Codes box	**Choose**	*Merge*
		Choose	*Define*
		Choose	*the End Record option in the Common Merge Codes box*

Your screen should look like Figure 12-16.

Figure 12-16

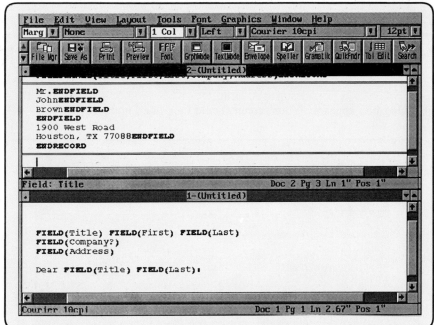

Complete records 2 and 3 as displayed in Figure 12-17.

Figure 12-17

```
Mr.ENDFIELD

GeorgeENDFIELD

JohnsonENDFIELD

ABC CompanyENDFIELD

3305 West University

San Antonio, TX 78232ENDFIELD

ENDRECORD
```
```
Ms.ENDFIELD

ElsaENDFIELD

MorelandENDFIELD

XYZ CompanyENDFIELD

1301 Washington

Houston, TX 77004ENDFIELD

ENDRECORD
```

Save the document as "ADDRESS.DTA". Close both documents before beginning the merge process.

■ MERGING FORM AND DATA FILES

During the merge operation, the text from the form file is combined with the fields of text from the data file. Each merged document is separated from the next with a hard page break [HPg].

The merged documents produced are first displayed on the screen. You can save this document or print it.

To perform a merge:

Press	Ctrl + F9		*Choose*	*Tools*
Press	1 or M to select the Merge option		*Choose*	*Merge*
			Choose	*Run*

The Run Merge dialog box appears. Your screen should look like Figure 12-18.

Figure 12-18

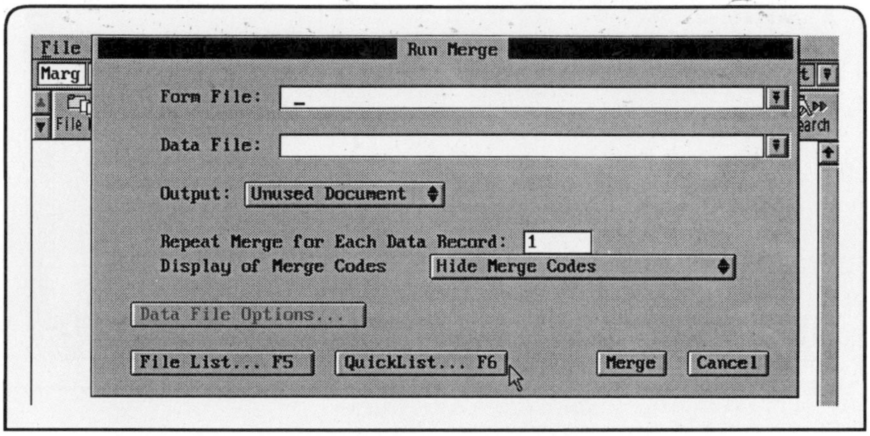

You can either type in the filename for the form file or use the File List and QuickList features to select a filename.

To enter the name of the form file:

Type	LETTER.FRM		*Type*	*LETTER.FRM*
Press	←Enter			

To enter the name of the data file:

Type	ADDRESS.DTA		*Type*	*ADDRESS.DTA*
Press	←Enter			

To begin the merge process:

Press	←Enter to select the Merge command button		*Click*	*the Merge command button*

The message "Merging Record: 1" appears on the status bar briefly while the documents are being merged. After the merge is completed:

Press	Home , Home , ↑		*Click*	*at the beginning of the document*

Except for the date, your screen should look like Figure 12-19.

Figure 12-19

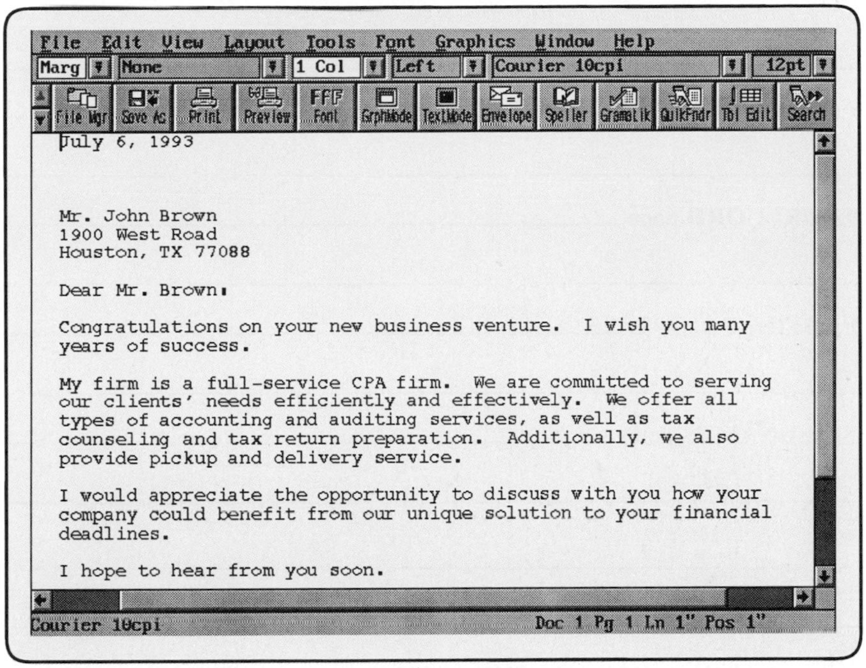

```
 File  Edit  View  Layout  Tools  Font  Graphics  Window  Help
Marg ▼ None              ▼ 1 Col ▼ Left ▼ Courier 10cpi            ▼  12pt ▼
```

July 6, 1993

Mr. John Brown
1900 West Road
Houston, TX 77088

Dear Mr. Brown:

Congratulations on your new business venture. I wish you many
years of success.

My firm is a full-service CPA firm. We are committed to serving
our clients' needs efficiently and effectively. We offer all
types of accounting and auditing services, as well as tax
counseling and tax return preparation. Additionally, we also
provide pickup and delivery service.

I would appreciate the opportunity to discuss with you how your
company could benefit from our unique solution to your financial
deadlines.

I hope to hear from you soon.

```
Courier 10cpi                              Doc 1 Pg 1 Ln 1" Pos 1"
```

To see all of the documents you can use the PAGE UP and PAGE DOWN keys or click on the down scroll arrow in the vertical scroll bar.

You may have an extra page at the bottom of the document that includes only the current date. This extra page is created if you have an extra hard return at the end of your data file. You can delete the extra page from your merge document using normal editing techniques. To avoid merging an extra page in the future, remove the extra hard return from the last record in your data file.

You can print the merged documents using the normal printing procedures.

You do not need to save the merged documents, because you can perform the merge again at any time. Close the document without saving changes.

EXERCISE 1

INSTRUCTIONS: Define the following concepts:

1. Document merge _____

   _____

2. Form file _____

   _____

3. Merge codes _____

   _____

4. Data file _____

   _____

5. Record _____

   _____

6.   Field _____

_____

7.   **FIELD** code _____

_____

8.   **ENDRECORD** code _____

_____

9.   **ENDFIELD** code _____

_____

10.   **FIELDNAMES** code _____

_____

EXERCISE 2

INSTRUCTIONS:			Circle T if the statement is true and F if the statement is false.
T	F	1.	A document merge is a procedure in which text from several documents is appended into one document.
T	F	2.	The form file manages the entire merge operation.
T	F	3.	Three sources of data for the document merge are data files, DOS delimited text files, and the keyboard.
T	F	4.	In the form file, there can be only one **FIELD** merge code in the document.
T	F	5.	In the data file, there is a corresponding field of text for each **FIELD** merge code.
T	F	6.	When inserting **FIELD** merge codes in the form file, you can place a "?" after the field name to avoid blank lines or spaces for fields that do not contain text.
T	F	7.	You cannot repeat the fields in a form file.
T	F	8.	The first merge code in the data file should be the **FIELDNAMES** code.
T	F	9.	When defining the record in the data file, you can enter a maximum of five fields.
T	F	10.	The order of the fields can be different in each record.

EXERCISE 3

INSTRUCTIONS:	1.	Create the following documents.
	2.	Spell check each document.
	3.	Save the letter in a form file using the name "CH12EX03.FRM".
	4.	Save the address list in a data file using the name "CH12EX03.DTA".
	5.	Print the form file and the data file.
	6.	Close both documents.
	7.	Merge the two documents.
	8.	Print the merge document.
	9.	Save the merge document in a file using the name "CH12EX03.MRG".
	10.	Close the document.

FORM FILE FOR EXERCISE 3

DATE

FIELD(Title) **FIELD**(First) **FIELD**(Middle) **FIELD**(Last)
FIELD(Address)

Dear **FIELD**(First):

As a preferred customer, you are invited to our special pre-July 4th
sale. It will be held on July 1-3 at all locations in town.

We will have all of our summer clothing on sale at 50% off regular
prices. For the best selection, be sure and get to one of our stores
early.

We look forward to seeing you!

Sincerely yours,

Tom Jackson
President

DATA FILE FOR EXERCISE 3

FIELDNAMES(Title;First;Middle;Last;Address)**ENDRECORD**

Ms.**ENDFIELD**
Susan**ENDFIELD**
K.**ENDFIELD**
Jackson**ENDFIELD**
1643 Main Street
St. Louis, MO 64072**ENDFIELD**
ENDRECORD

Mr.**ENDFIELD**
William**ENDFIELD**
A.**ENDFIELD**
Batsell**ENDFIELD**
P.O. Box 2299
St. Louis, MO 64033-2099**ENDFIELD**
ENDRECORD

EXERCISE 4

INSTRUCTIONS:
1. Create the following documents.
2. Spell check each document.
3. Save the letter in a form file using the name "CH12EX04.FRM".
4. Save the address list in a data file using the name "CH12EX04.DTA".
5. Print the form and data files.
6. Close both documents.
7. Merge the two documents.
8. Print the merge document.
9. Save the merge document in a file using the name "CH12EX04.MRG".
10. Close the document.

FORM FILE FOR EXERCISE 4

DATE

FIELD(Title) **FIELD**(First) **FIELD**(Last)
FIELD(Address)

Dear **FIELD**(Title) **FIELD**(Last):

We would like your help in contributing to the Annual Save the
Mongoose Fund. You have helped many causes in the past. We know
that once you read the enclosed information you will give generously.

This is a new cause, and we will not bother you again if you do not
want to help. Just return the enclosed envelope and mark "No."

Sincerely,

George Voegel
Chairman

Enclosures

DATA FILE FOR EXERCISE 4

FIELD NAMES(Title;First;Last;Address)**ENDRECORD**

Ms.**ENDFIELD**
Kelli**ENDFIELD**
McKinnon**ENDFIELD**
2467 California Avenue
Huntsville, AL 35804**ENDFIELD**
ENDRECORD

Mrs.**ENDFIELD**
Victoria**ENDFIELD**
Prestia**ENDFIELD**
9204 Sunset Drive
Flagstaff, AZ 86001**ENDFIELD**
ENDRECORD

Ms.**ENDFIELD**
Jennifer**ENDFIELD**
Price**ENDFIELD**
3829 Cherry Court
Little Rock, AR 72201**ENDFIELD**
ENDRECORD

Ms.**ENDFIELD**
Debbie**ENDFIELD**
Janezick**ENDFIELD**
212 Mountview Road
Durango, CO 81301**ENDFIELD**
ENDRECORD

EXERCISE 5

INSTRUCTIONS:

1. Create the following documents.
2. Spell check each document.
3. Save the letter in a form file using the name "CH12EX05.FRM".
4. Save the address list in a data file using the name "CH12EX05.DTA".
5. Print the form and data files.
6. Close both documents.

FORM FILE FOR EXERCISE 5

```
DATE


FIELD(Title) FIELD(First) FIELD(Last)
FIELD(Pos?)
FIELD(Company?)
FIELD(Address)

Dear FIELD(First):

As a long-time customer, you must be aware that we have been having
some financial difficulties.

The problems have gotten worse, and we will be forced to close our
doors for good at the end of May.  We thank you for your past
patronage.

Sincerely,


Zigmund Zachary

xx
```

DATA FILE FOR EXERCISE 5

```
Mr. James Washington          Ms. Jennifer Gartner
Director of Sales             Purchasing Agent
Nevada Lumber                 AAA Kitchen & Bath
1177 Wickshire Lane           2020 Smith Rd.
Reno, NV 89501                Amherst, MA 03031

Ms. Debbie Murphy             Dr. Michael Ellasser
300 Shadow Bend Road          348 East Main Street
Aztec, NM 87101               Asheboro, NC 27203

Mr. Steve Gobert
174 York Street
Columbus, IN 47201
```

EXERCISE 6

INSTRUCTIONS:
1. Add the following names and addresses to "CH12EX05.DTA".
2. Save the data file using the name "CH12EX06.DTA".
3. Merge the document with "CH12EX05.FRM".
4. Preview the merge document.
5. Print the merge document.
6. Close the document without saving changes.

DATA FILE FOR EXERCISE 6

Mr. Anthony Cacaccio
Sales Agent
914 Lawndale
Kansas City, KS 66110

Mr. Kevin Martins
Regional Manager
Park Lumber Company
865 Skyline Drive
Laramie, WY 82070

Ms. Laura Sundberiage
Barrington Lumber Company
1022 Pepper Road
Barrington, IL 60010

EXERCISE 7

INSTRUCTIONS:

1. Create the following documents.
2. Spell check each document.
3. Save the letter in a form file using the name "CH12EX07.FRM".
4. Save the address list in a data file using the name "CH12EX07.DTA".
5. Close the two documents.
6. Merge the two documents.
7. Print the merge document.
8. Close the merge document without saving changes.

FORM FILE FOR EXERCISE 7

DATE

FIELD(Title?) **FIELD**(First?) **FIELD**(Last?)
FIELD(Pos?)
FIELD(School?)
FIELD(Address?)

Dear **FIELD**(First?):

The Fall Conference for the National Business Teachers is just around
the corner. It will be held this year at Hilton Head, South
Carolina, November 10, 11, and 12.

I hope that you are planning to attend. The meetings sound exciting
and the exhibitions will be better than ever.

Read the enclosed brochure for all the details.

Sincerely,

Richard Dyer
President

xx

DATA FILE FOR EXERCISE 7

Mr. Richard Cardinali
Department Chairman
Central High School
Madison, WI 53701

Mr. Mark Hale
Department Chairman
Lincoln Community College
Tacoma, WA 98402

Ms. Courtney Fergusen
Secretarial Science Dept.
Bayside Community College
1200 East Coast Road
McLean, VA 22101

Mr. Jim Godell
Washington High School
233 Randolf Street
Wheeling, WV 26003

EXERCISE 8

INSTRUCTIONS:

1. Create the following documents.
2. Spell check each document.
3. Save the letter in a form file using the name "CH12EX08.FRM".
4. Save the address list in a data file using the name "CH12EX08.DTA".
5. Close both documents.
6. Merge the two documents.
7. Print the merge document.
8. Close the merge document without saving changes.

FORM FILE FOR EXERCISE 8

DATE

FIELD(Title) **FIELD**(First) **FIELD**(Last)
FIELD(Address)

Dear **FIELD**(Title) **FIELD**(Last):

This is to confirm your reservations to stay in the lodge during the family conference this August. You will be staying in room **FIELD**(Room number). You may arrive as early as 4:00 on Friday afternoon, the 12th, and we ask that you clear the room before you go to lunch on Sunday.

If you have any questions, please feel free to contact me. We hope that you and your family will enjoy your stay.

Sincerely,

Oran Miller
Retreat Director

DATA FILE FOR EXERCISE 8

Mr. Andrew Gibson
11300 Sinclair
San Marcos, TX 78134
#B-109

Mr. Benjamin Horwitz
2901 Lark Meadow
Bandera, TX 78078
#A-114

Ms. Melody Jackson
8611 Pine Ridge
New Braunfels, TX 78189
#A-120

Dr. Steve Knight
358 Spring Ridge
San Antonio, TX 78243
#B-115

EXERCISE 9

INSTRUCTIONS:

1. Create the following documents.
2. Save the letter in a form file using the name "CH12EX09.FRM".
3. Save the address list in a data file using the name "CH12EX09.DTA".
4. Print both documents.
5. Close both documents.
6. Merge the two documents.
7. Print the merge document.
8. Close the merge document without saving changes.

FORM FILE FOR EXERCISE 9

DATE

FIELD(Title) **FIELD**(First) **FIELD**(Last)
FIELD(Pos)
FIELD(Address)

Dear **FIELD**(Title) **FIELD**(Last):

This is to inform you that the sales promotion for next year will be announced next week at your area meeting. You will be receiving a video tape the day of the meeting. The tape contains a message from Edward in which he explains the new product line and all the new promotions for the coming year.

Along with the video tape you will also receive a meeting agenda. This will explain how the tape should be used at your meeting for maximum effectiveness.

You know how important promotions are in motivating sales, so please make sure that all your people attend.

Thank you and I know this is going to be a great new year!

Sincerely,

Mark Seymour
Southwest Regional Sales Manager

DATA FILE FOR EXERCISE 9

Mr. Brian Gilbert
Houston Area Sales Manager
7392 Southwest Frwy.
Houston, TX 77088

Mr. Lloyd Jones
San Antonio Area Sales Manager
1708 Point Park Dr.
San Antonio, TX 78243

Mr. Ben Madison
Austin Area Sales Manager
306 Ridgeway
Austin, TX 78765

Ms. Ann Maddox
Dallas Area Sales Manager
822 Greenridge
Dallas, TX 75297

CHAPTER THIRTEEN

ADVANCED MERGING TECHNIQUES

OBJECTIVES

In this chapter, you will learn to:
- ■ Merge from the keyboard
- ■ Create a merged list

■ CHAPTER OVERVIEW

In this chapter, the process for merging a document from the keyboard is described and illustrated. The process for creating a list of items with the Merge feature is also demonstrated.

■ MERGING FROM THE KEYBOARD

Although you always need a form file for a merge, you do not always need a data file. You can enter merge information directly from the keyboard. This means that you can type the text during the merge. This type of merge is useful when you need to create only one form letter from a form file. The **KEYBOARD** merge code pauses the merge to allow the user to enter information from the keyboard. Before starting this section, close any documents on your screen.

The KEYBOARD Merge Code

The **KEYBOARD** merge code pauses the merge so that you can enter data, and displays a prompt in the status bar. In the following example, you create a memo form using the **KEYBOARD** merge code.

To begin the memo:

Press	Shift + F6		**Choose**	Layout
Type	INTEROFFICE MEMORANDUM		**Choose**	Alignment
			Choose	Center
			Type	INTEROFFICE MEMORANDUM

To insert three blank lines:

Press	←Enter four times		**Press**	←Enter four times

To enter the headings for the memo:

Type	To:		*Type*	*To:*
Press	`Tab⇄` twice		*Press*	`Tab⇄` *twice*

To insert the **KEYBOARD** merge code:

Press	`Shift`+`F9`		*Choose*	*Tools*
Press	1 or F to select the Form option button		*Choose*	*Merge*
Press	2 or K to select the Keyboard option		*Choose*	*Define*
			Click	*the Form option button*
			Choose	*the Keyboard option*

The Parameter Entry dialog box appears. Your screen should look like Figure 13-1.

Figure 13-1

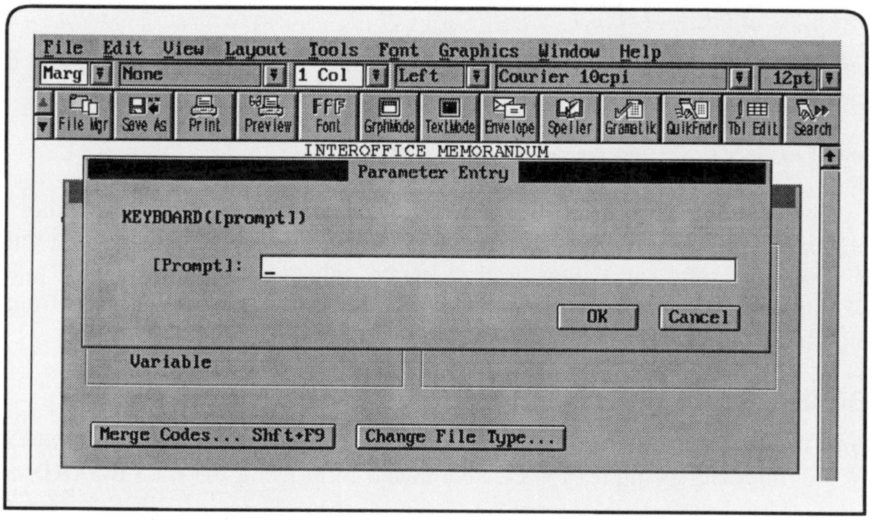

To enter the prompt message:

Type	Enter the person's name and press F9		*Type*	*Enter the person's name and press F9*
Press	`←Enter`		*Click*	*the OK command button*

Your screen should look like Figure 13-2.

Figure 13-2

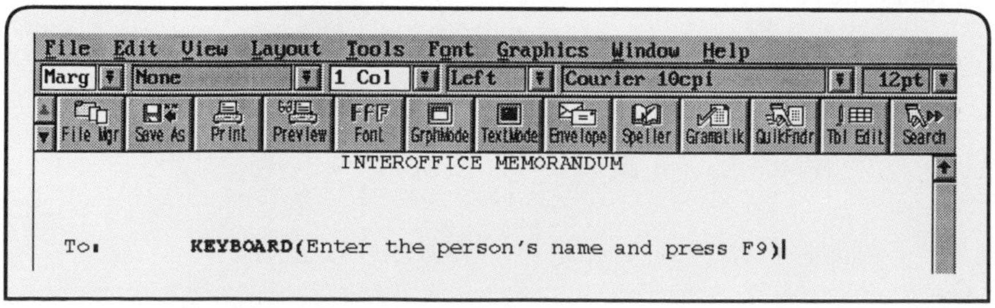

To create a blank line:

Press	[←Enter] twice		*Press*	[←Enter] twice

To create the second line of the memo:

Type   From:

Press   [Tab⇆]

Press   [Shift]+[F9]

Press   2 or K to select the Keyboard option

Type   Enter your name and press F9

Press   [←Enter]

Press   [←Enter] twice

Type   From:

Press   [Tab⇆]

Choose   Tools

Choose   Merge

Choose   Define

Choose   the Keyboard option

Type   Enter your name and press F9

Click   the OK command button

Press   [←Enter] twice

To create the Date line of the memo:

Type   Date:

Press   [Tab⇆]

Press   [Shift]+[F9]

Press   M or [Shift]+[F9] to select the Merge Codes command button

Press   D

Press   [←Enter] to select the Select command button

Press   [←Enter] twice

Type   Date:

Press   [Tab⇆]

Choose   Tools

Choose   Merge

Choose   Define

Click   the Merge Codes command button

Click   the down scroll arrow until the **DATE** code appears

Click   on the **DATE** code

Click   the Select command button

Press   [←Enter] twice

To create the Subject line:

Type   Subject:

Press   [Tab⇆]

Press   [Shift]+[F9]

Press   2 or K to select the Keyboard option

Type   Enter the subject of the memo and press F9

Press   [←Enter]

Type   Subject:

Press   [Tab⇆]

Choose   Tools

Choose   Merge

Choose   Define

Choose   the Keyboard option

Press	[←Enter] twice	Type	Enter the subject of the memo and press F9
		Click	the OK command button
		Press	[←Enter] twice

Your screen should look like Figure 13-3.

Figure 13-3

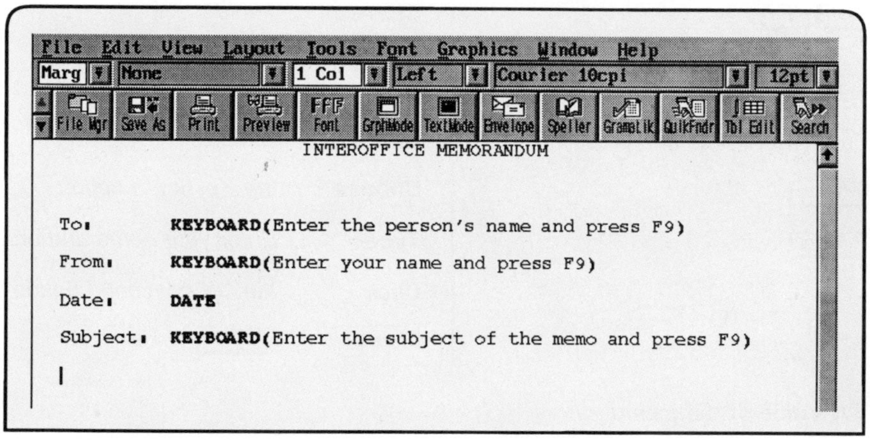

```
 File  Edit  View  Layout  Tools  Font  Graphics  Window  Help
 Marg ▼  None           ▼  1 Col ▼  Left  ▼  Courier 10cpi        ▼   12pt ▼
 File Mgr  Save As  Print  Preview  Font  GrphMode  TextMode  Envelope  Speller  GramaLik  QuikFndr  Tbl Edit  Search
                        INTEROFFICE MEMORANDUM

        To:      KEYBOARD(Enter the person's name and press F9)

        From:    KEYBOARD(Enter your name and press F9)

        Date:    DATE

        Subject: KEYBOARD(Enter the subject of the memo and press F9)

        |
```

Save the document as "MEMO.FRM". Close the document.

To illustrate a merge using the **KEYBOARD** code:

Press	[Ctrl] + [F9]	Choose	Tools
Press	1 or M to select the Merge option	Choose	Merge
		Choose	Run

You can type the form filename or click the Down Arrow button to search for the filename. To enter the form filename:

Type	MEMO.FRM	Type	MEMO.FRM

In a **KEYBOARD** merge the data file information is provided from the keyboard. To remove the data file filename:

Press	[Tab↹]	Click	the Data File text box
Press	[Delete]	Press	[Delete]

To begin the merge process:

Press	[←Enter] twice	Click	the Merge command button

The top part of your screen should look like Figure 13-4.

Figure 13-4

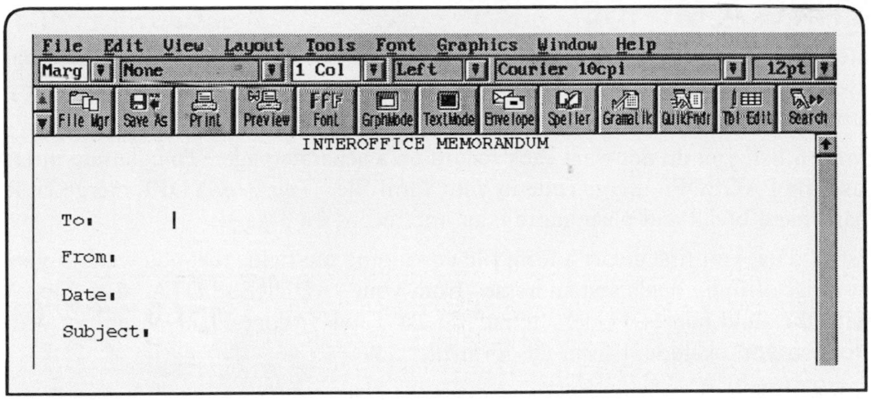

The form file text appears on the screen and the cursor is placed at the first pause for the recipient's name. Notice the message that appears in the status bar.

To enter the recipient's name:

Type	Michael Roberts
Press	⌨ F9

To continue the merge:

Type	Doug Travis
Press	⌨ F9
Type	Sales Figures
Press	⌨ F9

Except for the date, the top part of your screen should look like Figure 13-5.

Figure 13-5

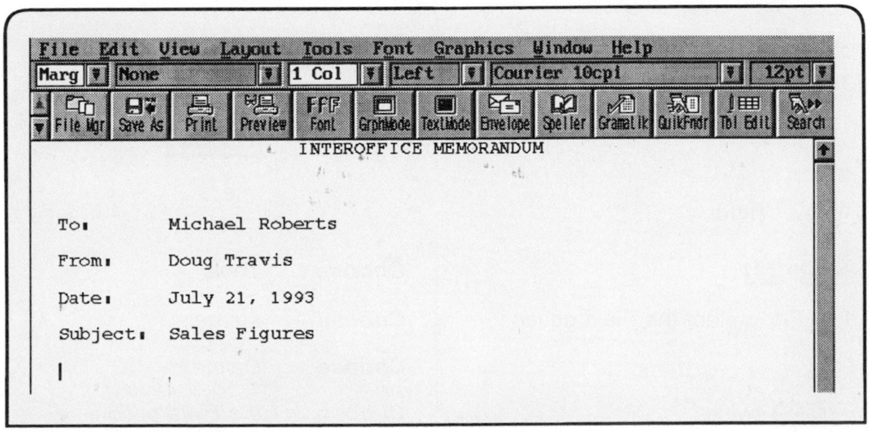

Close the document without saving changes.

■ CREATING A MERGED LIST

You can create a list of data using the Merge feature. When you create a data file, a hard page break [HPg] is placed between each record. This hard page break places each record on a separate page when you merge the form and data files.

When you create a list, you do not want each record on a separate page. To combine information in a list format, you use the PAGEOFF merge code in your form file. The **PAGEOFF** merge code allows you to remove the hard page break and place more than one record on a page.

To create a list of data, you first create a form file containing the fields that you want in your list. Suppose that you want a list of individuals and addresses from your "ADDRESS.DTA" data file. You will create a form file with the field names "Title", "First", "Last", and "Address". You do not want the company name in the list, so you exclude it from the form file.

To create the form file:

Press	Shift + F9		*Choose*	*Tools*
Press	1 or F to select the Form option button		*Choose*	*Merge*
Press	1 or F to select the Field option		*Choose*	*Define*
Type	Title		*Click*	*the Form option button*
Press	←Enter		*Choose*	*the Field option*
			Type	*Title*
			Click	*the OK command button*

To enter the "First" field:

Press	Spacebar		*Press*	*Spacebar*
Press	Shift + F9		*Choose*	*Tools*
Press	1 or F to select the Field option		*Choose*	*Merge*
Type	First		*Choose*	*Define*
Press	←Enter		*Choose*	*the Field option*
Press	Spacebar		*Type*	*First*
			Click	*the OK command button*
			Press	*Spacebar*

To create the "Last" field:

Press	Shift + F9		*Choose*	*Tools*
Press	1 or F to select the Field option		*Choose*	*Merge*
Type	Last		*Choose*	*Define*
Press	←Enter twice		*Choose*	*the Field option*
			Type	*Last*
			Click	*the OK command button*
			Press	*←Enter*

To create the "Address" field:

Press	Shift + F9	**_Choose_**	_Tools_
Press	1 or F to select the Field option	**_Choose_**	_Merge_
Type	Address	**_Choose_**	_Define_
Press	↵Enter	**_Choose_**	_the Field option_
		Type	_Address_
		Click	_the OK command button_

Your screen should look like Figure 13-6.

Figure 13-6

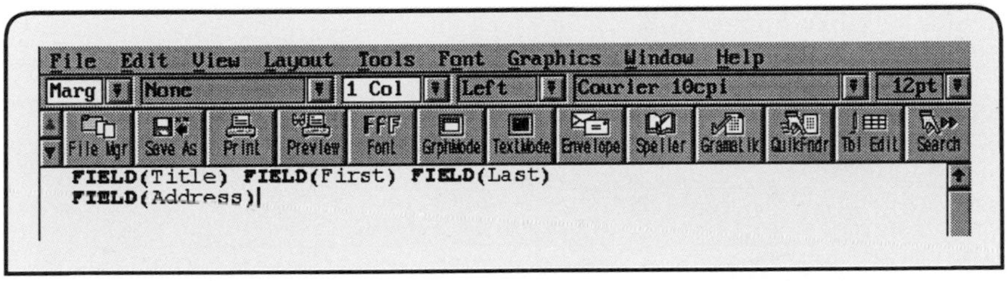

To place a blank line between each record:

Press	↵Enter twice	**_Press_**	_↵Enter twice_

To remove the hard page break from each record:

Press	Shift + F9	**_Choose_**	_Tools_
Press	3 or P to select the Page Off option	**_Choose_**	_Merge_
		Choose	_Define_
		Choose	_the Page Off option_

Your screen should look like Figure 13-7.

Figure 13-7

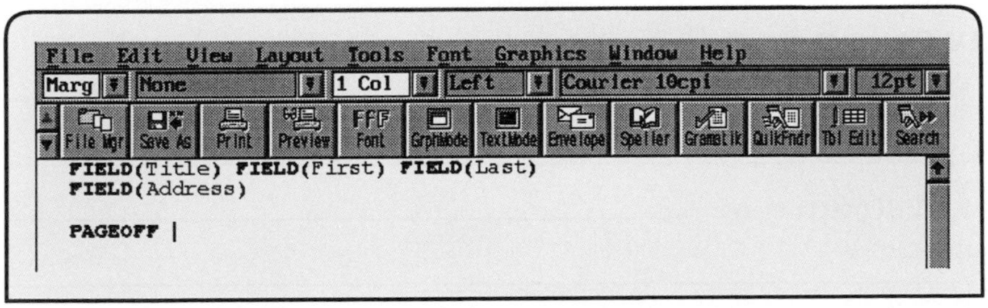

Save the document as "LIST.FRM". Close the document before beginning the merge process.

To merge the list:

Press	Ctrl + F9	**_Choose_**	_Tools_
Press	1 or M to select the Merge option	**_Choose_**	_Merge_
		Choose	_Run_

To enter the name of the form file:

Type	LIST.FRM	**Type**	*LIST.FRM*
Press	⏎Enter		

To enter the data filename and execute the merge:

Type	ADDRESS.DTA	**Click**	*in the Data File text box*
Press	⏎Enter	**Type**	*ADDRESS.DTA*
Press	⏎Enter to select the Merge command button	**Click**	*the Merge command button*

Your screen should look like Figure 13-8.

Figure 13-8

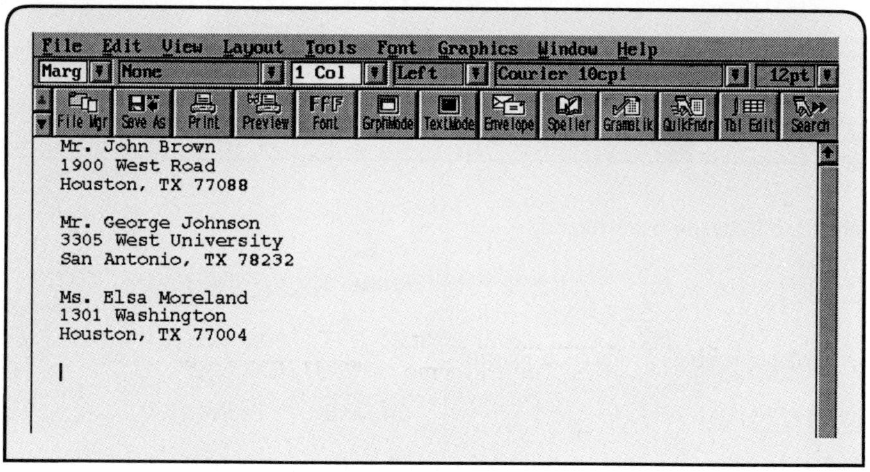

Close the file without saving changes.

EXERCISE 1

INSTRUCTIONS: Define the following concepts:

1. Keyboard merge _____

_____

2. **KEYBOARD** merge code _____

_____

3. **PAGEOFF** merge code _____

_____

EXERCISE 2

INSTRUCTIONS: Circle T if the statement is true and F if the statement is false.

T   F   1.   The **KEYBOARD** merge code pauses the merge so that you can enter text from the keyboard and prompts you with a message.

T   F   2.   By default, each record is placed on a separate page when you perform a merge.

T   F   3.   Data records can be combined in a list by using the **ENDRECORD** merge code.

T   F   4.   The **PAGEOFF** merge code tells WordPerfect not to place a hard page break after each record.

T   F   5.   You must use a data file if you are creating a list using merge.

EXERCISE 3

INSTRUCTIONS:
1. Create the following document using the **KEYBOARD** merge code to prompt you for the addressee's name and team ID.
2. Spell check the document.
3. Save the document as "CH13EX03.FRM". Close the document.
4. Send the memo to the following individuals.

     Mr. Jack Rather   Ms. Mary Ann Turbell
     Supervisor, South Team 10   Supervisor, North Team 9

5. Save each memo separately. Save the Rather memo as "CH13EX03.01". Save the Turbell memo as "CH13EX03.02".
6. Print both documents.
7. Close both documents.

FORM FILE FOR EXERCISE 3

```
                        MEMORANDUM


TO:    KEYBOARD(Addressee's name)
       KEYBOARD(Addressee's team ID)

FROM: Howard J. Dalrymple, Village Manager

DATE: DATE

RE:    Waste Recycling

Our community is about to undergo a severe test.  We will be asking
all residents to recycle paper, glass, and compostable materials.

You, as a supervisor of a Public Works team, must make sure that your
employees make a good effort to collect all materials and separate
them into the proper bins on the new trucks.  This is an important
event for our community and our country.  Please ask all employees to
make an extra effort during the first few weeks to help the residents
place the correct materials in the right container.
```

EXERCISE 4

INSTRUCTIONS:

1. Create the following document using the **KEYBOARD** merge code to prompt you for the addressee and address data.
2. Spell check the document.
3. Save the document as "CH13EX04.FRM".
4. Close the document.
5. Merge the document with the address information below.
6. Save each letter. Save the White letter as "CH13EX04.01". Save the Brunner letter as "CH13EX04.02".
7. Print each document.
8. Close each document.

FORM FILE FOR EXERCISE 4

DATE

KEYBOARD(Addressee's name)
KEYBOARD(Address)

Dear **KEYBOARD**(Addressee's first name):

There will be several Real Estate Property Law seminars at the next State Convention. As a member of the real estate division of your law firm, I want to encourage your attendance.

One seminar in particular, "Keeping Up With Property Law," should be very rewarding. The speaker, Mr. Bill Anderson, is excellent and he will be reviewing pertinent changes for the last year.

Please read over the Bar Convention brochure for more information about this and the many other fine seminars at this year's convention.

Sincerely,

Ronald O'Connor
Director, Continuing Legal Education

ADDRESSES FOR EXERCISE 4

Ms. Judy White
383 Parkway, Suite 34
Dallas, Texas 75223

Mr. Stephen Brunner
765-B Commerce
San Antonio, Texas 78213

EXERCISE 5

INSTRUCTIONS:

1. Create the following document using the **KEYBOARD** merge code to prompt you for the addressee and address data.
2. Spell check the document.
3. Save the document as "CH13EX05.FRM".
4. Close the document.
5. Merge the document with the address information below.
6. Save each letter. Save the Armstrong letter as "CH13EX05.01". Save the James letter as "CH13EX05.02". Save the Johnson letter as "CH13EX05.03". Save the McBrady letter as "CH13EX05.04".
7. Print each document.
8. Close each document.

FORM FILE FOR EXERCISE 5

DATE

KEYBOARD(Addressee's name)
KEYBOARD(Address)

Dear **KEYBOARD**(Addressee's first name):

As a valued customer, you have earned a 10% discount on your next purchase. I also want to let you know that we have received shipment of the newest Harold Jackson novel. It has been given wonderful reviews and I know you will want to add this book to your library.

Most exciting of all, Mr. Jackson will be at our location on August 15th to personally autograph your copy. He is a delightful gentleman and you won't want to miss this chance to meet him!

Sincerely,

Bob Greenburg
Owner, The Little Bookstore

ADDRESSES FOR EXERCISE 5

Mr. Allen Armstrong 1234 Broadway Houston, Texas 77055	Ms. Christina Johnson 6135 Archway Houston, Texas 77057
Mr. Mark James 12959 Oak Tree Way Houston, Texas 77245	Ms. Lynn McBrady 1212 Talley Road Houston, Texas 77198

EXERCISE 6

INSTRUCTIONS:

1. Create the following document using the **KEYBOARD** merge code to pause the merge.
2. Spell check the document.
3. Save the document as "CH13EX06.FRM".
4. Close the document.
5. Merge the document with the names and suite numbers listed below.
6. Save each memo. Save the Brown memo as "CH13EX06.01". Save the Roodman memo as "CH13EX06.02". Save the Carter memo as "CH13EX06.03". Save the Williams memo as "CH13EX06.04".
7. Print each document.
8. Close each document.

FORM FILE FOR EXERCISE 6

```
                          MEMORANDUM


TO:           KEYBOARD

SUITE:        KEYBOARD

FROM:         Madeline Howard, Head Office Manager

DATE:         DATE

SUBJECT:      Break Rooms


It has been brought to my attention that everyone is not doing his
part to keep the break rooms in good condition.

Also please keep track of what you leave in the refrigerators.  The
refrigerators are intended to give you a place to keep your food
during the day, not overnight.  It is your responsibility to remove
any uneaten food at the end of the day.

Thank you for your attention in this matter.
```

RECIPIENTS FOR EXERCISE 6

```
Henry Brown                      Barbara Carter
Suite 245                        Suite 353

Elizabeth Roodman                Frank Williams
Suite 249                        Suite 359
```

EXERCISE 7

INSTRUCTIONS:
1. Create the following form file to merge a list of items.
2. Save the document as "CH13EX07.FRM".
3. Close the document.
4. Create a data file using the addresses listed below.
5. Save the document as "CH13EX07.DTA". Close the document.
6. Merge the two documents.
7. Print the list.
8. Close the document without saving changes.

FORM FILE FOR EXERCISE 7

```
FIELD(First) FIELD(Last)
FIELD(Address)

PAGEOFF
```

DATA FILE FOR EXERCISE 7

```
Charles Edwards                      Arthur Jordan
11226 Timbercraft Drive              17209 Longwood
San Antonio, Texas 78244             Dallas, Texas 75387

Robert Garcia                        Thomas McDonald
4735 Valley Lane                     4414 Bellbrook
Houston, Texas 77077                 San Antonio, Texas 78253

Philip Howle                         Karen Ho
700 N.W. 34th St.                    7812 Windchase Drive
Austin, Texas 78749                  Ft. Worth, Texas 75213
```

EXERCISE 8

INSTRUCTIONS:
1.   Create the following form file to merge a list of items.
2.   Save the document as "CH13EX08.FRM".
3.   Close the document.
4.   Create a data file using the addresses listed below.
5.   Save the document as "CH13EX08.DTA". Close the document.
6.   Merge the two documents.
7.   Print the list.
8.   Close the document without saving changes.

FORM FILE FOR EXERCISE 8

```
FIELD(Title) FIELD(First) FIELD(Last)
FIELD(Company?)
FIELD(Address)

PAGEOFF
```

DATA FILE FOR EXERCISE 8

```
Mr. Donald Roberts              Mr. Allen Winters
Acme Company                    All Rite Paints, Inc.
209 West Avenue                 4332 S. Bonham
Rochester, New York 14699       Orem, Utah 84194

Ms. Joan Robinson               Mr. John Welch
8871 Business Park Blvd.        Long Construction Company
Plano, Texas 75077              18773 NW 45th Street
                                Redmond, Washington 98001
```

CHAPTER FOURTEEN

MACROS

OBJECTIVES

In this chapter, you will learn to:

- Create a macro
- Use a macro
- Assign a macro to a Button Bar
- Edit a macro
- Create an interactive macro
- Delete a macro

■ CHAPTER OVERVIEW

In this chapter, the procedures for creating, using, editing, and deleting a macro are described and illustrated. A method for creating an interactive macro is also demonstrated.

■ CREATING A MACRO

A **macro** is a set of recorded actions in WordPerfect. The macro commands represent the actions exactly as they are executed when you move the cursor, enter text, or choose options from the various menus.

Macros are especially useful when performing detailed, repetitive tasks. For example, you can use a macro to format many documents the same way, instead of tediously formatting each from scratch. A macro can insert an entire memo heading at the top of a document at the touch of a key. Or you can use a macro to add the same closing for most letters that you prepare. Rather than enter the same keystrokes each time you want to perform a task, you can create a macro to do the work for you.

You can create a macro by using the Macro Record feature. To begin recording a macro, press CTRL+F10 or choose Tools, Macro, and then the Record option from the Macro menu. You will be asked to enter a name for the macro. Each macro is stored in a file using the name you specified. WordPerfect adds a ".WPM" extension to all macro names and stores the macros in the "MACROS" subdirectory in the "WP60" directory. You can change the macro directory by pressing SHIFT+F1 to select the File Setup, Location of Files command.

There are two ways to name a macro. One way is to enter a name between one and eight characters long. The characters in a macro name should be either letters or numbers. You cannot use spaces in a macro name.

Another way to define a macro name is to hold down the ALT key and press a letter from A to Z or a number 0 through 9. The advantage of naming a macro in this way is that to use the macro, you simply press ALT and the letter or number.

Before starting this section, close any documents appearing on your screen.

Often, you may use the same closing for a letter. Suppose you want to record a macro that creates the closing for you.

To record a macro that inserts a closing into a document:

Press	Ctrl + F10		**Choose**	Tools
			Choose	Macro
			Choose	Record

The Record Macro dialog box appears. Your screen should look like Figure 14-1.

Figure 14-1

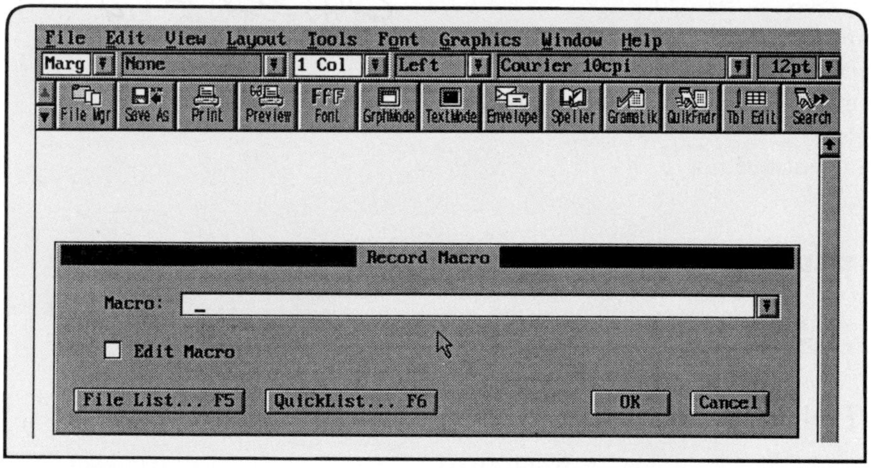

To enter the name for the macro:

Type	closing		**Type**	closing

To begin recording the macro:

Press	↵Enter		**Click**	the OK command button

The bottom part of your screen should look like Figure 14-2. Notice that the message "Recording Macro" appears on the status bar, indicating that WordPerfect is recording your actions.

Figure 14-2

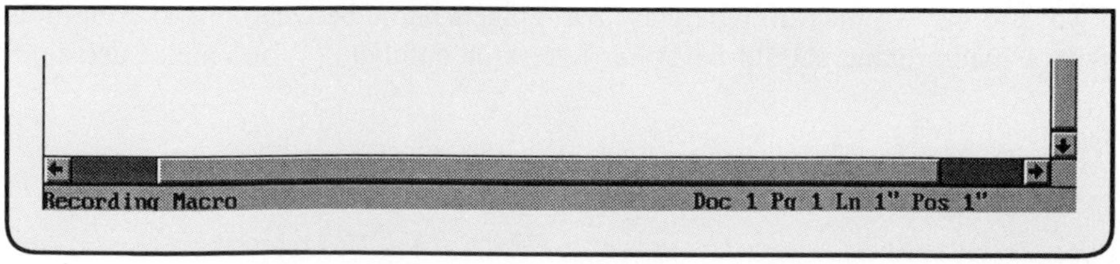

To enter the closing:

Type	Sincerely,		*Type*	*Sincerely,*
Press	⎵Enter four times		*Press*	*⎵Enter four times*
Type	Joseph Carson		*Type*	*Joseph Carson*
Press	⎵Enter twice		*Press*	*⎵Enter twice*
Type	Enclosure		*Type*	*Enclosure*

The top part of your screen should look like Figure 14-3.

Figure 14-3

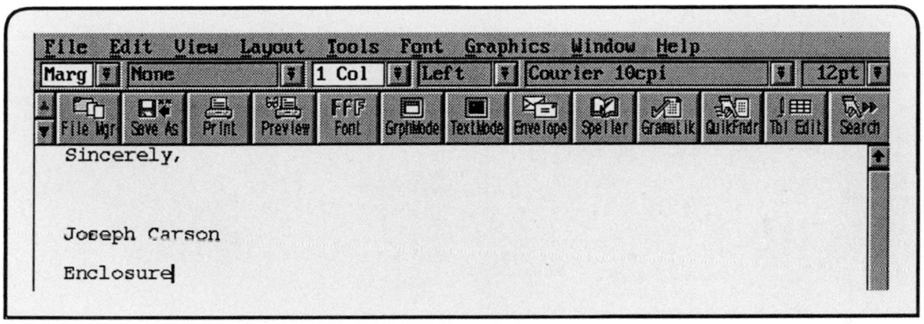

To stop recording keystrokes:

Press	Ctrl + F10		*Choose*	*Tools*
			Choose	*Macro*
			Choose	*Stop*

Briefly, the message "Compiling macro" appears on your screen. Notice that the message "Recording Macro" no longer appears on the status bar, indicating that WordPerfect is no longer recording your actions. The macro has been saved in the "C:\WP60\MACROS" directory using the name "CLOSING.WPM".

Close your document. Do not save any changes.

Suppose you want to create a macro that sets a standard format for a letter and you want to name it by holding down the ALT key and selecting a letter. This standard format sets a 1.5" left margin, a 2.5" top margin to allow space for the letterhead, full justification, and a Helve-WP (Type 1) 12 point font.

To record a macro to format a letter:

Press	Ctrl + F10		*Choose*	*Tools*
			Choose	*Macro*
			Choose	*Record*

To enter the name:

Press	Alt +F to create the macro name		*Press*	*Alt +F to create the macro name*
Press	⎵Enter		*Click*	*the OK command button*

You are now ready to select all of the format options for your letter. If you make an error, continue the process for creating the macro. You will learn how to edit or modify a macro in a later section.

To define the margins for the letter:

Press	Shift + F8		*Choose*	*Layout*
Press	2 or M to select the Margins option		*Choose*	*Margins*
Set	the left margin to 1.5"		*Set*	*the left margin to 1.5"*
Set	the top margin to 2.5"		*Set*	*the top margin to 2.5"*
Press	←Enter twice		*Click*	*the OK command button*

To set the letter justification:

Press	1 or L to select the Line option		*Choose*	*Layout*
Set	the Justification to Full		*Choose*	*Justification*
Press	←Enter twice		*Choose*	*Full*

To set the font:

Press	Ctrl + F8		*Click*	*the Font button on the Button Bar* 
				FFF Font
Set	the font to Helve-WP (Type 1)		*Set*	*the font to Helve-WP (Type 1)*
Press	←Enter		*Click*	*the OK command button*

The bottom part of your screen should look like Figure 14-4. Notice the change in the Pos indicator from 1" to 1.5" on the status bar, indicating the left margin is now 1.5". Also, the Ln value is now 2.5", corresponding to the top margin of 2.5". "Recording Macro" continues to appear on the left side of the status bar.

Figure 14-4

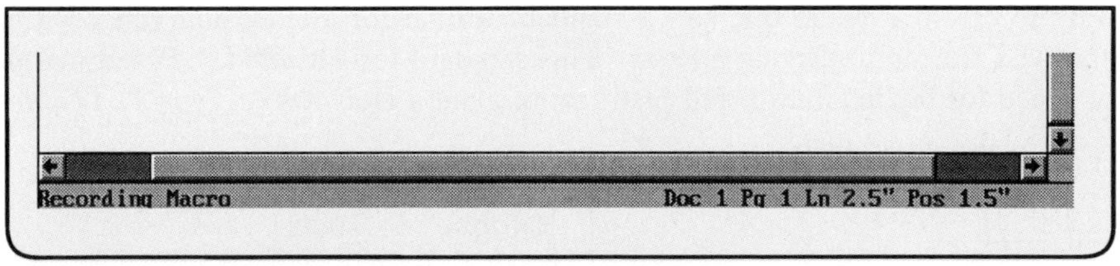

Recording Macro   Doc 1 Pg 1 Ln 2.5" Pos 1.5"

To stop recording keystrokes:

Press	Ctrl + F10		*Choose*	*Tools*
			Choose	*Macro*
			Choose	*Stop*

Notice that the message "Recording Macro" no longer appears on the status bar, indicating that WordPerfect is no longer recording your actions. The macro has been saved in the "C:\WP60\MACROS" directory using the name "ALTF.WPM".

Close your document without saving changes.

■ USING A MACRO

The instructions for using or executing a macro depend on the name you gave the macro when you created it. If you need to cancel the execution of the macro while it is processing, press the ESC key.

To use or execute your "CLOSING" macro:

Press	Alt + F10	**Choose**	Tools
		Choose	Macro
		Choose	Play

The Play Macro dialog box appears, and your screen should look like Figure 14-5.

Figure 14-5

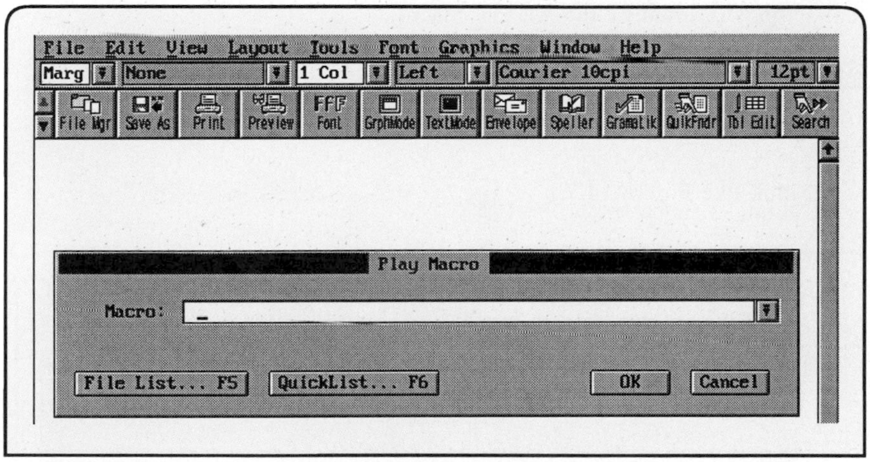

To enter the name of the macro:

Type	CLOSING	**Type**	CLOSING
Press	←Enter	**Click**	the OK command button

Note that when you enter the macro name, you do not have to include the ".WPM" extension. WordPerfect automatically adds the extension to the filename. The top part of your screen should look like Figure 14-6.

Figure 14-6

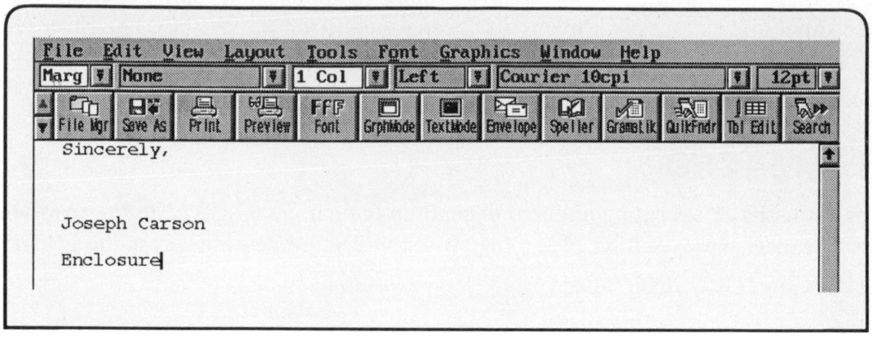

Close the document without saving the changes.

Open the "JOHNSON:LTR" file created in Chapter 3. To format the "JOHNSON.LTR" file using the ALT+F macro:

Press   Alt +F | *Press*   Alt +F

To see the format settings inserted by the ALT+F macro:

Press   Alt +F3 | *Choose*   *View*

                                                      Choose   *Reveal Codes*

Your screen should look like Figure 14-7.

Figure 14-7

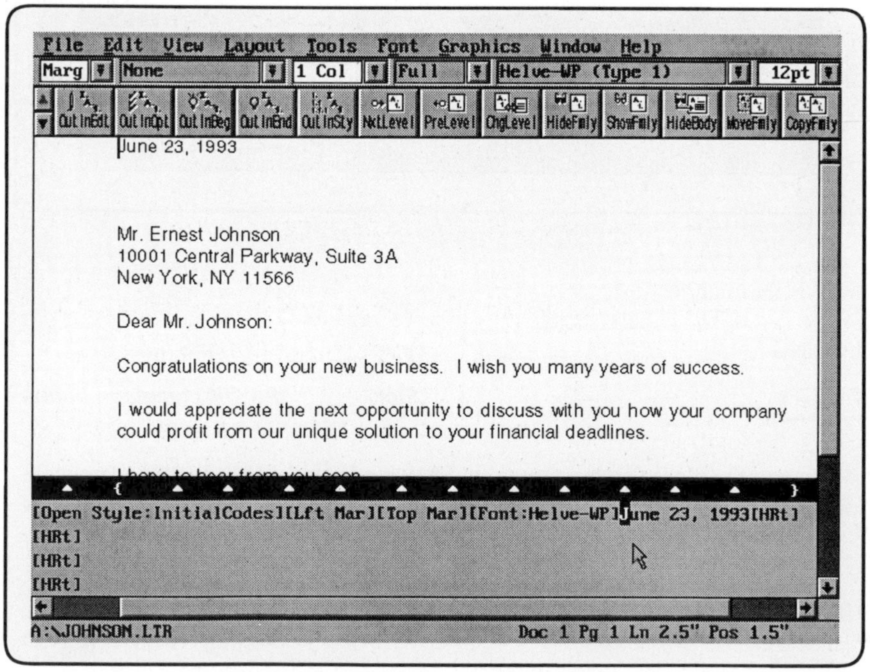

Turn Reveal Codes off, and close the document without saving the changes.

■ ASSIGNING A MACRO TO THE BUTTON BAR

You may use certain macros quite frequently. Rather than having to access the Macro Play feature each time you want to execute a macro, you can assign a macro to a Button Bar.

You use the Edit option from the Button Bar Setup menu to place a macro on a Button Bar. You can assign the macro to any Button Bar.

Suppose that you want to access the "CLOSING" macro frequently from the "MACROS" Button Bar. To select the "MACROS" Button Bar:

Choose	*View*
Choose	*Button Bar Setup*
Choose	*Select*

The Select Button Bar dialog box appears. Your screen should look like Figure 14-8.

Figure 14-8

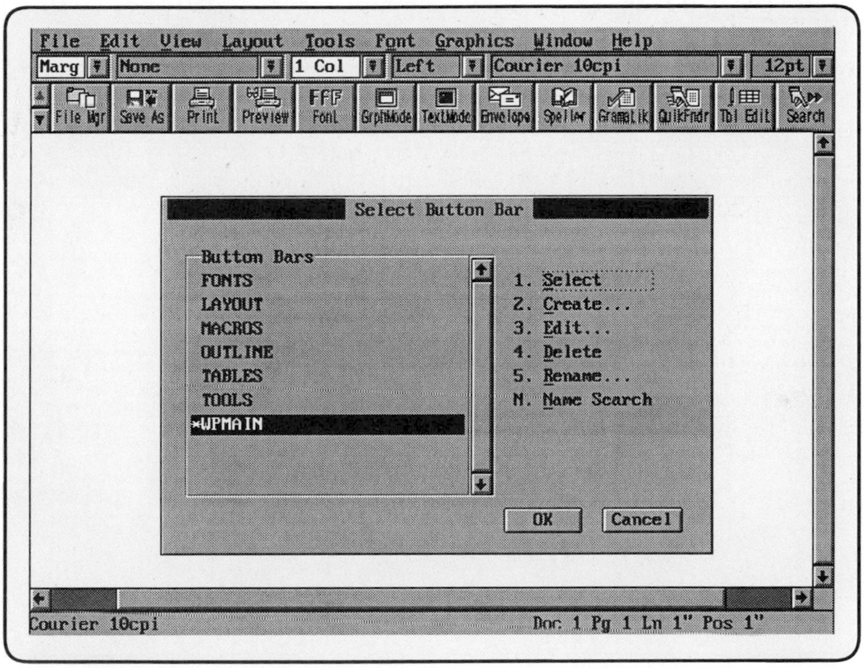

To select the "MACROS" Button Bar:

Press	the arrow keys to highlight the "MACROS" option in the Button Bars option box	*Highlight*	*the "MACROS" option in the Button Bars option box*
Press	1 or S to select the Select option	*Choose*	*the Select option*

The "MACROS" Button Bar appears. The top of your screen should look like Figure 14-9.

Figure 14-9

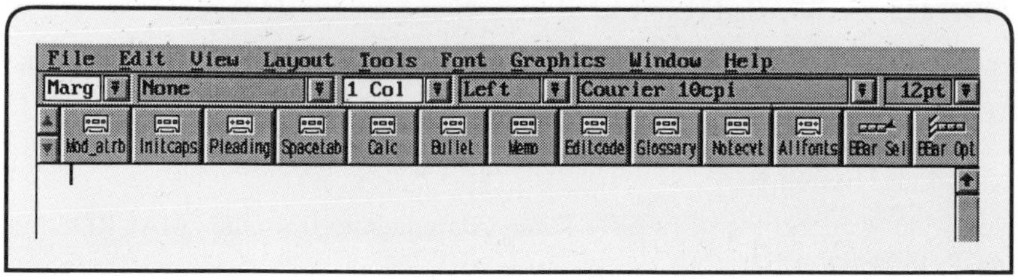

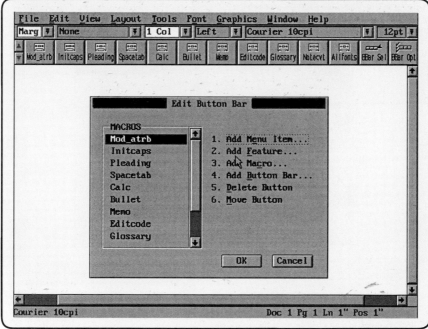

To add the "CLOSING" macro to the Button Bar:

Choose	*View*
Choose	*Button Bar Setup*
Choose	*Edit*

The Edit Button Bar dialog box appears, and your screen should look like Figure 14-10.

Figure 14-10

To add the macro to the Button Bar:

Press	3 or C to select the Add Macro option	***Choose***	*the Add Macro option*

The Macro Button List dialog box appears. Your screen should look like Figure 14-11.

Figure 14-11

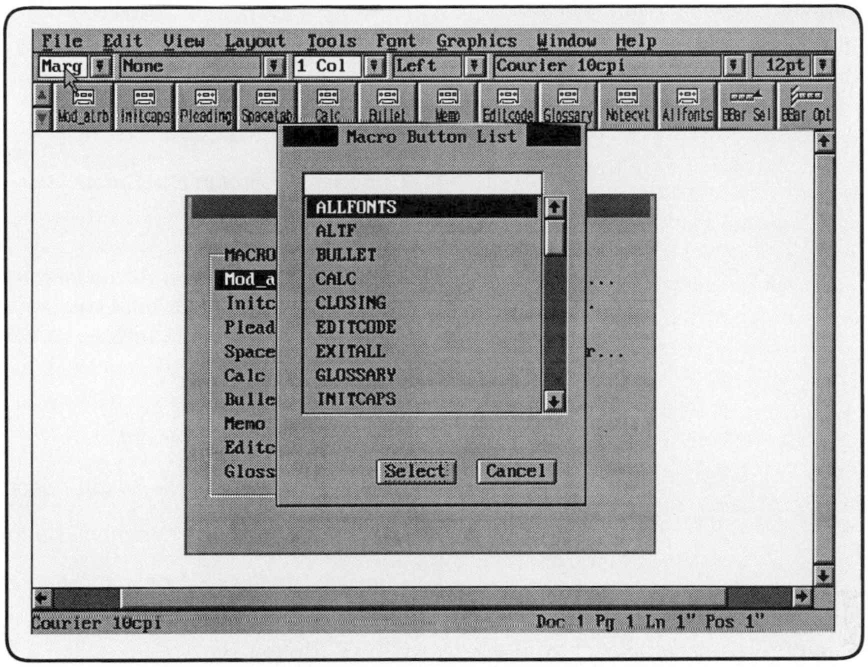

To choose the new Button Bar item:

Press	the Down Arrow key to select the "CLOSING" macro	*Highlight*	*the "CLOSING" macro*
Press	⏎Enter to select the Select command button	*Click*	*the Select command button*

The Closing macro appears in the MACROS list box. To accept the macro:

Press	F7	*Click*	*the OK command button*

The Closing macro has been added to the end of the "MACROS" Button Bar. The top part of your screen should look like Figure 14-12.

Figure 14-12

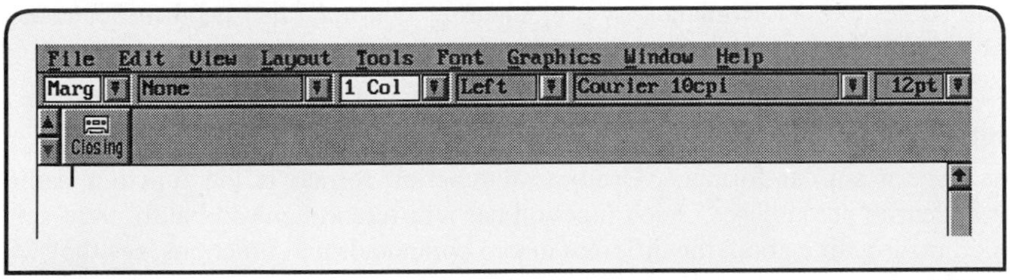

To run a macro that has been assigned to a Button Bar, you select the button. To run the Closing macro:

Click	*the Closing button on the Button Bar*

Close the document without saving changes.

You also use the Button Bar Setup feature to delete a macro from a Button Bar. To delete the "CLOSING" button from the "MACROS" Button Bar:

Choose	*View*
Choose	*Button Bar Setup*
Choose	*Edit*
Click	*the Down Arrow button on the scroll bar until you see the "Closing" macro in the MACROS option box*
Click	*on the "Closing" option in the MACROS option box*
Choose	*the Delete Button option*
Click	*the Yes command button*
Click	*the OK command button*

The "Closing" button has been deleted from the "MACROS" Button Bar.

The top part of your screen should look like Figure 14-13.

Figure 14-13

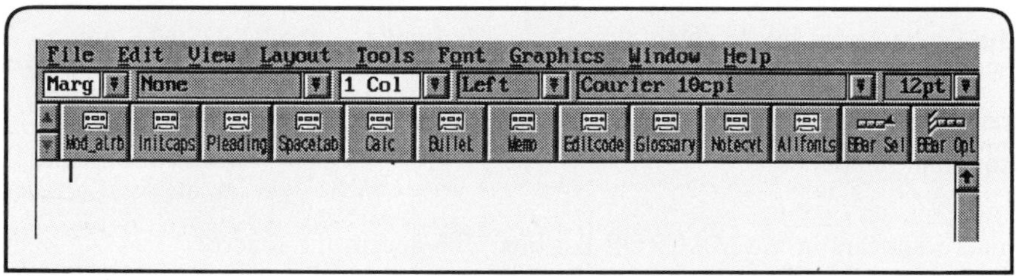

Select the "WPMAIN" Button Bar.

■ EDITING A MACRO

In some situations you may need to edit or change a macro that you created. For instance, it may be necessary to add some text or commands to your macro. You may also need to delete text or incorrect commands that exist in a macro.

You can open a macro file to modify the existing macro. Macro files are made up of a series of commands called **functions**. Every WordPerfect command has a corresponding function.

Most functions have a similar format. The typical function format is the function name followed by conditions that appear in parentheses. Each function has a different name and a different set of conditions. For more detailed information about the different macro commands and functions, see the "Macros" section of your WordPerfect Reference manual.

Suppose you forgot to include the title "Chief Executive Officer" for Mr. Carson in the letter closing. You can change the closing macro to include the title.

To edit the "CLOSING" macro:

Press	Ctrl + F10	*Choose*	*Tools*
Type	CLOSING (in the Macro text box)	*Choose*	*Macro*

| **Press** | ⎆Enter |
| **Press** | E to select the Edit command button |

Choose	*Record*
Type	*CLOSING (in the Macro text box)*
Click	*the Edit Macro check box until an X appears*
Click	*the OK command button*

Your screen should look like Figure 14-14.

Figure 14-14

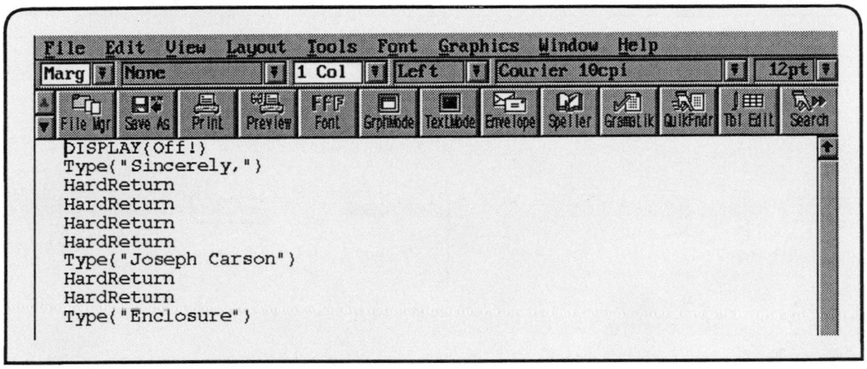

Notice that there are three functions in this macro. The DISPLAY (OFF!) function tells WordPerfect to not show the commands as it works through the macro. Each macro begins with a DISPLAY (OFF!) function, but it is not an essential part of the macro.

The Type function allows you to enter text as part of a macro. The Type function is followed by the string of text that you want the macro to insert in your document surrounded by parentheses. The string of text should appear in quotation marks.

To insert the HardReturn function:

| **Move** | the cursor after the ")" following the Type function for the text "Joseph Carson" |

| *Click* | *after the ")" following the Type function for the text "Joseph Carson"* |

Your screen should look like Figure 14-15.

Figure 14-15

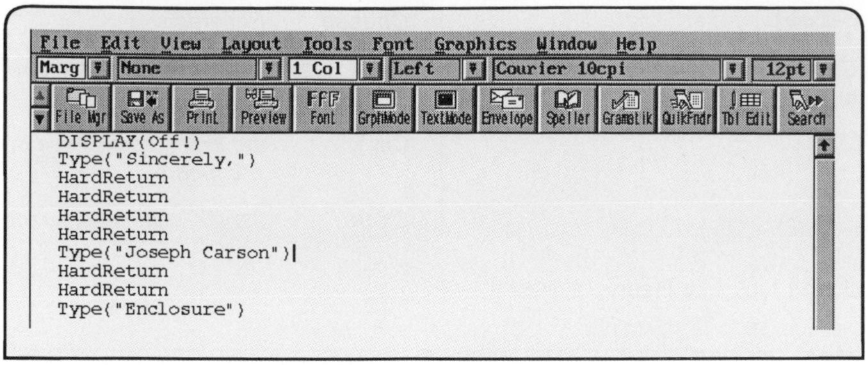

Press   [←Enter] to add a blank line

Type   HardReturn

Press   [←Enter] *to add a blank line*

Type   *HardReturn*

Your screen should look like Figure 14-16.

Figure 14-16

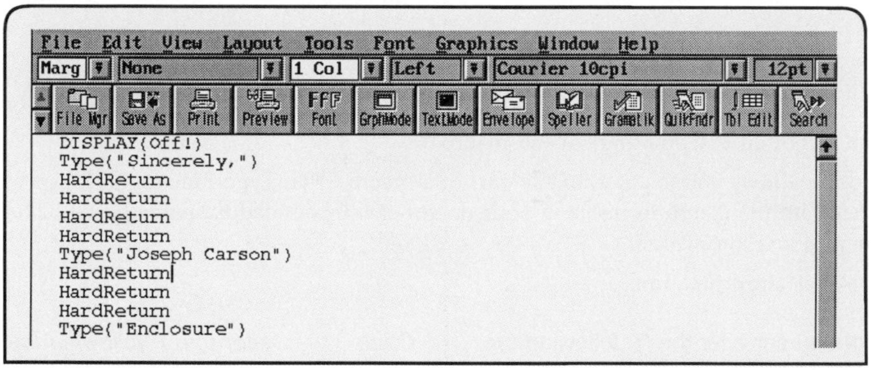

To add the text "Chief Executive Officer" after the HardReturn function, you use the Type function. To insert the Type function:

Press   [←Enter]

Type   Type("Chief Executive Officer")

Press   [←Enter]

Type   *Type("Chief Executive Officer")*

Your screen should look like Figure 14-17.

Figure 14-17

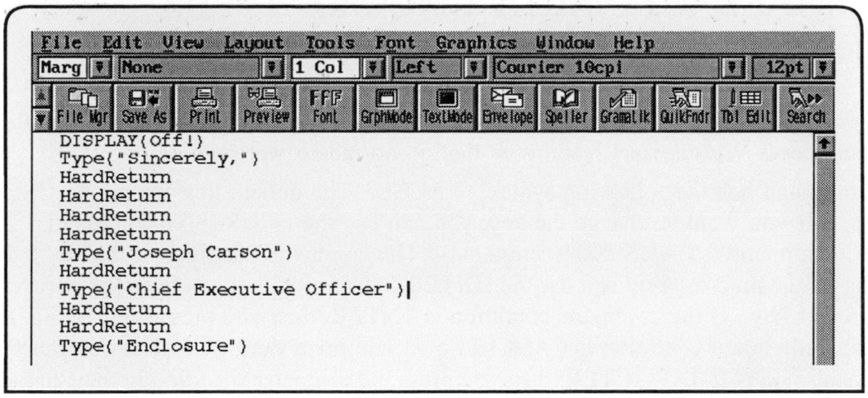

To save your macro:

Press	F7	**Choose**	*File*
Press	Y or ←Enter to select the Yes command button	**Choose**	*Close*
Press	N or ←Enter to select the No command button	**Click**	*the Yes command button*

To test the changes to the macro:

Press	Alt + F10	**Choose**	*Tools*
Type	CLOSING	**Choose**	*Macro*
Press	←Enter	**Choose**	*Play*
		Type	*CLOSING*
		Click	*the OK command button*

Your screen should look like Figure 14-18.

Figure 14-18

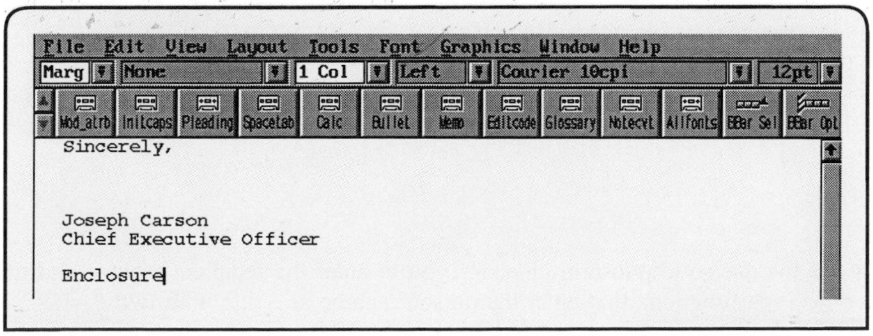

Close the document without saving changes.

■ CREATING AN INTERACTIVE MACRO

The "CLOSING" macro creates a closing for a letter. Sometimes you might want to enter different data in the closing. You can use macro programming commands to create an interactive macro.

The PAUSE command allows you to pause the macro until you press a specified key. While the macro is paused, you can access WordPerfect features as though no macro were running.

The PAUSE command has the following syntax: PAUSE. The default key for the PAUSE command is the ENTER key. If you want to change the key, you can use the PAUSESET command. The syntax for the PAUSESET command is PAUSESET(command). The command condition is the key that you want to end the pausing of the macro. You can use the ENTER key, which is the default key, or the ESC key, or any single character key. If the command condition is ENTER, then you press the ENTER key to resume the macro. If the command condition is CANCEL, then you press the ESC key to continue the macro. If the command condition is CHARACTER, then you press the character specified in the Character condition to resume the macro.

To add the PAUSE macro command to a macro, you edit the macro. To edit the Closing macro:

Press	Ctrl + F10		*Choose*	*Tools*
Type	CLOSING (in the Macro text box)		*Choose*	*Macro*
Press	⏎Enter		*Choose*	*Record*
Press	E to select the Edit command button		*Type*	*CLOSING (in the Macro text box)*
			Click	*the Edit Macro check box until an X appears*
			Click	*the OK command button*

Your screen should look like Figure 14-19.

Figure 14-19

Suppose you want the macro to pause in order for you to enter the recipient's name and title. You need to replace the two Type functions that enter the person's name and title with two PAUSE commands.

To replace the second Type function with a PAUSE command:

Move	the cursor to the left margin of the second Type function		*Click*	*at the left margin of the second Type function*

Your screen should look like Figure 14-20.

Figure 14-20

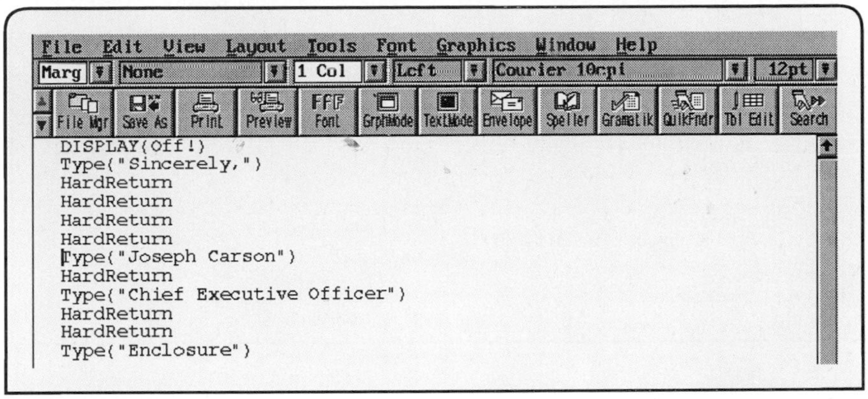

```
File  Edit  View  Layout  Tools  Font  Graphics  Window  Help
Marg ▼ None                   ▼ 1 Col ▼ Left ▼ Courier 10cpi        ▼   12pt ▼
File Mgr Save As  Print Preview  Font  GrphMode TextMode Envelope Speller Gramatik QuikFndr Tbl Edit Search
  DISPLAY(Off!)                                                          ↑
  Type("Sincerely,")
  HardReturn
  HardReturn
  HardReturn
  HardReturn
  Type("Joseph Carson")
  HardReturn
  Type("Chief Executive Officer")
  HardReturn
  HardReturn
  Type("Enclosure")
```

To remove the Type function:

Highlight   the Type function line   │   *Select*   *the Type function line*

Your screen should look like Figure 14-21.

Figure 14-21

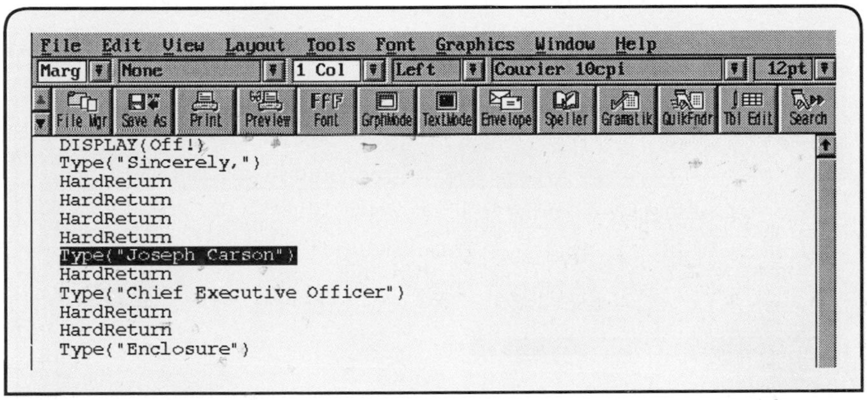

```
File  Edit  View  Layout  Tools  Font  Graphics  Window  Help
Marg ▼ None                   ▼ 1 Col ▼ Left ▼ Courier 10cpi        ▼   12pt ▼
File Mgr Save As  Print Preview  Font  GrphMode TextMode Envelope Speller Gramatik QuikFndr Tbl Edit Search
  DISPLAY(Off!)                                                          ↑
  Type("Sincerely,")
  HardReturn
  HardReturn
  HardReturn
  HardReturn
  Type("Joseph Carson")
  HardReturn
  Type("Chief Executive Officer")
  HardReturn
  HardReturn
  Type("Enclosure")
```

To add a PAUSE command that pauses the macro until the ENTER key is pressed:

Press   [Delete]   │   *Press*   [Delete]

Type   PAUSE   │   *Type*   *PAUSE*

Your screen should look like Figure 14-22.

Figure 14-22

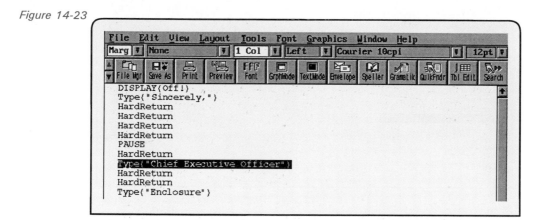

To replace the Type command for the text "Chief Executive Officer" with a PAUSE command:

Move	the cursor to the left margin of the Type command for the text "Chief Executive Officer"	***Click***	*at the left margin of the Type command for the text "Chief Executive Officer"*
Highlight	the line	***Select***	*the line*

Your screen should look similar to Figure 14-23.

Figure 14-23

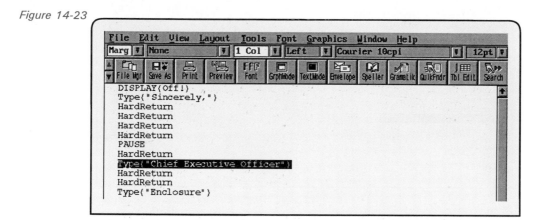

To add the PAUSE command:

Press	Delete	***Press***	Delete
Type	PAUSE	***Type***	*PAUSE*

Your screen should look similar to Figure 14-24.

Figure 14-24

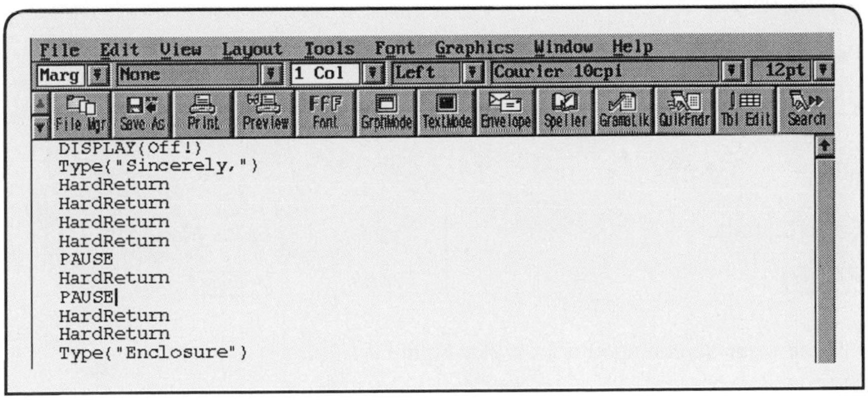

```
File  Edit  View  Layout  Tools  Font  Graphics  Window  Help
Marg ▼ None              ▼ 1 Col ▼ Left  ▼ Courier 10cpi        ▼ 12pt ▼
File Mgr Save As Print Preview  Font  GrphMode TextMode Envelope Speller GramBtik QuikFndr Tbl Edit Search
  DISPLAY(Off!)
  Type("Sincerely,")
  HardReturn
  HardReturn
  HardReturn
  HardReturn
  PAUSE
  HardReturn
  PAUSE|
  HardReturn
  HardReturn
  Type("Enclosure")
```

To save the macro under a different name:

Press   F10

Type   CLOSING2.WPM

Press   ←Enter

Choose   File

Choose   Save As

Type   CLOSING2.WPM

Click   the OK command button

Close the macro file.

To run the interactive macro:

Press   Alt + F10

Type   CLOSING2

Press   ←Enter

Choose   Tools

Choose   Macro

Choose   Play

Type   CLOSING2

Click   the OK command button

The top part of your screen should look like Figure 14-25.

Figure 14-25

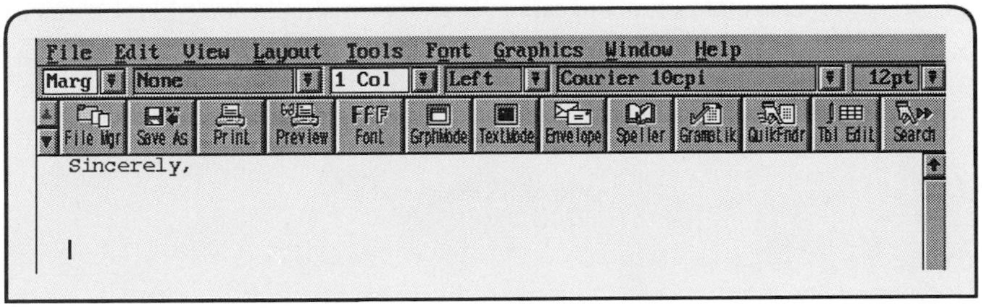

```
File  Edit  View  Layout  Tools  Font  Graphics  Window  Help
Marg ▼ None              ▼ 1 Col ▼ Left  ▼ Courier 10cpi        ▼ 12pt ▼
File Mgr Save As Print Preview  Font  GrphMode TextMode Envelope Speller GramBtik QuikFndr Tbl Edit Search
  Sincerely,


  |
```

When the macro pauses, you can enter the data and use WordPerfect commands. When you press the ENTER key, the macro continues.

To enter the closing name:

Type	Paula Jones		*Type*	*Paula Jones*
Press	⏎Enter		*Press*	⏎Enter

To enter the title:

Type	Sales Manager		*Type*	*Sales Manager*
Press	⏎Enter		*Press*	⏎Enter

The macro ends and your screen should look like Figure 14-26.

Figure 14-26

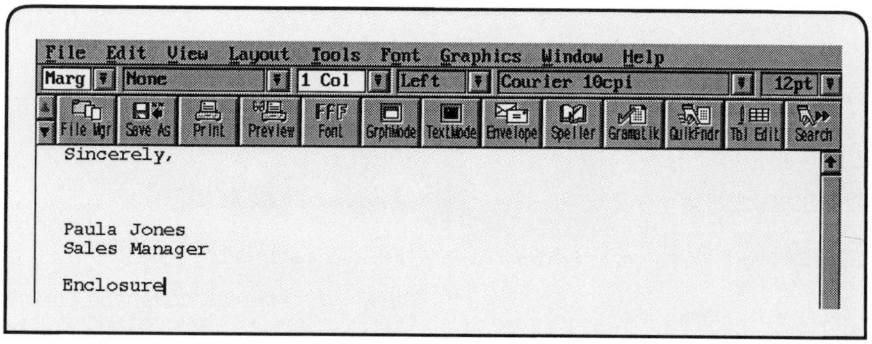

Close the document without saving changes.

For more information on the various macro commands, contact WordPerfect Corporation for a macros manual.

■ DELETING A MACRO

You can delete a macro by deleting the macro file.

To delete a macro:

Press	F5		*Choose*	*File*
			Choose	*File Manager*

The Specify File Manager List dialog box appears. Your screen should look like Figure 14-27.

Figure 14-27

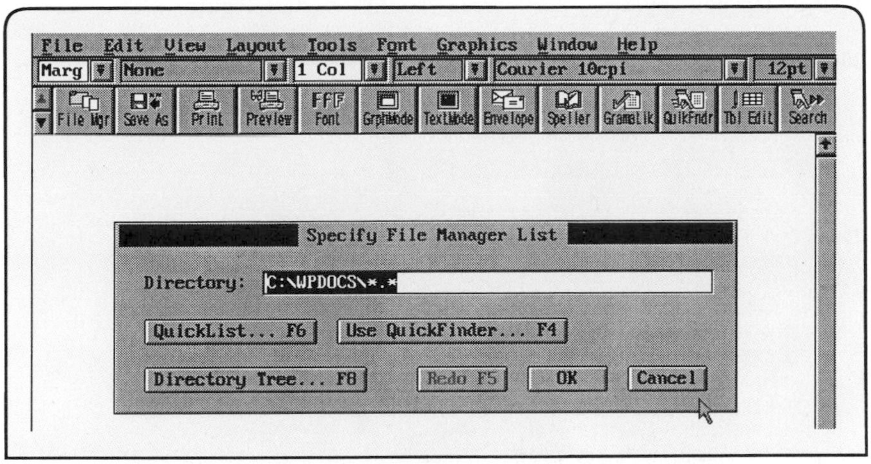

To use the QuickList option:

Press   F6

Click   *the QuickList command button*

The QuickList dialog box appears, and your screen should look like Figure 14-28.

Figure 14-28

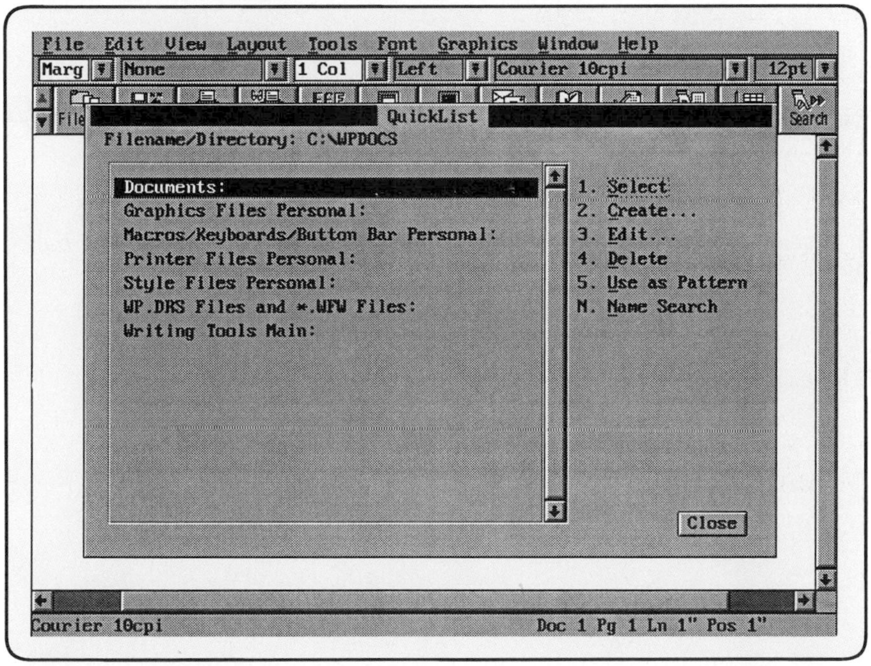

To select the proper directory:

Press   the Down Arrow key to highlight the "Macros/Keyboards/Button Bar Personal:" directory

Click   *on the "Macros/Keyboards/Button Bar Personal:" directory*

Press   1 or S to select the Select option

Choose   *the Select option*

The File Manager dialog box appears. Your screen should look like Figure 14-29.

Figure 14-29

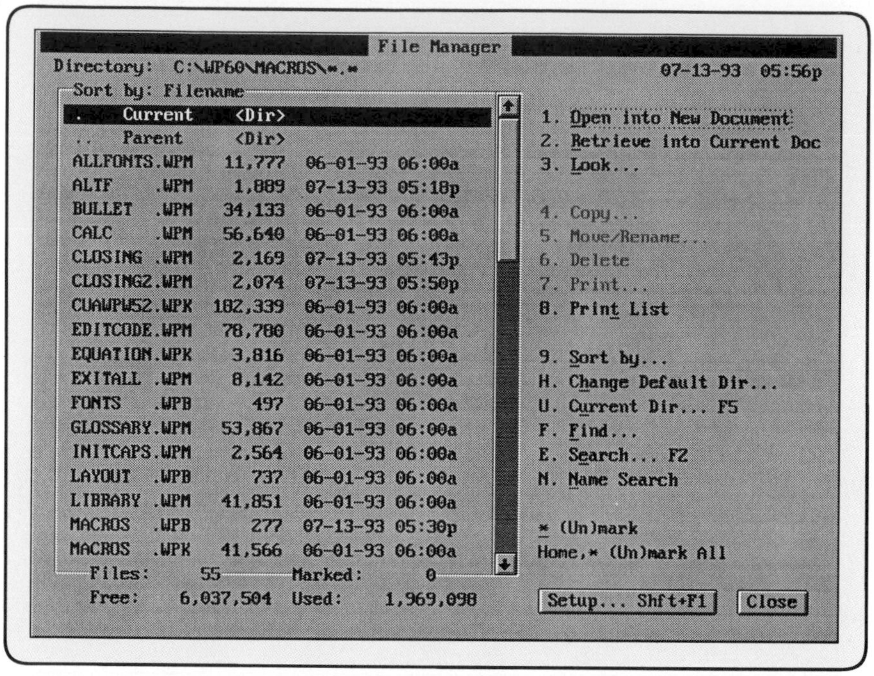

To delete the "CLOSING.WPM" file:

Press	the Down Arrow key to highlight the "CLOSING.WPM" filename	*Click*	*the "CLOSING.WPM" filename*
Press	6 or D to select the Delete option	*Choose*	*the Delete option*
Press	Y to select the Yes command button	*Click*	*the Yes command button*

Delete the "ALTF.WPM" macro file.

Close the File Manager dialog box.

EXERCISE 1

INSTRUCTIONS: Discuss the following concepts briefly:

1.   Macro feature _____

_____

2.   The process for recording a macro _____

_____

_____

3.   The steps for playing a macro _____

_____

_____

4.   The process for editing a macro _____

_____

_____

5.   The process for assigning a macro to a Button Bar _____

_____

_____

6.   The process for pausing a macro _____

_____

_____

7.   The steps for deleting a macro _____

_____

_____

EXERCISE 2

INSTRUCTIONS: Circle T if the statement is true and F if the statement is false.

T	F	1.	A macro is a set of recorded actions in WordPerfect.
T	F	2.	All macros must be named using an ALT key.
T	F	3.	WordPerfect adds a ".WPM" extension to all macro names.
T	F	4.	"Recording Macro" appears in the status bar when you are recording actions.
T	F	5.	"WEEKLY SALES DEMO.WPM" is a valid macro name.

T   F   6.   You can edit a macro by opening the macro file.
T   F   7.   Every menu command has a corresponding macro function.
T   F   8.   The HardReturn function places a hard page break in your document.
T   F   9.   When you add a macro to a Button Bar, the macro appears as a button.

EXERCISE 3

INSTRUCTIONS:

1. Create a macro to prepare the following heading and date for letters that are prepared on a routine basis. Boldface and center the heading. The name of the macro should be "COMPANY".
2. Execute the macro.
3. Print the document after the macro is executed.
4. Close the document without saving changes.

```
                Jackson, Kemp & Garza
              Certified Public Accountants
              829 Gessner Road, Suite 430
                  Richmond, VA 23489




current date
```

EXERCISE 4

INSTRUCTIONS:

1. Create a macro to include the following information at the closing of all letters for your firm. Name the macro using the ALT+A keys.
2. Execute the macro.
3. Print the document after the macro is executed.
4. Close the document without saving changes.

```
Cordially,



Susan K. Scanlan
Attorney at Law

SKS/df
```

EXERCISE 5

INSTRUCTIONS:

1. Create a macro that will create the letter heading shown below. This heading includes the current date, four returns, the inside address, and the salutation. Name the macro using the ALT+B keys.
2. Execute the macro.
3. Print the document after the macro is executed.
4. Close the document without saving changes.

```
current date


President of the United States
The White House
1600 Pennsylvania Avenue
Washington, D.C. 20013

Dear Mr. President:
```

EXERCISE 6

INSTRUCTIONS:

1. Create the following macro for the beginning paragraph of letters. Name the macro using the ALT+R keys.
2. After creating the macro, use it in the letter shown below.
3. Print the letter.
4. Save the letter in a file using the name "CH14EX06".
5. Close the letter.

MACRO TEXT FOR EXERCISE 6

```
Thank you for your letter of inquiry regarding a position at our
company.  At this time, we do not have any openings for someone with
your background.
```

Current date

Mr. Mark Robinson
1090 West Roslyn Road
Irvine, CA 92711

Dear Mr. Robinson:

Use the "ALT-R" macro.

Your background in Chemical Analysis could
be of value to us in the near future. We are
considering opening a Research and Development
department within the next year. We will call
you after this department is given permission
to exist.

Thank you for your interest in our company.

Sincerely,
ADAMS SOLVENTS

Marshall Smith
Director of Personnel

EXERCISE 7

INSTRUCTIONS:

1. Assign the ALT+R macro created in Exercise 6 to the "MACROS" Button Bar.
2. Type the following letter using the **"No Openings"** button on the "MACROS" Button Bar as the first paragraph.
3. Spell check the letter.
4. Preview the letter.
5. Print the letter.
6. Save the letter in a file using the name "CH14EX07".
7. Close the document.

```
current date


Mrs. Theo Reid
1647 Portage
River Edge, NJ 07661

Dear Mrs. Reid:

ALT+R

If anything does develop in your area of expertise, Survey Developer,
in the next six months, we will contact you to see if you are still
interested in pursuing a position with our company.

Thank you again for your interest in our company.

Very truly yours,



James Stutesman, Manager
Quantitative Measuring
```

EXERCISE 8

INSTRUCTIONS:

1. Create a macro for the full heading of the memorandum shown below. Boldface and center "**MEMORANDUM**". Use a 2" top margin. Place the cursor so that you are ready to start typing.
2. Name this macro "MEMOS".
3. Execute the macro.
4. Print the document after executing the macro.
5. Assign the macro to the "WPMAIN" Button Bar.
6. Close the document and do not save the changes.

```
                            MEMORANDUM

TO:

FROM:    Samuel E. Beckett

DATE:    current date

SUBJECT:
```

EXERCISE 9

INSTRUCTIONS:

1. Open the "MEMOS" macro created in Exercise 8.
2. After "Beckett", add a comma (,) and the word "**President**".
3. Save the macro using the same name. Close the document.
4. Execute the macro.
5. Print the document after executing the macro.
6. Close the document without saving the changes.

EXERCISE 10

INSTRUCTIONS:

1. Open the "MEMOS" macro.
2. Add a Pause command at the "To:" and "Subject:" lines to pause the macro until the ENTER key is pressed.
3. Save the macro using the same name. Close the document.
4. Execute the macro.
5. Address the memo to **Maria Campbell**. The subject of the memo is **New Products**. Add the following text to the memo after the macro executes.
6. Print the memo.
7. Save the memo as "CH14EX10".
8. Close the document.

```
The Fall product line is being announced July 22nd at B & J's
department store in Los Angeles.  Please notify all staff members of
the announcement date and location.

Invitations to the Fall line introduction will be distributed at a
later date.
```

CHAPTER FIFTEEN

ENVELOPES AND LABELS

OBJECTIVES

In this chapter, you will learn to:
- Change paper size and type
- Create envelopes
- Create envelopes using a macro
- Create envelopes with bar codes
- Create labels using a macro

■ CHAPTER OVERVIEW

In this chapter, the Paper Size/Type feature is discussed. The process of creating a paper size for an envelope is illustrated. The creation of bar codes for envelopes is demonstrated. The use of macros to print envelopes and label forms is also illustrated.

■ PAPER SIZE/TYPE

The **Paper Size/Type** feature in WordPerfect enables you to define a printer form for special sizes of paper that you want to use when printing your document. Your document can be an envelope or label, an invitation on 5" x 7" cards, or any printed material that requires special paper. You can also define a printer form so that the printer handles paper a certain way.

You can use the Paper Size/Type feature by pressing SHIFT+F8 and selecting the Page option from the Format dialog box or by choosing Page from the Layout menu. The existing forms are listed in the Paper Size/Type dialog box. WordPerfect has already created the standard 8.5" x 11" form for you. Depending on the type of printer selected, there may be other forms already defined for you. Most laser printers include a form for business envelopes. You will see all of the existing forms in the Paper Name list box. To use a new paper type, select the desired form from the Paper Name list box and use the Select option. Once you select a form, a Paper Size code is inserted into your document.

The Paper Size/Type feature enables you to create custom forms by adding new forms or editing existing forms. To add a new form, use the Create option in the Paper Size/Type dialog box. To edit an existing form, highlight the paper type from the Paper Name list box and use the Edit option.

When editing a form, you can specify the following attributes in the Edit Paper Size/Type dialog box:

Type of the paper, such as letterhead, envelope, etc.

Size of the paper.

Location of the paper. Continuous or manual (by hand) paper feed.

The Prompt to Load option. WordPerfect prompts you when it is ready to print the next form, so that you can put the form in the printer.

The orientation of the font. A **portrait font** type is shown on this page, where the text is printed down the length of the page. A **landscape font** type is used when text is printed across the length of the page. (Some printers may not be able to print landscape if they do not contain fonts for landscape printing.)

The Delete option deletes a paper type from the Paper Name list box. Once you delete a paper type, it is no longer available for any new documents that you create.

■ ENVELOPES

Printing addresses on envelopes is a word processing task that almost everyone must perform at one time or another. You can print on envelopes one at a time as needed. You can also print many addresses on envelopes by using a data file containing addresses. Either way, WordPerfect can do the job for you.

Envelopes do not use the standard 8.5" x 11" paper upon which you normally print letters and reports. A standard business envelope is 9.5" x 4.13", and a standard short envelope is 6.5" x 3.5". WordPerfect has defined the paper sizes for the most commonly used envelope sizes. However, you might have to create a paper size for an odd-sized envelope.

Before starting this section, be sure all documents are closed.

Creating an Envelope Form

Suppose you want to create an envelope to accompany the "JOHNSON.LTR" letter created in Chapter 3. You use 6.5" x 4.5" envelopes, which are not included as a standard form. If you want to print small envelopes using the address for the "JOHNSON.LTR" letter, you need to create the paper size for the 6.5" x 4.5" envelope form.

To select the Page Format feature:

| **Press** | Shift + F8 | **Choose** | Layout |
| **Press** | 3 or P to select the Page option | **Choose** | Page |

The Page Format dialog box appears. Your screen should look like Figure 15-1.

Figure 15-1

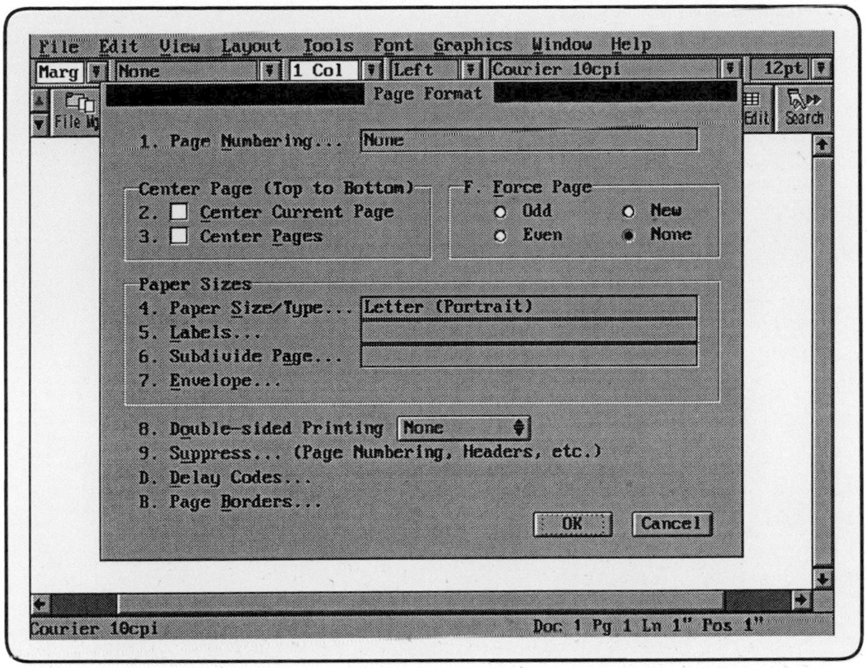

To select the Paper Size/Type features:

| **Press** | 4 or S to select the Paper Size/Type option in the Paper Sizes option box | **Choose** | *the Paper Size/Type option in the Paper Sizes option box* |

The Paper Size/Type dialog box appears. A list of paper types is displayed in the Paper Name list box. The paper types in the Paper Name list box depend on the printer that you have selected. Assuming you have selected the HP LaserJet Series II printer, your screen should look like Figure 15-2.

Figure 15-2

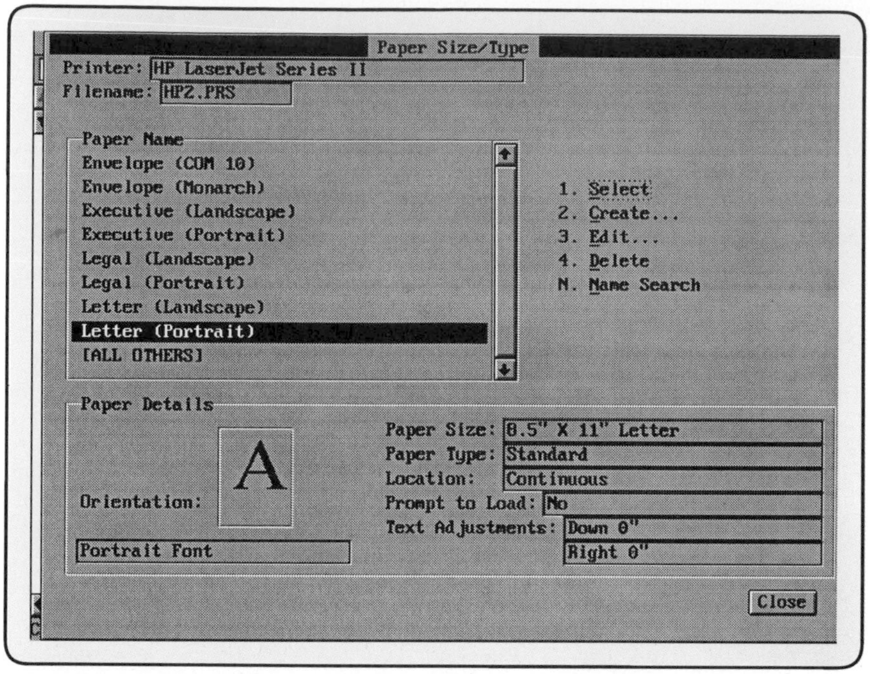

To create a new paper type for the small envelope and add it to the list:

Press   2 or C to select the Create option | ***Choose***   *the Create option*

The Create Paper Size/Type dialog box appears. Your screen should look like Figure 15-3.

Figure 15-3

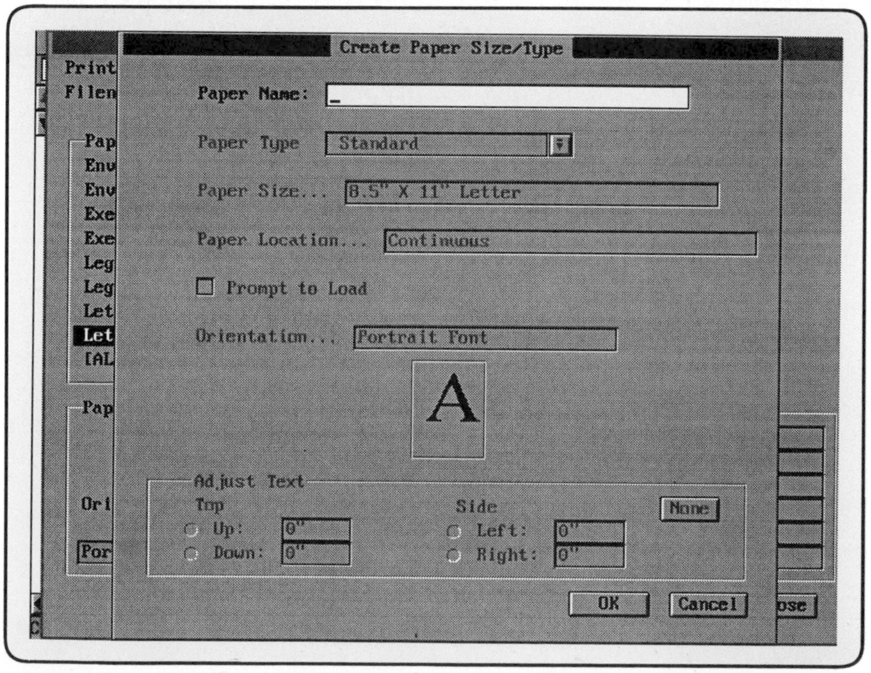

Notice that because the Paper Name text box is already selected, the other options are not numbered.

To begin defining your new paper form, you must first name it.

To name the new form:

Type	Small Envelope, 6.5x4.5	*Type*	*Small Envelope, 6.5x4.5*
Press	[←Enter]	*Double-click*	*in the Paper Name text box*

Notice that all the options become available for the Small Envelope form after it has been named.

You can select from various types of paper to define your form. The "Standard" paper type is the paper you normally would have loaded in your printer. If you do not find the type that you want, then select the option "Other".

To define the type for envelopes:

Press	2 or T to select the Paper Type text box	*Click*	*the Paper Type drop-down list button*
Type	E to highlight the Envelope option	*Double-click*	*on the Envelope option*
Press	[←Enter]		

Your screen should look like Figure 15-4.

Figure 15-4

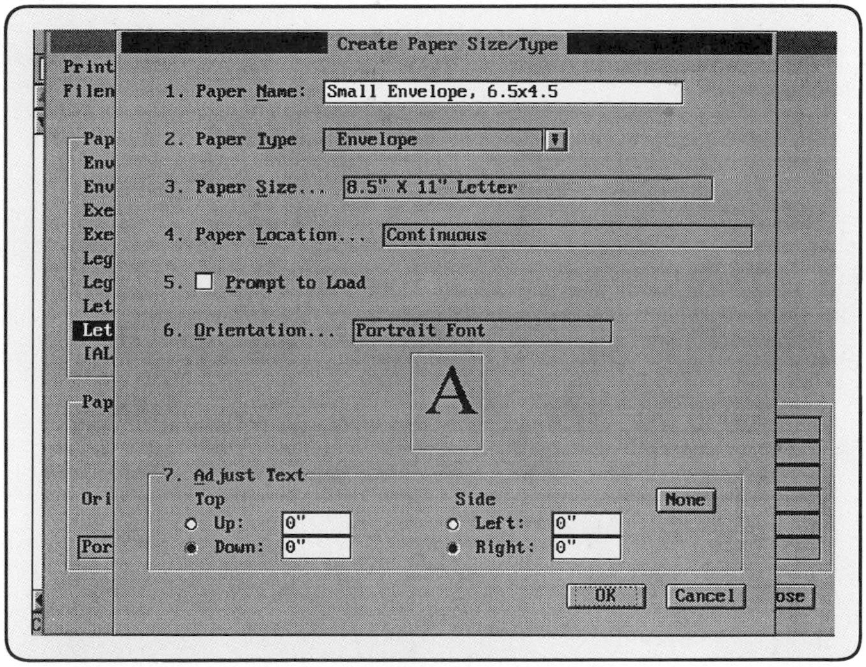

To change the paper size to that of a small envelope:

Press	3 or S to select the Paper Size option	*Choose*	*the Paper Size option*

The Define Paper Size dialog box appears. Your screen should look like Figure 15-5.

Figure 15-5

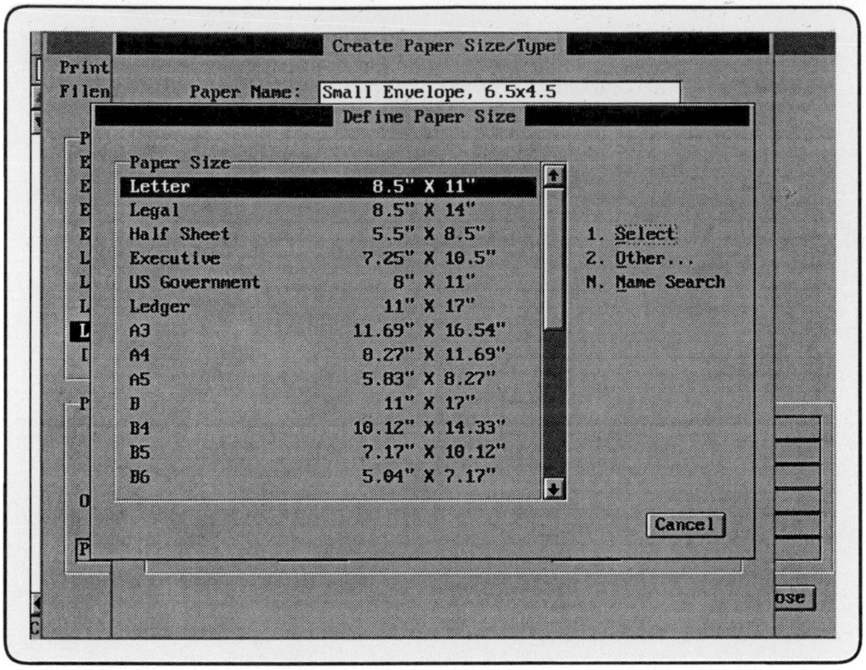

```
┌──────────────────────────────────────────────────────────┐
│                  Create Paper Size/Type                    │
│ Print                                                      │
│ Filen      Paper Name: │Small Envelope, 6.5x4.5 │          │
│                       Define Paper Size                    │
│  ┌─ Paper Size ─────────────────────────┐                  │
│  │ Letter              8.5" X 11"      │▲│                  │
│  │ Legal               8.5" X 14"      │ │                 │
│  │ Half Sheet          5.5" X 8.5"     │ │  1. Select      │
│  │ Executive           7.25" X 10.5"   │ │  2. Other...    │
│  │ US Government        8" X 11"        │ │  N. Name Search │
│  │ Ledger              11" X 17"        │ │                 │
│  │ A3                  11.69" X 16.54"  │ │                 │
│  │ A4                  8.27" X 11.69"   │ │                 │
│  │ A5                  5.83" X 8.27"    │ │                 │
│  │ B                   11" X 17"        │ │                 │
│  │ B4                  10.12" X 14.33"  │ │                 │
│  │ B5                  7.17" X 10.12"   │ │                 │
│  │ B6                  5.04" X 7.17"   │▼│                  │
│  └──────────────────────────────────────┘                 │
│                                          ┌──────┐          │
│                                          │Cancel│          │
│                                          └──────┘          │
└──────────────────────────────────────────────────────────┘
```

To see the paper sizes for the envelopes:

Press   ⬇ until you can see all the envelope sizes

Drag   *the scroll box in the Paper Size list box to the bottom of the vertical scroll bar*

Notice that 6.5" x 4.5" is not listed. You must use the Other option to define a custom size. Also notice that in the Paper Size list box, none of the options contain an underlined letter. To select an option, press an arrow key until the desired paper size is highlighted. Then press 1 or S to select the option or choose the Select option.

To select the Other option:

Press   2 or O to select the Other option

Choose   *the Other option*

The Define Other Paper Size dialog box appears. Your screen should look like Figure 15-6.

Figure 15-6

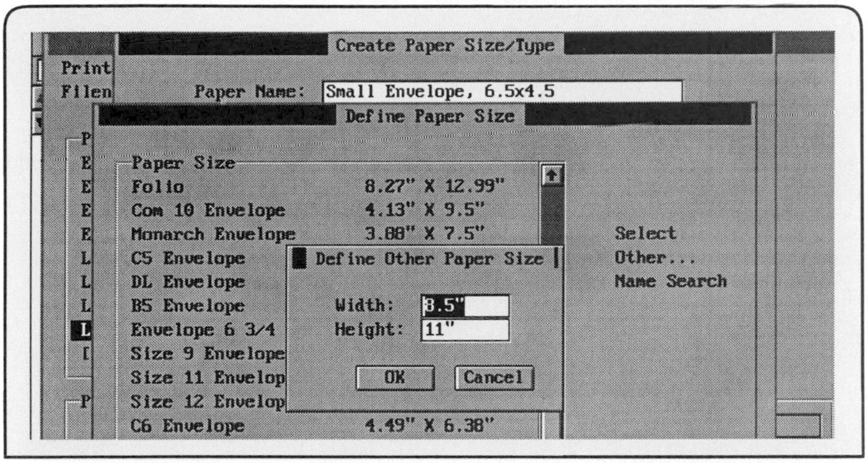

To enter the width (6.5") and height (4.5") of the new form:

Type	6.5 in the Width text box	*Type*	*6.5 in the Width text box*
Press	Tab⇄ to select the Height text box	*Click*	*in the Height text box*
Type	4.5	*Type*	*4.5*
Press	↵Enter	*Double-click*	*on the number in the Height text box*

Your screen should look like Figure 15-7.

Figure 15-7

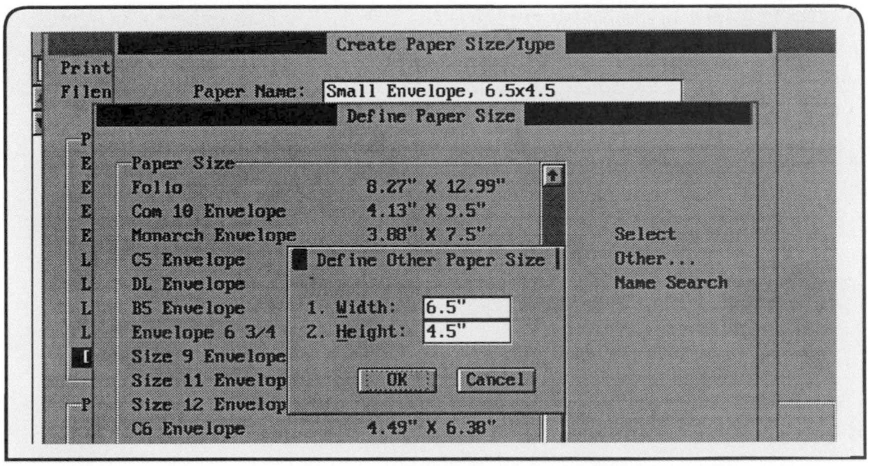

To complete the new paper size:

Press	↵Enter	*Click*	*the OK command button*

The Paper Location option in the Create Paper Size/Type dialog box tells the printer where it should look for the paper. A Manual Feed selection tells the printer that it should look in the manual paper feed slot for the paper. This means that you will hand feed each envelope into the printer. A Continuous selection indicates that paper is fed continuously into the printer either by a tractor feeder on a dot matrix printer or by a sheet feeder on a laser printer. For information on your printer, consult the owner's manual for your printer.

To change the paper location:

Press	4 or L to select the Paper Location option	**_Choose_**	_the Paper Location option_

The Paper Location dialog box appears. Your screen should look like Figure 15-8.

Figure 15-8

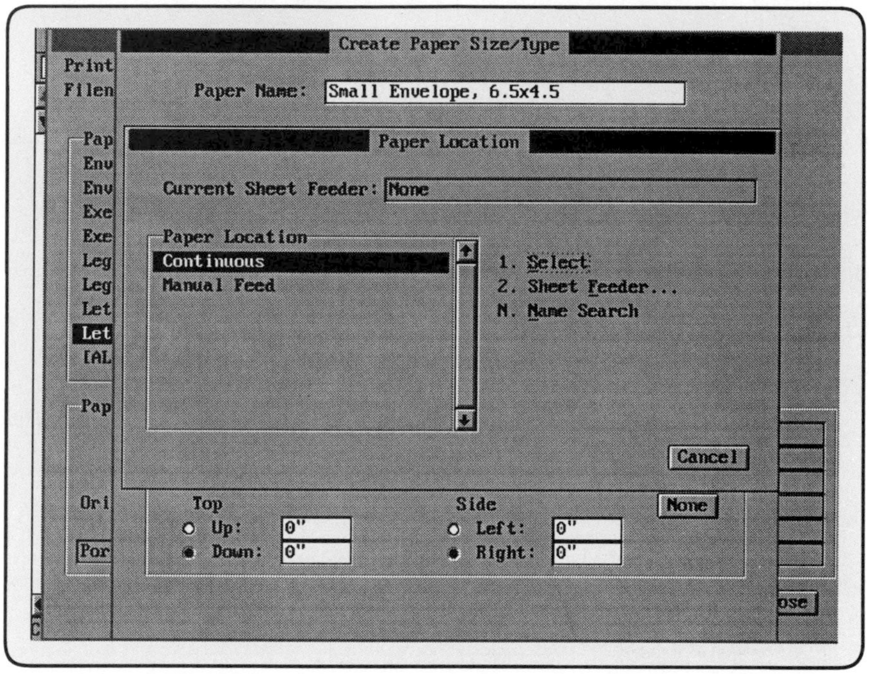

To select the Manual Feed option:

Press	⬇ to highlight the Manual Feed option in the Paper Location list box	**_Choose_**	_the Manual Feed option in the Paper Location list box_
Press	1 or S to select the Select option	**_Choose_**	_the Select option_

For additional information on the Create Paper Size/Type options, see the "Paper Size/Type" section in the WordPerfect Reference manual.

You must also specify a font orientation in the Orientation box. You can choose between a portrait or landscape font type.

Whether to choose a portrait or landscape font depends on how the envelope is fed into the printer. If the long side of the envelope is fed first, then choose a portrait font type. If the short side is fed first, then choose a landscape font type. In most cases, you would use a landscape font type.

In this example, the envelope will be fed short side first into a laser printer. To specify a landscape font type:

Press   6 or O to select the Orientation option | ***Choose***   *the Orientation option*

The Paper Orientation dialog box appears. Your screen should look like Figure 15-9.

Figure 15-9

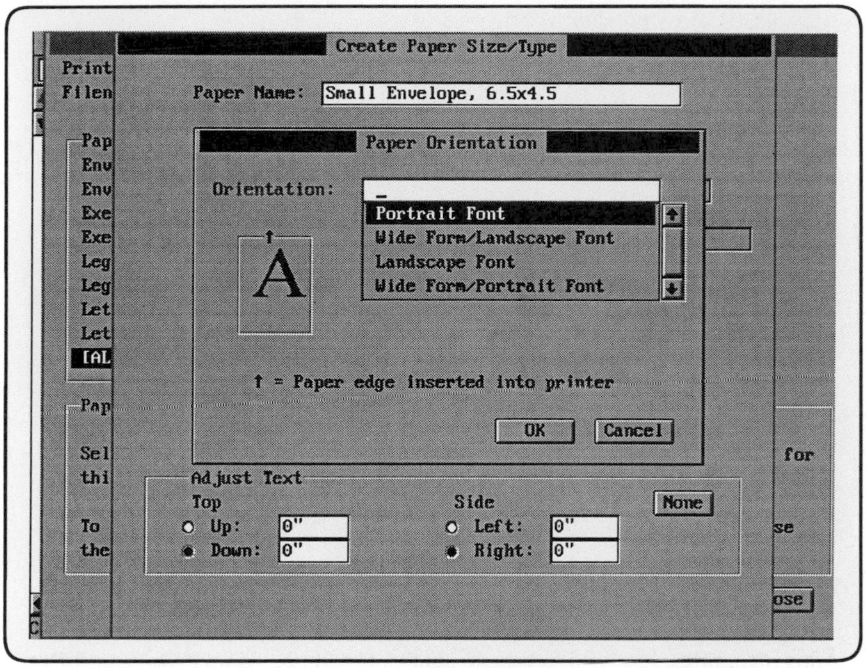

To select the Landscape Font option:

Press   L to highlight the Landscape Font option in the Orientation text box | ***Choose***   *the Landscape Font option in the Orientation text box*

Press   ⟵Enter | ***Click***   *the OK command button*

To return to the list of paper types:

Press   ⟵Enter | ***Click***   *the OK command button*

Your screen should look like Figure 15-10.

Figure 15-10

```
                              Paper Size/Type
   Printer: HP LaserJet Series II
   Filename: HP2.PRS

   ┌─Paper Name─────────────────────────────┐
     Envelope (COM 10)                    ▲
     Envelope (Monarch)                          1. Select
     Executive (Landscape)                       2. Create...
     Executive (Portrait)                        3. Edit...
     Legal (Landscape)                           4. Delete
     Legal (Portrait)                            N. Name Search
     Letter (Landscape)
     Letter (Portrait)
     Small Envelope, 6.5x4.5              ▼
   └────────────────────────────────────────┘

   ┌─Paper Details──────────────────────────────────────────┐
                              Paper Size: 6.5" X 4.5" Other
              ┌──────────┐    Paper Type: Envelope
              │    A     │    Location:   Manual Feed
              │          │    Prompt to Load: No
     Orientation:              Text Adjustments: Down 0"
     ┌──────────────────┐                        Right 0"
     │ Landscape Font   │
     └──────────────────┘
                                                    ┌───────┐
                                                    │ Close │
                                                    └───────┘
```

The new form definition that you created for small envelopes is highlighted in the list.

You can also create or select a paper size through the "LAYOUT" Button Bar.

Using an Envelope Form

When using an envelope paper size, you can use any of the WordPerfect features you would use for other documents. In this example, you will create a single envelope. However, you could create several envelopes by separating each address with a hard page break [HPg]. You could also merge envelopes by adding field codes to your envelope document and merging it with a data file.

To select the envelope definition that you created and exit the Page Format dialog box:

| **Press** | 1 or S to select the Select option | **Choose** | the Select option |
| **Press** | ⏎Enter | **Click** | the OK command button |

Now that the envelope form is selected, you can create your envelope document. When using small envelopes that are 6.5" x 4.5", the first line of the address should be 2.5" from the left edge of the envelope and 2.5" below the top edge of the envelope. This means that the left margin is set to 2.5". The right margin should be 0". The top margin should be 2.5" and the bottom margin should be set to 0".

Certain printers require a minimum margin on each side of the page. If you try to type in a value smaller than the minimum value, WordPerfect warns you that the specified value is invalid and adjusts the margins for you. For example, you cannot have a 0" margin on a laser printer. Most laser printers require a small margin on the edges of the page.

Assuming you have selected the HP LaserJet Series II printer, the minimum left margin is .24". The minimum right margin is .21". The minimum top margin is .195". The minimum bottom margin is .32". If you have selected a different printer, your margins may be different; but the basic steps remain the same.

To change the margins, press SHIFT+F8, then press 2 or M or choose the Margins option in the Format dialog box. To change the margins:

Press	2 or M to select the Margins option		*Choose*	*Layout*
Press	1 or L to select the Left Margin text box		*Choose*	*Margins*
Type	2.5		*Click*	*the Left Margin text box*
Press	[Tab⇆] to select the Right Margin text box		*Type*	*2.5*
Type	.21		*Click*	*the Right Margin text box*
Press	[Tab⇆] to select the Top Margin text box		*Type*	*.21*
Type	2.5		*Click*	*the Top Margin text box*
Press	[Tab⇆] to select the Bottom Margin text box		*Type*	*2.5*
Type	.32		*Click*	*the Bottom Margin text box*
Press	[↵Enter] three times		*Type*	*.32*
			Click	*the OK command button*

To enter the address information:

Type	Mr. Ernest Johnson		*Type*	*Mr. Ernest Johnson*
Press	[↵Enter]		*Press*	*[↵Enter]*
Type	10001 Central Parkway, Suite 3A		*Type*	*10001 Central Parkway, Suite 3A*
Press	[↵Enter]		*Press*	*[↵Enter]*
Type	New York, NY 11566		*Type*	*New York, NY 11566*

Preview the document so you can see a small envelope with the address properly placed on it. Your screen should look like Figure 15-11 if you use the Full Page option.

Figure 15-11

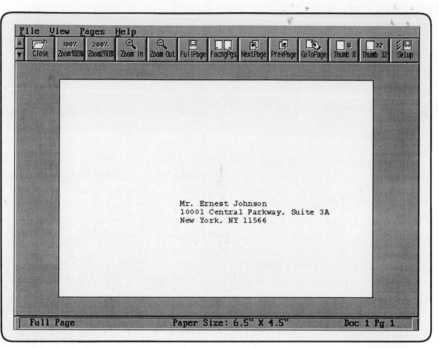

Return to the normal editing screen by pressing F7, clicking the Close button on the Button Bar, or choosing Close from the File menu.

Save the document as "JOHNSON.ENV".

Printing Envelopes

To print the envelope:

Press   Shift + F7   ***Click***   *the Print button on the Button Bar*

Press   ←Enter to select the Print   ***Click***   *the Print command button*
             command button

WordPerfect returns your document to your screen. Because you set the paper settings option to manual, your printer will not actually print the envelope until you manually feed it into the printer. Insert the envelope into the manual paper feed slot on the printer. It may take a few seconds for your printer to respond.

Once your envelope has printed, close the "JOHNSON.ENV" document.

Creating an Envelope Using a Predefined Paper Size

Because envelopes are created so often, WordPerfect provides an envelope feature that places an address in your document on an envelope. To select the envelope feature, press ALT+F12, choose Envelope from the Layout menu, or click on the Envelope button on the "WPMAIN" Button Bar.

Suppose you want to create an envelope for the "JOHNSON.LTR" document. First, open the "JOHNSON.LTR" file.

To create an envelope:

Press   Alt + F12 | *Click*   *the Envelope button on the Button Bar*

The Envelope dialog box appears. Your screen should look like Figure 15-12.

Figure 15-12

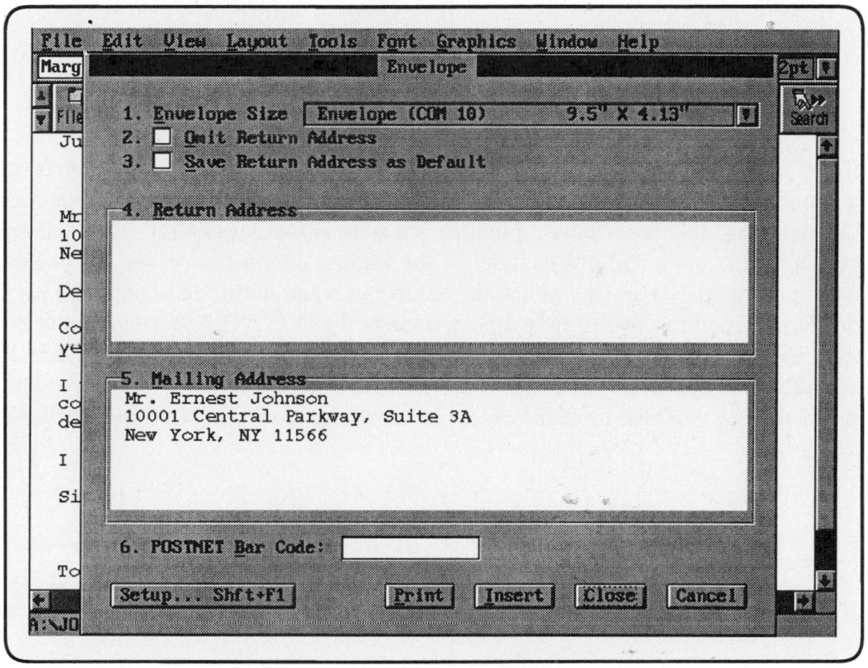

Notice the inside address from the "JOHNSON.LTR" file appears in the Mailing Address option box.
The following options are available in the WordPerfect Envelope dialog box:

The **Envelope Size** option is a drop-down list that contains all the envelope paper sizes available for the selected printer.

The **Omit Return Address** check box allows you to omit using a return address. If your return address is preprinted on your envelope, make sure this option is checked.

The **Save Return Address as Default** check box allows you to put your address in the Return Address option box by default. Every envelope you create after selecting this option will contain your return address.

The **Print** command button automatically sends the envelope to the printer.

If you would like the envelope to be included at the end of the document, click the **Insert** command button. If you do not click this command button, the envelope will be deleted after it is printed.

The **POSTNET Bar Code** text box allows you to type in the Bar Code for this letter. You can also press SHIFT+F1 or click the Setup command button to change the default bar code setting. You can choose for WordPerfect to read the zip code in the address and generate a POSTNET bar code automatically. The default setting is not to include a bar code.

To select the standard business envelope paper size:

| **Press** | 1 or E to select the Envelope Size drop-down list button | *Click* | *the Envelope Size drop-down list button* |
| **Press** | `←Enter` to select the Envelope (COM 10) 9.5" x 4.13" option | *Double-click* | *the Envelope (COM 10) 9.5" x 4.13" option* |

To print the envelope:

| **Press** | P to select the Print command button | *Click* | *the Print command button* |

Using a POSTNET Bar Code

WordPerfect offers you the option of using bar codes on your envelopes and in your text. By using a POSTNET Bar Code, you can speed mail sorting, increase delivery accuracy, and decrease your own postage costs. You can use this feature by typing the zip code in the POSTNET Bar Code text box. Then WordPerfect creates the bar code and places it below the address on your envelope. If you want to always use bar codes, you can press SHIFT+F1 or click the Setup command button to change the bar code settings. By default, WordPerfect requires you to type the zip code in the POSTNET Bar Code text box. However, you can choose to have the bar code automatically created. If you choose the Automatically Create Bar Code option, WordPerfect will create the bar code from the mailing address in your document. In the Envelope Setup dialog box, you also have the option of removing the POSTNET Bar Code option from the Envelope dialog box.

To create an envelope:

| **Press** | `Alt`+`F12` | *Click* | *the Envelope button on the Button Bar* |

To place a bar code on your envelope:

Press	6 or B to select the POSTNET Bar Code text box	*Click*	*in the POSTNET Bar Code text box*
Type	11566	*Type*	*11566*
Press	`←Enter`	*Double-click*	*in the POSTNET Bar Code text box*

So that the bar code will be created automatically the next time you use the Envelope button, you need to change the POSTNET Bar Code setup options.

To change the Setup options:

| **Press** | `Shift`+`F1` to select the Setup command button | *Click* | *the Setup command button* |

The Envelope Setup dialog box appears. Your screen should look like Figure 15-13.

Figure 15-13

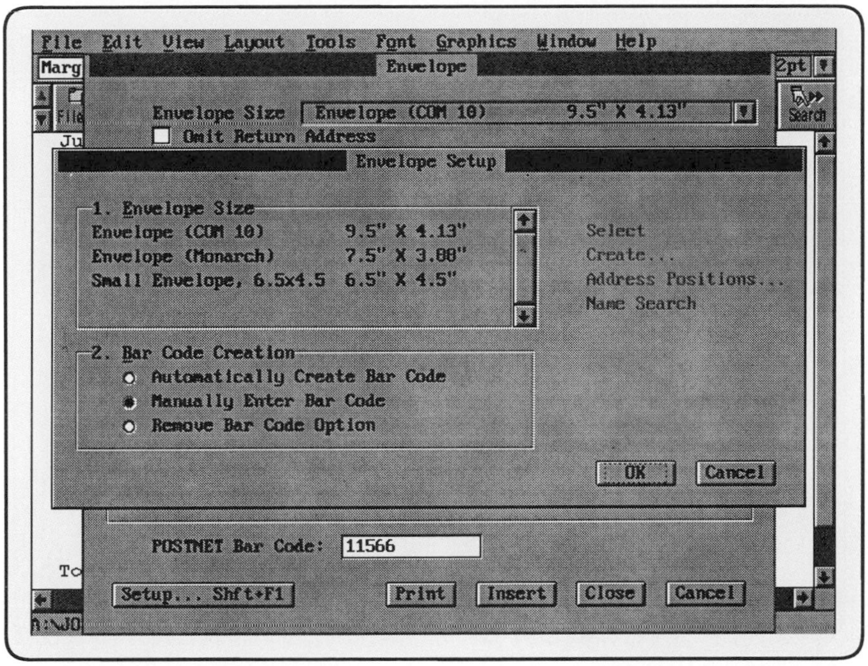

To change the Bar Code Creation options:

Press	2 or B to select the Bar Code Creation option box	*Choose*	*the Bar Code Creation option box*
Press	1 or A to select the Automatically Create Bar Code option button	*Click*	*the Automatically Create Bar Code option button*
Press	⏎Enter	*Click*	*the OK command button*

To insert the envelope into the document:

Press	⏎Enter to select the Insert command button	*Click*	*the Insert command button*

The envelope is put on a page by itself at the end of your letter. Your screen should look like Figure 15-14.

Figure 15-14

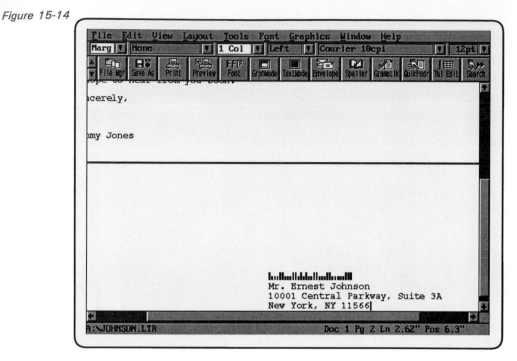

Close the document without saving changes.

■ LABELS

If you need to print many addresses for envelopes, it is quicker to print them on labels. Dot matrix printers use labels that pass through on a tractor feed. Laser printers use labels on sheets that enter the printer through the sheet feeder. If you use a laser printer, be sure to buy labels specifically made for laser printers. Using labels made for a copier in a laser printer may damage your printer.

Labels come in many different sizes. You must tell WordPerfect when it is printing with paper that is not standard 8.5" x 11" paper. In this section, creating a label paper type with a macro is demonstrated.

Creating a Label Paper Type

Label paper types require many changes in the Paper Size/Type feature. Because labels are difficult to create manually, WordPerfect provides several paper sizes already created from which to select the type of label you are using.

To select a label paper type:

Press	Shift + F8	*Choose*	*Layout*
Press	3 or P to select the Page option	*Choose*	*Page*
Press	5 or L to select the Labels option in the Paper Sizes option box	*Choose*	*the Labels option in the Paper Sizes option box*

The Labels dialog box appears. Your screen should look like Figure 15-15.

Figure 15-15

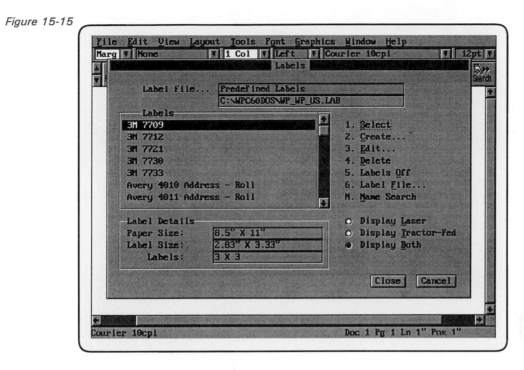

This dialog box provides you with a definition for most Avery and 3M brand labels. To select a label paper type, highlight the paper type using the arrow keys and press a 1 or S to select the paper type, or click on the paper type and choose the select option.

To select the Avery label paper type, number 5161:

Press	⬇ to highlight the Avery 5161 Address paper type	*Click*	*the down arrow button in the vertical scroll bar until you can see the Avery 5161 Address paper type*
Press	1 or S to select the Select option	*Click*	*the Avery 5161 paper type*
		Choose	*the Select option*

The Labels Printer Info dialog box appears. Your screen should look like Figure 15-16.

Figure 15-16

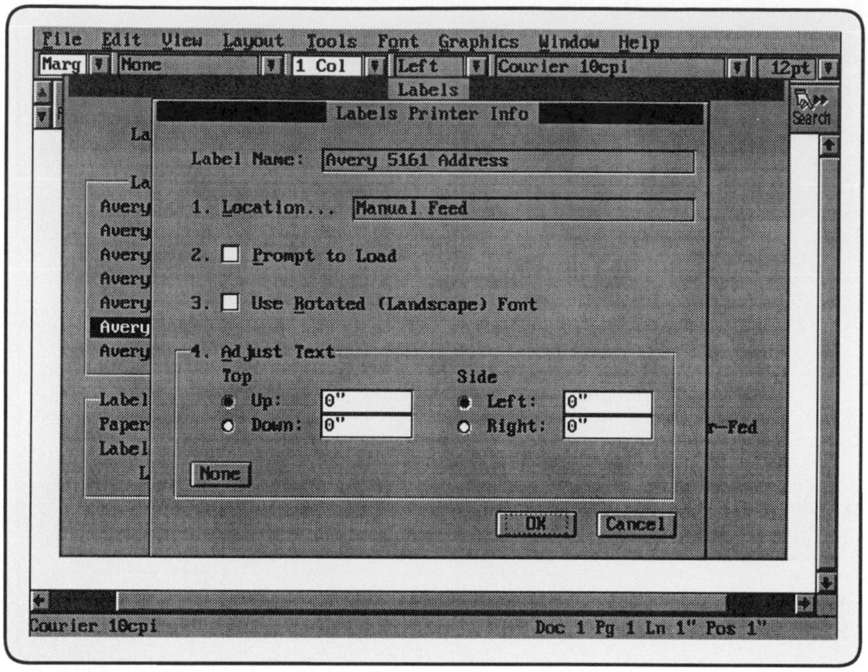

If your labels are continuous feed, you will need to change your paper location. To use continuous feed labels:

Press	1 or L to select the Location option	***Choose***	*the Location option*
Press	[↑] to highlight the Continuous option in the Paper Location list box	***Click***	*on the Continuous option in the Paper Location list box*
Press	1 or S to select the Select option	***Choose***	*the Select option*

To accept the changes in the Labels Printer Info dialog box:

| **Press** | [←Enter] | ***Click*** | *the OK command button* |

To select the new page format and return to the document:

| **Press** | [←Enter] twice | ***Click*** | *the OK command button* |

Using a Label Paper Type

When using a label paper type, you can use any of the WordPerfect features you would use in other documents. You could create a single label or create several labels by separating each address with a hard page break [HPg]. In this example, you will merge the labels with the data file "ADDRESS.DTA" by adding field codes to your labels document.

Notice that the "Ln" and "Pos" indicators in the status bar have changed to reflect the margins defined in the labels paper type.

You are now ready to enter the field merge codes into the form file that you are creating. You will use the "ADDRESS.DTA" document created in Chapter 13 as the data file. The fields in "ADDRESS.DTA" are Title, First, Last, Company, and Address.

To enter the "Title" field merge code into the form file:

Press	Shift + F9		**Choose**	Tools
Press	1 or F to select the Form option button		**Choose**	Merge
Press	1 or F to select the Field option		**Choose**	Define
Type	Title		**Click**	the Form option button
Press	↵Enter		**Choose**	the Field option
			Type	Title
			Click	the OK command button

To enter the "First" field merge code into the form file:

Press	Spacebar		**Press**	Spacebar
Press	Shift + F9		**Choose**	Tools
Press	1 or F to select the Field option		**Choose**	Merge
Type	First		**Choose**	Define
Press	↵Enter		**Choose**	the Field option
			Type	First
			Click	the OK command button

To enter the "Last" field merge code:

Press	Spacebar		**Press**	Spacebar
Press	Shift + F9		**Choose**	Tools
Press	1 or F to select the Field option		**Choose**	Merge
Type	Last		**Choose**	Define
Press	↵Enter		**Choose**	the Field option
			Type	Last
			Click	the OK command button

To enter the "Company" field merge code on a new line and avoid blank lines in the document if the Company field is empty:

Press	↵Enter		**Press**	↵Enter
Press	Shift + F9		**Choose**	Tools
Press	1 or F to select the Field option		**Choose**	Merge
Type	Company?		**Choose**	Define
Press	↵Enter		**Choose**	the Field option

Type	*Company?*
Click	*the OK command button*

To enter the "Address" field on a new line:

Press	⏎Enter
Press	Shift + F9
Press	1 or F to select the Field option
Type	Address
Press	⏎Enter

Press	⏎Enter
Choose	Tools
Choose	Merge
Choose	Define
Choose	the Field option
Type	Address
Click	the OK command button

The top part of your screen should look like Figure 15-17.

Figure 15-17

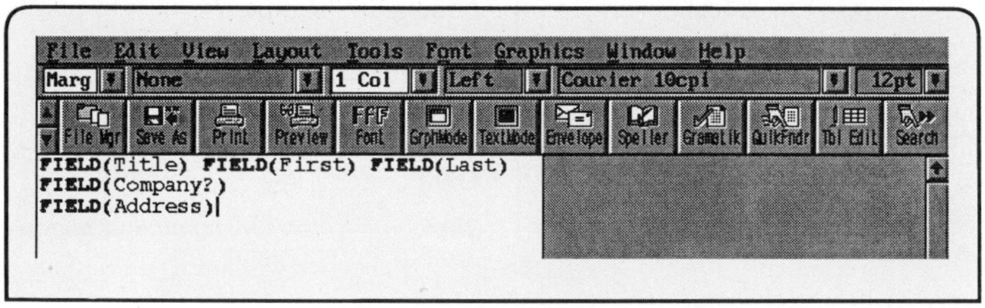

Save the document as "LABEL.FRM". Close the document.

Merge the "LABEL.FRM" (Form file) and "ADDRESS.DTA" (Data file) files. Move the cursor to the beginning of the document.

The top part of your screen should look like Figure 15-18.

Figure 15-18

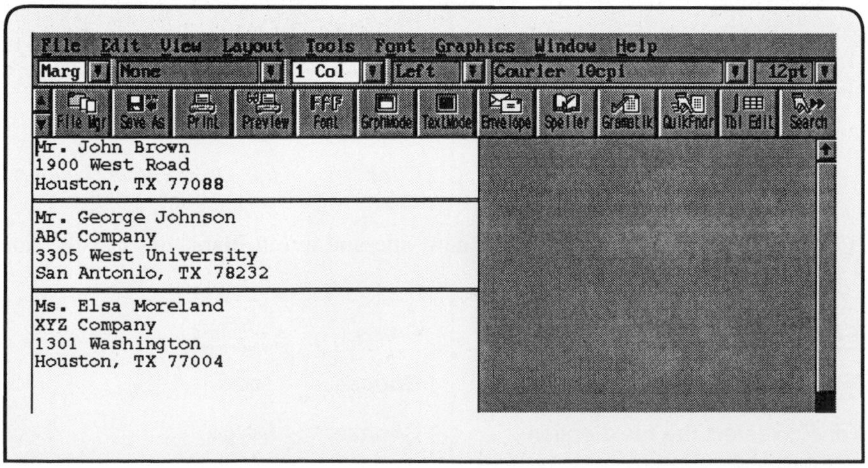

A hard page break is used to separate each address label. When the cursor is moved from one label to another, the page number in the status bar changes.

Use the Print Preview feature to see the layout of the labels on the page. Select the 100% option. The top part of your screen should look like Figure 15-19.

Figure 15-19

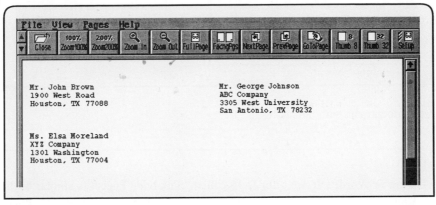

Return to the normal editing screen by pressing F7, clicking the Close button on the Button Bar, or choosing Close from the File menu.

If you wanted to insert a bar code at the end of the label for Mr. John Brown, you could use the Bar Code command in the text.

To place a bar code in the first label:

| **Press** | the arrow keys to place the cursor at the end of the zip code in the first label | *Click* | *at the end of the zip code in the first label* |

The top part of your screen should look like Figure 15-20.

Figure 15-20

The top part of your screen should look like Figure 15-20.

To insert the bar code command:

Press	⏎Enter	*Press*	*⏎Enter*
Press	Shift + F8	*Choose*	*Layout*
Press	7 or O to select the Other option	*Choose*	*Other*
Press	8 or R to select the Bar Code option	*Choose*	*the Bar Code option*
Type	77088	*Type*	*77088*
Press	⏎Enter	*Click*	*the OK command button*

The top part of your screen should look like Figure 15-21.

Figure 15-21

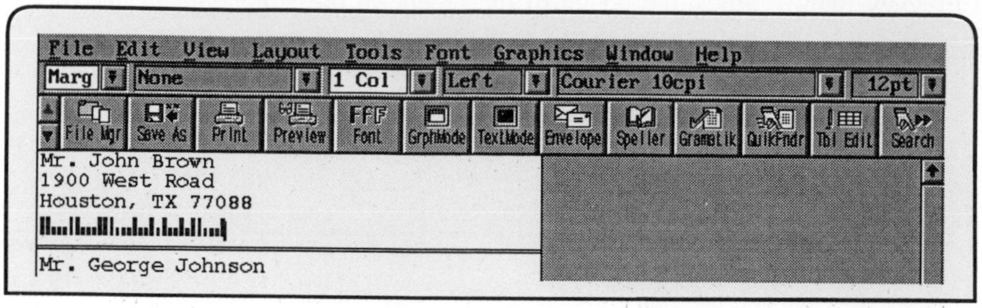

Close the merged document without saving it.

User Tip

A new feature in WordPerfect 6.0 for DOS called "Subdivide Page," is similar to the Labels feature. Using the Subdivide Page feature, you can subdivide a normal sheet of paper into sections. You can also create *logical* pages on one *physical* page.

To use the Subdivide Page feature, press SHIFT+F8, then press 3 or P to select the Page option. Press 6 or A to select the Subdivide Page option. You may also choose Page from the Layout menu, and then select Subdivide Page.

You may define the desired number of rows and columns.

The page remains subdivided until you turn off the feature by using the same keystrokes and selecting the Off command button.

For more information on this topic, see the "Subdivide Page" section in the WordPerfect Reference manual.

EXERCISE 1

INSTRUCTIONS: Define the following concepts:

1. Paper Size/Type feature _____

    _____

2. POSTNET Bar Code _____

    _____

3. Envelope size option _____

    _____

4. Landscape font _____

    _____

5. Portrait font _____

    _____

EXERCISE 2

INSTRUCTIONS: Circle T if the statement is true and F if the statement is false.

T   F   1.   The Paper Size/Type feature allows you to create paper types for special sizes of paper and to handle special printer instructions.

T   F   2.   A Manual Feed location setting in the Create Paper Size/Type dialog box tells WordPerfect that you are feeding the paper into the printer by hand.

T   F   3.   A Landscape font option causes the text to be printed across the length of the page.

T   F   4.   Some printers may not be able to print landscape fonts if they do not contain fonts for landscape printing.

T   F   5.   Once you have created a paper type, you cannot edit it. You must delete the form, then add a new one.

T   F   6.   You cannot use envelopes or labels to create form files for a merge document.

EXERCISE 3

INSTRUCTIONS:
1.   Create a document using the 9.5" x 4.13" standard business envelopes paper type.
2.   The address should start 4.5" from the left edge of the envelope and 2" from the top edge of the envelope.
3.   Create an envelope for each of the following addresses. Separate each address with a hard page break.
4.   Preview the envelopes.
5.   Print the envelopes.
6.   Save the document as "CH15EX03".
7.   Close the document.

```
Ms. Felice Avila              Mrs. Audree Walsh
Zurich Products Company       Sunrise Breakfast Company
615 West Main Street          1045 Collins Avenue
Houston, TX 77013             Miami, FL 33152

Mr. Ray Devery                Dr. Paul Thompson
Liberty Foundation            Super Visions Corporation
234 Park Avenue               8990 Roselle Road
New York, NY 10001            Schaumburg, IL 60172

Ms. Joan Young
Publications Press
4515 Harbor Lane
Saginaw, MI 48605
```

EXERCISE 4

INSTRUCTIONS:

1. Create the following mailing list as a data file. Save the file using the name "CH15EX04.DTA".
2. Create a form file using the small envelope paper type (6.5" x 3.5") and the field names in the data file "CH15EX04.DTA".
3. The address should start 3" from the left edge of the envelope and 2" from the top edge of the envelope.
4. Save the file as "CH15EX04.FRM". Close the document.
5. Merge the two documents.
6. Preview the merge document.
7. Print the Murphy envelope only.
8. Save the merge document in a file using the name "CH15EX04.ENV".
9. Close the document.

```
Ms. Gerry Goncher          Ms. Grace Morgan
Traffic Programmer         Lab Assistant
Semper Corporation         Computer Wizards
888 West Wayne             6321 North Route 37
Omaha, NB 66108            Louisville, KY 40201

Mr. Jack Carroll           Ms. Debbie Murphy
Finer Lawn Products        International Products
2288 North Holland         1401 Frontage Road
Concord, NH 03301          New Orleans, LA 70113
```

EXERCISE 5

INSTRUCTIONS:

1. Create the following mailing list as a data file. Save the file using the name "CH15EX05.DTA". Close the document.
2. Merge the mailing list with a form file for standard business envelopes. The name of the form file should be "CH15EX05.FRM".
3. Preview the merge document.
4. Print the envelopes using plain paper inserted manually.
5. Save the merge document in a file using the name "CH15EX05.ENV".
6. Close the document.

```
Mr. Larry Haffner                Ms. Dolores Samson
247 Einstein Street              620 Braintree Lane
Anchorage, AK 99502              Brookline, MA 02146

Mr. William Neumann              Mr. Michael Oester
Engineering and Maintenance      Canonsburg Chemical Company
Absolute Corporation             639 Newton Boulevard
135 Pecos Circle Drive           Canonsburg, PA 15317
Escanaba, MI 49829
```

EXERCISE 6

INSTRUCTIONS: 1. Create a form file using the 3M 7730 label paper type to merge with "CH15EX04.DTA". The form file name should be "CH15EX06.FRM".
2. Close the document.
3. Merge the documents to create labels.
4. Preview the document.
5. Print the labels.
6. Do not save the merge document.

EXERCISE 7

INSTRUCTIONS: 1. Create the following mailing list as a data file using the name "CH15EX07.DTA". Close the document.
2. Create a form file with the following letter. The name of the form file should be "CH15EX07.FRM". Close the document.
3. Merge the two documents.
4. Print the merged letters.
5. Save the merged letters in a file using the name "CH15EX07.LTR".
6. Create a form file for the addresses using the 3M 7730 Label paper type. Save the file as "CH15EX07.LAB". Close the document.
7. Merge the labels and the data file. Print the labels on a sheet of paper.
8. Close the document.

```
Ms. Faith Anderson              Mr. Stewart Straka
635 Bothwell Drive              Personnel Specialist
Tuscaloosa, AZ 35401            Moraine Empire Steel
                                2278 W. Highland Avenue
                                Jackson, MS 39205


Mr. William Mahaffey            Mr. Kent Barron
University Press                Personnel Consultant
Parkland University             234 West Park Avenue
Iron Mountain, MI 49801         Cleveland, OH 44101
```

Current date

Inside Address

Dear (title and last name):

The Executive Board of the Nationwide Personnel Association will have its monthly meeting at Iron Mountain, Michigan. As usual the meeting will be held the last weekend of the month.

I hope that you have received the material dealing with "Termination." We all have problems when someone is fired. One of the outcomes of our meeting will be to develop a seminar to be presented around the country.

Bring your ideas for someone who could conduct this seminar. We also need to develop a marketing plan for the seminar.

See you at the end of the month.

Very truly yours,

Martin Q. Ryan
President N.P.A.

xx

EXERCISE 8

INSTRUCTIONS:

1. You have purchased a box of 3M labels. The product number is 7721. The labels are page labels that are continuously fed into the printer.
2. Using the new label type, create a form file for the addresses in the "CH15EX07.DTA" file. Save the form file as "CH15EX08.FRM". Close the document.
3. Merge the two documents.
4. Preview the merged labels.
5. Print the labels on a sheet of paper.
6. Save the merged labels in a file using the name "CH15EX08.LAB". Close the document.

CHAPTER SIXTEEN

SORTING AND SELECTING

OBJECTIVES

In this chapter, you will learn to:
- Sort by lines
- Sort with more than one key
- Sort a portion of a document
- Sort paragraphs
- Sort a merge data file
- Select specific records from a merge data file

■ CHAPTER OVERVIEW

With the Sort feature, you can organize names, dates, and numbers into alphabetical or numerical order. The data may appear in lines or paragraphs in a WordPerfect document. You can also sort a merge data file or part of a document. This chapter covers sorting lines and paragraphs in a document, portions of a document, and merge data files.

You can also use the Sort feature to select records from a list of items or a merge data file. This chapter illustrates the process for selecting records using the Sort feature.

Create the document in Figure 16-1. This document contains the last name, first name, city, state, and zip code of several individuals. Before entering the text, delete all existing tabs. Then set left tabs at 2", 3.5", 5", and 6". When performing a sort, it is important to have only one TAB separating each column of data.

Figure 16-1

Adams	Joseph	New York	NY	10014
Konkel	Joel	Santa Cruz	CA	12100
Aaron	Sandra	San Antonio	TX	78221
Adams	Jennifer	New York	NY	10061
Fernandez	Jose	Miami	FL	33471
Nguyen	Alfred	San Antonio	TX	78201
Kainer	Donna	Newark	NJ	90122
Adams	Charles	San Antonio	TX	78216
Cernosky	Elena	Miami	FL	33201
Mogab	John	New York	NY	10042
Travis	Doug	New Haven	CT	50088
Chesser	Linda	San Jose	CA	12001
Aguilar	Maria	Provo	UT	01155

Save the document as "COLUMN.SRT". You should *always save* your document before sorting.

■ LINE SORT

Suppose you want to sort the "COLUMN.SRT" document by city. Each horizontal line represents a record. When the file is sorted, all data appearing on a line will stay together.

To enter the Sorting feature:

Press   Ctrl + F9   **Choose**   *Tools*

Press   2 or S to select the Sort option   **Choose**   *Sort*

The Sort (Source and Destination) dialog box appears. Your screen should look like Figure 16-2.

Figure 16-2

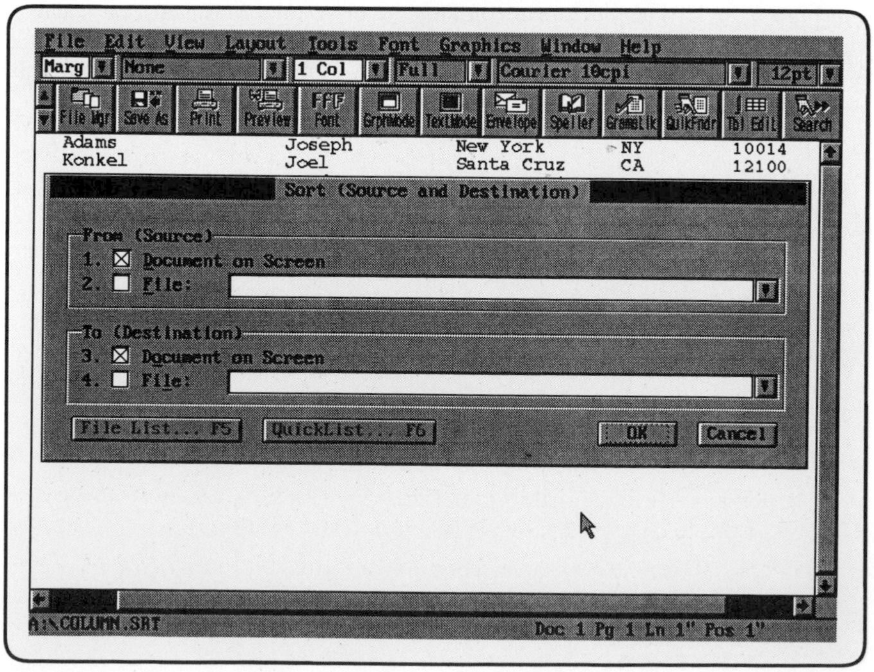

You may choose to sort the document appearing on the screen or you can sort a document on a disk. Most often, you will choose to sort the document on the screen. Please note in Figure 16-2 that an X appears in the #1 and #3 check boxes. This means that the file to be sorted is presently on the screen and that the sorted output data should also be displayed on the screen.

To accept these defaults:

Press   `←Enter` | ***Click***   the OK command button

The Sort dialog box appears on the screen. Your screen should look like Figure 16-3.

Figure 16-3

Adams	Joseph	New York	NY	10014
Konkel	Joel	Santa Cruz	CA	12100
Aaron	Sandra	San Antonio	TX	78221
Adams	Jennifer	New York	NY	10061
Fernandez	Jose	Miami	FL	33471
Nguyen	Alfred	San Antonio	TX	78201
Kainer	Donna	Newark	NJ	90122
Adams	Charles	San Antonio	TX	78216
Cernosky	Elena	Miami	FL	33201
Mogab	John	New York	NY	10042
Travis	Doug	New Haven	CT	50088
Chesser	Linda	San Jose	CA	12001
Aguilar	Maria	Provo	UT	01155

A:\COLUMN.SRT   Doc 1 Pg 1 Ln 2.67" Pos 6.2"

Sort

1. Record Type [Line   ▲▼]

2. Sort Keys (Sort Priority)   Key Type Ord Field   Word
                                    Add   1   Alpha ↑   1   1
                                    Edit
                                    Delete
                                    Insert

3. Select Records: [   ]
4. ☐ Select Without Sorting
5. ☐ Sort Uppercase First   [Perform Action] [View] [Close] [Cancel]

By default, the Record Type default is the Line option. Because the data are separated by tabs and there are no blank lines between each record, you can use the Line option to sort the document. If the data are separated by spaces or commas and blank lines appear between each record, use the paragraph option to sort the document. The third alternative for a Record Type is called "Merge Data File". Both paragraph sorting and merge sorting are discussed in greater detail later in this chapter. You can also sort a segment of a document by blocking part of the document before choosing the Sort feature.

Keys are fields, words, or phrases by which a document is sorted. For example, suppose you want to sort a document by the city in which people live. The sort key is whatever column or field contains the city names.

When sorting, you must create a key that identifies the field that is to be sorted, like *city* in the example above. This is done by counting the fields from left to right. In the current document, *city* is the third column. Thus, it is field 3. This number is entered into the Field box in the Sort Keys box. **In a Line Sort, fields must be separated by single tabs.**

Also associated with each key definition is the type of data appearing in the key field. Text in the field can be alphanumeric (containing letters and numbers) or numeric (only numbers).

The location of a word in the key field is also needed for the sort. If the desired field contains more than one word, then you must select one of those words by which to sort the data. This number is positive if you count from left to right in the field. The number is negative if you count from right to left, from the end of the field to the beginning. **In a Line Sort, words are separated by spaces**.

If you would like to sort by date, you treat each part of the date as a separate word in a field. For the sort to work properly, the parts of the date must be separated by slashes (1/1/93) or dashes (1-1-93). To insert the dash character, it is not enough to simply press the hyphen on the keyboard. You must use a "Hard hyphen" created by pressing HOME, then the hyphen on the keyboard. **If the date is separated by pressing just the - key, WordPerfect will not recognize the numbers as a date**.

In the "COLUMN.SRT" document, there are five fields: last name, first name, city, state abbreviation, and zip code. Each field has one or two words in it. All of the fields are alphanumeric (can contain alphabetic or numeric characters), except for the zip code, which is numeric. Note that because the zip codes are all five digits, you can consider the zip code an alphanumeric field if you so desire. If the numeric values varied in length, such as dollar amounts, you would need to use the numeric type to sort them properly.

The Select Records option in the Sort dialog box lets you define a subset of the document to be sorted. This option is covered later in this chapter.

The default Sort Priority for the Sort feature shows that the Key 1 criteria are: alphabetical, in ascending order, first field, and first word. This setting appears to the right of the second option in the Sort dialog box. Thus, with no change to the sorting priority, the data will be sorted according to the last names of the individuals.

Suppose you want to sort the "COLUMN.SRT" document by city only.

To change Key 1 to sort by city:

Press	2 or K to select the Sort Keys option	**Choose**	*the Sort Keys option*
Press	2 or E to select the Edit option	**Choose**	*the Edit option*

The Edit Sort Key dialog box appears. Your screen should look like Figure 16-4.

Figure 16-4

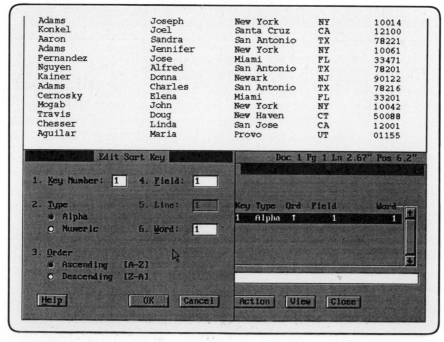

The Key Number is 1. This will not be changed. It simply means that it is the first level criterion. The Type is Alpha and does not need to be changed. The Order is Ascending and does not need to be changed.

To change the Field to identify the column containing city names, which is the third field in the document:

Press	4 or F to select the Field text box		***Click***	*on the number in the Field text box*
Type	3		***Type***	*3*
Press	⏎Enter		***Double-click***	*in the Field text box*

You do not need to change the Line or Word setting, because you will only sort by the first word in the city field. Later in this chapter, the use of the Line option will be discussed.

Your screen should look like Figure 16-5.

Figure 16-5

```
Adams       Joseph      New York     NY    10014
Konkel      Joel        Santa Cruz   CA    12100
Aaron       Sandra      San Antonio  TX    78221
Adams       Jennifer    New York     NY    10061
Fernandez   Jose        Miami        FL    33471
Nguyen      Alfred      San Antonio  TX    78201
Kainer      Donna       Newark       NJ    90122
Adams       Charles     San Antonio  TX    78216
Cernosky    Elena       Miami        FL    33201
Mogab       John        New York     NY    10042
Travis      Doug        New Haven    CT    50088
Chesser     Linda       San Jose     CA    12001
Aguilar     Maria       Provo        UT    01155
```

```
                  Edit Sort Key                    Doc 1 Pg 1 Ln 2.67" Pos 6.2"

1. Key Number:  1    4. Field:  3

2. Type              5. Line:   1        Key Type Ord  Field       Word
   ● Alpha                                1  Alpha  ↑    1           1
   ○ Numeric         6. Word:   1

3. Order
   ● Ascending  [A-Z]
   ○ Descending [Z-A]

   [Help]          [ OK ]  [Cancel]     [Action] [View] [Close]
```

To return to the Sort dialog box:

Press	⏎Enter to select the OK command button		***Click***	*the OK command button*

To perform the sorting procedure:

Press	Tab⇄ twice to select the Perform Action command button		***Click***	*the Perform Action command button*
Press	⏎Enter			

Briefly, a message appears on the screen indicating how many records are being examined. In a few seconds, your screen should look like Figure 16-6.

Figure 16-6

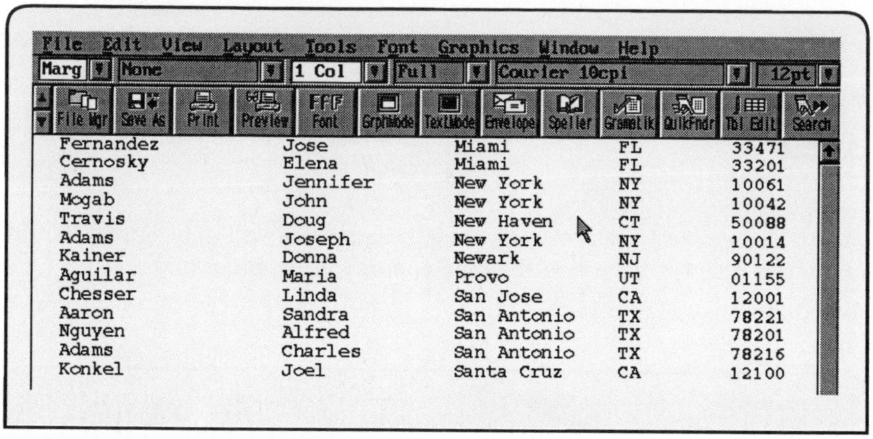

Notice that the third column, which is the city, is now in alphabetical order by the first word only. However, problems exist when the city is two words. Notice that the cities beginning with "New" and "San" are not in the correct order. This problem is solved in the next section.

■ SORTING WITH MORE THAN ONE KEY

There are times when you need to sort a document using more than one key. The example in the previous section where the document was sorted by city is such a case. Because the names of some cities contain more than one word, two keys must be defined to sort the document. The first key should sort by the first word in the city field, and the second key should sort by the second word.

To sort the "COLUMN.SRT" document by the first and then the second words of the city:

Press	Ctrl + F9		**Choose**	Tools
Press	2 or S to select the Sort option		**Choose**	Sort
Press	↵Enter		**Click**	the OK command button

Notice the previous Sort Priority. WordPerfect will retain previous selections until you exit the software.

To add a second level key:

Press	2 or K to select the Sort Keys option		**Choose**	the Sort Keys option
Press	1 or A to select the Add option		**Choose**	the Add option

In the Edit Sort Key dialog box, a 2 appears in the Key Number text box.

To define Key 2 as the second word of the city field:

Press	4 or F to select the Field text box		**Click**	on the number in the Field text box
Type	3		**Type**	3
Press	↵Enter		**Double-click**	on the Field text box

Press	6 or W to select the Word text box	*Click*	*on the number in the Word text box*
Type	2	*Type*	*2*
Press	⏎Enter twice	*Click*	*the OK command button*

Your screen should look like Figure 16-7.

Figure 16-7

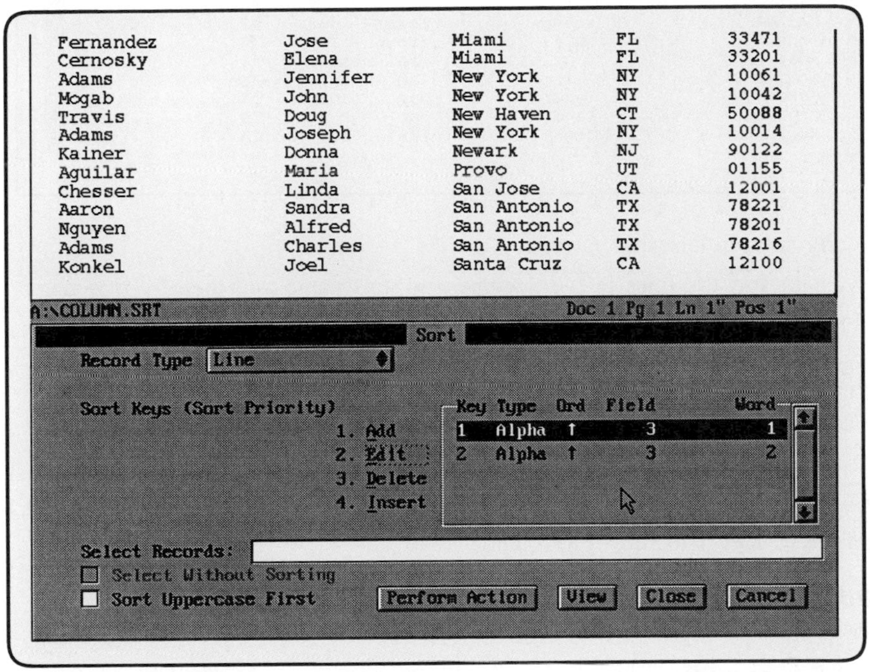

To begin the sort process:

| **Press** | Tab⇥ twice to select the Perform Action command button | *Click* | *the Perform Action command button* |
| **Press** | ⏎Enter | | |

The top part of your screen should look like Figure 16-8.

Figure 16-8

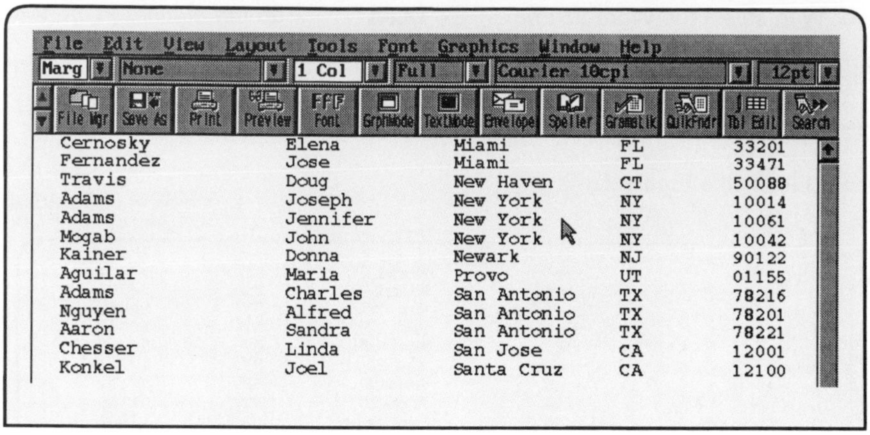

Notice that the city column is sorted correctly.

Suppose you want to sort the lines in the document by last name and then by first name. To sort the "COLUMN.SRT" document by last name and then first name:

Press	Ctrl + F9	*Choose*	*Tools*
Press	2 or S to select the Sort option	*Choose*	*Sort*
Press	←Enter	*Click*	*the OK command button*

To change the field of Key 1 to sort by last name (field 1):

Press	2 or K to select the Sort Keys option	*Choose*	*the Sort Keys option*
Press	2 or E to select the Edit option	*Choose*	*the Edit option*
Press	4 or F to select the Field text box	*Click*	*on the number in the Field text box*
Type	1	*Type*	*1*
Press	←Enter twice	*Double-click*	*in the Field text box*
		Click	*the OK command button*

To change the field of Key 2 to sort by first name (field 2):

Press	↓ to highlight the Key 2 criteria	*Click*	*on the Key 2 criteria*
Press	2 or E to select the Edit option	*Choose*	*the Edit option*
Press	4 or F to select the Field text box	*Click*	*on the number in the Field text box*
Type	2	*Type*	*2*
Press	←Enter	*Double-click*	*in the Field text box*
Press	6 or W to select the Word text box	*Click*	*on the number in the Word text box*
Type	1	*Type*	*1*
Press	←Enter twice	*Click*	*the OK command button*

Type	1		*Type*	*1*
Press	⏎Enter twice		*Click*	*the OK command button*

Your screen should look like Figure 16-9.

Figure 16-9

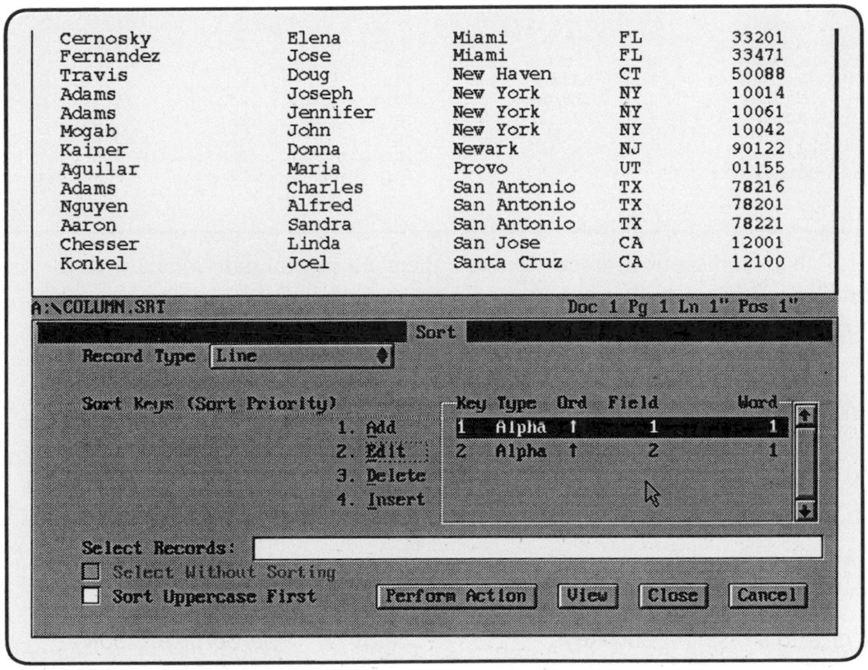

To begin the sort process:

Press	Tab⇆ twice to select the Perform Action command button		*Click*	*the Perform Action command button*
Press	⏎Enter			

The top part of your screen should look like Figure 16-10.

Figure 16-10

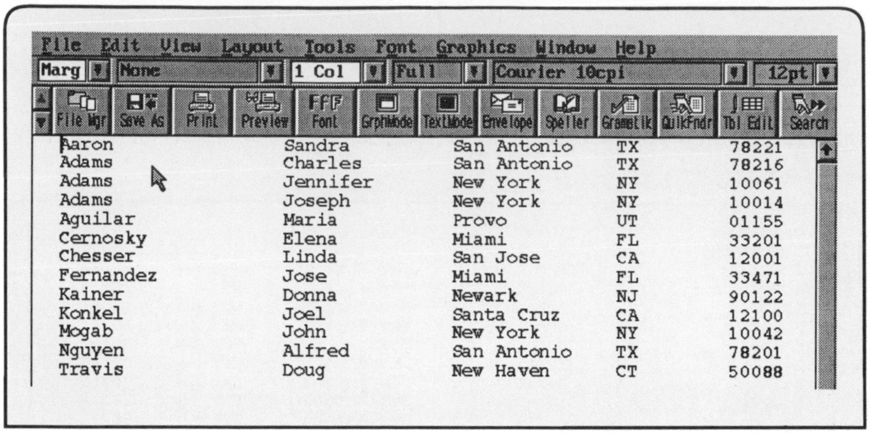

Notice that field 1 is in alphabetical order. Because there are several individuals with the same last name, "Adams," WordPerfect then alphabetized by first name, which is field 2.

Save your document using the name "COLUMN2.SRT".

■ SORTING A PORTION OF A DOCUMENT

You can also sort a portion or subset of a document by highlighting the records before choosing the Sort feature. The following example shows this process.

Suppose you want to sort the addresses for those individuals whose last names begin with "A" in ascending order by zip code.

To highlight those individuals whose last names begin with "A":

| **Move** | the cursor before the "A" in "Aaron" | *Click* | *before the "A" in "Aaron"* |
| **Highlight** | the first five records | *Select* | *the first five records* |

The top part of your screen should look like Figure 16-11.

Figure 16-11

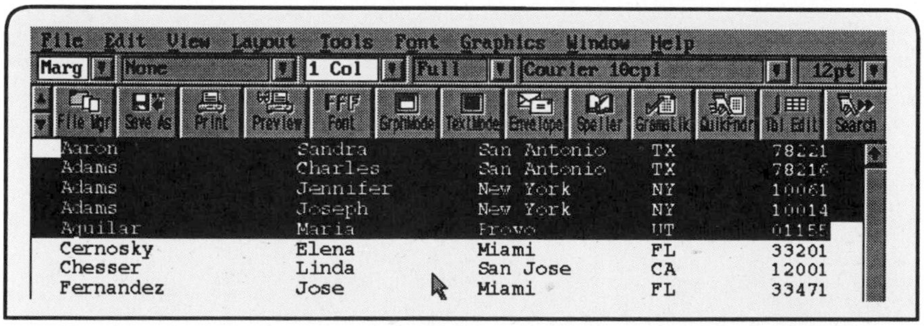

To sort the selected lines in ascending order by zip code:

| **Press** | Ctrl + F9 | *Choose* | *Tools* |
| | | *Choose* | *Sort* |

WordPerfect knows that you are entering the Sorting process and immediately displays the selected records and the Sort dialog box. Two sort keys appear in the Sort Keys box. For this sort, only one key is needed. The Delete option deletes a sort key. In this example, Key 2 is the unnecessary sort key.

To delete the second sort key:

Press	2 or K to select the Sort Keys option	*Click*	*on the Key 2 criteria to select them*
Press	⬇ to highlight Key 2	*Choose*	*the Delete option*
Press	3 or D to select the Delete option		

To change the type of Key 1 to numeric:

Press	2 or E to select the Edit option	*Choose*	*the Edit option*
Press	2 or T to select the Type options	*Click*	*the Numeric option button in the Type option*
Press	2 or N to select the Numeric option button		

To change the field of Key 1 to sort by zip code, which is the fifth field:

Press	4 or F to select the Field text box	*Click*	*on the number in the Field text box*
Type	5	*Type*	*5*
Press	⏎Enter twice	*Click*	*the OK command button*

Your screen should look like Figure 16-12.

Figure 16-12

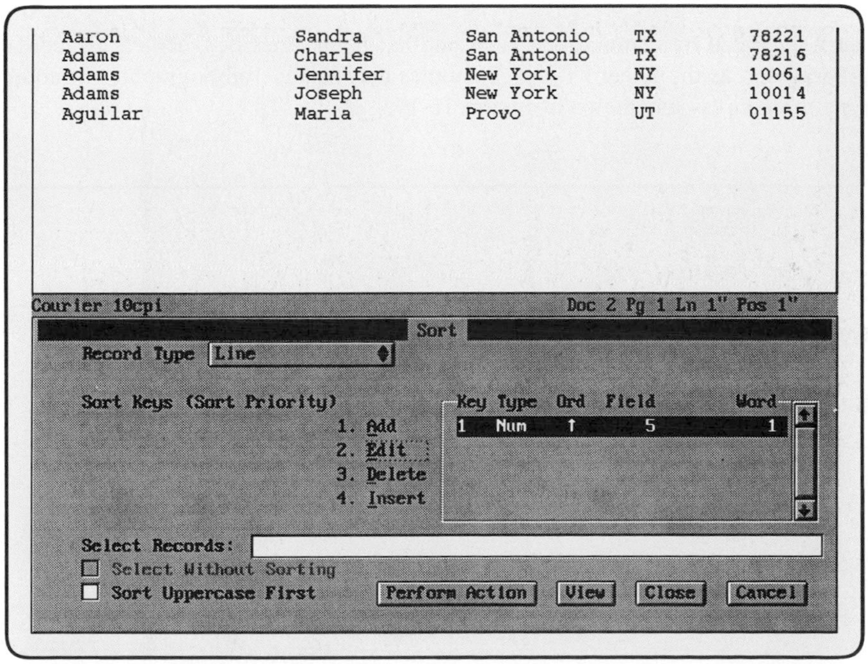

```
Aaron          Sandra         San Antonio    TX      78221
Adams          Charles        San Antonio    TX      78216
Adams          Jennifer       New York       NY      10061
Adams          Joseph         New York       NY      10014
Aguilar        Maria          Provo          UT      01155




Courier 10cpi                              Doc 2 Pg 1 Ln 1" Pos 1"
                                    Sort
        Record Type  Line        ↕

        Sort Keys (Sort Priority)    Key Type  Ord  Field      Word
                         1. Add      1  Num     ↑      5          1
                         2. Edit
                         3. Delete
                         4. Insert

        Select Records:
        ☐ Select Without Sorting
        ☐ Sort Uppercase First    Perform Action  View  Close  Cancel
```

To begin the sort process:

Press   Tab twice to select the Perform   ***Click***   *the Perform Action command*
                 Action command button   *button*

The top part of your screen should look like Figure 16-13.

Figure 16-13

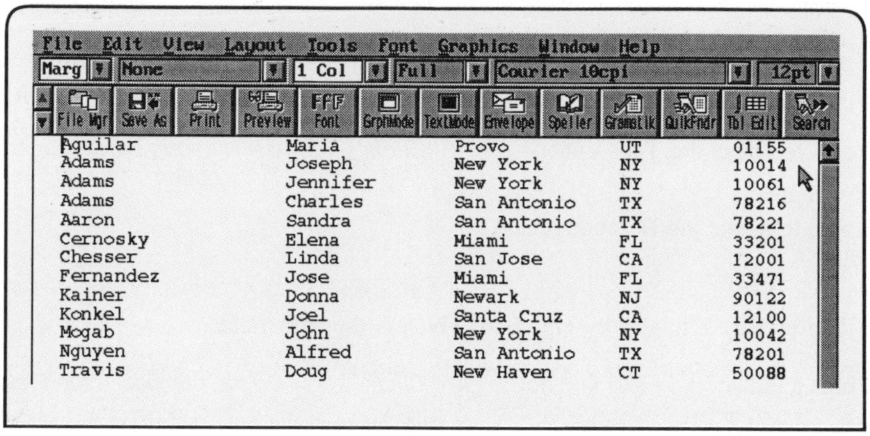

Notice that the zip codes are now in ascending order for those people who have a last name starting with the letter "A."

Save your document using the name "COLUMN3.SRT". Close the document.

■ SORTING PARAGRAPHS

When text appears separated by commas or spaces and has blank lines between each record, the data can be sorted using Paragraph as the Record Type. Examples may include bibliographies or address lists. For our example, type the address list shown in Figure 16-14.

Figure 16-14

Mr. Bill McBride
P. O. Box 1267
Houston, Texas 77077

Ms. Alexandra Simonton
123 Maple Ave.
San Antonio, Texas 78232

Dr. Joanne S. Podraza
7530 Moline
Bellaire, Texas 77401

Mrs. Tai Tang
5608 Belcrest
Philadelphia, Pennsylvania 19119

Dr. Chris Kindsvatter
8214 Forest Knoll
Millers Landing, Maryland 21107

Save the file using the name "PARAGRAF.SRT".

To sort the address list numerically by zip code, enter the sorting procedure:

Press	Ctrl + F9	Choose	Tools
Press	2 or S to select the Sort option	Choose	Sort
Press	←Enter	Click	the OK command button

Notice the Record Type has automatically changed to Paragraph.

To sort the list numerically by zip code, you must determine where the zip code appears in each record. In the address list, the zip code is on the third line and is the last word. In most cases, it is the third word, but for cities containing two words, the zip code is the fourth word. This inconsistency will require a change in the numbering pattern. It will be demonstrated below.

To establish the Sorting Priority to be in zip code order:

Press	2 or K to select the Sort Keys option	Choose	the Sort Keys option
Press	2 or E to select the Edit option	Choose	the Edit option
Press	4 or L to select the Line text box	Click	on the number in the Line text box
Type	3	Type	3
Press	←Enter	Click	on the number in the Word text box
Press	6 or W to select the Word option	Type	-1
Type	-1	Double-click	on the number in the Word text box
Press	←Enter		

Your screen should look like Figure 16-15.

Figure 16-15

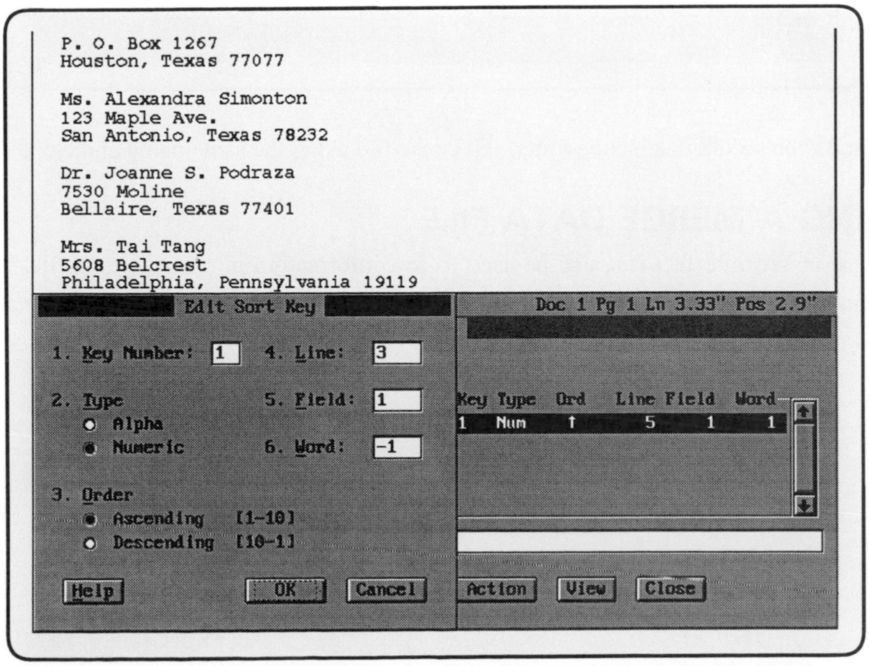

The Line text box shows a 3 because the zip code appears in the third line of each record. The negative one appearing in the Word text box instructs WordPerfect to count words from right to left. Thus, it will not matter if the zip code appears as the third or fourth word. Notice the Type is still set to be Numeric because of the Sorting procedure completed earlier in this chapter. Unless tabs appear in the data, the number in the Field text box may be ignored.

To perform the sort:

Press   ⌸Enter

Press   Tab⇄ twice to select the Perform Action command button

Press   ⌸Enter

Click   the OK command button

Click   the Perform Action command button

Your screen should look like Figure 16-16.

Figure 16-16

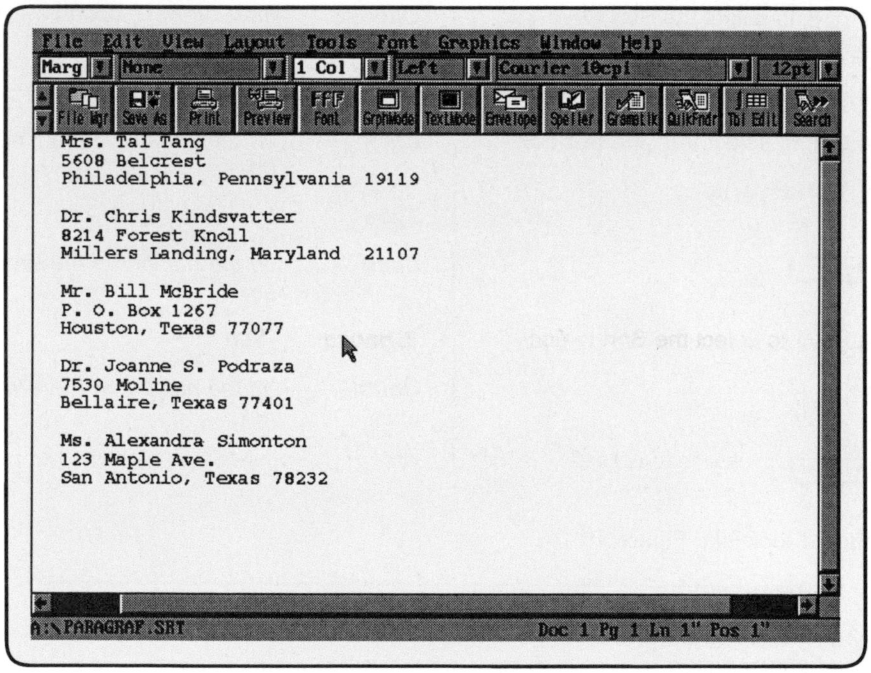

```
 File  Edit  View  Layout  Tools  Font  Graphics  Window  Help
Marg ▼ None          ▼ 1 Col ▼ Left ▼ Courier 10cpi          ▼ 12pt ▼
 File Mgr Save As  Print  Preview  Font  GrphMode TextMode Envelope Speller Grmetlk QuikFndr Tbl Edit Search
       Mrs. Tai Tang
       5608 Belcrest
       Philadelphia, Pennsylvania 19119

       Dr. Chris Kindsvatter
       8214 Forest Knoll
       Millers Landing, Maryland  21107

       Mr. Bill McBride
       P. O. Box 1267
       Houston, Texas 77077

       Dr. Joanne S. Podraza
       7530 Moline
       Bellaire, Texas 77401

       Ms. Alexandra Simonton
       123 Maple Ave.
       San Antonio, Texas 78232


 A:\PARAGRAF.SRT                        Doc 1 Pg 1 Ln 1" Pos 1"
```

The records should be sorted in zip code order.   Save the file using the same name and close the document.

■ SORTING A MERGE DATA FILE

The Sort feature in WordPerfect can also be used to sort information in a merge data file.

Open the document "ADDRESS.DTA" that you created in Chapter 12. Your screen should look like Figure 16-17.

Figure 16-17

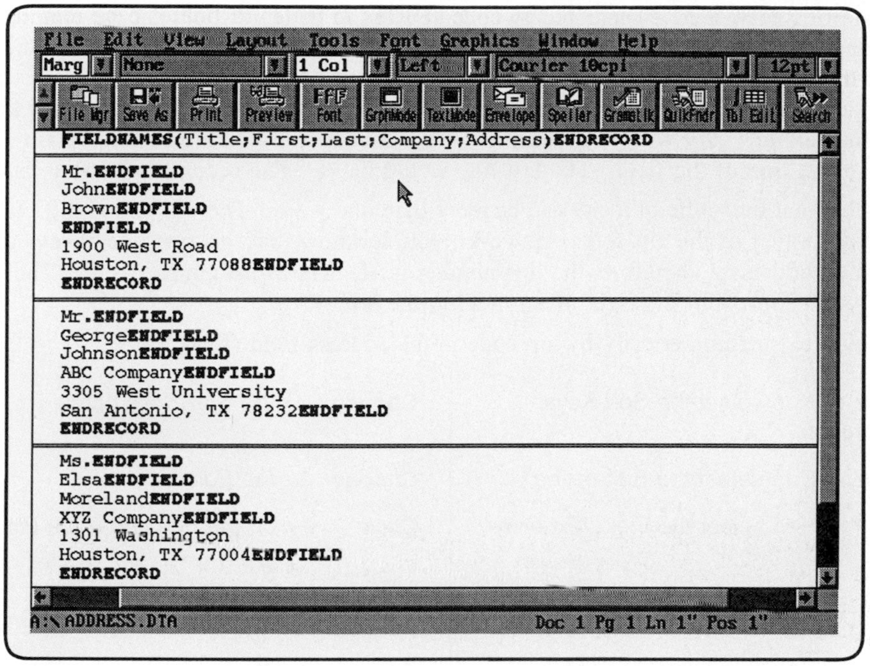

Suppose you want to sort the addresses in ascending order by zip code.

To sort by zip code:

Press	Ctrl + F9
Press	2 or S to select the Sort option
Press	↵Enter

Choose	*Tools*
Choose	*Sort*
Click	*the OK command button*

Notice the Record Type has automatically changed to Merge Data File and remembers the priority settings of the previous sorting procedure.

Your screen should look like Figure 16-18.

Figure 16-18

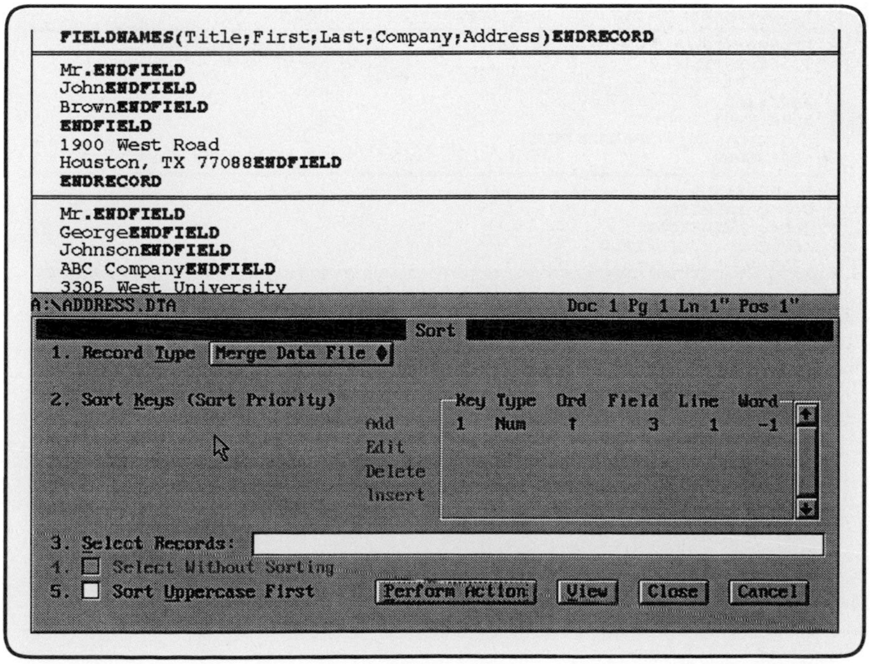

In a merge data file, each field is separated by an **ENDFIELD** code. A field can have more than one line in it. For example, the address field has two lines of text. You must enter the number of the line in the Line text box in the Sort Keys text box. The line number is positive if you count from the top of the field down to the bottom. The line number is negative if you count from the bottom of the field to the top. For example, if address lines vary with some having suite numbers, and you are sorting by zip code, you will need to use the last line of the field. The last line would be -1. The second to last line is -2.

It is also possible that the name of a city can be more than one word. Therefore, it is difficult to know the exact line word number of the zip code. However, you do know that the zip code always appears last in the last line in an address. Therefore, the line number is -1. The word number is -2. The word number is negative if you count from the right of the field to the left.

To change Key 1 to sort numerically by zip code in the address field (field 5):

Press	2 or K to select the Sort Keys option	**Choose**	the Sort Keys option
Press	2 or E to select the Edit option	**Choose**	the Edit option
Press	4 or F to select the Field text box	**Click**	on the number in the Field text box
Press	5	**Type**	5
Press	⏎Enter	**Click**	on the number in the Line text box
Press	5 or L to select the Line text box	**Type**	-1
Press	-1	**Click**	on the number in the Word text box
Press	⏎Enter	**Type**	-1
Press	6 or W to select the Word text box	**Click**	the OK command button
Type	-1		
Press	⏎Enter twice		

Your screen should look like Figure 16-19.

Figure 16-19

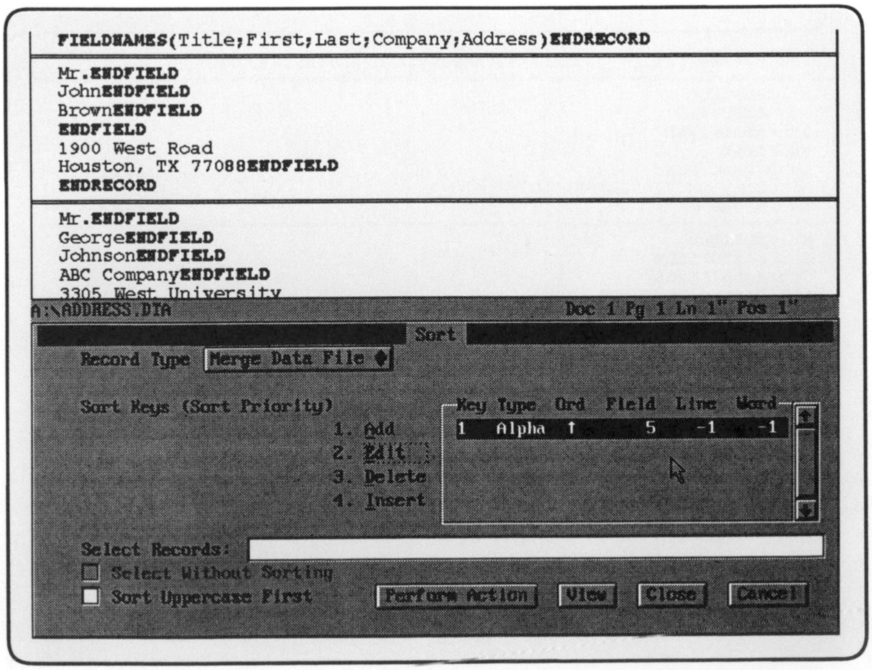

To begin the sort process:

Press	⌜Tab⇄⌟ twice to select the Perform Action command button
Press	⌜←Enter⌟

Click	*the Perform Action command button*

Notice that the zip codes are now in ascending order. Your screen should look like Figure 16-20.

Figure 16-20

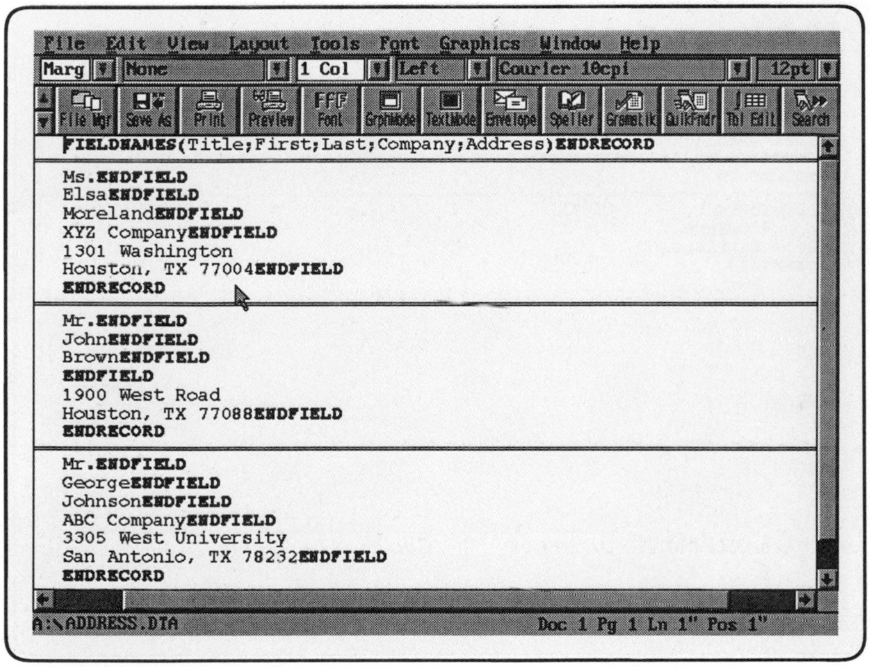

Save the document as "MERGE.SRT".

■ SELECTING RECORDS

Some of your lists or merge data files might be quite large. At times, you may want to select only a portion of the records in that list or merge data file. The Select Records feature in the Sort dialog box allows you to select records based on certain criteria.

Suppose you want to select the records of the people who live in Houston from the "MERGE.SRT" document.

To begin the sorting procedure and select only the Houston records:

Press	⌜Ctrl⌟ + ⌜F9⌟
Press	2 or S to select the Sort option
Press	⌜←Enter⌟

Choose	*Tools*
Choose	*Sort*
Click	*the OK command button*

To select only those records containing the word "Houston", you first place the cursor in the Select Records text box. You can use a global key. A **global key** lets you specify text that may appear anywhere in the record. The global key is specified as "keyg" in a selection statement. To find "Houston" anywhere in the record, the statement will look like this "keyg=Houston".

To select only those records containing the word "Houston":

Press	3 or S to select the Select Records text box		*Click*	*in the Select Records text box*
Type	keyg=Houston		*Type*	*keyg=Houston*

Your screen should look like Figure 16-21.

Figure 16-21

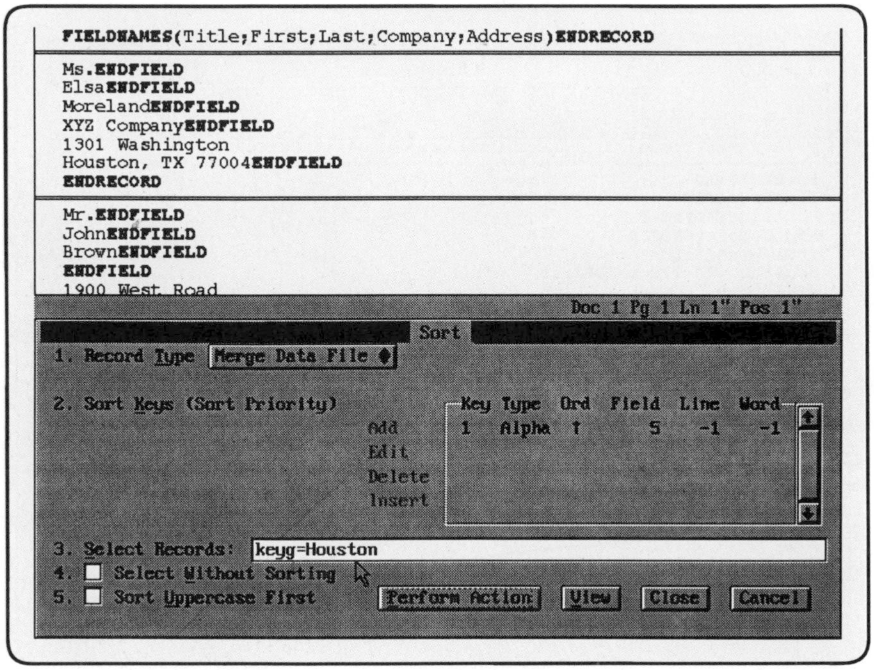

To perform the selection process:

Press	[←Enter] twice		*Click*	*the Perform Action command button*

The record for San Antonio should have been removed. Notice that the document still has the name "MERGE.SRT." It is important to have saved the original address list because the records eliminated during the selection procedure are now gone from the file and cannot be recovered. Save the file using the name "CITY.SRT". Close the document.

Using the global key to select records is the fastest, easiest way to isolate particular records. Another method is to use the Select Record text box to specify particular criteria.   For example, the selection statement could consist of the key number and the criterion, or data you want to select.   To select the records containing "Houston", the first key should be Field 5, Line -1, Word 1.

The key number is entered as text "key1" through "key9". After you enter the key number in the selection statement, you need to enter an operator or symbol. The following operators can be used as part of your selection statement and will appear in the left side of the Sort dialog box when you choose the Select Records text box.

Operator	Description
=	Specifies records with the same value. For example, key1=Houston searches for records that contain the text "Houston" in key1.
| (OR)	Allows you to select records that meet any of several conditions. For example, key1=Houston|key1=Dallas searches for records containing the text "Houston" or "Dallas" in key1.
& (AND)	Allows you to select records that must meet several conditions. For example, key1=Houston&key2=77024 searches for records containing the text "Houston" in key1 and the number "77024" in key2.
<>	Specifies records that do not match the following criteria. For example, key1<>Houston selects records that do not contain the text "Houston" in key1.
>	Specifies records that are greater than the criteria. For example, key1>77024 selects records with a numeric value greater than "77024" in key1. If the criteria were a word rather than a number, the > operator searches for records that are alphabetically "greater than" the word in the criteria. For example, "B" is greater than "A."
<	Specifies records that are less than the criteria. For example, key1<77024 selects records with a numeric value less than "77024" in key1. If the criteria were a word rather than a number, the < operator searches for records that are alphabetically "less than" the word in the criteria. For example, "Y" is less than "Z."
>=	Specifies records that are greater than or equal to the criteria. For example, key1>=77024 selects records with a numeric value greater than or equal to "77024" in key1. If the criteria were a word rather than a number, the >= operator searches for records that are alphabetically greater than or equal to the word in the criteria.
<=	Specifies records that are less than or equal to the criteria. For example, key1<=77024 selects records with a numeric value less than or equal to "77024" in key1. If the criteria were a word rather than a number, the <= operator searches for records that are alphabetically less than or equal to the word in the criteria.

Note: Spaces may be placed between the phrases in the criteria statements.

EXERCISE 1

INSTRUCTIONS: Define the following concepts:

1.   Sort feature _____

_____

2.   Line sort _____

_____

3.   Keys _____

_____

4.   Fields _____

_____

5.   Words _____

_____

6.   Merge Data File sort _____

_____

7.   Paragraph sort _____

_____

8.   Select Records feature _____

_____

9.   Select Records operators _____

_____

10.   Global key _____

_____

EXERCISE 2

INSTRUCTIONS: Circle T if the statement is true and F if the statement is false.

T   F   1.   With the Sort feature, you can sort lines, paragraphs, merge data files, or blocked text.

T   F   2.   You can perform a line sort if there are no blank lines between the text.

T   F   3.   You cannot perform a paragraph sort if there are blank lines between the text.

T   F   4.   You should always save your document before sorting.

T   F   5.   Keys are words, fields, or phrases by which a document is sorted.

T   F   6.   Numeric keys are made up of letters or numbers.

T   F   7.   If you want to sort by the last word in a field of a merge data file, then the word number of the key should be -1.

T   F   8.   If the key occurs in the second to last line of a field in a merge data file, then the line number should be -2.

T   F   9.   When you use the Select Records feature, you must define a key and create a selection statement.

T   F   10.   The & operator in a Select Records statement indicates that either of two conditions can be met for the record to be selected.

EXERCISE 3

INSTRUCTIONS: 1.   Create the following document. Set your own tabs. The order of the data in the columns is **last name**, **first name**, **middle initial**, **city**, **state**, and **zip code**.

2.   Save the document in a file using the name "CH16EX03".

3.   Sort the document by state abbreviation.

4.   Print the document.

5.   Sort the document in descending order by zip code.
6.   Print the document.
7.   Sort the document in ascending order by last name, first name, and middle initial.
8.   Print the document.
9.   Sort the document by city within each state. Make sure that the zip codes are in ascending order within each city.
10.   Print the document.
11.   Sort the individuals that live in California by last name, first name, and middle initial.
12.   Print the document.
13.   Close the document without saving changes.

```
Smith       Albert    D   Seattle         WA   93006
Thompson    Sally     W   Minneapolis     MN   55455
Jackson     Thomas    C   Omaha           NE   65532
Smith       Albert    B   San Francisco   CA   95476
James       Susan     W   Chicago         IL   60672
Garcia      Mary      L   Laredo          TX   76549
Baker       Dave      M   Dallas          TX   75543
Yee         Teresa    M   Oxnard          CA   93321
Allen       William   X   San Francisco   CA   75436
Jackson     Mary      D   Durham          NC   23498
Baker       Dale      T   New Bern        NC   23653
Martinez    Anna      B   Del Rio         TX   78890
```

EXERCISE 4

INSTRUCTIONS:
1.   Create the following document. Set your own tabs.
2.   Print the document.
3.   Sort the document in ascending order by last names.
4.   Print the document.
5.   Save the document in a file using the name "CH16EX04".
6.   Close the document.

```
                    MONTHLY SALES REPORT

Walters        Phil         Rockford      IL    3,432
Koch           Victor       Elgin         IL    4,372
McFarland      Marilyn      DeKalb        IL    6,175
Kohlmeyer      Paulette     Indianapolis  IN    5,329
Zwerger        William      Evansville    IN    3,778
Wyrwicz        Norbert      Plymouth      IN    4,309
Paskalides     James        LaPorte       IN    2,909
Tkemetarovic   Joseph       Ames          IA    4,588
Hijjawi        Syed         Ottumwa       IA    5,272
Fatah          Renee        Des Moines    IA    6,377
Sherrell       Wilhelmina   Lewiston      ID    5,440
Bishop         Robert       Moscow        ID    3,970
```

EXERCISE 5

INSTRUCTIONS:
1. Open the document "CH16EX04".
2. Sort the amount column in descending order.
3. Print the document.
4. Save the document in a file using the name "CH16EX05".
5. Close the document.

EXERCISE 6

INSTRUCTIONS:
1. Create the following document. Set your own tabs.
2. Sort the document in ascending order by zip code.
3. Add the title "**SELECTED SALES PERSONNEL**" to the top of the document. Make the title three lines above the first line of the list.
4. Print the document.
5. Save the document in a file using the name "CH16EX06".
6. Close the document.

Irwin	Tom	Albany	GA	31701
Jorandy	Gwen	Moline	IL	61265
Lorek	Austin	Albany	GA	31702
Nix	Madie	Albany	GA	31701
Rau	John	Albany	GA	31701
Cassidy	Ian	Moline	IL	61265
Shapiro	Robert	Portland	ME	04101
Cloyd	Johan	Albany	GA	31702
Kahle	Jerry	Portland	ME	04102
Peterman	Tim	Chicago	IL	60616
Panagakis	Angela	Moline	IL	61265

EXERCISE 7

INSTRUCTIONS:
1. Create the following document. Set your own tabs.
2. Sort by country and then by year in descending order.
3. Print the document.
4. Save the document in a file using the name "CH16EX07".
5. Sort by last name and then first name in ascending order.
6. Print the document.
7. Close the document without saving changes.

```
            SELECTED OLYMPIC GOLD MEDAL WINNERS

      (Name, Year, Event, and Country Represented)

   Carl Lewis           1988      100-Meters       USA
   Volker Beck          1980      400-Meters       GDR
   Sergi Bubka          1988      Pole Vault       USSR
   John Walker          1976      1,500-Meters     NZ
   Carl Lewis           1988      Long Jump        USA
   Tapio Korjus         1988      Javelin          FIN
   Lasse Viren          1976      5,000-Meters     FIN
   Steve Lewis          1988      400-Meters       USA
   Sergei Litinov       1988      Hammer Throw     USSR
   Mark Todd            1988      Equestrian       NZ
```

EXERCISE 8

INSTRUCTIONS:

1. Create a merge data file using the mailing list shown below. The field names should be **Title**, **First**, **Last**, **Position**, and **Address**. Name the file "CH16EX08.DTA".
2. Sort the merge data file by zip code in ascending order.
3. Print the document.
4. Save the document in a file using the name "CH16EX08".
5. Close the document.

```
Ms. Geri Bitting              Mr. Delmar Cotes
1122 Inverrary                1216 Houbolt Avenue
High Point, NC 27260          Durham, NC 27702

Mr. William Komarek           Ms. Gina Sterr
Director of Financial Planning   Vice President
101 Bar Harbor Road           1266 Main Street
Charlotte, NC 28202           Asheville, NC 28801

Mr. Mike Isermann             Ms. Norma Aguilar
Decision Support Manager      Chief Financial Officer
1520 South Belmont            9911 South San Felipe Drive
High Point, NC 27261          San Louis Obispo, CA 02211

Mrs. Margaret Brinkman
Director of Marketing
347 Pleasant Hill
Durham, NC 27701
```

EXERCISE 9

INSTRUCTIONS:

1. Create the following merge data file. Name the file "CH16EX09.DTA". The field names should be **Name**, **Department**, and **Magazine**. Each field corresponds to one line.
2. Sort the document by date of magazine in descending order.
3. Print the document.

4. Sort the document by department in ascending order.
5. Print the document.
6. Sort the document by last name and then first name in ascending order.
7. Print the document.
8. Close the document without saving changes.

```
Janet Harborow                      Linda Chesser
Marketing Department                Accounting Department
PC Magazine, 7/1/92                 PC World, 5/1/94

John Mogab                          Donna Gail Kainer
Internal Auditing                   Information Systems
Computers in Accounting, 6/1/92     ComputerWorld, 4/22/94

Doug Travis                         Joel Konkel
Research & Development              Information Systems
Communications of the ACM, 6/1/94   InfoWorld, 4/30/94
```

EXERCISE 10

INSTRUCTIONS:

1. Open the file "CH16EX08.DTA".
2. Select only the records from **Durham, NC**.
3. Save the file as "CH16EX10".
4. Print the file.
5. Close the file.

EXERCISE 11

INSTRUCTIONS:

1. Open the file "CH16EX08.DTA".
2. Select the records for people from **Durham** or from **High Point**. *Note: Since the desired data appear in the same field, only one key is needed for the selection statement. Also the selection statement only requires using the word "High". The word "Point" does not need to be used at all.*
3. Save the file as "CH16EX11".
4. Print the file.
5. Close the file.

CHAPTER SEVENTEEN

CREATING AND USING COLUMNS

OBJECTIVES

In this chapter, you will learn to:

- Create newspaper-style columns
- Create newspaper-style columns with the Ribbon
- Create parallel columns

■ CHAPTER OVERVIEW

There may be times when you want to include columns in a document. WordPerfect allows you to have parallel and newspaper-style columns. This chapter illustrates the process for creating these types of columns using the Columns feature.

■ NEWSPAPER-STYLE COLUMNS

In WordPerfect you can create **newspaper-style columns**, in which text continues from column to column. To create columns, press ALT+F7 and select Columns or choose the Columns option under the Layout menu.

Whenever you want to use columns in a document, you need to determine:

1. The type of column
2. The number of columns
3. The distance between each column
4. The width of each column

A Column Definition code is placed in your document with the values for each of these attributes. The definition continues in effect until another column definition is specified. You can mix regular text paragraphs with columns on the same page of text.

To show the use of newspaper-style columns, suppose the State Financial Society needs to prepare a story for a newsletter to announce two job appointments.

Center and boldface the words "CHAPTERS ADD ASSISTANTS" and press ENTER twice. The top part of your screen should look like Figure 17-1.

Figure 17-1

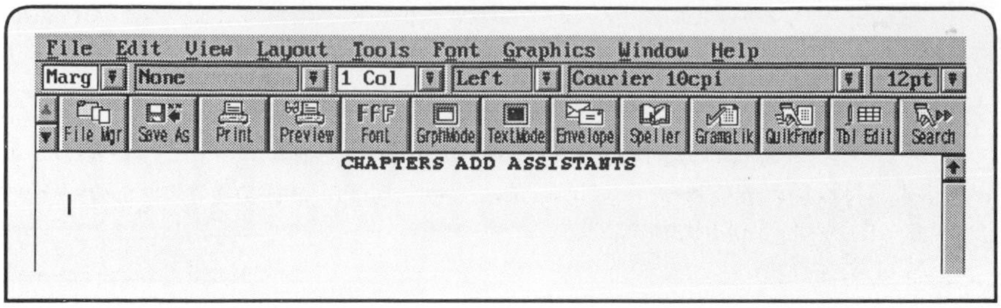

To define the characteristics for the columns:

Press	Alt + F7	***Choose***	*Layout*
Press	1 or C to select the Columns option	***Choose***	*Columns*

The Text Columns dialog box appears. Your screen should look like Figure 17-2.

Figure 17-2

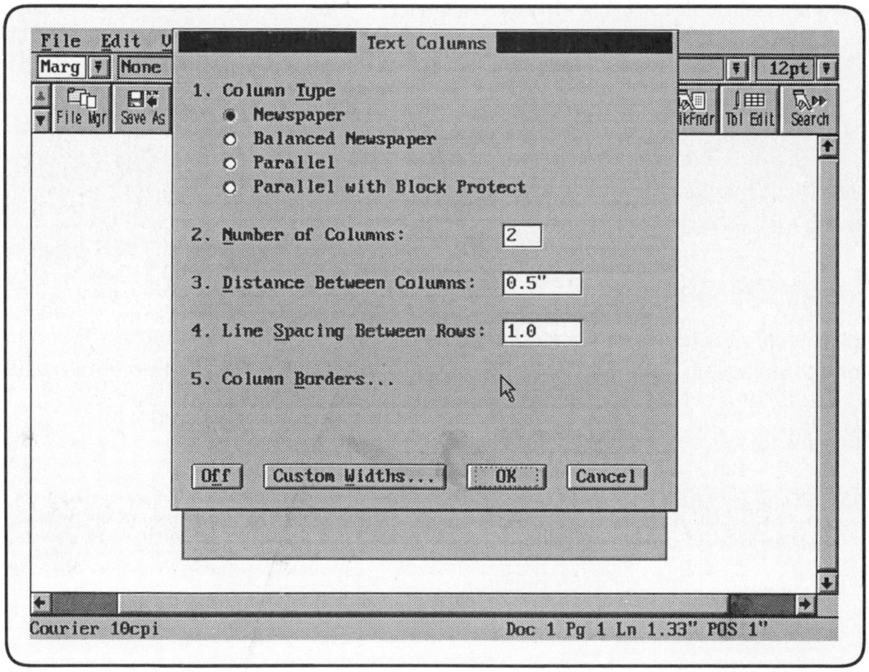

Note that the default settings for columns in WordPerfect are newspaper-style columns and two columns to a page. Unless you change the distance between columns, WordPerfect assumes a value of approximately one-half inch. You can have a maximum of 24 columns in a document.

To change the number of columns to three columns:

Press	2 or N to select the Number of Columns text box	***Click***	*in the Number of Columns text box*
Type	3	***Type***	*3*
Press	←Enter		

The width of each column is based on the number of columns that you defined and the current margins for the document. You can change the width for each column through this dialog box. Press W for Custom Widths or click the Custom Widths command button. Highlight the appropriate column and press E for Edit or click on the Edit command button. A dialog box appears in the lower right corner of the screen and you can press 1 or W to select the text box containing the current width. Type in the new width and press ENTER or click the OK command button. You should not set the column widths so wide that they will be out of the bounds of the document margins.

To see the current column widths:

Press	W for Columns Widths	**_Click_**	_the Custom Widths command button_

Your screen should look like Figure 17-3.

Figure 17-3

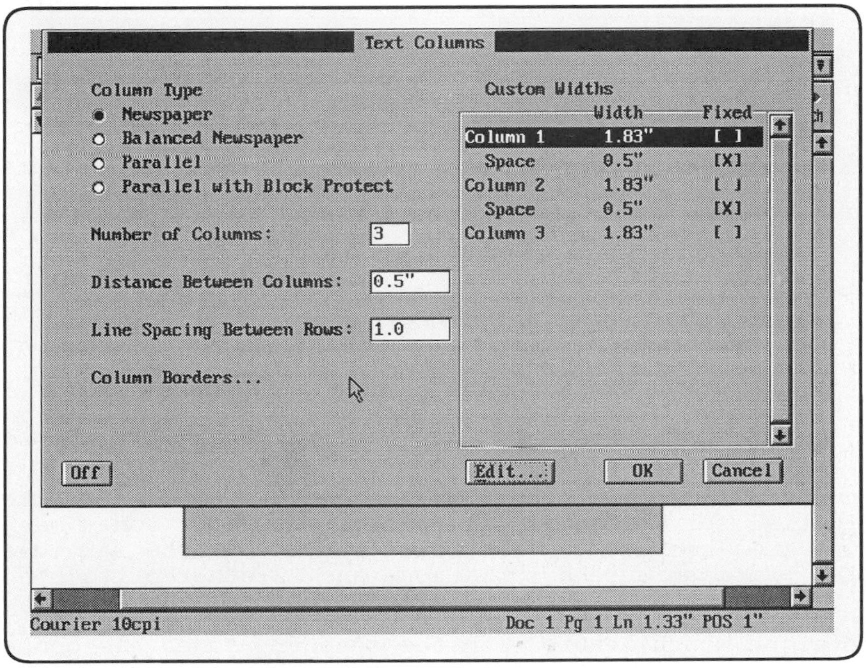

Notice that you now have three equally spaced columns.

To leave the columns evenly spaced and change the Number of Columns option to two columns again:

Press	Tab⇥	**_Click_**	_in the Number of Columns text box_
Press	2 or N to select the Number of Columns text box	**_Type_**	_2_
Type	2	**_Press_**	⏎Enter
Press	⏎Enter		

Notice that you now have two equally spaced columns.

The Distance Between Columns option is calculated for you at approximately one-half inch. However, you can change the value by selecting the Distance Between Columns text box.

To return to your document:

Press   ⌐←Enter⌐   ***Click***   *the OK command button*

Once you have defined the columns, you can enter text using the Columns feature. By default, the columns are turned on when you choose OK from the Text Columns dialog box.

The bottom part of your screen should look like Figure 17-4.

Figure 17-4

```
Courier 10cpi                          Col 1 Doc 1 Pg 1 Ln 1.33" Pos 1"
```

Notice that a "Col" indicator is displayed before the document indicator on the status bar.

Enter the text in Figure 17-5 in your document.

Figure 17-5

```
    Two chapters recently have hired executive secretaries to support
growing activities.  The Southwest and the Southeast Texas chapters
are the first to take advantage of the newly revised Chapter
Assistance Program.


    Susan Jones began duties as executive secretary of the Southwest
Chapter on June 1.  She has over 14 years experience in bookkeeping
and secretarial services.  For the past five years, Jones has
conducted a home bookkeeping service.  Presently, she services two
civic clubs, an insurance association, and 22 other private accounts.


    In her eight-month tenure with the chapter, Jones has concentrated
her efforts in the area of CPE and dues billing.  She says she is
working on transferring the chapter records to a computer.


    Doris Brown became the Southeast Texas executive secretary on
November 10.  Owner of Brown Business Services, a marketing-
management company, Brown brings to the chapter position a wide range
of business and community experience.


    Brown also has been associated for more than 15 years with the
Greater Orange Area Chamber of Commerce.  She has served on the
Chamber Board of Directors Committee, the Executive Committee, the
Civic Affairs Division, and the Convention Visitors Bureau.


    With Brown's support, the chapter hopes to develop CPE programs
and later expand to other areas.
```

Your screen should look like Figure 17-6.

Figure 17-6

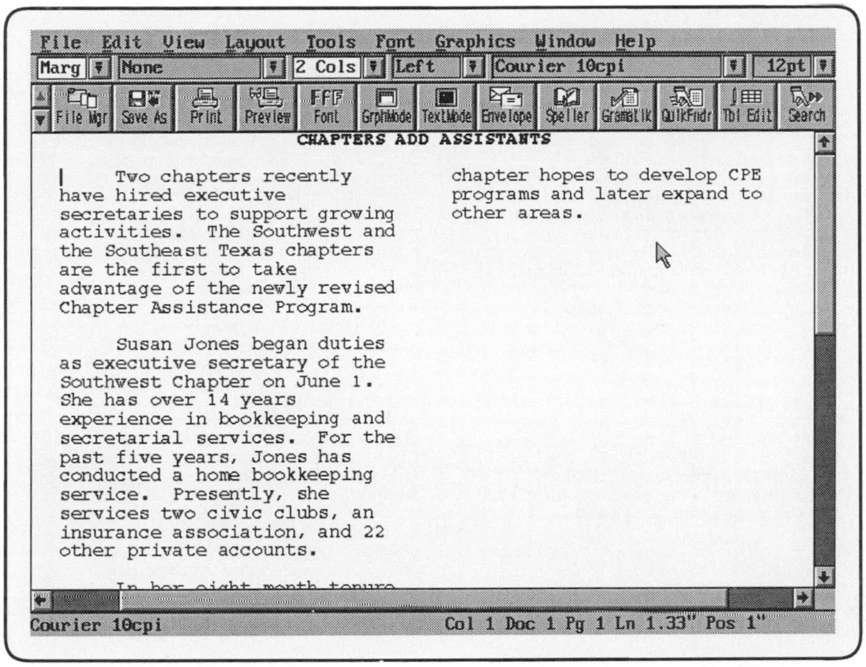

A Soft Page break code [SPg] is placed in the document when you enter text beyond the bottom margin of a column. The cursor is then moved to the top of the next column. You can choose to break a column at another location by inserting a column break. To insert a column break, press CTRL+ENTER. The text following the column break will move to the next column.

To move the fourth paragraph beginning with "Doris Brown" to the second column:

| **Move** | the cursor to the left margin of the fourth paragraph | ***Click*** | *at the left margin of the fourth paragraph* |
| **Press** | Ctrl + ←Enter | ***Press*** | *Ctrl + ←Enter* |

Your screen should look like Figure 17-7.

Figure 17-7

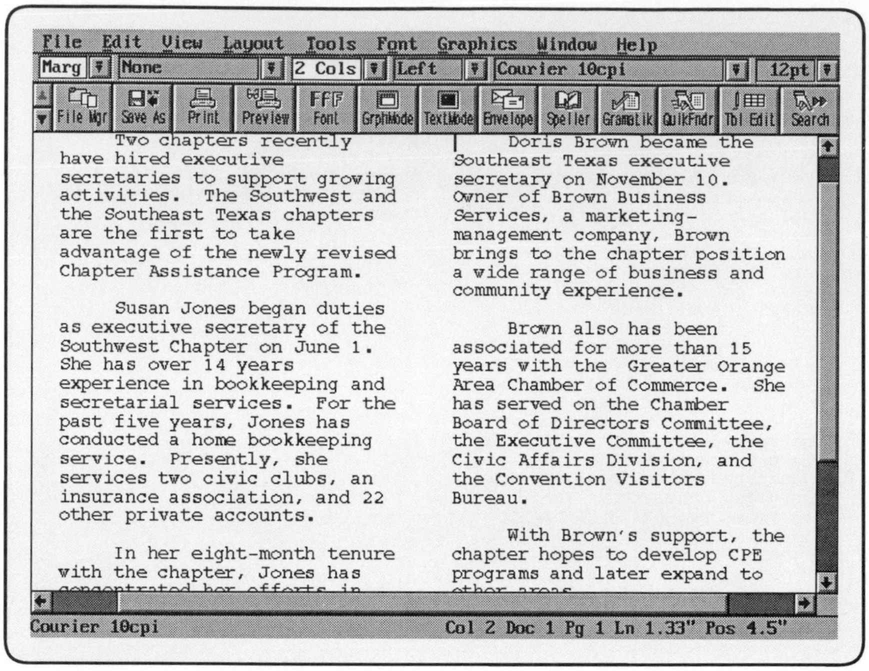

Once you have typed text in the columns, you can move the cursor to a different column by pressing ALT+RIGHT ARROW key to move right one column, ALT+LEFT ARROW key to move left one column or by moving the mouse pointer to the desired column and clicking.

To turn off the Columns feature, you must first move the cursor to the end of the column text.

To turn off the Columns feature:

Press	Home , Home , ↓	*Click*	*at the end of the document*
Press	Alt + F7	*Choose*	*Layout*
Press	1 or C to select the Columns option	*Choose*	*Columns*
Press	F to select the Off command button	*Click*	*the Off command button*
Press	↵Enter		

This step places a Column Definition Off code [Col Def:Off] in the document. Notice that the "Col" indicator no longer appears on the status bar. The bottom part of your screen should look like Figure 17-8.

Figure 17-8

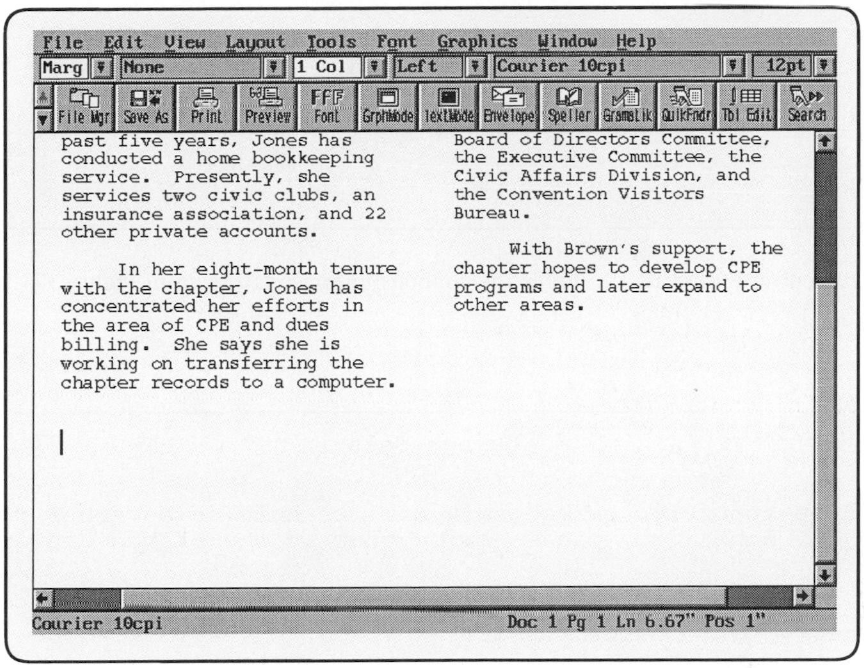

Save the document as "NEWSCOL" and close it.

■ CREATING NEWSPAPER-STYLE COLUMNS WITH THE RIBBON

You can easily create newspaper-style columns with the mouse by using the Ribbon.

To view the Ribbon, if it is not presently on the screen:

Choose	*View*
Choose	*Ribbon*

The Columns button on the Ribbon allows you to use the default settings for newspaper-style columns. You can select up to 24 evenly spaced newspaper-style columns. The Columns button looks like this:

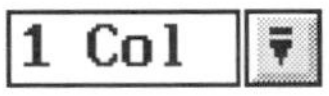

To create three newspaper-style columns:

Click	*the down arrow to the right of the Columns button on the Ribbon*
Double-click	*3 Cols*

The top part of your screen should look like Figure 17-9.

Figure 17-9

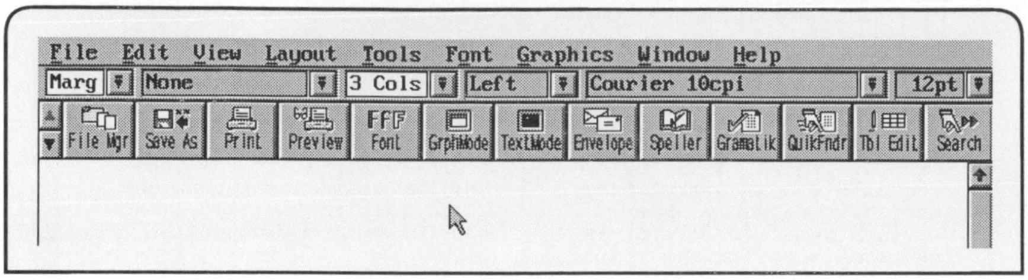

Create the document in Figure 17-10. Force the columns to break as shown in Figure 17-11 by inserting column breaks.

Figure 17-10

Garage Sale

The employee-sponsored garage sale will be held on November 12. If you have any donations, please bring them in one of the appropriate containers.

Alex Newberry has donated his 1965 Mustang convertible to be auctioned off.

All proceeds will be donated to Saint Mary's Orphanage.

Volunteers for the garage sale can sign up with Denise Newcastle. Several times are available in the morning.

Refreshments will be provided for volunteers by Chez Tim - Bakery and Cafe.

Volunteer Hours

Our company has volunteered 700 hours so far this year.

If you do volunteer work and would like someone in the company to match your hours, please turn in the name of the organization and the time that you serve. Libby Street coordinates all volunteer hours.

Keep up the good work!

Your screen should look like Figure 17-11.

Figure 17-11

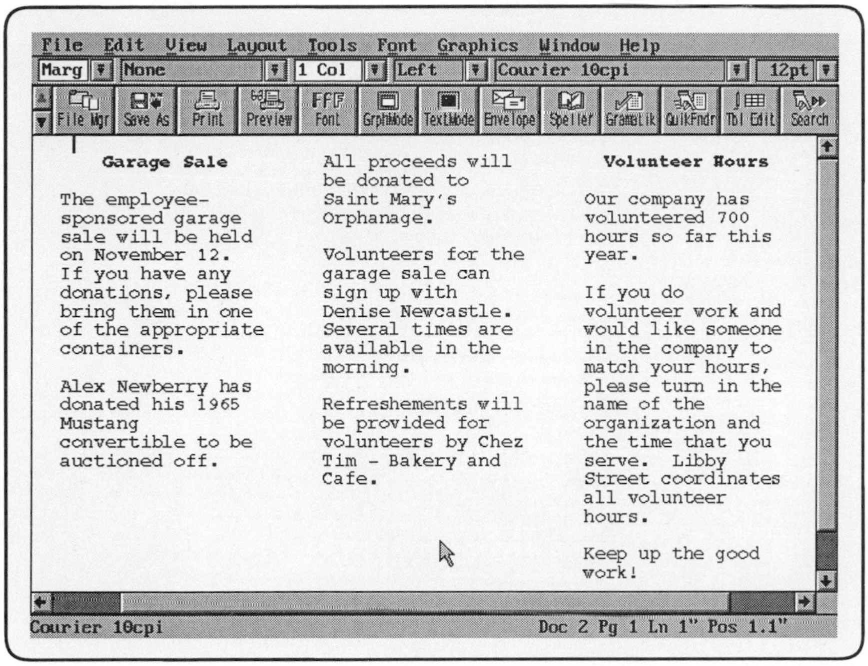

To turn off the columns using the Ribbon:

Click	*at the end of the document*
Click	*the down arrow to the right of the Columns button on the Ribbon*
Double-click	*1 Col*

Save the document as "RIBBON.DOC". Close the document.

■ PARALLEL COLUMNS

Parallel columns are columns in which the text is printed exactly as it is entered into each column. When one column is full, the text does *not* roll over into the next column. Figure 17-12 illustrates a document created with parallel columns.

Figure 17-12

NAME	SKILLS DESCRIPTION	AGE
Abrams, K	Programming in various database packages. Expert in network hardware and software. Works well with others.	35
Donaldson, M.	Speaks 32 languages. Speaks and reads 17 languages. Expert in German, Russian, Czech, Polish, French, Italian, Mandarin, Spanish, and Japanese. Thesis in British history. Has an unobtrusive demeanor.	45

There are two types of parallel columns:

Parallel - A column of text can be split onto two pages when the text extends below the bottom margin.

Parallel with Block Protect - An attempt is made to hold sets of items together on the same page. This type of column was used in the example in Figure 17-12.

As with newspaper-style columns, you must define the characteristics for parallel columns before you use them.

To show the use of parallel columns, assume that you want to prepare a traveling schedule for your supervisor. Your completed document will look similar to Figure 17-13 shown below.

Figure 17-13

	ITINERARY	
DATE	CITY	ACCOMMODATIONS
April 20, 1994	Dallas, Texas	Holiday Inn
April 25, 1994	San Francisco, California	Ramada Inn
April 28, 1994	Los Angeles, California	Holiday Inn

To begin the process, center and boldface the word "ITINERARY" and press ENTER twice.

To define parallel columns:

Press	Alt + F7		*Choose*	*Layout*
Press	1 or C to select the Columns option		*Choose*	*Columns*
Press	1 or T to select Column Type		*Choose*	*the Parallel option button*
Press	3 or P to select Parallel			

To change the Number of Columns option to three columns and return to the document:

Press	2 or N to select the Number of Columns text box		*Click*	*in the Number of Columns text box*
Type	3		*Type*	*3*

To accept three parallel columns:

Press	←Enter twice		*Click*	*the OK command button*

The width of each column is based on the number of columns that you defined and the current margins for the document. As with the newspaper columns described in the previous section, you can change the width of each column and adjust the distance between columns.

Once you have defined the characteristics of the parallel columns, you can start using the parallel columns.

As you enter text into the columns, press CTRL+ENTER to advance the cursor to the next column.

To center a heading over the first column:

Press	Shift + F6		*Choose*	*Layout*
Type	DATE		*Choose*	*Alignment*
			Choose	*Center*
			Type	*DATE*

To move the cursor to the next column:

Press	Ctrl + ←Enter		*Press*	*Ctrl + ←Enter*

To center a heading over the second column:

Press	Shift + F6		*Choose*	*Layout*
Type	CITY		*Choose*	*Alignment*
			Choose	*Center*
			Type	*CITY*

To move to the next column:

Press   [Ctrl] + [↵Enter]   *Press*   [Ctrl] + [↵Enter]

To center a heading over the third column:

Press   [Shift] + [F6]   *Choose*   Layout

Type   ACCOMMODATIONS   *Choose*   Alignment

                                                  Choose   Center

                                                  Type   ACCOMMODATIONS

To move to the next column:

Press   [Ctrl] + [↵Enter]   *Press*   [Ctrl] + [↵Enter]

The top part of your screen should look like Figure 17-14.

Figure 17-14

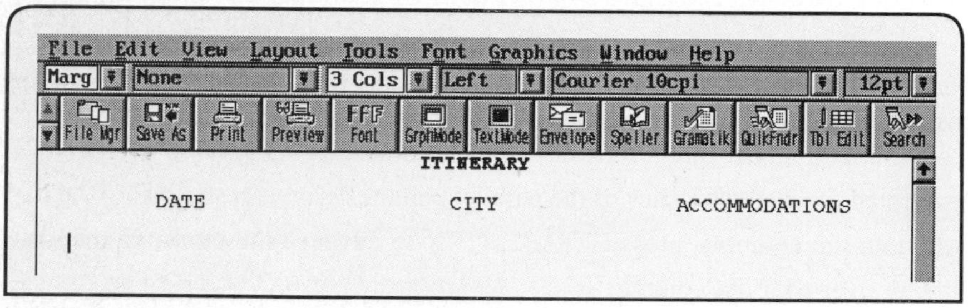

Inserting a column break in the last column moved the cursor to the first column of a new column set. In Reveal Codes, each block of columns is separated by a [HCol] code.

In This Book

To insert a column break, you have been instructed to press CTRL+ENTER. For the remainder of this book, the steps for inserting a column break are abbreviated as "Insert a break."

To place the first entry in the schedule:

Type   April 20, 1994

Insert   a break

Type   Dallas, Texas

Insert   a break

Type   Holiday Inn

Insert   a break

The top part of your screen should look like Figure 17-15.

Figure 17-15

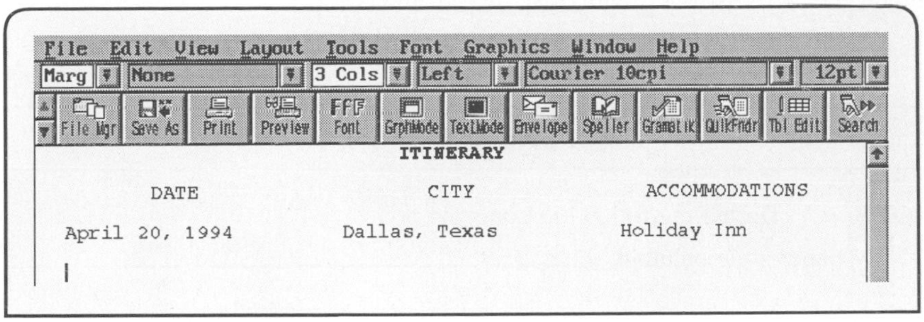

To add the second entry in the schedule:

Type	April 25, 1994
Insert	a break
Type	San Francisco, California
Insert	a break
Type	Ramada Inn
Insert	a break

To insert the third entry in the schedule:

Type	April 28, 1994
Insert	a break
Type	Los Angeles, California
Insert	a break
Type	Holiday Inn
Insert	a break

Once you have typed text in the columns, you can move the cursor by pressing ALT+RIGHT ARROW key to move right one column, ALT+LEFT ARROW key to move left one column or by moving the mouse to the appropriate column and clicking.

You must move the cursor below the columns before you turn off the Columns feature.

To turn off the Column feature:

Move	the cursor to the bottom of the document	*Click*	*at the end of the document*
Press	Alt + F7	*Choose*	*Layout*
Press	1 or C to select the Columns option	*Choose*	*Columns*
Press	F to select the Off command button	*Click*	*the Off command button*
Press	↵Enter		

This step places a [Col Def] code in the document. Notice that the "Col" indicator no longer appears on the status bar.

Save the document as "PARALCOL" and close the document.

EXERCISE 1

INSTRUCTIONS: Define the following concepts:

1. Newspaper-style columns _____

    _____

2. Column type _____

    _____

3. Column Width _____

    _____

4. Number of columns _____

    _____

5. Distance between columns _____

    _____

6. Columns feature _____

    _____

7. Parallel columns _____

    _____

8. Parallel columns with block protect _____

    _____

EXERCISE 2

INSTRUCTIONS: Circle T if the statement is true and F if the statement is false.

T   F   1.   Newspaper-style columns allow text to continue from column to column on a page.

T   F   2.   When using columns, you need to define the left and right margins in each column.

T   F   3.   You can have a maximum of 10 columns in a document.

T   F   4.   Inserting a column break breaks a column of text before the end of the page and moves the text to the next column.

T   F   5.   Word wrap does not occur within a column. You must press ENTER after every line of text.

T   F   6.   In parallel columns, text does not roll over into the next column when one column is full.

T   F   7.   When you turn the Columns feature on, a "Col" indicator is displayed before the page indicator on the status bar.

T   F   8.   Inserting two page breaks turns the Columns feature off.

EXERCISE 3

INSTRUCTIONS:

1.   Create the following newspaper-style document. Both columns are of equal width.

2.   Save the document in a file using the name "CH17EX03".

3.   Print the document.

4.   Close the document.

OUR TRAINING COMMITMENT

Napier & Judd, Inc. understands that analysis and communication of information are vital to your business. We are committed to helping you develop the computer skills you need to enhance productivity and business success. We have trained more than 40,000 executives, managers, professionals, and clerical employees. We provide the highest quality instructors, materials and facilities.

ABOUT OUR COURSES

Our emphasis is on quality. Participant ratings for our courses are excellent. We consistently receive very high ratings for presentation skills, knowledge of subject matter, course materials, and our facilities.

Each instructor has extensive training and business experience. All courses are "hands-on." You will be assigned your own IBM compatible 80386 microcomputer with a VGA monitor.

EXERCISE 4

INSTRUCTIONS:

1.   Create the following two-column document. Break the columns so that they are approximately the same length.

2.   Boldface and center the title "**1993 LEGISLATIVE UPDATE**" at the top of the page.

3.   Preview, print, and save the document in a file using the name "CH17EX04".

4.   Close the document.

The following bill has been passed by the State Legislature and approved by the Governor.

SENATE BILL 1004

1. This bill extends the insurance for survivors that are disabled children over the age of 18. Under this bill, the monthly survivor benefits will continue to be paid for a disabled child who is not able to engage in any active physical or mental endeavor.

2. Removes the age 70 participation limit. Currently a person employed and age 70 would not be eligible to take benefits reserved for retirement. This change will now allow persons regardless of age to take part in the retirement system payout.

3. Adds and compounds a 4 percent automatic annual increase for all retirees.

HIGHEST AWARD FOR FINANCIAL REPORTING--OUR NEWSLETTER.

The Governor's Office has just been informed that this Newsletter has been awarded the prestigious Golden Pen Award.

This award is given to those newsletters that are found to be extremely factual and full of spirit and involvement.

The Golden Pen Award is recognized by the profession as the highest award given to non-professional newsletters.

The award was presented to James L. Smirk, Deputy Director of Finance.

There are over 20,000 newsletters in the United States that are published on a regular basis. We were one of 20 selected. Congratulations to all who have helped with the information gathering.

WORKSHOPS

The State University is sponsoring two workshops dealing with Financial Planning for Retirement.

The first will be held on May 20, at the Capital Coliseum. The title is "Planning for the Future." This session will be from 1 to 3 in the afternoon.

The second will be held June 20, an all-day affair, 8 a.m. to 4 p.m. It is entitled "Seven Common Problems to Avoid."

Reserve your space now. Call 1-800-555-9999.

Current reinvestment rate of your Funds is 8.2 percent.

EXERCISE 5

INSTRUCTIONS:
1. Create the following three-column document. Break the columns so that they are approximately the same length.
2. Place the titles "**HAWTHORNE HERALD**" and "**(Inside the Office)**" on the first and second lines of the page. Boldface and center the titles.
3. Preview, print, and save the document in a file using the name "CH17EX05".
4. Close the document.

Announcing:

Three new employees have joined our ranks.

Tom Brown is the new assistant to **George Bear.** Tom will coordinate the work flow between the production area and the Dock. Glad to have you with us, Tom.

Phyllis Freemont is the new Office Receptionist. She is the new voice that you now hear over the P.A. system, the telephone and the intercom. Phyllis is married and has three children. This is her second position with our company. She was here five years ago as a student intern. Happy to have you back with us, Phyllis.

Finally, but not least, **Carrie Troester.** Carrie comes to us with a new MBA in Finance. She will be in charge of the Accounting Office. Carrie was with the Temeer Corporation

for five years while she went to school part time to obtain her new degree. She has vast experience in the area of Accounting. We wish her well.

CONFERENCE TRAVEL

Bill Walton is making a presentation to the local Rotary at the September 15 meeting in Hoffman Hills. Bill will be talking about the Changing Office and its impact on the workers, production and savings.

Another traveler is **Gordon Rich.** Gordon is going to Boston for the Annual Office Equipment and Furniture Show. Gordon will be presenting his paper on "**Ergonomics.**" As you may know, Gordon is considered the leading authority on this field. This is Gordon's fourth trip to speak this year.

NEW PAYROLL SYSTEM

Carrie Troester has announced that we will be receiving our pay every two weeks. This will start the beginning of October. This is a benefit that was asked for during our last wage negotiation.

FOR SALE:

86 T-Bird, low mileage. Call Sally in Graphics.

4-Bedroom home in Flint Creek. Call Jim Arrowsmith in Communications.

Appliances: Refrig., Elec. Range, Washer, Dryer, Ice Maker. Call Howard Timms in Personnel.

If you have any news that you would like printed, give it to Sharon in Personnel.

EXERCISE 6

INSTRUCTIONS:

1. Open the document "CH17EX05".
2. Place the second title "**(Inside the Office)**" a double space below the first title.
3. Change "**Announcing:**" to all capital letters.
4. In the first column, delete the sentence that begins with "**Phyllis is married . . .**".
5. Delete the last sentence about Carrie Troester in the second column.
6. Delete the last sentence about Gordon Rich -- "**This is . . .**".
7. Add the following text before "**CONFERENCE TRAVEL**".

> **OUR PRESIDENT'S DAY**
>
> In honor of **Thomas J. Wakins**, our president, Wednesday, October 18
> will be a day off with pay.

8. Readjust any spacing to create a more attractive document. Add or delete
line spacing as needed.
9. Preview and print the document.
10. Save the document in a file using the name "CH17EX06".
11. Close the document.

EXERCISE 7

INSTRUCTIONS:

1. Create the following document using parallel columns.
2. Use three columns.
3. Centered column headings are: **Day, Date, and Destination/Comments**.
4. The main title is "**MEDIEVAL CASTLES**". It is centered and boldface.
5. The secondary title is "**(France, Portugal, and Spain in October)**". It is
a double space below the main title.
6. Preview and print the document.
7. Save the document in a file using the name "CH17EX07".
8. Close the document.

MEDIEVAL CASTLES
(France, Portugal, and Spain in October)

Day	Date	Destination/Comments
Sunday	Oct. 8	Bordeaux, France. Arrive from your city by noon-Bordeaux time.
Monday	Oct. 9	Bordeaux/Dordogne Visit Ice Age Caves and local castles.
Tuesday	Oct. 10	The Castle of Begnac. The castle sits atop a 500 foot high bluff.

Figure 18-7

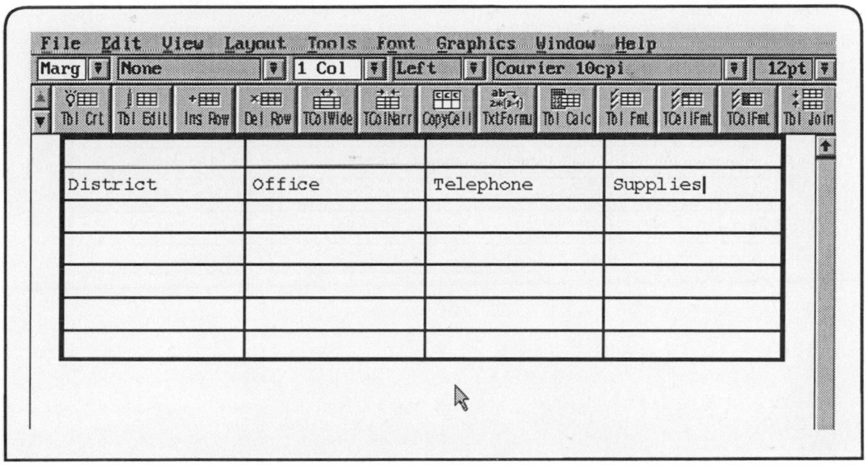

Complete the table in Figure 18-8. Add the dollar signs and commas. Later in this chapter, you will learn a method for automatically formatting the numbers. To move the cursor forward a cell, press TAB or click on that cell. To move the cursor to a previous cell, press SHIFT+TAB or click on that cell. If you accidentally press ENTER, press BACKSPACE to return the row back to its original height. (Pressing ENTER inserts a hard return, moves the cursor to the next line in the cell, and expands the length of the cell.)

Figure 18-8

District	Office	Telephone	Supplies
Central	$38,000.50	$2,310.00	$11,810.98
Eastern	31,645.61	4,412.31	7,881.22
Midwest	53,760.75	3,708.78	8,544.65
Mountain	48,145.25	6,974.96	5,221.88
Western	40,746.41	8,418.77	10,550.29

Save the file using the name "TABLE.DOC". It is a good idea to save tables often. Then if some of your editing changes do not perform as expected, you can retrieve another copy of the previously saved table.

■ EDITING A TABLE

After you create a table, you may want to change or edit its appearance. You can use the Table Editing feature to enhance the appearance of the table. If you are using the mouse, you can use the "TABLES" Button Bar to format and edit the table. The second column in the following instructions uses the "TABLES" Button Bar.

Check for the "Cell" prompt on the status bar to make sure the cursor is in the table. If the cursor is not in the table, move the cursor to any cell in the table.

Press   Alt + F11 | **Click**   on the Tbl Edit button in the
                                                      Button Bar

Your screen should look like Figure 18-9.

Figure 18-9

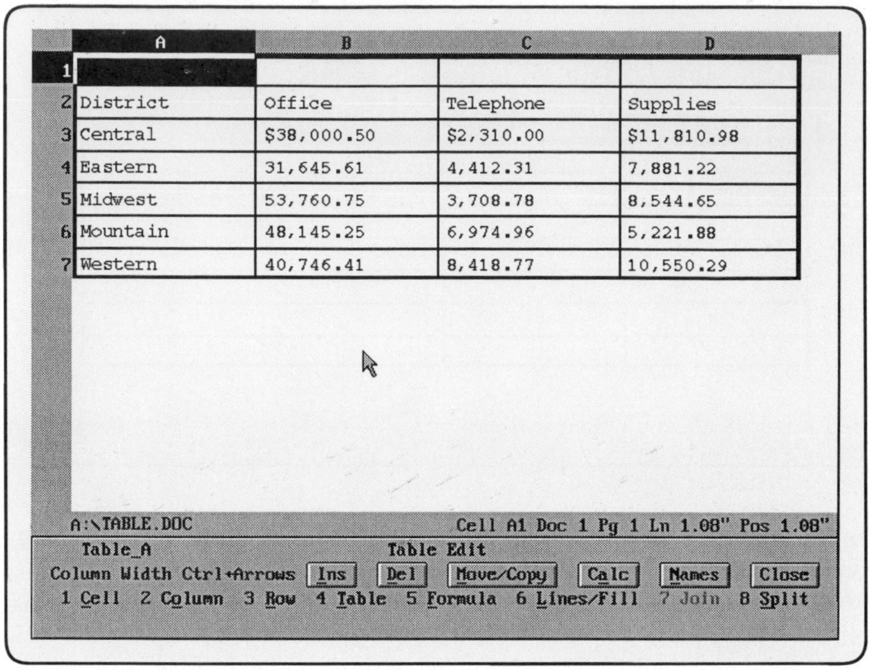

The Table Edit menu and related buttons on the "TABLES" Button Bar are described below:

Ctrl+Arrows - With this key combination, the column widths can be quickly adjusted. You may also use the "TColWide" and the "TColNarr" buttons on the Button Bar.

Ins - With this command button, columns or rows can be inserted above or below the present cursor position. You may also use the "Ins Row" button on the Button Bar.

Del - With this command button, contents of cells, columns or rows can be deleted. You may also use the "Del Row" button on the Button Bar.

Move/Copy - This command button permits the contents of a cell, row, column, or block of data to be moved or copied to a new location. You may also use the "CopyCell" button on the Button Bar to assist with duplicating data.

Calc - If any numeric data have changed in the table, this command updates the calculations. The "Tbl Calc" button on the Button Bar performs the same function.

Names - With this command, you can refer to a range of cells with a specified name. This topic is discussed in greater detail in the next chapter.

Close - The Close command permits you to exit the Table Edit mode with the mouse.

Cell - This option allows you to change the appearance, size, and alignment, of text in a cell. You can also shade and lock a cell using this option. The "TCellFmt" button on the Button Bar also displays the Cell Format dialog box.

Column - This option allows you to change appearance, size, or alignment of text in a column. You can also adjust the column width and margins or determine the number of decimal places for a column. The "TColFmt" button on the Button Bar also displays the Column Format dialog box.

Row - This option allows you to set margins, height, and the number of lines that will be permitted per row. In addition, Header Rows are established in this option.

Table - This option allows you to change appearance, size, or alignment of text in an entire table. You can also adjust the column width and margins and determine the number of decimal places for numeric data. The alignment of the table relative to the left and right margins can also be adjusted here. The "Tbl Fmt" button on the Button Bar also displays the Table Format dialog box.

Formula - Tables can contain mathematical formulas. This option allows you to create formulas and place them in one or more cells. This feature is discussed more thoroughly in the next chapter.

Lines/Fill - The lines around a table can be changed in appearance and in degrees of thickness. Shading and patterns may also be applied to selected cells. Use the Block feature to change the appearance of more than one cell.

Join - When cells are highlighted, this option joins several cells, columns, or rows together.

Split - When cells are highlighted, this option splits a column or row.

Joining Cells

Suppose you want to enter the company name and title of the table in the first row. You need only one cell in the first row for the entire table heading. You can use the Join option to join the four cells into one cell that stretches from the left margin to the right margin of the table. You must first enter the Table Edit mode, then select the cells that you want to join, and finally choose the Join option.

To join the first row of cells:

Move	the cursor to cell A1	*Click*	*on cell A1*
Press	F12	*Drag*	*to select all the cells in the first row*
Press	End to highlight the first row of cells	*Choose*	*the Join option*
Press	7 or J to select the Join option	*Click*	*the Yes command button*
Press	Y to select the Yes command		

Move the cursor to cell A3. Your screen should look like Figure 18-10.

Figure 18-10

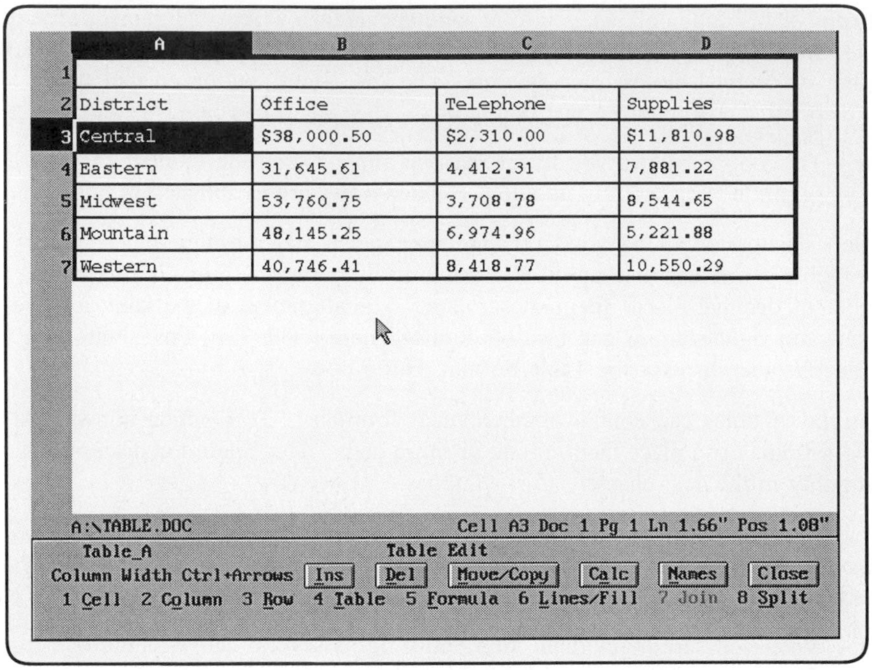

	A	B	C	D
1				
2	District	Office	Telephone	Supplies
3	Central	$38,000.50	$2,310.00	$11,810.98
4	Eastern	31,645.61	4,412.31	7,881.22
5	Midwest	53,760.75	3,708.78	8,544.65
6	Mountain	48,145.25	6,974.96	5,221.88
7	Western	40,746.41	8,418.77	10,550.29

```
A:\TABLE.DOC                        Cell A3 Doc 1 Pg 1 Ln 1.66" Pos 1.08"
   Table_A                          Table Edit
Column Width Ctrl+Arrows  [Ins]  [Del]  [Move/Copy]  [Calc]  [Names]  [Close]
   1 Cell  2 Column  3 Row  4 Table  5 Formula  6 Lines/Fill  7 Join  8 Split
```

The Join option works only when cells have been blocked.

To enter the heading:

Press	F7	**Click**	*the Close command button*
Move	the cursor to cell A1	**Click**	*on cell A1*
Type	JOHNSON PARTNERS	**Type**	*JOHNSON PARTNERS*
Press	↵Enter	**Press**	*↵Enter*
Type	DISTRICT EXPENSE REPORT	**Type**	*DISTRICT EXPENSE REPORT*
Press	↵Enter	**Press**	*↵Enter*
Type	First Quarter	**Type**	*First Quarter*

Your screen should look like Figure 18-11.

Figure 18-11

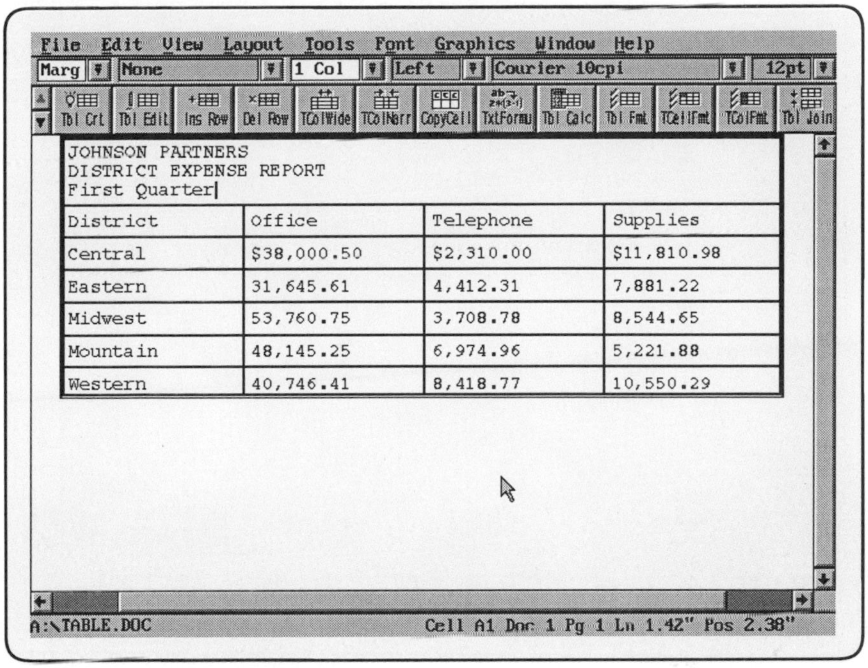
File Edit View Layout Tools Font Graphics Window Help
Marg None 1 Col Left Courier 10cpi 12pt
Tbl Crt Tbl Edit Ins Row Del Row TColWide TColNarr CopyCell TxtFormu Tbl Calc Tbl Fmt TCellFmt TColFmt Tbl Join
JOHNSON PARTNERS
DISTRICT EXPENSE REPORT
First Quarter
District Office Telephone Supplies
Central $38,000.50 $2,310.00 $11,810.98
Eastern 31,645.61 4,412.31 7,881.22
Midwest 53,760.75 3,708.78 8,544.65
Mountain 48,145.25 6,974.96 5,221.88
Western 40,746.41 8,418.77 10,550.29
A:\TABLE.DOC
Cell A1 Doc 1 Pg 1 Ln 1.42" Pos 2.38"

Boldfacing and Centering Text

You can format text in a table by choosing the Cell option in the Table Edit mode. Through this option, the table heading can be boldfaced and centered.

To apply boldfacing and centering to the first two rows of the table:

Press	Alt + F11	***Click***	*the Tbl Edit button on the Button Bar*
Press	F12 to turn the Block feature on	***Drag***	*across rows 1 and 2*
Press	↓ to highlight the second row	***Choose***	*the Cell option*
Press	1 or C to select the Cell option		

The Cell Format dialog box appears on the screen. Your screen should look like Figure 18-12.

Figure 18-12

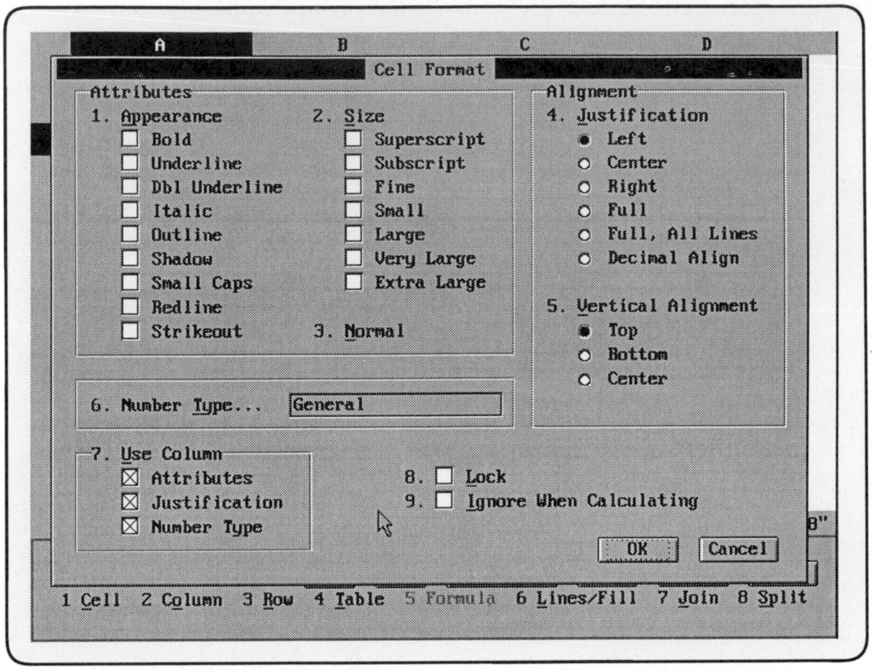

The "TCellFmt" button on the "TABLES" Button Bar will only work on individual cells. It is not possible to select a group of cells and use the "TCellFmt" button. If you do so, only the last cell highlighted will receive the formats.

The Cell Format dialog box gives you broad formatting capabilities for the data in your table. These options are described below:

> **Attributes -** This option allows you to change the appearance of the text in the cell (i.e., bold, underline, and italics). You can also change the size of the text in the specified cells.

> **Alignment -** You can change the justification of the cell contents to left, full, center, right, or decimal align. You can also adjust the vertical alignment of the text to be at the top, bottom, or center of the cell.

> **Number Type -** You can make numeric data appear differently.

> **Use Column -** This option allows you to format cells according to decisions made about the columns.

> **Lock -** When this check box has an X in it, it means that the data in the cell cannot be changed.

> **Ignore When Calculating -** When this check box has an X in it, it means that the cell will not be used for calculation. This is important when a year such as "1994" appears at the top of a numeric column.

To center the text in rows 1 and 2:

Press	1 or A to select the Appearance option	*Click*	*the Bold check box in the Appearance option until an X appears*
Press	1 or B to place an X in the Bold check box		

To center the text in the two rows:

Press	4 or J to select the Justification options	*Click*	*the Center option button in the Justification options*
Press	2 or C to select the Center option button		

To accept the cell formats:

Press	⏎Enter	*Click*	*the OK command button*

The top of your screen should look like Figure 18-13.

Figure 18-13

```
                  A              B              C              D
        ┌──────────────────────────────────────────────────────────┐
        │              JOHNSON PARTNERS                             │
    1   │           DISTRICT EXPENSE REPORT                         │
        │                First Quarter                             │
    2   │  District   │   Office    │  Telephone  │   Supplies      │
    3   │ Central     │ $38,000.50  │ $2,310.00   │ $11,810.98      │
    4   │ Eastern     │ 31,645.61   │ 4,412.31    │ 7,881.22        │
    5   │ Midwest     │ 53,760.75   │ 3,708.78    │ 8,544.65        │
    6   │ Mountain    │ 48,145.25   │ 6,974.96    │ 5,221.88        │
    7   │ Western     │ 40,746.41   │ 8,418.77    │ 10,550.29       │
        └──────────────────────────────────────────────────────────┘
```

The text in rows 1 and 2 is now boldfaced and centered.

Decimal Aligning Numeric Data

You can also format the numbers in the cells. To format the data in cell B3 to be decimal aligned:

Move	the cursor to cell B3	*Click*	*on cell B3*
Press	1 or C to select the Cell option	*Choose*	*the Cell option*
Press	4 or J to select the Justification options	*Click*	*the Decimal Align option button in the Justification options*
Press	6 or D to select the Decimal Align option button	*Click*	*the OK command button*
Press	⏎Enter		

Your screen should look like Figure 18-14.

Figure 18-14

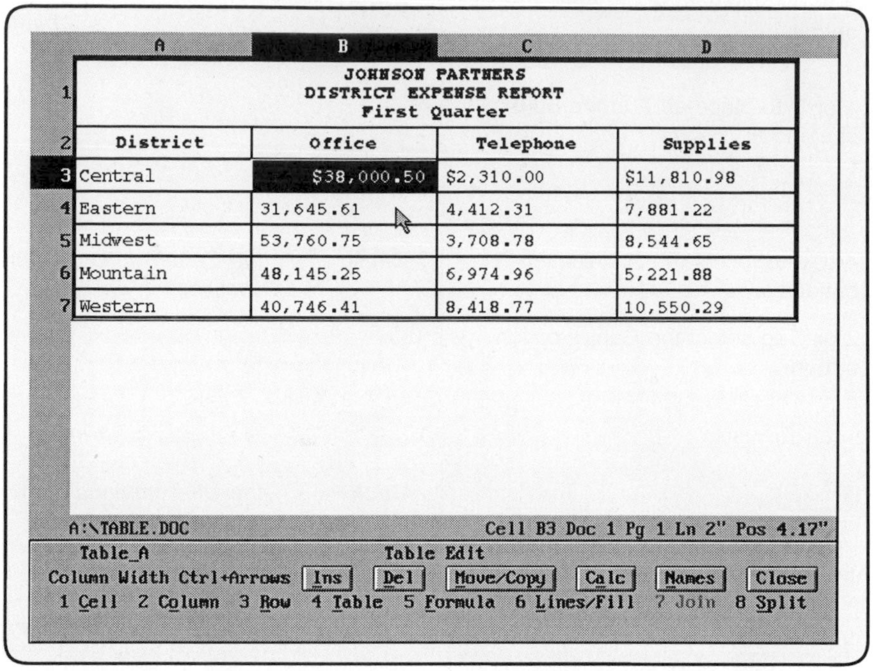

	A	B	C	D
1		JOHNSON PARTNERS DISTRICT EXPENSE REPORT First Quarter		
2	District	Office	Telephone	Supplies
3	Central	$38,000.50	$2,310.00	$11,810.98
4	Eastern	31,645.61	4,412.31	7,881.22
5	Midwest	53,760.75	3,708.78	8,544.65
6	Mountain	48,145.25	6,974.96	5,221.88
7	Western	40,746.41	8,418.77	10,550.29

A:\TABLE.DOC   Cell B3 Doc 1 Pg 1 Ln 2" Pos 4.17"

Table_A   Table Edit
Column Width Ctrl+Arrows [Ins] [Del] [Move/Copy] [Calc] [Names] [Close]
   1 Cell 2 Column 3 Row 4 Table 5 Formula 6 Lines/Fill 7 Join 8 Split

Notice that the number in cell B3 is right justified and aligned on the decimal point.

You can also format an entire column at a time. To decimal align the data in column B:

Move	the cursor to any cell in column B	*Click*	*on any cell in column B*
Press	2 or O to select the Column option	*Choose*	*the Column option*

The Column Format dialog box appears. To change the Justification to decimal align:

Press	4 or J to select the Justification options	*Click*	*the Decimal Align option button in the Justification options*
Type	6 or D to select the Decimal Align option button	*Click*	*the OK command button*
Press	⏎Enter		

The top part of your screen should look like Figure 18-15.

Figure 18-15

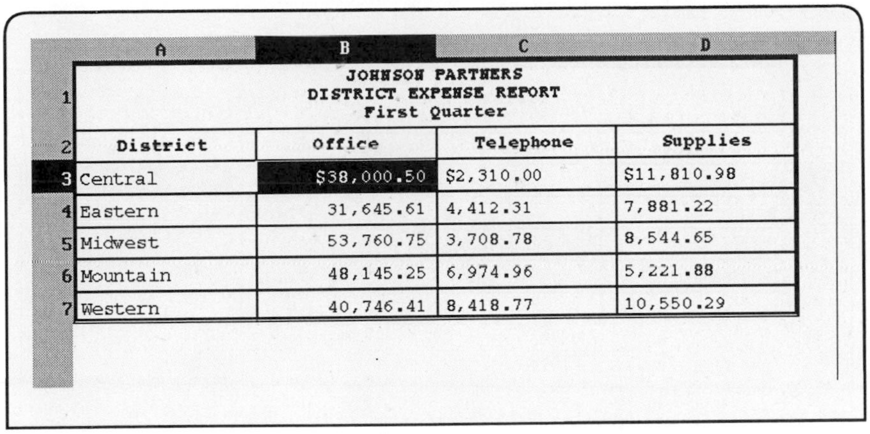

Notice that the "Office" column title stayed boldfaced and centered. This cell was formatted with the Cell feature. Column formats do not affect cells that were formatted using the Cell feature.

To format the numeric data in columns C and D to be decimal aligned:

Move	the cursor to cell C3	*Select*	*one cell in columns C and D*
Press	F12	*Choose*	*the Column option*
Press	→	*Click*	*the Decimal Align option button in the Justification options*
Press	2 or O to select the Column option	*Click*	*the OK command button*
Press	4 or J to select the Justification options		
Press	6 or D to select the Decimal Align option button		
Press	←Enter		

The top part of your screen should look like Figure 18-16.

Figure 18-16

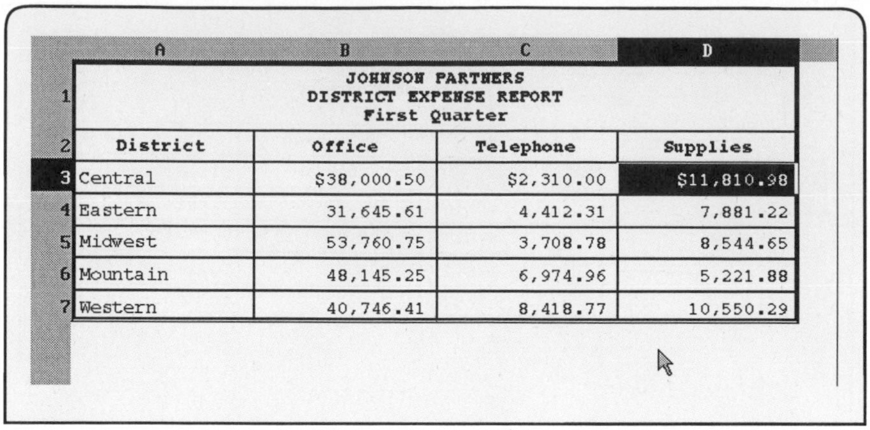

	A	B	C	D
		JOHNSON PARTNERS **DISTRICT EXPENSE REPORT** **First Quarter**		
2	**District**	**Office**	**Telephone**	**Supplies**
3	Central	$38,000.50	$2,310.00	$11,810.98
4	Eastern	31,645.61	4,412.31	7,881.22
5	Midwest	53,760.75	3,708.78	8,544.65
6	Mountain	48,145.25	6,974.96	5,221.88
7	Western	40,746.41	8,418.77	10,550.29

In This Book

For the remaining portion of this chapter, you are asked simply to select or highlight the cells in the table. You can use either the keyboard or mouse method for selecting the cells.

Changing the Appearance of Lines in a Table

You can also change the style of the lines surrounding the cells. To change the lines above and below the column titles so they are thicker:

Highlight	cells A2 through D2	*Highlight*	*cells A2 through D2*
Press	6 or L to select the Lines/Fill option	*Choose*	*the Lines/Fill option*
Press	5 or T to select the Top option	*Choose*	*the Top option*
Press	⬇ until "Thick Line" is highlighted	*Choose*	*the Thick Line option*
Press	1 or S to select the Select option	*Choose*	*the Select option*
Press	6 or B to select the Bottom option	*Choose*	*the Bottom option*
Press	⬇ until "Thick Line" is highlighted	*Choose*	*the Thick Line option*
Press	1 or S to select the Select option	*Choose*	*the Select option*
Press	←Enter	*Click*	*the Close command button*
Press	F7	*Click*	*the Close command button*

The top part of your screen should look similar to Figure 18-17.

Figure 18-17

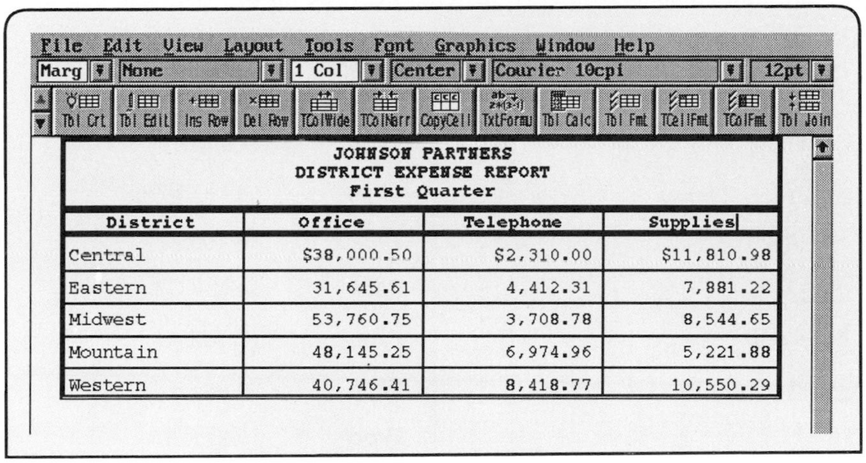

Inserting Rows in a Table

You can add more information to a table by inserting rows or columns. When you are in the Table Edit mode, you can use the Ins command button to insert rows or columns. You can delete rows and columns using the Del command button.

When you are in the normal document editing screen, you can also add a row to a table by pressing CTRL+INSERT. A new row is created above the present location of the cursor. To insert a row below the last row in the table, you must be in the Table Edit mode. You can delete the current row by pressing CTRL+DELETE and answering Yes to the dialog box.

Suppose you want to insert a row to include the Southern district. To insert a row alphabetically between Mountain and Western:

Move	the cursor to any cell in row 7		*Click*	*on any cell in row 7*
Press	Ctrl + Insert		*Click*	*the Ins Row button on the Button Bar*

You may also insert rows with the Insert Rows option under Tables in the Layout menu. The top part of your screen should look like Figure 18-18.

Figure 18-18

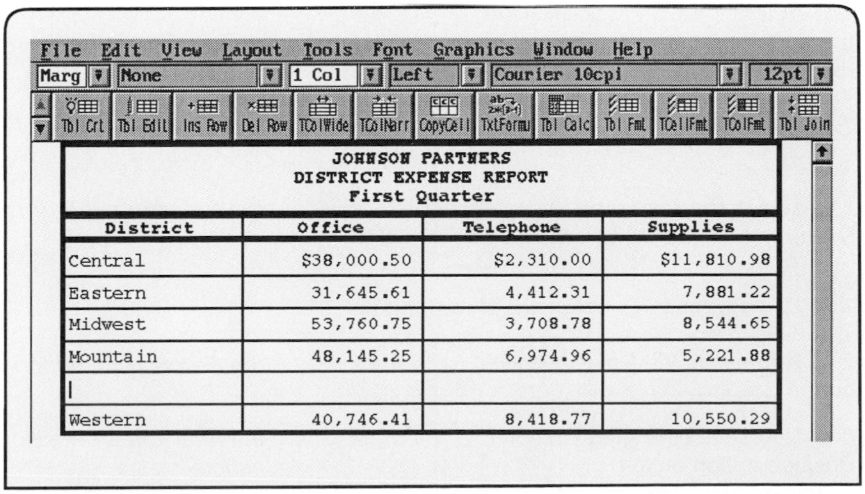

An empty row with four columns is inserted between the rows for the Mountain and Western districts. To enter data for the Southern district:

Move	the cursor to cell A7		*Click*	*on cell A7*
Type	Southern		*Type*	*Southern*
Press	[Tab↹]		*Click*	*on cell B7*
Type	34,706.21		*Type*	*34,706.21*
Press	[Tab↹]		*Click*	*on cell C7*
Type	11,142.46		*Type*	*11,142.46*
Press	[Tab↹]		*Click*	*on cell D7*
Type	15,211.75		*Type*	*15,211.75*

The top part of your screen should look like Figure 18-19.

Figure 18-19

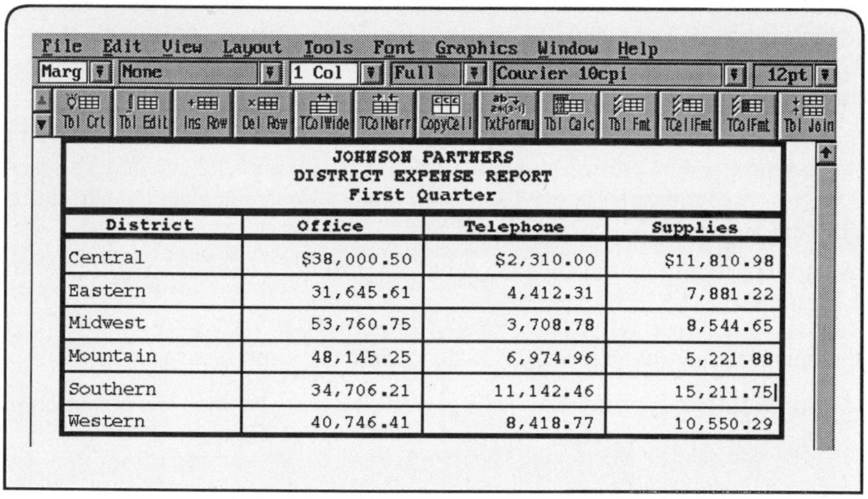

Notice that the information is formatted using the formats you previously defined.

To add a row to the bottom of the table:

Move	the cursor to any cell in the last row		*Click*	*on any cell in the last row*
Press	[Alt]+[F11]		*Click*	*the Tbl Edit button on the Button Bar*
Press	I to select the Ins command button		*Click*	*the Ins command button*

The Insert dialog box appears. To select the Rows option:

Press	2 or R to select the Rows option button		*Click*	*the Rows option button*
Press	5 or A to select the After Cursor Position option button		*Click*	*the After Cursor Position option button*
Press	[←Enter]		*Click*	*the OK command button*

A new row is added to the bottom of the table. This row will be used for the totals.

Performing Vertical Calculations in a Table

You can perform calculations on the numbers in a table. Suppose you want to sum the numbers in the office, telephone, and supplies columns to obtain a total for these expense categories.

You must be in the Table Edit mode to perform calculations on a table. You need to create a formula to calculate these totals. One of the easiest formulas you can create is one that sums a column. This is done by typing a plus sign (+) in the Formula text box.

| **Move** | the cursor to cell B9 | **Click** | on cell B9 |
| **Press** | 5 or F to select the Formula option | **Choose** | the Formula option |

The Table Formula dialog box appears. Your screen should look like Figure 18-20.

Figure 18-20

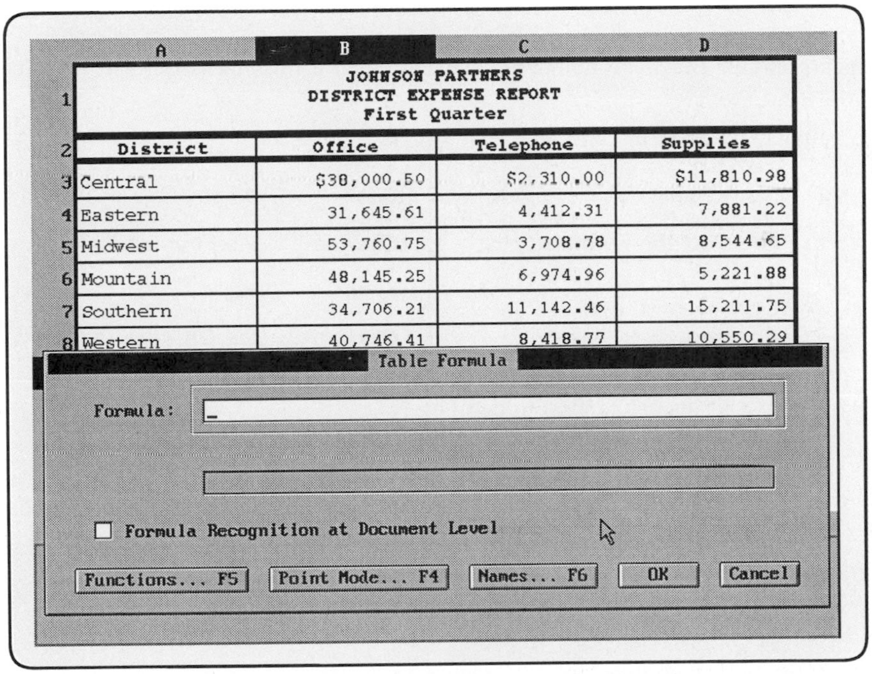

There are three types of "automatic" formulas, called **functions**. By placing a +, =, or * in the cell, you can get a subtotal (+), total (=), or grand total (*) for the column. The grand total function sums totals. The total function sums subtotals. The subtotal function sums the numbers.

To insert the subtotal function in cell B9:

| **Type** | + | **Type** | + |
| **Press** | ⏎Enter twice | **Click** | the OK command button |

The top part of your screen should look like Figure 18-21.

Figure 18-21

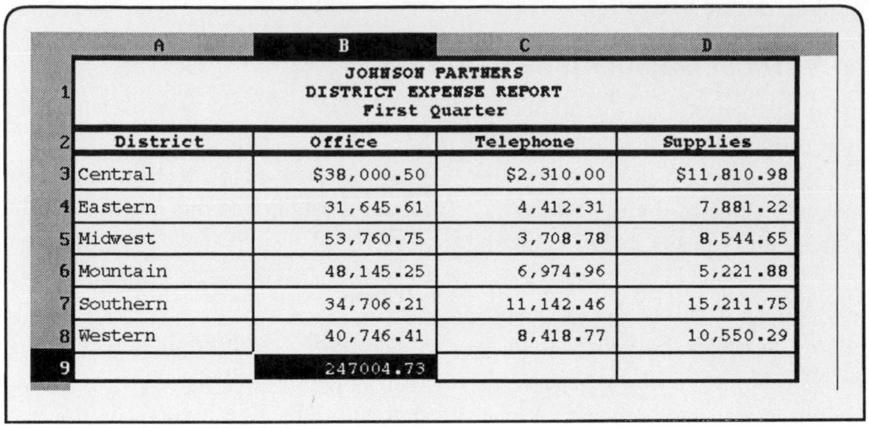

	A	B	C	D
1	JOHNSON PARTNERS DISTRICT EXPENSE REPORT First Quarter			
2	District	Office	Telephone	Supplies
3	Central	$38,000.50	$2,310.00	$11,810.98
4	Eastern	31,645.61	4,412.31	7,881.22
5	Midwest	53,760.75	3,708.78	8,544.65
6	Mountain	48,145.25	6,974.96	5,221.88
7	Southern	34,706.21	11,142.46	15,211.75
8	Western	40,746.41	8,418.77	10,550.29
9		247004.73		

The total appears in cell B9. The number calculated when a formula is defined for a cell is called the **result**.

To insert the subtotal function in cell C9:

Move	the cursor to cell C9	***Click***	*on cell C9*
Press	5 or F to select the Formula option	***Choose***	*the Formula option*
Type	+	***Type***	*+*
Press	[↵Enter] twice	***Click***	*the OK command button*

Repeat the steps above to insert the total in cell D9.

To add a title to the row:

Press	[F7]	***Click***	*the Close command button*
Move	the cursor to cell A9	***Click***	*on cell A9*
Type	Total	***Type***	*Total*

The top part of your screen should look like Figure 18-22.

Figure 18-22

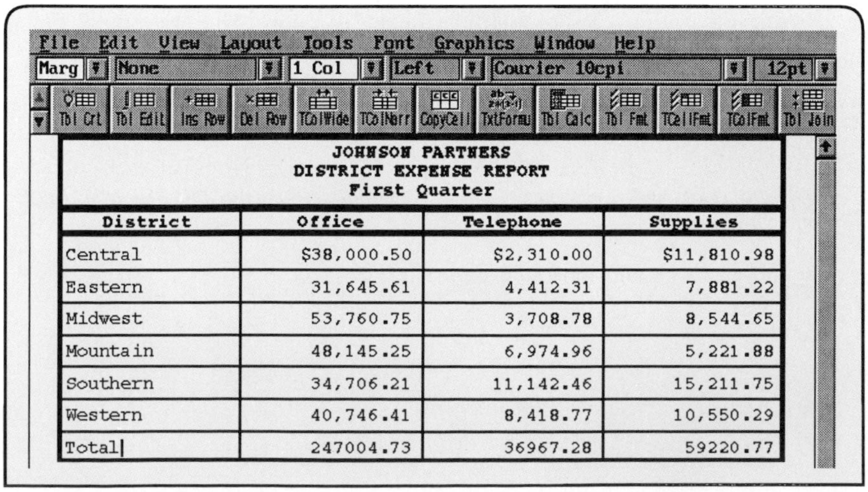

JOHNSON PARTNERS DISTRICT EXPENSE REPORT First Quarter			
District	Office	Telephone	Supplies
Central	$38,000.50	$2,310.00	$11,810.98
Eastern	31,645.61	4,412.31	7,881.22
Midwest	53,760.75	3,708.78	8,544.65
Mountain	48,145.25	6,974.96	5,221.88
Southern	34,706.21	11,142.46	15,211.75
Western	40,746.41	8,418.77	10,550.29
Total	247004.73	36967.28	59220.77

Changing Number Formats

The totals for the expense categories now appear on the screen. Because the row was added to the end of the table rather than inserted in the middle, you will need to add dollar signs and commas to format the numbers.

To add dollar signs and commas to the Total row:

Press	Alt + F11		**Click**	*the Tbl Edit button on the Button Bar*
Highlight	cells B9 through D9		**Select**	*cells B9 through D9*
Press	1 or C to select the Cell option		**Choose**	*the Cell option*
Press	6 or T to select the Number Type option		**Choose**	*the Number Type option*

The Number Type Formats dialog box appears on the screen. Your screen should look like Figure 18-23.

Figure 18-23

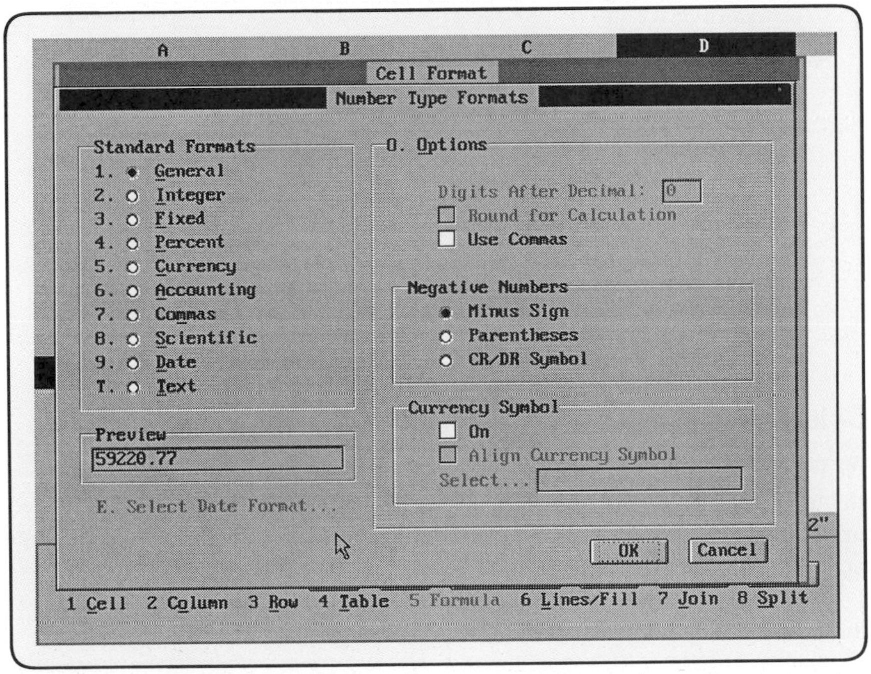

The Number Type Formats dialog box allows you to specify the way your numbers will display in the table.

To change the format to currency:

Press	5 or C to select the Currency option button in the Standard Formats box		**Click**	*the Currency option button in the Standard Formats box*

Notice the Preview text box. It shows how the number will display in the table.

To accept the format:

Press	←Enter		**Click**	*the OK command button*

Notice the Number Type option now shows Currency. To accept the changes and close the Cell Format dialog box:

| **Press** | ⏎Enter | **Click** | *the OK command button* |

Your screen should look like Figure 18-24.

Figure 18-24

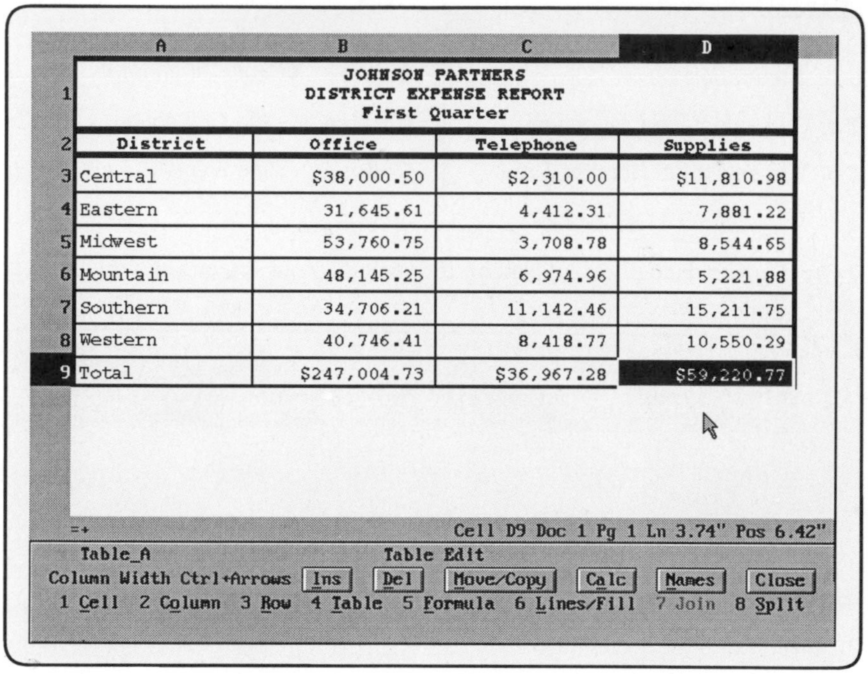

Inserting Columns in a Table

Suppose you want to add a column so you can determine total expenses for each district.

To add columns to a table, you must be in the Table Edit mode. Columns may be inserted to the left or right of the current cursor position. You can also divide a column in half by using the Split option.

To split the Supplies column into two columns:

Move	the cursor to cell D2	**Click**	*on cell D2*
Highlight	the Supplies column	**Highlight**	*the Supplies column*
Press	8 or S to select the Split option	**Choose**	*the Split option*

The Split Cell dialog box appears on the screen. To select the Columns option button and close the dialog box:

Press	1 or C to select the Columns option button	**Click**	*the Columns option button*
Type	2	**Type**	*2*
Press	⏎Enter twice	**Click**	*the OK command button*

Your screen should look like Figure 18-25.

Figure 18-25

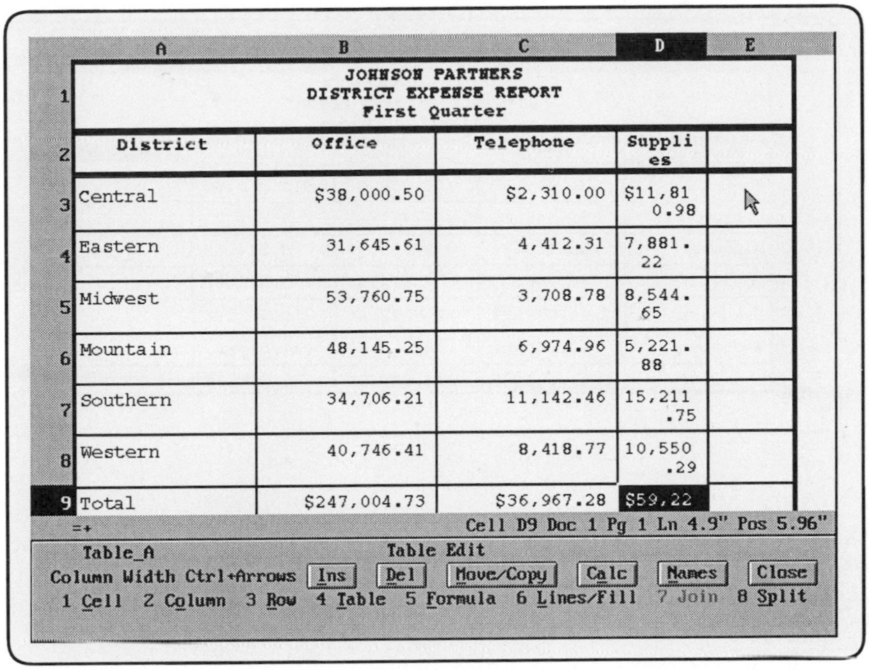

A fifth column is added to the right side of the table. The width of the Supplies column is smaller to make room for the new column. You can change the width of a column by pressing CTRL+LEFT or RIGHT ARROW. If you are in the normal editing screen, you can change the width of columns by clicking on the "TColWide" or "TColNarr" buttons on the "TABLES" Button Bar.

To change the width of column 1:

Move	the cursor to cell A2	*Click*	*on cell A2*
Press	[Ctrl]+[←] several times	*Press*	*[Ctrl]+[←] several times*

Another method is available to adjust the width of several columns at a time. To change the width of column B through column E:

Highlight	cells B2 through E2	*Highlight*	*cells B2 through E2*
Press	2 or O to select the Column option	*Choose*	*the Column option*
Press	8 or W to select the Width text box in the Columns box	*Click*	*in the Width text box in the Columns box*
Type	1.30	*Type*	*1.30*
Press	[←Enter] twice	*Click*	*the OK command button*

The top part of your screen should look similar to Figure 18-26.

Figure 18-26

	A	B	C	D	E
1		JOHNSON PARTNERS DISTRICT EXPENSE REPORT First Quarter			
2	District	Office	Telephone	Supplies	
3	Central	$38,000.50	$2,310.00	$11,810.98	
4	Eastern	31,645.61	4,412.31	7,881.22	
5	Midwest	53,760.75	3,708.78	8,544.65	
6	Mountain	48,145.25	6,974.96	5,221.88	
7	Southern	34,706.21	11,142.46	15,211.75	
8	Western	40,746.41	8,418.77	10,550.29	
9	Total	$247,004.73	$36,967.28	$59,220.77	

Performing Horizontal Calculations in a Table

You can create formulas to do calculations that the functions cannot. The four operators that you can use to create a formula are:

+   Add

-   Subtract

*   Multiply

/   Divide

The cell location is used in place of numbers in the formula, for example, B3+C3. WordPerfect then uses the amount in each location cell referenced in the formula for the calculation.

To create a formula to compute the total expenses for each district, you need to add Office, Telephone, and Supplies expenses.

To create the formula for the Central District and close the Table Formula dialog box:

Move	the cursor to cell E3	**Click**	on cell E3
Press	5 or F to select the Formula option	**Choose**	the Formula option
Type	B3+C3+D3	**Type**	B3+C3+D3
Press	⏎Enter twice	**Click**	the OK command button

When you enter the cell locations in a formula, you may use uppercase or lowercase letters. The top part of your screen should look like Figure 18-27.

Figure 18-27

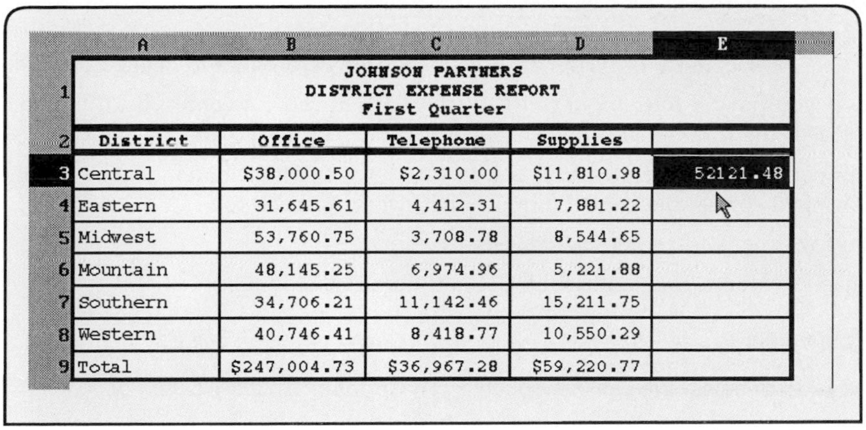

Look at the status bar on your screen. Notice the status bar displays the formula.

When the calculation is completed, the result of the formula is displayed in the cell. You can copy the same formula to several rows or columns.

To copy the formula in cell E3 to the other cells below it in the column:

Press	M to select the Move/Copy command button	***Click***	*the Move/Copy command button*
Press	P to select the Copy command button	***Click***	*the Copy command button*
Press	2 or D to select the Down option button	***Click***	*the Down option button*
Type	6	***Type***	*6*
Press	⏎Enter twice	***Click***	*the OK command button*

The top part of your screen should look like Figure 18-28.

Figure 18-28

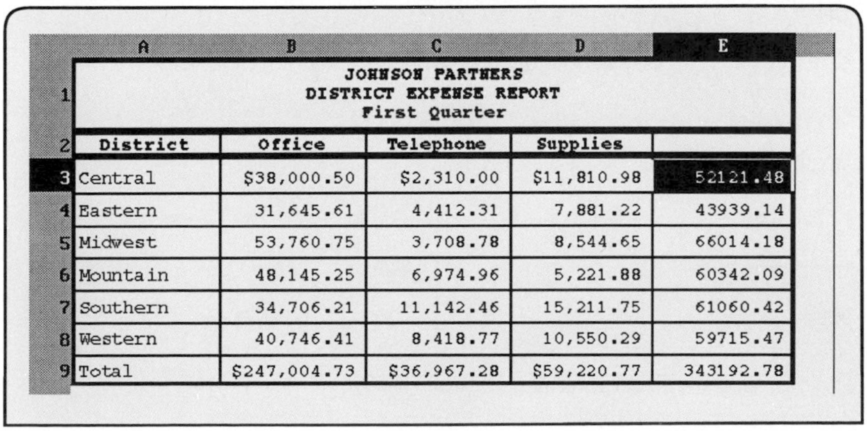

Make sure the cursor is in cell E4. The results of the copied formulas are displayed in column E. Notice that the cell location (on the left side of the status bar) in the copied formula is B4+C4+D4. When you copy formulas to other cells, WordPerfect uses **relative cell references** to change formulas in a table.

For example, if you have a formula in cell C4 that refers to cell B4 (one cell to the left) and copy that formula to cell D4, the formula will reference cell C4 (one cell to the left).

Check the cell locations in the copied formulas as you move down the column. The cell locations in each formula are changed so that the copied formulas will work for each row.

Notice that you will need to add dollar signs and commas.

To add commas to column E and close the Column Format dialog box:

Move	the cursor to cell E3		*Click*	*on cell E3*
Press	2 or O to select the Column option		*Choose*	*the Column option*
Press	6 or T to select the Number Type option		*Choose*	*the Number Type option*
Press	7 or M to select the Commas option button in the Standard Format box		*Click*	*the Commas option button in the Standard Format box*
Press	⏎Enter twice		*Click*	*the OK command button twice*

To add a dollar sign to the first cell in column E and close the Cell Format dialog box:

Move	the cursor to cell E3		*Click*	*on cell E3*
Press	1 or C to select the Cell option		*Choose*	*the Cell option*
Press	6 or T to select the Number Type option		*Choose*	*the Number Type option*
Press	5 or C to select the Currency option button in the Standard Format box		*Click*	*the Currency option button in the Standard Format box*
Press	⏎Enter twice		*Click*	*the OK command button twice*

Follow the steps above to format cell E9 with a dollar sign.

To see the formula in cell E4:

Move	the cursor to cell E4		*Click*	*on cell E4*

To add a title to the column:

Press	F7		*Click*	*the Close command button*
Move	the cursor to cell E2		*Click*	*on cell E2*
Type	Total		*Type*	*Total*

The top part of your screen should look like Figure 18-29.

Figure 18-29

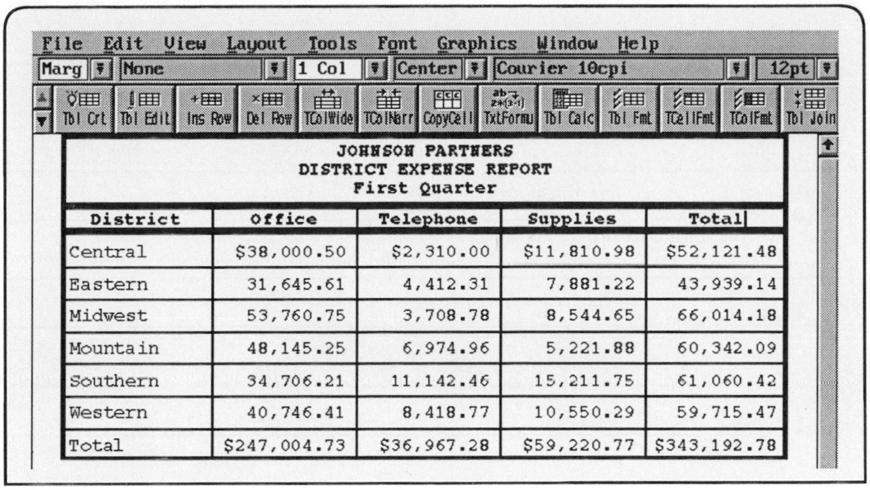

JOHNSON PARTNERS
DISTRICT EXPENSE REPORT
First Quarter

District	Office	Telephone	Supplies	Total
Central	$38,000.50	$2,310.00	$11,810.98	$52,121.48
Eastern	31,645.61	4,412.31	7,881.22	43,939.14
Midwest	53,760.75	3,708.78	8,544.65	66,014.18
Mountain	48,145.25	6,974.96	5,221.88	60,342.09
Southern	34,706.21	11,142.46	15,211.75	61,060.42
Western	40,746.41	8,418.77	10,550.29	59,715.47
Total	$247,004.73	$36,967.28	$59,220.77	$343,192.78

Save the document using the name "ENHANCED.TBL".

Recalculation in a Table

If any of the numeric data change in a table, WordPerfect will not automatically recalculate the totals. However, a feature is available to recompute the totals.

To demonstrate this feature:

Move	the cursor to cell B3	***Click***	*on cell B3*
Delete	the current contents of the cell	***Delete***	*the current contents of the cell*
Type	$50,000.00	***Type***	*$50,000.00*

Notice that no totals have changed. To recalculate the data:

Press	Alt+F11	***Click***	*the Tbl Calc button on the Button Bar*
Press	A to select the Calc command button		

In a few seconds, all the totals related to cell B3 will be updated.

Close the document without saving the changes.

EXERCISE 1

INSTRUCTIONS: Define the following concepts:

1. Tables feature ______________________________

____

2. Row ______________________________

____

3.   Column _____

_____

4.   Cell _____

_____

5.   Insert feature _____

_____

6.   Formula feature _____

_____

7.   Move/Copy _____

_____

8.   Functions _____

_____

9.   Relative Cell References _____

_____

10. Column Format _____

_____

11. Cell Format _____

_____

12. Number Type Formats _____

_____

EXERCISE 2

INSTRUCTIONS: Circle T if the statement is true and F if the statement is false.

T   F   1.   Columns have numeric names, and rows have alphabetic names.
T   F   2.   A table is a grid that is organized into columns and rows.
T   F   3.   The Join option only works when cells are blocked.
T   F   4.   Columns run horizontally.
T   F   5.   A cell occurs where each column and row meet.
T   F   6.   You can move from cell to cell by pressing the TAB key.
T   F   7.   As long as the Table Def code exists, you cannot delete the Cell, Row, or Tbl Off codes.

T	F	8.	The Move/Copy command button does not allow you to copy mathematical formulas.
T	F	9.	The Lock option enables you to prevent changes to a cell or column.
T	F	10.	There are four operators that you can use when creating a formula: +, -, *, and =.

EXERCISE 3

INSTRUCTIONS:

1. Create the following table. The data are for sales of three products by region.
2. The company information and column titles should be centered and boldfaced. The row titles should be left justified and boldfaced. The sales data should be right justified.
3. Insert a row between the North and East regions. The row title is "**Central**". Use the following values, from left to right, for the cells in the Central row: **17,000, 6,000,** and **3,000**.
4. Add a column at the end of the table and title it "**Total Regional Sales**".
5. The values in the "**Total Regional Sales**" column are calculated by summing the sales values for each product in a region.
6. Add a row at the end of the table and title it "**Total Product Sales**".
7. Calculate the values for the cells in the "**Total Product Sales**" row by summing the sales for the products in each region.
8. Make the lines above and below the column titles thicker.
9. Print the document.
10. Save the document in a file using the name "CH18EX03".
11. Close the document.

JACKSON APPLIANCE INC. REGIONAL SALES REPORT Second Quarter			
Region	**Washing Machines**	**Toasters**	**Mowers**
North	$65,000	$10,000	$8,000
East	50,000	20,000	12,000
South	25,000	5,000	2,000
West	31,000	16,000	4,000

EXERCISE 4

INSTRUCTIONS:

1. Create the following document using the Tables feature.
2. Center the column headings.
3. Place a double line border around the outer edge of the table. All lines inside the table are single.
4. Center the table from top to bottom on the page using the Center Page option under the Page option from the Layout menu.
5. Preview the document.
6. Print the document.
7. Save the document in a file using the name "CH18EX04".
8. Close the document.

TEN MOST POPULOUS CITIES IN THE WORLD

City	Country	Population
Tokyo	Japan	25,434,000
Mexico City	Mexico	16,901,000
San Paolo	Brazil	14,911,000
New York City	United States	14,598,000
Seoul	South Korea	13,665,000
Osaka-Kobe	Japan	13,562,000
Buenos Aires	Argentina	10,750,000
Calcutta	India	10,462,000
Bombay	India	10,137,000
Rio de Janeiro	Brazil	10,116,000

EXERCISE 5

INSTRUCTIONS:

1. Create the following table.
2. Starting with "**Steven J. Ross**", shade every other row in the table.
3. Decimal align the third column.
4. Center the document from top to bottom on the page using the Center Page option under the Page option on the Layout menu.
5. Center the column and table headings.
6. Preview the document.
7. Print the document.
8. Save the document in a file using the name "CH18EX05".
9. Close the document.

THE TEN HIGHEST PAID CHIEF EXECUTIVES		
Name	Company	Total Pay
Craig O. McCaw	McCaw Cellular	$53,994,000
Steven J. Ross	Time Warner	34,200,000
Donald A. Pels	Lin Broadcasting	22,791,000
Jim P. Manzi	Lotus Development	16,363,000
Paul Fireman	Reebok International	14,606,000
Ronald K. Richey	Torchmark	12,666,000
Martin S. Davis	Paramount	11,635,000
Roberto C. Goizueta	Coca-Cola	10,715,000
Michael D. Eisner	Walt Disney	9,589,000
August A. Busch, III	Anheuser-Busch	8,816,000

EXERCISE 6

INSTRUCTIONS:

1. Open the document "CH18EX05".
2. Change the title to "**THE 20 HIGHEST-PAID CHIEF EXECUTIVES**".
3. Add a blank line after the title.
4. Put a double line border under the column titles.
5. Add the following ten lines at the bottom of the table.
6. Starting with "**James R. Moffett**", shade every other line.
7. Add the note "**Data: Standard & Poor's Compustat Services, Inc.**" a double space below the table.
8. Preview the document.
9. Print the document.
10. Save the document in a file using the name "CH18EX06".
11. Close the document.

William G. McGowan	MCI	8,666,000
James R. Moffett	Freeport McMoran	7,300,000
Donald E. Peterson	Ford Motor	7,147,000
P. Roy Vagelos	Merck	6,764,000
W. Michael Blumenthal	Unisys	6,511,000
S. Parker Gilbert	Morgan Stanley	5,510,000
Harry A. Merlo	Louisiana-Pacific	5,314,000
Rueben A. Mark	Colgate-Palmolive	5,004,000
Robert J. Pfeiffer	Alexander & Baldwin	4,943,000
William P. Stiritz	Ralston Purina	4,854,000

Data: Standard & Poor's Compustat Services, Inc.

EXERCISE 7

INSTRUCTIONS:

1. Create the following letter and table.
2. The title of the table is centered and boldfaced.
3. The column headings are centered. There is a thick line under the title.
4. Use the Math feature to calculate column 4. The formula is **(B3-C3)/C3*100**.
5. Spell check the document.
6. Preview the document.
7. Print the document.
8. Save the document in a file using the name "CH18EX07".
9. Close the document.

current date

Mr. George Evans
Director of Sales
Eastwood Merchandise Company
1098 West Huron Street
Cleveland, OH 44101

Dear Mr. Evans:

Here is the list of top salespeople for the year. I hope that you will
notice the improvement of some of the salespeople over last year's
figures.

EASTWOOD MERCHANDISE COMPANY SALES LEADERS FOR 19--			
Name	This Year	Last Year	% of Change
James Bradford	$250,000	$200,000	25.00
Lenore Berger	387,000	302,000	28.15
Horace Grant	250,557	175,000	43.18
Dina Reynolds	450,000	275,000	63.64
Lincoln Tyler	315,500	150,750	109.29

These five people will be honored at the Annual Meeting for all
salespeople. They will be awarded plaques and, of course, they will be
substantially rewarded by their commissions.

Sincerely,

Neil Smith
Regional Sales Director

xx

EXERCISE 8

INSTRUCTIONS:
1. Create the following table.
2. Boldface the state names in the first column.
3. Change the state nicknames in the second column to small print.
4. Shade the column headings line using the Tables Cell feature.
5. When done, remove all lines from the table.

6. Preview the document.
7. Print the document.
8. Save the document in a file using the name "CH18EX08".
9. Close the document.

TRIVIA INFORMATION ABOUT
SELECTED STATES

Name	Nickname	Flower
Alabama	Heart of Dixie	Camellia
Alaska	The Last Frontier	Forget-me-not
Hawaii	The Aloha State	Yellow Hibiscus
Indiana	The Hoosier State	Peony
Kentucky	The Bluegrass State	Goldenrod
New Jersey	Garden State	Purple Violet
Pennsylvania	Keystone State	Mountain Laurel
Texas	The Lone Star State	Bluebonnet

EXERCISE 9

INSTRUCTIONS:

1. Open the document "CH18EX08".
2. Change the initial font to Bodoni-WP (Type 1) 10 point.
3. Add a column to the end of the table. The column heading should be "**Abbr**". Enter the two-letter state abbreviation for each state. The abbreviations are listed below:

    AL, AK, HI, IN, KY, NJ, PA, TX

4. The last column should be in italics.
5. Put the lines back into the table. Put a double line around the outer edges of the table.
6. Preview the document.
7. Print the document.
8. Save the document in a file using the name "CH18EX09".
9. Close the document.

EXERCISE 10

INSTRUCTIONS:

1. Create the following table.
2. Enlarge the first column to fit the names.
3. The title of the table is boldfaced and centered.
4. The column headings are centered, shaded, and aligned at the bottom of the cell.
5. Double lines are placed around the outside of the table, the title, the Names column, and the Totals column.
6. Center the data in columns 3 and 4. Decimal align columns 2, 5, and 6.
7. Compute the totals by using this formula, **B3+E3**.
8. Preview the document.
9. Print the document.
10. Save the document in a file using the name "CH18EX10.01".
11. Add the following names to the end of the table:

Farrel, S.	**595**	**8**	**4**	**250**
Vasquez, J.	**595**	**5**	**7**	**175**

12. Add a Totals row that sums each column, including the Totals column.
13. Format the Totals row so the numbers display a dollar sign and commas.
14. Shade the Totals row and column using the Tables Cell feature.
15. Preview the document.
16. Print the document.
17. Save the document in a file using the name "CH18EX10.02".
18. Close the document.

CONFERENCE REGISTRATION					
Names	Fees	Mtg's Pvt.	Mtg's Group	Meals	Totals
Barnes, G.	$595	4	8	$250	
Cartier, J.	595	5	7	175	
Franklin, R.	595	6	6	225	
Hoard, R.T.	595	2	10	100	
Lytle, R.S.	595	3	9	240	
Mansfield, T.	595	0	12	360	

CHAPTER NINETEEN

ADVANCED TABLE FEATURES

OBJECTIVES

In this chapter, you will learn to:

- ■ Use advanced functions in formulas
- ■ Create a range name

■ CHAPTER OVERVIEW

At times you may want to perform more sophisticated calculations in your table besides sum, total, or grand total. This chapter illustrates the use of advanced table functions. The process of creating a range name is also demonstrated.

■ USING ADVANCED FUNCTIONS IN FORMULAS

WordPerfect 6.0 for DOS has 101 special functions. Each one performs some unique calculation and has a specific structure that you must use. To see a full explanation and example of each function, consult "Appendix Q" in the WordPerfect Reference manual.

In this chapter, some of the functions will be demonstrated. Within a table, you might want to perform the complex functions found in a spreadsheet, such as averaging a series of numbers or using the SUM function. The advanced functions are predefined formulas that you can use in your table calculations.

The table illustrated in Figure 19-1 was created in the previous chapter. It calculates the total office, telephone, and supplies expenses of a company. To determine the totals for each column and row, you could have used the SUM function. In this chapter, rather than finding the total expenditures for each category, you will learn how to determine the average cost of each expense.

Figure 19-1

JOHNSON PARTNERS DISTRICT EXPENSE REPORT First Quarter				
District	**Office**	**Telephone**	**Supplies**	**Total**
Central	$38,000.50	$2,310.00	$11,810.98	$52,121.48
Eastern	31,645.61	4,412.31	7,881.22	43,939.14
Midwest	53,760.75	3,708.78	8,544.65	66,014.18
Mountain	48,145.25	6,974.96	5,221.88	60,342.09
Southern	34,706.21	11,142.46	15,211.75	61,060.42
Western	40,746.41	8,418.77	10,550.29	59,715.47
Total	$247,004.73	$36,967.28	$59,220.77	$343,192.78

Open the "ENHANCED.TBL" file created in Chapter 18. You may wish to display the "TABLES" Button Bar if it is not presently on the screen.

Before using the AVE(list) function to get an average for each expense column, insert a row below the Total row at the bottom of the table.

To insert a row below the Totals row:

Press	Alt + F11		*Click*	*the Tbl Edit button on the Button Bar*
Move	the cursor to any cell in row 9		*Click*	*on any cell in row 9*
Press	I to select the Ins command button		*Click*	*the Ins command button*
Press	2 or R to select the Rows option button		*Click*	*the Rows option button*
Press	5 or A to select the After Cursor Position option button		*Click*	*the After Cursor Position option button*
Press	←Enter		*Click*	*the OK command button*

The bottom part of your screen should look like Figure 19-2.

Figure 19-2

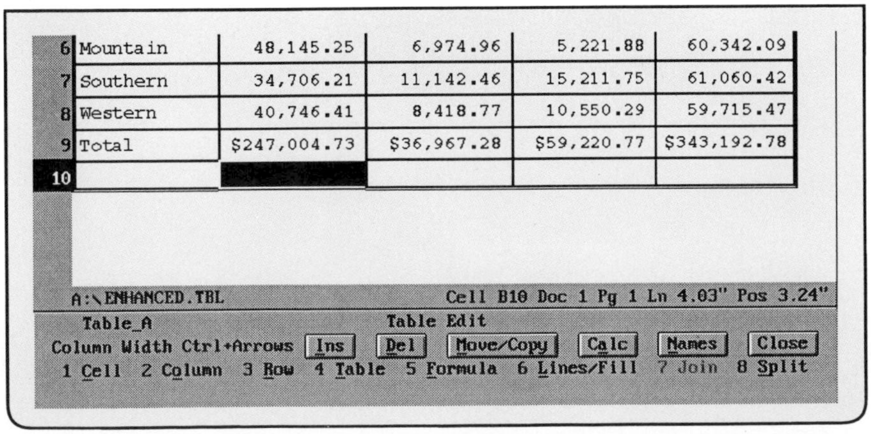

6	Mountain	48,145.25	6,974.96	5,221.88	60,342.09
7	Southern	34,706.21	11,142.46	15,211.75	61,060.42
8	Western	40,746.41	8,418.77	10,550.29	59,715.47
9	Total	$247,004.73	$36,967.28	$59,220.77	$343,192.78
10					

A:\ENHANCED.TBL   Cell B10 Doc 1 Pg 1 Ln 4.03" Pos 3.24"
Table_A   Table Edit
Column Width Ctrl+Arrows [Ins] [Del] [Move/Copy] [Calc] [Names] [Close]
1 Cell 2 Column 3 Row 4 Table 5 Formula 6 Lines/Fill 7 Join 8 Split

To view the functions:

Move	the cursor to cell B10	*Click*	*on cell B10*
Press	5 or F to select the Formula option	*Choose*	*the Formula option*
Press	[F5] to select the Functions command button	*Click*	*the Functions command button*

The Table Functions dialog box appears. For a complete description of all the functions, consult "Appendix Q" in the WordPerfect Reference manual. Your screen should look like Figure 19-3.

Figure 19-3

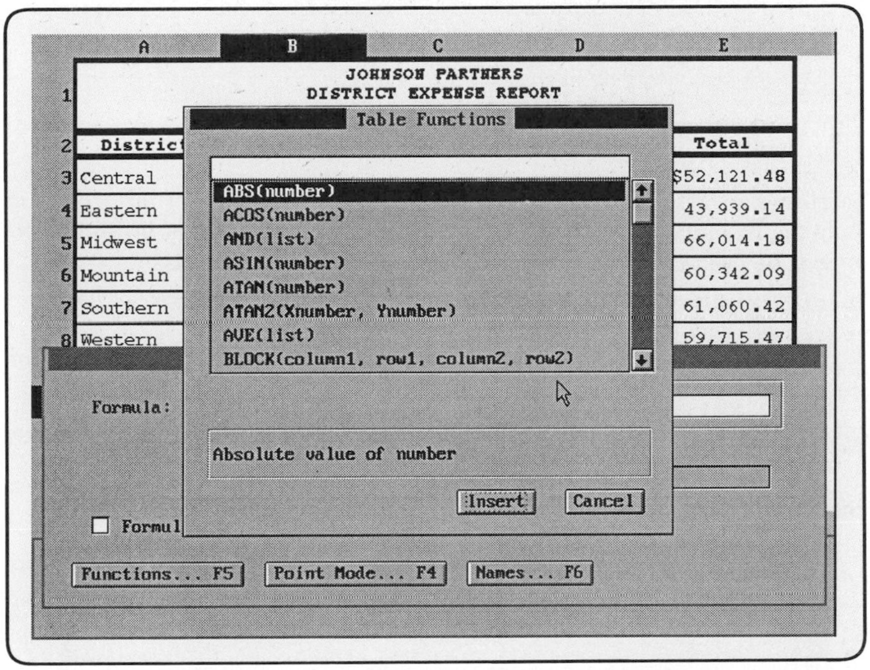

To insert the AVE(list) function:

Press	⬇ six times to highlight the AVE(list) function	*Click*	*the AVE(list) function*
Press	[←Enter] to select the Insert command button	*Click*	*the Insert command button*

The Table Formula dialog box appears on the screen. The bottom of your screen should look like Figure 19-4.

Figure 19-4

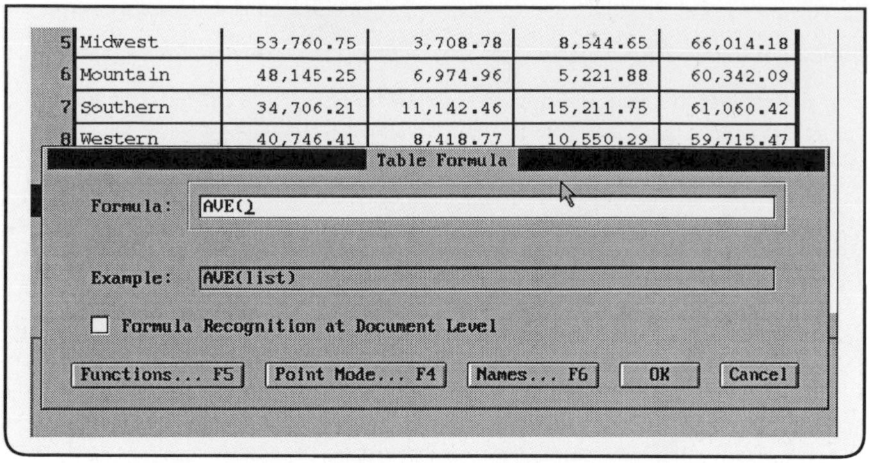

5	Midwest	53,760.75	3,708.78	8,544.65	66,014.18
6	Mountain	48,145.25	6,974.96	5,221.88	60,342.09
7	Southern	34,706.21	11,142.46	15,211.75	61,060.42
8	Western	40,746.41	8,418.77	10,550.29	59,715.47

Table Formula

Formula: AVE()

Example: AVE(list)

☐ Formula Recognition at Document Level

[Functions... F5] [Point Mode... F4] [Names... F6] [OK] [Cancel]

Notice that the characters "AVE( )" are in the Formula text box, and that there is an example of the function syntax in the Example text box. You wish to compute the average of the data in cells B3 through B8. The colon will be used to indicate that you want to use a block of cells.

To complete the AVE(list) function and close the Table Formula dialog box:

Type	B3:B8 (within the parentheses of the function)	**Type**	B3:B8 *(within the parentheses of the function)*
Press	⟵Enter twice	**Click**	*the OK command button*

Your screen should look like Figure 19-5.

Figure 19-5

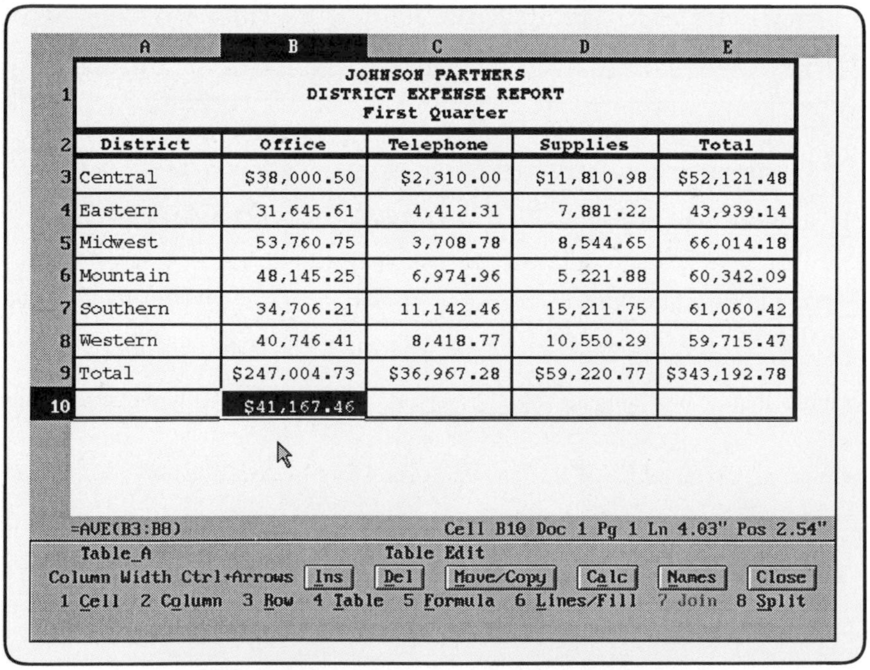

	A	B	C	D	E
1		JOHNSON PARTNERS DISTRICT EXPENSE REPORT First Quarter			
2	District	Office	Telephone	Supplies	Total
3	Central	$38,000.50	$2,310.00	$11,810.98	$52,121.48
4	Eastern	31,645.61	4,412.31	7,881.22	43,939.14
5	Midwest	53,760.75	3,708.78	8,544.65	66,014.18
6	Mountain	48,145.25	6,974.96	5,221.88	60,342.09
7	Southern	34,706.21	11,142.46	15,211.75	61,060.42
8	Western	40,746.41	8,418.77	10,550.29	59,715.47
9	Total	$247,004.73	$36,967.28	$59,220.77	$343,192.78
10		$41,167.46			

=AVE(B3:B8)   Cell B10 Doc 1 Pg 1 Ln 4.03" Pos 2.54"

Table_A   Table Edit
Column Width Ctrl+Arrows [Ins] [Del] [Move/Copy] [Calc] [Names] [Close]
1 Cell 2 Column 3 Row 4 Table 5 Formula 6 Lines/Fill 7 Join 8 Split

The average displays a number with two decimal places because that was the format of the numbers in the Total row. When the new row was added to the bottom of the table, it received the formatting of the row above it. If you wish to see a different number of decimal places in an average, use the Cell Format dialog box described in the previous chapter.

Follow the steps above to place the formula in cells C10 and D10. Be sure to change the formula to cells C3:C8 and D3:D8, respectively. Then put the title "Average" in cell A10. Your screen should look like Figure 19-6.

Figure 19-6

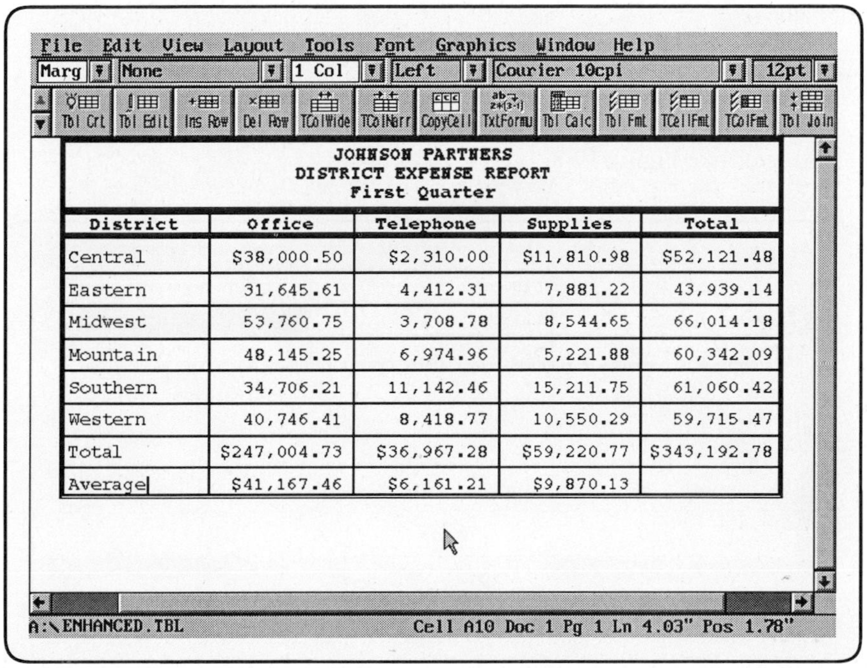

You could also have used the Move/Copy command button to copy the contents of cell B10 to cells C10 and D10. Save the file using the name "AVERAGE.TBL". Close the file.

Suppose you want to set up a table that calculates the monthly payment for an installment loan. Create the table in Figure 19-7.

Figure 19-7

Principal	$18,000.00	Monthly Payment
Interest Rate	12%	
Term in Months	60	

To calculate the monthly payment:

Move	the cursor to cell C2	*Click*	*on cell C2*
Press	Alt + F11	*Click*	*the Tbl Edit button on the Button Bar*
Press	5 or F to select the Formula option	*Choose*	*the Formula option*

Press	F5 to select the Functions command button		**Click**	the Functions command button
Press	P to instantly scroll down to the functions beginning with the letter P		**Click**	the down scroll arrow until the PMT(rate%, PV, periods, FV [,type]) function is highlighted
Press	↓ until the PMT(rate%, PV, periods, FV [,type]) function is highlighted		**Click**	the Insert command button
Press	↵Enter to select the Insert command button			

Your screen should look like Figure 19-8.

Figure 19-8

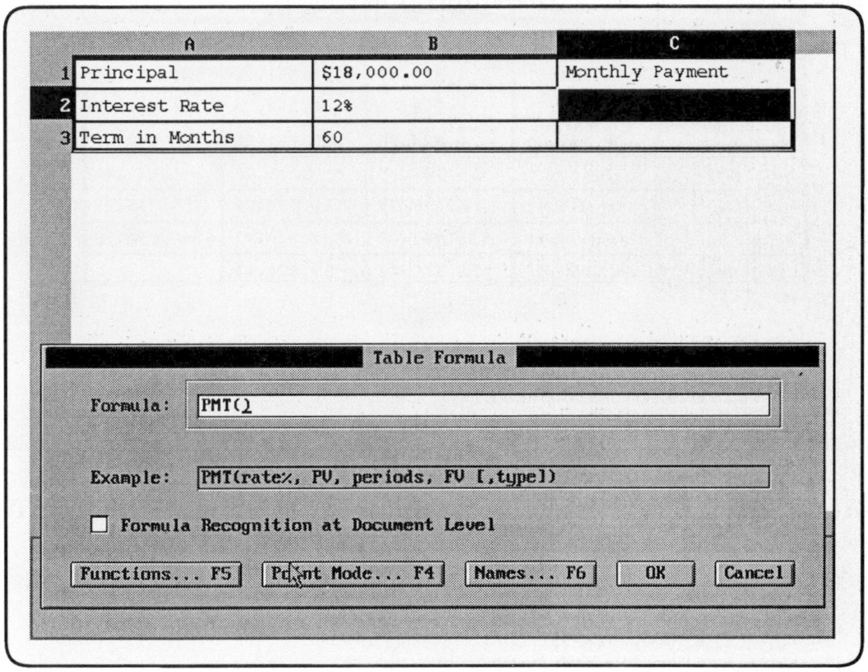

Notice the example in the Table Formula dialog box. Each component of the PMT function is described below:

PMT   is the name of the function. It is used to calculate the payment for a loan or investment.

rate%   is the rate of interest in percent format (e.g., 10%). If payments will be made monthly, the rate is divided by 12. If payments are to be made quarterly, the rate is divided by 4. If only one payment is made per year, it is not divided by anything.

PV   means "Present Value". It means the total amount of the loan or investment.

periods   is used to determine the length of the debt or investment.

FV   means "Future Value". It means the ending value of the loan or investment. If the payment is being computed for a loan, the FV will be 0. If payment is being computed for an investment, the FV will be the anticipated value of the investment.

type   is an optional component of the function. If a zero is included for the type, it means payments are made at the end of each period. A non-zero value means payments are to be made at the beginning of each period.

For this exercise, the rate appears in cell B2 and will be divided over 12 months. The PV appears in cell B1, the period appears in cell B3, and the FV will be zero.

To compose the elements of the PMT function and close the dialog box:

Type	B2/12,B1,B3,0	*Type*	*B2/12,B1,B3,0*
Press	⏎Enter twice	*Click*	*the OK command button*

The monthly payment should appear in cell C2. Your table should look like Figure 19-9.

Figure 19-9

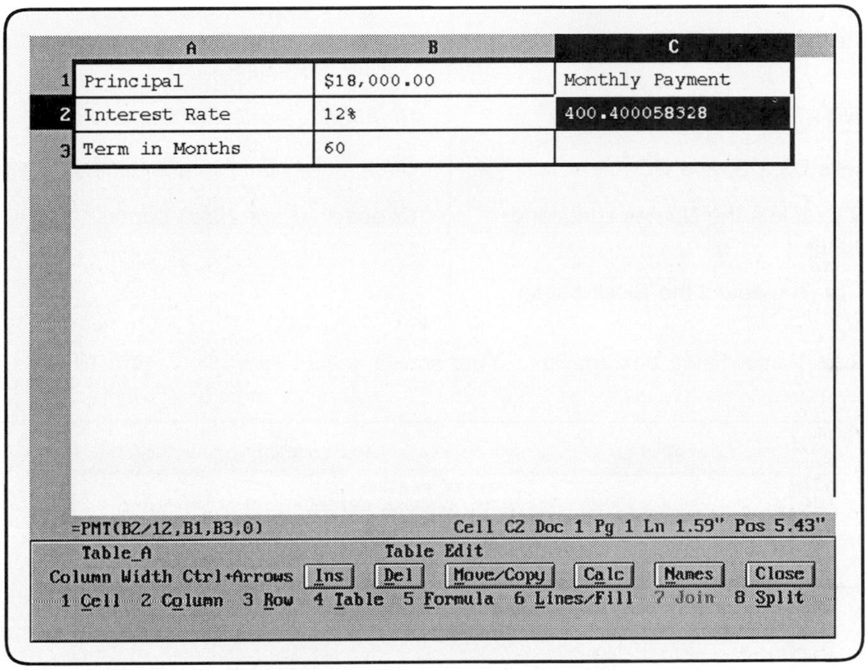

	A	B	C
1	Principal	$18,000.00	Monthly Payment
2	Interest Rate	12%	400.400058328
3	Term in Months	60	

=PMT(B2/12,B1,B3,0)   Cell C2 Doc 1 Pg 1 Ln 1.59" Pos 5.43"

Table_A   Table Edit
Column Width Ctrl+Arrows Ins   Del   Move/Copy   Calc   Names   Close
  1 Cell 2 Column 3 Row 4 Table 5 Formula 6 Lines/Fill 7 Join 8 Split

To format the result to two decimal places and close the dialog boxes:

Press	1 or C to select the Cell option	*Choose*	*the Cell option*
Press	6 or T to select the Number Type option	*Choose*	*the Number Type option*
Press	3 or F to select the Fixed option button	*Click*	*the Fixed option button*
Press	⏎Enter twice	*Click*	*the OK command button twice*

Save the document as "PMT.TBL".

If you choose to change the rate, principal, or term, the table will not automatically recalculate. To view an updated monthly payment, you may press ALT+F11 and then choose the Calc command button. You may also click the "Tbl Calc" button on the Button Bar or choose Calculate All from the Tables option under the Layout menu.

Close the document.

■ CREATING A RANGE NAME

When working with complex tables and formulas, you may find it useful to create range names in your tables. **Range names** allow you to use the name rather than the cell address when you are referring to a block of cells in your formula. For example, when you created "ENHANCED.TBL" in the previous chapter, you created the formula B3+C3+D3 to compute the total expenses for the Central district. Rather than having to name each cell in the formula, you could name cells B3 through D3, and use that name in the formula.

Open the "ENHANCED.TBL" document.

To name the range of cells B3 through D3:

Move	the cursor to cell B3		*Click*	*the Tbl Edit button on the Button Bar*
Press	Alt + F11		*Highlight*	*cells B3, C3, and D3*
Highlight	cells B3, C3, and D3		*Click*	*the Names command button*
Press	N to select the Names command button		*Choose*	*the Block option*
Press	1 or B to select the Block option			

The Create Block Name dialog box appears. Your screen should look like Figure 19-10.

Figure 19-10

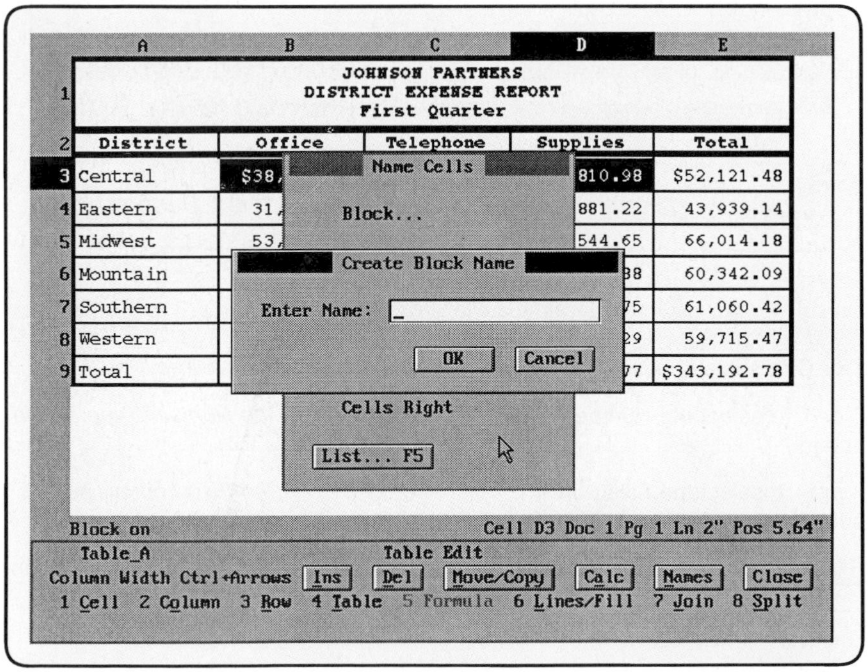

To enter the name:

Type	Central		*Type*	*Central*
Press	↵Enter		*Click*	*the OK command button*

To change the formula in cell E3:

Move	the cursor to cell E3	*Click*	*on cell E3*
Press	5 or F to select the Formula option	*Choose*	*the Formula option*
Press	⌞F5⌟ to select the Functions command button	*Click*	*the Functions command button*
Type	SUM (to highlight the SUM(list) function)	*Type*	*SUM (to highlight the SUM(list) function)*
Press	⌞←Enter⌟ to select the Insert command button	*Click*	*the Insert command button*

Now the SUM(list) function is in the Formula text box.

To insert the range name into the formula:

Press	⌞F6⌟ to select the Names command button	*Click*	*the Names command button*

The List Table Names dialog box appears. Your screen should look like Figure 19-11.

Figure 19-11

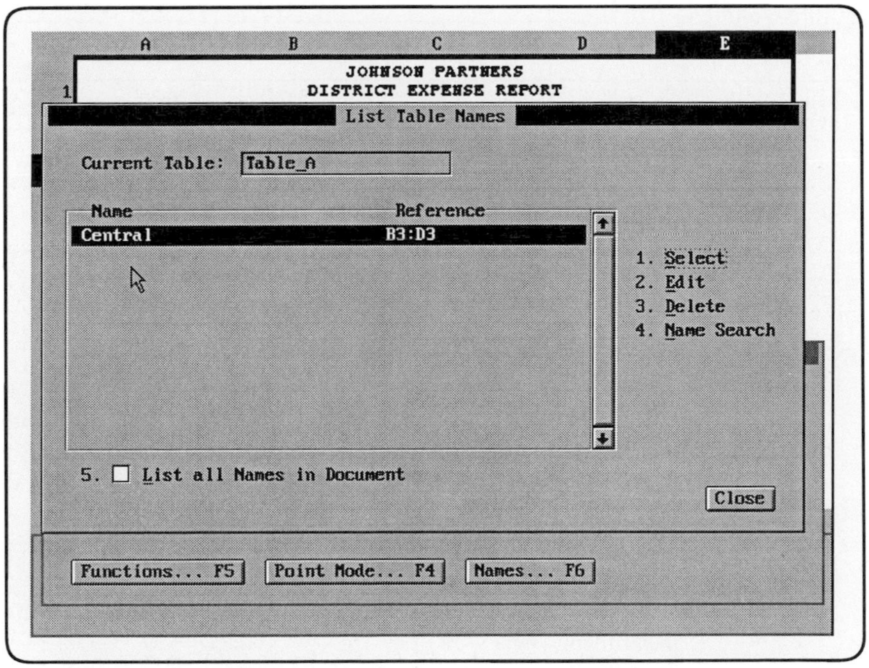

To select the "Central" name:

Press	1 or S to select the Select option	*Choose*	*the Select option*

To complete the formula:

Press	⌞←Enter⌟ twice	*Click*	*the OK command button*

Notice that the number did not change, but the formula listed in the status bar is different.
Close the document without saving changes. Select the "WPMAIN" Button Bar.

EXERCISE 1

INSTRUCTIONS: Define the following concepts:

1.   Table functions _____

_____

2.   SUM function _____

_____

3.   AVE function _____

_____

4.   PMT function _____

_____

5.   Present Value _____

_____

6.   Future Value _____

_____

7.   Range name _____

_____

EXERCISE 2

INSTRUCTIONS: Circle T if the statement is true and F if the statement is false.

T   F   1.   WordPerfect 6.0 has about 50 built-in functions.

T   F   2.   When the AVE function is placed in a cell, it knows automatically to average the numbers immediately above it.

T   F   3.   The correct format for displaying a list of numbers for the AVE function is "B3:B8".

T   F   4.   The Move/Copy command cannot be used to copy functions from one cell to another.

T   F   5.   The PMT function offers a method for computing a monthly payment for an installment loan.

T   F   6.   The PMT function may require as many as six different numbers to complete its structure.

T   F   7.   The "type" is a required part of the PMT function.

T   F   8.   "PV" stands for "Previous Value" in the PMT function.

T   F   9.   A range name can be a single word and can replace a block of cell addresses.

T   F   10.   Once a range name is created, the name automatically replaces a block of cells in a formula.

EXERCISE 3

INSTRUCTIONS:

1. Open "CH18EX03" created in the previous chapter. If you have not created it, you should do so at this time.
2. Insert a row below the last row of the table.
3. Use the AVE function to determine the average sales for each product.
4. Type "**Average**" in cell A9.
5. Save the document in a file using the name "CH19EX03".
6. Print the document.
7. Close the document.

EXERCISE 4

INSTRUCTIONS:

1. Open the file called "CH18EX04" created in the previous chapter. If you have not created the file, you should do so at this time.
2. Insert two rows below the data for Rio de Janeiro.
3. In cell C12, insert the SUM function to determine the total population of the noted cities.
4. In cell C13, insert the AVE function to determine the average population of the noted cities.
5. In cells A12 and A13, type "**Total Population**" and "**Average**", respectively.
6. Print the document.
7. Save the document in a file using the name "CH19EX04".
8. Close the document.

EXERCISE 5

INSTRUCTIONS:

1. Open "CH18EX06" created in the previous chapter. If you have not created the file, you should do so at this time.
2. Insert two rows below the last row.
3. In cell C23, determine the average of the top five salaries.
4. In cell A23, type "**Average of the Top Five**".
5. In cell C24, determine the average of the lowest five salaries.
6. In cell A24, type "**Average of the Lowest Five**".
7. Preview the document.
8. Print the document.
9. Save the document in a file using the name "CH19EX05".
10. Close the document.

EXERCISE 6

INSTRUCTIONS: 1.   Create the following table.

Installment Loan Payment Schedule		
Principal		Monthly payment
Interest		
Term		

2. Determine the monthly payment for a loan in which the principal amount is $20,000, the rate is 12%, and the term is 48 months. The monthly payment should appear in cell C3.
3. Print the document.
4. Save the document in a file using the name "CH19EX06".
5. Close the document.

EXERCISE 7

INSTRUCTIONS: 1.   Open the file called "CH18EX07" created in the previous chapter. If you have not created the file, you should do so at this time.
2. Insert a row at the bottom of the table.
3. Use the SUM function to determine the total sales for each year.
4. Create a range name for each year. The range name for this year is called **"Current"**. The range name for last year is called **"Previous"**.
5. Insert the range names in the SUM functions found in cells B8 and C8.
6. Print the document.
7. Save the document in a file using the name "CH19EX07".
8. Close the document.

CHAPTER TWENTY

DESKTOP PUBLISHING: RETRIEVING AND EDITING GRAPHICS BOXES

OBJECTIVES

In this chapter, you will learn to:
- Retrieve an image
- Create and edit captions
- Change the border style of graphics boxes
- Change the border spacing of graphics boxes
- Change the fill style of graphics boxes
- Attach graphics to a document
- Change the horizontal and vertical positions of graphics boxes
- Change the size of a graphics box
- Use the mouse to change the box size and position
- Identify other graphics boxes

■ CHAPTER OVERVIEW

WordPerfect includes many of the capabilities that are found in desktop publishing software packages. For example, you can place graphics images in your document. You can include borders, captions, and enhancements to the images in your document.

In this chapter, the procedures for retrieving graphic images are described and illustrated. Methods for sizing graphics boxes, attaching graphics boxes to a document, creating captions, and changing the vertical and horizontal positions of graphics boxes are also discussed.

Once you have created a graphic, WordPerfect offers options to enhance or modify the appearance of the graphics box. For example, you can specify a new type of border, change the caption location, and add a fill style to the graphics box. This chapter also describes the procedures for using these graphics options.

■ RETRIEVING AN IMAGE

Many software packages, including WordPerfect, have generic graphic images already made for you. WordPerfect 6.0 has 30 graphic images that come with the software package. WordPerfect graphics have the extension ".WPG" and are stored in the "C:\WP60\GRAPHICS" directory when you install the WordPerfect program. We will use several of these images in this chapter.

Open the document called "NEWSCOL" that you created in Chapter 17.

Suppose you want to place a picture of some hot air balloons in the newspaper-style document that you created earlier.

To retrieve a graphic image that already exists in WordPerfect:

Move	the insertion point to the left margin of the second paragraph in Column 1	***Click***	*at the left margin of the second paragraph in Column 1*
Press	Alt + F9	***Choose***	*Graphics*
		Choose	*Retrieve Image*

If you used the keystroke method, the Graphics dialog box appears on the screen. Your screen should look like Figure 20-1. If you are using the mouse method, the Retrieve Image File dialog box appears on the screen as shown in Figure 20-2.

Figure 20-1

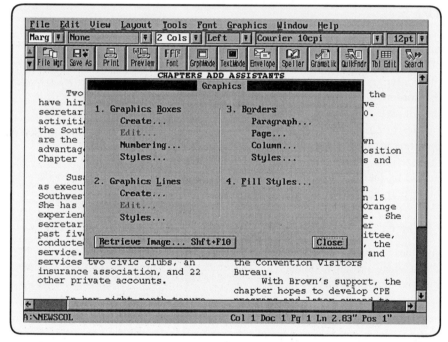

To retrieve the "HOTAIR.WPG" image:

Press   R or Shift + F10 to select the Retrieve Image command button

The top part of your screen should look like Figure 20-2.

Figure 20-2

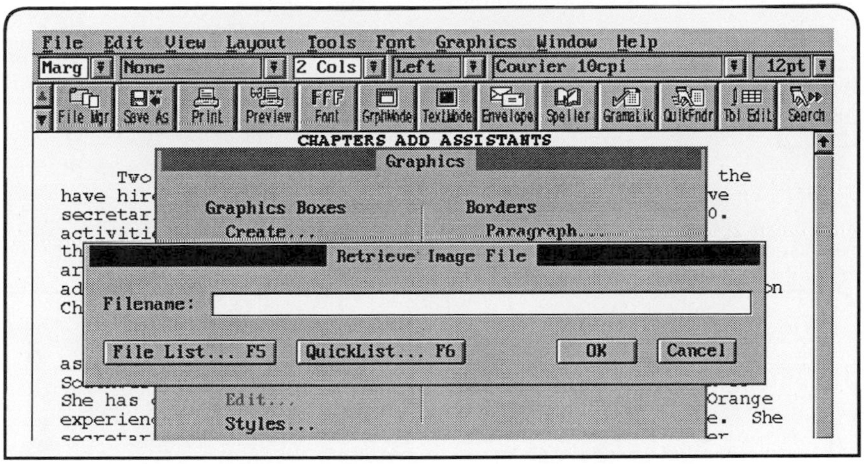

To view the list of WordPerfect graphics:

Press	[F5] to select the File List command button	*Click*	*the File List command button*
Press	[←Enter] to accept the C:\WP60\GRAPHICS*.* directory	*Click*	*the OK command button*

The File List dialog box containing the available graphics appears on the screen. Your screen should look similar to Figure 20-3.

Figure 20-3

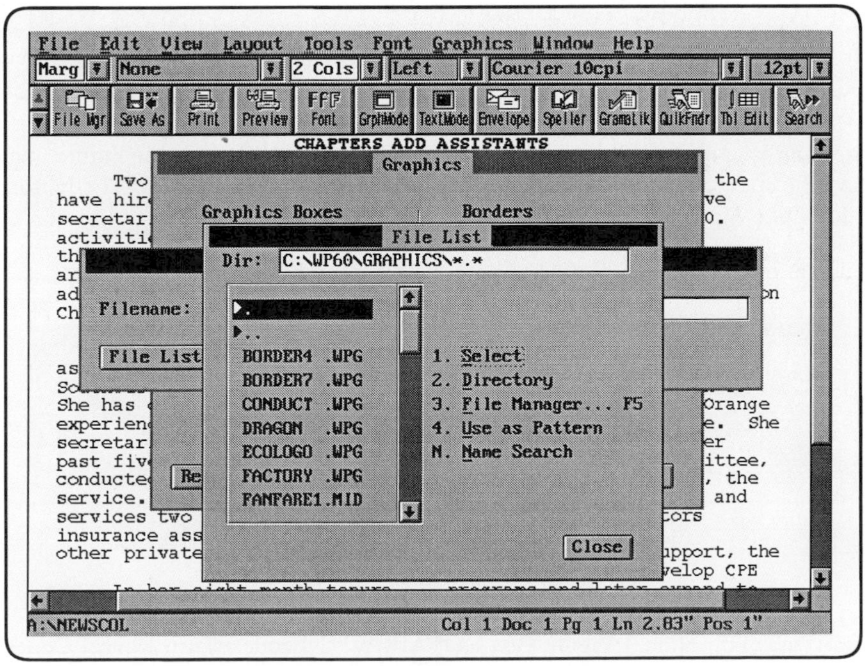

To select the graphic image of the hot air balloons:

Press	⬇ until "HOTAIR.WPG" is highlighted	***Click***	*the down scroll arrow until "HOTAIR.WPG" is highlighted*
Press	⬅Enter	***Double-click***	*the "HOTAIR.WPG" choice*

In a few seconds, your screen should look like Figure 20-4.

Figure 20-4

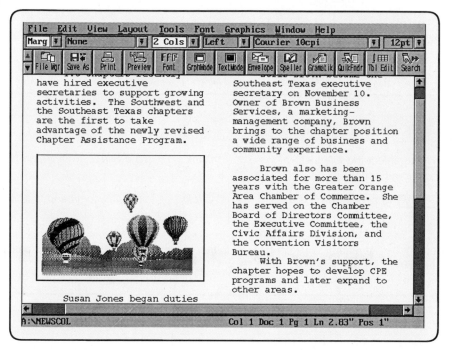

When you retrieve an image, WordPerfect numbers the graphics box. To view the Figure number and code, turn on the Reveal Codes feature and place the cursor on the Figure Box code. The bottom part of your screen should look like Figure 20-5.

Figure 20-5

```
                 Susan Jones began duties
    {     ▲     ▲     ▲     ▲     ▲     }   {     ▲     ▲     ▲     ▲     ▲     }
[HRt]
[Box (Para):Edit Num 1;Figure Box;HOTAIR.WPG;][Lft Tab]Susan Jones began duti
es[SRt]
as executive secretary of the[SRt]
A:\NEWSCOL                              Col 1 Doc 1 Pg 1 Ln 2.83" Pos 1"
```

Notice the [Box (Para):Edit Num 1;Figure Box;HOTAIR.WPG;] code. Turn Reveal Codes off.

■ CREATING AND EDITING CAPTIONS

The Caption option allows you to attach a heading below, above, or beside a graphics box.

To create a caption for the "HOTAIR.WPG" graphics box:

Press	Alt + F9	***Choose***	*Graphics*
Press	1 or B to select the Graphics Boxes option	***Choose***	*Graphics Boxes*
Press	2 or E to select the Edit option	***Choose***	*Edit*

The Select Box to Edit dialog box appears. Your screen should look like Figure 20-6.

Figure 20-6

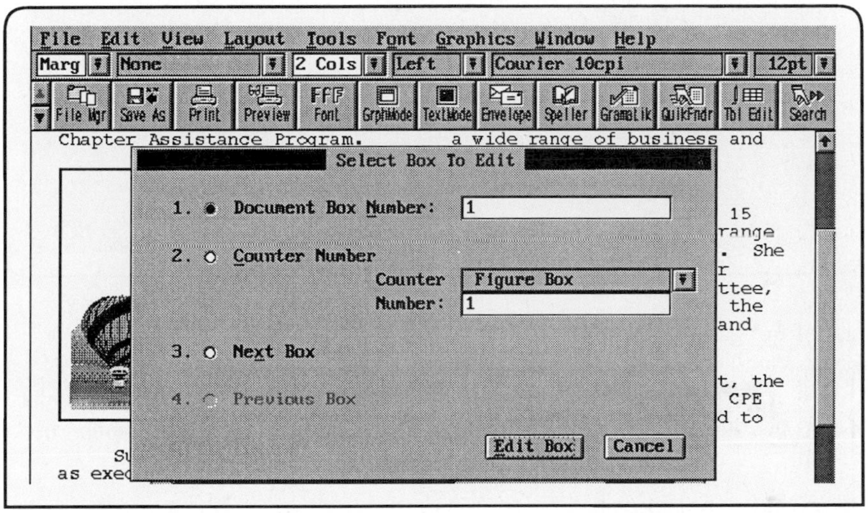

To edit the figure:

Press	E or ←Enter to select the Edit Box command button	***Click***	*the Edit Box command button*

The Edit Graphics Box dialog box appears. Your screen should look like Figure 20-7.

Figure 20-7

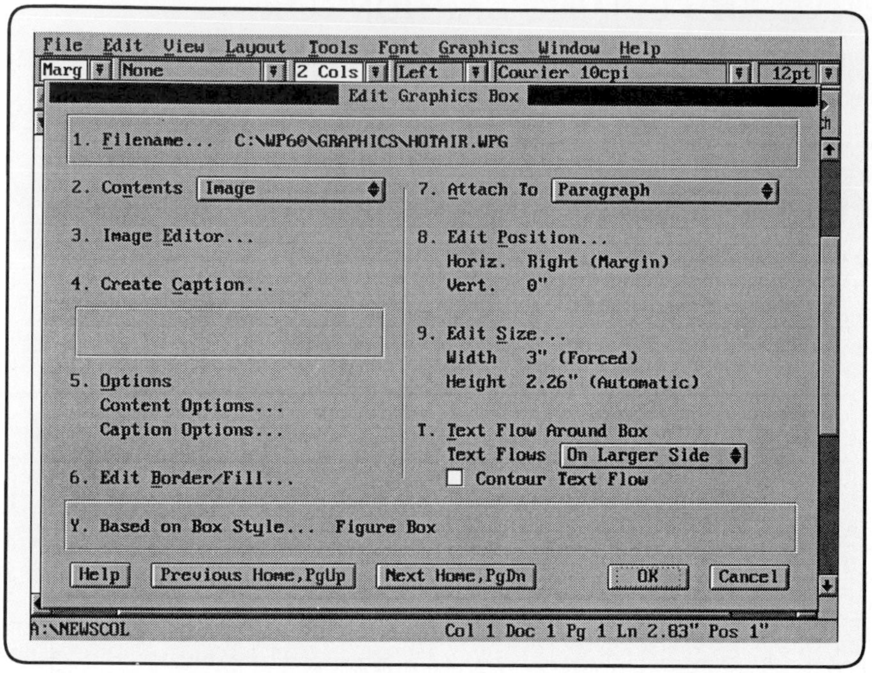

Notice the name of the graphic image listed beside the Filename option.

To create a caption:

Press   4 or C to select the Create Caption option

Choose   the Create Caption option

The current caption appears. The top part of your screen should look like Figure 20-8.

Figure 20-8

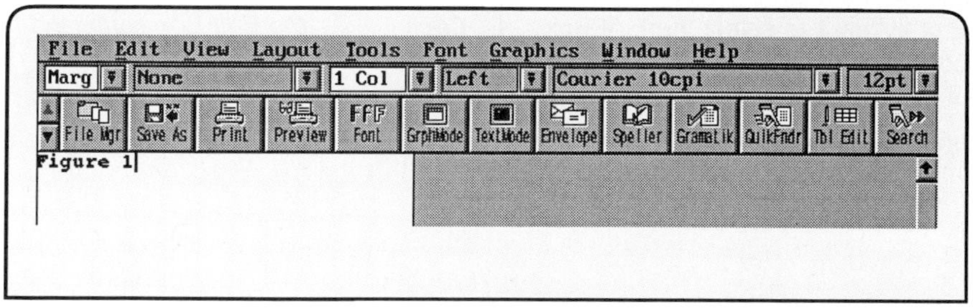

Notice that the text "Figure 1" appears on the screen. WordPerfect assumes that you want to use the caption "Figure 1". Suppose you want to use a different caption.

To delete the text "Figure 1":

Press   ⟨←Backspace⟩

Press   ⟨←Backspace⟩

To enter the caption "Up, Up, and Away!":

Type   Up, Up, and Away!

Type   *Up, Up, and Away!*

| **Press** | F7 | | ***Press*** | F7 |
| **Press** | ↵Enter | | ***Click*** | the OK command button |

Your screen should look like Figure 20-9.

Figure 20-9

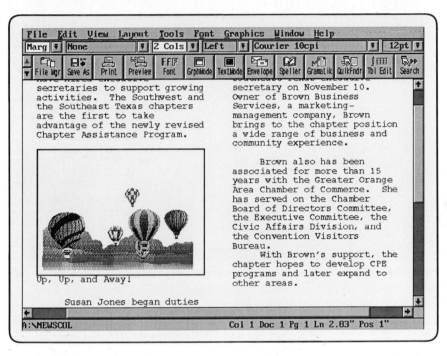

Notice that the caption appears below and outside the graphics box.

Editing a Caption

The Options choice in the Edit Graphics Box dialog box is divided into two selections. The Content Options choice consists of options to change the position of the text in the Caption Box. The Caption Options choice consists of options on where the caption will be placed in or around the graphics box. You can also change the caption format in the Caption Options dialog box. The Caption Position options will vary according to the type of box you have defined.

Suppose you want to place the caption beside the "HOTAIR.WPG" graphic, inside the border, and rotate the text of the caption. To select the Caption Position option:

Press	Alt + F9		***Choose***	*Graphics*
Press	1 or B to select the Graphics Boxes option		***Choose***	*Graphics Boxes*
Press	2 or E to select the Edit option		***Choose***	*Edit*
Press	↵Enter		***Click***	the Edit Box command button
Press	5 or O to select the Options option		***Choose***	the Options option
Press	2 or C to select the Caption Options option		***Choose***	the Caption Options option

The Caption Options dialog box appears, and your screen should look like Figure 20-10.

Figure 20-10

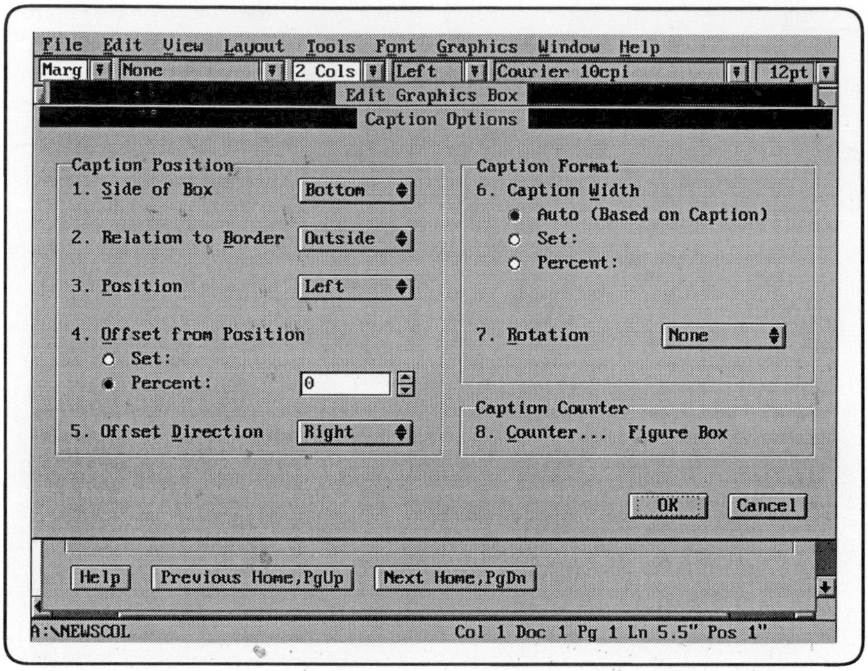

To place the caption on the side of the graphic box:

Press	1 or S to select the Side of Box pop-up list button in the Caption Position option box	*Hold down*	*the mouse button on the Side of Box pop-up list button in the Caption Position option box*
Press	L to select the Left option	*Choose*	*the Left option*

To place the caption inside the graphic border:

Press	2 or B to select the Relation to Border pop-up list button	*Hold down*	*the mouse button on the Relation to Border pop-up list button*
Press	I to select the Inside option	*Choose*	*the Inside option*

To change the position of the caption:

Press	3 or P to select the Position pop-up list button	*Hold down*	*the mouse button on the Position pop-up list button*
Press	C to select the Center option	*Choose*	*the Center option*

To rotate the caption and exit the dialog boxes:

Press	7 or R to select the Rotation pop-up list button in the Caption Format option box	*Hold down*	*the mouse button on the Rotation pop-up list button in the Caption Format option box*
Press	⬇ to select the 90° option	*Choose*	*the 90° option*
Press	←Enter three times	*Click*	*the OK command button twice*

Now that your caption has changed, your screen should look like Figure 20-11.

Figure 20-11

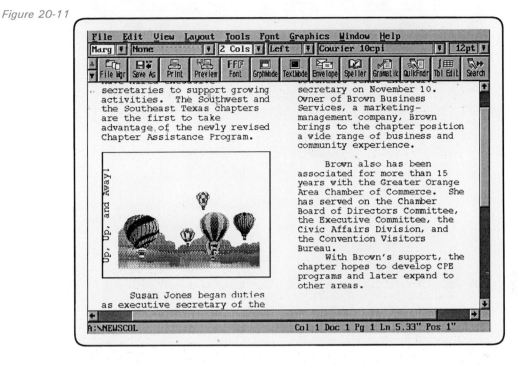

For more information on creating and editing graphics captions, see the WordPerfect Reference manual.

■ CHANGING THE BORDER STYLE OF GRAPHICS BOXES

You can change the default settings for any of the eight graphics box types. The other box types are described in greater detail later in this chapter. Once options are changed, any future boxes of a particular type are changed to reflect the new options.

To select the Edit Graphics Box dialog box:

Press	Alt + F9	**Choose**	*Graphics*
Press	1 or B to select the Graphics Boxes option	**Choose**	*Graphics Boxes*
Press	2 or E to select the Edit option	**Choose**	*Edit*
Press	↵Enter	**Click**	*the Edit Box command button*

The Edit Border/Fill option lets you change the appearance of the borders around a graphics box. You can change the border style for each side of the box.

To change the Border Styles for the graphics box:

Press	6 or B to select the Edit Border/Fill option	**Choose**	*the Edit Border/Fill option*

The Edit Graphics Box Border/Fill dialog box appears. Your screen should look like Figure 20-12.

Figure 20-12

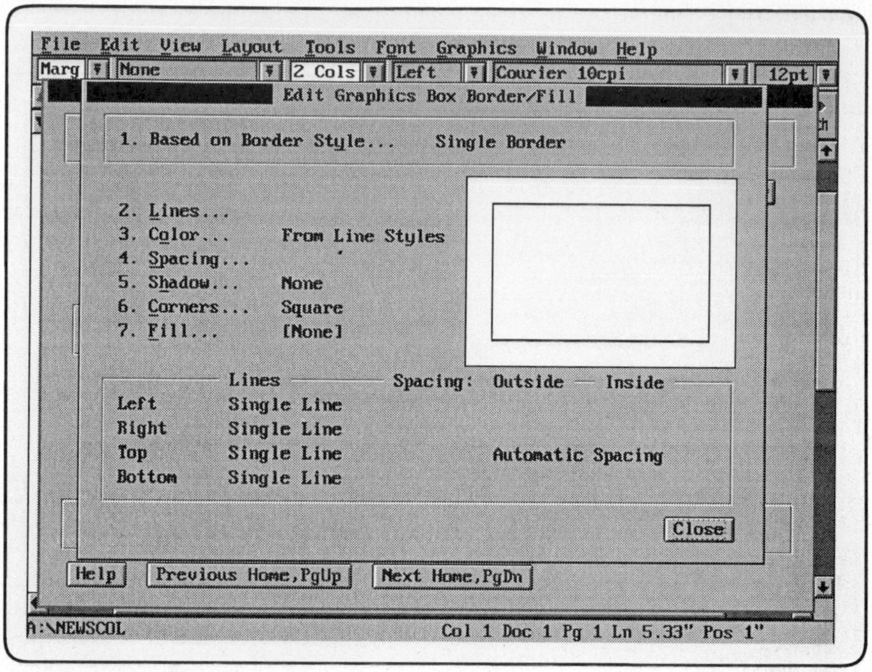

WordPerfect contains several border styles already defined. You can choose to have no border, a single line, a double line, a dashed line, a dotted line, a thick line, an extra thick line, a thin line-thick line border, and a thick line-thin line border.

Suppose you want to change the border style of the "HOTAIR.WPG" graphics box to a Thin Thick Border with a shadow.

To change the border style:

Press	1 or Y to select the Based on Border Style option	**Choose**	*the Based on Border Style option*

The Border Styles dialog box appears. Your screen should look like Figure 20-13.

Figure 20-13

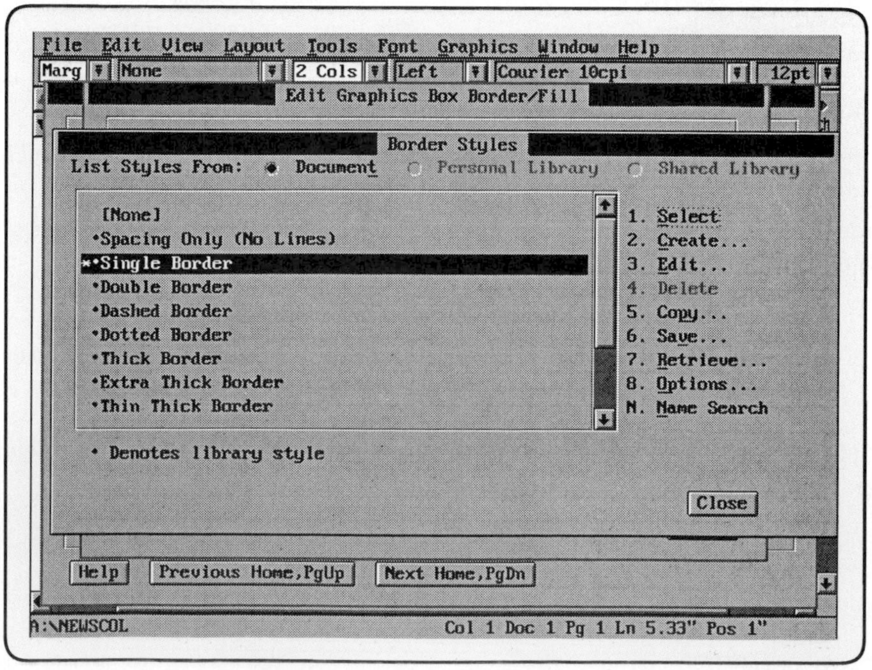

To select the Thin Thick Border style:

Press	⬇ six times to select the Thin Thick border	***Choose***	*the Thin Thick Border option*
Press	1 or S to select the Select option	***Choose***	*the Select option*

Notice the example border in the Edit Graphics Box Border/Fill dialog box. Note that you can also change the border option for each individual line.

To create a shadow:

Press	5 or H to select the Shadow option	***Choose***	*the Shadow option*

The Shadow dialog box appears, and your screen should look like Figure 20-14.

Figure 20-14

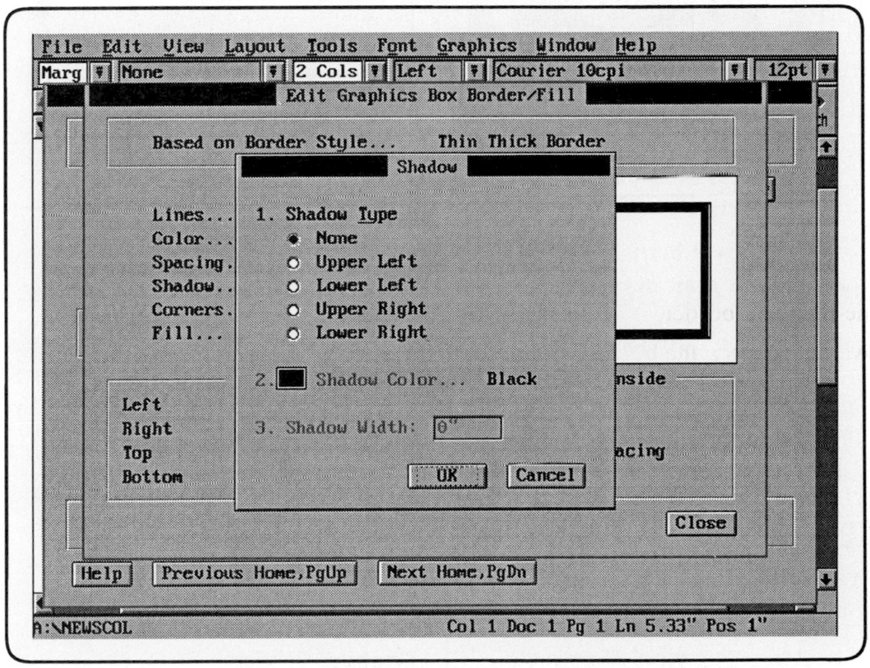

To change the Shadow option and exit the dialog boxes:

Press	1 or T to select the Shadow Type option	***Click***	*the Lower Right option button*
Press	5 or O to select the Lower Right option button	***Click***	*the OK command button*
Press	⏎Enter three times	***Click***	*the Close command button*
		Click	*the OK command button*

Your screen should look like Figure 20-15.

Figure 20-15

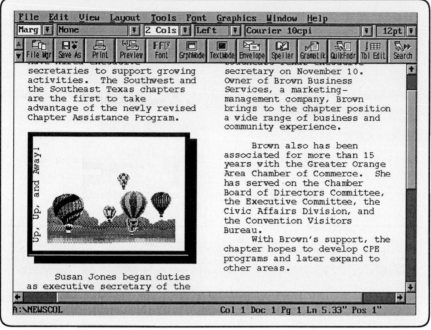

■ CHANGING THE BORDER SPACING OF GRAPHICS BOXES

The Border Spacing option is divided into two selections. The Outside Border Spacing option concerns the space between the text in the document and the outer box borders. The Inside Border Spacing option concerns the space between the border of the box and the text or image inside. Notice that you can change the space on the left, right, top, and bottom of the box.

To change the Outside Border Spacing option:

Press	Alt + F9	*Choose*	*Graphics*
Press	1 or B to select the Graphics Boxes option	*Choose*	*Graphics Boxes*
Press	2 or E to select the Edit option	*Choose*	*Edit*
Press	↵Enter	*Click*	*the Edit Box command button*
Press	6 or B to select the Edit Border/Fill option	*Choose*	*the Edit Border/Fill option*
Press	4 or S to select the Spacing option	*Choose*	*the Spacing option*

The Border Spacing dialog box appears. Your screen should look like Figure 20-16.

Figure 20-16

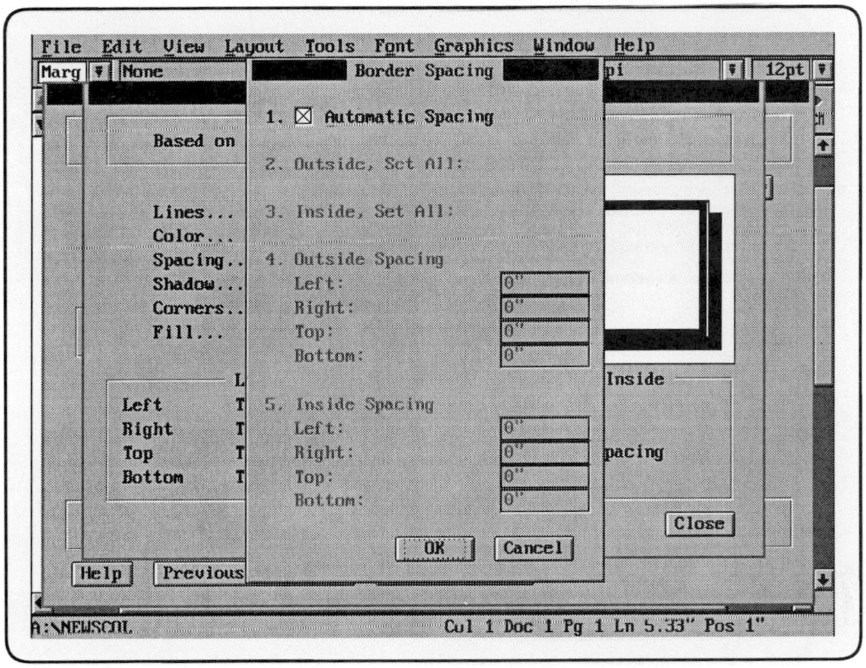

To change the Inside Spacing to .1":

Press	1 or A to remove the X in the Automatic Spacing check box		*Click*	*the Automatic Spacing check box until the X disappears*
Press	5 or N to select the Inside Spacing option		*Choose*	*the Inside Spacing option*
Type	.1		*Type*	*.1*
Press	[Tab↹] to move the cursor to the Right text box		*Click*	*in the Right text box*
Type	.1		*Type*	*.1*
Press	[Tab↹] to move the cursor to the Top text box		*Click*	*in the Top text box*
Type	.1		*Type*	*.1*
Press	[Tab↹] to move the cursor to the Bottom text box		*Click*	*in the Bottom text box*
Type	.1		*Type*	*.1*
Press	[↵Enter] four times		*Click*	*the OK command button*
			Click	*the Close button*
			Click	*the OK command button*

Your screen should look like Figure 20-17.

Figure 20-17

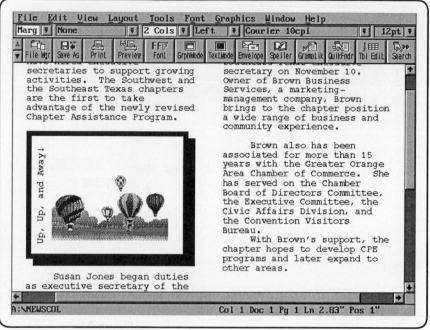

Notice that the graphic is smaller within the graphics box. You want to leave the outside border spacing at 0". If you wanted to change the outside border spacing, you would press 4 or S to select the Outside Spacing option and press the TAB key to select each text box, or you would click on the appropriate text box.

In This Book

Earlier in the chapter, you were told the instructions for selecting a graphics box to edit. For the remainder of the book, you will only be told to edit the graphics box.

■ CHANGING THE FILL STYLE OF GRAPHICS BOXES

The Fill Style option allows you to determine a shading for the graphics box. You enter a percentage value for the shading. A value of 100% means black and 0% means white.

Suppose you want to shade the "HOTAIR.WPG" graphics box. To change the fill style percentage to 10:

Edit	the "HOTAIR.WPG" graphics box	*Edit*	*the "HOTAIR.WPG" graphics box*
Press	6 or B to select the Edit Border/Fill option	*Choose*	*the Edit Border/Fill option*
Press	7 or F to select the Fill option	*Choose*	*the Fill option*

The Fill Style and Color dialog box appears. The top part of your screen should look like Figure 20-18.

Figure 20-18

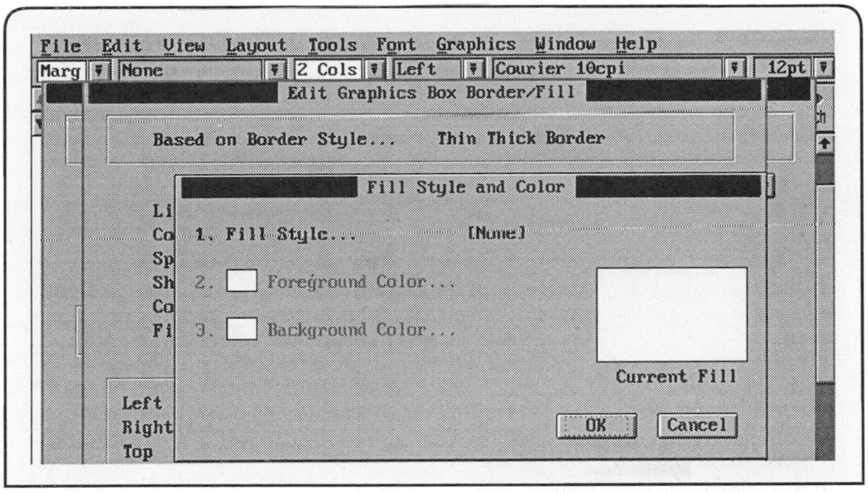

To select the fill style:

Press 1 or Y to select the Fill Style option | ***Choose*** *the Fill Style option*

The Fill Styles dialog box appears. Your screen should look like Figure 20-19.

Figure 20-19

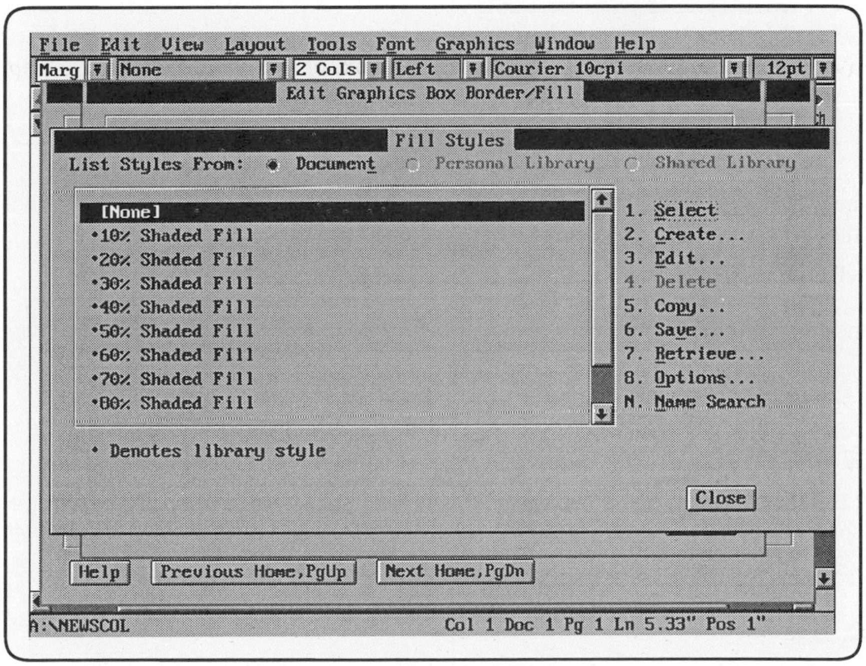

To change the fill style and exit the dialog boxes:

Press ⬇ twice to select the 10% Shaded Fill option | ***Choose*** *the 10% Shaded Fill option*

Press 1 or S to select the Select option | ***Choose*** *the Select option*

Press [←Enter] three times | ***Click*** *the OK command button*

Click	the Close command button
Click	the OK command button

Your screen should look like Figure 20-20.

Figure 20-20

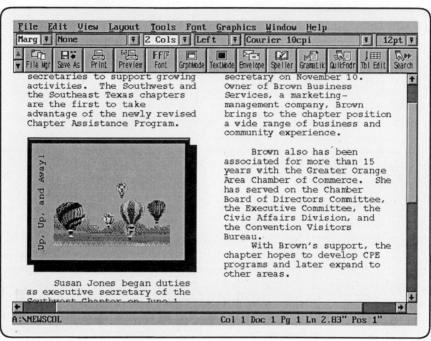

After seeing the graphic, suppose you want to change the border style to a double line with no shadow border, place the caption outside the border, and have no fill style.

To make the changes:

Edit	the "HOTAIR.WPG" graphics box	***Edit***	*the "HOTAIR.WPG" graphics box*
Press	5 or O to select the Options option	***Choose***	*the Options option*
Press	2 or C to select the Caption Options option	***Choose***	*the Caption Options option*
Press	2 or B to select the Relation to Border pop-up list button	***Hold down***	*the mouse button on the Relation to Border pop-up list button*
Press	O to select the Outside option	***Click***	*the Outside option*
Press	⏎Enter	***Click***	*the OK command button*
Press	6 or B to select the Edit Border/Fill option	***Choose***	*the Edit Border/Fill option*
Press	1 or Y to select the Based on Border Style option	***Choose***	*the Based on Border Style option*
Press	⬆ five times to select the Double Border option	***Choose***	*the Double Border option*
Press	1 or S to select the Select option	***Choose***	*the Select option*

Press	7 or F to select the Fill option	*Choose*	*the Fill option*
Press	1 or Y to select the Fill Style option	*Choose*	*the Fill Style option*
Press	↑ twice to select the [None] option	*Choose*	*the [None] option*
Press	1 or S to select the Select option	*Choose*	*the Select option*
Press	←Enter three times	*Click*	*the OK command button*
		Click	*the Close command button*
		Click	*the OK command button*

You do not have to turn the shadow option off. WordPerfect does it for you automatically when you choose a different border style. Your screen should look like Figure 20-21.

Figure 20-21

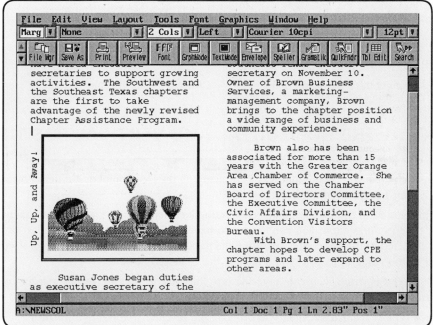

■ ATTACHING A GRAPHICS BOX TO A DOCUMENT

In the Edit Graphics Box dialog box, you may attach the graphics box to a document in several different ways. The choice made here will determine how the graphics box will "move" on the page. It can be treated as a *character* in a line, fixed on the *page*, associated with a *paragraph*, or have a *fixed page position*.

The default attachment for the graphics box is a paragraph attachment. This means that the graphics box is fixed at a particular position within the paragraph.

To change the attachment so that the graphics box will be attached to the page:

Edit	the "HOTAIR.WPG" graphics box		*Edit*	*the "HOTAIR.WPG" graphics box*
Press	7 or A to select the Attach To pop-up list button		*Hold down*	*the mouse button on the Attach To pop-up list button*
Press	A to select the Page option		*Choose*	*Page*

To return the attachment to Paragraph:

Press	7 or A to select the Attach To pop-up list button		*Hold down*	*the mouse button on the Attach To pop-up list button*
Press	P to select the Paragraph option		*Choose*	*Paragraph*

■ CHANGING THE HORIZONTAL AND VERTICAL POSITION OF GRAPHICS BOXES

You can change the placement of a graphics box by changing the Horizontal or Vertical Position in the Edit Graphics Box dialog box or by dragging it with the mouse.

The Edit Position option in the Edit Graphics Box dialog box depends on the selected attachment type. If the attachment type is *Paragraph*, you can choose to have the box lined up with the left or right edge of the paragraph, centered in the paragraph, or filling the paragraph margins. For example, if you wanted the figure centered in the paragraph, you would choose the Centered option.

If the attachment type is *Page*, you can have the box lined up in relation to the margins of the page or columns. You can also set the position any number of inches from the left margin.

If the attachment type is *Character*, then you do not need to enter a horizontal position.

By default, the graphics box appears against the right margin of the column and at the top line of the paragraph. To edit the horizontal position of the graphics box:

Press	8 or P to select the Edit Position option		*Choose*	*the Edit Position option*

The Paragraph Box Position dialog box appears:

Press	1 or H to select the Horizontal Position pop-up list button		*Hold down*	*the mouse button on the Horizontal Position pop-up list button*
Press	L to select the Left option		*Choose*	*Left*

To edit the vertical position of the graphics box:

| **Press** | 3 or D to select the Distance from Top of Paragraph text box | *Click* | *in the Distance from Top of Paragraph text box* |
| **Type** | 1 | *Type* | *1* |

Your screen should look like Figure 20-22.

Figure 20-22

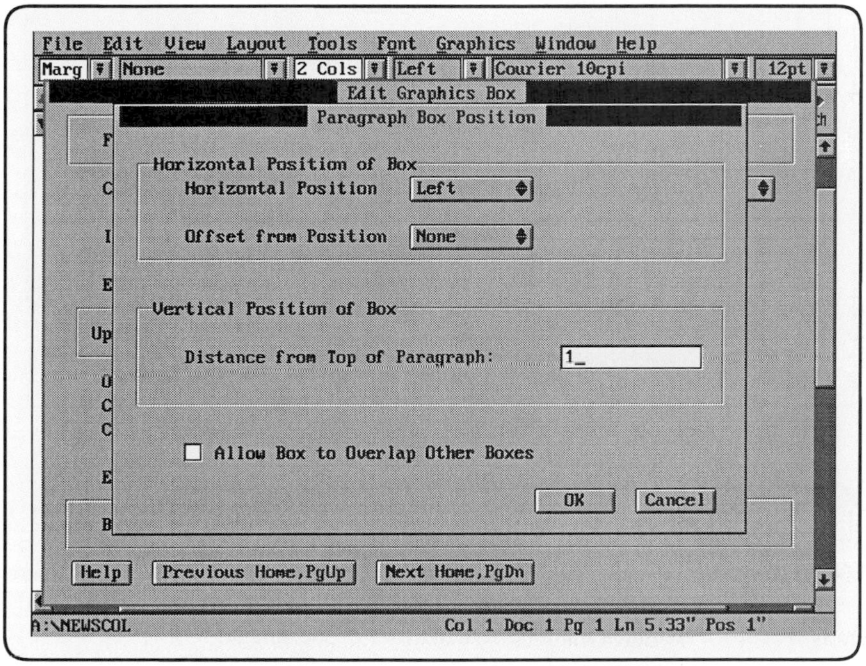

To return to the document:

| **Press** | [↵Enter] three times | *Click* | *the OK command button twice* |

The graphics box should now appear against the left margin, and be several lines lower than the top of the paragraph. Your screen should look similar to Figure 20-23.

Figure 20-23

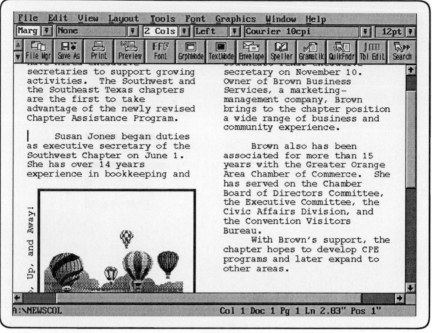

■ CHANGING THE SIZE OF A GRAPHICS BOX

You can also change the size of a graphics box by using the options in the Edit Graphics Box dialog box. You can set both the width and the height of the graphics box, or you can choose to have WordPerfect automatically set either or both the width and height of the graphics box. When you first retrieve an image, WordPerfect automatically calculates the height and width of the image.

To change the size of the "HOTAIR.WPG" graphics box to be 2" by 2":

Edit	the "HOTAIR.WPG" graphics box	*Edit*	*the "HOTAIR.WPG" graphics box*
Press	9 or S to select the Edit Size option	*Choose*	*the Edit Size option*

The Graphics Box Size dialog box appears. Your screen should look like Figure 20-24.

Figure 20-24

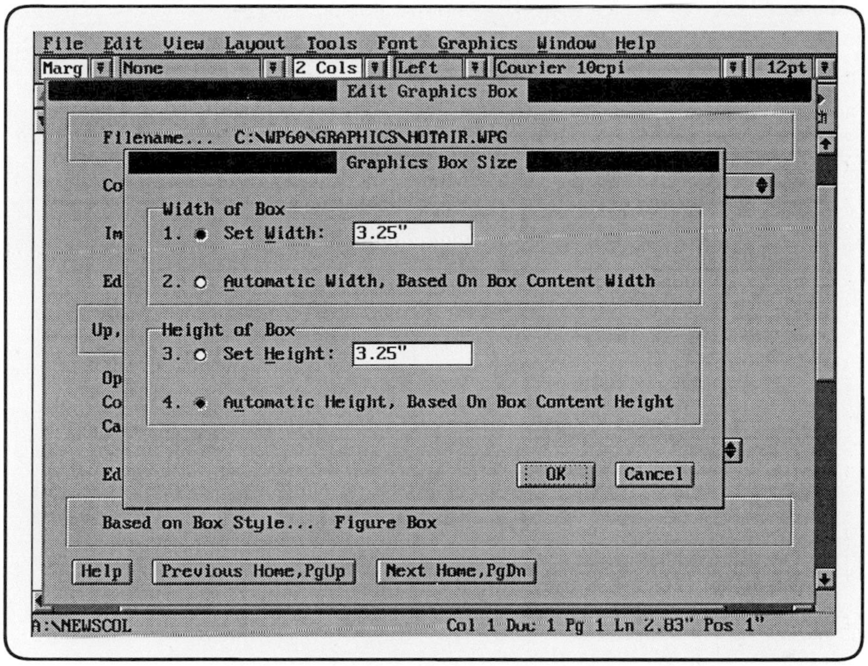

To set the width and height, and return to the document:

Press	1 or W to select the Set Width text box		*Click*	*in the Set Width text box*
Type	2		*Type*	*2*
Press	⏎Enter		*Click*	*in the Set Height text box*
Press	3 or H to select the Set Height text box		*Type*	*2*
Type	2		*Click*	*the OK command button twice*
Press	⏎Enter three times			

Your screen should look like Figure 20-25.

Figure 20-25

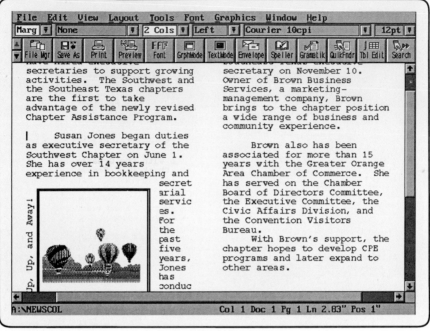

Currently the size of the "HOTAIR.WPG" graphics box causes the paragraph to wrap incorrectly. This error can be corrected by making the box smaller.

To change the size of the graphics box to 1.3":

Edit	the "HOTAIR.WPG" graphics box
Press	9 or S to select the Edit Size option
Press	1 or W to select the Set Width text box
Type	1.3
Press	[←Enter]
Press	3 or H to select the Set Height text box
Type	1.3
Press	[←Enter] three times

Edit	*the "HOTAIR.WPG" graphics box*
Choose	*the Edit Size option*
Click	*in the Set Width text box*
Type	*1.3*
Click	*in the Set Height text box*
Type	*1.3*
Click	*the OK command button twice*

Your screen should look like Figure 20-26.

Figure 20-26

```
 File  Edit  View  Layout  Tools  Font  Graphics  Window  Help
 Marg ▼ None              ▼ 2 Cols ▼ Left    ▼ Courier 10cpi        ▼  12pt ▼
 File Mgr  Save As  Print  Preview  Font  GrphMode  TextMode  Envelope  Speller  GramaTik  QuikFndr  Tbl Edit  Search

   secretaries to support growing      secretary on November 10.
   activities.  The Southwest and      Owner of Brown Business
   the Southeast Texas chapters        Services, a marketing-
   are the first to take               management company, Brown
   advantage of the newly revised      brings to the chapter position
   Chapter Assistance Program.         a wide range of business and
                                       community experience.
   |    Susan Jones began duties
   as executive secretary of the          Brown also has been
   Southwest Chapter on June 1.        associated for more than 15
   She has over 14 years               years with the Greater Orange
   experience in bookkeeping and       Area Chamber of Commerce.  She
                      secretarial      has served on the Chamber
                      services.        Board of Directors Committee,
                      For the          the Executive Committee, the
                      past five        Civic Affairs Division, and
                      years,           the Convention Visitors
                      Jones has        Bureau.
                      conducted a         With Brown's support, the
                      home             chapter hopes to develop CPE
                      bookkeeping      programs and later expand to
                      service.         other areas.
   Presently, she services two
   civic clubs, an insurance

 A:\NEWSCOL                        Col 1 Doc 1 Pg 1 Ln 2.83" Pos 1"
```

Save the document as "graphics".

■ USING THE MOUSE TO CHANGE THE BOX SIZE AND POSITION

You can also size and move a graphics box using the mouse. To size a graphics box using the mouse, drag a sizing handle while the mouse pointer appears as a double-pointing arrow. **Sizing handles** are the small black squares on the sides of the graphics box.

To change the size of the "HOTAIR.WPG" graphics box:

Click   *on the "HOTAIR.WPG" graphics box*

Your screen should look like Figure 20-27.

Figure 20-27

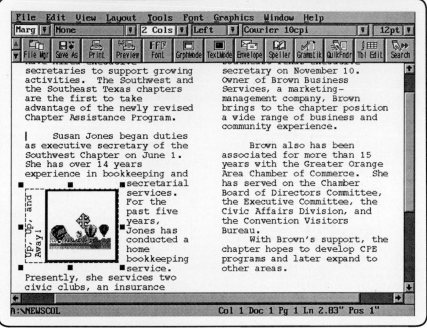

Notice a dashed line appears around the graphics box and sizing handles appear on each side and in each corner of the graphics box. When the mouse pointer is placed over one of the sizing handles, it becomes a double-pointing arrow and is used to resize the graphics box.

To make the "HOTAIR.WPG" graphics box wider:

> **Move**   *the mouse pointer to the middle sizing handle on the right side of the image until the mouse pointer appears as a double-pointing arrow*

Your screen should look like Figure 20-28.

Figure 20-28

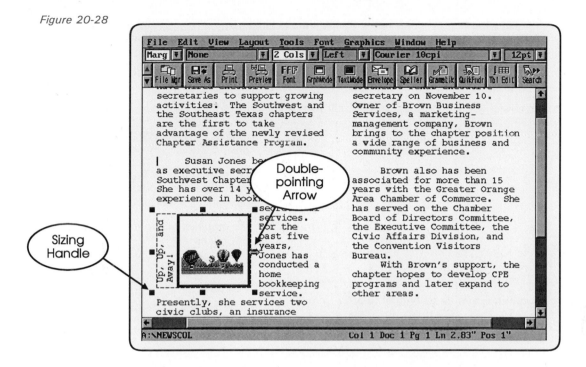

To size the graphics box:

Drag	*the mouse pointer to the right about 1/2"*
Release	*the mouse button*

Your screen should look similar to Figure 20-29.

Figure 20-29

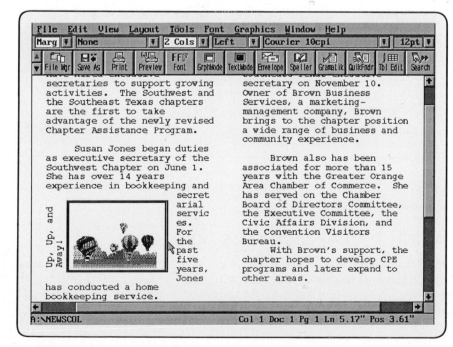

The graphics box can also be resized vertically by moving the mouse pointer to a sizing handle in the top or bottom center of the box. If one of the corner sizing handles is used, the graphics box is resized proportionally both vertically and horizontally.

You can also move a graphics box using the mouse. Click on the graphics box and drag it while the mouse pointer appears as a move pointer (four arrows).

To move "HOTAIR.WPG" graphics box to the right margin of Column 1:

Click	*on the "HOTAIR.WPG" graphics box*
Move	*the mouse pointer to the center of the image (the mouse pointer appears with four arrows)*
Drag	*the graphics box to the right margin of Column 1*
Release	*the mouse button*

Your screen should look similar to Figure 20-30.

Figure 20-30

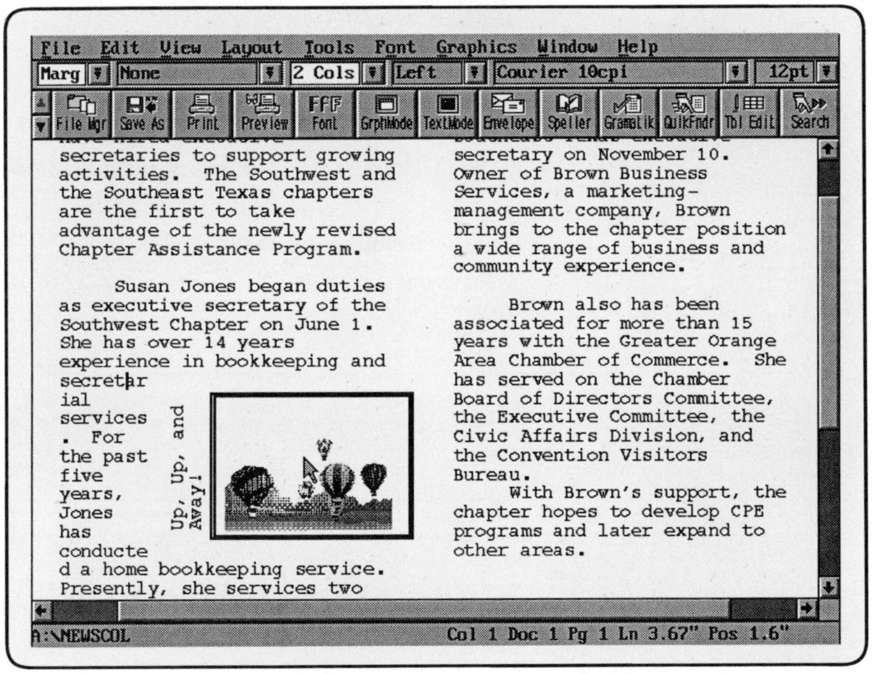

The graphics box can also be moved vertically using the mouse method.

Close the document without saving changes.

■ CREATING OTHER GRAPHICS BOXES

The Graphics feature allows you to place other types of graphics boxes into your document. Within a graphics box, you can enter text and WordPerfect will word wrap any text that you include in the box. You can also place text outside the box and specify whether text should wrap around the box. You can change the location, appearance, and size of the graphics box at any time.

The eight box types available in WordPerfect include:

Figure - Place graphic images and pictures in this type of box.

Table - This box holds WordPerfect tables and other tables containing numbers.

Text - This box holds text. It is used when you want to draw special attention to certain text on the page. Text boxes are discussed in Chapter 21.

User - This is a "miscellaneous" box. If you cannot place an image in any other type of box, then use this one.

Equation - Place equations in this box. Chapter 23 explains equations in further detail.

Button - This box is used for a Hypertext link to graphically illustrate a particular keystroke in your document. For more information about the Hypertext feature, consult the WordPerfect Reference manual.

Watermark - This box contains a Watermark, which is a light graphic image appearing behind the text in the document. Watermarks are discussed in greater detail in Chapter 22.

Inline Equation - This type of box is used to insert an equation in a line of text.

You can also leave a box empty for the purpose of creating white space in a document. WordPerfect numbers each box according to its type and place in the document. Each box type has a menu of options that you can use to modify the contents and appearance of the box.

EXERCISE 1

INSTRUCTIONS: Define the following concepts:

1. Graphics feature _____

_____

2. Figure box _____

_____

3. Horizontal Position _____

_____

4. Vertical Position _____

_____

5. Sizing Handles _____

_____

6. Equation box _____

_____

7.   Caption _____

_____

8.   Attachment options _____

_____

9.   Border style _____

_____

EXERCISE 2

INSTRUCTIONS: Circle T if the statement is true and F if the statement is false.

T   F   1.   The Graphics feature allows you to combine pictures or text into your document.

T   F   2.   There are four box types available when using the Graphics feature: Figure, Table, Text, and User.

T   F   3.   Figure boxes can be used for graphic images and pictures.

T   F   4.   Table boxes can be used to display mathematical and scientific equations.

T   F   5.   Text boxes can be used for WordPerfect tables, maps, and statistical data.

T   F   6.   If the attachment type is "Paragraph," then you must enter the amount of vertical space from the top of the paragraph for the Vertical Position option.

T   F   7.   The Caption option allows you to attach headings to a graphics box.

T   F   8.   Attachment types determine how the graphics box moves within the document.

T   F   9.   Moving a graphics box is done by placing the mouse pointer over the sizing handles and dragging the mouse.

EXERCISE 3

INSTRUCTIONS: 1.   Create the following document.
2.   Place a picture of a lighthouse scene between the two paragraphs in the document. The name of the WordPerfect graphic is "LIGHTHS.WPG".
3.   Save the document in a file using the name "CH20EX03".
4.   Print the document.
5.   Close the document.

Using graphic images to enhance the appearance of a document has become very popular. A lighthouse scene is shown below.

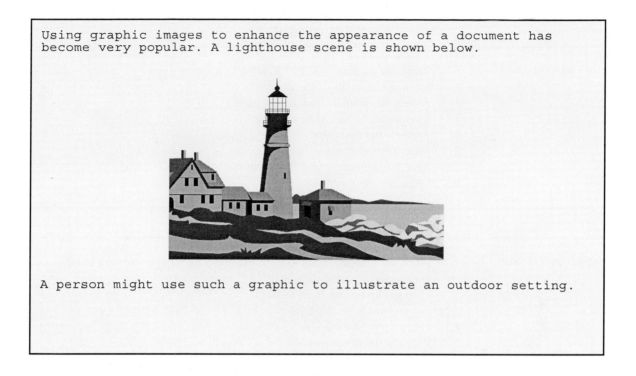

A person might use such a graphic to illustrate an outdoor setting.

EXERCISE 4

INSTRUCTIONS:

1. Create the following document. Use the graphic "SKIER1.WPG".
2. Use the caption "Artist's Drawing". Place it below the picture.
3. Set the height and width of the graphic to 3 inches.
4. Set the attachment type to paragraph.
5. Set the horizontal position to left.
6. Center the page from top to bottom.
7. Print the document.
8. Save the document in a file using the name "CH20EX04".
9. Close the document.

This graphic is a drawing of a downhill skier. Its design is different from most of the other WordPerfect 6.0 images.

You can access the 30 graphics files that come with WordPerfect by pressing ALT+F9. If you are using the mouse, you can use the Retrieve Image feature under the Graphics menu.

Artist's Drawing

EXERCISE 5

INSTRUCTIONS:
1. Place the graphic "SKIPPER.WPG" on a new page.
2. Change the width of the picture to 6".
3. Attach the graphics box to the page.
4. Change the border style to thick.
5. Preview the document.
6. Print the document.
7. Save the document in a file using the name "CH20EX05".
8. Close the document.

EXERCISE 6

INSTRUCTIONS:
1. Place the graphic "HOTROD.WPG" on a new page. Set the height to 4" and center it on the page.
2. Change the border style to single.
3. Put a shadow on the border.
4. Use a 10% Shaded Fill.
5. Preview the document.
6. Print the document.
7. Save the document in a file using the name "CH20EX06".
8. Close the document.

EXERCISE 7

INSTRUCTIONS:
1. Create the following document.
2. Place a picture of a sun chair in the document. The name of the WordPerfect graphic is "SUMMRCNR.WPG".
3. Change the border to a dotted line border.
4. Make a shadow border in the lower left.
5. Use the 10% Shaded Fill option.

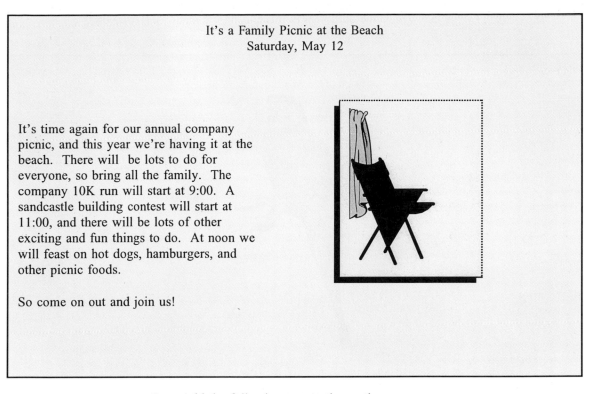

It's a Family Picnic at the Beach
Saturday, May 12

It's time again for our annual company picnic, and this year we're having it at the beach. There will be lots to do for everyone, so bring all the family. The company 10K run will start at 9:00. A sandcastle building contest will start at 11:00, and there will be lots of other exciting and fun things to do. At noon we will feast on hot dogs, hamburgers, and other picnic foods.

So come on out and join us!

6.   Add the following text as the caption.

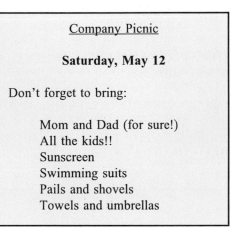

Company Picnic

Saturday, May 12

Don't forget to bring:

Mom and Dad (for sure!)
All the kids!!
Sunscreen
Swimming suits
Pails and shovels
Towels and umbrellas

7.   Save the document in a file using the name "CH20EX07".
8.   Print the document.
9.   Close the document.

EXERCISE 8

INSTRUCTIONS: 1.   Create the following document. Use the "PARROT.WPG" graphics file.
2.   Eliminate the borders around the parrot graphics box. Make the box 3" by 3".
3   Attach the graphics box to the page, and center the box between the margins.
4.   Preview and print the document.

5.   Save the document in a file using the name "CH20EX08".
6.   Close the document.

THE AVIARY CLUB
WILL
MEET NEXT TUESDAY

THE MEMBERS OF THE AVIARY CLUB WILL HOLD THEIR NEXT MONTHLY MEETING AT 10:15 A.M. IN THE MELLON LIBRARY.

ALL MEMBERS ARE REQUESTED TO TRY TO BRING A FRIEND TO THE MEETING.

REFRESHMENTS WILL BE SERVED. THE FILM, "THE GREAT CONDOR," WILL BE SHOWN. ROBERT J. THIEDA, CURATOR OF THE NATURAL SCIENCE MUSEUM, WILL SPEAK.

CHAPTER TWENTY-ONE

DESKTOP PUBLISHING: EDITING GRAPHIC IMAGES

OBJECTIVES

In this chapter, you will learn to:

- Change the brightness and contrast of a graphic image
- Change the scale of a graphic image
- Move a graphic image
- Rotate a graphic image
- Use the black and white options
- Flip a graphic image vertically and horizontally
- Overlay text on a graphic image

■ CHAPTER OVERVIEW

Whenever you include a graphic image in a document, you may want to edit the graphic. The Image Editor in WordPerfect allows you to rotate, scale, and move a graphic image within the box that contains it. You can also change the fill style of a graphic image, make it black and white, or change the brightness and contrast of the image.

In this chapter, editing graphic images is described and illustrated. Some of the topics on editing graphic images include rotating, moving, scaling, and changing a graphic image to black and white. The process of overlaying text on a graphic image is also discussed.

■ CHANGING THE BRIGHTNESS AND CONTRAST

You can adjust both the brightness and the contrast of a graphic image in your document. By adjusting the brightness of your image, you can change the density of the color of the image. Changing the contrast will change the difference between the light and dark areas of the graphic image. You can change the brightness of a graphic image by typing a number in the Brightness text box, or pressing the comma (,) or the period. You can also select the Brightness option from the Color Adjust option in the Edit menu, or by clicking on the "Brightns" button on the Button Bar.

Open the "GRAPHICS" document.

To change the brightness of the image:

Edit	the "HOTAIR.WPG" graphics box	*Edit*	*the "HOTAIR.WPG" graphics box*
Press	3 or E to select the Image Editor option	*Choose*	*the Image Editor option*

The Image Editor screen appears. Your screen should look like Figure 21-1.

Figure 21-1

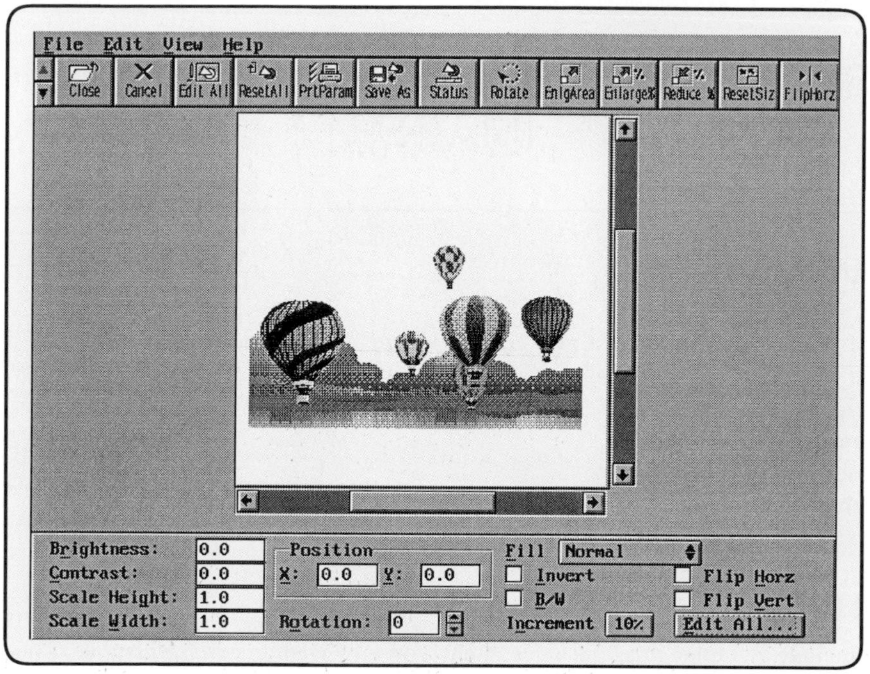

The Image Editor has a menu and a Button Bar that allows you to edit graphic images. The status box at the bottom of the Image Editor indicates the position of your image in the graphics box, the scale of your graphic image, the number of degrees your graphic image has been rotated, and the increment of change currently selected.

To make the image darker:

Press	R to select the Brightness text box	*Click*	*the down triangle button on the Button Bar to view the other buttons*
		Click	*the Brightns button on the Button Bar* 

To enter the number to change the Brightness:

Type	-.2	*Type*	*-.2*
Press	↵Enter	*Click*	*the OK command button*

Your screen should look like Figure 21-2.

Figure 21-2

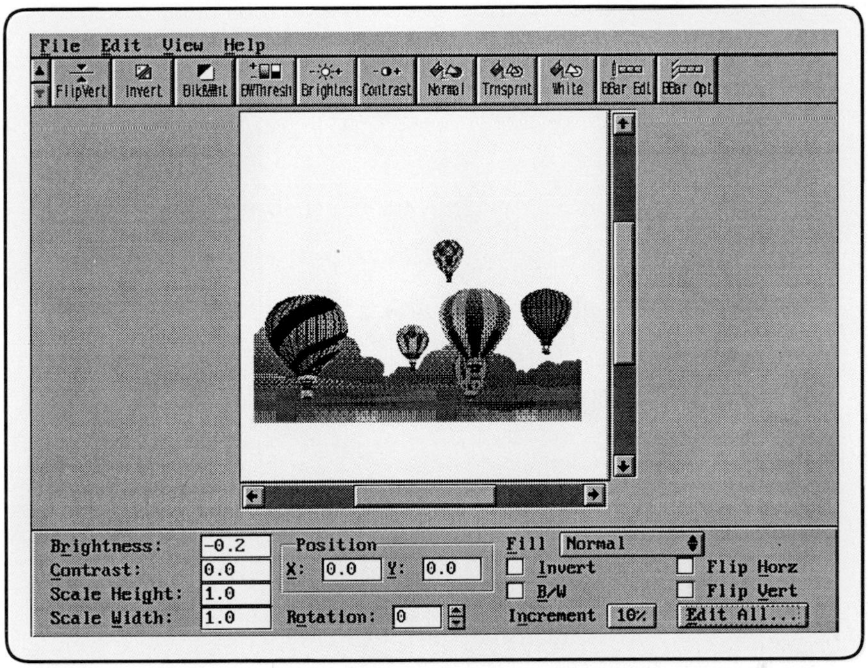

You can change the contrast of an image by typing a number in the Contrast text box or by pressing the greater than (>) and less than (<) symbols. You can also choose the Contrast option from the Color Adjust option in the Edit menu, or click on the "Contrast" button on the Button Bar.

To increase the contrast:

Press	C to select the Contrast text box	*Click*	*the Contrast button on the Button Bar* 

If you are using the mouse or menu methods, the Contrast dialog box appears.

To change the contrast:

Type	.2	*Type*	*.2*
Press	←Enter	*Click*	*the OK command button*

Your screen should look like Figure 21-3.

Figure 21-3

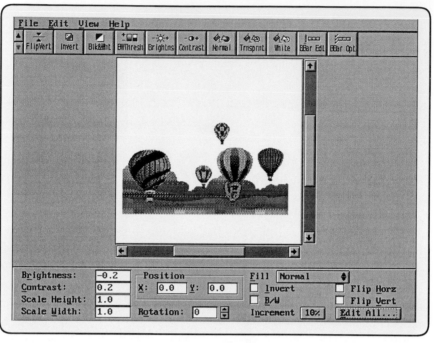

■ CHANGING THE SCALE OF A GRAPHIC IMAGE

Suppose you want to reduce the size of the "HOTAIR.WPG" image. You can enlarge or reduce an image in a horizontal or vertical direction by typing a number in the Scale Height and Scale Width text boxes in the status box.

If you want to enlarge an image by the increment percentage, you may choose from among three methods. Press the PAGE UP key, choose Enlarge % from the Position option in the Edit menu, or click the "Enlarge%" button on the Button Bar. Likewise, there are three methods for reducing an image using the increment percentage. You may press the PAGE DOWN key, choose Reduce % from the Position option in the Edit menu, or click the "Reduce%" button on the Button Bar.

Assume you want the image to be scaled to 75% of the original size, both horizontally and vertically. First, you must increase the percentage of change so that you can scale the image easily.

The Increment feature allows you to specify by what percentage you want to affect the graphic image when you use certain editing features. For example, if the increment percentage is 10% and you choose to scale the graphic image using the keyboard, it would be scaled by 10% in the graphics box. To change the increment percentage feature, press the INSERT key. Note that the default increment percentage is 10%.

To increase the increment percentage to 25%:

Press   [Insert] | *Choose*   *the Increment option*

The bottom of your screen should look like Figure 21-4.

Figure 21-4

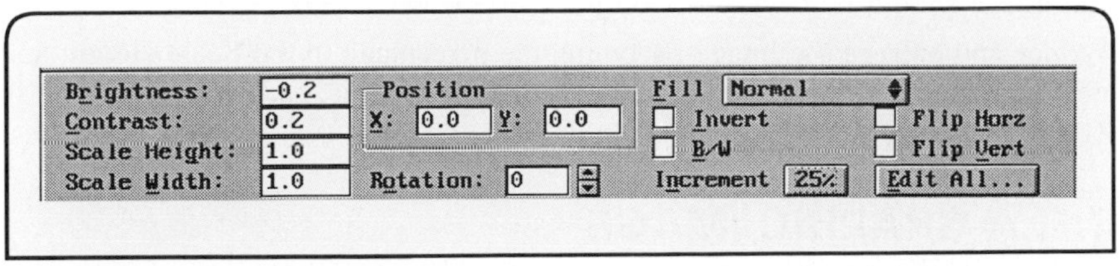

Notice the increment percentage displays 25%.

To reduce the "HOTAIR.WPG" image by 25%:

Press   Page Down   *Click*   *the up triangle button on the Button Bar*

        Click   *the Reduce% button on the Button Bar*

Your screen should look like Figure 21-5.

Figure 21-5

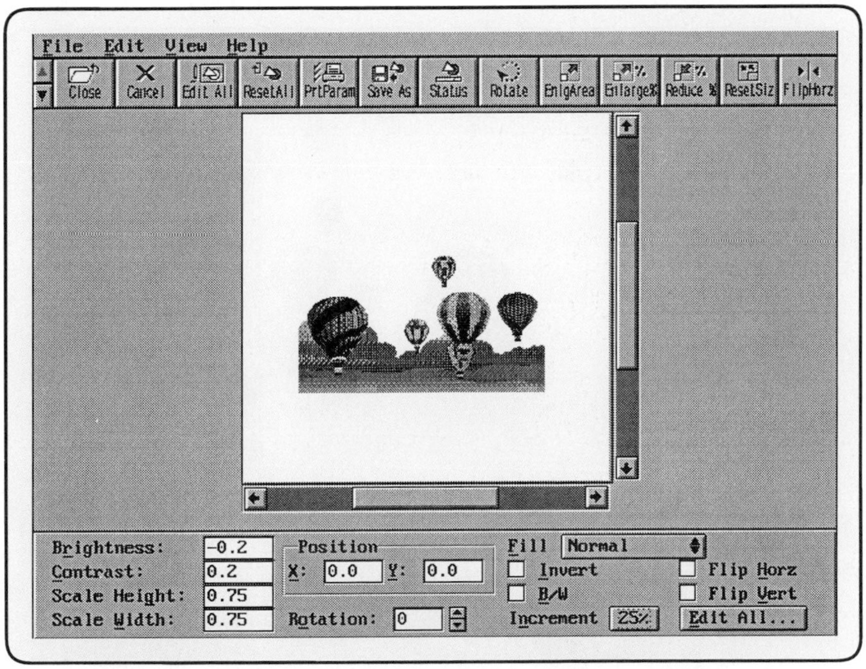

Notice that the Scale Height and Scale Width indicators have changed to .75".

You can enlarge the image by pressing the PAGE UP key, using the Enlarge % choice from the Position option in the Edit menu, or by clicking the "Enlarge%" button on the Button Bar.

To enlarge the image by 25%:

Press   Page Up   *Click*   *the Enlarge% button on the Button Bar*

Now the graphic image should be back to its original size.

You can also reduce and enlarge the image by typing the percentage in the Scale Height and Scale Width text boxes. For more details on how to enlarge an area of the graphic, see the "Scaling an Image" section of the WordPerfect Reference manual.

■ MOVING A GRAPHIC IMAGE

Assume that you want to move the "HOTAIR.WPG" image to another location in the box. You can move an image vertically or horizontally within the box by pressing the RIGHT ARROW, LEFT ARROW, UP ARROW, or DOWN ARROW keys, or by dragging the scroll boxes in the figure box. You can also type a number in the X Position text box and a number in the Y Position text box.

To move the image up and to the right:

Press	→	*Click*	*the left arrow button on the horizontal scroll bar*
Press	↑	*Click*	*the down arrow on the vertical scroll bar*

The graphic moves up and to the right by 25%, the current increment percentage.

Your screen should look similar to Figure 21-6.

Figure 21-6

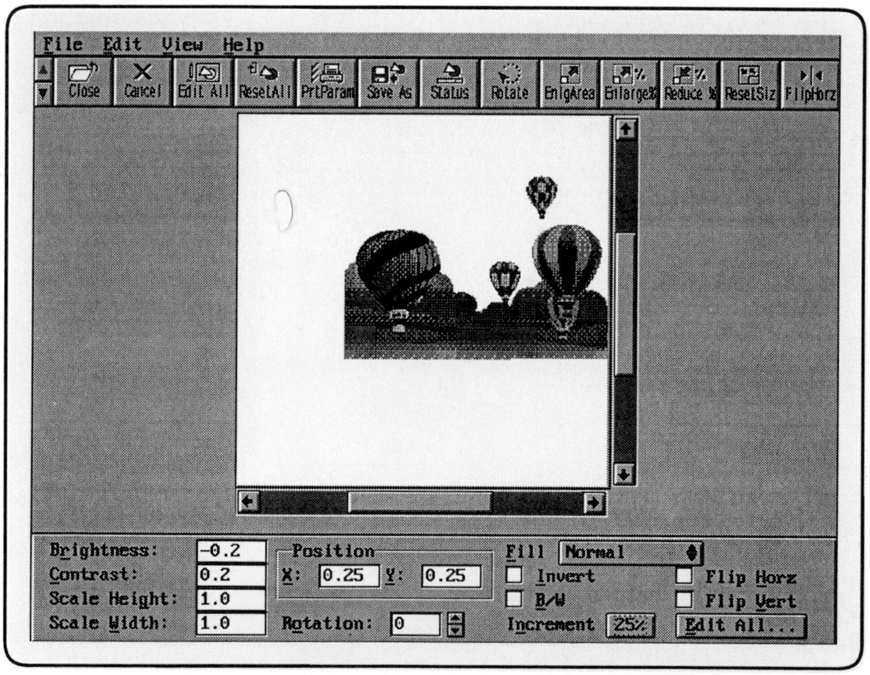

Notice the X and Y positions of the image have changed.

■ ROTATING A GRAPHIC IMAGE

Suppose you want to rotate the "HOTAIR.WPG" graphic image. The Rotate option allows you to rotate the image in a circle.

To rotate an image, you can use the plus (+) and minus (-) keys, choose Rotate from the Edit Position menu, or click the "Rotate" button on the Button Bar. When you rotate an image using the keyboard, the figure is rotated by the increment percentage.

To rotate the graphic image to the left 10%:

Press	Insert	***Click***	*the Increment option button three times*
Press	-	***Click***	*the Rotate button on the Button Bar* 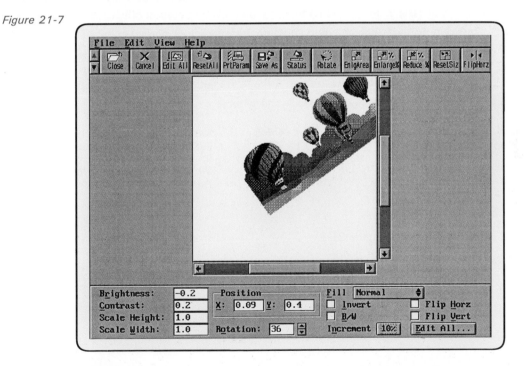
	or	***Drag***	*the Rotate bar up and to the left until the Rotation text box on the status bar displays 36*
Press	O to select the Rotation text box in the status box		*or*
Type	36	***Click***	*in the Rotation text box*
Press	↵Enter	***Type***	*36*
		Press	↵Enter

Your screen should look like Figure 21-7.

Figure 21-7

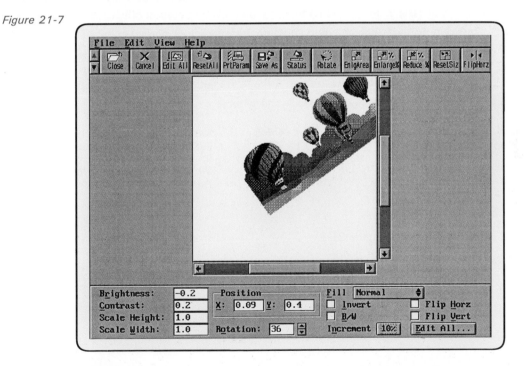

To rotate the image 10% to the right:

Press	+	***Click***	*the Rotate button on the Button Bar*

	or	***Drag***	the Rotate bar down and to the right until the Rotation text box in the status box displays 0	
Press	O to select the Rotation text box in the status box		*or*	
Type	0	***Click***	in the Rotation text box in the status box	
Press	`←Enter`	***Type***	0	
		Press	`←Enter`	

The "HOTAIR.WPG" graphic image should now be back in its original position.

■ USING THE BLACK AND WHITE OPTIONS

Most WordPerfect graphic images appear in color on the screen. However, many printers cannot print color documents. Most printers adapt the color graphic images and print them in varying shades of gray. WordPerfect has two features that help you print graphic images when you do not have a color printer and prefer not to print using a gray scale.

The Black and White feature changes any graphic image colors in the picture to black. If the image has a number of colors in it, the Black and White option may not have the desired effect.

The Fill feature offers options to change all colors to white, transparent, or normal color. The Fill feature does not affect black and white pictures.

The Black and White feature is located in the Attributes option in the edit menu, and the Fill feature is located in the Edit menu. You can also click on the "Blk&Wht" button on the Button Bar.

To change the picture of the hot air balloons to black and white:

Press	B to place an X in the B/W check box	***Click***	the down triangle button on the Button Bar
		Click	the Blk&Wht button on the Button Bar

Your screen should look similar to Figure 21-8.

Figure 21-8

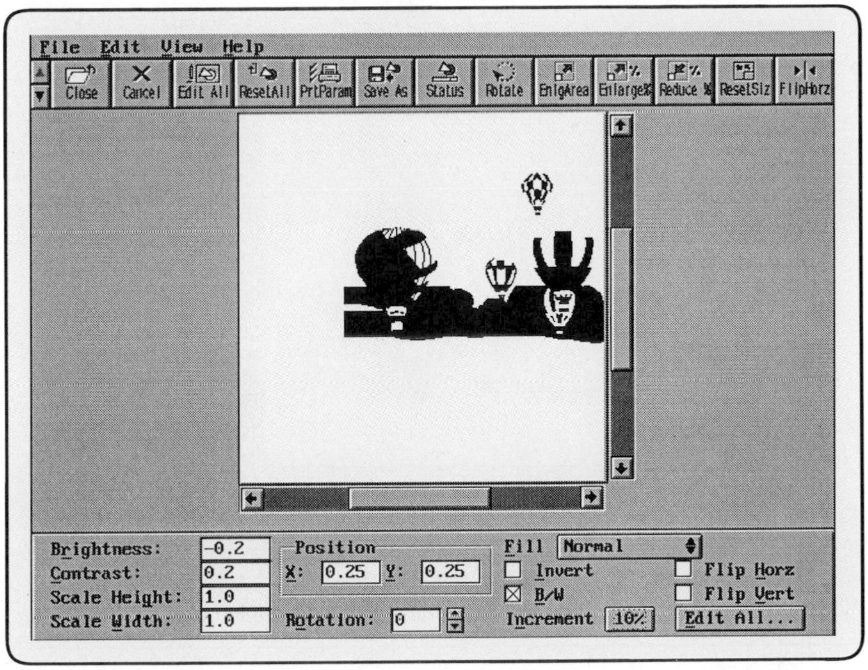

Because there are many colors in the hot air balloons, the Black and White feature makes the graphic too dark.

Suppose you decided that you did not like any of the changes you have made to the image so far. You could reset the changes by choosing Reset All from the Edit menu or by clicking on the "ResetAll" button on the Button Bar. To change the image back to normal:

Press   Ctrl + Home

Click   *the up triangle button on the Button Bar*

Click   *the ResetAll button on the Button Bar*

■ FLIPPING A GRAPHIC IMAGE VERTICALLY AND HORIZONTALLY

There may be times when you need to flip a graphic image on its axis, or make a mirror image of the graphic. WordPerfect offers both horizontal and vertical mirroring options. You can flip an image by placing an X in the Flip Horz check box, by choosing Flip Horizontal from the Attributes option in the Edit menu, or by clicking on the "FlipHorz" button on the Button Bar.

To flip the "HOTAIR.WPG" graphic horizontally:

Press   H to place an X in the Flip Horz check box

Click   *the Flip Horz check box until an X appears*

Your screen should look like Figure 21-9.

Figure 21-9

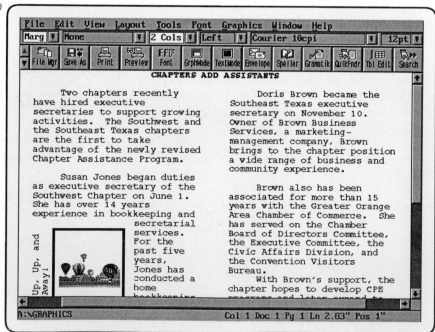

Notice that the largest balloon is now on the right side of the graphic image. You can flip a graphic image vertically by placing an X in the Flip Vert check box. You can also choose Flip Vertical from the Attributes option in the Edit menu, or by clicking the "FlipVert" button on the Button Bar.

To return to your document:

Press   F7 twice

Click   *the Close button on the Button Bar*

Click   *the OK command button*

Your screen should look like Figure 21-10.

Figure 21-10

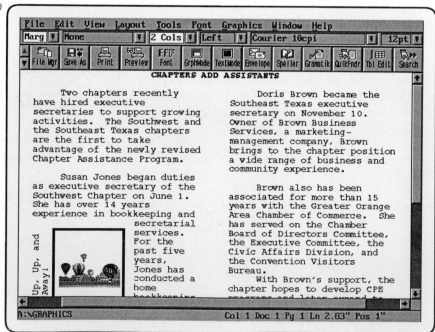

Save the document as "GRAPHICS.EDT".

■ OVERLAYING TEXT ON A GRAPHIC IMAGE

WordPerfect offers several graphic images that you may want to customize by placing text over the graphic image. The Text Flow Around Box options provide the capability to overlay text on a graphic image. Place your cursor at the left margin of the first paragraph in column 2.

To create a text box for the text overlay:

Press	Alt + F9	***Choose***	*Graphics*
Press	1 or B to select the Graphics Boxes option	***Choose***	*Graphics Boxes*
Press	1 or C to select the Create option	***Choose***	*Create*
Press	2 or N to select the Contents pop-up list button	***Hold down***	*the mouse button on the Contents pop-up list button*
Press	T to select the Text option	***Choose***	*the Text option*
Press	3 or E to select the Create Text option	***Choose***	*the Create Text option*

The Text Editor appears, and your screen should look like Figure 21-11.

Figure 21-11

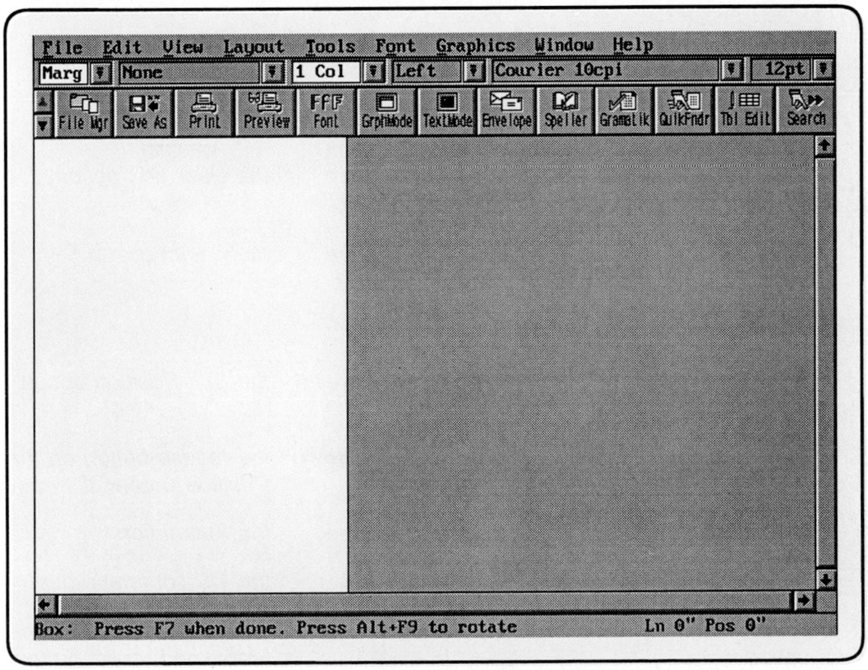

To create the graphic and edit its box style:

Press	Alt + F9	***Choose***	*Graphics*
Press	1 or B to select the Graphics Boxes option	***Choose***	*Graphics Boxes*
Press	1 or C to select the Create option	***Choose***	*Create*

Press   Y to select the Based on Box Style   **Choose**   *the Based on Box Style option*
option

The Graphics Box Styles dialog box appears. Your screen should look like Figure 21-12.

Figure 21-12

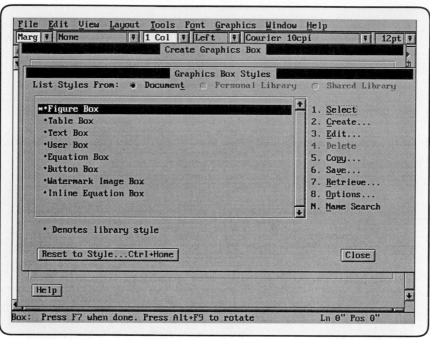

Press   ⬇ three times to select the User   **Choose**   *the User Box option*
Box option

Press   1 or S to select the Select option   **Choose**   *the Select option*

To edit the box position and the flow of text around the box:

Press   8 or P to select the Edit Position   **Choose**   *the Edit Position option*
option

Press   1 or H to select the Horizontal   **Hold down**   *the mouse button on the Horizontal*
Position pop-up list button   *Position pop-up list button*

Press   F to select the Full option   **Choose**   *the Full option*

Press   ⏎Enter   **Click**   *the OK command button*

Press   T to select the Text Flow Around   **Hold down**   *the mouse button on the Text*
Box option   *Flows pop-up list button*

Press   1 or F to select the Text Flows   **Choose**   *the Through Box option*
pop-up list button

Press   T to select the Through Box option

To retrieve the graphic image:

Press	1 or F to select the Filename option	*Choose*	*the Filename option*
Press	F5 to select the File List command button	*Click*	*the File List command button*
Press	←Enter	*Click*	*the OK command button*
Press	↓ until "LIGHTHS.WPG" is selected	*Select*	*"LIGHTHS.WPG"*
Press	1 or S to choose the Select option	*Choose*	*the Select option*
Press	←Enter	*Click*	*the OK command button*

The graphic image now appears in the Text Editor. Your screen should look like Figure 21-13.

Figure 21-13

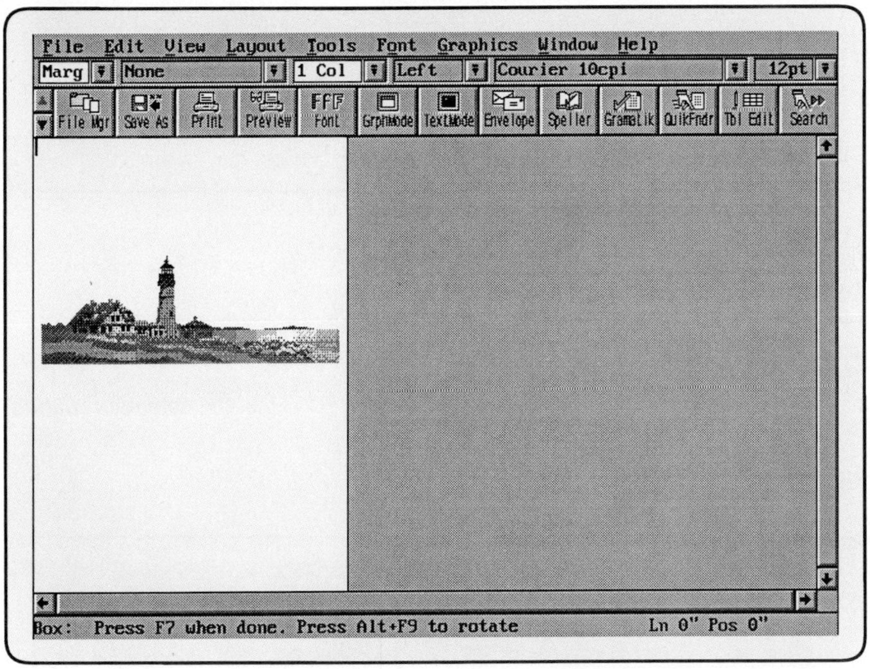

To enter the text and format the text box:

Type	We wish smooth sailing for Susan and Doris as they come on board with us.	*Type*	*We wish smooth sailing for Susan and Doris as they come on board with us.*
Press	←Enter eleven times	*Press*	*←Enter eleven times*
Press	Shift + F6	*Choose*	*Layout*
Type	Welcome!	*Choose*	*Alignment*
		Choose	*Center*
		Type	*Welcome!*

Your screen should look like Figure 21-14.

Figure 21-14

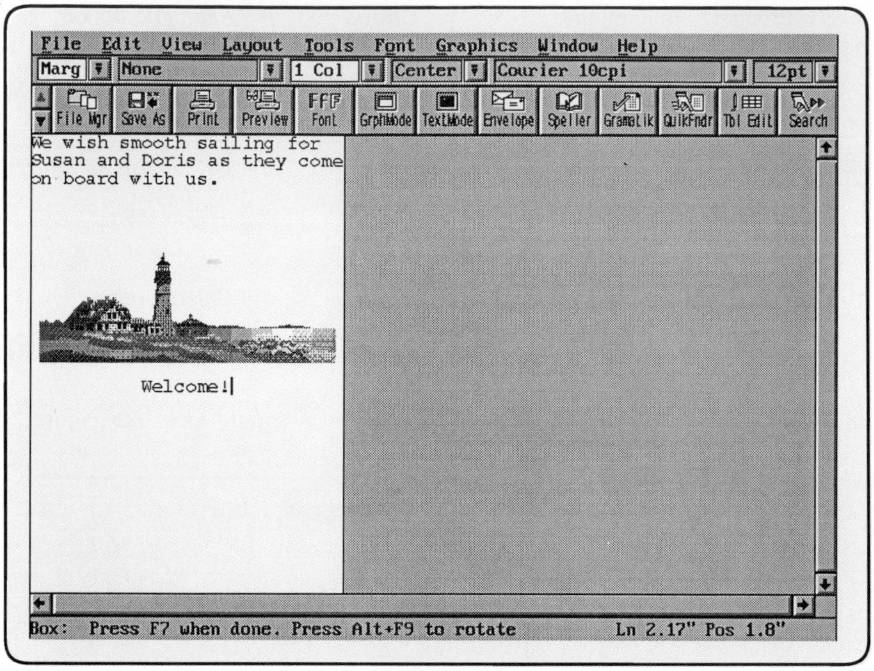

To return to the document:

Press	F7		**Choose**	*File*
Press	←Enter		**Choose**	*Exit*
			Click	*the OK command button*

Your screen should look like Figure 21-15.

Figure 21-15

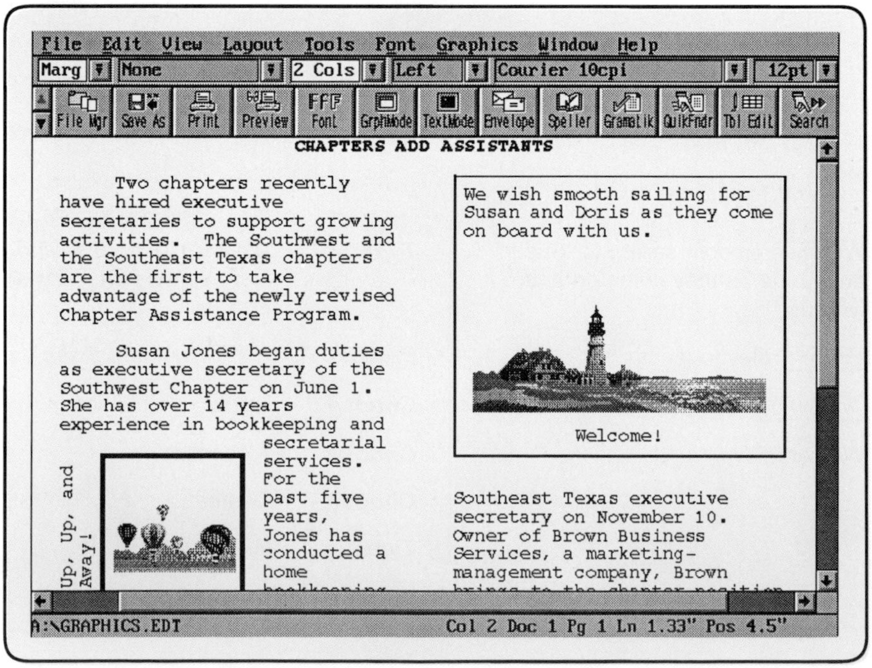

Save the document as "GRAPHICS.TXT". Close the document.

For more detailed information on the other Image Editor features see the "Graphics: Editing Images" section of the WordPerfect Reference manual.

EXERCISE 1

INSTRUCTIONS: Define the following concepts:

1. Image Editor _____

    _____

2. Rotate option _____

    _____

3. Scale option _____

    _____

4. Move option_____

    _____

5. Black and White option _____

    _____

6. Fill Style option _____

    _____

7. Text Flow Around Box option _____

    _____

EXERCISE 2

INSTRUCTIONS: Circle T if the statement is true and F if the statement is false.

T	F	1.	The Image Editor allows you to draw pictures and charts in WordPerfect.
T	F	2.	The Rotate option allows you to rotate the image in the graphics box.
T	F	3.	In the Image Editor, pressing the RIGHT ARROW key rotates the image to the right.
T	F	4.	The Scale option allows you to enlarge or reduce the graphics box on the page.
T	F	5.	The Increment feature allows you to specify by what percentage you want to affect the graphic image when you use the keyboard to make it black and white.
T	F	6.	You can scale a graphic image horizontally but not vertically.
T	F	7.	You can scale an image by pressing the arrow keys.
T	F	8.	The Move option allows you to move the image within the graphics box.
T	F	9.	Pressing the CTRL+UP ARROW key moves the image up.

T	F	9.	Pressing the CTRL+UP ARROW key moves the image up.
T	F	10.	You can only move an image up or down in the graphics box.
T	F	11.	If you turn off the Text Flow Around Box option then you can place one graphic image on another image or place text on a graphic image.

EXERCISE 3

INSTRUCTIONS:

1. Create the following document.
2. Place a picture of the wizard in the document where indicated. The name of the WordPerfect graphic for the wizard is "WIZARD.WPG". Make the graphics box 3.25" by 3.25", and center it horizontally on the page.
3. Save the document in a file using the name "CH21EX03".
4. Print the document.
5. Rotate the graphic image 25% to the right.
6. Print the document.
7. Rotate the graphic image back to its original position.
8. Rotate the graphic image 10% to the left.
9. Print the document.
10. Rotate the graphic image back to its original position.
11. Scale the graphic image to 50% of its original size.
12. Print the document.
13. Scale the graphic image back to its original size.
14. Move the graphic image to the left 1/2" and down 1".
15. Print the document.
16. Move the graphic image back to its original position.
17. Print the document.
18. Close the document without saving changes.

MERLIN
Come join us for the Senior class play,
Saturday night at the Moody Auditorium.

"MERLIN" is the story of the man behind the name and the myth.
It was written by the Senior class.
Tickets are $1.50.

EXERCISE 4

INSTRUCTIONS:

1. Create the following document. Use the "FISHTROP.WPG" graphic image.
2. The size of the graphics box is 4" x 4". Center the graphics box horizontally on the page. Rotate the figure 315°. Reduce the size of the graphic by 30%.
3. Preview and print the document.
4. Save the document in a file using the name "CH21EX04".
5. Close the document.

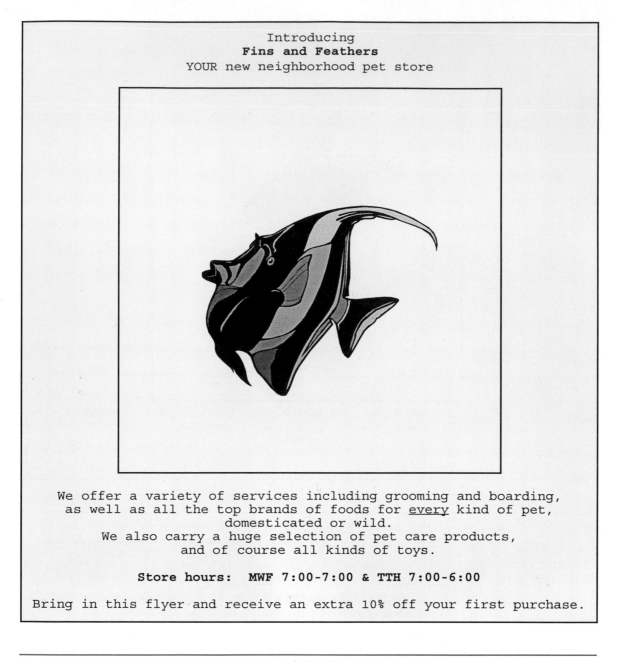

Introducing
Fins and Feathers
YOUR new neighborhood pet store

We offer a variety of services including grooming and boarding,
as well as all the top brands of foods for <u>every</u> kind of pet,
domesticated or wild.
We also carry a huge selection of pet care products,
and of course all kinds of toys.

Store hours: MWF 7:00-7:00 & TTH 7:00-6:00

Bring in this flyer and receive an extra 10% off your first purchase.

EXERCISE 5

INSTRUCTIONS:

1. Create the following document. Use the "CONDUCT.WPG" graphic image.
2. Left align the graphics box on the page. The size of the graphics box is 3" x 3". Remove all borders from the graphics box.
3. Place the caption on the right and center it vertically.
4. Preview and print the document.
5. Save the document in a file using the name "CH21EX05".
6. Close the document.

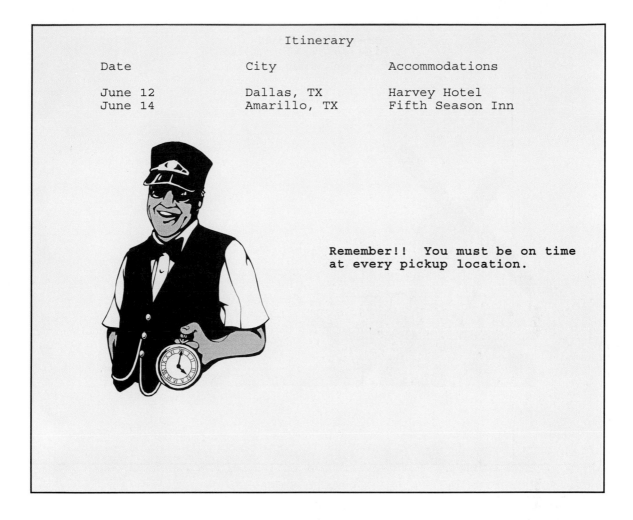

```
                         Itinerary

Date                  City               Accommodations

June 12               Dallas, TX         Harvey Hotel
June 14               Amarillo, TX       Fifth Season Inn




                                    Remember!!  You must be on time
                                    at every pickup location.
```

EXERCISE 6

INSTRUCTIONS:

1. Create the following document. Use the "WINDMILL.WPG" graphic.
2. Center the graphic vertically and horizontally on the page.
3. Remove all the borders.
4. Enlarge the graphic image by 25%.
5. Center and boldface the caption "Great Vacations!" above the graphic.
6. Preview and print the document.
7. Save the document in a file using the name "CH21EX06".
8. Close the document.

EXERCISE 7

INSTRUCTIONS:

1.   Create a graphics box using the "LIGHTHS.WPG" graphic image. Attach the graphic to the page, center the graphics box between the left and right margins, and change the size to 5" wide and 5" tall. Remove all borders from the graphics box. Turn on the Through Box option in the Text Flow Around Box feature.

2.   Center the following caption above the graphics box:

"Worldwide Travel - We bring you close to nature!"

3.   Create a second graphics box using the "JEEP.WPG" graphic image. This graphics box is also attached to the page. Set the vertical position to 4". Do not change the size of the graphic. Remove all borders from the graphics box.

4.   Save the document as "CH21EX07".

5.   Print the document.

6.   Close the document.

Worldwide Travel - We bring you close to nature!

EXERCISE 8

INSTRUCTIONS:

1. Create the following document by opening the document "CH21EX04".
2. Edit the "FISHTROP.WPG" graphic image. Change the X position of the graphic image to -.3", and the Y position to .29". Change the Text Flow Around Box feature to Through Box.
3. Create another graphics box that contains the "PARROT.WPG" graphic image. The graphics box is 2" by 2". Change the Horizontal position to Right with an Offset from Position set to Left 1.7". Change the Vertical position of the box to a Distance from Top of Paragraph of 1.15". Remove the graphics box borders.
4. Change its X position to .6".
5. Save the file using the name "CH21EX08".
6. Print the document.

Introducing
Fins and Feathers
YOUR new neighborhood pet store

We offer a variety of services including grooming and boarding,
as well as all the top brands of foods for <u>every</u> kind of pet,
domestic or wild.
We also carry a huge selection of pet care products,
and of course all kinds of toys.

Store hours: MWF 7:00-7:00 & TTH 7:00-6:00

Bring in this flyer and receive an extra 10% off your first
purchase.

CHAPTER TWENTY-TWO

DESKTOP PUBLISHING: ADVANCED GRAPHIC FEATURES

OBJECTIVES

In this chapter you will learn to:
- Create vertical and horizontal lines
- Edit vertical and horizontal lines
- Create borders around text
- Place a watermark behind the text on a page

■ CHAPTER OVERVIEW

In this chapter, creating and editing graphic lines is demonstrated. You also are shown how to place a border around selected text. A new feature called Watermarks is discussed.

■ CREATING LINES

Open the "GRAPHICS.EDT" document created in Chapter 21. Suppose you want to place a horizontal line below the "CHAPTERS ADD ASSISTANTS" text.

Horizontal Lines

To create a horizontal line:

Move	the cursor to Ln 1.17" Pos 1"		*Click*	*below the main heading (Ln 1.17" Pos 1")*
Press	Alt + F9		*Choose*	*Graphics*
Press	2 or L to select the Graphics Lines option		*Choose*	*Graphics Lines*
Press	1 or C to select the Create option		*Choose*	*Create*

The Create Graphics Line dialog box appears. Your screen should look like Figure 22-1.

Figure 22-1

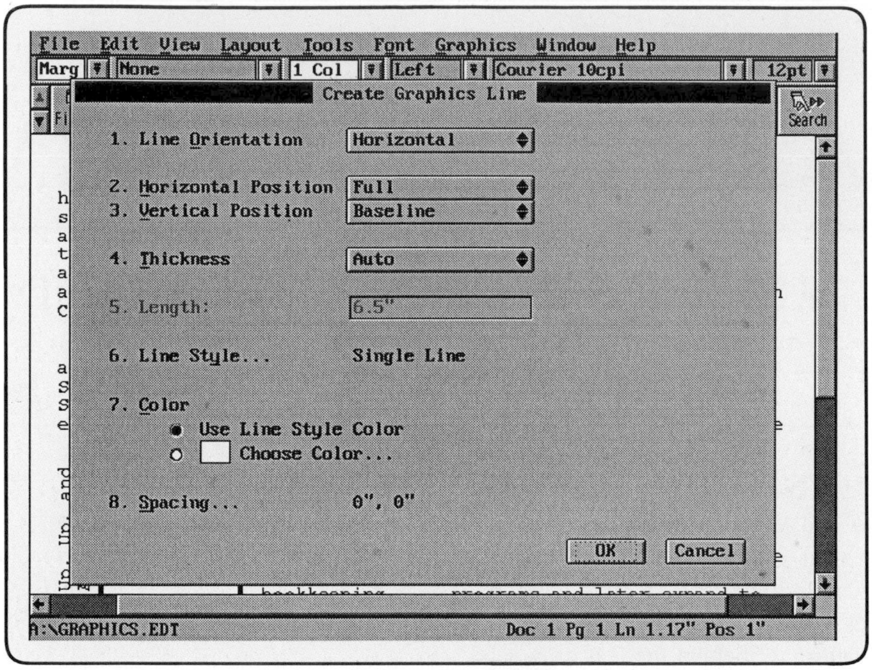

The Line Orientation option allows you to choose either a horizontal or vertical line.   By default, the line is horizontal. The Horizontal Position option allows you to position the line across the page. You can start the line at the left or right margin, center the line, or extend the line from margin to margin (Full option). You can also set the line to begin a certain number of inches from the left side of the page.

The Vertical Position option allows you to position the graphic line on the current line (Baseline) or to set a specific position on the page where the line should be printed (Set). The Thickness option allows you to accept an automatic 0.013" thick line or set the desired thickness.

The Length option allows you to define the length and thickness of the line. If the Horizontal Position option is defined as Full, the line length is set automatically based on the left and right margins and cannot be changed. If any of the other options are chosen for the horizontal position, the line length can be shortened.

By default, the Line Style option is a single line. Some of the other options include double, dashed, dotted, thick, and extra thick. The Color option allows you to specify shading for the line. You may choose varying shades of many different colors. These color choices will not print in color unless you have a color printer; however, they will display in color on the screen.

To accept the default settings:

Press   ⏎Enter | ***Click***   *the OK command button*

The top part of your screen should look like Figure 22-2.

Figure 22-2

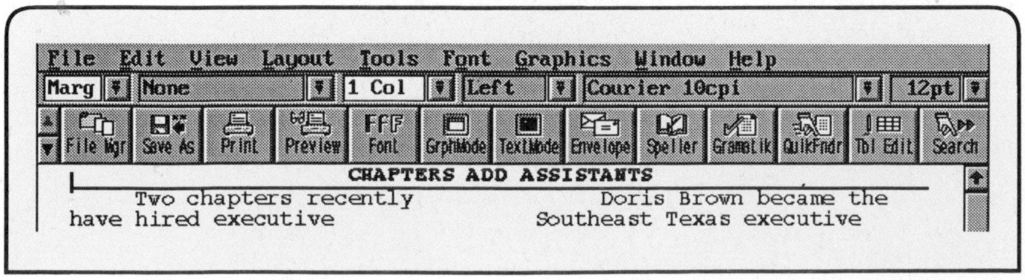

Notice that the line extends from the left margin to the right margin.

Vertical Lines

Suppose you want a vertical line between the columns in your document. To create the vertical line:

Move	the cursor to the beginning of the first paragraph in Column 1		*Click*	*at the left margin of the first paragraph in Column 1*
Press	Alt + F9		*Choose*	*Graphics*
Press	2 or L to select the Graphics Lines option		*Choose*	*Graphics Lines*
Press	1 or C to select the Create option		*Choose*	*Create*
Press	1 or O to select the Line Orientation option		*Hold down*	*the mouse button on the Line Orientation pop-up list button*
Press	V to select the Vertical option		*Choose*	*the Vertical option*

The Horizontal Position option allows you to position the line slightly to the left of the left margin, slightly to the right of the right margin, between columns, or set at a specific position.

To select the Horizontal Position option:

Press	2 or H to select the Horizontal Position options		*Hold down*	*the mouse button on the Horizontal Position pop-up list button*
Press	B to select the Between Columns option		*Choose*	*the Between Columns option*

Your screen should look like Figure 22-3.

Figure 22-3

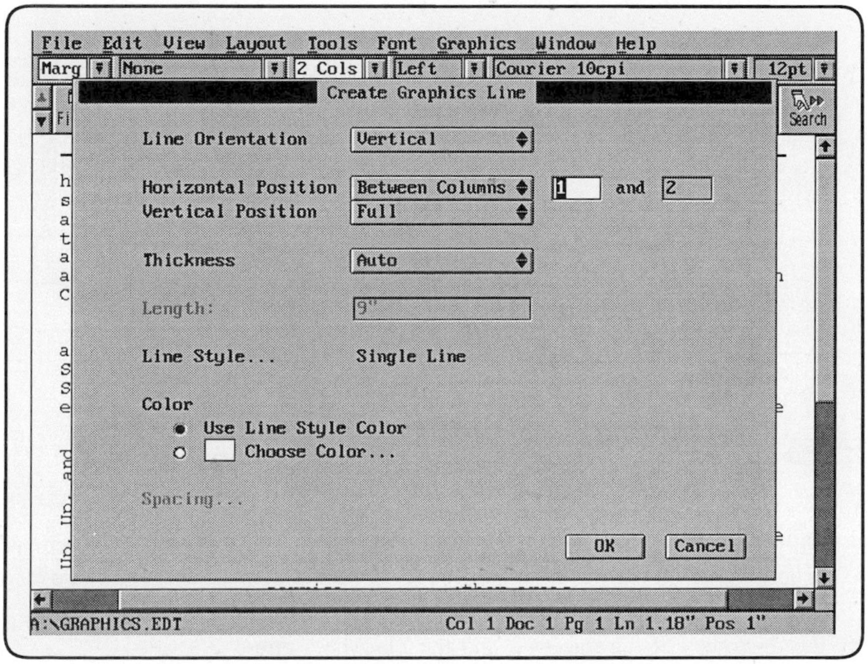

The default setting places the line between columns 1 and 2.

To accept this horizontal position:

| **Press** | [↵Enter] | **Double-click** | *in the text box for column 1* |

The Vertical Position option allows you to position the line at the top or bottom margin, centered between margins, extended the full length of the margins, or set to a specific position from the top of the page. By default, the vertical line would extend from the top margin to the bottom margin.

To select the Vertical Position option:

| **Press** | 3 or V to select the Vertical Position options | **Hold down** | *the mouse button on the Vertical Position pop-up list button* |
| **Press** | S to select the Set option | **Choose** | *the Set option* |

Your screen should look like Figure 22-4.

Figure 22-4

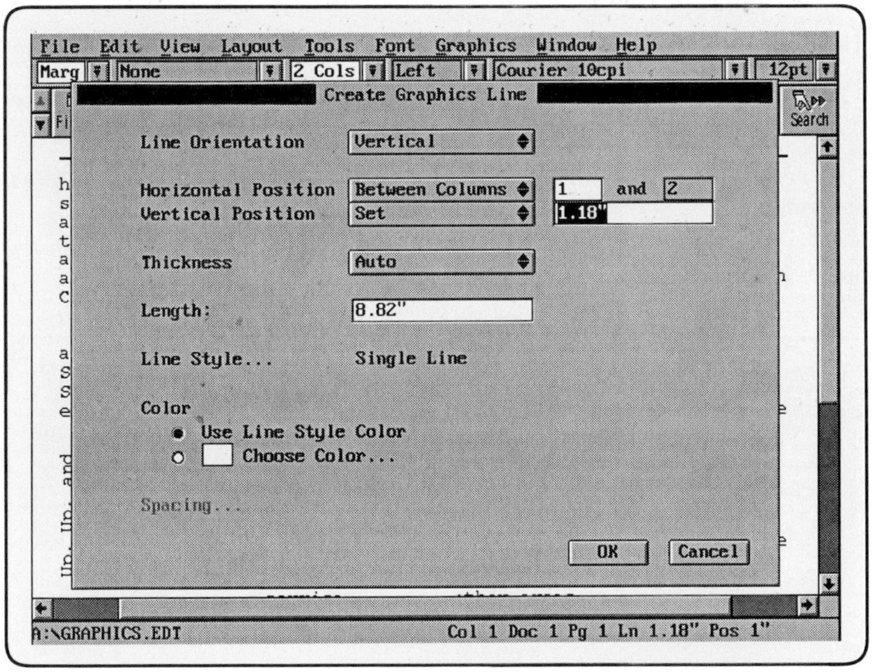

To specify that you want the line to begin where the cursor is located:

| **Press** | [↵Enter] | **Double-click** | *in the Vertical Position text box* |

Notice that the Length option automatically changed. The line measures from the cursor position to the bottom margin. If you wanted a shorter line, the Length option allows you to define how long you want the line to be.

You can specify the thickness of the line by using the Thickness option.

The Line Style option allows you to specify shading for the line. By default, the Line Style option is a single line. Some of the other options include double, dashed, dotted, thick, and extra thick.

The Color option allows you to specify shading for the line. You may choose varying shades of many different colors. These color choices will not print in color unless you have a color printer; however, they will display in color on the screen.

To accept the defaults for thickness, style, and color, and return to the document:

Press   ⟨←Enter⟩ | ***Click***   *the OK command button*

Your screen should look like Figure 22-5.

Figure 22-5

```
 File  Edit  View  Layout  Tools  Font  Graphics  Window  Help
[Marg ▼][None          ▼][2 Cols ▼][Left  ▼][Courier 10cpi    ▼][12pt ▼]
  ⌐¬   ⌐¬    ⌐¬    ⌐¬    FFF   ⌐¬    ■    ⌐¬    ⌐¬    ⌐¬    ⌐¬    ⌐¬
File Mgr Save As Print Preview Font Grphmode TextMode Envelope Speller Grammlik QuikFndr Tbl Edit Search
                        CHAPTERS ADD ASSISTANTS                          ▲
      Two chapters recently          Doris Brown became the
  have hired executive           Southeast Texas executive
  secretaries to support growing  secretary on November 10.
  activities.  The Southwest and  Owner of Brown Business
  the Southeast Texas chapters    Services, a marketing-
  are the first to take           management company, Brown
  advantage of the newly revised  brings to the chapter position
  Chapter Assistance Program.     a wide range of business and
                                  community experience.
      Susan Jones began duties
  as executive secretary of the       Brown also has been
  Southwest Chapter on June 1.    associated for more than 15
  She has over 14 years           years with the Greater Orange
  experience in bookkeeping and   Area Chamber of Commerce.  She
                      secretarial has served on the Chamber
                      services.    Board of Directors Committee,
                      For the      the Executive Committee, the
                      past five    Civic Affairs Division, and
                      years,       the Convention Visitors
                      Jones has    Bureau.
                      conducted a     With Brown's support, the
                      home         chapter hopes to develop CPE
                      bookkeeping  programs and later expand to  ▼
 ◄                                                            ►
A:\GRAPHICS.EDT                    Col 1 Doc 1 Pg 1 Ln 1.18" Pos 1"
```

■ EDITING LINES

After you insert a line, you may need to modify it. Suppose you want to change the thickness of the horizontal line.

When you choose to edit a line, you need to determine the number of the line. In Reveal Codes, you will see that the horizontal line is called [Graph Line:1;Horiz]. The vertical line is called [Graph Line:2;Vert]. You may also edit a line by double-clicking on it.

To edit the horizontal line:

Press   ⟨Alt⟩ + ⟨F9⟩ | ***Double-***   *on the horizontal line*
                                    click

Press   2 or L to select the Graphics
              Lines option

Press   2 or E to select the Edit option

Press   1 or N to select the Graphics
              Line Number text box

Type   1

Press   [←Enter] twice

You can also enter the Select Graphics Line To Edit dialog box by choosing Edit from the Graphics Lines option under the Graphics option on the menu.

The Edit Graphics Line dialog box appears. Your screen should look like Figure 22-6.

Figure 22-6

```
  File  Edit  View  Layout  Tools  Font  Graphics  Window  Help
 Marg ▼ None            ▼ 2 Cols ▼ Left  ▼ Courier 10cpi          ▼ 12pt ▼
 ▲ ▼ Fi                    Edit Graphics Line                         Search
                                                                        ▲
      h    1. Line Orientation    Horizontal      ♦
      s
      a    2. Horizontal Position Full            ♦
      t    3. Vertical Position   Baseline        ♦
      a
      a    4. Thickness           Auto            ♦
      C
           5. Length:             6.5"
      a
      S    6. Line Style...       Single Line
      S
      e    7. Color
                 ● Use Line Style Color
                 ○ ☐ Choose Color...

           8. Spacing...          0", 0"

      [ Previous Home,PgUp ]  [ Next Home,PgDn ]      [ OK ]  [ Cancel ]
                                                                        ▼
 ◄                                                                   ►  ▲▼
 A:\GRAPHICS.EDT              Col 1 Doc 1 Pg 1 Ln 1.18" Pos 1"
```

To change the thickness of the horizontal line:

Press	4 or T to select the Thickness option	***Hold down*** *the mouse button on the Thickness pop-up list button*
Press	S to select the Set option	***Choose*** *Set*
Type	.05	***Type*** *.05*
Press	[←Enter]	***Double-click*** *in the Thickness text box*

Your screen should look like Figure 22-7.

Figure 22-7

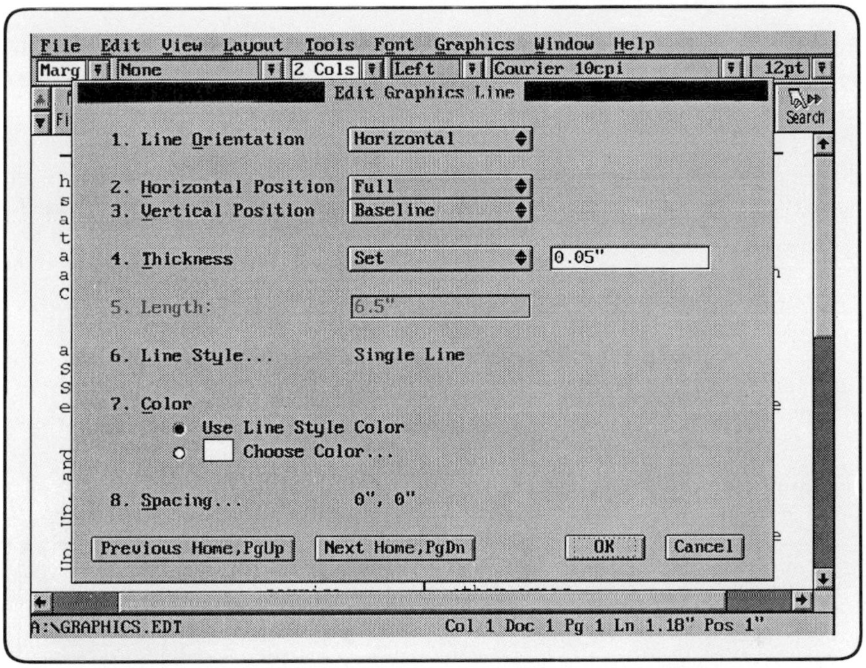

To return to the document:

Press   ⏎Enter   │   ***Click***   *the OK command button*

Notice that the horizontal line is thicker. The top part of your screen should look like Figure 22-8.

Figure 22-8

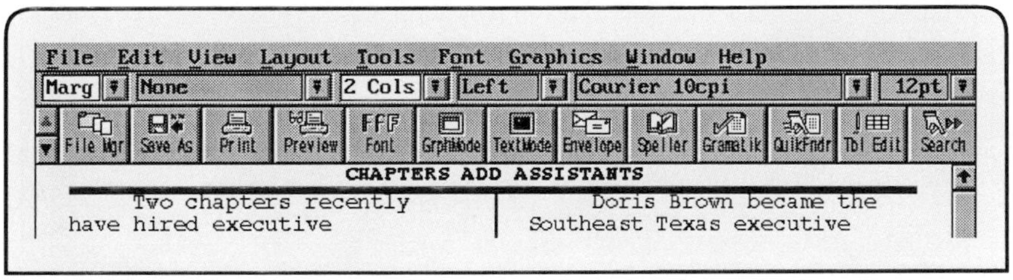

To return to the document... (figure image)

Save the document as "GRAPHICS.LIN".

You can also size and move a graphic line using the mouse. To edit a line using the mouse, select the line by clicking on it.

To move the line, position the mouse pointer over the line so that it appears as a move pointer (four pointing arrows) and drag the line in the desired direction.

To size the line, position the mouse pointer over one of the sizing handles so that it appears as a double-pointing arrow. Drag a sizing handle in the desired direction. (Remember that a sizing handle is a small square box that appears when a graphic line is selected.)

■ CREATING BORDERS AROUND TEXT

At times, you may want to draw attention to particular text by placing a border around the text. A border is a square or rectangle that encloses a page, paragraph, column, or section of selected text.

To enclose the last paragraph of the document in a border:

Move	the cursor to the beginning of the last paragraph in column 2		***Click***	*at the left margin of the last paragraph in column 2*
Press	Alt + F9		***Choose***	*Graphics*
Press	3 or O to select the Borders option		***Choose***	*Borders*
Press	1 or P to select the Paragraph option		***Choose***	*Paragraph*

The Create Paragraph Border dialog box appears. Your screen should look like Figure 22-9.

Figure 22-9

```
 File  Edit  View  Layout  Tools  Font  Graphics  Window  Help
 Marg ▼ None              ▼ 2 Cols ▼ Left  ▼ Courier 10cpi      ▼  12pt ▼

 File Mgr Save As Print Preview Font GrphMode TextMode Envelope Speller Gramatik QuikFndr Tbl Edit Search

        services.        Board of Directors Committee,
        For the          the Executive Committee, the
        past five        Civic Affairs Division, and
                         the Convention Visitors

           ┌──────────── Create Paragraph Border ────────────┐
           │                                                 │ rt, the
           │  1. Border Style...  Single Border              │ p CPE
           │                                                 │ and to
        Presentl│  2. Fill Style...    [None]                │
        civic cl│                                            │
        associat│  3. Customize...                           │
        private │                                            │
           │  ┌─────┐              ┌──────┐  ┌────────┐      │
           In  │  │ Off │              │  OK  │  │ Cancel │      │
        with the │  └─────┘              └──────┘  └────────┘   │
        concentrated her efforts in └─────────────────────────┘
        the area of CPE and dues
        billing.  She says she is
        working on transferring the
        chapter records to a computer.

 A:\GRAPHICS.LIN                    Col 2 Doc 1 Pg 1 Ln 4.55" Pos 4.5"
```

You may change the Border Style making a change in the appearance of the lines around the text. You may also change the Fill Style, which permits shading in the white space around the text within the border. By default, the border line is single and there is no fill style. You may also customize the border in various ways, including adjusting margins within the border and rounding the corners of the border. For more information about customizing a border, consult the WordPerfect Reference manual.

To accept the default border options and return to the document:

Press	←Enter		***Click***	*the OK command button*

The bottom of your screen should look like Figure 22-10.

Figure 22-10

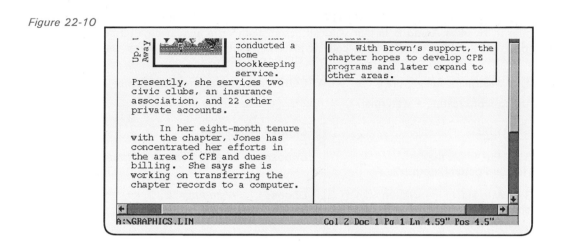

You may also create a border through the Format menu by choosing SHIFT+F8, 1 or L for Line, and 5 or B for Borders. The menu method would be to choose Layout, Line, and Paragraph Borders.

If you wish to place a border around more than one paragraph but less than a whole page or column, you may highlight the text before selecting the border options.

Save the document using the same name. Close the document.

■ USING WATERMARKS

Watermarks are a new feature in WordPerfect 6.0. A watermark is a graphic image that appears faintly behind a page of text. A watermark is used in Figure 22-11.

Figure 22-11

You can create up to two watermarks on each page of text. They are called Watermark A and Watermark B and are similar to Headers A and B in that you can designate them to appear on alternating pages. A watermark appears on the page on which the code is placed and all subsequent pages, unless otherwise specified.

Before creating a watermark image, open the "NEWSCOL" document created in Chapter 17.

To begin the process of creating a watermark:

Press	Shift + F8		*Choose*	*Layout*
Press	5 or H to select the Header/Footer/Watermark		*Choose*	*Header/Footer/Watermark*
Press	3 or W to select the Watermarks option		*Choose*	*Watermark A*
Press	1 or A to select the Watermark A option			

The Watermark A dialog box appears on the screen. Your screen should look like Figure 22-12.

Figure 22-12

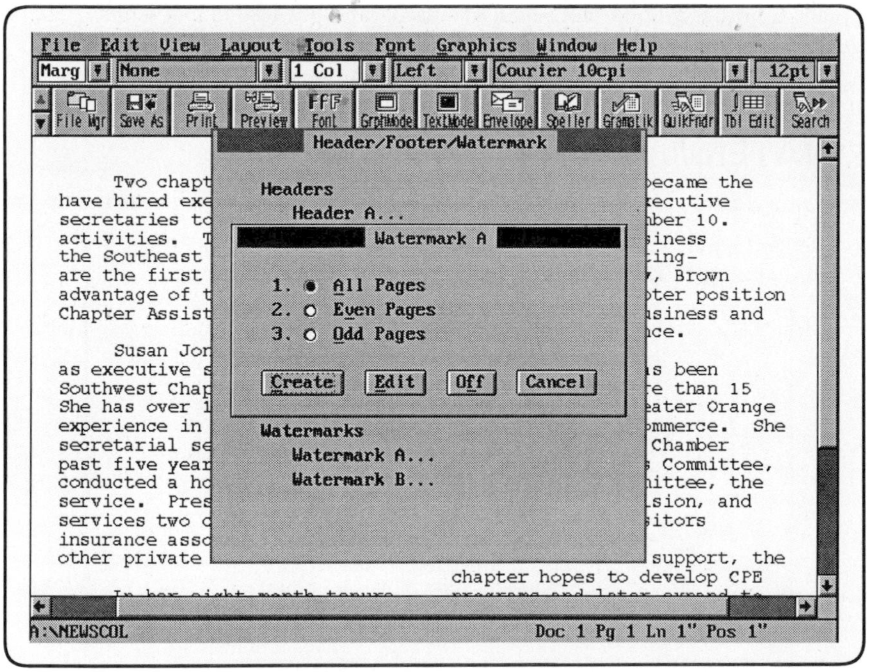

You may choose to have the watermark appear on all pages, even pages, or odd pages. The default is to appear on all pages. The default is appropriate for our needs.

To select the desired watermark:

Press	←Enter to select the Create command button		*Click*	*the Create command button*

The Watermark A editing screen appears. Your screen should look like Figure 22-13.

Figure 22-13

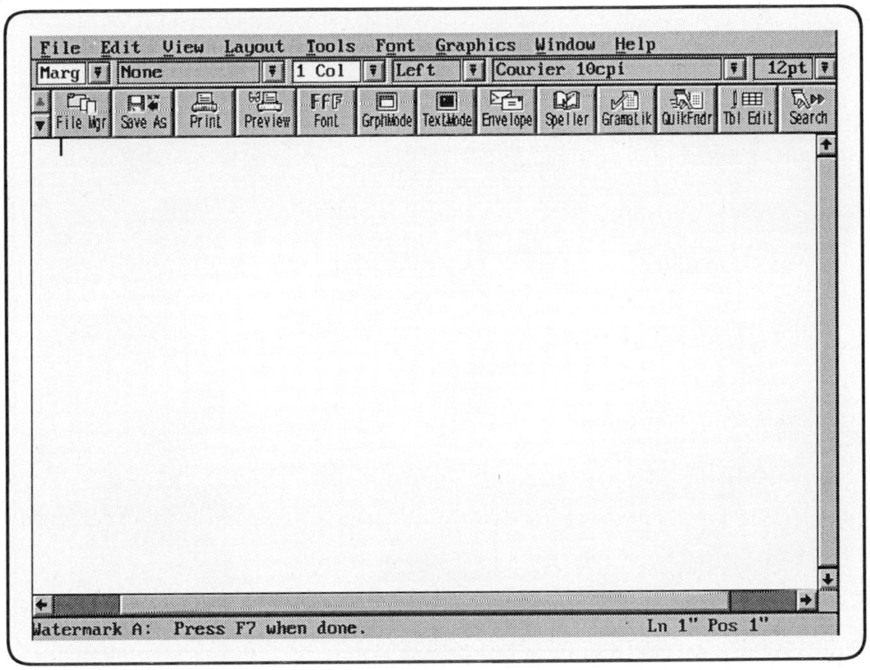

To retrieve one of the WordPerfect graphic images:

Press	Alt + F9	**Choose**	*Graphics*
Press	Shift + F10 to select the Retrieve Image command button	**Click**	*the Retrieve Image command button*
Press	F5 to select the File List command button	**Click**	*the File List command button*
Press	↵Enter	**Click**	*the OK command button*
Press	↓ until "PENPUSH.WPG" is highlighted	**Click**	*the down scroll arrow until "PENPUSH.WPG" is highlighted*
Press	↵Enter	**Choose**	*the Select option*
Press	F7 to exit from the Watermark editing screen	**Press**	*F7 to exit from the Watermark editing screen*

The watermark will not display on the screen in any of the viewing modes. When you preview the document in full page mode, it should look like Figure 22-14.

Figure 22-14

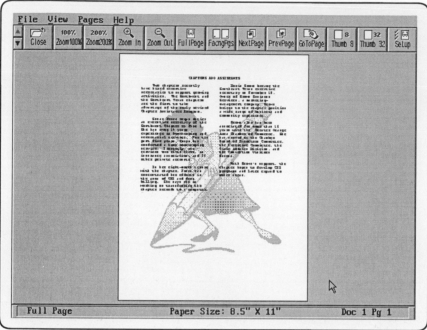

For more information about editing a watermark image, consult the WordPerfect Reference manual. Save the file using the name "WATRMARK.DOC". Close the file.

EXERCISE 1

INSTRUCTIONS: Define the following concepts:

1.   Graphics Line feature _____

    _____

2.   Horizontal Position option _____

    _____

3.   Vertical Position option _____

    _____

4.   Line Style option _____

    _____

5.   Thickness option _____

    _____

6. Color option _____

_____

7. Borders _____

_____

8. Border Styles _____

_____

9. Fill Styles _____

_____

10. Watermarks _____

_____

EXERCISE 2

INSTRUCTIONS: Circle T if the statement is true and F if the statement is false.

T   F   1.   The Graphics Lines feature allows you to create and edit horizontal and vertical lines.

T   F   2.   Lines cannot be shaded.

T   F   3.   If the Horizontal Position option is set to "Full," the length of the line is automatically set to extend from the left to the right margin.

T   F   4.   When creating lines, you can set the horizontal position, vertical position, line length, line thickness, and shading of the line.

T   F   5.   When creating vertical lines, the Vertical Position option allows you to position the line at either the top or bottom margins.

T   F   6.   When creating horizontal lines, the Horizontal Position option allows you to position the line on the baseline or at a set position.

T   F   7.   A border can only be placed around single paragraphs.

T   F   8.   The appearance of the border can be changed to include rounded corners.

T   F   9.   It is possible to add shading to the interior of a border.

T   F   10. You can create as many watermark images as you wish on a single page of text.

EXERCISE 3

INSTRUCTIONS: 1.   Create the following newspaper-style document. Use the "WINRACE.WPG" graphic.

2.   The horizontal lines at the top of the document should be full. The thickness is 0.25". Shading is 10%.

3.   The size of the graphic is 1.5" x 2.5". Change the borders to reflect the illustration. Center the graphic horizontally.

4.   Print the document.

5.   Save the document in a file using the name "CH22EX03".

6.   Close the document.

THE LATEST NEWS

We want everyone to help us reduce the amount of mail that is coming into the office. It is always an uphill battle trying to control it!

Please try to use the computer mail system. This system was designed to reduce the paper flow in the office. Since we have instituted this system, we have reduced internal paper usage by 50%. We can do better!

Our next goal is to try to reduce the mail. Not all incoming mail is for product orders. We are receiving too much "junk mail." If you have any customers that send us more information than we need, please ask them to send you only the essential information.

We would like to take this opportunity to welcome the new employees. In the Word Processing department, **Ginny Moritz** has been with us for three weeks. Ginny has seven years of experience in the field of word processing.

In the Executive Division, **Tom Sheerer** has just been employed to help with the traffic. Tom has been a Traffic Manager for the past 10 years with the Dibow Company.

The new face you see in the Payroll department belongs to **Jorge Escobar**. Jorge has just graduated from MidState University with a B.S. in Accounting.

We wish all these new employees "good luck" with their new positions. We know they've joined a winning team.

EXERCISE 4

INSTRUCTIONS:

1. Create the letterhead illustrated below. Use the "WINDMILL.WPG" graphic.
2. The width of the horizontal lines is 0.1".
3. The size of each graphic is 1" x 1".
4. Print the document.
5. Save the document in a file using the name "CH22EX04".
6. Close the document.

   THE INTERNATIONAL TRAVEL SOCIETY

EXERCISE 5

INSTRUCTIONS:

1. Create the following document. Use the "SKIPPER.WPG" graphic for the watermark.
2. The horizontal lines for the heading are full and 0.05" wide.
3. The height of the graphic is 0.5".
4. Print the document.
5. Save the document in a file using the name "CH22EX05".
6. Close the document.

THE DAILY NAVIGATOR

EXERCISE 6

INSTRUCTIONS:

1. Create the following document. Use the following graphics: "HOTAIR.WPG", and "LIGHTHS.WPG".

2. Use horizontal lines that are .25" thick and use 50% shading for the heading. Place vertical lines between the columns. The vertical lines should extend to the bottom of the page.

3. Print the document.

4. Save the document in a file using the name "CH22EX06".

5. Close the document.

THE COMPANY NEWSLETTER

We take this time to express congratulations to the staff members with newborn babies. Betty Sue was born on July 4 to Tom and Mary Brown. Tim Ryan was born on May 7 to Gene and Rose Gunther.

Do you have an idea that can be used by the company?

We are willing to pay for any sound ideas that will save us money. Cash awards will be based on the amount of money saved in one year.

Management is really serious about this idea. They will pay 1 percent of any saved amount.

The rumors that have been going around the office about new computers are really true.

Everyone in the company will be given a new computer for their desktops by the end of the year. We will be connected to each other by something called a LAN.

The new LAN will allow us to talk to one another on the computer as easily as on the phone. In fact, if you have a computer at home and a modem, you will be able to get your messages over the phone-modem at home. This will allow us to leave detailed messages to each other and receive answers back without coming into the office.

There is also another feature on this system that will allow us to check each other's calendars to set up meetings that will not conflict with each other.

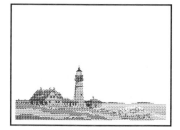

As you may have heard, the company will be merging with a company from West Germany. We will become a multinational organization in just a short time. This will have definite advantages for those who own stock in the company. It is expected that the stock will split at least 3 to 1 in our favor.

It will mean many positions will be available for transfer. There will be a procedure for you to follow if you would like an overseas assignment.

EXERCISE 7

INSTRUCTIONS:
1. Create the following document. Use the graphic "TIGERHD.WPG".
2. The size of the graphic is 1.75" x 2.5". Display the graphic in black and white. Position the graphic against the left margin.
3. The horizontal lines above and below the heading should be centered and 5" long.
4. Place a border around the last section entitled "**MOVING??**".
5. Print the document.
6. Save the document in a file using the name "CH22EX07".
7. Close the document.

THE WEEKLY CLARION

CONTRACT NEGOTIATIONS
Once again, we are troubled with the type of contract negotiated by our bargaining team with management.

Have you read the section on Overtime Pay? If we follow this contract, we will be receiving less for working overtime now than at any previous time.

Management has given us some good benefits, but in this case, they have stripped us of a very lucrative increase in our weekly paychecks.

Ask your local negotiator how this new clause of **not paying for overtime until after 40 hours are worked** came to be.

There are some really good items in this new contract. I would like to personally thank everyone for basically a fine contract. If the overtime section can be reworked, we could have the best contract ever.

MOVING??
If you plan to move out of the area in the next year, you should contact Jim O'Donnell for help. Jim moves all the executives and is very good. He offers great rates as well!

CHAPTER TWENTY-THREE

EQUATION EDITOR

OBJECTIVES

In this chapter, you will learn to:
- Create an equation
- Use the Commands Palette
- Save an equation
- Use an equation
- Print an equation
- Edit an equation

■ CHAPTER OVERVIEW

Some documents require complex equations. For example, you may need to include an equation for the average salary for a group of employees. This equation would look like Figure 23-1.

Figure 23-1

$$\mu = \frac{\sum\limits_{i=1}^{n} SAL}{N}$$

The Equation Editor feature allows you to create and edit mathematical and scientific equations. Once you create an equation, you can save the equation to be used in other documents as well. These topics are discussed and illustrated in this chapter.

■ CREATING AN EQUATION

The Equation Editor feature allows you to include mathematical and scientific equations in a document. This feature does not calculate the equation for you. Instead, it helps you create the complex characters that make up an equation so that you do not have to draw them manually.

Each equation is placed in a graphics box in your document. You create the equation that is placed in that box.

Suppose you need to create an equation that adds the variable A to the quantity of 6 minus the variable Y divided by another variable, Z. Your completed equation will look like Figure 23-2.

477

Figure 23-2

$$A + \frac{6-Y}{Z}$$

To create a graphics box for the equation:

Press	Alt + F9	*Choose*	*Graphics*
Press	1 or B to select the Graphics Boxes option	*Choose*	*Graphics Boxes*
Press	1 or C to select the Create option	*Choose*	*Create*
Press	Y to select the Based on Box Style option	*Choose*	*the Based on Box Style option*

The Graphics Box Styles dialog box appears on the screen. Your screen should look like Figure 23-3.

Figure 23-3

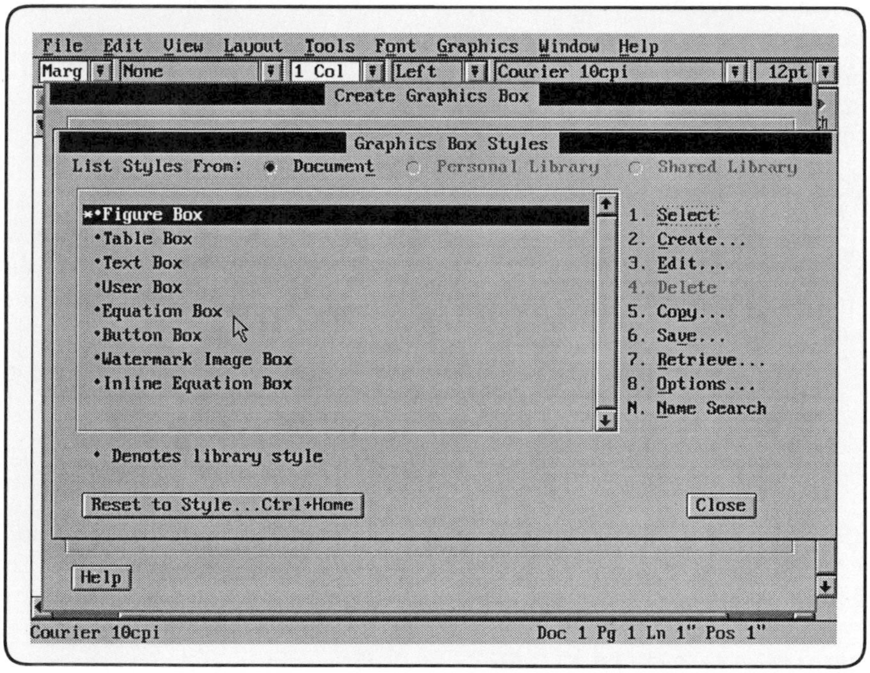

Press	↓ until the Equation Box option is highlighted	*Choose*	*the Equation Box option*
Press	1 or S to choose the Select option	*Choose*	*the Select option*
Press	3 or E to select the Create Equation option	*Choose*	*the Create Equation option*

The Equation Editor appears on the screen. Your screen should look like Figure 23-4.

Figure 23-4

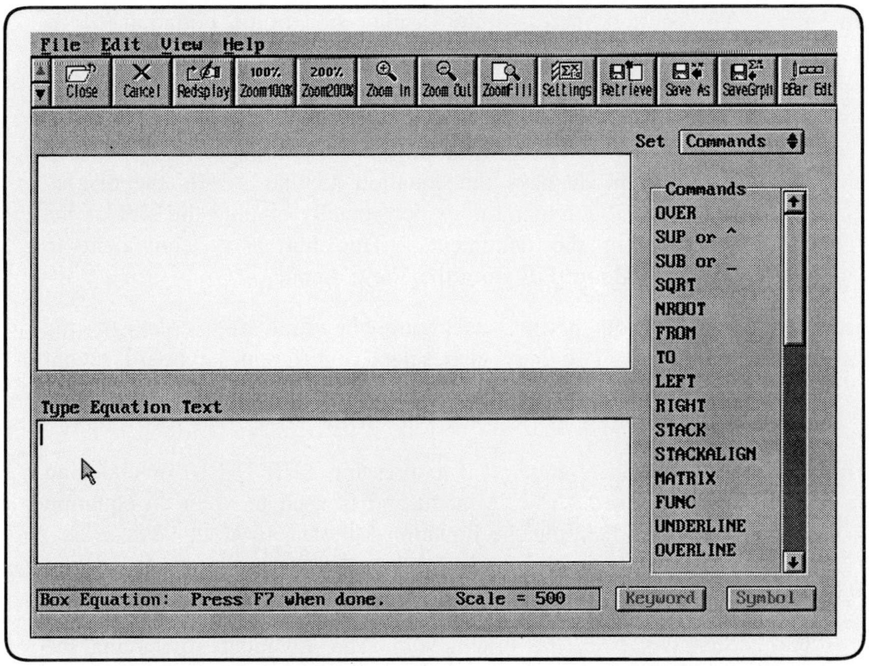

The Equation Editor is divided into three panes. The display pane at the top of the screen shows how the equation will look when printed. The editing pane at the bottom of the screen is where you create and edit an equation. The commands palette on the right side of the screen provides lists of commands and symbols that you use to build an equation.

The following list describes the commands available on the Equation Editor Button Bar, which appears above the top of the display pane and the command palette.

Button	Purpose
Close	This button is equivalent to pressing F7 or choosing Close from the File menu. It is used to exit the Equation Editor screen.
Cancel	This button is the same as pressing the ESC key or choosing Cancel from the File menu. It displays previously deleted data.
Redisplay	This button draws the commands and symbols entered in the editing pane in the display pane. This button is equivalent to pressing CTRL+F3, F9, or choosing Redisplay from the View menu.
Zoom 100%	This button allows you to view the size of the equation as it will appear in the printed document. It is equivalent to choosing 100% from the View menu.
Zoom 200%	This button allows you to see a view of the equation that is twice its normal size. It is equivalent to choosing 200% from the View menu. Zoom 200% does not change the actual size of the equation in the printed document.

Button	Purpose
Zoom In	This button increases the display size of an equation. It is equivalent to choosing Zoom In from the View menu.
Zoom Out	This button decreases the display size of an equation. It is equivalent to choosing Zoom Out from the View menu.
Zoom Fill	This button displays the equation so that it fills the display pane. This command does not actually change the size of the equation in the document. This button is equivalent to choosing Zoom Fill from the View menu.
Settings	This button permits changing the font and color of the equation. You may also select a different keyboard layout with this option. It is equivalent to pressing SHIFT+F1 or selecting Settings from the File menu.
Retrieve	This button is equivalent to pressing SHIFT+F10 or choosing Retrieve from the File menu and is used to open an equation stored on disk into the Equation Editor.
Save As	This button allows you to save the equation as text with its own filename. It is equivalent to pressing F10 or choosing Save As from the File menu. The advantage of saving the equation as a text file is that it can later be edited in the Equation Editor.
SaveGrph	This button allows you to save the equation as a graphics file with a .WPG extension. It is equivalent to choosing Save As Image from the File menu. If the equation is saved as an image, you will not be able to edit it in the Equation Editor. You would need to use the Image Editor. For more information about this topic, consult the WordPerfect Reference manual.
BBar Edt	This button allows you to change the buttons appearing on the Equation Editor Button Bar.
BBar Opt	This button allows you to change the display of the Button Bar on the screen.

In most cases, you can type an equation just as you would say it. Let's say that you need to create an equation that adds the variable A to the quantity 6 minus the variable Y divided by another variable, Z.

To create the equation:

Type   A+6-Y over Z | *Type*   *A+6-Y over Z*

The bottom part of your screen should look like Figure 23-5.

Figure 23-5

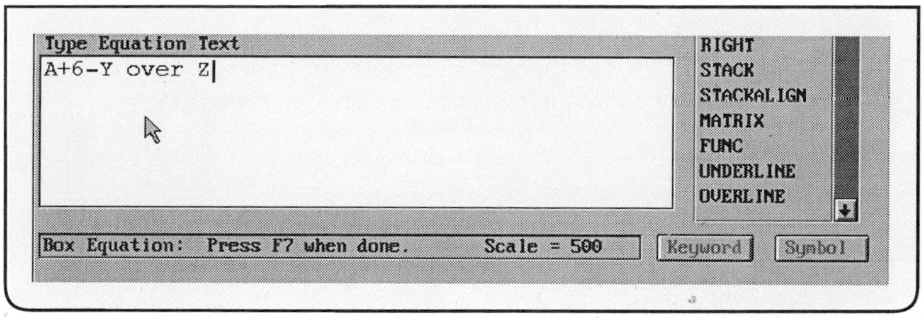

The text you typed is displayed in the editing pane. To see the equation in the display pane:

Press   Ctrl + F3

or

F9

Click   the Redisplay button on the Button Bar

The top part of your screen should look like Figure 23-6.

Figure 23-6

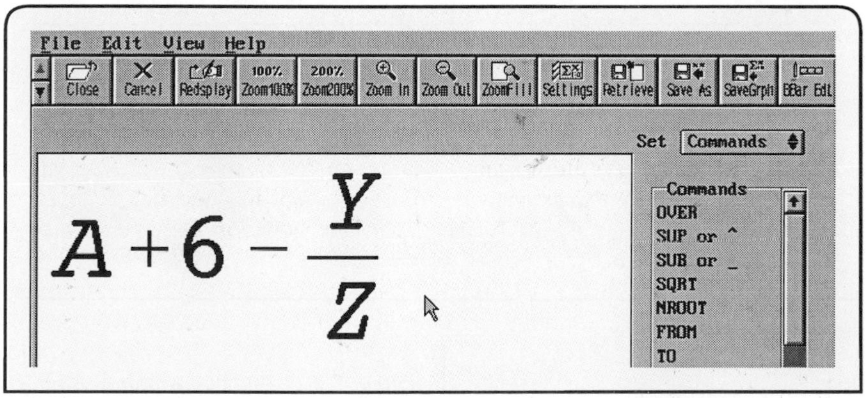

The equation appears in the display pane, but this is not the correct formula. The "OVER" command makes a fraction. It places the character to the left of the command over the character to the right. Only the "Y" is over the "Z". You want the entire "6 - Y" over the "Z".

To have WordPerfect recognize (6 - Y) as a single character to the left of the "OVER" command, you must place braces { } around the characters.

To edit the equation:

Move	the cursor before the "6" in the equation in the editing pane		**Click**	before the "6" in the equation in the editing pane
Type	{		**Type**	{
Move	the cursor after the letter "Y" in the editing pane		**Click**	after the letter "Y" in the editing pane
Type	}		**Type**	}

The bottom part of your screen should look like Figure 23-7.

Figure 23-7

```
Type Equation Text                              RIGHT
A+{6-Y}| over Z                                 STACK
                                                STACKALIGN
                                                MATRIX
                                                FUNC
                                                UNDERLINE
                                                OVERLINE
Box Equation:  Press F7 when done.    Scale = 602   Keyword   Symbol
```

To display the edited equation:

Press   [Ctrl]+[F3]

or

[F9]

Click   the Redisplay button on the Button Bar

The top part of your screen should look like Figure 23-8.

Figure 23-8

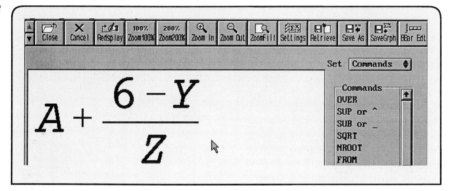

To return to the normal editing screen:

Press   [F7]

Click   the Close button on the Button Bar

Press   [←Enter]

Click   the OK command button

The top part of your screen should look like Figure 23-9.

Figure 23-9

```
File  Edit  View  Layout  Tools  Font  Graphics  Window  Help
Marg ▼ None        ▼ 1 Col ▼ Left ▼ Courier 10cpi          ▼  12pt ▼
File Mgr Save As Print Preview Font GrphMode TextMode Envelope Speller GramatIk QuikFndr Tbl Edit Search

                        A + 6−Y
                            Z
```

The equation appears in your document. The equation is much smaller in the document than in the Equation Editor. By default, equation boxes are centered horizontally in the document and no borders are displayed. You can change the box position and the box options of an equation box in the same way that you change the box position and options of other graphics boxes. This topic was discussed in Chapter 20.

Save the document as "EQUATE1". Close the document.

■ USING THE COMMANDS PALETTE

At times, you might need to create an equation that requires the use of scientific and mathematical symbols. WordPerfect provides a Commands Palette that contains such symbols.

Suppose you want to create the equation for computing the average age for all of the people in a class. This equation looks like Figure 23-10.

Figure 23-10

$$\mu = \frac{\Sigma x_i}{N}$$

In This Chapter

Equations are given to you for the purpose of examples and exercises. Although the format is provided, an explanation of each character will not accompany the formula. For more detailed information about the equation symbols, see "Appendix C, Equation Commands" in the WordPerfect Reference manual.

To create the equation:

Press	Alt + F9	*Choose*	*Graphics*
Press	1 or B to select the Graphics Boxes option	*Choose*	*Graphics Boxes*
Press	1 or C to select the Create option	*Choose*	*Create*
Press	Y to select the Based on Box Style option	*Choose*	*the Based on Box Style option*
Press	↓ four times until Equation Box is highlighted	*Double-click*	*on the Equation Box option*
Press	1 or S to choose the Select option	*Choose*	*the Create Equation option*
Press	3 or E to select the Create Equation option		

The Equation Editor appears on the screen.

To move the cursor to the current Commands palette:

Press	F5	*Click*	*on the first command in the palette list*

The top part of your screen should look like Figure 23-11.

Figure 23-11

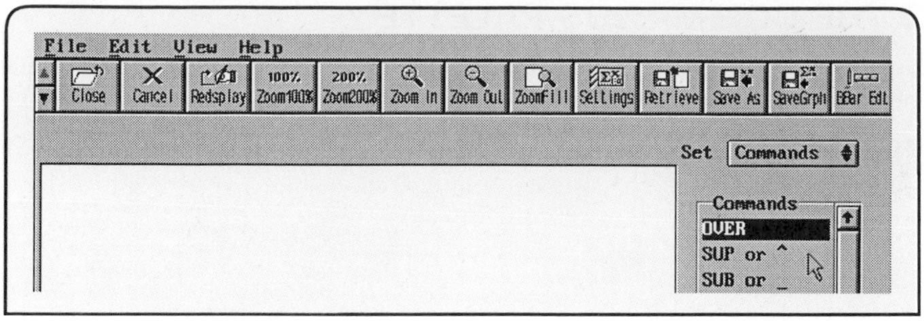

The name of the current palette appears in the Set box. The current palette is "Commands". You can view other commands in this palette by pressing the UP ARROW or DOWN ARROW keys or by using the scroll bar.

A definition of each command or symbol appears in the left corner of the status bar. For example, if the current palette selection is "OVER", the message "Fraction: x OVER y" appears in the left corner of the status bar.

There are eight command palettes. You can view them by pressing F5 again or by clicking and holding down on the palette pop-up list.

The following is a description of each of the palettes:

Palette	Purpose
Commands	This set displays a set of commands that are represented by words. All commands in this palette format the text of the equation.
Large	This set displays large and small mathematical, scientific, bracket, and brace symbols.
Symbols	This set displays many commonly used symbols.
Greek	This set displays upper- and lowercase Greek symbols and their variants.
Arrows	This set displays many geometric shapes as well as a variety of arrow designs.
Sets	This command palette shows set symbols, relational operators and other characters. Where symbols indicate a keyword on the status line, that word can be typed in the editing window.
Other	This set shows various accent marks and different positions of ellipses.
Functions	This set displays various mathematical functions, such as log, exp, sin, and cos.

Before creating the equation, change to the Greek palette:

Press   F5   *Hold down*   the mouse button to view the Set pop-up list

Press   ↓ three times to select the "Greek" palette   *Choose*   the Greek palette

Press   ←Enter

The Greek symbols are displayed in the palette on the right side of your screen. The top part of your screen should look like Figure 23-12.

Figure 23-12

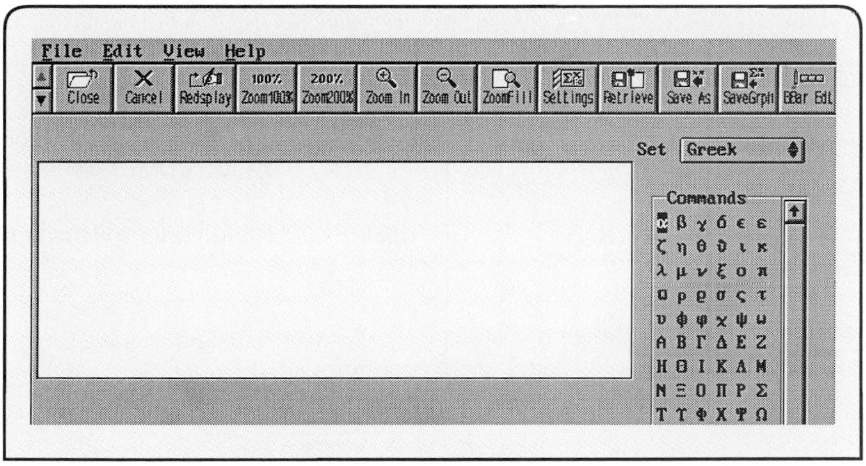

The names of the symbols are shown on the status bar. To select the "mu" symbol:

Press	⬇ twice	***Click***	*on the μ (mu) symbol*
Press	➡ once	***Click***	*the Keyword command button*
Press	⏎Enter to select the Keyword command button		

The bottom part of your screen should look like Figure 23-13.

Figure 23-13

The Keyword command button places the name of the symbol in the editing pane. The Symbol command button places the actual symbol in the editing pane.

To continue the formula:

Type	=	***Type***	*=*
Type	{	***Type***	*{*

To select the "SMALLSUM" symbol from the Large palette:

Press	F5 twice		*Hold down*	*the mouse button to view the Set pop-up list*
Press	↑ twice to select the Large palette		*Choose*	*the Large palette*
Press	↵Enter		*Click*	*on the Small Sum symbol (the first symbol in the second column)*
Press	→ to select the Small Sum symbol		*Click*	*the Keyword command button*
Press	↵Enter to select the Keyword command button			

The bottom part of your screen should look like Figure 23-14.

Figure 23-14

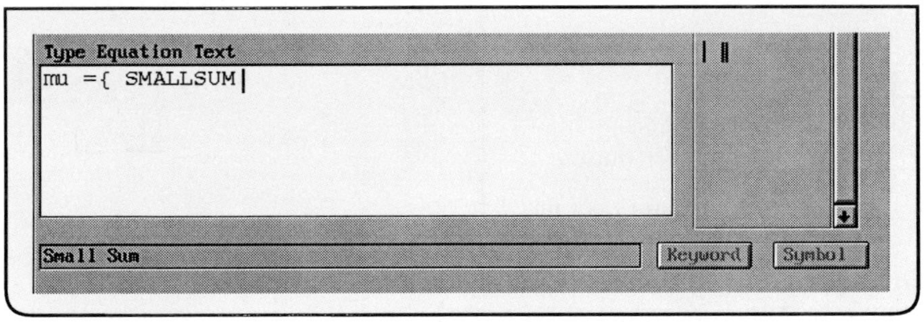

Type   X | *Type*   *X*

The X in the equation includes a subscript "i" which can be created using the "SUB" command.
To select the SUB command:

Press	F5 twice		*Hold down*	*the mouse button to view the Set pop-up list*
Press	↑ to select the Commands palette		*Choose*	*the Commands palette*
Press	↵Enter		*Click*	*on the SUB or _ command*
Press	↓ twice to select the SUB or _ command		*Click*	*the Keyword command button*
Press	↵Enter to select the Keyword command button		*Type*	*i*

Type	i		Type	}
Type	}		Type	over N
Type	over N			

The bottom part of your screen should look like Figure 23-15.

Figure 23-15

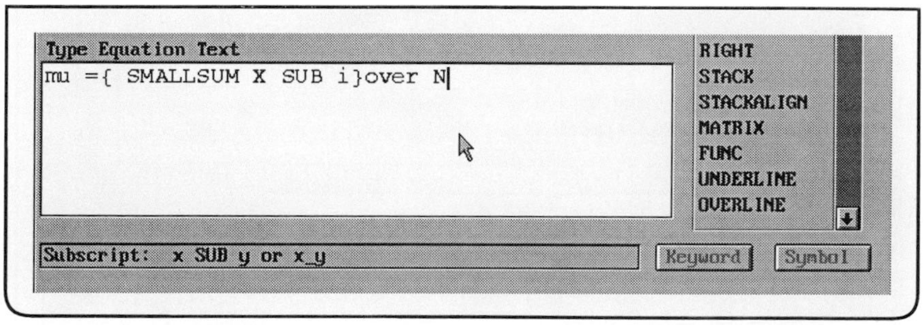

To display the equation:

Press Ctrl + F3 or F9

Click *the Redisplay button on the Button Bar*

The top part of your screen should look like Figure 23-16.

Figure 23-16

■ SAVING AN EQUATION

After you create an equation, you may want to save the equation so that you can use it in other documents. Saving an equation is not the same as saving the entire document. To save an equation, you must remain in the Equation Editor screen. To save a document, you must be in the normal editing screen.

To save the equation that you have created to a separate file:

Press F10

Click *the Save As button on the Button Bar*

The Save Equation dialog box appears. Your screen should look like Figure 23-17.

Figure 23-17

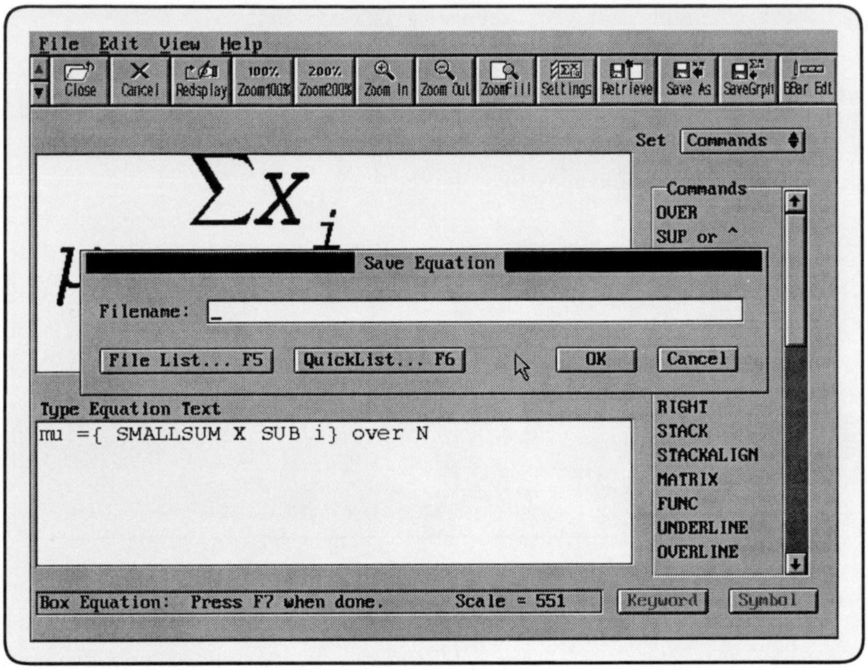

WordPerfect does not automatically add an extension to the equation filename when you save the file. However, when retrieving an equation file, it may be helpful to use the same extension consistently. A suggested extension is "EQN".

Type	**AVG.EQN**		*Type*	*AVG.EQN*
Press	⏎Enter to select the OK command button		*Click*	*the OK command button*

The equation is saved in the default directory.

To exit from the Equation Editor screen and return to the normal editing screen:

Press	F7		*Click*	*the Close button on the Button Bar* 
Press	⏎Enter		*Click*	*the OK command button*

Close the document without saving changes.

■ USING AN EQUATION IN A DOCUMENT

This section shows how an equation fits into a document containing text. Create the document shown in Figure 23-18. In the last paragraph, make sure the i in X_i is a subscript.

Figure 23-18

```
Suppose you need to know the average age of the students in a
WordPerfect class.  The average age can be computed by summing the
ages of all the people in the class and dividing by the number of
students.

The formula for computing the average for a group of items is:




where u is the symbol for the arithmetic mean, Xᵢ represents the value
for each of the items for which you are computing the mean, and N is
the number of items.
```

Suppose you want to insert the equation saved in the file "AVG.EQN" in the middle of your document. To move to the location where you want to insert the equation and then enter the Equation Editor:

Move	the cursor to the second line after the line beginning "The formula"	*Click*	*at the second line after the line beginning "The formula"*
Press	[Alt]+[F9]	*Choose*	*Graphics*
Press	1 or B to select the Graphics Boxes option	*Choose*	*Graphics Boxes*
Press	1 or C to select the Create option	*Choose*	*Create*
Press	Y to select the Based on Box Style option	*Choose*	*the Based on Box Style option*
Press	[↓] until the Equation Box option is highlighted	*Double-click*	*on the Equation Box option*
Press	1 or S to choose the Select option	*Choose*	*the Create Equation option*
Press	3 or E to select the Create Equation option		

To retrieve the equation saved in the file "AVG.EQN":

Press	[Shift]+[F10]	*Click*	*the Retrieve button on the Button Bar* 

Type	the path and filename for the equation	*Type*	*the path and filename for the equation*
Press	[←Enter]	*Click*	*the OK command button*

You could edit the equation and save it again before returning to the normal editing screen.

To return to the normal editing screen:

Press	[F7]	*Click*	*the Close button on the Button Bar* 
			[Close icon]
Press	[←Enter]	*Click*	*the OK command button*

The top part of your screen should look like Figure 23-19.

Figure 23-19

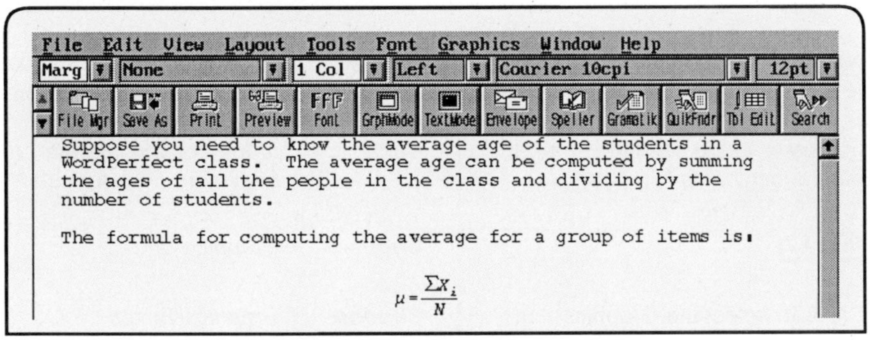

You can replace the "u" in the first line of the last section with the Greek "mu" symbol. You could create an equation consisting of only one character, the mu symbol. However, WordPerfect also has special character sets that contain many mathematical and scientific symbols. Using the WordPerfect Characters feature is much simpler and faster for one symbol.

To delete the "u" from the document and enter the WP Characters feature:

Move	the cursor before the "u" in the first line of text after the equation	*Click*	*before the "u" in the first line of text after the equation*
Press	[Delete]	*Press*	*[Delete]*
Press	[Ctrl]+[W]	*Choose*	*Font*
		Choose	*WP Characters*

The WordPerfect Characters dialog box appears on the screen. Your screen should look like Figure 23-20.

Figure 23-20

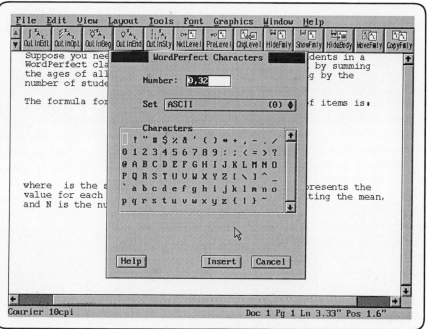

To access the Greek character set:

Press	⬇ to select the Set pop-up list option	***Hold down***	*the mouse button to view the Set pop-up list*
Press	↵Enter to view the pop-up list	***Choose***	*Greek*
Press	G to select Greek		

To select the "mu" symbol:

Press	3 or C to select the Characters list box	***Click***	*on the μ symbol in the Characters list box*
Press	⬇ once		
Press	→ nine times		

Your screen should look like Figure 23-21.

Figure 23-21

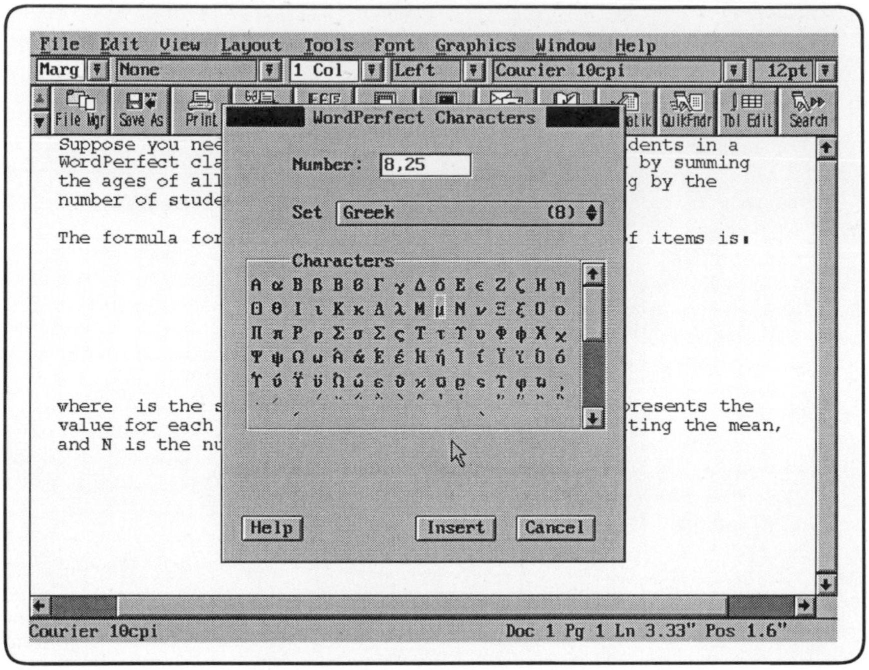
File Edit View Layout Tools Font Graphics Window Help
WordPerfect Characters
Number: 8,25
Set Greek (8)
Characters
Help
Insert
Cancel
Courier 10cpi
Doc 1 Pg 1 Ln 3.33" Pos 1.6"

Notice the text "8,25" appears in the Number text box. The μ symbol is number 25 in the eighth character set.

To insert the symbol and close the dialog box:

Press	Enter	***Click***	*the Insert command button*

The bottom part of your screen should look like Figure 23-22.

Figure 23-22

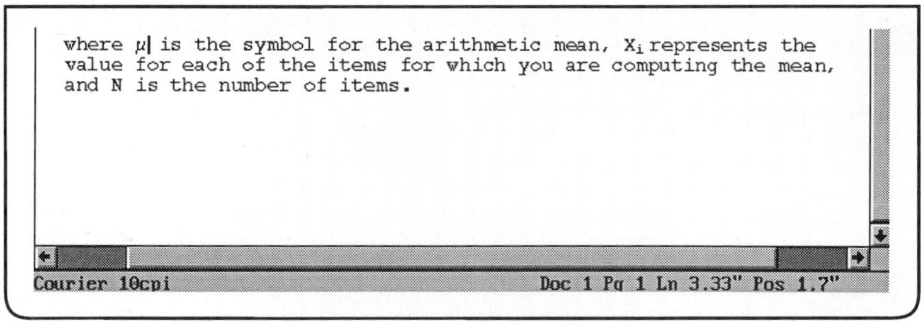
where μ is the symbol for the arithmetic mean, Xi represents the
value for each of the items for which you are computing the mean,
and N is the number of items.
Courier 10cpi
Doc 1 Pg 1 Ln 3.33" Pos 1.7"

Notice that the μ symbol appears in the document. Save the document as "EQUATE2".

■ PRINTING AN EQUATION

When you send an equation to your printer, WordPerfect uses the printer settings to reproduce the equation you see on the screen.

If your printer can print graphics, you should have no problem printing equations. If your printer cannot print graphics, characters that cannot be printed will be replaced with a space.

Print the document.

■ EDITING AN EQUATION

Each equation in a document is numbered by WordPerfect. When editing an equation, you are asked to enter the equation number.

To edit equation 1:

Move	the cursor onto the Equation Box code in Reveal Codes		***Double-click***	*on the equation for computing averages*
Press	Alt + F9			
Press	1 or B to select the Graphics Boxes option			
Press	2 or E to select the Edit option			

If you used the keyboard method, the Select Box To Edit dialog box appears on the screen and your screen should look like Figure 23-23. If you used the mouse method, the Edit Graphics Box dialog box appears on your screen.

Figure 23-23

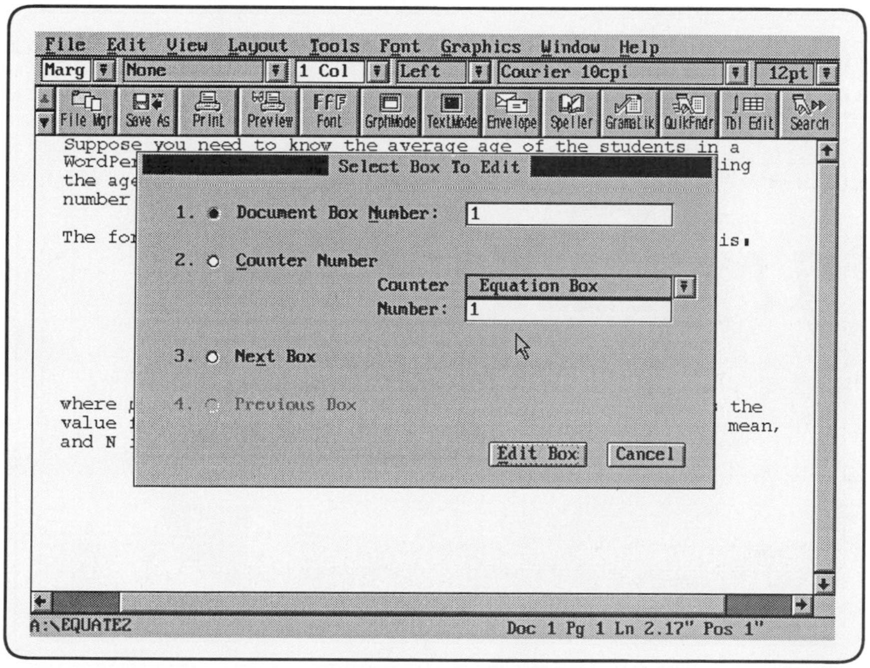

Notice that the second option is called Counter Number. It indicates that Equation Box Number 1 will be edited if no other selection is made.

To accept the default and enter the Equation Editor screen:

Press	↵Enter to select the Edit Box command button		***Choose***	*the Edit Equation option*

Press   3 or E to select the Edit Equation option

To change "over" to a "/" in the equation:

Move   the cursor before the text "over"   *Click*   *before the text "over"*

Press   Delete four times   *Press*   Delete *four times*

Type   /   *Type*   /

To display the equation:

Press   Ctrl + F3 or F9   *Click*   *the Redisplay button on the Button Bar*

Your screen should look like Figure 23-24.

Figure 23-24

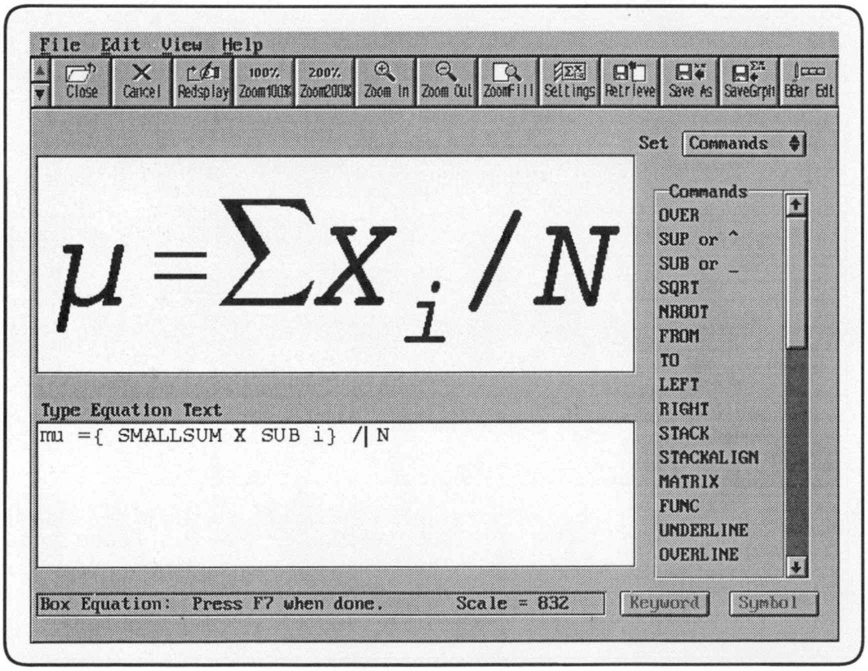

You cannot use the spacebar to add a space between characters in the display of your equation. To create a space between characters in your equation, you insert a tilde (~).

To add a space before and after the equal sign in this equation:

Move   the cursor before the = sign   *Click*   *before the = sign*

Type   ~   *Type*   ~

Move	the cursor after the = sign		*Click*	*after the = sign*
Type	~		*Type*	*~*

To view the changes in the equation:

Press	Ctrl + F3 or F9		*Click*	*the Redisplay button on the Button Bar* 

Your screen should look like Figure 23-25.

Figure 23-25

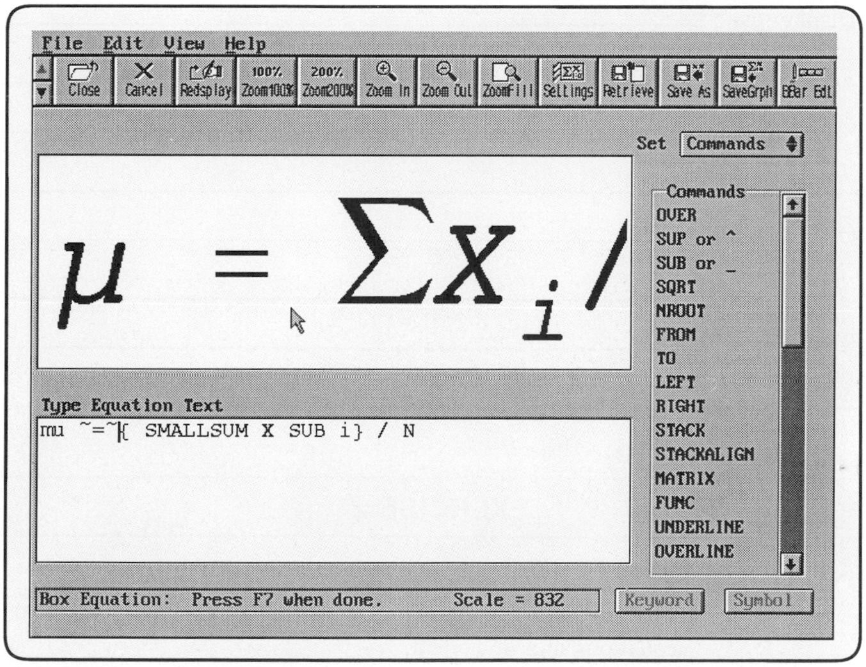

To return to the normal editing screen:

Press	F7		*Click*	*the Close button on the Button Bar* 
Press	↵Enter		*Click*	*the OK command button*

Save the document as "EQUATE3". Close the document.

EXERCISE 1

INSTRUCTIONS: Define the following concepts:

1. Equation feature _____

   _____

2. Equation Editor _____

   _____

3. Editing pane _____

   _____

4. Display pane _____

   _____

5. Commands palette _____

   _____

6. OVER command _____

   _____

7. Redisplay button _____

   _____

EXERCISE 2

INSTRUCTIONS: Circle T if the statement is true and F if the statement is false.

T   F   1.   The Equation feature allows you to include mathematical or scientific equations in a document.

T   F   2.   The Equation Editor can create and calculate equations for you.

T   F   3.   The Equation Editor is divided into four parts: the editing pane, the display pane, the Commands palette, and the calculation window.

T   F   4.   The Commands palette shows how the equation will look when printed.

T   F   5.   The display pane provides lists of commands and symbols that you use for building an equation.

T   F   6.   The "OVER" command creates the horizontal line for a fraction.

T   F   7.   To recognize (5 x T x W) as a single character to the left of the OVER command, place brackets [ ] around the characters.

T   F   8.   Saving an equation saves the document, too.

T   F   9.   You must use a tilde (~) to create a space in an equation.

T   F   10.   It is not possible to alter the font appearance of an equation.

EXERCISE 3

INSTRUCTIONS:

1. Create the following formula that computes the interest owed on a loan for a specific time period.

$$I = P \times \frac{R}{12}$$

2. Save the formula in a file using the name "INTEREST.EQN".
3. Print the formula.
4. Close the document.
5. Create the following document and insert the formula as indicated.
6. Save the document in a file using the name "CH23EX03".
7. Print the document.
8. Close the document.

```
Sometimes it is necessary to compute the amount of interest due for a
loan during a specific month.  The following formula can be used to
calculate the interest due for a particular month.
```

$$I = P \times \frac{R}{12}$$

```
The letter I is the variable for Interest.  P is the variable for the
Principal or loan amount owed.  R is the annual interest rate, for
example, 10%.  The annual interest rate is divided by 12, because you
need to calculate the monthly interest amount rather than the annual
interest amount.
```

EXERCISE 4

INSTRUCTIONS:

1. Create the following document.
2. Use the "SMALLSUM" symbol from the Large palette for the voltage formula. Save the formula in a file using the name "VOLTAGE.EQN".
3. Use the name "CIRCLE.EQN" for the second equation.
4. Print the document.
5. Save the document in a file using the name "CH23EX04".
6. Close the document.

Loop Equations:

Kirchoff's Voltage Law

$$\Sigma Erises = \Sigma Vdrops$$

Area of a Circle

$$A = \pi r^2$$

EXERCISE 5

INSTRUCTIONS:
1. Create the following financial formulas.
2. Save the Present Value of an Annuity formula as "PV.EQN". Save the Future Value of an Annuity formula as "FV.EQN".
3. Print the document.
4. Save the document in a file using the name "CH23EX05".

The Present Value of an Annuity formula allows you to determine the present value of an investment based on a number of equal payments (p), discounted at a specific interest rate (i), over a certain period of time (n).

$$p \times \frac{1-(1+i)^{-n}}{i}$$

The Future Value of an Annuity formula allows you to determine the future value of an investment based on a number of equal payments (p), earning a periodic interest rate (i), over a certain period of time (n).

$$p \ x \ \frac{(1+i)^n-1}{i}$$

EXERCISE 6

INSTRUCTIONS:

1. Create the following statistical equations. Use the "SQRT" command to create the square root symbol. Use the "sigma" command in the Greek palette for the character σ. Use the "mu" command in the Greek palette for the character μ.
2. Save the first equation as "STDDEV.EQN". Save the second formula as "VARIANCE.EQN".
3. Print the document.
4. Save the document in a file using the name "CH23EX06".
5. Close the document.

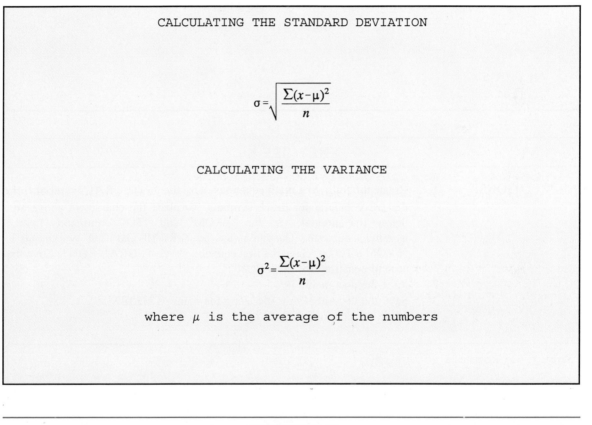

CALCULATING THE STANDARD DEVIATION

$$\sigma = \sqrt{\frac{\Sigma(x-\mu)^2}{n}}$$

CALCULATING THE VARIANCE

$$\sigma^2 = \frac{\Sigma(x-\mu)^2}{n}$$

where μ is the average of the numbers

EXERCISE 7

INSTRUCTIONS:

1. Create the following math equations. Use the "SQRT" command in the Commands palette to create the square root symbol. Use the vertical line in the Large palette to create the vertical line in the second equation. Use the "sigma" and "mu" characters from the Greek palette for the characters σ and μ respectively. Save the first equation as "DENSITY.EQN". Save the second equation as "INEQUAL.EQN".
2. Print the document.
3. Save the document in a file using the name "CH23EX07".
4. Close the document.

Standard Density Function

$$\frac{1}{\sqrt{2\pi}} e^{-\frac{1}{2}U^2}$$

Tchebycheff's Inequality Formula

$$P \ (\ |x-\mu| \ \geq \ k\sigma) \ \leq \ \frac{1}{k^2}$$

EXERCISE 8

INSTRUCTIONS:

1. Create the following math equations. Use the "INTEGRAL" symbol from the Large palette for the $\int$ symbol. To place the characters above and below the integral, use the "FROM" and "TO" commands in the Commands palette. The syntax for the "FROM" and "TO" commands is "FROM a TO b". Save the first equation as "INTEGRAL.EQN". Save the second equation as "LOG.EQN".

2. Print the document.

3. Save the document in a file using the name "CH23EX08".

4. Close the document.

Integral Formula

$$\int_a^b f(x)d(x)$$

Logarithmic Rule

$$\int \frac{1}{x} \ dx \ = \ 1nx+c \ (x>0)$$

CHAPTER TWENTY-FOUR

DOCUMENT STYLE SHEETS AND TYPESETTING FEATURES

OBJECTIVES

In this chapter, you will learn to:
- Create and use a style
- Edit a style
- Save styles
- Retrieve a style
- Delete a style
- Use typesetting features

■ CHAPTER OVERVIEW

There may be times when you want to use the same format within a document. At other times, you may require the use of the same format for several different documents. To repeat a format, you can use the Styles feature. In this chapter, the procedures for creating, editing, saving, retrieving, and deleting a style sheet or format are described and illustrated.

You may also need to adjust special features in your document such as letterspacing and word spacing, line height, and kerning. These typesetting features are also discussed and illustrated.

■ CREATING AND USING A STYLE

A **style** allows you to repeat formats easily. A style can have text and any number of format codes associated with it. A style is placed into the document as a code. You can use several styles within one document.

Create the document in Figure 24-1.

Figure 24-1

```
Beginning:  Word Processing Basics.  Create, modify, save, and print
documents.  Topics include pull-down menus, file retrieval,
scrolling, deleting, search and replace, text enhancements, reveal
codes, line spacing, tabs, margin settings, pagination, headers and
footers, and page format options.  The block, switch and move
functions are also covered.  No prior knowledge of word processing is
required.

Dates:       April 18     May 16       June 18

Intermediate:  Form Letters, Merge, and Macros.  This course covers
macros, math calculations, text columns, the table feature, the
document merge feature, sorting, creating, and editing a graphic
image, forms fill-in, creating mailing labels using the merge
feature, and file conversion.  A preview of style sheets and
generating an index is also presented.

Dates:       April 19     May 17       June 19

Advanced:  Graphics, Style Sheets, and Indexing.  This course is
currently in the planning stage.  ABC Can Company plans to offer this
class in July.
```

Save the document using the name "SCHEDULE".

Suppose you want to create styles that will do the following:

1.   Boldface the words "Beginning:", "Intermediate:", and "Advanced:".

2.   Italicize and underline the names of the courses, like "Word Processing Basics".

3.   Italicize the lines containing the dates.

To access the Styles feature:

Press   Alt + F8 | *Choose*   *Layout*
                                            | *Choose*   *Styles*

The Style List dialog box appears. Your screen should look like Figure 24-2.

Figure 24-2

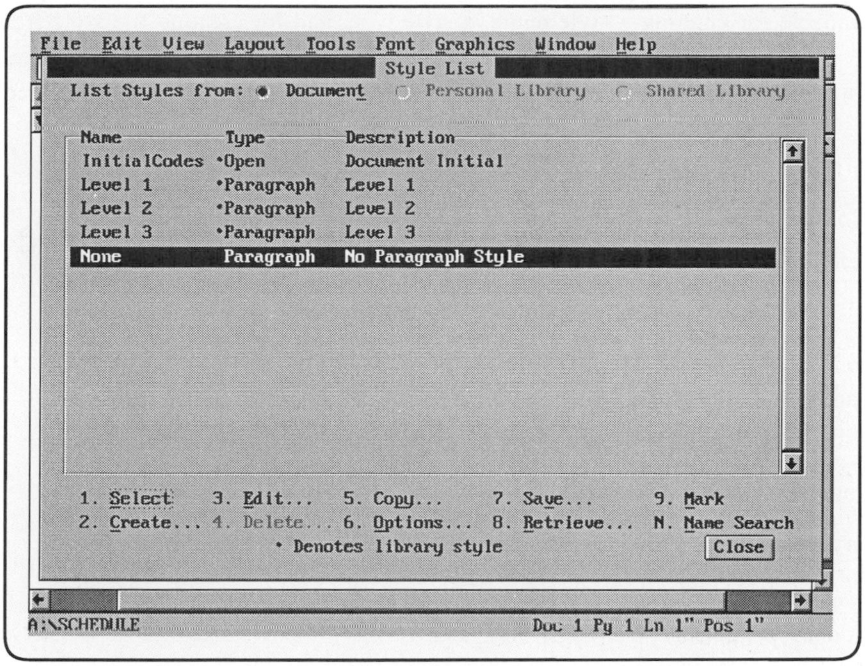

Notice that five styles automatically appear in the Style List dialog box. These styles are the default styles available in WordPerfect. The default styles are saved in a file called "LIBRARY.STY" in the "C:\WP60" directory. The default styles will automatically appear when you press ALT+F8 or choose Styles from the Layout menu. You can change the default style sheet and the default styles directory if you press SHIFT+F1 and select Location of Files or choose Location of Files from the Setup option under the File menu.

To create a style:

Press   2 or C to select the Create option   *Choose*   *the Create option*

The Create Style dialog box appears. Your screen should look like Figure 24-3.

Figure 24-3

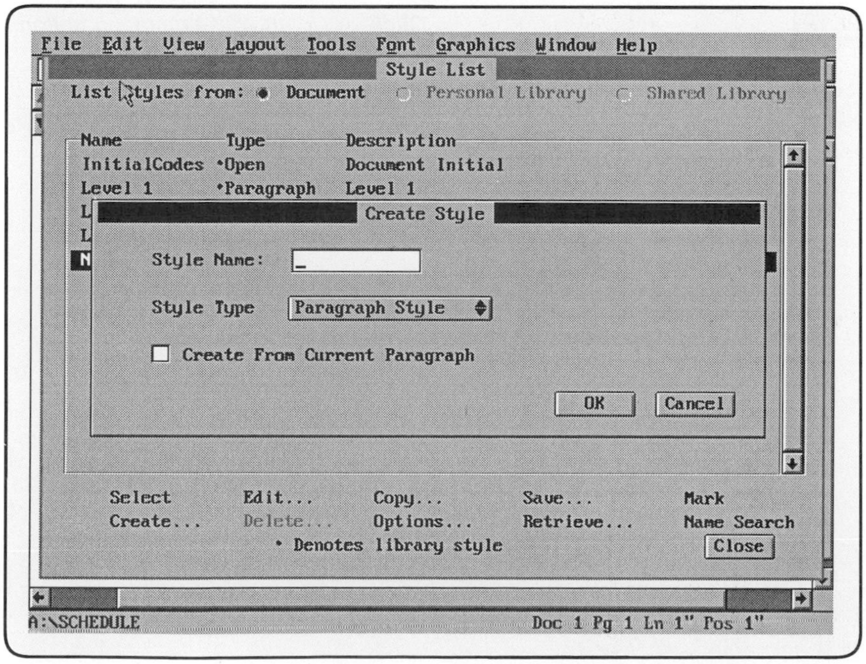

Options are available for entering a style name, a style type, and for creating the style from the current paragraph.

You can give a style a name by typing the name in the Style Name text box. Twelve characters will fit in the Style Name text box. The name can contain spaces.

To name the style:

Type	Course Level		*Type*	*Course Level*
Press	[↵Enter]		*Press*	[↵Enter]

There are three types of styles:

Paragraph - This style type uses On and Off codes to turn on the features defined with the style, and then turns off the style at a later point in the text. This style affects paragraphs or blocked text. Use this style type for headings and whole paragraphs.

Character - This style type uses On and Off codes to turn on the features defined with the style, and then turns off the style at a later point in the text. This style type affects blocked text or text you are about to type. Use this style type for phrases or blocked text.

Open - An Open style type turns on the features associated with the style once. These features are used to the end of the document.

The default setting for the style type is Paragraph. To change the type of style to Character:

Press	2 or T to select the Style Type pop-up list button		*Hold down*	*the Style Type pop-up list button*
Press	C to select the Character Style option		*Choose*	*the Character Style option*

To accept the style settings and insert the formatting codes:

Press	[↵Enter]		*Click*	*the OK command button*

The Edit Style dialog box appears. Your screen should look like Figure 24-4.

Figure 24-4

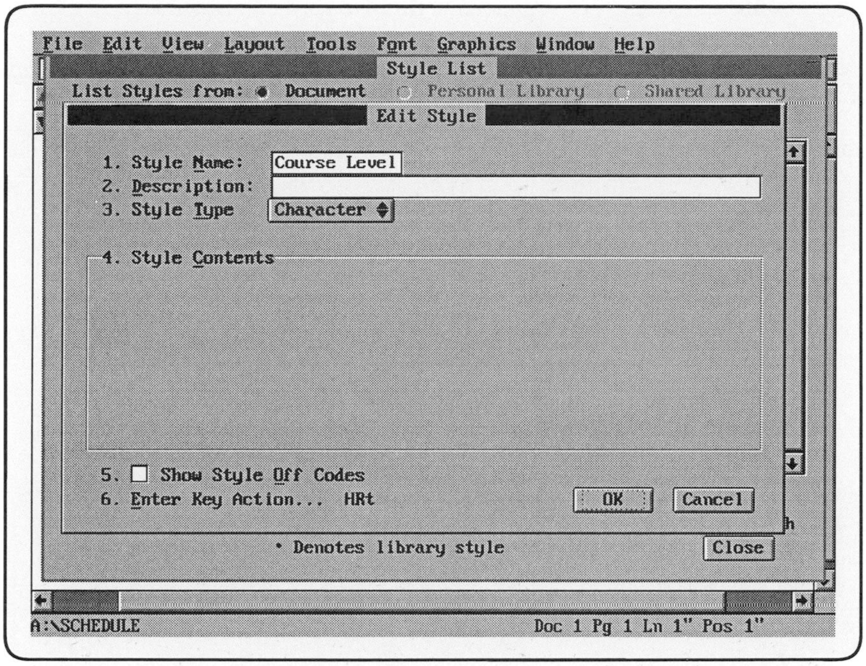

The Edit Style dialog box allows you to enter a description for the style, change the style type, associate feature codes and text with a style, and determine how the ENTER key operates in the style.

The Description text box is used to enter text that describes the style that you are creating. A description of the style is helpful, because a name cannot tell all the features that a particular style can perform. Approximately 48 characters will fit in the Description text box.

Recall that style types affect how these codes operate in the document. The codes in the Open style type are on until the end of the document. The codes in the Paragraph and Character style types are on in a document until the Style Off code is reached. The codes and text are placed in a style in the same way that they are placed in a document.

The Show Style Off Codes check box allows you to turn certain codes on when the style is turned off. This option places a Comment code in the Style Contents. Whatever formatting codes are above the comment take place when the style is turned on. Those below the Comment code take effect when the style is turned off. Otherwise, when a style is turned off, any document setting that was changed when the style was turned on is returned to its original value.

The Enter Key Action option allows you to change how the ENTER key works when you are using that particular style.

Insert a Hard Return - A hard return code is placed in your document when you press the ENTER key while using the style, and the style remains on. This option is only available when you are using the Character type style.

Turn Style Off - A Style Off code is placed in your document when you press the ENTER key while using this style.

Turn Style Off and Back On - A Style Off code is placed in your document when you press the ENTER key. The style then turns on again.

Turn Style Off and Link to: - A Style Off code is placed in your document, and then another style that you specify is turned on.

To enter the description:

Press	2 or D to select the Description text box		*Click*	*in the Description text box*
Type	Bold Course Levels		*Type*	*Bold Course Levels*
Press	[←Enter]		*Press*	[←Enter]

To activate the Style Contents section:

Press	4 or C to select the Style Contents option box		*Choose*	*the Style Contents option box*

The Style Contents section becomes active, and your screen should look like Figure 24-5.

Figure 24-5

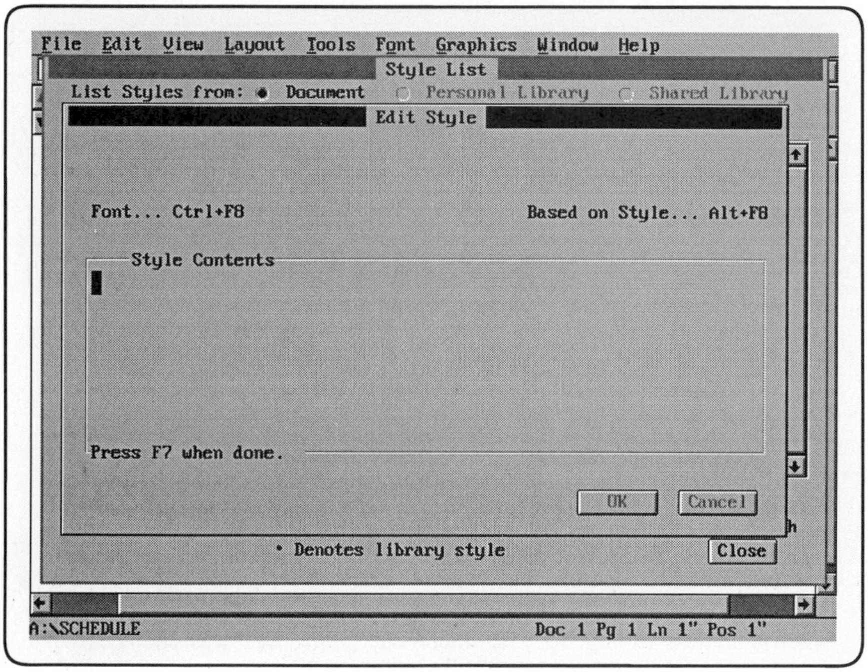

To place a Bold On code [Bold On] in the Style Contents:

Press	[F6]		*Choose*	*Font*
			Choose	*Bold*

Your screen should look like Figure 24-6.

Figure 24-6

To close the Edit Style dialog box:

Press	F7	**Choose**	File
Press	↵Enter	**Choose**	Exit
		Click	the OK command button

Your screen should look like Figure 24-7.

Figure 24-7

The Course Level style is now shown in the Style List dialog box.

You must now create two more styles for the course title and the date lines. To create the Course Title style:

Press	2 or C to select the Create option	*Choose*	*the Create option*
Type	Course Title	*Type*	*Course Title*
Press	⏎Enter	*Press*	*⏎Enter*
Press	2 or T to select the Style Type pop-up list button	*Hold down*	*the Style Type pop-up list button*
Press	C to select the Character Style option	*Choose*	*the Character Style option*
Press	⏎Enter	*Click*	*the OK command button*
Press	2 or D to select the Description text box	*Click*	*in the Description text box*
Type	Italicize and Underline Course Titles	*Type*	*Italicize and Underline Course Titles*
Press	⏎Enter	*Press*	*⏎Enter*
Press	4 or C to select the Style Contents option box	*Choose*	*the Style Contents option box*
Press	Ctrl +I	*Choose*	*Font*
Press	F8	*Choose*	*Italic*
		Choose	*Font*
		Choose	*Underline*

The top of your screen should look like Figure 24-8.

Figure 24-8

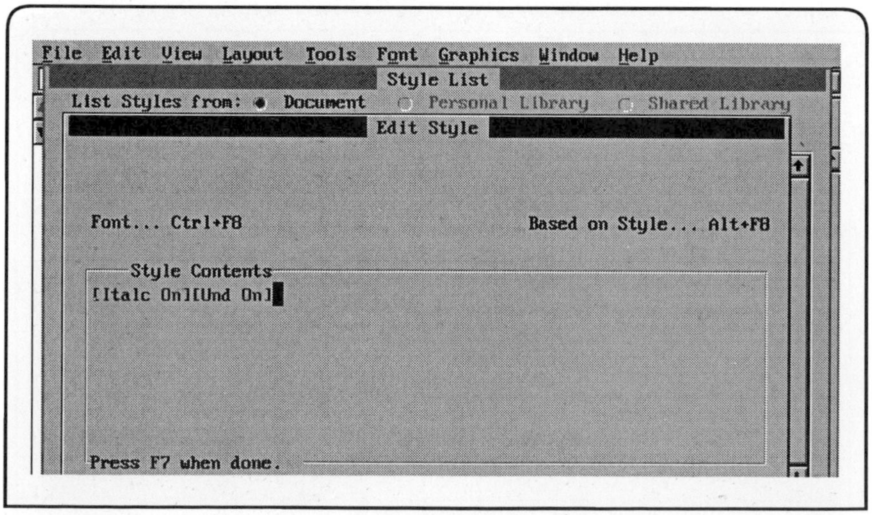

To return to the list of styles:

Press	F7	*Choose*	*File*
Press	⏎Enter	*Choose*	*Exit*
		Click	*the OK command button*

The Course Title style now appears in the list.

To create a style for the date lines:

Press	2 or C to select the Create option		***Choose***	*the Create option*
Type	Dates		***Type***	*Dates*
Press	[←Enter] twice		***Click***	*the OK command button*
Press	2 or D to select the Description text box		***Click***	*in the Description text box*
Type	Italicize Date Lines		***Type***	*Italicize Date Lines*
Press	[←Enter]		***Press***	*[←Enter]*
Press	4 or C to select the Style Contents option box		***Choose***	*the Style Contents option box*
Press	[Ctrl]+I		***Choose***	*Font*
Press	[F7]		***Choose***	*Italic*
Press	[←Enter]		***Choose***	*File*
			Choose	*Exit*
			Click	*the OK command button*

Your screen should look like Figure 24-9.

Figure 24-9

```
 File  Edit  View  Layout  Tools  Font  Graphics  Window  Help
                          Style List
     List Styles from: ● Document   ○ Personal Library   ○ Shared Library

     Name           Type        Description
     Course Level   Character    Bold Course Levels
     Course Title   Character    Italicize and Underline Course Titles
     Dates          Paragraph    Italicize DATe Lines
     InitialCodes  •Open         Document Initial
     Level 1       •Paragraph    Level 1
     Level 2       •Paragraph    Level 2
     Level 3       •Paragraph    Level 3
     None           Paragraph    No Paragraph Style




     1. Select    3. Edit...   5. Copy...    7. Save...     9. Mark
     2. Create... 4. Delete... 6. Options... 8. Retrieve... N. Name Search
                     • Denotes library style              [ Close ]

 A:\SCHEDULE                              Doc 1 Pg 1 Ln 1" Pos 1"
```

Notice that the Style Type for the Dates style is Paragraph. The Dates style now appears in the list.

To return to your document:

Press	[F7]		***Click***	*the Close command button*

To use the Course Level style:

Highlight	the text "Beginning:"		*Select*	*the text "Beginning:"*
Press	Alt + F8		*Choose*	*Layout*
			Choose	*Styles*

To turn on the Course Level style:

Press	↑ seven times to highlight Course Level		*Click*	*on Course Level*
Press	1 or S to select the Select option		*Choose*	*the Select option*

Repeat the steps to select and turn on the Course Level style for the "Intermediate:" and "Advanced:" text. Your screen should look like Figure 24-10.

Figure 24-10

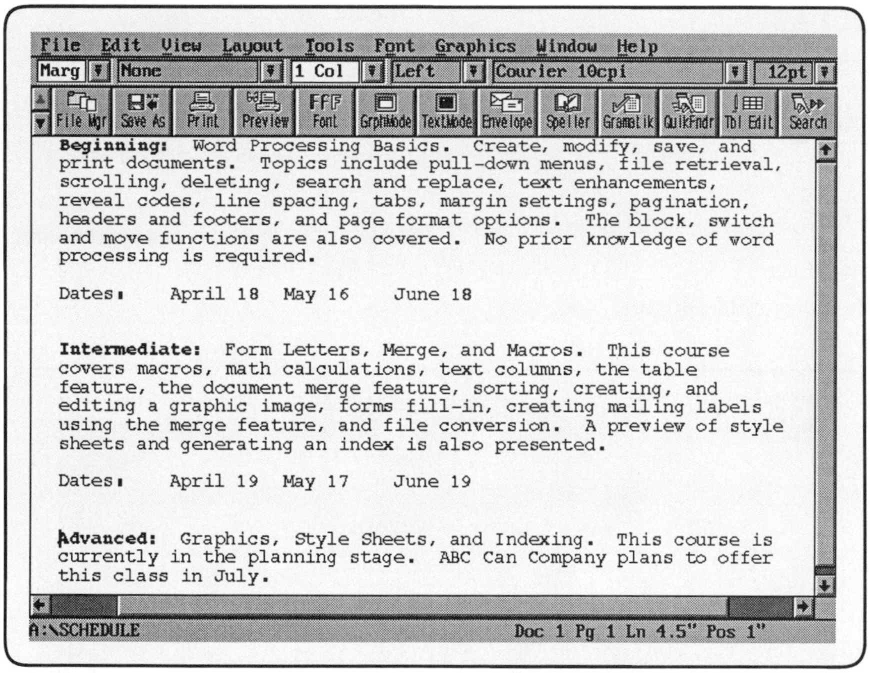

The course levels are now boldfaced.

Display the Reveal Codes to see the Char Style On and Off codes. When you move the cursor on top of the Char Style On code, the code expands to show the codes that you placed in the Style Contents section. When you move your cursor on top of the Style Off code, the code expands to show the contents of the Style Contents Off section. Turn off the Reveal Codes feature.

To use the Course Title style:

Highlight	the text "Word Processing Basics."		*Select*	*the text "Word Processing Basics."*
Press	Alt + F8		*Choose*	*Layout*
Press	↑ six times to select Course Title		*Choose*	*Styles*
Press	1 or S to select the Select option		*Click*	*on Course Title*
			Choose	*the Select option*

Repeat the steps to select and turn on the Course Title style for the "Form Letters, Merge, and Macros" and "Graphics, Style Sheets, and Indexing" text, including the periods that follow them.

To use the Dates style:

Highlight	the date line for the Beginning class	*Select*	*the date line for the Beginning class*
Press	Alt + F8	*Choose*	*Layout*
Press	↑ five times to select Dates	*Choose*	*Styles*
Press	1 or S to select the Select option	*Click*	*on Dates*
		Choose	*the Select option*

Repeat the steps to select and turn on the Dates style for the line containing the dates for the Intermediate class.

Your screen should look like Figure 24-11.

Figure 24-11

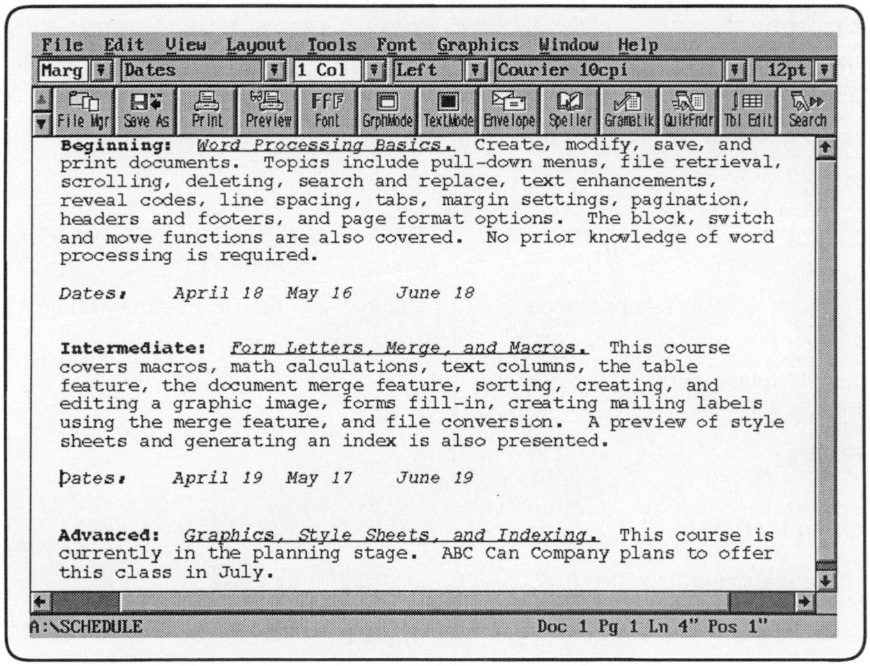

Suppose you want to place the title "WordPerfect 6.0 for DOS" at the top of the schedule. Assume that you want the text to be centered and in the Helve-WP (Type 1) 14 point boldface font style.

To create a style for the format of the heading:

Press	Alt + F8	*Choose*	*Layout*
Press	2 or C to select the Create option	*Choose*	*Styles*
Type	Title	*Choose*	*the Create option*
Press	↵Enter twice	*Type*	*Title*
Press	2 or D to select the Description text box	*Click*	*the OK command button*

Type	Helve-WP (Type 1) 14 pt Boldfaced and Centered	*Click*	*in the Description text box*
Press	`←Enter`	*Type*	*Helve-WP (Type 1) 14 pt Boldfaced and Centered*
		Press	`←Enter`

To change the font to Helve-WP (Type 1) 14 point boldface:

Press	4 or C to select the Style Contents option box	*Choose*	*the Style Contents option box*
Press	`Ctrl`+`F8`	*Choose*	*Font*
Press	1 or F to select the Font drop-down list box	*Choose*	*Font*
Press	H to highlight the Helve-WP (Type 1) font	*Click*	*the Font drop-down list box*
Press	`←Enter`	*Click*	*on the Helve-WP (Type 1) font (you may have to scroll down to see the option)*
Press	2 or S to select the Size text box	*Click*	*in the Size text box*
Type	14	*Type*	*14*
Press	`←Enter`	*Click*	*the Bold check box until an X appears*
Press	3 or A to select the Appearance option box	*Click*	*the OK command button*
Press	1 or B to place an X in the Bold check box		
Press	`←Enter`		

To insert a [Cntr on Mar] code:

Press	`Shift`+`F6`	*Choose*	*Layout*
		Choose	*Alignment*
		Choose	*Center*

Your screen should look like Figure 24-12.

Figure 24-12

```
 File  Edit  View  Layout  Tools  Font  Graphics  Window  Help
                            Style List
    List Styles from: ● Document  ○ Personal Library  ○ Shared Library
                            Edit Style

     Indent... F4        Dbl Indent... Shft+F4    Mark Text... Alt+F5

     Font... Ctrl+F8   ' Format... Shft+F8     Based on Style... Alt+F8

        ┌─Style Contents─────────────────────────────────────┐
        │ [Font:Helve-WP][Font Size:14pt][Bold On][Cntr on Mar]│
        │                                                      │
        │                                                      │
        │                                                      │
        │                                                      │
        │ Press F7 when done.                                  │
        └──────────────────────────────────────────────────────┘
                                          [  OK  ]  [ Cancel ]

                    • Denotes library style            [ Close ]

 A:\SCHEDULE                          Doc 1 Pg 1 Ln 4" Pos 1"
```

To return to the list of styles:

Press	F7	**Choose**	*File*
Press	↵Enter	**Choose**	*Exit*
		Click	*the OK command button*

The Title style now appears in the Style List dialog box.

To return to your document:

Press	F7	**Click**	*the Close command button*

You have already formatted existing text with a style by selecting the text and then selecting the Course Level, Course Title, and Dates styles. You can also select a style first and then type the text.

Turn on Reveal Codes. To position the cursor where the heading is to be typed:

Move	the cursor to the beginning of the document	**Click**	*at the beginning of the document*
Place	the cursor on the [Char Style On:Course Level] code in front of the text "Beginning:"	**Click**	*on the [Char Style On:Course Level] code in front of the text "Beginning:"*
Press	↵Enter three times	**Press**	*↵Enter three times*
Move	the cursor to the beginning of the document	**Click**	*at the beginning of the document*

Turn Reveal Codes off.

To select a style before entering the text:

Press	Alt + F8	**Choose**	*Layout*
		Choose	*Styles*

To turn on the Title style:

Press	⬇ to select Title		*Click*	*on Title*
Press	1 or S to select the Select option		*Choose*	*the Select option*

To enter the heading:

Type	WordPerfect 6.0 for DOS		*Type*	*WordPerfect 6.0 for DOS*

The top part of your screen should look like Figure 24-13.

Figure 24-13

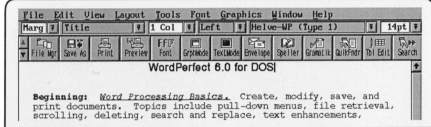

Format codes that affect an entire document are normally placed in a group at the beginning of a document. By including these codes in a style, you can easily select the style to format the entire document. Because the format codes will affect the entire document, the style should be placed in an Open style type.

Suppose you want to format the schedule with 2" left and right margins, 1.5" top margin, 1" bottom margin, full justification, page numbering, and a font set to Helve-WP (Type 1) 12 point. When adding format codes to your style, select the Layout menu options as you would in a normal document or press the appropriate function keys.

To create the Format style:

Press	Alt + F8		*Choose*	*Layout*
Press	2 or C to select the Create option		*Choose*	*Styles*
Type	Format		*Choose*	*the Create option*
Press	↵Enter		*Type*	*Format*
Press	2 or T to select the Style Type pop-up list button		*Press*	*↵Enter*
Press	O to select the Open Style option		*Hold down*	*the Style Type pop-up list button*
Press	↵Enter		*Choose*	*the Open Style option*
Press	2 or D to select the Description text box		*Click*	*the OK command button*
Type	Margins, justification, font, and page numbering		*Click*	*the Description text box*
Press	↵Enter		*Type*	*Margins, justification, font, and page numbering*
Press	4 or C to select the Style Contents option box		*Choose*	*the Style Contents option box*

To insert the format codes for the style:

Set	the left and right margins at 2" and the top margin at 1.5"	*Set*	*the left and right margins at 2" and the top margin at 1.5"*
Set	full justification	*Set*	*full justification*
Set	page numbering at the bottom center of every page	*Set*	*page numbering at the bottom center of every page*
Set	Helve-WP (Type 1) 12 pt as the font	*Set*	*Helve-WP (Type 1) 12 pt as the font*

Your screen should look like Figure 24-14.

Figure 24-14

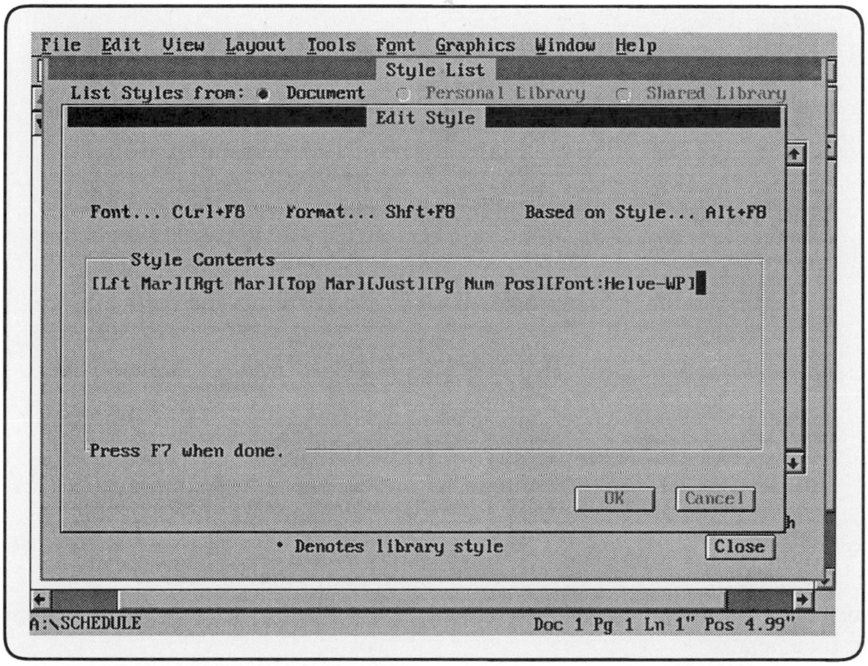

To return to your document:

Press	F7	*Choose*	*File*
Press	↵Enter	*Choose*	*Exit*
Press	F7	*Click*	*the OK command button*
		Click	*the Close command button*

Turn on Reveal Codes. To format the entire document:

Move	the insertion point to the beginning of the document	*Click*	*at the beginning of the document*
Place	the cursor on the [Para Style:Title;] code	*Click*	*on the [Para Style:Title;] code*
Press	Alt + F8	*Choose*	*Layout*
		Choose	*Styles*

To turn on the Format style:

| **Press** | ⬆ five times to select Format | ***Click*** | *on Format* |
| **Press** | 1 or S to select the Select option | ***Choose*** | *the Select option* |

Turn off Reveal Codes. Your screen should look like Figure 24-15.

Figure 24-15

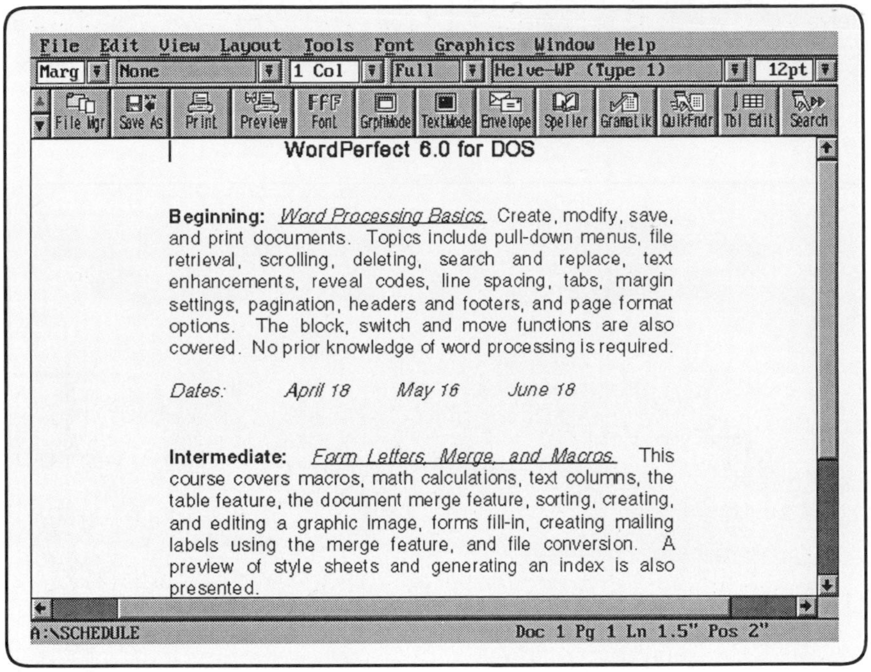

Notice that the text is in Helve-WP (Type 1) 12 point and the document margins and justification have changed.

Preview the document. Select full page. Notice that a page number appears at the bottom of the page. Return to your document.

■ EDITING A STYLE

When you want to edit a style, select the Style feature and change the information as necessary. The text in your document will reflect the changes wherever the edited style is used.

Suppose you want to change the Course Title style so that the titles are no longer in italics. Instead the titles are to be boldfaced and underlined.

To edit the Course Title style:

Press	Alt + F8	***Choose***	*Layout*
Press	⬆ seven times to select Course Title	***Choose***	*Styles*
Press	3 or E to select the Edit option	***Click***	*on Course Title*
Press	2 or D to select the Description text box	***Choose***	*the Edit option*

Type	Boldface and Underline Course Titles		**Click**	*in the Description text box*
Press	⏎Enter		**Type**	*Boldface and Underline Course Titles*
			Press	⏎Enter

To delete the [Italc On] code and replace it with the [Bold On] code:

Press	4 or C to select the Style Contents option box		**Choose**	*the Style Contents option box*
Press	Delete		**Press**	Delete
Press	F6		**Choose**	*Font*
			Choose	*Bold*

Your screen should look like Figure 24-16.

Figure 24-16

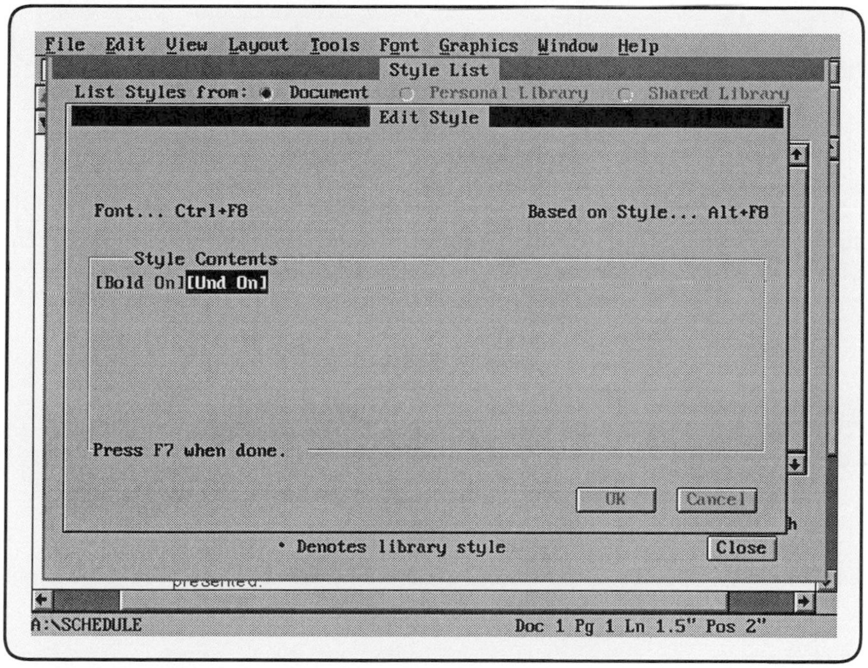

To return to your document:

Press	F7		**Choose**	*File*
Press	⏎Enter		**Choose**	*Exit*
Press	F7		**Click**	*the OK command button*
			Click	*the Close command button*

Your screen should look like Figure 24-17.

Figure 24-17

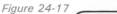

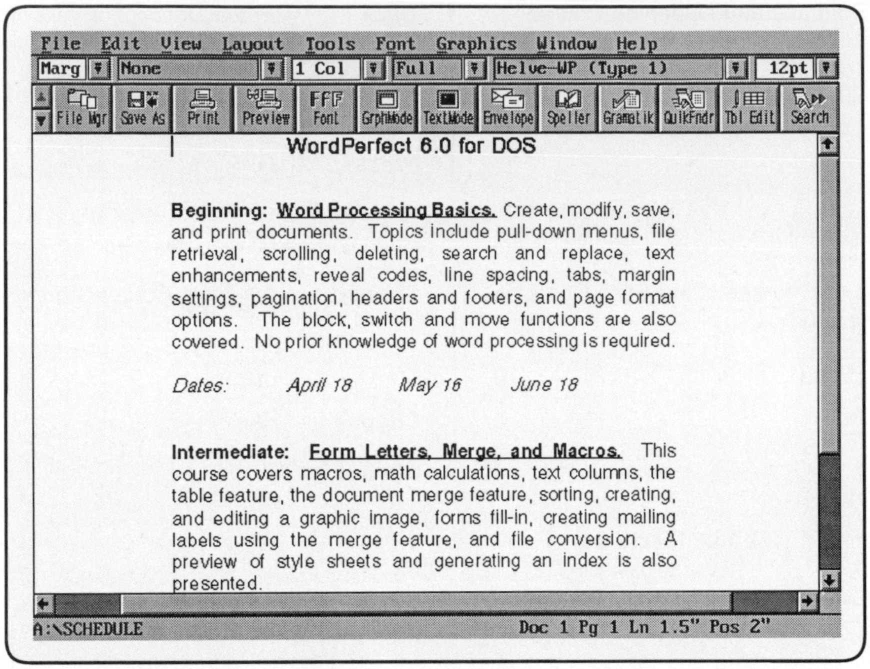

Notice that the course titles are boldfaced and underlined.

■ SAVING STYLES

Once you create a list of styles, you may want to use the same styles to format other documents. By saving the list as a style library, you can retrieve the list into any WordPerfect document.

Suppose you want to save the styles that you created for use with other documents.

To save a list of styles:

Press	Alt + F8		**Choose**	*Layout*
Press	7 or V to select the Save option		**Choose**	*Styles*
			Choose	*the Save option*

The Save Styles dialog box appears. Your screen should look like Figure 24-18.

Figure 24-18

```
 File  Edit  View  Layout  Tools  Font  Graphics  Window  Help
                              Style List
  List Styles from: ● Document    ○ Personal Library    ○ Shared Library

 ┌Name────────Type────────Description─────────────────────────────┐
  Course Level  Character    Bold Course Levels
  Course Title  Character    Boldface and Underline Course Titles
 ┌──────────────────────── Save Styles ──────────────────────────┐
 │                                                                │
 │   Filename: ▁                                                  │
 │                                                                │
 │         ⊠ Save User Created Styles                             │
 │         ☐ Save WP System Styles                                │
 │                                                                │
 │   ┌File List... F5┐  ┌QuickList... F6┐      ┌OK┐  ┌Cancel┐      │
 └────────────────────────────────────────────────────────────────┘

    Select       Edit...      Copy...      Save...      Mark
    Create...    Delete...    Options...   Retrieve...  Name Search
                  • Denotes library style                 ┌Close┐

 A:\SCHEDULE                          Doc 1 Pg 1 Ln 1.5" Pos 2"
```

To name the style library file:

Type	SCHED.STY		*Type*	*SCHED.STY*
Press	←Enter		*Click*	*the OK command button*

The ".STY" filename extension is not necessary, but it can help you quickly identify files that contain styles. The styles are now saved in the "SCHED.STY" file. They can be retrieved into any other WordPerfect document. The styles are saved in the "C:\WP60" directory by default. To change the location where styles are stored, use the Location of Files option under the Setup option in the File menu.

To return to your document:

Press	F7		*Click*	*the Close command button*

Save the document as "STYSCHED". Close the document.

■ RETRIEVING A STYLE

You can retrieve a list of styles that was saved at an earlier time. The new styles appear in the Style List dialog box.

To retrieve a list of styles:

Press	Alt + F8		*Choose*	*Layout*
Press	8 or R to select the Retrieve option		*Choose*	*Styles*
			Choose	*the Retrieve option*

The Retrieve Styles dialog box appears. Your screen should look like Figure 24-19.

Figure 24-19

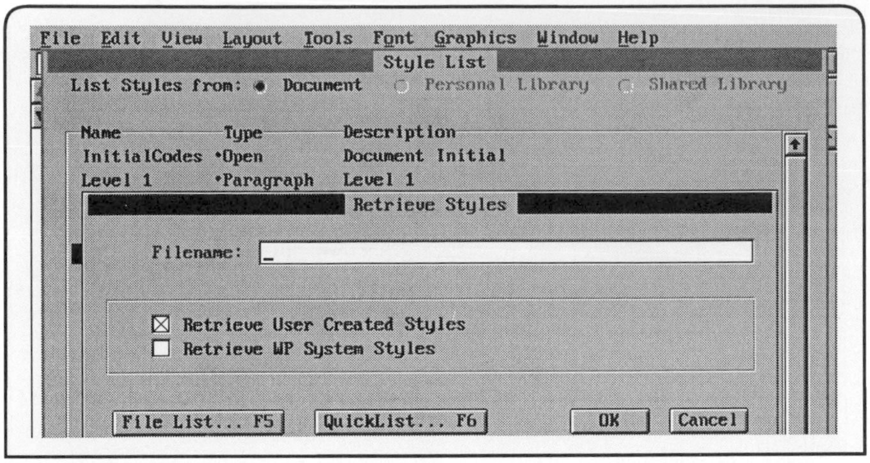

To enter the filename of the styles:

Type	SCHED.STY		*Type*	*SCHED.STY*
Press	⏎Enter		*Click*	*the OK command button*

Your screen should look like Figure 24-20.

Figure 24-20

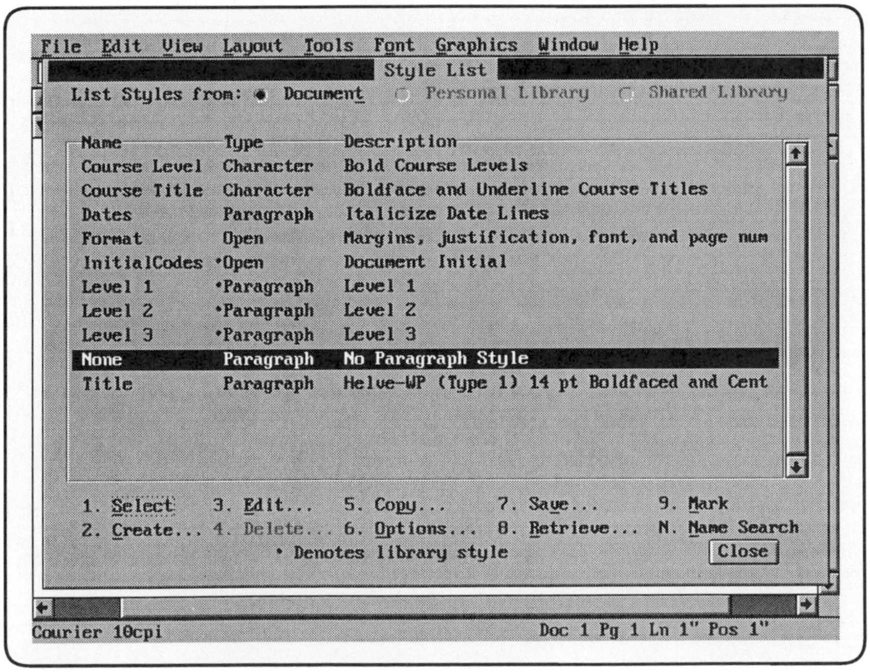

Now you can apply these styles to your document without having to recreate the styles. Close the Style List dialog box.

■ DELETING A STYLE

There are two options available to you when deleting a style. These options are described below:

Including Codes - The style is deleted from the list, and all references to the style are removed from the document. No codes are placed back into the document.

Leaving Codes - The style is deleted from the list, and all style codes referring to this style are removed from the document. However, all format and feature codes contained in the style are placed into the document at the location of each style code.

Retrieve the "STYSCHED" document. Be sure to use the File Retrieve command and *not* the File Open command.

To delete the Dates style including the codes:

Press	Alt + F8		***Choose***	*Layout*
Press	↑ seven times to select Dates		***Choose***	*Styles*
Press	4 or D to select the Delete option		***Choose***	*Dates*
			Choose	*the Delete option*

The Delete Style dialog box appears. The top of your screen should look like Figure 24-21.

Figure 24-21

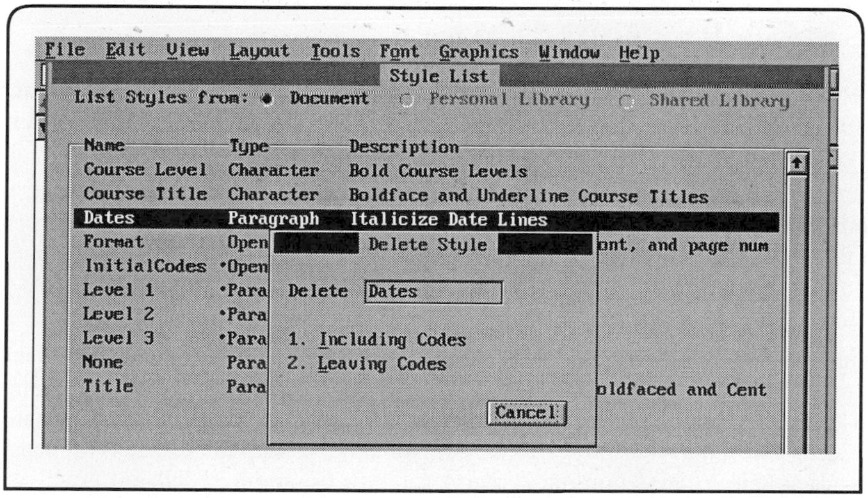

To delete the codes:

Press	1 or I to select the Including Codes option		***Choose***	*the Including Codes option*

Notice the Dates style has been deleted from the Style List dialog box. To return to your document:

Press	F7		***Click***	*the Close command button*

Your screen should look like Figure 24-22.

Figure 24-22

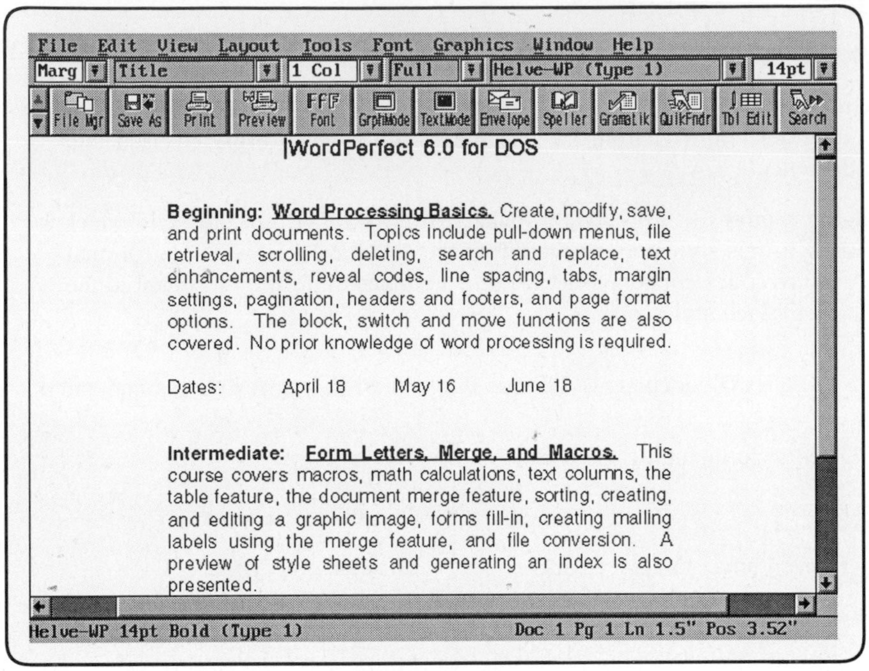

File   Edit   View   Layout   Tools   Font   Graphics   Window   Help

Marg ▾ Title   ▾ 1 Col ▾ Full ▾ Helve-WP (Type 1)   ▾ 14pt ▾

File Mgr Save As Print Preview Font Grphode TextHode Envelope Speller Gramtik QuikFndr Tbl Edit Search

|WordPerfect 6.0 for DOS

Beginning: <u>Word Processing Basics.</u> Create, modify, save, and print documents. Topics include pull-down menus, file retrieval, scrolling, deleting, search and replace, text enhancements, reveal codes, line spacing, tabs, margin settings, pagination, headers and footers, and page format options. The block, switch and move functions are also covered. No prior knowledge of word processing is required.

Dates: April 18   May 16   June 18

Intermediate: <u>Form Letters, Merge, and Macros.</u> This course covers macros, math calculations, text columns, the table feature, the document merge feature, sorting, creating, and editing a graphic image, forms fill-in, creating mailing labels using the merge feature, and file conversion. A preview of style sheets and generating an index is also presented.

Helve-WP 14pt Bold (Type 1)   Doc 1 Pg 1 Ln 1.5" Pos 3.52"

The dates are no longer italicized and the style code is deleted from your document.

Close the document without saving changes.

■ USING TYPESETTING FEATURES

When you create newsletters, manuscripts, and large reports, the appearance of the text on each page is very important. WordPerfect provides several typesetting features that allow you to change the amount of space between letters, between words, and between lines of text.

Suppose you create a monthly corporate newsletter. When you create the newsletter using the default settings in WordPerfect, there is not enough space between the headings and the following paragraphs, the words are too far apart, and the letters in each word are too close together. You can change each of these options using the WordPerfect Typesetting feature. To use the typesetting features, press SHIFT+F8 or choose Other from the Layout menu.

Before beginning this section, create the document in Figure 24-23. To format the document properly, set the font to Roman-WP (Type 1) 12 point, use two equally spaced newspaper-style columns, and set the justification to full. The newsletter heading is Roman-WP (Type 1) 14 point boldfaced and is centered. Boldface each section heading. Force the second column to begin with the "Issue Awareness Committee" section. Indent each item in the list in the "Issue Awareness Committee" section.

Figure 24-23

THE COMPANY NEWSLETTER

New Employees

Welcome!   We have several new employees this month. Please extend a welcome to Julia Brown, Finance; Oliver Hunt, Human Services; and James Sharp, PC Support.

Happy Birthday!

A warm Happy Birthday wish to all of our employees with June birthdays. This month's birthday bunch includes Doris Boyd, Mark Cohn, Ross James, Samantha Cooley, and Belinda Meyers. The monthly birthday celebration will be held in Conference Room 2 on the 15th.

Annual Meeting

The annual meeting of the stockholders is June 28-July 2. All meetings and conferences will be held at the Boliver Hotel. There are still rooms available if you would like accommodations at the hotel rather than having to commute. You can obtain a room for a special discount of $50 per night. Please contact Janice Johnson if you would like more information.

Issue Awareness Committee

The IAC has distributed packets containing important employee information to each employee. Each packet should contain:

New insurance forms for medical, life, and disability plans

Information on the company 401K plan

Stock and money market fund options

Company-provided day care information

Carpool matching forms

Please turn in your completed copy of each of these forms to your direct supervisor by June 30. If you need a form, please contact Mike Rogers, the IAC chair.

Brown Bag Seminar

A lunch seminar will be presented on June 12. The topic this month is "Advanced Graphic Features in WordPerfect 6.0 for DOS." The workshop will begin promptly at 11:45.

Save the document as "NEWSLET".

Leading Adjustment

To change the amount of space between lines:

Move	the cursor to the beginning of Column 1	*Click*	*at the beginning of Column 1*
Press	Shift + F8	*Choose*	*Layout*
Press	7 or O to select the Other option	*Choose*	*Other*

The Other Format dialog box appears. Your screen should look like Figure 24-24.

Figure 24-24

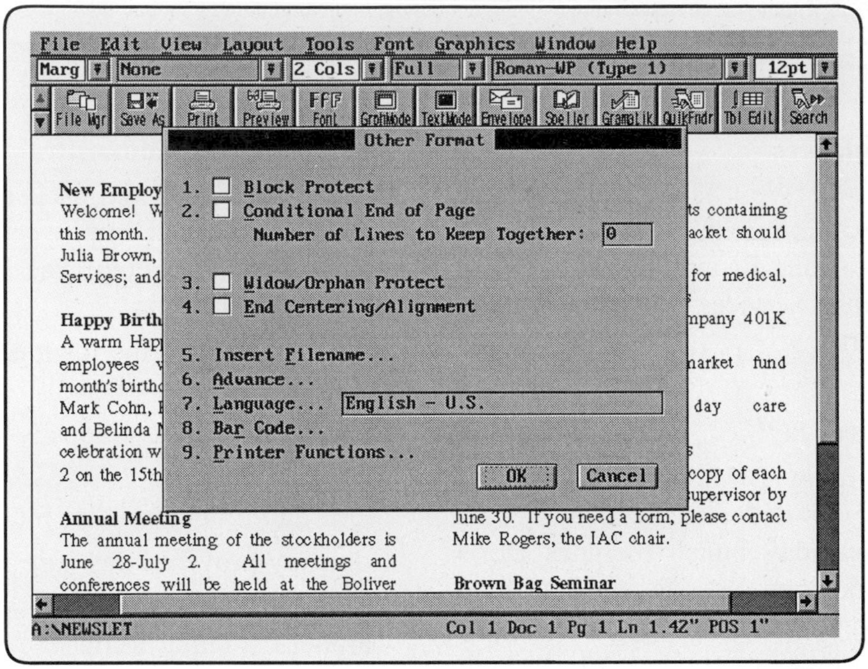

To adjust the line height:

| **Press** | 9 or P to select the Printer Functions option | **Choose** | the Printer Functions option |

The Printer Functions dialog box appears on the screen. Your screen should look like Figure 24-25.

Figure 24-25

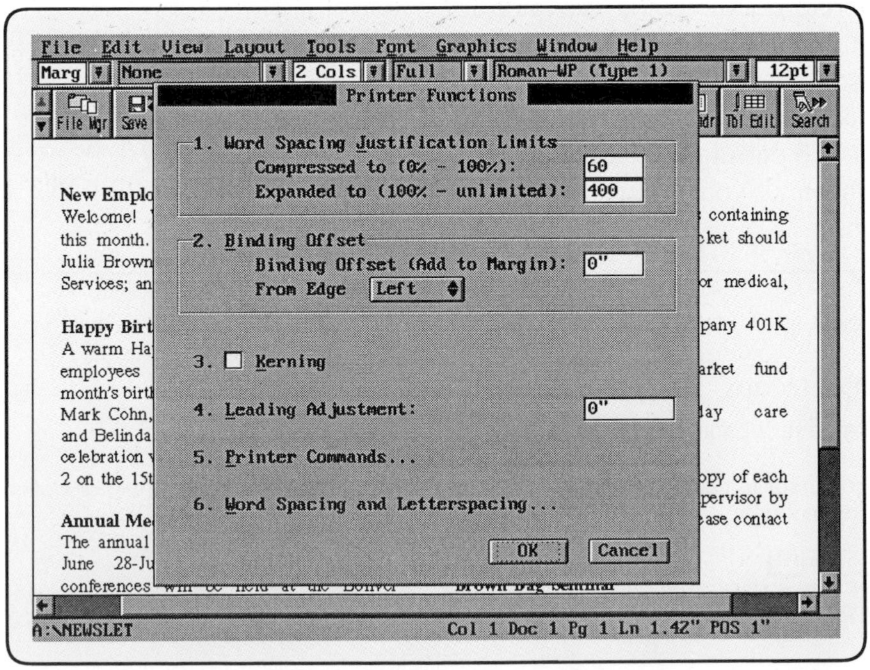

Several Printer Functions are available. Each feature is described in the following list:

Word Spacing Justification Limits - adjusts the spacing between words in your document. This feature is important when full justification is used. If your justified text is too close together, then you should increase the percentage under the Compressed To option. If the justified text is too far apart, then you decrease the number in the Expanded To option.

Binding Offset - adjusts the left and right margins to accommodate for binding two-sided documents, and changes the amount of spacing between the letters in your document.

Kerning - Manual kerning allows you to change the spacing between individual letter pairs in your document. Unlike letterspacing, manual kerning affects letters on a selected basis. Letterspacing affects large portions of the document, not individual letter pairs.

Leading Adjustment - specifies an amount of space to be added to or subtracted from the line height, thus changing the amount of white space between the lines of type.

Printer Commands - sends special commands to your printer that WordPerfect might not normally support.

Word Spacing and Letterspacing - compresses or expands the justified text in your document.

To change the leading adjustment between lines:

Press	4 or L to select the Leading Adjustment text box	*Click*	*in the Leading Adjustment text box*
Type	.05	*Type*	*.05*
Press	[←Enter]	*Click*	*the OK command button*

To return to the document:

| **Press** | [←Enter] three times | *Click* | *the OK command button* |

Your screen should look like Figure 24-26.

Figure 24-26

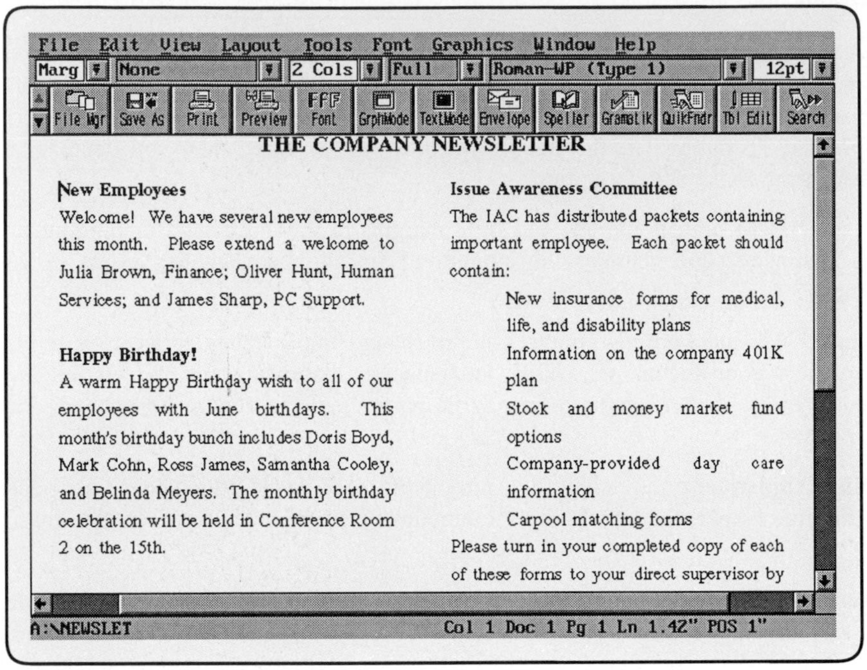

File Edit View Layout Tools Font Graphics Window Help
Marg None 2 Cols Full Roman-WP (Type 1) 12pt
File Mgr Save As Print Preview Font GrphMode TextMode Envelope Speller Gramatik QuikFndr Tbl Edit Search
THE COMPANY NEWSLETTER
New Employees
Welcome! We have several new employees this month. Please extend a welcome to Julia Brown, Finance; Oliver Hunt, Human Services; and James Sharp, PC Support.
Happy Birthday!
A warm Happy Birthday wish to all of our employees with June birthdays. This month's birthday bunch includes Doris Boyd, Mark Cohn, Ross James, Samantha Cooley, and Belinda Meyers. The monthly birthday celebration will be held in Conference Room 2 on the 15th.
Issue Awareness Committee
The IAC has distributed packets containing important employee. Each packet should contain:
New insurance forms for medical, life, and disability plans
Information on the company 401K plan
Stock and money market fund options
Company-provided day care information
Carpool matching forms
Please turn in your completed copy of each of these forms to your direct supervisor by
A:\NEWSLET
Col 1 Doc 1 Pg 1 Ln 1.42" POS 1"

Notice the extra space between each line.

Word Spacing and Letterspacing

The Word Spacing and Letterspacing options allow you to change the amount of space between the words or letters in your document.

The Word Spacing Justification Limits option changes the spacing between words only when full justification is used. You can change the amount of space between words, or the amount of space between letters, regardless of the justification, using the Word Spacing and Letterspacing option.

The Kerning option changes the spacing between letters for specific letter pairs.

Suppose you want to *decrease* the amount of space between words and *increase* the amount of space between letters in the newsletter. To change the amount of letterspacing and word spacing in the body of the newsletter:

Move	the cursor to the left margin of Column 1	***Click***	*at the left margin of Column 1*
Press	Shift+F8	***Choose***	*Layout*
Press	7 or O to select the Other option	***Choose***	*Other*
Press	9 or P to select the Printer Functions option	***Choose***	*the Printer Functions option*
Press	6 or W to select the Word Spacing and Letterspacing option	***Choose***	*the Word Spacing and Letterspacing option*

The Word Spacing and Letterspacing dialog box appears on the screen. Your screen should look like Figure 24-27.

Figure 24-27

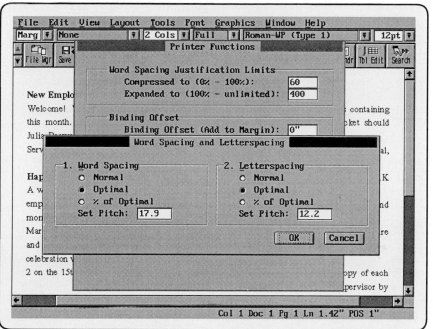

Four settings can be used to change the Word Spacing option. The Normal option instructs WordPerfect to change the word spacing to what the printer manufacturer considers appropriate. The Optimal option instructs WordPerfect to set the word spacing to what WordPerfect considers optimal. The % of Optimal option allows you to increase or decrease the amount of word spacing based on a percentage of what WordPerfect considers optimal. The Set Pitch option allows you to change the word spacing based on a certain numbers of characters per inch.

To change the amount of space between words to 95% of optimal:

Press	1 or W to select the Word Spacing option	*Click*	*the % of Optimal option button in the Word Spacing box*
Press	3 or P to select the % of Optimal option	*Type*	*95*
Type	95	*Double-click*	*in the % of Optimal text box*
Press	⏎Enter		

Like the Word Spacing option, four settings can be used to change the Letterspacing option. The Normal option instructs WordPerfect to change the letterspacing to what the printer manufacturer considers appropriate for that font. The Optimal option instructs WordPerfect to set the letterspacing to what WordPerfect considers optimal. The % of Optimal option allows you to increase or decrease the amount of letterspacing based on a percentage of what WordPerfect considers optimal. The Set Pitch option allows you to change the letterspacing based on a certain numbers of characters per inch.

To increase the Letterspacing option to 110% of optimal:

| Press | 2 or L to select the Letterspacing option | *Click* | *the % of Optimal option button in the Letterspacing box* |
| Press | 3 or P to select the % of Optimal option | *Type* | *110* |

Type	110	**Double-click**	*in the % of Optimal text box in the Letterspacing box*
Press	⏎Enter		

To accept the word spacing and letterspacing changes and return to the document:

Press	⏎Enter *four times*	**Click**	*the OK command button three times*

The words should appear closer together and the letters within each word should appear to be farther apart. Your screen should look like Figure 24-28.

Figure 24-28

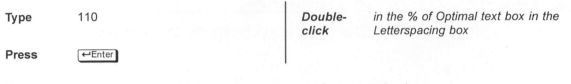

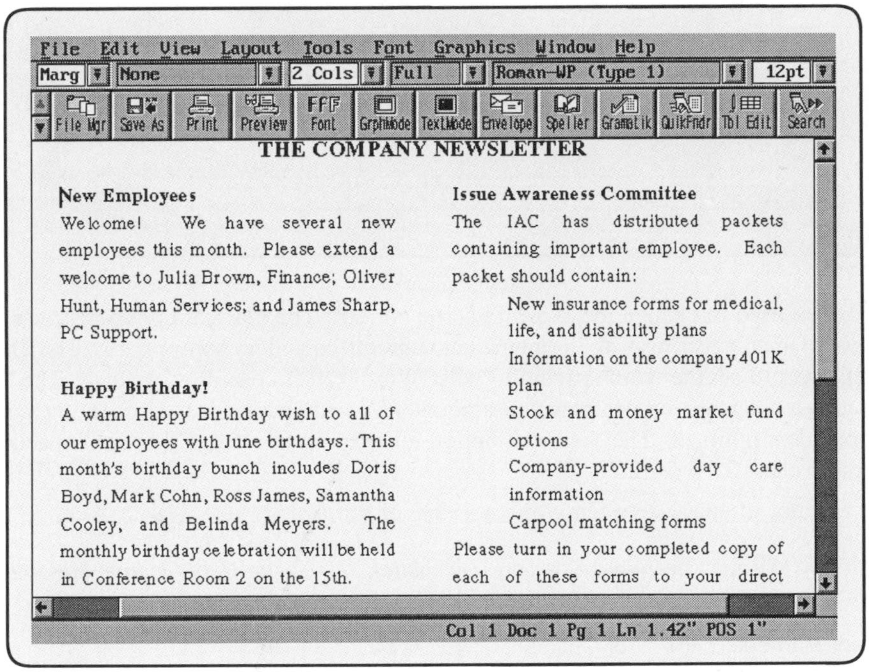

Kerning

The Kerning option allows you to manually increase or decrease the amount of space between two characters. Notice the title of the newsletter. The two "T"s in the word "NEWSLETTER" are very close together because you are using a Roman-WP (Type 1) font. To add space between these two characters only, you can use the Manual Kerning option in the Printer Functions dialog box.

To add space between the two "T"s in the title:

Move	the cursor between the two "T"s in the word "NEWSLETTER" in the title of the document	**Click**	*between the two "T"s in the word "NEWSLETTER" in the title of the document*
Press	Shift + F8	**Choose**	*Layout*
Press	7 or O to select the Other Option	**Choose**	*Other*
Press	9 or P to select the Printer Functions option	**Choose**	*the Printer Functions option*
Press	3 or K to place an X in the Kerning check box	**Click**	*in the Kerning check box until an X appears*

To accept the kerning choice and return to your document:

Press [←Enter] three times | ***Click*** *the OK command button twice*

The top part of your screen should look like Figure 24-29.

Figure 24-29

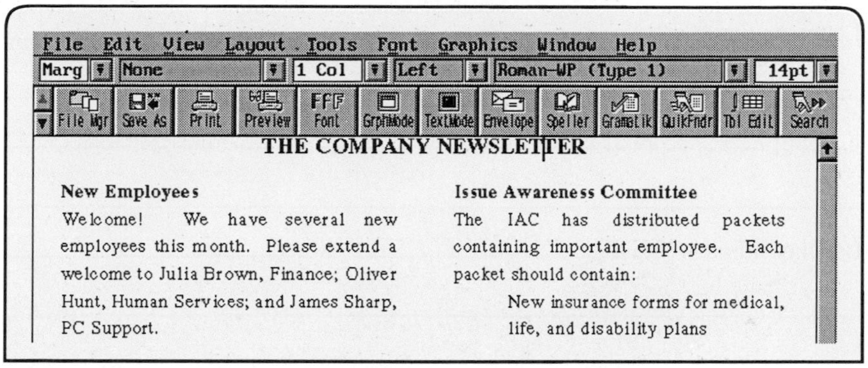

To turn the Kerning feature off after the double Ts, place your cursor at the end of the title and follow the same steps to remove the X from the Kerning check box.

Save the document as "NEWSLET1". Close the document.

EXERCISE 1

INSTRUCTIONS: Define the following concepts:

1. Styles feature _____

2. Edit Styles _____

3. Style name _____

4. Style type _____

5. Style description _____

6. Style codes _____

7. Paragraph type _____

8. Open type _____

9.   Character type _____

_____

10.   Word spacing _____

_____

11.   Letterspacing _____

_____

12.   Kerning _____

_____

13.   Leading adjustment _____

_____

EXERCISE 2

INSTRUCTIONS:			Circle T if the statement is true and F if the statement is false.
T	F	1.	The Styles feature helps you control repeating formats in a document.
T	F	2.	The Edit Style dialog box allows you to associate format codes and text with a style.
T	F	3.	There are two types of styles that you can create: Paragraph and Open.
T	F	4.	The Paragraph style type turns on the features associated with the style once. The features are used to the end of the document.
T	F	5.	The Open style type uses On and Off codes to turn on the features defined with the style, and then turns off the style at a later point in the text.
T	F	6.	There are two options when deleting a style: Leaving Codes and Including Codes.
T	F	7.	The Leaving Codes option places all format codes contained in the style at the location of each style code.
T	F	8.	The Including Codes option deletes the style codes from the document.
T	F	9.	A style can have text and any number of format codes associated with it.
T	F	10.	You can change the amount of space between words using the Kerning feature.
T	F	11.	The Letterspacing feature changes the amount of space between a specific pair of characters.
T	F	12.	The Leading Adjustment feature can change the amount of space between lines.

EXERCISE 3

INSTRUCTIONS:
1.   Create the following document.
2.   Print the document.
3.   Create a style to center and boldface the title "CONSULTING SPECIALTIES".
4.   Create a style to boldface and underline the headings.
5.   Use the styles on the document.

6. Print the document.
7. Save the final document in a file using the name "CH24EX03".
8. Save the styles in a file using the name "CH24EX03.STY".

```
CONSULTING SPECIALTIES

Information Systems Consulting

        Information Systems Assessment
        Information Systems Planning

Software and Hardware Selection

        Requirements Analysis
        System Evaluation
        Implementation Assistance

Systems Development

        Database Applications
        Multi-User Applications
        Distributed Processing

Local Area Network Consulting

        Selection
        Installation
        Training
```

EXERCISE 4

INSTRUCTIONS:
1. Create the following styles for a very short letter (body of letter contains less than 75 words).
2. Set the left and right margins to 1.75".
3. Set justification to left.
4. Turn on hyphenation.
5. If possible, set the initial font to Roman-WP (Type 1) 14 point.
6. Save the style in a file using the name "SHORT.STY".
7. Close the document.

EXERCISE 5

INSTRUCTIONS:
1. Retrieve your styles for a short letter, "SHORT.STY", that you created in Exercise 4.
2. Create the following document using the short letter style.
3. Save the letter in a file using the name "CH24EX05".
4. Print the letter.
5. Close the document.

```
current date


Johnston and Hovell Company
855 N. Lafayette Street
Sioux Falls, SD   57101

Ladies and Gentlemen:

This will acknowledge that we have received your Purchase Order
#23AB421 for 100 gross of "OOO" springs.

We are currently back ordered on this part and do not expect to make
shipment for six more weeks.  Please advise.

Sincerely,

ROLF SPRING COMPANY



Robert R. Rolf
Vice President

xx
```

EXERCISE 6

INSTRUCTIONS:

1. Create the following styles for a left-bound manuscript.
2. Change the left margin to 1.5". The right margin remains the same. The body of the document is double spaced. Page numbers are placed at the top right of the page and start on the second page. Suppress the page number on the first page only. Turn on hyphenation. Set justification to left.
3. The title starts at the 2" line on the page and is centered.
4. Side headings are underlined.
5. Save the styles in a file using the name "LEFTMAN.STY".
6. Close the document.

EXERCISE 7

INSTRUCTIONS:

1. Retrieve the styles for a left-bound manuscript "LEFTMAN.STY" that you created in Exercise 6.
2. Create the document on the next page using the left-bound style.
3. Save the document in a file using the name "CH24EX07".
4. Print the document.
5. Close the document.

PREPARING FOR A SPEECH

The person who does not get excited before giving a speech is a rare individual. Almost everyone is on the verge of panic. This is especially true for first time speakers, or those students in speech class. Everyone is fearful of the unknown. How does my voice sound? Am I prepared enough? Are my notes easy to read? How sincere am I? Do I believe in what I am saying?

These and other questions will always race through your mind–you may also feel it in your stomach. The result may be near hysteria at the podium. Here are some time-worn suggestions to help ease the panic and make your talk interesting.

Overcoming Fear

Always select a subject with which you are very familiar. If this is not possible, make sure you have adequate time to prepare. Set up a schedule for gathering data. Try to incorporate the information into real life situations. You can do this by relating it to examples or your own personal experiences.

Make contact with your audience. You need not look people directly in the eye, but a good trick is to look at their foreheads.

If you are not using a voice amplifier, make certain everyone can hear you. Practice talking in an empty room with a tape recorder in the back. Check it out to see how you sound.

Be yourself. Whenever possible talk from your background. Be honest, be enthusiastic. Try to make your speech enjoyable for yourself and it will be enjoyable for your listeners.

Make Your Talk Interesting

A good speech should inform the listeners. Use facts and references to set the framework. Be careful though, not to use too many. Be selective. Use round numbers. Leave out insignificant details and incidents.

Try to confine your speech to only three or four main points. Remember your audience. They do not know your subject as well as you do. Make the last point clear by using anything that will add clarity -- charts, graphs, pictures. Always make sure that those in the back of the room can clearly see your visuals.

If possible, try to use humor. This is a powerful tool if you are up to it. Search your library for books on stories or jokes that relate to the point you are trying to make.

Conclude your talk by summing up the points clearly and concisely. Remember, a good speaker always finishes his speech before the audience finishes listening.

EXERCISE 8

INSTRUCTIONS:

1. Retrieve the short letter styles "SHORT.STY" that you created in Exercise 4.
2. Edit the style to change the left and right margins of the letter to 1.5".
3. Turn off hyphenation.
4. Enter the document shown below. Save it in a file using the name "CH24EX08".
5. Print the document.
6. Close the document.

```
current date


Taylor and Holmes Electronics
1201 West Moss Avenue
Red Bank White Oak, TN 37415

Dear Sir or Madam:

We find that your account is 60 days overdue.  Is there a problem
with our merchandise?  If not, why have you not responded to our last
three notices?

If we do not hear from you within ten days, we will be forced to
report this matter to the Red Bank White Oak Credit Bureau.

Respectfully yours,



James Arthur Dillon
Accounts Manager

xx
```

EXERCISE 9

INSTRUCTIONS:

1. Open the document "CH24EX07".
2. Edit the style so that the side headings are boldfaced instead of underlined.
3. Change the left and right margins to 2".
4. Move the page numbers to the bottom center of the page.
5. Print preview the document.
6. Print the document.
7. Save the document in a file using the name "CH24EX09".
8. Save the style changes in the file "LEFTMAN.STY".
9. Close the document.

EXERCISE 10

INSTRUCTIONS: 1.   Create the following styles for an invoice. A sample invoice is shown below.

```
                          Norma Dijkstra, PC
                          One Riverway Plaza
                   1800 Davis Boulevard, Suite 1550
                     New Orleans, LA 82110-0998


                              INVOICE


Company: Name                                    current date
         Address

Contact: Name                                Invoice:  #nnnn
                                             Total:    $99,999.99

Paragraph describing invoice activity and the period of invoice - in
italics.

   Class Date    Location                              Amount
   mm/dd/yy      Course location                    $nn,nnn.nn
```

2.   Create an open style for the invoice heading and addressee section. This style should do the following:

    a.   Set the left and right margins to 1.5". Set the bottom margin to 0.5".

    b.   Set justification to left.

    c.   Set the initial font to Helve-WP (Type 1) 12 pt.

    d.   Boldface and center the following text, which is the invoice heading:

        Norma Dijkstra, PC
        One Riverway Plaza
        1800 Davis Boulevard, Suite 1550
        New Orleans, LA 82110-0998

        INVOICE

    e.   Set tabs for the invoice addressee section. This is the section that contains the company name, address, date, and invoice number. Use your own discretion for tab spacing.

3.   Create a paired style for a paragraph describing the invoice activity and period. This paragraph is in italics.

4.   Create another open style for the itemized class section of the invoice located at the bottom. This style should do the following:

    a.   Set tabs for the column headings. Use your own discretion for tab spacing. The column headings should be boldfaced and underlined.

    b.   Set tabs for the column data. The amount column should have a decimal tab. Use your own discretion for tab placement.

5.   Save the style in a file using the name "INVOICE.STY".

6.   Create the following two invoices. Keep the two invoices in one document. Place a page break between each one. Use the "INVOICE.STY" style to create the invoices. Print the invoices. Save the document in a file using the name "CH24EX10".

```
Company:  ABC Training Services          current date
          1100 Sam Houston Parkway
          Suite 1500
          Aberdeen, TX 79220

Contact:  Mr. John J. McPherson          Invoice:  #901000
                                         Total:    $9,721.87

For training services rendered during the period of April 1, 1994 to
June 30, 1994.  Payment due thirty days after receipt.  The following
classes were taught during the period:

4/3/94      Moynihan Oil Company, Houston        1,200.00

4/11/94     Best Metal Products, Los Angeles     3,521.87

5/5/94      Allied Health Services, New Orleans  2,500.00

6/3/94      Allied Health Services, New Orleans  2,500.00
```

```
Company:  Hemlock PC Seminars            current date
          One Peachtree Plaza
          Suite 3400
          Atlanta, GA 79220

Contact:  Ms. Janice K. Hemlock          Invoice:  #901205
                                         Total:    $22,533.44

For training services rendered during the period of May, 1994.
Payment due fifteen days after receipt.  The following classes were
taught during the period:

5/3/94      Caladium Airlines, New York City     6,000.00

5/10/94     Caladium Airlines, Los Angeles       6,500.55

5/12/94     Percy Shelley Insurance, Miami       3,600.00

5/16/94     Caladium Airlines, Houston           1,110.44

5/23/94     Monstrosity Shoes, New York City     5,322.45
```

EXERCISE 11

INSTRUCTIONS:

1. Create the following document. Set the font to Roman-WP (Type 1) 12 point and the justification to full.
2. Change the leading adjustment to .03".
3. Change the Word Spacing feature to 95% of optimal.
4. Save the document as "CH24EX11".
5. Print the document.
6. Close the document.

NEW EXPENSE GUIDELINES

So that the XYZ Company does not have to cut more significant areas of our budget, we have revised our expense guidelines. Please begin implementing these new guidelines immediately.

- All employees must use the company mileage schedule for travel expenses. Departments that were previously using special schedules must convert to the corporate schedule effective today.
- All client expenses must be approved in advance by your department supervisor. Client expenses include client lunches, entertainment, and transportation expenses. If you think you will be incurring expenses during a client meeting, have the expenses approved. If the expenses are unnecessary, then you can discard the approval form.
- Office supplies will be cut back to a minimum. For example, we will no longer order four types of legal pads. Each department will use the same legal pads. Special orders must be requested through your department supervisor. If a department exceeds its office supply budget, employees will be asked to compensate the difference.
- We will no longer order preformatted diskettes or special mouse pads as part of our computer supplies.
- An immediate freeze has been placed on all purchases of office equipment. Department needs will be examined on an individual basis.

Thank you for your cooperation in implementing these guidelines. By cutting our travel and office expenses we may be able to avoid cuts in more important areas.

EXERCISE 12

INSTRUCTIONS:

1. Open the document "CH24EX07". If you have not created the document yet, do so at this time.
2. Change the leading adjustment to .05".
3. Change the word spacing to 98% of optimal and the letterspacing to 103% of optimal.
4. Save the document as "CH24EX12".
5. Print the document.
6. Close the document.

CHAPTER TWENTY-FIVE

OUTLINES

OBJECTIVES

In this chapter, you will learn to:
- Create an outline
- Edit an outline
- Hide and show outline families
- Use the Outline Edit Mode

■ CHAPTER OVERVIEW

An **outline** is a way of organizing the ideas and information that you want to present in a long document or report. The WordPerfect Outline feature allows you to create several types of outlines. The procedures for creating and editing an outline are described in this chapter.

■ CREATING AN OUTLINE

An outline is made up of paragraph numbers. In WordPerfect you can have up to eight levels of numbers within a document. An example of an outline is shown in Figure 25-1.

```
I.    INTRODUCTION
II.   HARDWARE
      A.   Keyboard
      B.   Monitor
           1.   Monochrome
                a.   No Graphics Capability
                b.   MGA
                c.   MVGA
           2.   Color
                a.   CGA
                b.   EGA
                c.   VGA
      C.   CPU
           1.   8088 Processor
           2.   80286 Processor
           3.   80386 Processor
           4.   80486 Processor
```

The levels in this outline are displayed through numbers and letters. Several other numbering styles are available and are discussed later in this chapter.

Viewing the Outline Button Bar

Both an Outline Bar and an Outline Button Bar are available. The Outline Bar is discussed later in this chapter.

To use the Outline Button Bar:

Choose	*View*
Choose	*Button Bar Setup*
Choose	*Select*
Select	*OUTLINE*
Choose	*the Select option*

If you choose to turn on the Outline Button Bar, the top of your screen should look like Figure 25-2.

Figure 25-2

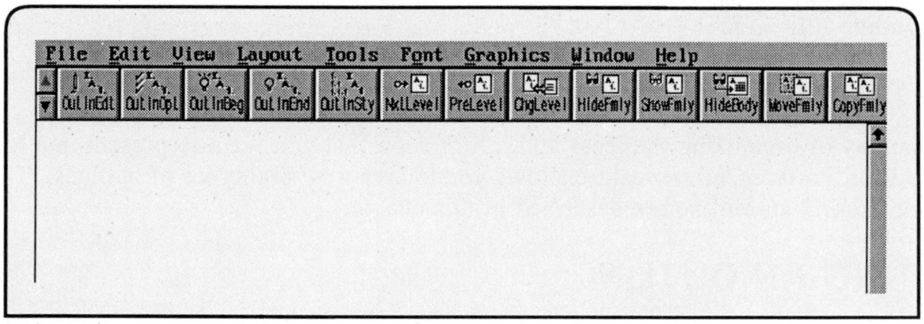

Creating an Outline

To start using the Outline feature:

Press	Ctrl + F5		**Click**	the OutlnBeg button on the Button Bar

If you used the keystroke method, the Outline dialog box appears on the screen. Your screen should look like Figure 25-3. If you used the menu method, the Outline Style List dialog box appears on the screen.

Figure 25-3

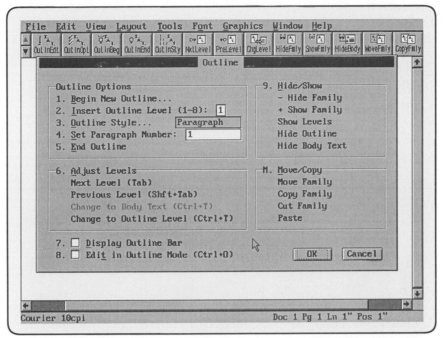

To begin a new outline:

Press   1 or B to select the Begin New
             Outline option

The Outline Style List dialog box appears on the screen. Your screen should look like Figure 25-4.

Figure 25-4

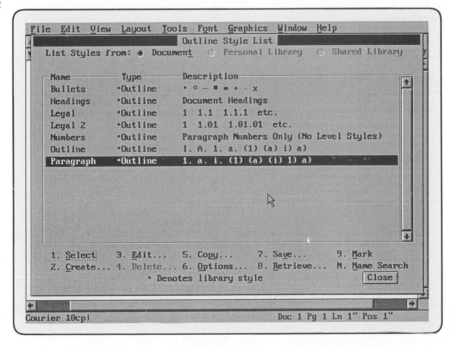

The default is to do a paragraph-style outline. However, you may also choose from among six other numbering styles.

To change to the Outline numbering style:

Press	⬆ once to highlight the Outline option	**Choose**	*the Outline option*
Press	1 or S to choose the Select option	**Choose**	*the Select option*

A Roman numeral one appears on the screen. Turn Reveal Codes on to see the Paragraph Style code [Para Style:Level 1;]. The bottom of your screen should look like Figure 25-5.

Figure 25-5

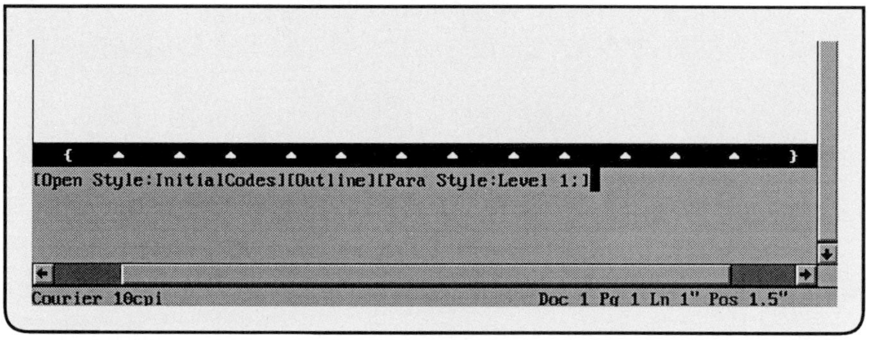

Remove the Reveal Codes from the screen. Now that the Outline feature is active, WordPerfect is ready to help you create an outline by inserting the numbers and letting you type the headings. After typing the information for the first heading, press ENTER to insert another first-level number. Pressing ENTER a second time will create a blank line. Press TAB to insert a second level. Press SHIFT+TAB to return to a higher level.

To enter the text for the first outline level:

Type	INTRODUCTION	**Type**	*INTRODUCTION*

To enter another first-level paragraph number:

Press	⏎Enter twice	**Press**	⏎Enter *twice*
Type	HARDWARE	**Type**	*HARDWARE*

The top part of your screen should look like Figure 25-6.

Figure 25-6

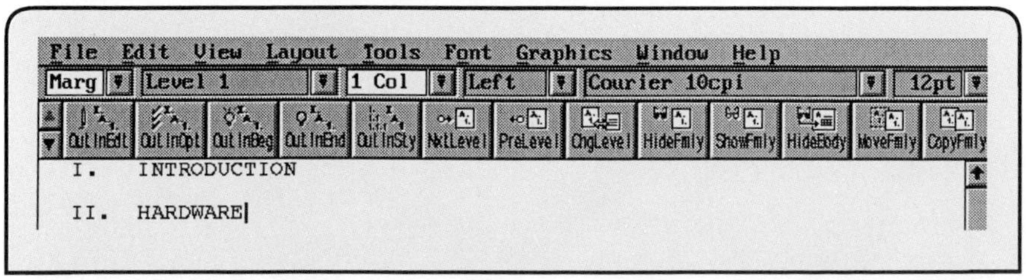

Pressing the TAB key or clicking the "NxtLevel" button on the Button Bar moves the number to the next tab stop and updates the number to the next level. If you want to move the number back a level, press SHIFT+TAB or click the "PreLevel" button on the Button Bar.

To insert a second-level paragraph number:

Press	`←Enter`		*Press*	`←Enter`
Press	`Tab↹`		*Click*	the NxtLevel button on the Button Bar 

The top part of your screen should look like Figure 25-7.

Figure 25-7

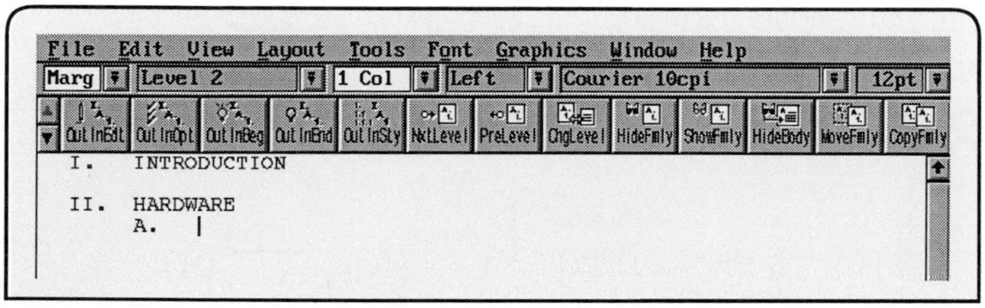

To enter the text for the second outline level:

Type	Keyboard		*Type*	Keyboard

The top part of your screen should look like Figure 25-8.

Figure 25-8

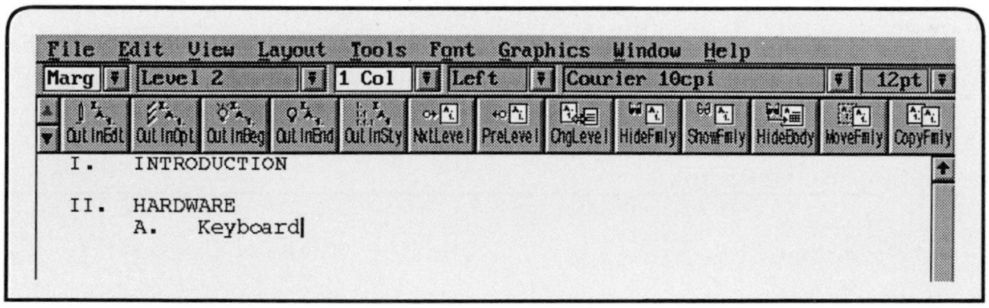

Press ENTER to add a paragraph at the same level. Use the TAB key and the SHIFT+TAB keys to change the level numbers.

To insert another second-level paragraph number:

Press	`←Enter`		*Press*	`←Enter`
Type	Monitor		*Type*	Monitor

To insert a third-level paragraph number:

Press	`←Enter`		*Press*	`←Enter`
Press	`Tab↹`		*Click*	the NxtLevel button on the Button Bar 
Type	Monochrome		*Type*	Monochrome

To insert a fourth-level paragraph number:

Press	[←Enter]		***Press***	[←Enter]
Press	[Tab↹]		***Click***	*the NxtLevel button on the Button Bar*
Type	No Graphics Capability		***Type***	*No Graphics Capability*
Press	[←Enter]		***Press***	[←Enter]
Type	MGA		***Type***	*MGA*
Press	[←Enter]		***Press***	[←Enter]
Type	MVGA		***Type***	*MVGA*
Press	[←Enter]		***Press***	[←Enter]

To return to the third level:

Press	[Shift]+[Tab↹]		***Click***	*the PreLevel button on the Button Bar*

Use TAB, and SHIFT+TAB or the "NxtLevel" and "PreLevel" button on the Button Bar to complete the remaining items in the outline shown in Figure 25-9. Remember that TAB advances one paragraph level (moves to the right) and that SHIFT+TAB reduces one paragraph level (moves to the left).

Figure 25-9

```
        2.  Color
            a. CGA
            b. EGA
            c. VGA
    C. CPU
        1.  8088 Processor
        2.  80286 Processor
        3.  80386 Processor
        4.  80486 Processor

III.  SOFTWARE
      A. Word Processing
      B. Spreadsheet
      C. Graphics
      D. Database

IV.   CONCLUSION
```

To turn off the Outline feature:

Press	[Ctrl]+[F5]		***Click***	*the OutlnEnd button on the Button Bar*
Press	5 or E to select the End Outline option			

Adding a Title to an Outline

Suppose you want to add the title "COMPUTER BOOK" to the top of the outline.

Press	Home, Home, Home, ↑ to place the cursor at the beginning of the document. Be sure the cursor is on the [Outline:Outline] code	***Click***	*at the beginning of the document. Be sure the cursor is on the [Outline:Outline] code*
Press	←Enter twice	***Press***	*←Enter twice*
Move	the cursor to the beginning of the document	***Click***	*at the beginning of the document*
Press	Shift + F6	***Choose***	*Layout*
Type	COMPUTER BOOK	***Choose***	*Alignment*
		Choose	*Center*
		Type	*COMPUTER BOOK*

Save the document using the name "BOOKOUT".

Your screen should look like Figure 25-10.

Figure 25-10

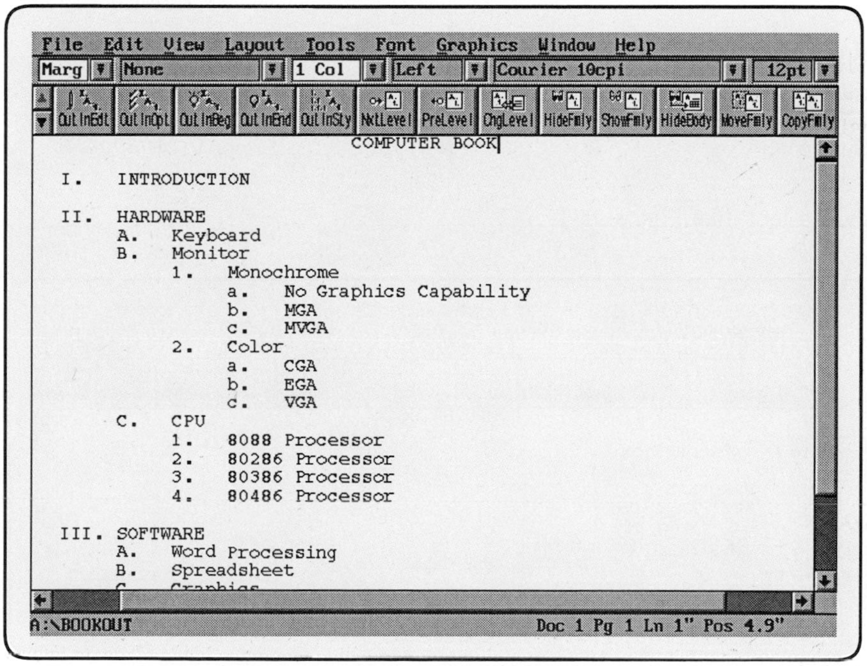

```
 File  Edit  View  Layout  Tools  Font  Graphics  Window  Help
Marg ▼ None                ▼ 1 Col ▼ Left   ▼ Courier 10cpi        ▼  12pt ▼
Out InEdt Out InOpt Out InBeg Out InEnd Out InSty NxtLevel PreLevel ChgLevel HideFmly ShowFmly HideBody MoveFmly CopyFmly
                              COMPUTER BOOK

    I.    INTRODUCTION

    II.   HARDWARE
          A.   Keyboard
          B.   Monitor
               1.   Monochrome
                    a.   No Graphics Capability
                    b.   MGA
                    c.   MVGA
               2.   Color
                    a.   CGA
                    b.   EGA
                    c.   VGA
          C.   CPU
               1.   8088 Processor
               2.   80286 Processor
               3.   80386 Processor
               4.   80486 Processor

    III. SOFTWARE
          A.   Word Processing
          B.   Spreadsheet
          C.   Graphics
A:\BOOKOUT                              Doc 1 Pg 1 Ln 1" Pos 4.9"
```

■ EDITING AN OUTLINE

WordPerfect defines a **family** in an outline as the paragraph number on the current line plus the paragraph numbers under that line. Any text included on these levels is also considered part of the family. Whenever you edit an outline, the paragraph numbers are automatically updated to reflect any changes you make.

To add more items in the Software family:

Move	the cursor to the end of the line "D. Database"		*Click*	*at the end of the line "D. Database"*
Press	⏎Enter		*Press*	*⏎Enter*
Type	Desktop Publishing		*Type*	*Desktop Publishing*

Suppose you want to add an item under "VGA" in the Color Monitor family.

Move	the cursor to the end of the line "c. VGA"		*Click*	*at the end of the line "c. VGA"*
Press	⏎Enter		*Press*	*⏎Enter*
Press	Tab⇄		*Click*	*the NxtLevel button on the Button Bar*
Type	Regular		*Type*	*Regular*
Press	⏎Enter		*Press*	*⏎Enter*
Type	Super-VGA		*Type*	*Super-VGA*

Your screen should look like Figure 25-11.

Figure 25-11

```
 File  Edit  View  Layout  Tools  Font  Graphics  Window  Help
 Marg ▼  Level 5        ▼  1 Col ▼  Left    ▼  Courier 10cpi        ▼    12pt ▼
 OutInEdt OutInOpt OutInBeg OutInEnd OutInSty NxtLevel PreLevel ChgLevel HideFmly ShowFmly HideBody MoveFmly CopyFmly
                          COMPUTER BOOK

     I.    INTRODUCTION

     II.   HARDWARE
           A.   Keyboard
           B.   Monitor
                1.   Monochrome
                     a.   No Graphics Capability
                     b.   MGA
                     c.   MVGA
                          (1)   Regular
                          (2)   Super-VGA
                2.   Color
                     a.   CGA
                     b.   EGA
                     c.   VGA
           C.   CPU
                1.   8088 Processor
                2.   80286 Processor
                3.   80386 Processor
                4.   80486 Processor

     III.  SOFTWARE
           A    Word Processing

 A:\BOOKOUT                              Doc 1 Pg 1 Ln 3" Pos 4.4"
```

Move, Copy, and Delete Family options are available in WordPerfect. These options make it very easy for you to move, copy, or delete complete outline families. With these "group" options, you can edit your outline. Suppose you want to copy the family associated with "SOFTWARE".

To copy the family:

Move	the cursor to any position in the heading called "III. SOFTWARE"		*Click*	*in the "III. SOFTWARE" heading*
Press	Ctrl + F5		*Click*	*the CopyFmly button on the Button Bar*  CopyFmly
Press	M to select the Move/Copy option			
Press	2 or C to select the Copy Family option			

The status line shows the message "Move cursor; press **Enter** to retrieve." The bottom of your screen should look similar to Figure 25-12.

Figure 25-12

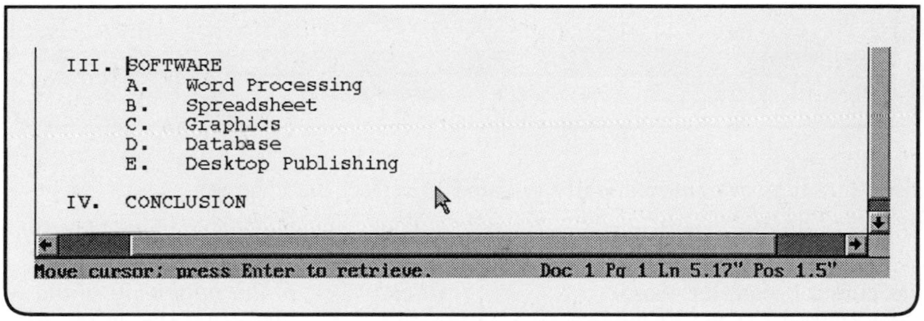

```
III.  SOFTWARE
      A.   Word Processing
      B.   Spreadsheet
      C.   Graphics
      D.   Database
      E.   Desktop Publishing

IV.   CONCLUSION

Move cursor; press Enter to retrieve.          Doc 1 Pg 1 Ln 5.17" Pos 1.5"
```

To place a copy of the Software family between the Introduction and the Hardware family:

Move	the cursor before the word "HARDWARE"		*Click*	*at the beginning of the word "HARDWARE"*
Press	↵Enter		*Click*	*the down triangle on the left side of the Button Bar*
			Click	*the PasteFam button on the Button Bar*  PasteFam

You cannot use the mouse to drag an outline family to a new location. You must use the pointer-movement keys.

Your screen should look like Figure 25-13.

Figure 25-13

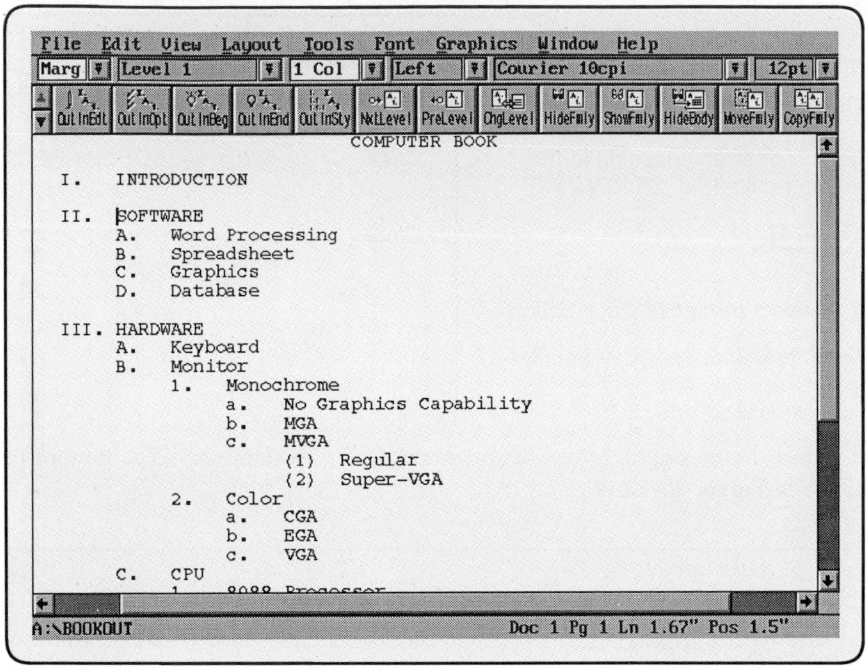

Notice the outline numbers are automatically updated to reflect the change.

The original Software family is still in the outline. To delete the original Software family:

Move	the cursor before the word "SOFTWARE" in the IV. heading	***Click***	*at the beginning of the word "SOFTWARE" in the IV. heading*
Press	Ctrl + F5	***Click***	*the Cut Fmly button on the Button Bar* 
Press	M to select the Move/Copy option		
Press	3 or T to select the Cut Family option		

Your screen should look like Figure 25-14.

Figure 25-14

```
 File  Edit  View  Layout  Tools  Font  Graphics  Window  Help
Marg ▼  Level 1        ▼ 1 Col  ▼ Left    ▼ Courier 10cpi         ▼ 12pt ▼
▲  ╎↗ᴸ   ╎↗ᴸ₊   ᵒᴸ₊   ᵒᴸ   ↗ᴸ₊   ↦ᴸ   ↤ᴸ   ↦₄ᴸ   ↦ᴸ   ₆₄ᴸ   ↦ᴸ   ↦ᴸ   ↦ᴸ
▼ OutInEdt OutInOpt OutInBeg OutInEnd OutInSty NxtLevel PreLevel ChgLevel HideFmly ShowFmly HideBody MoveFmly CopyFmly
              C.    Graphics                                              ↑
              D.    Database

        III. HARDWARE
              A.    Keyboard
              B.    Monitor
                    1.    Monochrome
                          a.    No Graphics Capability
                          b.    MGA
                          c.    MVGA
                                (1)   Regular
                                (2)   Super-VGA
                    2.    Color
                          a.    CGA
                          b.    EGA
                          c.    VGA
              C.    CPU
                    1.    8088 Processor
                    2.    80286 Processor
                    3.    80386 Processor
                    4.    80486 Processor

        IV.   CONCLUSION
                                                                         ▼
◄                                                                        ►
A:\BOOKOUT                            Doc 1 Pg 1 Ln 5.83" Pos 1.5"
```

After you edit an outline, family paragraph numbers automatically update.

Changing the Numbering Style

You might not want to use the automatic outline numbering scheme provided by WordPerfect. The Outline dialog box lets you change the numbers and other outline features according to your specifications.

To display the Outline dialog box:

Move	the cursor to the first line of the outline data	***Click***	*in the first line of the outline data*
Press	Ctrl + F5	***Click***	*the up triangle on the left side of the Button Bar*
		Click	*the OutlnOpt button on the Button Bar*

The Outline dialog box appears.

The current numbering style is displayed in the third option. By selecting the third option, you can see each of the seven styles and the corresponding numbering pattern. You may edit any of the predefined formats. You can also create your own outline format and save it. Consult the WordPerfect Reference manual for additional information about these topics.

To change the current definition to Legal:

Press	3 or O to select the Outline Style option	***Choose***	*the Outline Style option*
Press	↑ three times to select the Legal option	***Click***	*the Legal option*
Press	1 or S to choose the Select option	***Choose***	*the Select option*

Your screen should look like Figure 25-15.

Figure 25-15

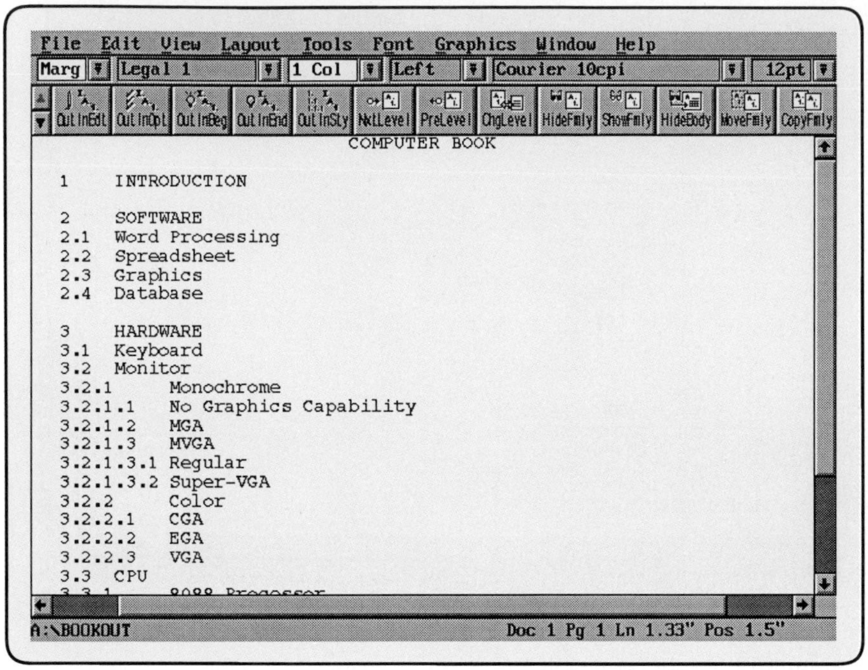

```
 File  Edit  View  Layout  Tools  Font  Graphics  Window  Help
Marg ▼ Legal 1        ▼  1 Col ▼  Left   ▼  Courier 10cpi         ▼  12pt ▼
▲  ↓↑,   ↕↑,   ↔↑,   ↔↑,   ↕↑,   ↔⤢  ⤢↔  ⤢↔  ⤢↔  ᵇᵈ↔  ⤢↔  ↔↔  ↔↔
▼ Out InEdt Out InOpt Out InBeg Out InEnd Out InSty NxtLevel PreLevel ChgLevel HideFmly ShowFmly HideBody MoveFmly CopyFmly
                              COMPUTER BOOK                              ↕

        1      INTRODUCTION

        2      SOFTWARE
        2.1    Word Processing
        2.2    Spreadsheet
        2.3    Graphics
        2.4    Database

        3      HARDWARE
        3.1    Keyboard
        3.2    Monitor
        3.2.1      Monochrome
        3.2.1.1    No Graphics Capability
        3.2.1.2    MGA
        3.2.1.3    MVGA
        3.2.1.3.1 Regular
        3.2.1.3.2 Super-VGA
        3.2.2      Color
        3.2.2.1    CGA
        3.2.2.2    EGA
        3.2.2.3    VGA
        3.3    CPU
        3.3.1      8088 Processor
A:\BOOKOUT                          Doc 1 Pg 1 Ln 1.33" Pos 1.5"
```

Save the document as "BOOKOUT2".

Change the numbering style back to Outline.

■ HIDING AND SHOWING FAMILIES

You may want to create a very detailed outline for yourself but need only the topic headings for some other person. It is possible to "hide" lower levels of an outline for viewing or printing purposes.

To hide the subheadings under "Software":

Move the cursor to the line containing "II. Software"

Press ⌨Ctrl + F5

Press 9 or H to select the Hide/Show option

Press 1 or ⌨- to select the Hide Family option

Click in the line containing "II. Software"

Click the HideFmly button on the Button Bar

The A. through D. subsections of the "Software" division should be gone. The extra hard return is also hidden. Your screen should look like Figure 25-16.

Figure 25-16

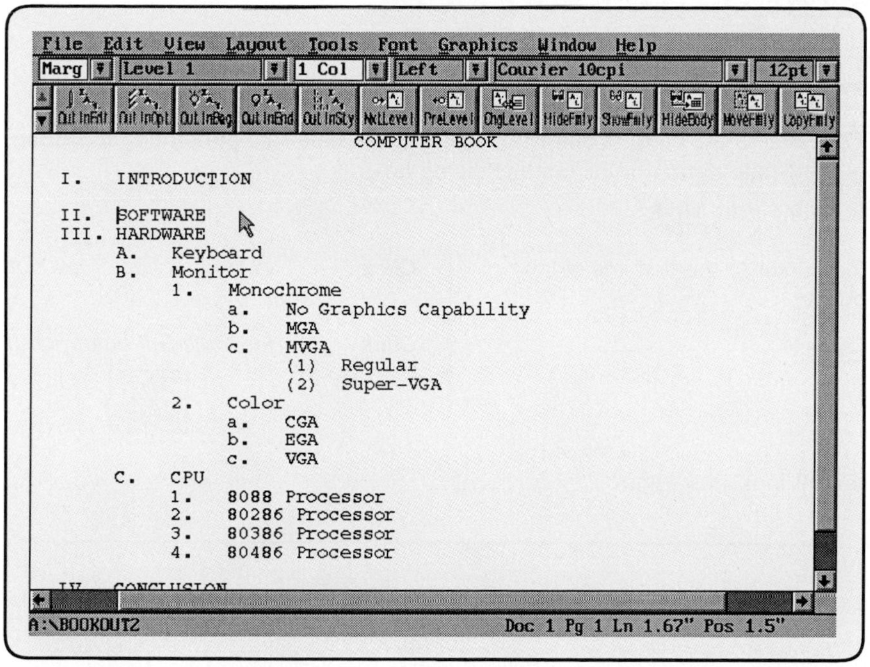

To display the A. through D. subsections:

Press	Ctrl + F5		
		Click	*the ShowFmly button on the Button Bar*
Press	9 or H to select the Hide/Show option		
Press	2 or + to select the Show Family option		

If you choose to add extra hard returns after completing an outline, you should press CTRL+A, then press ENTER. In doing so, an extra space appears without displaying another outline level.

To place an extra space between "II. SOFTWARE" and "A. Word Processing":

Move	the cursor to the end of the line containing "SOFTWARE"	**Click**	*at the end of the line containing "SOFTWARE"*
Press	Ctrl +A	**Press**	*Ctrl +A*

The Compose dialog box appears.

Press	←Enter	**Press**	*←Enter*

A blank line should appear between "II. SOFTWARE" and "A. Word Processing".

■ USING THE OUTLINE EDIT MODE

The Outline feature includes something called the "Edit Mode". When Outline Edit Mode is turned on, you can use many keystrokes to easily edit outline families. In addition, an Outline Bar appears near the top of the screen. It can be used with a mouse and performs the same actions as the keystrokes. You may press CTRL+O to access the Outline Edit Mode, click the "OutlnEdt" button on the Button Bar, or select the Edit in Outline Mode option in the Outline dialog box.

To access the Outline Edit Mode:

Move	the cursor to the first line of the outline		*Click*	*in the first line of the outline*
Press	Ctrl +O		*Click*	*the OutlnEdt button on the Button Bar* 

Your screen should look like Figure 25-17.

Figure 25-17

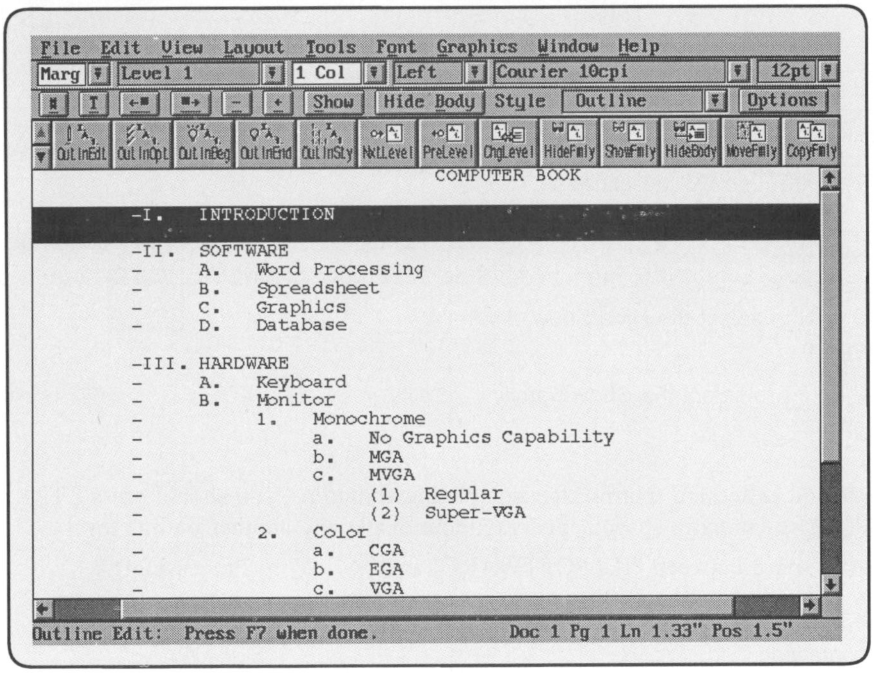

The table below lists the Edit Mode keystrokes and their purpose.

Keystroke	**Purpose**
↑, ↓, →, or ←	Highlights an entire outline family.
→	Shows any hidden items in the current level.
PAGE UP or Alt +↑ and PAGE DOWN or Alt +↓	Highlights the next family in the desired direction.

Keystroke	Purpose
[Ctrl]+[→] or [Tab↹] and [Ctrl]+[←] or [Shift]+[Tab↹]	Changes all items in a highlighted family to the next or previous numbering level.
[Ctrl]+[↑] or [Ctrl]+[↓]	Moves a highlighted family up or down.
[Ctrl]+[Delete], [↵Enter]	Cuts a highlighted family from the outline. When the cursor is moved to a new location, pressing ENTER makes the section reappear.
[Ctrl]+[Insert], [↵Enter]	Copies a highlighted family. When the cursor is moved to a new location, pressing ENTER makes the section reappear.
[Delete], [Backspace], or [Ctrl]+X	Removes a highlighted family from the outline.
[Ctrl]+C	Copies a highlighted family.
[Insert], or [Ctrl]+V	Pastes a cut or copied outline family.

The Outline Bar has many of the same features as the Outline Button Bar and is described below.

Button	Purpose
#	Changes normal text to an outline item.
T	Changes the current outline item to normal text.
←■	Changes all items in the current family to the previous level.
■→	Changes all items in the current family to the next level.
—	Hides the current outline family.
+	Makes a hidden outline family reappear.
Show	Shows all levels of an outline.
Hide Body/Show Body	Hides or shows normal text between outline items.
Style	Changes the numbering style of the outline.
Options	Opens the Outline dialog box permitting moving or copying portions of the outline.

To exit the Outline Edit Mode:

Press   F7 | *Press*   F7

Close the document without saving changes.
Return to the default Button Bar.

EXERCISE 1

INSTRUCTIONS: Define the following concepts:

1.   Outline _____

_____

2.   Outline Style _____

_____

3.   Family _____

_____

4.   Move Family_____

_____

5.   Copy Family_____

_____

6.   Cut Family _____

_____

7.   Hide Family _____

_____

8.   Show Family _____

_____

9.   Edit Mode _____

_____

EXERCISE 2

INSTRUCTIONS: Circle T if the statement is true and F if the statement is false.

T   F   1.   An outline is a way of organizing the ideas and information that you want to present in a long document or report.

T   F   2.   Outlines are made up of paragraph numbers.

T   F   3.   You can have up to nine levels of outline numbers within a document.

T   F   4.   Press TAB to advance one paragraph level.

T   F   5.   Press ENTER to advance one number in the same paragraph level.

T   F   6.   If you want to move the paragraph number back a level, press SHIFT+TAB.

T   F   7.   An outline family is the paragraph number on the current line plus the paragraph numbers under that line or level.

T   F   8.   There are Move, Copy, Delete, and Add Family options available in WordPerfect.

T   F   9.   In the Outline dialog box, you can choose between the Paragraph, Outline, Legal, Letter, and Bullets numbering styles or you can make your own style.

T   F   10.   The Edit Mode permits quick keystrokes for moving and copying outline families.

EXERCISE 3

INSTRUCTIONS: 1.   Create the following outline using the Outline feature.

```
            A MARKETING STUDY OF CONSUMER SHOPPING

I.      Introduction
II.     Types of Stores
        A.      The Mall
                1.Suburban
                2.Inner City
        B.      The Strip Center
        C.      The Boutique
                1.Mom-and-Pop Stores
                2.The Eclectic Boutique
        D.      The Gourmet Store
III.    Shopper Personalities
        A.      The Sale Hunter
        B.      The Gourmet
        C.      The Browser
        D.      The Catalog Shopper
IV.     Conclusion
```

2.   Save the document in a file using the name "CH25EX03.OT1".

3.   Print the document.

4.   Add the following information after Section III.

```
IV.     Shopping Seasons
        A.      Valentine's Day
        B.      Easter
        C.      Mother's Day
        D.      Father's Day
        E.      Fall
        F.      Christmas
```

5.   Print the document.
6.   Change the outline style to Paragraph.
7.   Print the document.
8.   Change the outline style to Bullets.
9.   Print the document.
10. Move the "**Shopper Personalities**" family immediately after the "**Introduction**" family.
11. Print the document.
12. Save the document in a file using the name "CH25EX03.OT2".
13. Close the document.

EXERCISE 4

INSTRUCTIONS: 1.   Create the following outline using the Outline feature.
2.   Preview the document.
3.   Print the document.
4.   Save the document in a file using the name "CH25EX04".
5.   Close the document.

```
          SELECTED TOPICS OUTLINE FOR WORD PROCESSING


I.     TYPING LETTERS
       A.    Personal Letters
       B.    Business Letters
             1.    Modified block style
             2.    Block style

II.    TYPING BUSINESS CORRESPONDENCE
       A.    Memorandums
       B.    Letters on Executive-size Paper
       C.    Reports
       D.    Tables

III.   STATISTICAL COMMUNICATIONS
       A.    Business Forms
       B.    Statistical Reports
       C.    Administrative Forms
```

EXERCISE 5

INSTRUCTIONS: 1.   Create the following outline using the Outline feature.
2.   Preview the document.
3.   Print the document.
4.   Save the document in a file using the name "CH25EX05".
5.   Close the document.

```
                        OUTLINE STRUCTURE


I.    PRIMARY HEADINGS IN ALL CAPITAL LETTERS
      A.    Identify Major Divisions of an Outline
            1.    Primary headings by Roman numerals
            2.    Secondary headings by capital letters
                  a.    Subdivisions by
                  b.    Arabic numerals or
                  c.    Small letters or
                  d.    Parentheses surrounding Arabic numerals or
                  e.    Parentheses surrounding small letters or
                  f.    Right parentheses next to Arabic numerals or
                  g.    Right parentheses next to small letters
      B.    Spacing the Outline
            1.    Double-space before the main headings
            2.    Single-space between subdivisions

II.   THE SENTENCE STRUCTURE
      A.    Identify Divisions as Topics
      B.    Punctuating and Spacing the Outline
            1.    Punctuate complete sentences as in normal writing
            2.    Use regular sentence spacing
```

EXERCISE 6

INSTRUCTIONS: 1.   Create the following outline using the Outline feature.
2.   Preview the document.
3.   Print the document.
4.   Save the document in a file using the name "CH25EX06".
5.   Close the document.

LEFT - BOUND MANUSCRIPTS

I. MARGINS AND SPACING
   A. Margins
      1. Left Margin 1½"
      2. Top, bottom, and right margins 1"
      3. Top, first page: 12 pitch 2"; 10 pitch 1½"
      4. Additional pages: 1"
   B. Spacing
      1. General Style: double spacing, 5-space paragraph indentions
      2. Business Style: single spacing with blocked paragraphs
      3. Always leave 2 lines of a paragraph at the top and bottom of each page
      4. Quoted material: single-space quotes of four or more lines; indent from left margins all lines of quote

II. PAGE NUMBERING
    A. First Page: Optional, but if used, centered at bottom of the page
    B. Other Pages: Typed even at the right top margin

EXERCISE 7

INSTRUCTIONS:

1. Open the document "CH25EX06".
2. Under Division I, move the "**Spacing**" family before the "**Margins**" family.
3. Change the text for Division I to "**SPACING AND MARGINS**".
4. Change the numbering style to Bullets.
5. Preview the document.
6. Print the document.
7. Save the document in a file using the name "CH25EX07".
8. Close the document.

EXERCISE 8

INSTRUCTIONS:
1. Create the following outline using the Outline feature.
2. Preview the document.
3. Print the document.
4. Save the document in a file using the name "CH25EX08".
5. Close the document.

```
                              AUSTRALIA

I.    PEOPLE
      A.    Age distribution
            1.    Age 0-14 approx. 22%
            2.    Age 15-59 approx. 62%
            3.    Age 59+ approx. 15%
      B.    Ethnic groups
            1.    Europeans 93%
            2.    Asians 5%
            3.    Aborigines 1.5%
      C.    Languages
            1.    English
            2.    Aboriginal
      D.    Religions
            1.    Anglican 26%
            2.    Protestant 25%
            3.    Roman Catholic 25%

II.   GEOGRAPHY
      A.    Area
            1.    2,966,200 sq. mi.
            2.    Almost as large as continental U.S.
      B.    Location:  SE of Asia
      C.    Neighbors
            1.    North
                  a.    Indonesia
                  b.    Papua, New Guinea
            2.    East
                  a.    Solomons
                  b.    Fiji
                  c.    New Zealand

III.  GOVERNMENT TYPE
      A.    Democratic federal state system
            1.    Head of State:  Queen Elizabeth
            2.    Head of Government:  Prim Min. Robert Lee Hawke
            3.    Local Division
                  a.    6 states
                  b.    2 territories
```

EXERCISE 9

INSTRUCTIONS:

1.   Open the document "CH25EX08".
2.   Copy the entire document to a new document. Make the following changes to Document 2.
3.   Delete the "**Neighbors**" family.
4.   Add the following family under Division III, subdivision 3a, "**6 states**":
     (1) New South Wales
     (2) Victoria
     (3) Queensland
     (4) South Australia
     (5) West Australia
     (6) Tasmania
5.   Add the following family under Division III, subdivision 3b, "**2 territories**":
     (1) Australian Capital Territory
     (2) Northern Territory
6.   Preview the document.
7.   Print the document.
8.   Save the document in a file using the name "CH25EX09". Close the document.
9.   Close the "CH25EX08" document without saving any changes.

EXERCISE 10

INSTRUCTIONS:

1.   Open the document "CH25EX09".
2.   Move the "**Geography**" family before the "**People**" family.
3.   Delete the "**Religions**" family.
4.   Change the numbering style to Paragraph.
5.   Preview the document.
6.   Print the document.
7.   Save the document in a file using the name "CH25EX10".
8.   Close the document.

CHAPTER TWENTY-SIX

FOOTNOTES AND ENDNOTES

OBJECTIVES

In this chapter, you will learn to:
- Create footnotes
- Create endnotes

■ CHAPTER OVERVIEW

Footnotes and endnotes are a method of documenting sources of quotations, facts, and ideas in a report. A **footnote** appears at the bottom of the page that contains its reference. **Endnotes** appear at the end of the document.

In this chapter, the procedures for creating and editing footnotes and endnotes are described.

■ FOOTNOTES

The Footnote feature is used by pressing CTRL+F7 or choosing the Footnote option from the Layout menu. As you create, edit, add, or delete a footnote, WordPerfect manages the numbering of the footnote and the format of the page so the footnote will fit.

Create the document shown in Figure 26-1.

Figure 26-1

CHAPTERS ADD ASSISTANTS

Southwest Chapter
   Susan Jones began duties as executive secretary of the Southwest Chapter on June 1. She has over 14 years experience in bookkeeping and secretarial services. For the past five years, Jones has conducted a home bookkeeping service.
   In her eight-month tenure with the chapter, Jones has concentrated her efforts in the area of CPE and dues billings. She says she is working on transferring the chapter records to a computer.
Southeast Chapter
   Doris Brown became the Southeast Texas executive secretary on November 10. Owner of Brown Business Services, a marketing-management company, Brown brings to the chapter position a wide range of business and community experience.
   Brown also has been associated for more than 15 years with the Greater Orange Area Chamber of Commerce. She has served on the Chamber Board of Directors Committee, the Executive Committee, the Civic Affairs Division, and the Convention Visitors Bureau.

Format the document in the following manner:

Set	the left and right margins to 2"	*Set*	*the left and right margins to 2"*
Set	the line spacing to double	*Set*	*the line spacing to double*

Save the document using the name "footnote".

Creating a Footnote

To view the Notes dialog box:

Move	the cursor after the word "Jones" on the first line of the first paragraph	*Click*	*after the word "Jones" on the first line of the first paragraph*
Press	Ctrl + F7	*Choose*	*Layout*
		Choose	*Footnote*

If you are using the keyboard method, the Notes dialog box appears, and your screen should look like Figure 26-2. If you are using the mouse method, the Footnote menu appears.

Figure 26-2

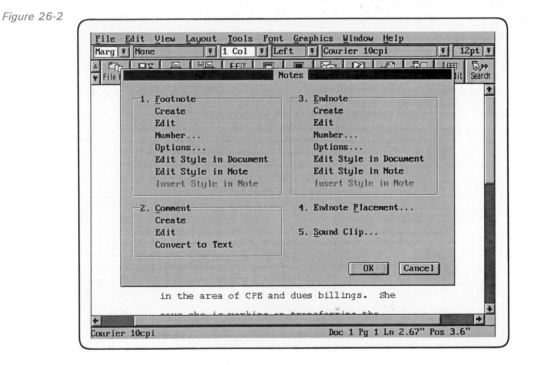

To begin a footnote:

Press	1 or F to select the Footnote option box	*Choose*	*Create*
Press	1 or C to select the Create option		

You are placed in the Footnote screen, and the top part of your screen should look like Figure 26-3.

Figure 26-3

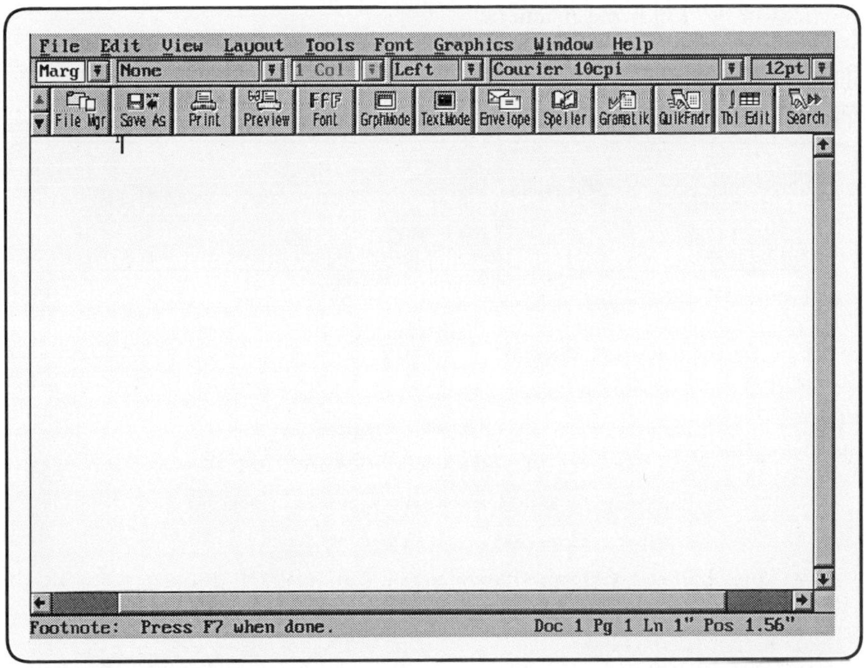

Notice the word "Footnote" appears in the status bar.

A footnote number is already provided for you. All you need to do is type the text of the footnote.

Type	Southwest Chapter, Main Office, (806) 498-5833	***Type***	*Southwest Chapter, Main Office, (806) 498-5833*
Press	F7 to exit the Footnote screen	***Choose***	*File*
		Choose	*Exit*

The top part of your screen should look like Figure 26-4.

Figure 26-4

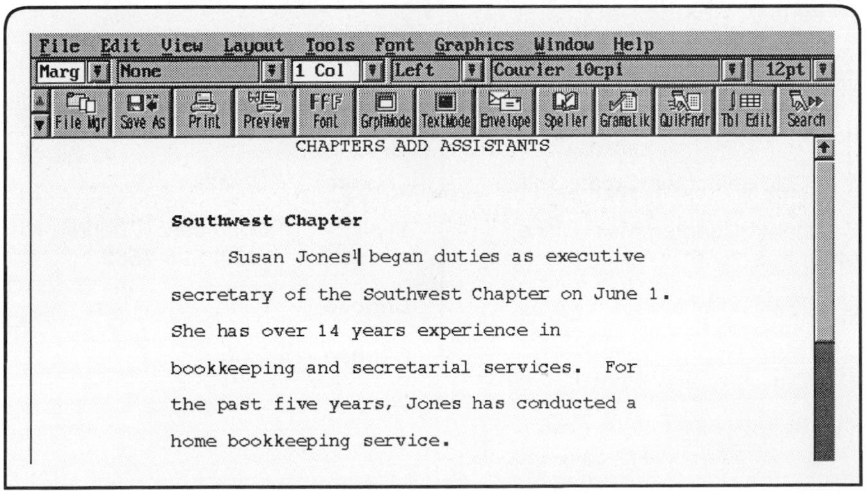

The Footnote code is represented by a number 1 on the screen.

Turn on the Reveal Codes feature, and place the cursor on the [Footnote] code.

Your screen should look like Figure 26-5.

Figure 26-5

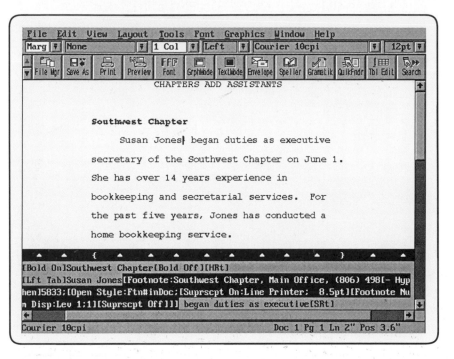

A Footnote code is placed in the document. The first part of the footnote text is shown. This makes finding a particular footnote easier for you.

Turn off the Reveal Codes feature.

To create another footnote:

Move	the cursor after the word "Brown" on the first line of the third paragraph		*Click*	*after the word "Brown" on the first line of the third paragraph*
Press	Ctrl + F7		*Choose*	*Layout*
Press	1 or F to select the Footnote option box		*Choose*	*Footnote*
Press	1 or C to select the Create option		*Choose*	*Create*
Type	Southeast Chapter, Main Office, (409) 898-1569		*Type*	*Southeast Chapter, Main Office, (409) 898-1569*
Press	F7		*Choose*	*File*
			Choose	*Exit*

Your screen should look like Figure 26-6.

Figure 26-6

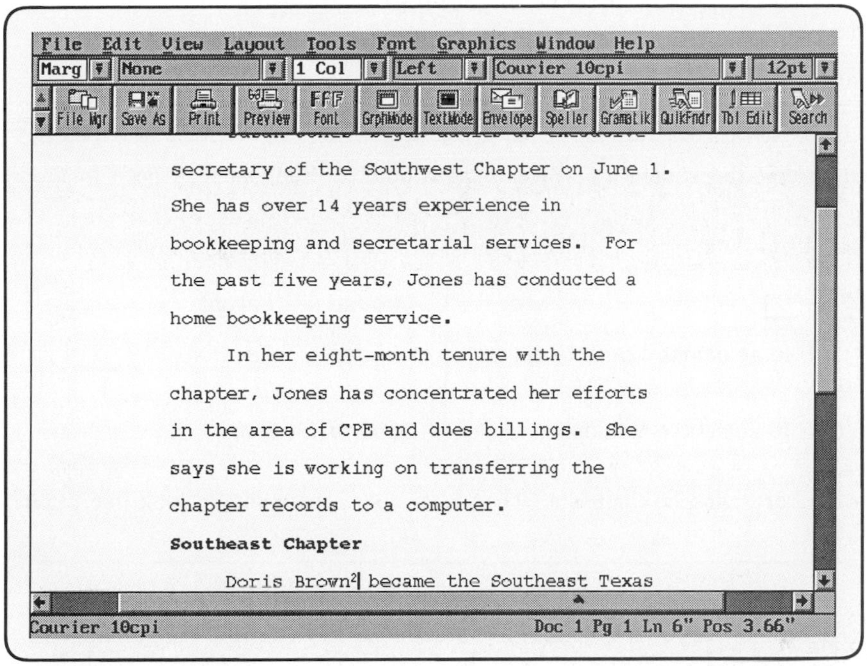

The Footnote code is represented by a number 2 on the screen.

Preview the document in Full Page Mode. Your screen should look like Figure 26-7.

Figure 26-7

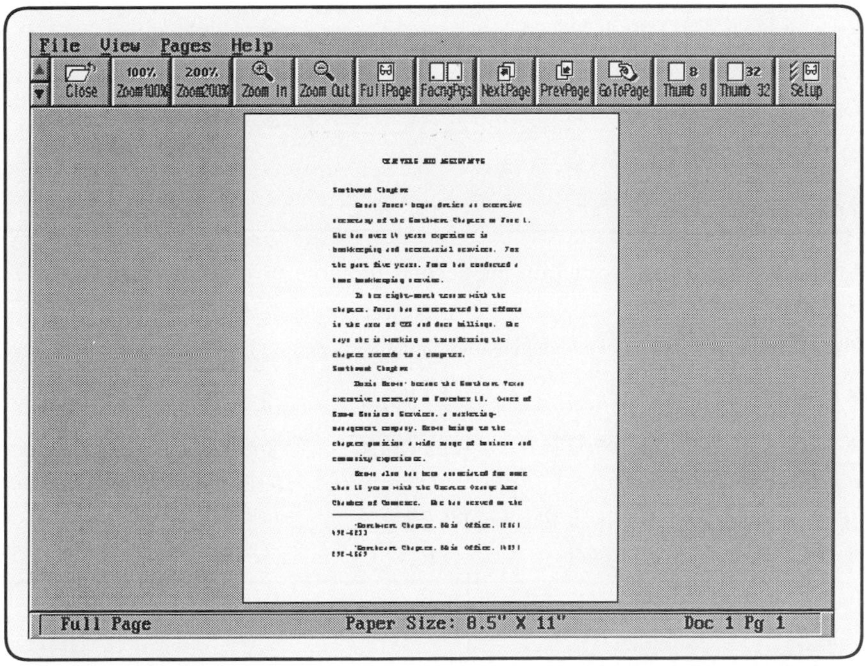

Notice that the footnotes appear at the bottom of the page. Text that did not fit on the first page has been moved to the second page to make room for the footnotes.

Return to your document.

Editing a Footnote

You may need to edit the contents of an existing footnote. Suppose you need to modify the second footnote.

To edit the second footnote:

Press	Ctrl + F7		***Choose***	*Layout*
Press	1 or F to select the Footnote option box		***Choose***	*Footnote*
Press	2 or E to select the Edit option		***Choose***	*Edit*

The Footnote Number dialog box appears. The top of your screen should look like Figure 26-8.

Figure 26-8

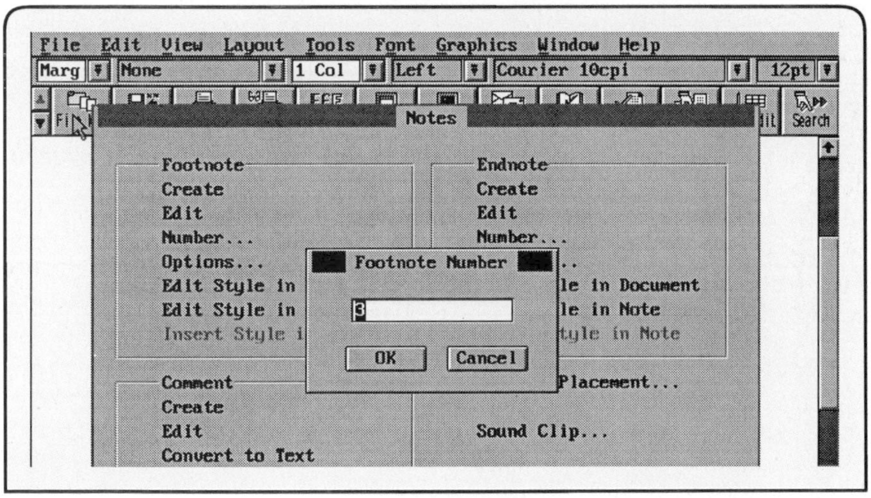

Your cursor does not have to be located on the second footnote in order to modify it. You open each footnote by its number.

To edit footnote 2:

Type	2		***Type***	*2*
Press	↵Enter		***Click***	*the OK command button*

The top part of your screen should look like Figure 26-9.

Figure 26-9

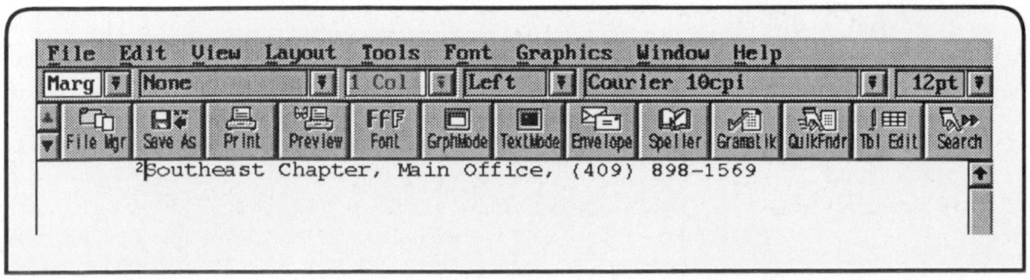

To change the last digit in the phone number from "9" to "8":

Move	the cursor before the last 9		*Click*	*before the last 9*
Press	Delete		*Press*	*Delete*
Type	8		*Type*	*8*
Press	F7		*Choose*	*File*
			Choose	*Exit*

Changing the Footnote Format

You can change the way WordPerfect numbers the footnotes and formats them on the page. This is done by selecting Options under the Footnote option from the Layout menu. A Footnote Option code (its appearance will vary depending on the option you are changing) is placed in your document. The option changes are in effect from the location of the code until the end of the document. Place the code at the beginning of the document if you want all footnotes to reflect your option changes. You can also place your Footnote Option code in a document style.

Suppose you want to have the line separating the text on a page from the footnote to extend from margin to margin (rather than a half-line as shown in Figure 26-7).

To change the Footnote options:

Move	the cursor to the beginning of the document		*Click*	*at the beginning of the document*
Press	Ctrl + F7		*Choose*	*Layout*
Press	1 or F to select the Footnote option box		*Choose*	*Footnote*
Press	4 or O to select the Options option		*Choose*	*Options*

The Footnote Options dialog box appears. Your screen should look like Figure 26-10.

Figure 26-10

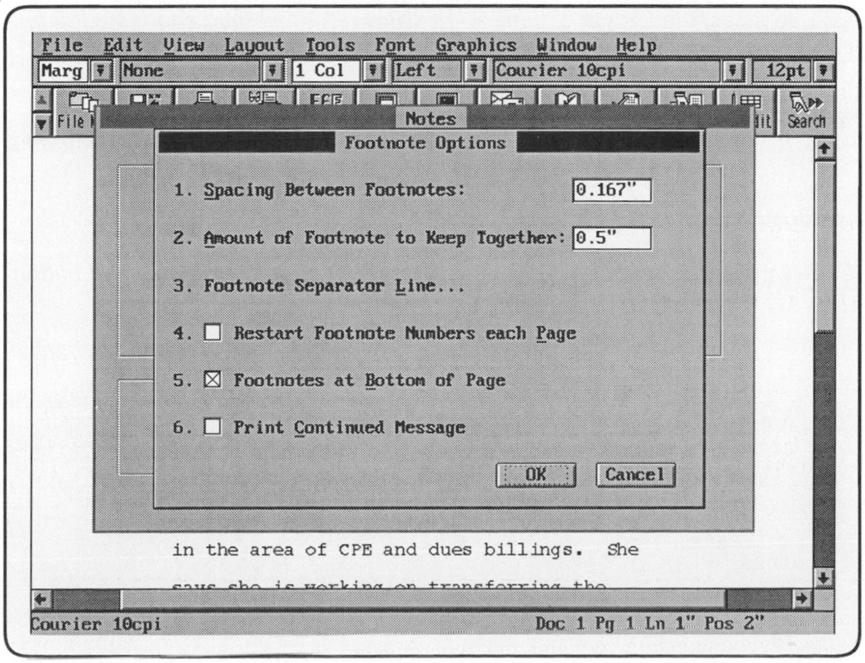

For detailed information regarding each of these options, see "Footnotes and Endnotes" in the WordPerfect Reference manual.

To change the footnote separator line:

| **Press** | 3 or L to select the Footnote Separator Line option | **Choose** | *the Footnote Separator Line option* |

The Footnote Separator Line dialog box appears. Your screen should look like Figure 26-11.

Figure 26-11

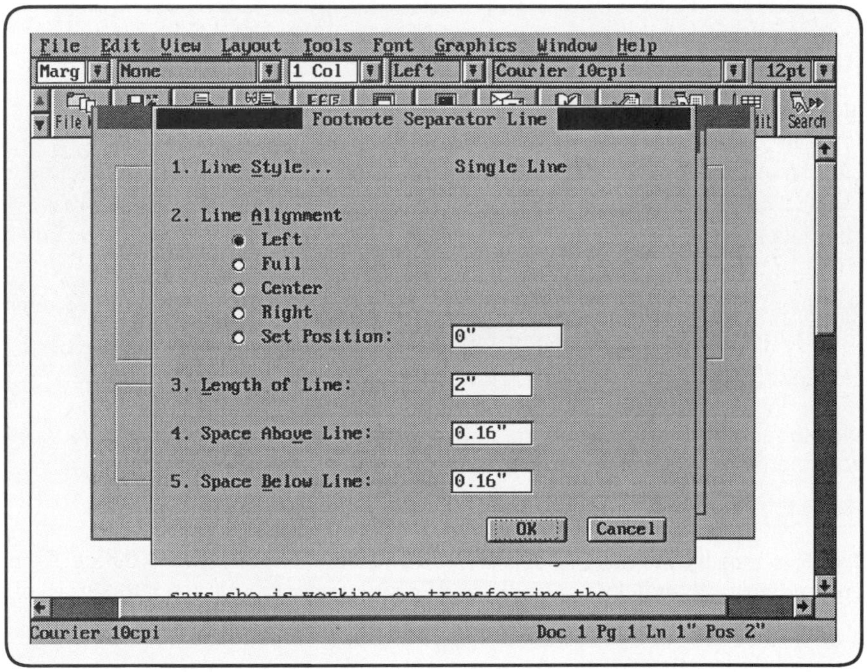

To have a line print from margin to margin:

Press	3 or L to select the Length of Line text box	**Click**	*in the Length of Line text box*
Type	6.5	**Type**	*6.5*
Press	⏎Enter	**Click**	*the OK command button*

To return to your document:

| **Press** | ⏎Enter three times | **Click** | *the OK command button* |

Preview the document. Notice that a line appears from margin to margin. Your screen should look like Figure 26-12.

Figure 26-12

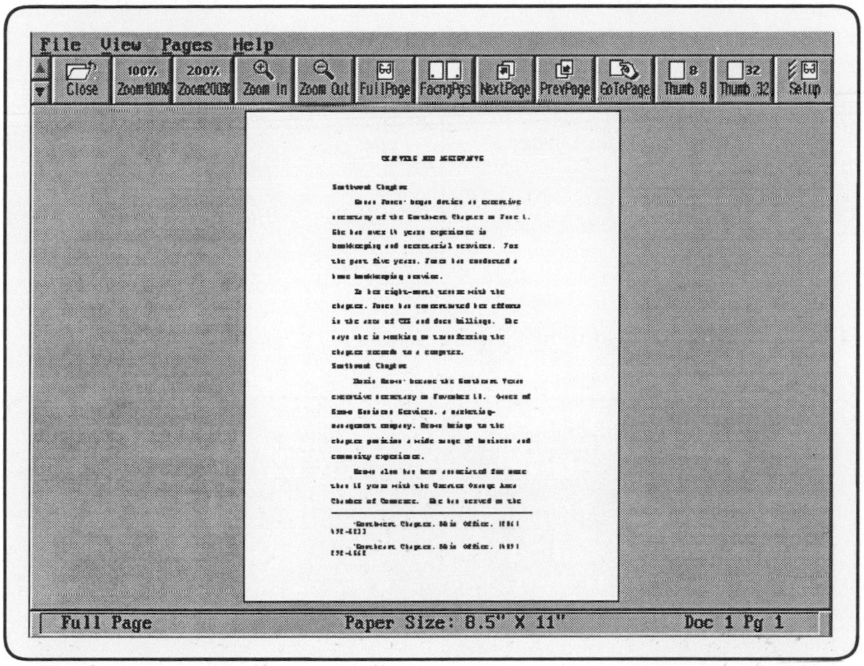

Return to your document. Save the document as "footnte2". Close the document.

■ ENDNOTES

The Endnote feature is used by pressing CTRL+F7 or by choosing the Endnote option from the Layout menu. As you create, edit, add, or delete an endnote, WordPerfect manages the numbering of the endnote and places it at the end of the document.

Open the "FOOTNOTE" document.

To create an endnote:

Move	the cursor after the word "Jones" on the first line of the first paragraph	***Click***	*after the word "Jones" on the first line of the first paragraph*
Press	⌨Ctrl + F7	***Choose***	*Layout*
Press	3 or E to select the Endnote option box	***Choose***	*Endnote*
Press	1 or C to select the Create option	***Choose***	*Create*

The top part of your screen should look like Figure 26-13.

Figure 26-13

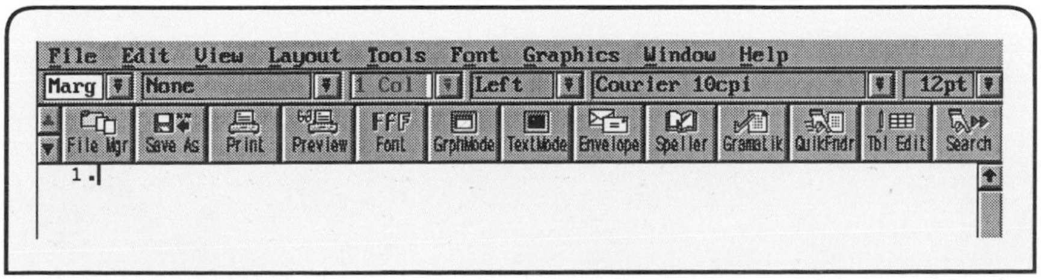

You are placed in the Endnote screen. The word "Endnote" appears in the status bar.

An endnote number is already provided for you. All you need to do is type the text of the endnote.

Press	the ⌨Spacebar⌨ twice		***Press***	*the* ⌨Spacebar⌨ *twice*
Type	Southwest Chapter, Main Office, (806) 498-5833		***Type***	*Southwest Chapter, Main Office, (806) 498-5833*
Press	⌨F7⌨		***Choose***	*File*
			Choose	*Exit*

The top part of your screen should look like Figure 26-14.

Figure 26-14

The Endnote code is represented by a number 1 on the screen.

Turn on the Reveal Codes feature, and place the cursor on the [Endnote] code.

The bottom part of your screen should look like Figure 26-15.

Figure 26-15

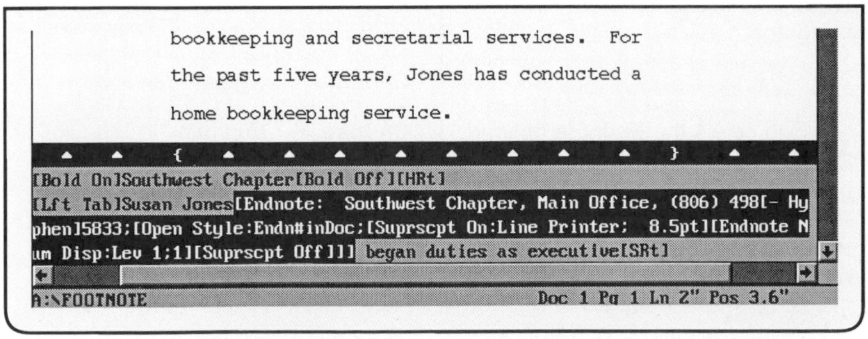

An Endnote code is placed in the document. The first part of the endnote text is shown. This makes finding a particular endnote easier for you.

Turn off the Reveal Codes feature.

To create another endnote:

Move	the cursor after the word "Brown" on the first line of the third paragraph	*Click*	*after the word "Brown" on the first line of the third paragraph*
Press	Ctrl + F7	*Choose*	*Layout*
Press	3 or E to select the Endnote option box	*Choose*	*Endnote*
Press	1 or C to select the Create option	*Choose*	*Create*
Press	the Spacebar twice	*Press*	*the Spacebar twice*
Type	Southeast Chapter, Main Office, (409) 898-1569	*Type*	*Southeast Chapter, Main Office, (409) 898-1569*
Press	F7	*Choose*	*File*
		Choose	*Exit*

The bottom part of your screen should look like Figure 26-16.

Figure 26-16

In her eight-month tenure with the chapter, Jones has concentrated her efforts in the area of CPE and dues billings. She says she is working on transferring the chapter records to a computer.
Southeast Chapter
Doris Brown[2] became the Southeast Texas

A:\FOOTNOTE   Doc 1 Pg 1 Ln 6" Pos 3.66"

The Endnote code is represented by a number 2 on the screen.

You can place a Hard Page code at the end of your document to force the endnotes to begin on a separate page.

To place the endnotes on a separate page:

Move	the cursor to the end of the document	*Click*	*at the end of the document*
Insert	a page break	*Insert*	*a page break*

Preview page 2 of the document in 100% Zoom. Your screen should look like Figure 26-17.

Figure 26-17

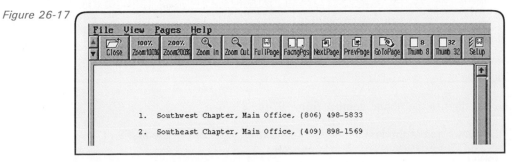

File View Pages Help

Close Zoom100% Zoom200% Zoom In Zoom Out FullPage FacngPgs NextPage PrevPage GoToPage Thumb 8 Thumb 32 Setup

    1. Southwest Chapter, Main Office, (806) 498-5833

    2. Southeast Chapter, Main Office, (409) 898-1569

Notice that the endnotes appear on a separate page. Return to your document.

Editing an Endnote

You may need to edit the contents of an existing endnote. Suppose you need to modify the second endnote.
To edit the second endnote:

Press	Ctrl + F7		***Choose***	*Layout*
Press	3 or E to select the Endnote option box		***Choose***	*Endnote*
Press	2 or E to select the Edit option		***Choose***	*Edit*

The Endnote Number dialog box appears. Your screen should look similar to Figure 26-18.

Figure 26-18

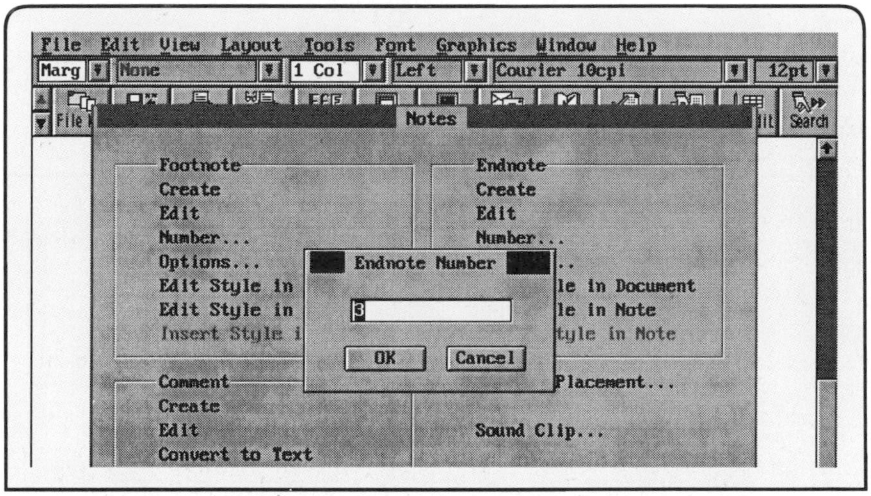

Your cursor does not have to be located on the second endnote in order to modify it. You open each endnote by its number.

To edit endnote 2:

Type	2		***Type***	*2*
Press	←Enter		***Click***	*the OK command button*

The top part of your screen should look like Figure 26-19.

Figure 26-19

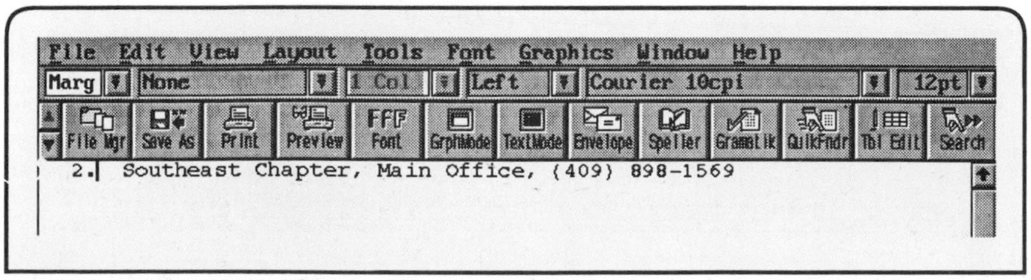

To change the last digit in the phone number from "9" to "8":

Move	the cursor before the last 9		***Click***	*before the last 9*
Press	Delete		***Press***	*Delete*

Type	8		*Type*	*8*
Press	F7		*Choose*	*File*
			Choose	*Exit*

Changing the Endnote Format

You can change the way WordPerfect numbers the endnotes. This is done by pressing CTRL+F7 and choosing Number, or by choosing Number under the Endnote option from the Layout menu. An Endnote Number Method code [Endnote Num Meth] is placed in your document. The number changes are in effect from the location of the code until the end of the document. Place the code at the beginning of the document if you want all endnotes to reflect your changes. You could also place your Endnote Option code in a document style.

Suppose you want to change the numbers (1, 2, etc.) for the endnotes to letters (a, b, etc.).

To change the endnote numbers:

Move	the cursor to the beginning of the document		*Click*	*at the beginning of the document*
Press	Ctrl + F7		*Choose*	*Layout*
Press	3 or E to select the Endnote option box		*Choose*	*Endnote*
Press	3 or N to select the Number option		*Choose*	*New Number*

The Set Endnote Number dialog box appears. Your screen should look like Figure 26-20.

Figure 26-20

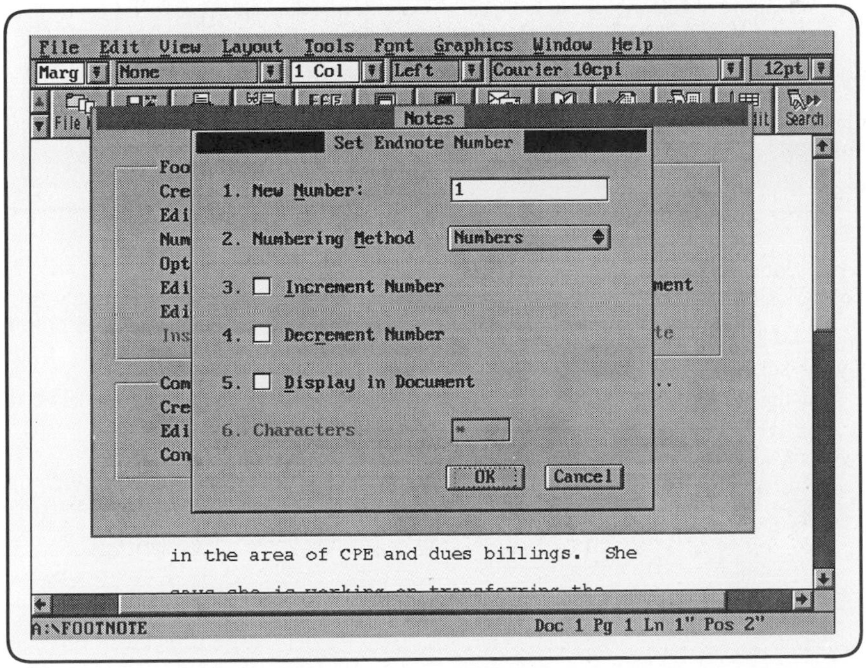

For detailed information regarding each of these options, see "Footnotes and Endnotes" in the WordPerfect Reference manual.

To change the Numbering Method option:

Press	2 or M to select the Numbering Method pop-up list button	*Click*	*the Numbering Method pop-up list button*
		Hold down	*the mouse button to view the pop-up list*

To select letters:

Press	E to select Lower Letters	*Choose*	*Lower Letters*

Your screen should look like Figure 26-21.

Figure 26-21

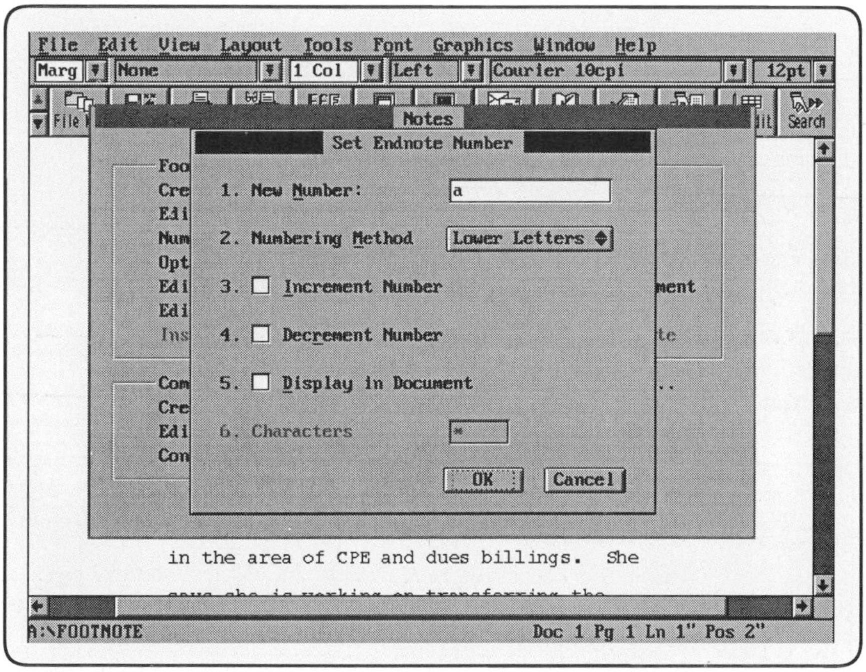

To return to your document:

Press	⏎Enter twice	*Click*	*the OK command button*

Preview page 2 of the document. Notice that a letter appears next to each endnote. The top part of your screen should look like Figure 26-22.

Figure 26-22

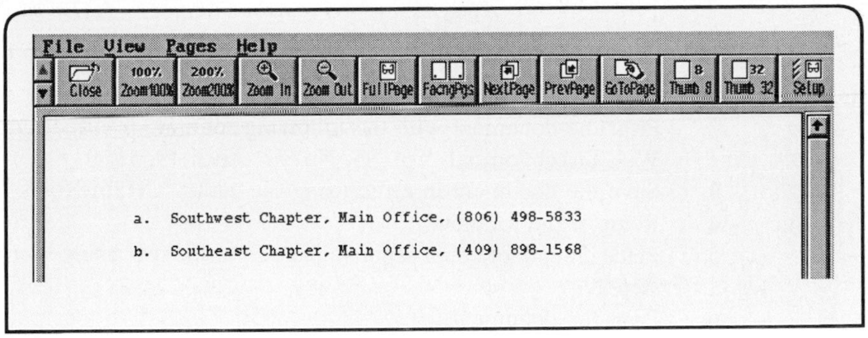

```
File  View  Pages  Help
Close  100%  200%  Zoom In  Zoom Out  FullPage  FacngPgs  NextPage  PrevPage  GoToPage  Thumb 8  Thumb 32  SetUp
    Zoom100%  Zoom200%



        a.   Southwest Chapter, Main Office, (806) 498-5833
        b.   Southeast Chapter, Main Office, (409) 898-1568
```

Return to your document. Save the document as "ENDNOTE". Close the document.

EXERCISE 1

INSTRUCTIONS: Define the following concepts:

1.   Footnotes _____

_____

2.   Endnotes _____

_____

EXERCISE 2

INSTRUCTIONS: Circle T if the statement is true and F if the statement is false.

T	F	1.	Footnotes and endnotes are a method of documenting sources of quotations, facts, and ideas in a report.
T	F	2.	Footnotes are usually listed at the end of the document.
T	F	3.	Endnotes are usually listed at the end of the page where they are used.
T	F	4.	WordPerfect manages the numbering of the footnotes and endnotes for you.
T	F	5.	You cannot change a footnote. You must delete it first, and then add a new one.
T	F	6.	If you look closely, you can see the actual endnote at the bottom of each page on the normal editing screen.
T	F	7.	You can change the way WordPerfect numbers the footnotes and formats them on the page.
T	F	8.	Your cursor must be at the top of the document in order to edit an endnote.
T	F	9.	WordPerfect formats the pages for you so that the footnotes will fit.

EXERCISE 3

INSTRUCTIONS: 1.   Create the following document.
2.   Print the document with the following footnote information:
Wall Street Journal, Vol. 85, No. 77, April 19, 1990, p.1.
3.   Save the document in a file using the name "CH26EX03".
4.   Remove the footnote.
5.   Place an endnote on a separate page from the text using the information in step 2.
6.   Print the document.
7.   Close the document without saving any changes.

The following quote appeared in the Wall Street Journal concerning Eastern Airlines:

Eastern Airlines was turned over to a trustee by a bankruptcy judge, who took control of the financially battered carrier away from Texas Air and Chairman Frank Lorenzo. Named as trustee was Martin R. Shugrue, who was ousted last year as president of Continental Airlines, Texas Airline's other airline unit. Unsecured creditors sought a trustee because they blamed management for Eastern's ever growing losses.[1]

EXERCISE 4

INSTRUCTIONS: 1.   Create the following document using footnotes. The footnotes are listed in the second box. The footnotes should appear at the bottom of the page separated by a 2" line from the body of the text.
2.   Spell check the document.
3.   Preview the document.
4.   Print the document.
5.   Save the document in a file using the name "CH26EX04".
6.   Close the document.

Springer defined "Ergonomics as the study of humans at work."[1] Yet, we have a different definition from Popham, "..ergonomics integrates both the physiological and psychological factors involved in creating an effective work area."[2]

1. T. J. Springer, "Ergonomics: The Real Issue," Office Administration and Automation, May, 1984, p. 69.

2. Estelle L. Popham, Rita Sloan Tilton, J. Howard Jackson, and J. Marshall Hanna, Secretarial Procedures and Administration, Cincinnati: South-Western Publishing Co., 1983), p. 26.

EXERCISE 5

INSTRUCTIONS:

1. Create the following document using footnotes. The footnotes are listed in the second box. The footnotes should appear at the bottom of the page separated by a 2" line from the body of the text.
2. Spell check the document.
3. Preview the document.
4. Print the document.
5. Save the document in a file using the name "CH26EX05".
6. Close the document.

In his Pulitzer Prize-winning book, Dumas Malone makes the following statement about Thomas Jefferson:

Jefferson would not have placed on a select list the bill on this subject (slavery), for it was merely a digest of existing laws. By the time that the revisors submitted their formal report they did not need to recommend that the importation of slaves be prohibited. The Assembly had already seen to that, and, according to Jefferson's later account, the action was taken on his motion.[1]

Accordingly, Jefferson proposed discontinuance of the slave trade before the American Revolution. Before he could make his statement to the House, it was introduced in 1778.[2]

---

1. Dumas Malone, <u>Jefferson the Virginian</u>, (Boston, Little, Brown and Company, 1948), p. 264.

2. Ford, I, 51-52: Hening IX, 471-72. As given in the <u>Delegates Journal</u>, the legislative history is as follows: On October 14, 1778, it was ordered that leave be given to bring in a bill to prevent the future importation of slaves, and that the committee of trade prepare and bring in the same. On October 15, Richard Kello of Southhampton presented a bill. This passed the House of Delegates on October 22, under a slightly different title. On October 27, as amended by the Senate, it was agreed to. Jefferson did not appear in the House until November 30.

EXERCISE 6

INSTRUCTIONS:

1. Open the document "CH26EX05".
2. Add the following sentence to the end of footnote 2 (do not include the double quotes):
"I have found no evidence of his intimacy with any member of the committee of trade."
3. Spell check the document.
4. Preview the document.
5. Print the document.
6. Save the document in a file using the name "CH26EX06".
7. Close the document.

EXERCISE 7

INSTRUCTIONS:

1. Create the following document using endnotes. Double-space the document. The endnotes are listed in the second box. Place the endnotes on a separate page at the end of the document. The title "ENDNOTES" should be centered and placed above the endnotes.
2. Spell check the document.
3. Preview the document.
4. Print the document.
5. Save the document in a file using the name "CH26EX07".
6. Close the document.

The Modern Language Association[1] has recommended using endnotes. These endnotes should appear at the end of a paper, and they should be listed in order of citation. They should appear under a heading "Endnotes." In either footnotes or endnotes, the number used to identify each should be a superior (raised) figure at the point of reference in the text.

At one time, only footnotes were acceptable as documentation of a reference. This presented problems with providing enough room at the bottom of the page to accommodate the material in the footnotes.

Endnotes and textual citation are similar. In each, the author, publication date, and page number(s) (if needed) of the material cited are given. The list is usually presented in alphabetic order on a separate page at the end of the report. Seybold and Young[2] strongly endorse this procedure because it is easy to use with a typewriter or personal computer.

---

1. <u>MLA Handbook for Writers of Research Papers</u>. New York: Modern Language Association, 1984, pp. 26-28.

2. Seybold, Catherine and Bruce Young. <u>The Chicago Manual of Style</u>. 13th ed. Chicago: The University of Chicago Press, 1982, p. 400.

EXERCISE 8

INSTRUCTIONS:

1. Create the following document using endnotes. Place the endnotes on a separate page at the end of the document. The title "ENDNOTES" should be centered and placed at the top of the page.
2. Spell check the document.
3. Preview the document.
4. Print the document.
5. Save the document in a file using the name "CH26EX08".
6. Close the document.

THE STRUCTURE OF EVERYDAY LIFE[1]

In Braudel's book, he comments that the present world population is over 4 billion people. Comparing this with the very approximate figures of the past shows that this number is five times the population of 1800, twelve times that of 1300.[2]

Cologne, at the intersection of two Rhine waterways, one up, and the other down-stream, and important over land routes, was the largest town in Germany in the fifteenth century. Despite this fact, it numbered only 20,000 people.[3]

In 1451, a plague killed 21,000 people in and around Cologne; over the next few years, 4,000 marriages were celebrated.[4]

Increases and declines therefore alternated in the short term, regularly compensating each other. Those most vulnerable - young children and the aged were always at risk.

Endnotes

1. Fernand Braudel, The Structure of Everyday Life, New York; Harper & Row Publishers, 1979.

2. If anyone accepts the figure of 350 million for 1300 and 1,000 million for 1800. These are the figures on which the calculations are based.

3. Heinrick Bechtel, Wirtschaftsgeschichte Deutschlands, Vol. 16, 1952, pp. 25-26.

4. Erich Schonfelder, Die Wirtschaftliche Entwicklung, translated in 1970, says 30,000 deaths.

CHAPTER TWENTY-SEVEN

PREPARING TABLES OF CONTENTS, INDEXES, AND LISTS

OBJECTIVES

In this chapter, you will learn to:
- Create, define, and generate a table of contents
- Create, define, and generate an index
- Create, define, and generate a list

■ CHAPTER OVERVIEW

When you prepare reports or long documents, you may need to make a table of contents, an index, or a list of items such as figures, maps, or tables. In this chapter, the procedures for creating, defining, and generating a table of contents, index, and list are described and illustrated.

■ TABLES OF CONTENTS

A **table of contents** appears at the front of large reports or books. It lists the headings of each chapter and the sections that divide each chapter. Several levels of subsections can be listed in the table of contents, depending on the level of detail you want to maintain. A page number is defined for each item in the table of contents. An example of a table of contents is shown at the front of this book.

The WordPerfect Table of Contents feature creates a table of contents automatically from a document that you prepare. A maximum of five levels of headings can be maintained. The first level is placed at the left margin. Levels two through five are placed at the next four Tab stops. You can specify how you would like the numbers to appear for each level.

Create the document in Figure 27-1. Set the initial font to Helve-WP (Type 1) 12 point. To create the text beneath each heading, use the Indent feature. Insert a page break between each Roman numeral heading. Save the document as "INFORM.RPT".

Figure 27-1

I.   Introduction

      Last year a decision was made to install new information processing equipment at the corporate office. The target date for installation and full operation is August 1.

(page break)

II.   History

      Prior to the installation of the information processing equipment last August, the document preparation group consisted of seven individuals. There are now five people in the department.

(page break)

III. New Information Processing Equipment

      A. Future Installations

          The company is beginning to install additional information processing systems in all of the organization's departments.

      B. Long-Range Plans

          The consultant that assisted us in the design and installation of the initial information processing equipment will work with us on a continuing basis to determine our long-term needs.

Creating a table of contents involves three steps. First, you must mark the headings or text in your document that you want to display in the table of contents. You can do this as you are creating your document or after you are finished entering the text. To mark text for the table of contents, highlight the text, press ALT+F5 and 1 or C or choose the Mark option under Table of Contents in the Tools menu. Then enter a table of contents level number (1 through 5) for the text.

The second step in creating a table of contents is to specify where you would like the table placed in the document and to define how the numbers should appear for each level in the table.

The third step is to use the Generate feature to display the table of contents.

Marking Table of Contents Entries

To mark the first heading, "I. Introduction":

Highlight	the heading "I. Introduction"	*Select*	*the heading "I. Introduction"*
Press	Alt + F5	*Choose*	*Tools*
		Choose	*Table of Contents*
		Choose	*Mark*

If you used the keystroke method, the Mark Text dialog box appears. Your screen should look like Figure 27-2. If you used the menu method, the Mark Table of Contents dialog box appears and your screen should look like Figure 27-3.

Figure 27-2

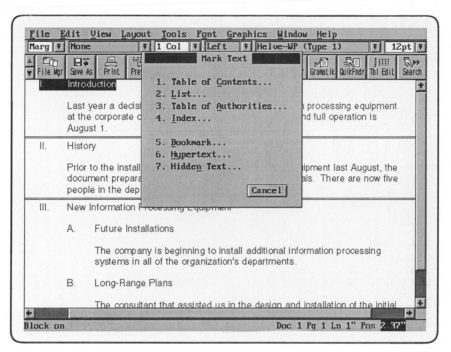

Press   1 or C to select the Table of Contents option

The Mark Table of Contents dialog box appears. Your screen should look like Figure 27-3.

Figure 27-3

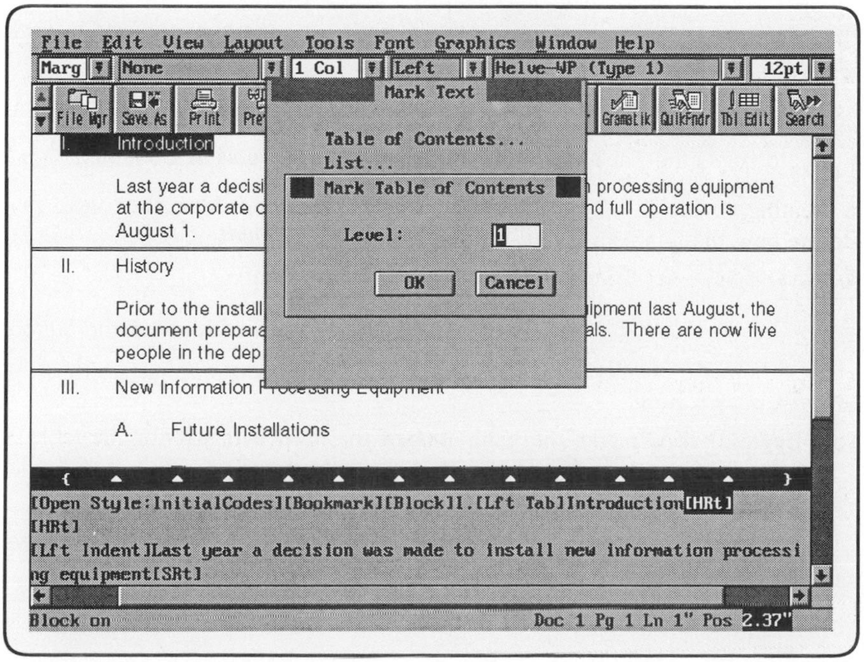

To enter the level:

Type	1 (if it is not already in the Level text box)	*Type*	*1 (if it is not already in the Level text box)*
Press	⏎Enter	*Click*	*the OK command button*

To display the codes that mark the text for the table of contents, turn on the Reveal Codes feature. Move the cursor to the code before "I. Introduction".

A [Mrk Txt ToC Begin:1] code indicates the beginning of a table of contents marker. Move the cursor to the code after "I. Introduction". A [Mrk Txt ToC End:1] code indicates the end of the text that is to be placed in the table of contents.

Turn off the Reveal Codes feature.

To mark the second heading, "II. History":

Highlight	the heading "II. History"	*Select*	*the heading "II. History"*
Press	Alt + F5	*Choose*	*Tools*
Press	1 or C to select the Table of Contents option	*Choose*	*Table of Contents*
Type	1 (if it is not already in the Level text box)	*Choose*	*Mark*
Press	⏎Enter	*Type*	*1 (if it is not already in the Level text box)*
		Click	*the OK command button*

Use the steps above to mark the third heading, "III. New Information Processing Equipment".

The "A. Future Installations" heading is a subheading to the section, and needs to be marked as a level-two heading.

To mark the subheading, "A. Future Installations":

Highlight	the subheading "A. Future Installations"	*Select*	*the subheading "A. Future Installations"*
Press	Alt + F5	*Choose*	*Tools*
Press	1 or C to select the Table of Contents option	*Choose*	*Table of Contents*
Type	2	*Choose*	*Mark*
Press	⏎Enter	*Type*	*2*
		Click	*the OK command button*

Turn on the Reveal Codes feature.

A [Mrk Txt ToC Begin:2] code marks the beginning of the level-two text for the table of contents. A [Mrk Txt ToC End:2] marks the end of the text.

Turn off the Reveal Codes feature.

Use the steps above to mark the subheading, "B. Long-Range Plans" for entry in the second level of the table of contents.

Defining the Space for a Table of Contents

After marking the text, you must tell WordPerfect where to place the table in the document and how to format the page numbers.

To create a separate page for the table of contents at the beginning of the document:

Move	the cursor to the beginning of the document (Make sure the cursor is on the [Mrk Txt ToC Begin:1] code)		*Click*	*at the beginning of the document (Make sure the cursor is on the [Mrk Txt ToC Begin:1] code)*
Insert	a page break		*Insert*	*a page break*
Move	the cursor to the beginning of the document		*Click*	*at the beginning of the document*

The top part of your screen should look like Figure 27-4.

Figure 27-4

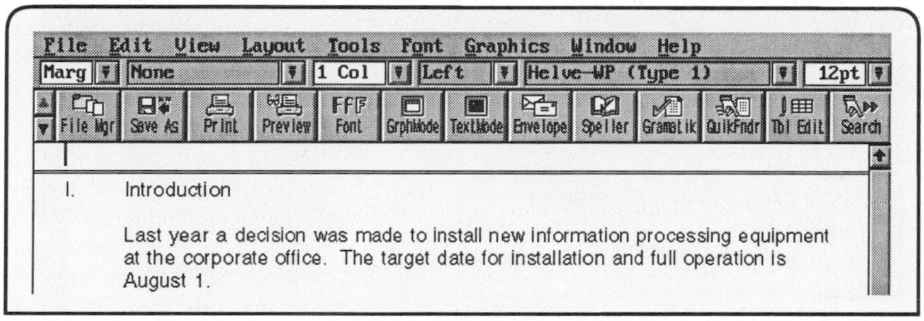

To define the table of contents:

Press	Alt + F5		*Choose*	*Tools*
			Choose	*Table of Contents*
			Choose	*Define*

If you used the keyboard method, the Mark dialog box appears. Your screen should look like Figure 27-5. If you used the menu method, the Define Table of Contents dialog box appears and your screen should look like Figure 27-6.

Figure 27-5

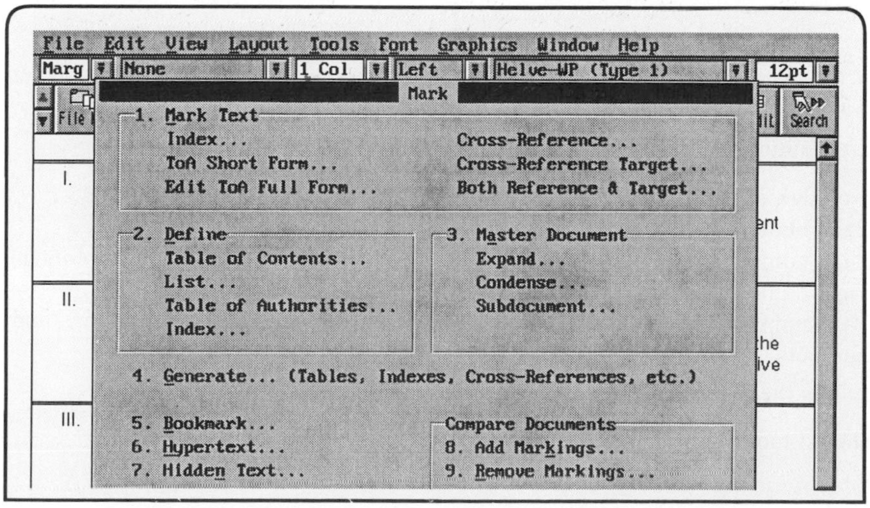

Press   2 or D to select the Define option

Press   1 or C to select the Table of
Contents option

The Define Table of Contents dialog box appears.   Your screen should look like Figure 27-6.

Figure 27-6

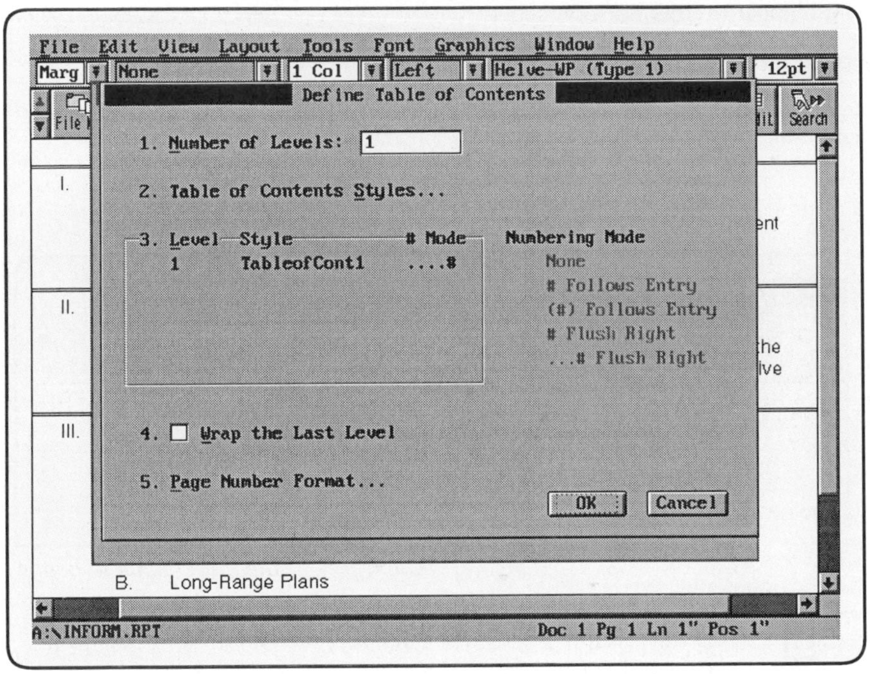

To change number of levels to 2:

Press   1 or N to select the Number of
Levels text box

Type   2

Press   [←Enter]

Click   *in the Number of Levels text box*

Type   *2*

Double-   *in the Number of Levels text box*
click

You can select the number of levels to be displayed, the page numbering style, and whether the last level should be word wrapped. You can also define a page number format.

There are five page numbering styles that you can choose:

1. No page numbers.
2. Page numbers directly following the text in the table of contents.
3. Page numbers in parentheses directly following the text in the table of contents.
4. Page numbers against the right margin (flush right).
5. Page numbers flush right with dots (leaders) placed between the headings and the numbers.

The default style is the last choice mentioned above.

Your screen should look like Figure 27-7.

Figure 27-7

```
 File  Edit  View  Layout  Tools  Font  Graphics  Window  Help
 Marg ▼  None            ▼  1 Col ▼  Left  ▼  Helve-WP (Type 1)        ▼  12pt ▼
                      Define Table of Contents                              Search
 File
                                                                        ↑
    I.      1. Number of Levels: 2

            2. Table of Contents Styles...        ▷

            3. Level─Style────────# Mode─┐ Numbering Mode
                  1    TableofCont1    ....#       None                      ent
   II.            2    TableofCont2    ....#       # Follows Entry
                                                   (#) Follows Entry
                                                   # Flush Right             he
                                                   ...# Flush Right          ive

   III.     4. ☐ Wrap the Last Level

            5. Page Number Format...
                                              ┌────────┐  ┌────────┐
                                              │  OK  : │  │ Cancel │
                                              └────────┘  └────────┘

          B.    Long-Range Plans
 A:\INFORM.RPT                          Doc 1 Pg 1 Ln 1" Pos 1"
```

To return to the document and accept the default page numbering style:

Press [←Enter] twice	**Click** *the OK command button*

Turn on the Reveal Codes feature.   Move the cursor to the [Def Mark] code.   The [Def Mark:ToC,2:Dot Ldr #] code is placed in the document where the table will be located.   This code indicates the table of contents will have two levels.   Each level will be formatted with the page numbers flush right and preceded by dot leaders.

Turn off the Reveal Codes feature.

Generating a Table of Contents

Once the text is marked and the space for the table of contents is defined, the last step is to generate the table of contents.

To generate a table of contents:

Press [Alt] + [F5]	**Choose** *Tools*
Press 4 or G to select the Generate option	**Choose** *Generate*

The Generate dialog box appears.   The top of your screen should look like Figure 27-8.

Figure 27-8

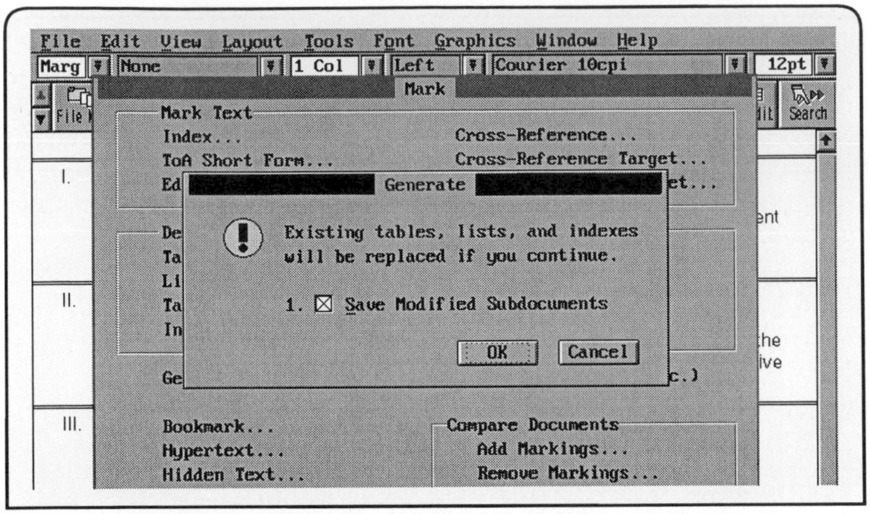

You are warned that any existing tables, lists, and indexes will be replaced. Press ENTER or click the OK command button to accept the warning and continue with the generation process. Choosing Cancel will return you to your document without generating the table of contents.

To generate the table of contents:

Press   ⟨←Enter⟩ to select the OK command button | ***Click***   *the OK command button*

A Generate in Progress box appears on the screen showing the progress of the table generation. When complete, the table of contents is displayed. Your screen should look like Figure 27-9.

Figure 27-9

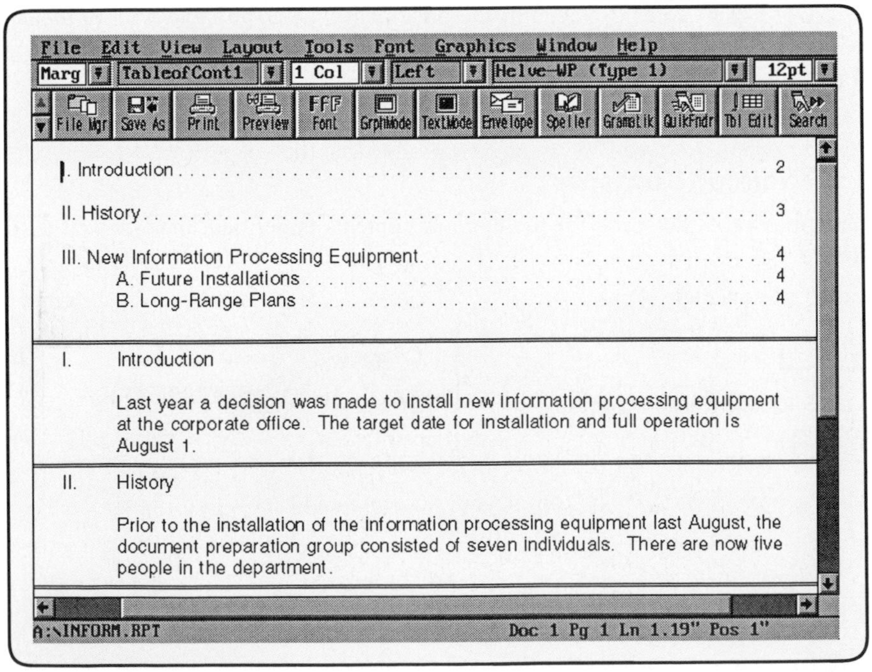

Turn on the Reveal Codes feature.

Notice that several codes have been automatically added to format the text in the table of contents. Page numbers for the table of contents are displayed at the right margin.

Turn off the Reveal Codes feature. Save the document as "TOC". Close the document.

■ INDEXES

An **index** appears at the end of a long report or book. It matches key words and phrases to page numbers in the report or book. An example of an index appears at the back of this book.

The procedure for creating an index is very similar to that of a table of contents. First, you mark the words or phrases that you want in the index. Then specify where you want the index to be placed in the document and how you want the page numbers to appear. You can choose one of five numbering styles. Finally, you display the index through the Generate feature.

Open the document "INFORM.RPT" created earlier in this chapter.

Marking Text for an Index

You can create your own index-topic heading, or you can select text in the document and use it as an index heading. For example, suppose you want to include the phrase "information processing" as an index heading. The phrase appears five times in the report.

There are two types of "information processing" included in the report: "equipment" and "systems." It would probably be best to list "Information Processing" in the index as a heading, with "equipment" and "systems" as subheadings.

To mark the text "information processing" for the index:

Highlight	the text "information processing" in the first paragraph		*Select*	*the text "information processing" in the first paragraph*
Press	Alt + F5		*Choose*	*Tools*
Press	4 or I to select the Index option		*Choose*	*Index*
			Choose	*Mark*

The Mark Index dialog box appears. Your screen should look like Figure 27-10.

Figure 27-10

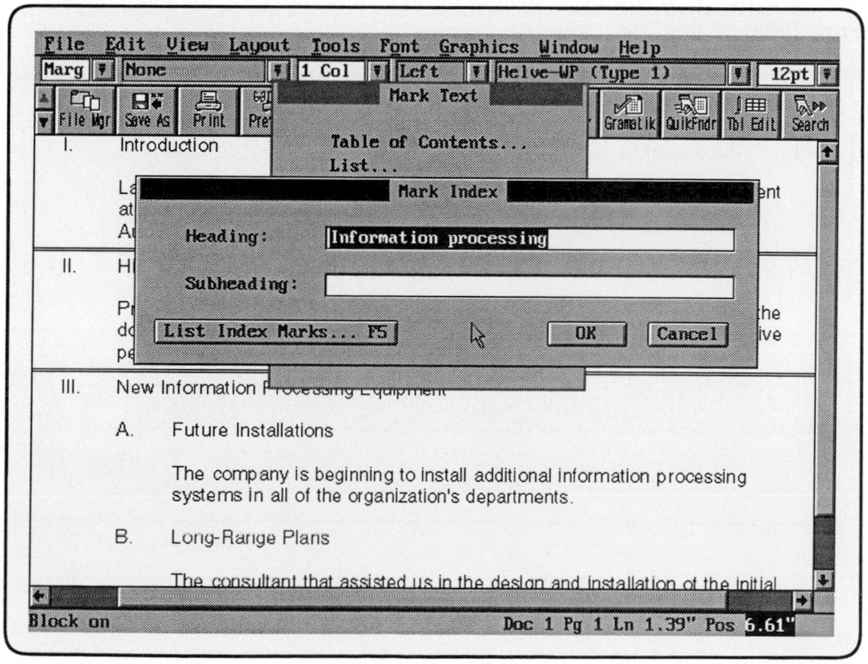

The highlighted word is offered as an index heading.

To accept the highlighted word and enter a subheading:

Press	Tab⇄ to select the Subheading text box		*Click*	*in the Subheading text box*
Type	equipment		*Type*	*equipment*
Press	↵Enter twice		*Click*	*the OK command button*

Turn on the Reveal Codes feature. Move the cursor to the [Index] code before the word "information". The [Index:Information processing;equipment] code is placed in the document for the heading and subheading.

Turn off the Reveal Codes feature.

To enter the heading, "Information processing" and the subheading, "systems":

Select	the text "information processing" in the third section		*Select*	*the text "information processing" in the third section*
Press	Alt + F5		*Choose*	*Tools*
Press	4 or I to select the Index option		*Choose*	*Index*
			Choose	*Mark*

To accept the highlighted word and enter the subheading:

Press	Tab⇄ to select the Subheading text box		*Click*	*in the Subheading text box*
Type	systems		*Type*	*systems*
Press	↵Enter twice		*Click*	*the OK command button*

Defining the Space for an Index

You can specify where the index will be located in the document and how the page numbers should appear through the Define Index dialog box.

To create a separate page for the index at the end of the document:

Move	the cursor to the end of the document		*Click*	*at the end of the document*
Insert	a page break		*Insert*	*a page break*

The bottom part of your screen should look like Figure 27-11.

Figure 27-11

The consultant that assisted us in the design and installation of the initial information processing equipment will work with us on a continuing basis to determine our long-term needs.

A:\INFORM.RPT   c 1 Pg 3 Ln 3.14" Pos 1"

To define the space for the index:

Press			***Choose***	*Tools*
Press	2 or D to select the Define option		***Choose***	*Index*
Press	4 or I to select the Index option		***Choose***	*Define*

The Define Index dialog box appears. Your screen should look like Figure 27-12.

Figure 27-12

```
 File  Edit  View  Layout  Tools  Font  Graphics  Window  Help
Marg ▼ None            ▼ 1 Col ▼ Left  ▼ Helve-WP (Type 1)         ▼  12pt ▼
                              Mark
 File              Define Index                            Search

   II.    ┌Level───────Current Style──┐  ┌Numbering Mode───────────┐
          │ Heading      Index1       │  │ 1. ○ None                │
          │ Subheading   Index2       │  │ 2. ○ # Follows Entry     │
          └───────────────────────────┘  │ 3. ○ (#) Follows Entry   │
                                          │ 4. ○ # Flush Right       │
          6. Index Level Styles...       │ 5. ● ...# Flush Right     │
   III.                                   └──────────────────────────┘

          7. ☒ Combine Sequential Page Numbers (Example: 51-62)

          8. Page Number Format...

          9. Concordance Filename: [                              ]

          [ File List... F5 ] [ QuickList... F6 ]      [  OK  ] [ Cancel ]
                                                                      sis

 ←                                                                    →
A:\INFORM.RPT                            c 1 Pg 3 Ln 3.14" Pos 1"
```

The Define Index feature allows you to determine the numbering format for the index or suggest an optional concordance file. A **concordance file** is a special file that you can create. The concordance file contains a list of all the index entries that you want to define for your document. You simply type each index entry on separate lines. WordPerfect compares this list with the document and creates an index. For more information on how to use a concordance file, see the "Concordance" section in the WordPerfect Reference manual.

The page numbering formats and suggested default are the same as the formats available for the Table of Contents feature.

To select the numbering style in which the numbers appear directly after the text:

Press	2 or F to select the # Follows Entry option button	**Click**	*the # Follows Entry option button*
Press	⟨←Enter⟩	**Click**	*the OK command button*

Turn on the Reveal Codes feature.   Move the cursor to the [Def Mark] code.   The [Def Mark:Index,# Follows;] code is placed in the document where the index will be located.   This code indicates the Index will be formatted with the page numbers directly following the index entries.

Turn off the Reveal Codes feature.

Generating an Index

Once the text is marked and the space for the index is defined, the third step is to generate the index.

To generate the index:

Press	⟨Alt⟩+⟨F5⟩	**Choose**	*Tools*
Press	4 or G to select the Generate option	**Choose**	*Generate*

You are warned that any existing tables, lists, and indexes will be replaced.   Press ENTER or click on the OK command button to accept the warning and continue with the generation process.   Choosing Cancel will return you to your document without generating the index.

To generate the index:

Press	⟨←Enter⟩ to select the OK command button	**Click**	*the OK command button*

A Generate in Progress box appears on the screen showing the progress of the index generation.   When complete, the index is displayed.   Your screen should look like Figure 27-13.

Figure 27-13

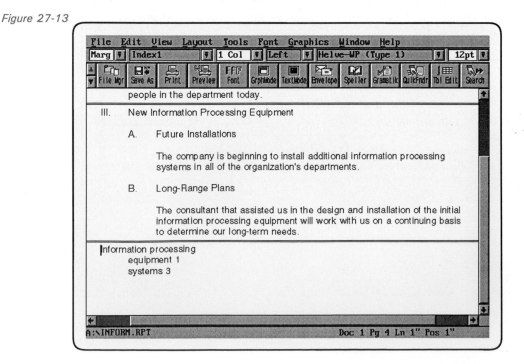

Turn on the Reveal Codes feature.

Notice that several codes have been automatically added to format the text in the index. Each index entry is separated from the page number by a space.

Turn off the Reveal Codes feature. Save the document as "INDEX". Close the document.

■ LISTS

You can create a list of figures, tables, maps, or illustrations that are used in a long report or book. A page number is placed with each item on the list so you can easily find it in the text. A list can appear at the front or back of the report or book. The entries appear in the order in which they are presented in the document.

The procedure for creating a list is very similar to that of a table of contents or an index. First, you mark the text that you want in the list. Then you specify where you want the list located in the document and how you want the page numbers to appear. You can choose one of five numbering styles. Last, you display the list through the Generate feature.

Open the document "INFORM.RPT" created earlier in this chapter.

Creating a List

Suppose you want to make a list of the first-level headings in your document.

To mark the first heading, "I. Introduction":

Highlight	the heading "I. Introduction"		*Select*	*the heading "I. Introduction"*
Press	Alt + F5		*Choose*	*Tools*
Press	2 or L to select the List option		*Choose*	*List*
			Choose	*Mark*

The Mark Text for List dialog box appears. The top part of your screen should look like Figure 27-14.

Figure 27-14

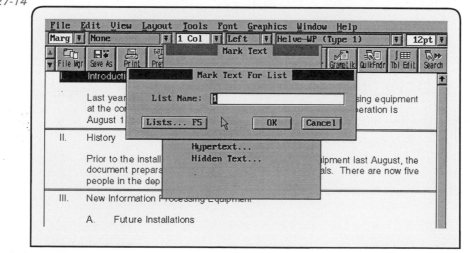

To enter the list name:

Type	1 (if it is not already in the text box)		*Type*	*1 (if it is not already in the text box)*
Press	↵Enter		*Click*	*the OK command button*

To display the codes that mark the text for the list, turn on the Reveal Codes feature. Move the cursor to the [Mrk Txt List Begin] code. A [Mrk Txt List Begin:1] code is placed before the text and a [Mrk Txt List End:1] code after the text to indicate a list 1 marker.

Turn off the Reveal Codes feature.

To mark the second heading, "II. History":

Select	the heading "II. History"		*Select*	*the heading "II. History"*
Press	Alt + F5		*Choose*	*Tools*
Press	2 or L to select the List option		*Choose*	*List*
Press	↵Enter to accept the entry in List 1		*Choose*	*Mark*
			Type	*1 (if it is not already in the text box)*
			Click	*the OK command button*

Complete the steps above to mark the heading, "III. New Information Processing Equipment".

Defining the Space for a List

After marking the text, you must tell WordPerfect where to place the list in the document and how to format the list.

To create a separate page for the list at the end of the document:

Move	the cursor to the end of the document		*Click*	*at the end of the document*
Insert	a page break		*Insert*	*a page break*

To define the list:

Press	Alt + F5		*Choose*	*Tools*
Press	2 or D to select the Define option		*Choose*	*List*
Press	2 or L to select the List option		*Choose*	*Define*

The Define List dialog box appears. Your screen should look like Figure 27-15.

Figure 27-15

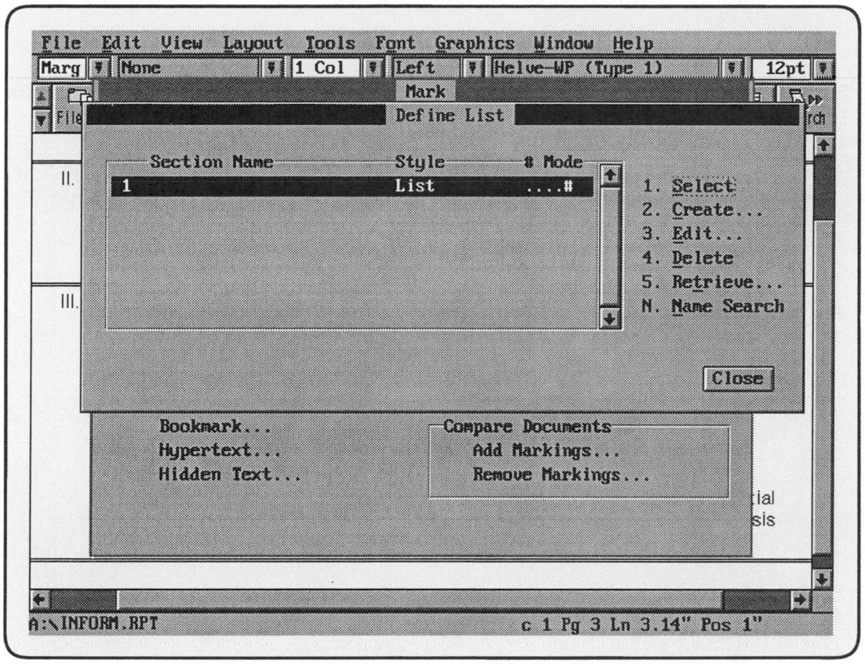

The possible page numbering styles are the same as those for the table of contents. To select a page numbering style:

Press	3 or E to select the Edit option	***Choose***	*the Edit option*
Press	6 or R to select the # Flush Right option	***Click***	*the # Flush Right option button*
Press	[←Enter]	***Click***	*the OK command button*

Recall that you can have up to 10 lists per document. To indicate that this is the first list for the document:

Press	1 or S to choose the Select option	***Choose***	*the Select option*

Turn on the Reveal Codes feature.

A [Def Mark:List,1:Flsh Rt #] code is placed in the document where the list will be located. This code indicates the list is List 1 and that each item in the list will be formatted with the page numbers following the item flush right.

Turn off the Reveal Codes feature.

Generating a List

Once the text is marked and space for the list is defined, you need to generate the list.

To generate a list:

Press	[Alt]+[F5]	***Choose***	*Tools*
Press	4 or G to select the Generate option	***Choose***	*Generate*
Press	[←Enter]		

A counter shows the progress of the list generation. When completed, the list is displayed. Your screen should look like Figure 27-16.

Figure 27-16

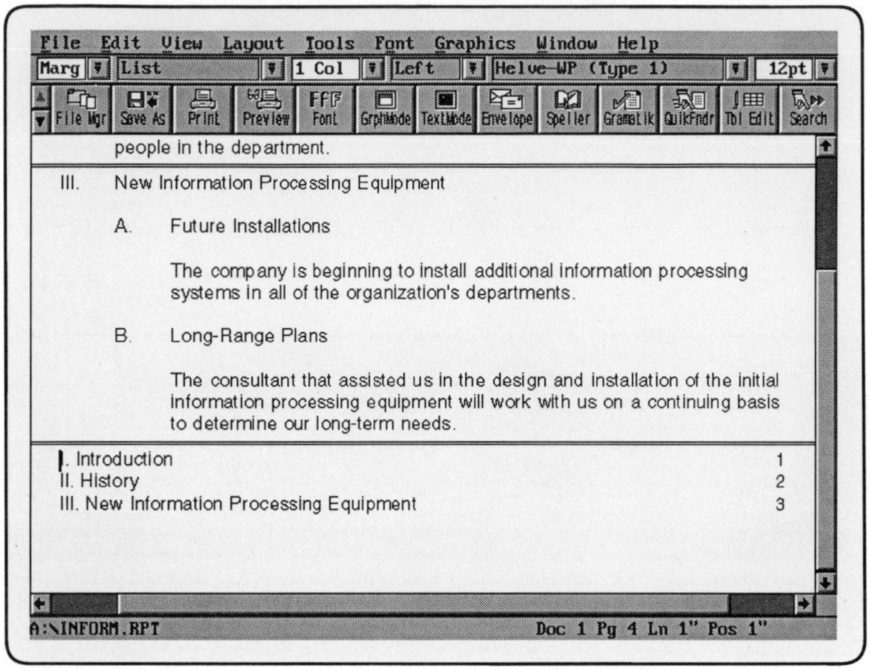

Turn on the Reveal Codes feature.

Notice that several codes have been automatically added to format the text in the list. Page numbers are flush right.

Turn off the Reveal Codes feature. Save the document as "LIST". Close the document.

Tip Box

Documents composed of several sections or chapters can become quite large and cumbersome. The computer may slow down in processing time as it interprets commands in such a large file. In addition, searching for particular information can be time consuming.

WordPerfect offers a feature in which a master document is created to manage smaller subdocuments. Each subdocument would be a chapter or section of the larger report.

The master document itself is quite small and only includes formatting codes to be applied to the whole document, as well as instructions for the order of the subdocuments. You can use the Cross Reference feature and each part being referenced may be in separate chapters. When the master document is generated, all cross references are accurately maintained and page numbering for the large document is efficiently managed.

You might have noticed master documents, subdocuments and cross references being mentioned in the figures in this chapter. For more information about these topics, consult the "Cross Reference" and the "Master Document" sections in the WordPerfect Reference manual.

EXERCISE 1

INSTRUCTIONS: Define the following concepts:

1.   Table of contents _____

_____

2.   Indexes _____

_____

3.   Lists _____

_____

4.   Mark text feature _____

_____

5.   Define feature _____

_____

6.   Generate feature _____

_____

EXERCISE 2

INSTRUCTIONS: Circle T if the statement is true and F if the statement is false.

T   F   1.   WordPerfect can manage a maximum of six levels of headings in a table of contents.

T   F   2.   When creating a table of contents, the next step after marking the headings and text in the document is actually generating the table of contents.

T   F   3.   The first step in creating a table of contents, index, or list is to specify where you would like the table, index, or list placed in the document and how the numbers should appear.

T   F   4.   An index matches key words and phrases to page numbers.

T   F   5.   An index appears at the front of a long report or book.

T   F   6.   The Define Index dialog box allows you to change the page numbering style.

T   F   7.   You can create up to 20 lists in a WordPerfect document.

T   F   8.   An index is made up of a heading and a subheading.

T   F   9.   The Define List code is placed before each item of text that should appear in the list.

T   F   10.   You can create a table of contents, index, or list with no page numbers.

EXERCISE 3

INSTRUCTIONS:

1. Create the following document. Use the Indent feature to align the paragraphs under the headings.
2. Save the document in a file using the name "CH27EX03.01".
3. Place a page break between each section.
4. Create a table of contents of the Roman numeral headings using the default page numbering style.
5. Place the table of contents on a separate page at the beginning of the document.
6. Create an index for the words "**quality**" and "**committee**".
7. Place the index on a separate page at the end of the document.
8. Print the document.
9. Save the document in a file using the name "CH27EX03.02".
10. Close the document.

```
I.     Introduction

       In a recent announcement, the president of the company
       indicated the importance of improving the quality of our
       services.  A task force has been organized to consider ways for
       enhancing our quality efforts.
(page break)
II.    History

       Our company has consistently been among the producers of
       quality services for our industry.  However, there is always
       room for improvement.  In the last industry update report, we
       placed fourth among 20 companies in quality.  While this is a
       very high rating, we slipped from number two to number four.
(page break)
III.   Quality Task Force Members

       The individuals assigned to the quality task force are the
       chief operating officer, the controller and division vice
       presidents.  There are a total of eight people on the
       committee.  The president has asked the group to report their
       results by October 31.
```

EXERCISE 4

INSTRUCTIONS:

1. Create the following document.
2. Use double-spacing.
3. Create a two-level table of contents of the underlined headings. Use the default page numbering style.
4. Print the document.
5. Save the document in a file using the name "CH27EX04".
6. Close the document.

```
                              IMPRESSIONS


Visual Impressions


     First Impressions.  Whenever we meet someone for the first
time, a first impression is made.  As you are introduced, you form a
judgment about that person.  The way the person behaves or dresses
may affect your impression.  Your first impression may accept or
reject the person without knowing anything else but his or her name.


     Letter Impressions.  When you write a letter, the reader views
the document as his or her first impression of you and the company
you represent.  The placement on the page, the quality of the paper,
the correctness of format, grammar, punctuation, and spelling all
create impressions.  The recipient of the letter makes judgments
based on a piece of paper about you and your company.


     Effective Images.  Always try to develop an effective image
with the written document.  Make sure that placement, formatting,
grammar, punctuation, and spelling are correct.  The use of good-
quality paper adds to a good impression.  Demonstrate your ability to
make effective good impressions for your company in everything you
do.
```

EXERCISE 5

INSTRUCTIONS:

1. Create the following document.
2. Double-space the document.
3. Create a table of contents using two levels. You may choose the page numbering style.
4. Create an index of the following words:

paycheck	**commissions**
Overtime	**Personnel Board**
holiday	**vacation**
terminated	**retirement**

5. Print the document.
6. Save the document in a file using the name "CH27EX05".
7. Close the document.

PAYROLL PROCEDURES

Change in Compensation Procedures

Payroll schedule changes. All employees will begin receiving their paycheck every two weeks commencing July 28. This is the regular payday for that time period. After July 28, you will receive 1/26th of your pay every two weeks.

Exempt personnel. Those employees who are scheduled to receive their pay once a month will continue to do so. These employees will receive their commissions every two weeks instead of once a month. This will begin on July 28.

Part-time personnel. All part-time personnel will continue to receive their checks once a month. If there is sufficient interest in changing this procedure, it will be considered by the Personnel Board.

Payroll Compensation

Overtime hours. Overtime pay will begin each day after a worker has worked his or her regular hours. This is changed from working 37 1/2 hours before receiving overtime pay.

Rate of pay. All overtime pay will be compensated at the rate of one and one-half times that of the regular pay.

Weekend pay. All employees (regardless of company status) will be paid at the rate of twice their regular hourly pay if they work four or more hours per day on the weekend.

Holiday pay. Any employee that must work on a regularly scheduled holiday will be compensated at the rate of three times his or her regular hourly rate.

Vacation pay. All employees will be paid their regular pay for 37 1/2 hours (normal work week) for vacation pay. The regular vacation pay will be issued according to the schedule of vacation pay for years worked.

Separation Pay

Separation pay for leaving company. Employees will receive one week's pay for every three years of service upon termination.

Terminated employees. Any employee terminated by request of the company will receive two weeks' severance pay. If terminated because of inappropriate conduct, no pay will be received.

Retirement pay. All employees who retire at age 70 after serving at least 10 years with the company will be eligible for the regular retirement plan.

Questions About New Procedures

If you have questions about any of the above procedures, please check with your foreman, supervisor, or manager.

EXERCISE 6

INSTRUCTIONS:
1. Create the following document. Double-space the document.
2. Create a table of contents on a separate page with the heading "**Table of Contents**". Use flush right numbers with dot leaders.
3. Create an index of the following words and place the page numbers in parentheses:

literature	**extensive vocabulary**
audience	**listener**
intelligence	**dictionary**

4. Print the document.
5. Save the document in a file using the name "CH27EX06".
6. Close the document.

Good Vocabulary

How is your vocabulary? A good vocabulary is very important to business people. Those individuals with extensive vocabulary usually receive greater benefits. Words help you think. Reading good literature will help you increase your vocabulary.

Vocabulary Recognition

We all recognize someone who has an extensive vocabulary. The greater our recognition of the words, the greater our understanding. Occasionally, someone with a very extensive vocabulary will try to impress everyone by overusing it. You must always consider your audience when using your vocabulary. If you send the reader or listener to the dictionary with every other word, you are not communicating, you are confusing that person.

Vocabulary Power

There is a high correlation between intelligence and vocabulary. This will usually translate to one's position within the firm. Just having a large, useful vocabulary is not enough. Hard work is the major criterion for promotion. Having a good vocabulary and being able to use it at the proper time will only enhance your position and power.

Word Power

Good managers read, speak, listen and write well. They did not automatically get this way. Most are avid readers. They either join book clubs or read learned professional journals extensively.

Everyone can acquire word power. Become a reader. Take an interest in using new words in the proper context and place. Acquire an interest in the dictionary. Learn to look up words you do not know. Learn to pronounce and use them. As you gain confidence, you will find that your appetite will become insatiable for more. Once you start, you may never want to stop.

EXERCISE 7

INSTRUCTIONS:

1. Create the following document.
2. Create a list of the first-level headings and place the page numbers in parentheses. Generate the list on a separate page at the beginning of the document.
3. Print the document.
4. Save the document in a file using the name "CH27EX07".
5. Close the document.

```
I.      Introduction
        A.      Changes
        B.      Trends
(page break)
II.     Getting Acquainted
        A.      Creating a document
        B.      Editing a document
        C.      Printing a document
(page break)
III.    Capabilities of WP Software
        A.      Editing Features
        B.      Formatting
        C.      Print Enhancements
        D.      Strikeover
(page break)
IV.     Database
(page break)
V.      Spreadsheets
```

EXERCISE 8

INSTRUCTIONS:

1. Create the following document. Place page breaks as they appear in the copy. Use double-spacing.
2. Display page numbers in the upper right corner of each page.
3. After entering the text, mark the text. Use side headings and paragraph introductions as items in the table of contents.
4. Define a table of contents page. Place the numbers against the right margin with dots between the headings and the numbers.
5. Place the title "TABLE OF CONTENTS" centered at the top of the page.
6. Print the document.
7. Save the document in a file using the name "CH27EX08".

AUSTRALIA

Introduction

Australia was founded over 200 years ago when British prisoners were exiled to this land. It was their punishment to create a new way of life on a continent whose only inhabitants were Aborigines. **(Page Break)**

Early History

British sea captain, James Cook. He was the first to reach the east coast of Australia in 1770. He claimed the land for the Crown.

Colonies. By 1856 six separate colonies were established. New South Wales and Tasmania were founded mostly by convicts. Victoria was founded by business people from Europe. Even today, Melbourne can remember its founding through the grid pattern of its streets. **(Page Break)**

Some Basic Facts

Size. Australia is roughly the size of the United States if you exclude Hawaii and Alaska.

Continent. Australia is the only nation that is a continent. This also means that it is the smallest of all continents. **(Page Break)**

Unusual Facts

Australia is the flattest and the driest continent. Less than 10 percent of the land is usable for growing crops.

Rocks. The oldest known fragment of the earth's crust is found in Jack Hills. It is estimated to be 4.3 billion years old. **(Page Break)**

Statistical Information

Per Capita. Australians have it better than most. The per capita income is $14,458. This is one of the highest in the world.

Citizenry. The life expectancy is 76 years. This is one of the world's longest.

Literacy. The literacy rate is considered 100 percent. This is an amazing statistic considering that the Aborigines have a very difficult time being accepted by many white people, and they resist efforts to be educated.

Workforce. The workers of this country earn six weeks of vacation annually. **(Page Break)**

CHAPTER TWENTY-EIGHT

FILE MANAGER AND QUICKFINDER

OBJECTIVES

In this chapter, you will learn to:
- Use the File Manager feature
- Use the QuickFinder feature

■ CHAPTER OVERVIEW

In this chapter, alternative methods for opening a document are shown. In addition, the QuickFinder feature is explained. QuickFinder is a fast method for indexing multiple files.

■ USING THE FILE MANAGER FEATURE

Document files that share a common trait should be organized and stored in the same directory, just as paper files are stored in a large file cabinet. In the cabinet, certain areas are dedicated to files concerning the same topic. On a computer, these areas are called **directories**. For example, all files concerning the same company, ABC Can Company, could be stored in a directory named "ABCCAN".

On the computer, you can refer to a directory in two ways:

1. It can be the name of a disk drive. For example, "A:".
2. It can be the name of another directory on a floppy or hard disk. For example, "\WPDOCS".

The backslash (\) indicates a directory and a colon (:) indicates a disk drive. The full name of a file, or **pathname**, is specified as a drive letter, a colon, a backslash, the name of the directory if one is used, another backslash, and then the filename. For example, if you save the "PRACTICE" document on drive A in the "WPDOCS" directory, then the pathname for the document is "A:\WPDOCS\PRACTICE".

Suppose you saved the "PRACTICE" document on the hard disk using the "WPDOCS" directory. Then the pathname for using the "PRACTICE" document file is "C:\WPDOCS\PRACTICE".

The File Manager feature lists the files stored in a directory. You can switch to different directories and view files stored in each one. Other abilities include opening, deleting, renaming, moving, printing, and copying files.

The status bar at the bottom of the File Manager indicates the number of files in the current directory and the number of bytes available on the drive.

The following list describes the commands available in File Manager.

Open into New Document displays the file in the normal editing screen. Here you can edit the document as usual.

Retrieve into Current Doc allows you to bring the contents of one file into another file.

Look at the selected file. You can view a text file, a graphics file, or hear a sound file. You can also select **Look** for a directory to view the files stored in it.

Copy the current file to a new or existing file. You can also copy a file into another directory by specifying a different pathname.

Move/Rename allows you to move a file to a new directory or to rename a file in the same directory. You are asked to enter a pathname and filename.

Delete the selected file or directory. Remember that a deletion is final; the file or directory will no longer exist.

Print part or all of the selected file. You can print a file without opening it.

Print List of the files in the current or another directory.

Sort by different criteria. Using this option, you can set up the File Manager to give you the information you want by default. You can sort by filename, extension, date and time, size, descriptive name, descriptive type, or no sort (arrange the files in the order they are saved on the disk). You can also have the File Manager list the descriptive names and types of the files listed.

Change Default Dir to create a new directory on a disk or drive. You can also change the default directory using this option.

Current Dir allows you to temporarily change to another directory without having to change the default directory. Use this option to look at the contents of any directory.

Find files in a directory. You can specify a filename, or WordPerfect can search through the document summaries, the first page, or the entire document to find a word or phrase. Using the Find feature results in a list of files that fit the criteria.

Search for a file in a directory. You can specify a filename, word, word pattern, or phrase found in the descriptive name or type.

Name Search to find a file by typing in the first few letters in its name.

(Un)Mark a file or several files. You can copy, delete, print, or move one or more files by marking them.

(Un)Mark All the files in a directory. You can copy, delete, print, or move all the files in a directory using the (Un)Mark All option.

For more information on any of the File Manager features, refer to your WordPerfect Reference manual. To open your "PRACTICE" document using the File Manager feature:

Press	F5		*Choose*	*File*
			Choose	*File Manager*

The Specify File Manager List dialog box appears. Your screen should look similar to Figure 28-1.

Figure 28-1

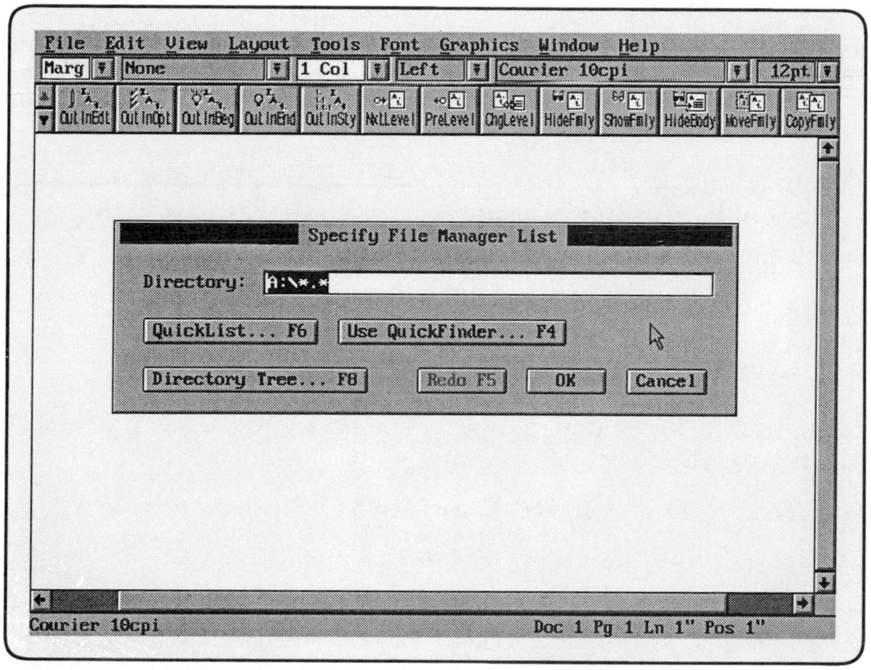

The directory listed in the Directory text box should be either "C:\WPDOCS" or "A:\" directory, whichever your default directory is.

To accept the directory:

Press   ⎗Enter | *Click*   *the OK command button*

The File Manager dialog box appears. Your screen should look like Figure 28-2.

Figure 28-2

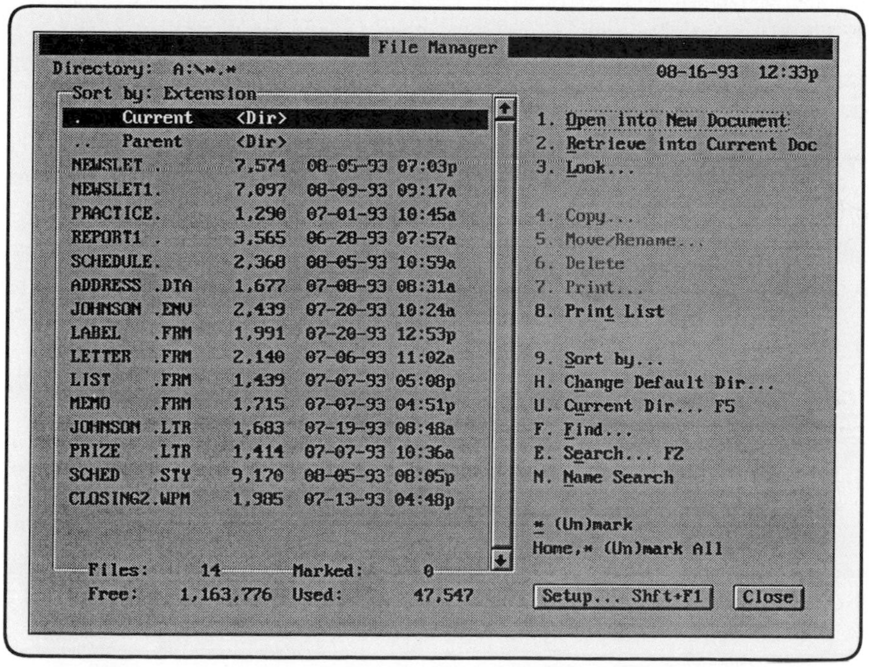

To open the "PRACTICE" document created in Chapter 2:

Press   ↓ to select the "PRACTICE" file | ***Click***   *on the "PRACTICE" file*

Your screen should look like Figure 28-3.

Figure 28-3

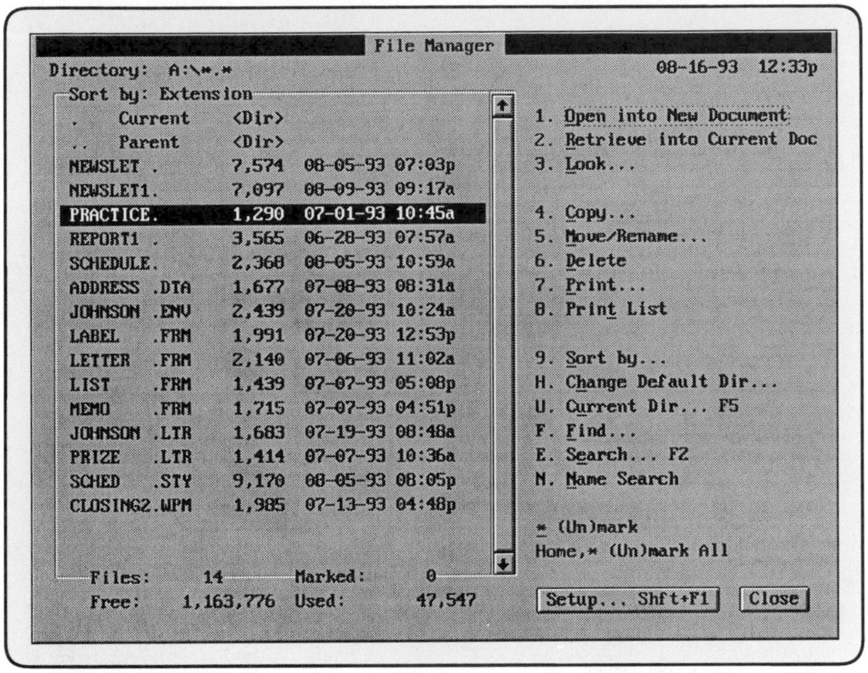

```
╔══════════════════════ File Manager ══════════════════════╗
║ Directory:  A:\*.*                          08-16-93  12:33p ║
║ ┌Sort by: Extension─────────────────┐                        ║
║ │  .    Current    <Dir>           ↑│  1. Open into New Document ║
║ │  ..   Parent     <Dir>            │  2. Retrieve into Current Doc ║
║ │ NEWSLET .      7,574  08-05-93 07:03p│  3. Look...                ║
║ │ NEWSLET1.      7,097  08-09-93 09:17a│                            ║
║ │ PRACTICE.      1,290  07-01-93 10:45a│  4. Copy...                ║
║ │ REPORT1 .      3,565  06-28-93 07:57a│  5. Move/Rename...         ║
║ │ SCHEDULE.      2,368  08-05-93 10:59a│  6. Delete                 ║
║ │ ADDRESS .DTA   1,677  07-08-93 08:31a│  7. Print...               ║
║ │ JOHNSON .ENV   2,439  07-20-93 10:24a│  8. Print List             ║
║ │ LABEL   .FRM   1,991  07-20-93 12:53p│                            ║
║ │ LETTER  .FRM   2,140  07-06-93 11:02a│  9. Sort by...             ║
║ │ LIST    .FRM   1,439  07-07-93 05:08p│  H. Change Default Dir...   ║
║ │ MEMO    .FRM   1,715  07-07-93 04:51p│  U. Current Dir... F5       ║
║ │ JOHNSON .LTR   1,683  07-19-93 08:48a│  F. Find...                ║
║ │ PRIZE   .LTR   1,414  07-07-93 10:36a│  E. Search... F2           ║
║ │ SCHED   .STY   9,170  08-05-93 08:05p│  N. Name Search            ║
║ │ CLOSING2.WPM   1,985  07-13-93 04:48p│                            ║
║ │                                   ↓│  * (Un)mark                 ║
║ │                                    │  Home,* (Un)mark All        ║
║ └Files:    14────Marked:      0─────┘                        ║
║   Free:   1,163,776  Used:      47,547    [Setup... Shft+F1] [Close] ║
╚══════════════════════════════════════════════════════════╝
```

Press   1 or O to select the Open into New Document option | ***Choose***   *the Open into New Document option*

The "PRACTICE" document now appears on your screen. Close the document.

■ USING THE QUICKFINDER FEATURE

QuickFinder is a utility that lets you maintain an index of files that are contained in directories, subdirectories, or disks. QuickFinder manages alphabetical lists of every word contained in each of the files specified.

You must create a QuickFinder Index before you can use QuickFinder to search your files.

To use the QuickFinder feature:

Press   F5 | ***Choose***   *File*

Press   F4 to select the Use QuickFinder command button | ***Choose***   *File Manager*

  | ***Click***   *the Use QuickFinder command button*

The QuickFinder File Indexer dialog box appears. The top of your screen should look like Figure 28-4.

Figure 28-4

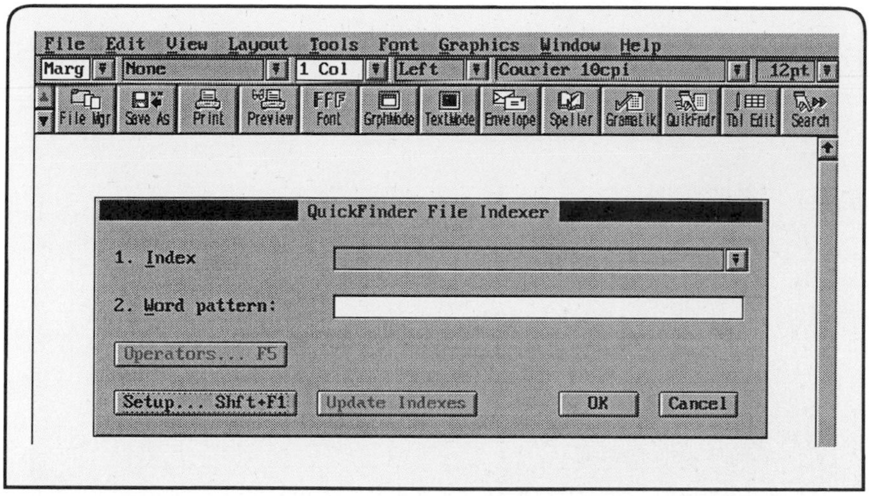

To set up an index:

Press   Shift + F1 to select the Setup | ***Click***   *the Setup command button*
command button

The QuickFinder File Indexes Setup dialog box appears. Your screen should look like Figure 28-5.

Figure 28-5

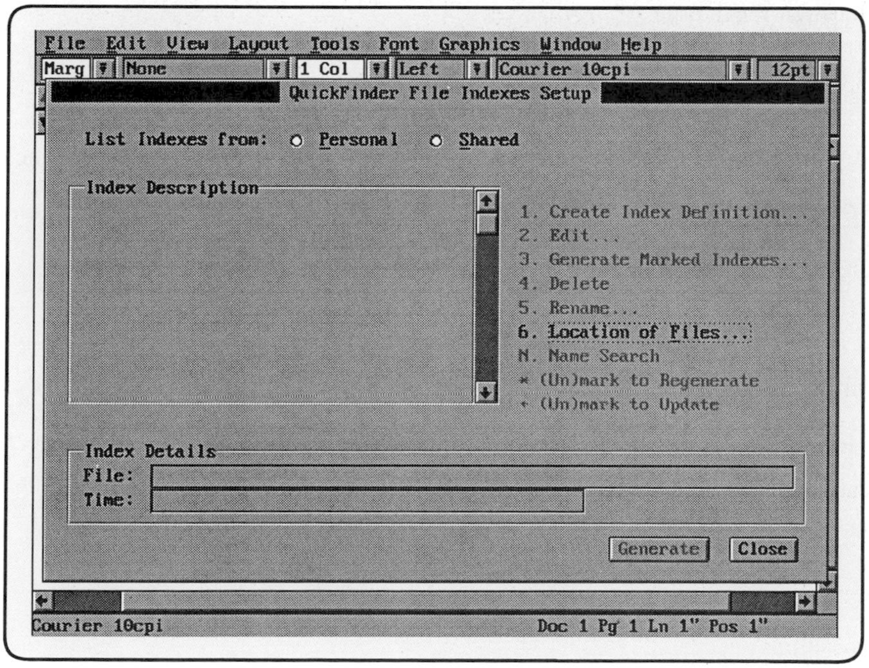

To create an Index:

Press   6 or F to select the Location of | ***Choose***   *the Location of Files option*
Files option

The QuickFinder Index Files dialog box appears. Your screen should look like Figure 28-6.

Figure 28-6

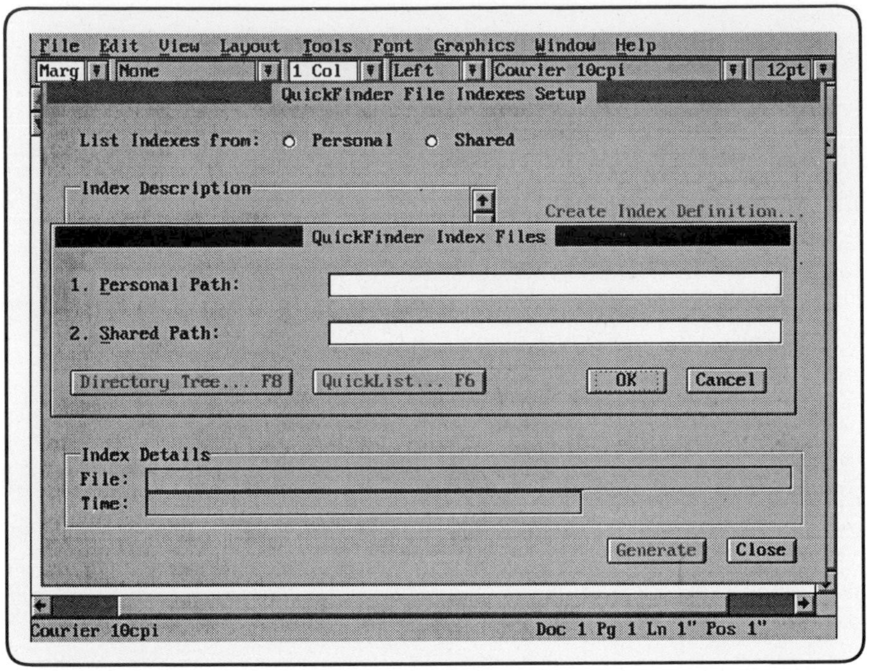

This dialog box allows you to determine where you want to save your QuickFinder Index.

To name the location for the file:

Press	1 or P to select the Personal Path text box	*Click*	*in the Personal Path text box*
Type	A:\ (or your default directory)	*Type*	*A:\ (or your default directory)*
Press	⏎Enter twice	*Click*	*the OK command button*

To define and describe the QuickFinder Index:

Press	1 or C to select the Create Index Definition option	*Choose*	*the Create Index Definition option*

The Create Index Definition dialog box appears. Your screen should look like Figure 28-7.

Figure 28-7

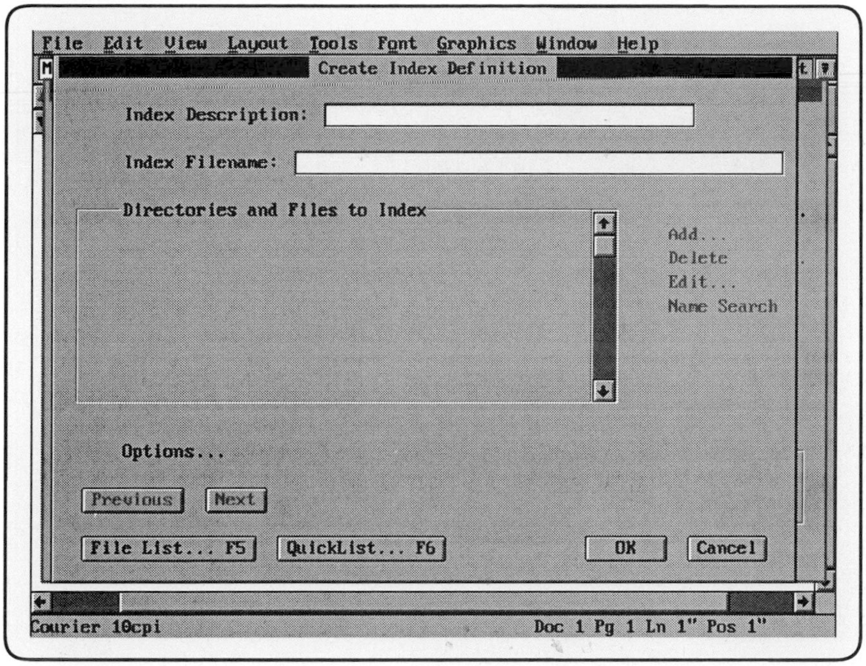

Now you will need to describe the index you are creating. Type a name in the Index Description text box. You may use several descriptive words. We will describe the index as "Johnson Documents".

To describe the index:

Type	Johnson Documents		*Type*	*Johnson Documents*
Press	[←Enter]		*Click*	*in the Index Filename text box*

To name the index:

Press	[←Enter] to accept the JohnsonD filename		*Press*	*[←Enter] to accept the JohnsonD filename*

Now you need to add the directories and files to index.

To add the directories and files:

Press	1 or A to select the Add option		*Choose*	*the Add option*

The Add QuickFinder Index Directory Pattern dialog box appears. Your screen should look like Figure 28-8.

Figure 28-8

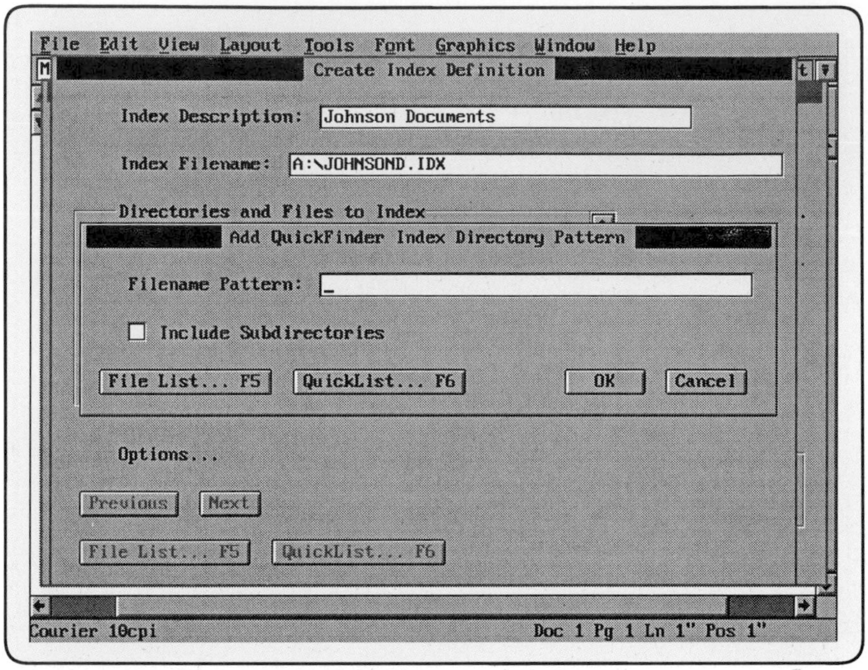

Notice the "Include Subdirectories" check box below the "Filename Pattern" text box. This option allows you to select the root directory on a specified drive. By placing an X in the check box, all subdirectories on that drive will be included in the index for "Johnson Documents".

To add the A:\ disk drive (or your default directory):

Type	A:\ (or your default directory)		*Type*	*A:\ (or your default directory)*
Press	⏎Enter		*Click*	*the Include Subdirectories check box until an X appears*
Press	2 or I to place an X in the Include Subdirectories check box		*Click*	*the OK command button*
Press	⏎Enter			

Each choice is reflected in the "Directories and Files to Index" list box, which appears in the middle of the Create Index Definition dialog box.

When all the desired drives and directories have been added to the "Directories and Files to Index" list box:

Press	Tab⇥		*Choose*	*the Options option*
Press	⏎Enter to select the Options option			

The QuickFinder Index Options dialog box appears. Your screen should look like Figure 28-9.

Figure 28-9

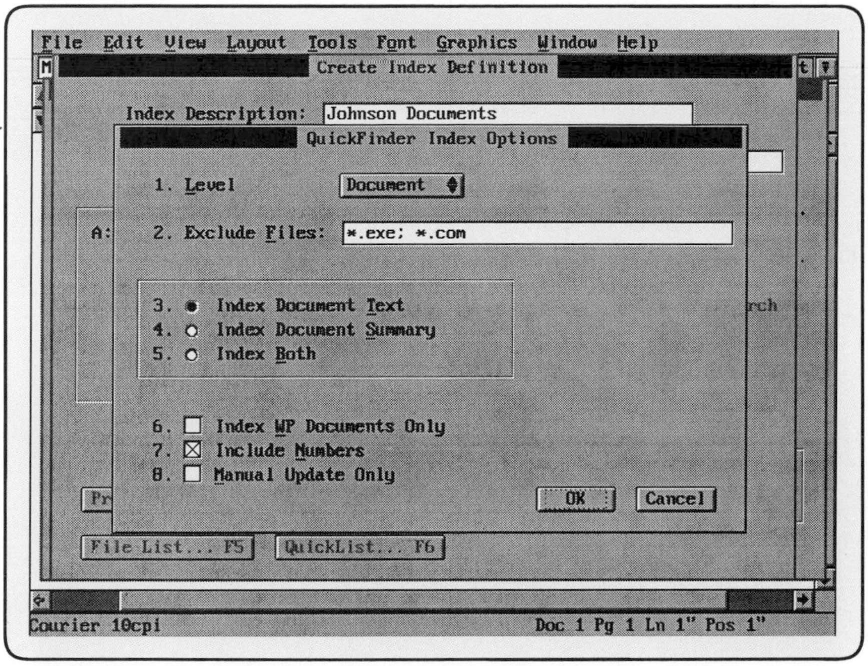

You can use the options in this dialog box to determine how QuickFinder will search for the files. For more information about the QuickFinder Index Options dialog box, refer to the "QuickFinder: Additional Information" section in your WordPerfect Reference manual.

To accept the default options and exit the Create Index Definition dialog box:

| **Press** | ⏎Enter twice | **Click** | *the OK command button twice* |

Now the "Johnson Documents" index description is listed in the Index Description list box in the QuickFinder File Indexes Setup dialog box.

To begin indexing the files:

| **Press** | 3 or G to select the Generate Marked Indexes option | **Choose** | *the Generate Marked Indexes option* |

It will take several minutes to index the files. The screen goes blank for a few seconds; then a screen indicating the progress of the indexing procedure appears.

When the indexing process is completed, the QuickFinder File Indexes Setup dialog box reappears.

To return to the document:

| **Press** | Tab⇆ | **Click** | *the Close command button* |
| **Press** | ⏎Enter twice | **Click** | *the OK command button* |

Now you can use the QuickFinder to search for files.

To use QuickFinder to search for all the documents containing the word, "JOHNSON":

| **Press** | F5 | **Choose** | *File* |
| **Press** | F4 to select the Use QuickFinder command button | **Choose** | *File Manager* |

Type	Johnson		***Click***	*the Use QuickFinder command button*
Press	[←Enter] twice		***Type***	*Johnson*
			Click	*the OK command button*

The File Manager dialog box appears with a list of files that contain the word, "JOHNSON". Your screen should look similar to Figure 28-10.

Figure 28-10

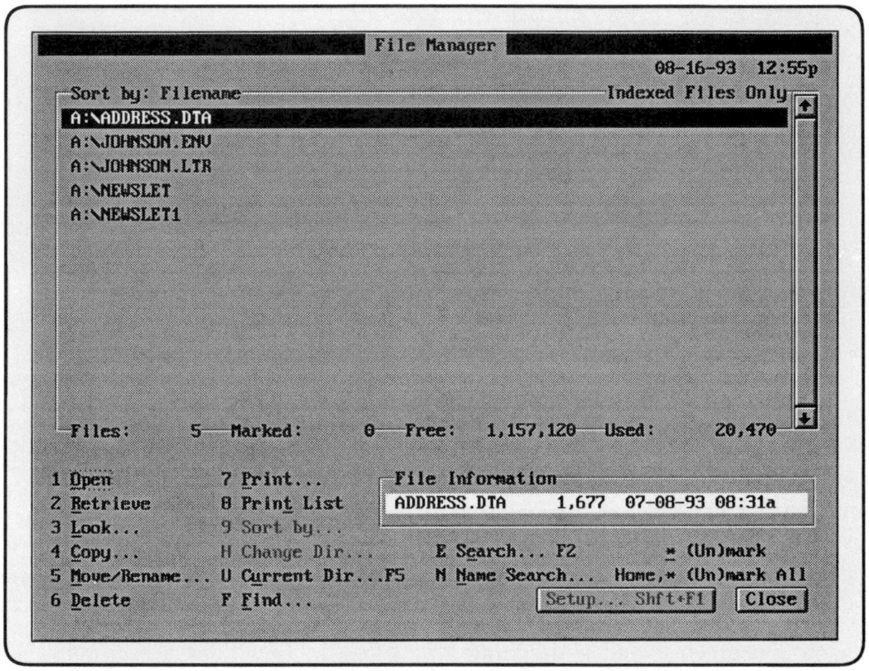

With the QuickFinder Index feature, the search for specified text is completed very quickly. The QuickFinder feature includes numerous additional options including updating, editing, deleting, moving, and renaming index entries. For more information on the QuickFinder feature, refer to "QuickFinder" in the WordPerfect Reference manual.

To return to the document:

Press	[F7]		***Click***	*the Close command button*

EXERCISE 1

INSTRUCTIONS: Define the following concepts:

1.   File Manager feature _____

_____

2.   Pathname _____

_____

3. QuickFinder _____

_____

4. Directories _____

_____

EXERCISE 2

INSTRUCTIONS: Circle T if the statement is true and F if the statement is false.

T F 1. Document files are stored in directories.

T F 2. A correct example of the pathname for a file is "C:\RESEARCH\WPFILE".

T F 3. You cannot delete a file using the File Manager feature.

T F 4. The File Manager feature lets you open a document for editing.

T F 5. You can edit a document in the Look screen of the File Manager.

T F 6. The backslash (\) indicates a drive and a colon indicates a directory.

T F 7. You can use QuickFinder to create indexes while you are in a WordPerfect document.

T F 8. QuickFinder can only index files contained in one directory.

EXERCISE 3

INSTRUCTIONS:
1. Use the standard method to open the file "PRACTICE".
2. Save the document using the standard method. Close the file.
3. Open the document file "PRACTICE" using the File Manager feature.
4. Move to the end of the document and type the sentence, "**You can open a document using the File Manager feature.**"
5. Save and close the document.

EXERCISE 4

INSTRUCTIONS:
1. List the files in the default directory using the File Manager.
2. Select the document "JOHNSON.LTR". (It was created in Chapter 3.)
3. View the document using the Look option.
4. Print "JOHNSON.LTR".
5. Exit the File Manager.

EXERCISE 5

INSTRUCTIONS:
1. List the files in the default directory by using the File Manager feature.
2. Select a document that you created for Chapter 3 ("CH03EX06").
3. Use the Look option to display the document. Use the scroll bars or the arrow keys to view the rest of the document.
4. Select another document and use Look to view and scroll through it.
5. Close the File Manager.

EXERCISE 6

INSTRUCTIONS:

1. Open QuickFinder.
2. Create an index called, "NORTHWEST DOCUMENTS".
3. Index the files.
4. Search for the word "NORTHWEST".
5. Exit QuickFinder.

EXERCISE 7

INSTRUCTIONS:

1. Open QuickFinder.
2. Create an index called, "ACCOUNTING DOCUMENTS".
3. Index the files.
4. Find all the files that have the words, "ACCOUNTING" and "JOHNSON" in them.
5. Exit QuickFinder.

EXERCISE 8

INSTRUCTIONS:

1. Open WordPerfect 6.0.
2. Use QuickFinder to access the index, "JOHNSON DOCUMENTS".
3. Search for the word, "JOHNSON".
4. Open the "JOHNSON.LTR" file.
5. Print the document.
6. Close the document.

APPENDIX A: PROOFREADER'S MARKS

DEFINED		EXAMPLES
Paragraph	¶	¶ Begin a new paragraph at this
Insert a character	∧	point. Ins͜rt a letter here.
Delete	ℛ	Delete ~~these words~~ ℛ Disregard
Do not change	*stet or*	the previous correction. To
Transpose	*tr*	transpose is to ‿around‿turn.
Move to the left	[	[Move this copy to the left.
Move to the right	]	]Move this copy to the right.
No paragraph	*No ¶*	*No ¶* Do not begin a new paragraph
Delete and close up	ℛ̃	here. Delete the hyphen from pre‑empt and close up the space.
Set in caps	*Caps or* ≡	≡a sentence begins with a capital
Set in lower case	*lc*	letter. This /Word should not
Insert a period	⊙	be capitalized. Insert a period⊙
Quotation marks	⌄ ⌄	⌄Quotation marks and a comma
Comma	∧	should be placed here∧ he said.
Insert space	#	Space between these/words. An
Apostrophe	⌄	apostrophe is whats⌄ needed here.
Hyphen	=	Add a hyphen to Afro=American. Close
Close up	⌒	up the extra spa⌒ce.
Use superior figure	⌄	Footnote this sentence.⌄ Set
Set in italic	*Ital. or* ___	the words, sine qua non, in italics.
Move up	⎡⎤	This word is too ⎡low.⎤ That word is
Move down	⎣⎦	too ⎣high.⎦

APPENDIX B: CONVERTING TO/FROM WORDPERFECT 6.0 FOR DOS

The most current version of the WordPerfect software package is WordPerfect 6.0 for DOS. You may have some documents that were created with an earlier version of WordPerfect, such as 4.2, 5.0, or 5.1. The different versions of WordPerfect use different document codes. You will want to update your documents so that WordPerfect 6.0 for DOS can work with them.

WordPerfect 6.0 for DOS files are saved in a WordPerfect 6.0 format. To use a WordPerfect 5.1 for DOS file in WordPerfect 6.0 DOS, open the old document in WordPerfect 6.0 for DOS. All document codes from WordPerfect 5.1 for DOS and WordPerfect 5.1 and 5.2 for Windows are compatible with WordPerfect 6.0 for DOS. You can also use your WordPerfect 6.0 for DOS files in WordPerfect 5.1 for DOS and WordPerfect 5.1 and 5.2 for Windows. Simply retrieve the WordPerfect 6.0 for DOS file into the WordPerfect 5.1 for DOS program, or into WordPerfect 5.1 or 5.2 for Windows.

If you are updating a document created in WordPerfect 5.0, 4.2, or earlier, open the document in WordPerfect 6.0 for DOS. When you select the file and click the Open command button, a Convert File Format dialog box appears on your screen. The name of the program in which the document was created should appear in the Convert File Format From drop down list box. If the program name is incorrect, you can select a program from the drop down list by clicking the down arrow next to the program name and scrolling through the list. When you have the correct program name selected, click the OK command button.

If you need to convert a WordPerfect 6.0 for DOS document to WordPerfect 5.0 or WordPerfect 4.2, change the File Format in the File, Save As command. To change the file format, click the down arrow of the Format drop down list box in the Save As dialog box and select the proper format. When you choose the OK command button, the file will be saved in the proper format.

For more information on converting files in WordPerfect 6.0 for DOS, see the "Conversion" section of the WordPerfect Reference manual.

APPENDIX C: USING THE SOUND, FAX, AND SHELL FEATURES IN WORDPERFECT 6.0 FOR DOS

One of the new features of WordPerfect 6.0 for DOS is the ability to use sound to enhance your documents. WordPerfect 6.0 for DOS can recognize two different types of sound files—MIDI files and Digital Audio files. MIDI files, or Musical Instrument Digital Interface files, are the standard file type for communication between computers and synthesizers. Digital Audio files store sounds that have been digitized and saved in a file. These files are much larger than MIDI files.

To access the sound capabilities of WordPerfect 6.0 for DOS, you must have a sound device in your computer (this is usually a card). Using a sound device, you can play, record, and use sound files in your documents. If you are unsure whether you have a sound device, choose Sound Clip from the Tools menu, and choose Type. If you have any sound devices, they will be listed in the Setup Sound Type dialog box. For more information about sound devices, refer to the "Sound" section in the WordPerfect Reference manual.

WordPerfect 6.0 for DOS also offers the capability of faxing documents directly from your computer via a modem or a fax server on a network.

You cannot use the Fax Services option unless you have a fax program installed on your computer or on the network server. Using the Fax Services capability in WordPerfect, you can send either an unrasterized file or a rasterized file. A rasterized file is one that has been converted to a faxable format. If you are unsure whether you have a fax program, choose Print/Fax from the File menu. If the Fax Services option is not available, you do not have a fax program installed or available to you. For more information on using the Fax Services, refer to the "Fax Services" section in the WordPerfect Reference manual.

Included with WordPerfect 6.0 for DOS is a feature called Shell. This feature provides a menu structure from which you can run WordPerfect and up to 40 different programs at the same time (the number would vary with your hard disk space and memory capacity). The Shell feature also allows you to use several clipboards to move information from one program to another. The advantages of running WordPerfect through the Shell feature are:

- the ability to run different programs simultaneously through the use of a menu system
- the ability to switch between the programs you have running
- the ability to open up to 80 different clipboards at a time
- the ability to cut and paste information between different programs

The use of the Shell feature is optional. If you would like more information about the Shell features, refer to the Shell User's Guide that accompanied your WordPerfect Reference manual.

COMMAND LIST

Command	Keyboard	Menu
Advance	Shift+F8,7,6	Layout, Other, Advance
Attributes	Ctrl+F8, 1-6	Font, Font
Backup File	Shift+F1,3,1, 1 or 2	File, Setup, Environment, Backup Options
Binding Offset	Shift+F8,7,9,2	Layout, Other, Printer Functions, Binding Offset
Block	Alt+F4 or F12	Edit, Block
Block Protect	Shift+F8,7,1	Layout, Other, Block Protect
Bookmark	Alt+F5,5 or Shift+F12	Edit, Bookmark
Borders Page	Shift+F8,3,B	Layout, Page, Page Borders
Paragraph Table	Alt+F9,3,1 Alt+F11,6	Graphics, Borders Layout, Tables, Edit
Button Bar		View, Button Bar
Capitalization of blocked text	Shift+F3,1-3	Edit, Convert Case
Center Page	Shift+F8,3,2 or 3	Layout, Page, Center Page
Columns, Newspaper	Alt+F7,1,1	Layout, Columns
Columns, Parallel	Alt+F7,1,1,3	Layout, Columns
Compose characters	Shift+F11	Font, WP Characters
Copy File	F5,F5,4	File, File Manager, Copy
Copy Text	Ctrl+F4	Edit, Copy
Cut Text	Ctrl+F4	Edit, Cut

Command	Keyboard	Menu
Date	Shift+F5	Tools, Date
Delay Codes	Shift+F8,3,D	Layout, Page, Delay Codes
Delete Codes	Alt+F3,3,1, Delete	View, Reveal Codes, Delete
Delete Files	F5,F5,6	File, File Manager, Delete
Delete Text	Backspace or Delete	
Directory Tree	F5,F8	File, File Manager, Directory Tree
Display Setup	Shift+F1	File, Setup
Display Mode	Ctrl+F3, 2-4	View, Text, Graphics, or Page Mode
Document Format	Shift+F8,4	Layout, Document
Document Window	Ctrl+F3,1	Window menu
Envelopes	Shift+F8,3,7 or Alt+F12	Layout, Envelope
Environmental Setup	Shift+F1,3	File, Setup, Environment
Equations	Alt+F9,1,1,Y	Graphics, Graphics Boxes, Create, Based on Box Style
Exit	F7	File, Exit
File List	F10,F5,Enter	File, File Manager, OK
File Manager	F5,F5	File, File Manager
Find File	F5,F5,F	File, File Manager, Find
Flush Right	Alt+F6	Layout, Alignment, Flush Right
Font	Ctrl+F8	Font, Font
Footnotes/Endnotes	Ctrl+F7,1 or 3	Layout, Footnote or Endnote

Command	Keyboard	Menu
Force Odd/Even pages	Shift+F8,3,F	Layout, Page, Force Page
Generate	Alt+F5,4	Tools, Generate
Go To	Ctrl+Home	Edit, Go to
Go to DOS	Ctrl+F1,1	File, Go to Shell, Go to DOS
Go to Shell	Ctrl+F1	File, Go to Shell
Grammatik	Alt+F1,3	Tools, Writing Tools, Grammatik
Graphics	Alt+F9,1	Graphics menu
Hard Page	Ctrl+Enter	
Hard Return	Enter	
Hard Space	Home+Spacebar	
Headers and Footers	Shift+F8,5, 1 or 2	Layout, Header/Footer/Watermark
Help	F1	Help menu
Hidden text	Alt+F5,7	Font, Hidden Text
Hyphenation	Shift+F8,1,6	Layout, Line, Hyphenation
Indent	F4 or Shift+F4	Layout, Alignment, Indent
Index	Alt+F5, 1,2 or 4	Tools, Index
Initial Codes	Shift+F8,4,1	Layout, Document, Initial Codes Setup
Initial Font	Shift+F8,4,3	Layout, Document, Initial Font
Initial Settings	Shift+F1	File, Setup

Command	Keyboard	Menu
Justification	Shift+F8,1,2	Layout, Justification
Kerning	Shift+F8,7,9,3	Layout, Other, Printer Functions, Kerning
Keyboard Layout	Shift+F1,4	File, Setup, Keyboard Layout
Labels	Shift+F8,3,5	Layout, Page, Labels
Landscape orientation	Shift+F8,3,4	Layout, Page, Paper Size/Type
Line Draw	Ctrl+F3,5	Graphics, Line Draw
Line Spacing	Shift+F8,1,3	Layout, Line, Line Spacing
List Files	F5,F5	File, File Manager, OK
Lists	Alt+F5,2 or 4	Tools, List
Location of Files	Shift+F1,5	File, Setup, Location of Files
Look	F5,F5,3	File, File Manager, OK, Look
Macro Play	Alt+F10	Tools, Macro, Play
Macro Record	Ctrl+F10	Tools, Macro, Record
Margins	Shift+F8,1	Layout, Margins
Mark Text	Alt+F5,1	
Master Document	Alt+F5,3	
Merge	Ctrl+F9,1	Tools, Merge, Run
Move Text	Ctrl+F4	Edit, Cut
New File		File, New
Open File	Shift+F10	File, Open
Outline	Ctrl+F5	Tools, Outline
Page Numbering	Shift+F8,3,1	Layout, Page, Page Numbering
Paper Size/Type	Shift+F8,3,4	Layout, Page, Paper Size/Type
Password	F10,F8	File, Save As, Password
Paste	Ctrl+V	Edit, Paste
POSTNET Bar Codes	Shift+F8,3,7,6	Layout, Envelope, POSTNET Bar Code
Print Job, Cancel	Shift+F7,6,C	File, Print/Fax, Control Printer, Cancel Job
Print Preview	Shift+F7,7	File, Print Preview
Print Quality	Shift+F7,G or T	File, Print/Fax, Graphics Quality or Text Quality
Print Setup	Shift+F7,1	File, Print/Fax, Setup
Printer Commands	Shift+F8,7,9,5	Layout, Other, Printer Functions, Printer Commands
Printer, Select	Shift+F7,S	File, Print/Fax, Select
QuickFinder	F5,F4	File, File Manager, Use QuickFinder
QuickList	F5,F6	File, File Manager, QuickList
Redisplay	Ctrl+F3,R	View, Screen Setup
Redline/Strikeout	Ctrl+F8,3	Font, Redline or Strikeout
Replace text	Alt+F2	Edit, Replace
Retrieve	Alt+F3 or F11	File, Retrieve
Reveal Codes	Alt+F12	View, Reveal Codes
Save	Ctrl+F12	File, Save
Save As	F10	File, Save As
Search	F2 or Shift+F2	Edit, Search
Sort	Ctrl+F9,2	Tools, Sort
Special Codes	Shift+F8,6,7	Layout, Character, Special Codes
Speller	Ctrl+F2	Tools, Writing, Tools, Speller
Spreadsheet, Import and Link	Alt+F7,5	Tools, Spreadsheet
Style	Alt+F8	Layout, Styles
Subdivide Page	Shift+F8,3,6	Layout, Page, Subdivide Page
Suppress	Shift+F8,3,9	Layout, Page, Supress
Switch Documents	Shift+F3	Window, Switch
Table of Contents, Define	Alt+F5,2,1	Tools, Table of Contents, Define
Table of Contents, Mark Text	Alt+F5,1	Tools, Table of Contents, Mark
Tables	Alt+F7,2	Layout, Tables
Tabs	Shift+F8,1,1	Layout, Tab Set
Thesaurus	Alt+F1,2	Tools, Writing, Tools, Thesaurus
Typeover	Insert	
Typesetting	Shift+F8,7,9	Layout, Other, Printer Functions
Undelete	Esc	Edit, Undelete
Undo	Ctrl+Z	Edit, Undo
Watermarks	Shift+F8,5,3	Layout, Header/Footer/Watermark
Word and Letterspacing	Shift+F8,7,9,6	Layout, Other, Printer Functions
WordPerfect Characters	Shift+F11	Font, WP Characters
Zoom	Ctrl+F3,7	View, Zoom